Patent Claim Drafting Practice

Tactics, Strategy, and Analysis

HOWARD A. SKAIST

AMERICAN BAR ASSOCIATION
Intellectual Property Law Section

Cover design by Amy Mandel, ABA Section of Intellectual Property Law; Jill Tedhams, ABA Design

Printed in the United States of America.

27 26 25 24 23   5 4 3 2 1

A catalog record for this book is available from the Library of Congress.

Discounts are available for books ordered in bulk. Special consideration is given to state bars, CLE programs, and other bar-related organizations. Inquire at Book Publishing, ABA Publishing, American Bar Association, 321 N. Clark Street, Chicago, Illinois 60654-7598.

www.shopABA.org

Contents

About the Author xii

Chapter 1
Introduction to Patent Claim Drafting Practice (PCDP) 1

1.1 PCDP Is a Complex and Challenging Task 2
Prior Art 7
Commercial Reasons for the Patent Filing 9
1.2 Business Strategy Drives Patent Strategy 13
1.21 Identify the Patent Strategy Objective 15
1.211 Claim Drafting Tactical and Strategy Illustrations 16
1.2111 Component Manufacturer 18
1.2112 System Integrator 31
1.2113 Network Provider 39
1.22 Anticipating Change in Patent Claim Drafting Strategy and/or Tactics 53
1.221 Illustrations 54
1.2211 Changes in Technology 54
1.2212 Changes in the Law 56
1.2213 Change in Business Strategy, Markets, Management, and/or Corporate Organization 60
1.3 Claim Breadth—Is Being Broad Always the Goal? 62
1.31 Drafting the Broadest Claims Possible—Advantages and Disadvantages 66
1.32 Searching the Prior Art Prior to Drafting—Advantages and Disadvantages 73

1.33 What Is Considered to Be Prior Art? 78
1.331 35 USC § 102/§ 103 PRE-AIA 78
1.332 35 USC § 102/§ 103 POST-AIA 99
1.3321 Claiming Priority to Pre-AIA Applications and Prior Art 106
1.333 Avoid Prior Art Admissions 110

Chapter 2
Introduction to Patent Claim Drafting Mechanics and to Various Claim Types **113**

2.1 What Is a Patent Claim? 113
2.11 Illustrative Claim Examples 119
2.111 Apparatus or Machine Claims 119
2.1111 Structural Versus Functional Limitations 127
2.112 Method or Process Claims 132
2.1121 Method of Using Claims 136
2.1122 Method of Making Claims 143
2.1123 Method Versus Apparatus 147
2.113 Composition of Matter Claims 153
2.114 Article of Manufacture Claims 161
2.1141 Beauregard Claims 161
2.115 Improvement Claims 166
2.1151 Jepson Claims 167
2.12 The Patent Claim Preamble 169
2.121 Theory of the Preamble 171
2.122 Examples of Preambles 172
2.13 The Patent Claim Transition Word 175
2.131 Theory of the Transition Word 176
2.132 Examples of Transition Words 183
2.14 The Patent Claim Body 185
2.141 Theory of the Claim Body 185
2.1411 Claim Elements/Limitations and their Relatonship 189
2.1412 Structure Versus Function Versus Process 191
2.1413 Inferential Claiming 192
2.1414 Interpreting Claims in Light of the Specification Versus Importing Limitations; Redefining Claim Terms Versus Importing Limitations 197

2.15 Independent Versus Dependent Claims 204
2.151 Theory of Dependent Claims 204
2.152 Adding a New Element Versus Further Clarifying an Existing Element or Limitation 210

Chapter 3
Introduction to Claim Construction and to Related Claim Drafting Principles 215

3.1 Legal Framework for Claim Construction 216
3.11 *Markman* Decision and *Markman* Hearings 216
ITC Investigation—Another Option 219
3.12 Intrinsic Evidence Versus Extrinsic Evidence 224
3.121 Pecking Order of Intrinsic Evidence 225
3.1211 Vitronics Decision 226
3.1212 Phillips *Decision* 229
3.122 Ordinary and Customary Meaning 234
3.1221 Use of Dictionaries 236
3.123 Patentee as Lexicographer 241
3.1231 Express Versus Implied Meaning of Claim Terms 243
3.1232 Categories of Claim Terminology 244
3.2 Claim Drafting Principles Based on *Markman* Framework and Type of Infringement 249
3.21 Direct, Literal Infringement 249
3.211 At the Start of Drafting, Consider the Types of Direct Infringement and the Business and Economic Considerations Surrounding the Invention 251
3.212 Make Claim Coverage Clear from the Face of the Claims 252
3.213 Use Words in the Claims Consistent with Their Understood Meaning 258
3.214 Use Words in the Claims with Broadly Understood Meanings where Appropriate 260
3.2141 Employ a Hierarchy of Claim Terms 262
3.215 Avoid Overly Specific Term Modifiers in the Independent Claims 268
3.216 Draft Short Claims 269

3.22 Indirect Infringement 272
3.221 A Claim for Indirect Infringement Is Harder to Prove Because It Requires Knowledge of the Patent and Knowledge That the Acts Contributed to or Induced Would Be Infringing; thus, Attempt to Draft Claims That Will Be Directly Infringed 274
3.2211 Contributory Infringement 275
3.2212 Inducing Infringement 284
3.23 Claim Drafting Principles Based on DOE Framework 292
3.231 Decision Examples 293
3.2311 Hilton-Davis Decision—Equivalence and More 293
3.2312 Festo *Decision—Prosecution History Estoppel* 299
3.2313 Dolly v. Spalding *Decision—Interpreting Claim Language to Exclude Equivalents* 301
3.2314 Wilson Sporting Goods *Decision—Prior Art Limit on Equivalency* 304
3.232 Focus on Literal Infringement Rather than the DOE When Drafting 307
3.233 Use Dependent Claims for Commercial Aspects Most Likely to Be Copied 307
3.234 Do Not Draft Claims in a Manner That Is Clearly Narrower than Needed and Easily Designed around Almost by Inspection of the Patent Claim 308
3.235 Rewriting Claims Versus Amending Claims 310

Chapter 4
PCDP Basics: Drilling Down on Claim Diversity 313

4.1 Employ a "Hedge" Strategy to Claiming—Use Patent Claim Diversity 314
4.11 The Patent Claims Should Expressly Recite the Broadest and Narrowest Embodiments of the Invention, Including Multiple Claims for Multiple Embodiments between the Broadest and the Narrowest 314
4.12 Examples of Varying Claim Types 318
4.121 Component Level Claims 319
4.1211 Illustrative Claim Example 320

4.122 System Level Claims 322

4.1221 Illustrative Claim Examples 326

4.123 Means Plus Function/Step Plus Function Claims 328

4.1231 Mas-Hamilton Decision 332

4.1232 Braun Medical *Decision* 334

4.1233 Williamson v. Citrix *Decision* 336

4.1234 Advantages and Disadvantages of Means Plus Function/Step Plus Function Claims 339

4.1235 Illustrative Claim Example—Functional Claiming With and Without Use of "Means" or "Step" 342

4.124 Structure Versus Function Revisited 347

4.125 Product-by-Process Claims 360

4.1251 Advantages and Disadvantages 361

4.1252 Illustrative Claim Example—Capturing Product-by-Process Infringement With and Without Product-By-Process Claims (e.g., 35 USC § 271(g)) 363

4.126 Method of Using Claims 369

4.1261 Illustrative Claim Example 371

4.1262 New Use of an Old Device 377

4.1263 Use Infringement of a System Claim (e.g., Server) *379*

4.127 Method of Making Claims 385

4.1271 Illustrative Claim Example 385

4.1272 Making a Device Capable of Infringing 388

4.128 Beauregard Claims 396

4.1281 Advantages and Disadvantages 397

4.1282 Examples of Various Approaches to Beauregard Claiming 398

4.129 Markush Group Claims 402

4.1291 Advantages and Disadvantages 405

4.1292 Examples—Claiming Subject Matter With and Without Markush Groups 407

4.130 Composition of Matter Claims 409

4.131 In General, Draft Claims of Varying Scope 413

4.1311 Examples of Broad Scope Claims 415

4.1312 Examples of Intermediate and Narrow Scope Claims 417

4.1313 Use Picture Claims 420

Chapter 5
More PCDP Basics 423

5.1 Claim Preambles Should Be Short and Avoid Introducing Limitations 424
5.11 For Method Claims, Avoid "A Method Comprising the Steps Of" 426
5.12 Avoid Preambles That Refer to Non-Statutory Subject Matter 426
5.13 Where the Preamble Ends Should Be Clear 427
5.14 List of Examples of Preambles 428
5.2 In the Predictable Arts, Use "Comprising" as the Transition Word 428
5.21 Use Varying Transitional Phrases to Vary Claim Scope in the Unpredicable Arts 432
5.211 "Consisting Of" and "Consisting Essentially Of" 432
5.3 Use Multiple Verbal Formulations or Approaches That Are Logically Consistent to Capture and Characterize the Inventive Concept 436
5.31 Identify Features of the Invention Independent of the Particular Embodiments 440
5.311 Illustrative Claim Example—Chair 441
5.312 Employ a Hierarchy of Claim Terms 443
5.313 Illustrative Example 444
5.32 Use Dependent Claims for Claim Differentiation and to Cover Commercial Embodiments 444
5.321 Illustrative Claim Example 446
5.4 Draft the Claims Before the Specification 448
5.41 Potential Written Description Issues 450
5.411 Use Express Definitions of Claim Terms 454
5.412 *Lizardtech* Decision 456
5.413 Negative Limitations 458
5.42 Avoid Potential Enablement Issues 459
5.43 Avoid Potential Indefiniteness Issues 460
5.44 Avoid Potential Patent Eligibility Issues 461
5.441 Illustrative Claim Example—Software: VisiCalc 465
5.442 Medical Diagnostic Methods 480
5.5 Have the Closest *Known* Prior Art in Mind when Drafting the Claims 483
5.51 Understanding Potential Inequitable Conduct Issues: *Therasense* 485

less familiar with the challenge of claim drafting sometimes see drafting patent claims as more of a commodity service that anyone with both technical training and legal training can perform. However, to the extent patent claim drafting is a commodity service, then it is more like gold or silver than like pork bellies.[7]

Patent attorneys are often perceived as "geeks," in part because patent claim drafting requires a technical degree of some kind (or the equivalent). Patent attorneys frequently majored in electrical engineering or physics in college, whereas others also destined to enter the legal profession may have majored in history, political science, or economics.

However, billions of dollars in value quite literally can be in play, depending on the language used in the claims of a given patent. To put a finer point on the subject, over many years, there have been lots of examples of incredibly valuable technology that, if better claimed, would have resulted in an incredibly valuable patent. Understanding what went wrong and what to do to provide appropriate patent protection requires understanding PCDP.

As an introductory point, first understand that the scope of legal rights granted by a patent is defined by the "claims" of the patent.[8] The claims of a patent are the numbered sentences at the very end of the patent. The claims

---

invention. For inventions in rapidly evolving fields, application filings are often made while the inventions are still in their nascent stages, i.e., early in the evolutionary process, necessitating inevitable and sometimes considerable fine tuning of claim language after the initial application filings have been made. Moreover, while an inventor is often aware of relevant prior art relating to the area he is developing, he is not always fully cognizant of all of the relevant prior art until after his application has been filed, thus again necessitating some fine tuning of claim language after the initial application filing has been made.").

7. Patent law may be thought of as involving several branches: patent prosecution, patent litigation, and patent licensing. Patent prosecution describes the process by which an inventor, usually through the help of an attorney, files an application with the U.S. Patent and Trademark Office (PTO) for examination to obtain a patent. Patent litigation focuses on patents once issued. A patent owner whose rights have been infringed may compel an accused infringer to stop the infringing activity and/or pay for damages arising from infringement that has occurred. Patent licensing allows patent owners to generate royalty income by allowing others to practice the invention. Yet another aspect may be thought of as a cross between litigation and prosecution. The America Invents Act (AIA) created several types of legal proceedings in the PTO that may take place after a patent has issued. These proceedings are a cross between litigation and prosecution, because while they take place in the PTO, they are inter partes, as in litigation. By contrast, patent prosecution is ex parte.

8. *See, e.g.*, Phillips v. AWH Corp., 415 F.2d 1303, 1312 (Fed. Cir. 2005) (en banc) ("It is a 'bedrock principle' of patent law that 'the claims of a patent define the invention to which the patentee is entitled the right to exclude.'"). *See also* Constant v. Advanced Micro-Devices, Inc., 848 F.2d 1560, 1571, 7 USPQ2d 1057, 1064 (Fed. Cir. 1988); Dollar Elec. Co. v. Syndevco, Inc., 205 USPQ 949, 959 (E.D. Mich. 1979), *aff'd*, 669 F.2d 1370, 214 USPQ 241 (6th Cir. 1982).

section of a patent begins with words, such as: "I claim," "We claim," or "What is claimed is," immediately followed by a colon. Following the colon are a succession of sequentially numbered partial sentences that complete the sentence that begins as "I claim," "We claim," or "What is claimed is."[9] Claims are, in effect, run-on sentences, since the only period in a claim occurs at the end of the claim.[10] Immediately following is a simple example of two patent claims. Claim 1 is referred to as an "independent claim" and claim 2 is referred to as a "dependent claim."[11]

EXAMPLE 1.1[12]

I claim:

1. An integrated circuit comprising: at least one metal conductor and at least one metal oxide semiconductor field effect transistor (MOSFET);

   wherein multiple contacts are coupled to the at least one metal conductor along a major axis of the at least one metal conductor to conduct current to or from the at least one metal conductor and to or from drain or source regions of the MOSFET; and

   wherein the at least one metal conductor is tapered along the major axis so that during current flow the current density in the at least one metal conductor is substantially constant along the major axis.

2. The integrated circuit of claim 1, wherein the at least one metal conductor is tapered to form the shape of a trapezoid.

---

9. *See In re* Fressola, 22 USPQ2d 1828 (Comm'r Pat. & Trademarks 1992), in which Commissioner Manbeck ruled that "[t]he single claim sentence requirement is within the PTO's statutory authority and is consistent with the statutory purpose of 35 U.S.C. § 112 2."

10. *See* section 5.94 discussing grammar in connection with patent claim drafting.

11. *See* Chapter 2 for a discussion of dependent and independent claims.

12. Illustrative example claims are presented throughout this book. The more important examples are numbered with the chapter in which the example appears and with the sequential number of the example in that chapter with these two numbers separated by a period, as shown here for Example 1.1. Thus, while most example claims have a number designation, as described, not all example claims appearing in this book are necessarily numbered. Also, for continuity and/or purposes of further explanation, and so on, some examples may be repeated in a later chapter. In those cases, they receive another number designation in the manner described despite being identical to a claim previously discussed in a prior chapter with a different number designation.

The main point here is that the scope of rights granted by a patent claim primarily turns on the exact words of the patent claims themselves.[13] Therefore, poor, sloppy, or not well-thought-out word selection may produce an undesirable result such that technology of value to the patentee is not *necessarily* covered by the claims of a patent. If that is the case, this will seriously reduce, if not completely eviscerate, the value of the patent at issue. There are many wonderful and troubling examples where this is precisely what happened, several of which are discussed later in this book.

As one quick example of the many that are legion, simply because a word of a patent claim had an "s" on the end, meaning that the particular element or limitation of the claim was plural, the accused product was held to not infringe the claims of the patent in suit.[14] The invention at issue and the accused product related to fireplaces. However, the claims referred to "rear walls" of a firebox that was part of the fireplace, rather than simply a "rear wall." The accused product had one rear wall. Ironically, the "s" was not in the patent claim as originally filed but was in the claim that ultimately issued. Therefore, little, almost innocuous, mistakes may, in certain circumstances, have a significant impact.[15]

Still, a similar point might be made in connection with other areas of law where the words used in a document, such as a contract, a will, a corporate merger agreement, or the like, if not carefully crafted, may lead to an undesirable outcome.[16]

PCDP is challenging, instead, because executing PCDP reasonably well requires an appreciation of several complex areas: the state of patent law, the state of the technology at issue, and the state of business/economic considerations often related to the technology at issue. Furthermore, these three topics are often "moving targets." To provide a few examples, new Supreme Court and/or federal circuit decisions often leave uncertain the full scope of legal

13. *See* section 2.1 and its subsections, which discusses patent claim types, the parts of a patent claim and the theory behind those parts; *see also* Chapter 3, which discusses principles of patent claim construction.

14. *See* Superior Fireplace v. Majestic Products, 270 F.3d 1358 (Fed. Cir. 2001).

15. There are also examples where mistakes in punctuation had dire consequences. *See* Cultor Corp. v. A.E. Staley, 224 F.3d 1328 (Fed. Cir. 2000), in which the federal circuit construed a claim narrowly based on a comma. *See* Allen Eng'g Corp. v. Bartell Indus., 299 F.3d 1336 (Fed. Cir. 2002), where a claim did not contain any punctuation at all at the end of the limitation and the federal circuit found the claim indefinite under 35 U.S.C. § 112 due to a truncated limitation.

16. It may be, however, that mistakes in patent claims are more "leveraged," in the sense that a patent claim is usually shorter than these examples of important legal documents that require custom drafting of language.

consequences and/or changes that may follow from those decisions. In addition, statutory changes, such as the America Invents Act (AIA), and/or regulatory changes, promulgated by the US Patent and Trademark Office (PTO), also frequently introduce change. Likewise, technological breakthroughs occurring on a weekly or daily basis may leave uncertain which technologies will remain and which will quickly be supplanted or become obsolete.

As a simple example, the movement from analog to digital modems had a significant effect on how computer networks operate. Not anticipating that change may have resulted in some patent claims that were of less value, if, for example, the claims recited analog modem technology rather than being broad enough to encompass both analog and digital modem technology.[17] Furthermore, changing economic and business conditions may also affect which technologies succeed in the marketplace and which do not. For example, difficulties in the economy may have slowed the adoption of solar technology and the adoption of more advanced cell phone networks, such as 5G and beyond. Similarly, the worldwide pandemic speeded up the adoption of technology that permits "virtual" meetings in place of "in-person" meetings. Understanding how a particular technology, especially one sought to be patented, may affect various markets, and how changes in various markets may impact the demand for the technology at issue and/or in what particular form the technology at issue will likely be sought (e.g., product demand) or deployed (e.g., product supply) may be particularly useful when drafting patent claims.

With this as background, this book will assist you in several respects. One goal is to provide up-to-date legal developments that likely affect good quality patent claim drafting.

Another goal is to provide guidance to you regarding how you may incorporate relevant technical and business knowledge to assist you in drafting patent claims of value. As you move through the sections of this book, it will become clear that considerations are discussed that amount to tools for creating excellent quality patent claims in light of legal considerations and for a variety of purposes, such as patent licensing and/or for other types of patent enforcement endeavors.

In other words, a universe of ways in which to craft a patent claim is available. To narrow this universe, useful tools include a good understanding of the

17. Likewise, there have been cases where the situation was reversed and because the claim was sufficiently broad to cover both analog and digital technology, the claim was held invalid because the analog technology predated the invention at issue. *Cf.* Personalized Media Commc'ns v. Apple, 952 F.3d 1336 (Fed. Cir. 2020) (claims avoided prior art because interpreted to mean only digital signals, rather than digital and analog signals).

technology at issue, including typical implementations, of typical competing technologies, as well as of relevant markets, including how the technology is likely to be sold or distributed, where it likely will be manufactured, and so on. With such tools, your challenge is to craft patent claims that will hopefully sail through the PTO, stand up to federal court and/or competitor scrutiny, and successfully extract the greatest amount of value through enforcement, such as via injunction, and/or in terms of damages, royalties, or other forms of valuable consideration.

In pursuit of this goal, we begin with a discussion regarding considerations that typically limit patent claim scope. It is a generally accepted principle that broad patent claims tend to provide more value than narrow patent claims.[18] As at least an initial premise, experience suggests two primary considerations appear to typically limit the scope of patent claims that are applied for and ultimately issue from the PTO.

The first of these considerations is the so-called prior art. As discussed later in detail, prior art has a specific legal meaning in this context (which changed when the relevant portion of the America Invents Act (AIA) went into force on March 16, 2013).[19] It is important that the implications of this change be fully understood to be able to draft quality patent claims. The second of these considerations, however, surprising to some, tends to be *self-imposed* claim limitations primarily derived from the commercial reasons for pursuing the patent filing.

Prior Art

Because prior art may limit claim scope, some amount of searching the prior art is frequently associated with drafting patent claims. Because the prior art is the practical limit on claim scope, knowing the prior art before drafting the claims and prior to taking a position before the PTO, in many instances, should provide an advantage; unfortunately, searches are notoriously poor while consuming valuable resources. In general, the higher the quality of the search, usually the more resources that are consumed.

Whether to search tends to be a contextually laden decision and is discussed in more detail in later sections of this book.[20] However, being able to obtain and study the best and most relevant prior art before developing or

18. *But see* section 1.31 discussing advantages and disadvantages of broad claims.

19. *See* section 1.33 and its subsections discussing in detail aspects of pre- and post-AIA statutes that provide the legal meaning of "prior art."

20. *See* section 1.32 discussing the advantages and disadvantages of searching.

drafting the patent claims is akin to knowing your opponent's argument or position before you draft your own argument. Rarely does the law provide this opportunity to an advocate, so, *if cost is not a factor*, it may be something to consider. Unfortunately, *cost usually is a factor*. Therefore, a search may not necessarily be undertaken, or the results, again, may be quite poor in that the best and most relevant prior art may not be uncovered, since only limited resources are usually allocated to this activity *at the time* the initial patent claims are prepared. Furthermore, despite the advantage just mentioned, in some circumstances, a search may not be needed and, if so, may unnecessarily add additional cost.[21] Still, two reasons to search for prior art are (1) if it turns out the exact subject matter has been done previously, knowing that early allows you to avoid the cost of pursuing a patent application; (2) knowing the best prior art allows you to draft original claims that decrease the likelihood that claim elements or limitations need to be added during prosecution and, consequently, avoid prosecution history estoppel.

As a result, as one might have inferred, some uncertainty as to the closest and most relevant prior art is likely to exist when the patent claims are submitted to the PTO. It is rarely clear at the time of filing a patent application that one has, in fact, found the best and most relevant prior art. One reason for this is because the cost of doing a completely comprehensive and thorough search would likely make pursuing a patent application prohibitively expensive. Online resources are improving so that, if needed, a useful and cost-effective search to at least uncover "low hanging fruit" may be undertaken. More typically, however, the most careful, thorough, and, therefore, costly, prior art searching is performed in conjunction with litigation or a similar type of patent assertion activity. Much more is usually at stake in a litigation (or licensing) situation than is at stake at the time an application is filed, explaining the greater allocation of resources for searching later. This may also at least partially explain why it is that new art is usually found and frequently does impact the patent claims in connection with an Inter Partes Review (IPR) or other post-grant proceeding in the PTO, for example. These proceedings frequently result from assertion of a patent. Certainly, if serious searching is undertaken prior to filing a patent application, the art found may, in fact, be highly relevant art. Typically, in this situation, an expansive and aggressive posture would be appropriate when drafting the patent claims.

---

21. Again, considerations for the decision to search are addressed in section 1.32.

To be more precise, however, regardless of whether a search is undertaken, it is usually considered good practice that the claims submitted be as expansive as reasonably possible to secure allowance of claims that will also stand up to close legal scrutiny (e.g., in light of the *known* prior art at the time of filing). Therefore, the claims should not be so broad that they are invalid as a matter of law in light of the *known* prior art. Likewise, it is a good practice for the patent drafter[22] to have a good faith argument for patentability over the *known* prior art at the time of filing.[23] Of course, there may also be some situations in which it may be best not to "swing for the fences,"[24] discussed later in some detail.

> It is usually considered good practice that the claims submitted be as expansive as reasonably possible to secure allowance of claims that will also stand up to close legal scrutiny (e.g., in light of the *known* prior art at the time of filing). The claims, however, should not be so broad that they are invalid as a matter of law in light of the *known* prior art. Likewise, it is a good practice for the patent drafter to have a good faith argument for patentability over the *known* prior art at the time of filing.

Commercial Reasons for the Patent Filing

It is a well-known fact that obtaining a patent is expensive. As the comic Henny Youngman quipped, when explaining why divorces are so expensive, "it is because they are worth it!" Individuals and/or entities would not seek to own a patent unless they believed there was something of value to be gained. Patentees expect the patent assets to be commercially valuable. Companies, such as Texas Instruments (TI), AT&T, and IBM, for example, have shown this to be true with patent licensing programs that have generated significant annual revenues. Likewise, companies such as Qualcomm and Rambus have

---

22. A variety of terms are used interchangeably throughout this book without loss of generality, such as *claim drafter*, *application drafter*, *patent drafter*, *patent practitioner*, and so on.

23. Drafting principles to avoid submitting claims that "read on" known prior art will be discussed in much more detail in section 5.5 and its subsections.

24. This topic is discussed in more detail in section 1.31, which addresses the advantages and disadvantages of broad claims.

been able to build successful licensing businesses around a portfolio of valuable patents. Nonetheless, it is also true that the value of a given patent filing, may, at best, be speculative, at the time the patent application is filed.

An expectation of commercial value plays into the patent process in several ways. Often, companies or individuals have more than one technical idea capable of being pursued and, due to limited financial and/or other resources, must limit the number of applications that receive resources in the form of time and money. Commercial value assessments are, therefore, employed to make patent application filing selections. In other words, some patent applications are not pursued so that others, believed to have more potential value, may be pursued. That is, typically the patentee has a commercial goal in mind that led to the proposed patent filing. A patent application drafter may let these commercial considerations limit, or at least strongly influence, the scope of the patent claims.

Although it may seem natural to allow such commercial reasons to dictate or limit claim scope, it is recommended that the commercial reasons for filing a patent application *not necessarily limit* the applied for claim scope. Certainly, the drafter should understand the commercial reasons behind the proposed filing, along with the inventive subject matter, and these considerations may also prove to be a helpful starting point when drafting the claims. Furthermore, as a minimum, the filed claims should address this commercial goal or goals.

However, again, experience has shown it would be wise to not permit commercial motivations to be a *strict* limit on the claim scope being pursued in the application. More specifically, due to some of the changes and uncertainties just discussed and discussed further later in this chapter, such as changes in the technology, changes in the law, changes in the economy, and even changes in the management of the company pursuing the patent application,[25] the motivations for filing the patent application years earlier may prove to be different from the commercial motivations for keeping and seeking to enforce the patent, once it issues.[26] Even at successful and patent savvy technology companies, it may be long after the patent application is filed, or even issued, that management gains a *full and complete* understanding of what makes the particular technology covered by the claims valuable in the market place.

As with the prior art, this existing uncertainty suggests taking a more expansive approach to patent claiming at the outset. It is, in essence, recommended that any and all claims that are capable of being pursued based on

---

25. *See* section 1.22 and its subsections, discussing these considerations.
26. It may take three to five years or even longer for a patent application to issue as a patent.

the technology be included in the application except where cost prohibitive; for example, typical claims to include are method claims, component claims, system claims, software claims, manufacturing claims, and so on.[27] Of course, some clients may not want to absorb the associated expense of filing with many claims, which dictates a more measured approach in which claim types are prioritized based on the situation.[28]

However, it is useful to recognize now that patents may be employed in a wide variety of circumstances, including to protect the patentee's competitive advantage against imitators, to have something to assert if a competitor with patents pursues the patentee with its patents, to obtain licensing revenue, and/or to obtain other value. A variety of different patent claims that vary in scope in diverse ways increases the likelihood that the full value of the patented technology will be extracted. Furthermore, patent claims to protect against imitation may be drafted differently from patent claims to provide defensive protection in the event a competitor asserts its patents. It follows with this potential for significantly varying claims, that the time to draft such claims to cover these possible eventualities *is better accomplished prior to filing*, rather than after the patent application has already been filed, prosecuted, and is about to issue, for example. Of course, it almost goes without saying that the patent claims must also be adequately supported by the specification of the patent application to avoid legal risks, such as want of written description or the risk that undesirable limitations will be "read" into the claims from the specification, as explained in more detail in later chapters.[29] These are yet additional reasons to consider and draft patent claims early that cover the *full* scope of the subject matter of the patent application.

> The preferred time to draft claims to fully cover the subject matter of a patent application is prior to filing, rather than after the patent application has already been filed, prosecuted, and is about to issue.

27. The types of claims available to include in a patent application are introduced in the subsections of section 2.11, and discussed in more detail in the sections of Chapter 4.

28. *See* the subsections of section 2.11, in which aspects of different claim types are introduced, and the sections of Chapter 4, in which these claim types are discussed in more detail.

29. *See* subsection 2.1414 and section 5.4 (including subsections), which discuss importing limitations from the specification into the claims, want of written description, and other claim drafting issues that constitute non-prior art claiming issues.

Some simple examples regarding the benefits of a more expansive approach to claim drafting, as suggested, may provide perspective. A patent attorney writing an application for a component manufacturer may make a regular practice of omitting patent claims to end-product apparatuses or systems that would incorporate such components. The reasoning might be that the manufacturer is not likely to sue its own customers or even potential customers, that is, companies that manufacture end products that include the component. Claims may, therefore, be limited to the component sold. Furthermore, it may be reasoned, how much does claiming the component in an end product typically add in terms of patentability?

For example, a memory manufacturer, your client, may choose to omit claims to devices that employ the memory being sold, such as desktop computers, servers, cell phones, tablets, and laptops. However, as one example of changing circumstances, a customer of your client that is an original equipment manufacturer (OEM) or perhaps a system integrator might acquire a memory manufacturing business allowing it to produce that component internally and reduce its costs. Now, the OEM that *was* a customer of your client has become a direct competitor of that client.

One might believe that, even here, patenting component claims directed to memory devices should be sufficient to handle the new situation, and this might be correct; however, keep in mind that memory is not the core business for this entity that has just become a competitor. Claims directed to the entity's core business may be more helpful if a dispute with your client develops.

In a different turn of events, perhaps a different OEM, which does not purchase the component from your client/the patentee, sues your client to reduce the supply of components to your client's customer/the different OEM's competitor, or, at least, to increase the costs of your client's customer/the different OEM's competitor. In such a case, having component claims in a patent owned by your client may prove less valuable against this OEM that is suing your client than having claims that cover an end product incorporating such a component. One reason is because typically the OEM suing your client will have obtained a contractual indemnity against patent infringement from its component supplier and, thus, may not be as concerned about defending a countersuit involving the component itself. However, as implied by the last example, a lawsuit that has the potential to threaten the core business of the aggressor may prove more worrisome and may even bring that company to the bargaining table before trial has concluded or even begun.

Likewise, this latter hypothetical situation may have implications related to international manufacturing and importation into the United States. For example, the company suing your client may purchase components manufactured abroad and, likewise, may have a system integrator then complete assembly of the end product abroad before being imported into the United States for sale to its customers. In this scenario, again, component claims may be of little use, since U.S. Customs would need to take apart the end product entering U.S. borders to find infringing components (which almost certainly will *not* occur) before being able to stop shipment into the United States; however, in contrast, claims directed to the end product may be sufficient to obtain an exclusion order that would keep the infringing end product from coming into the United States for sale. In short, many factors that are difficult to know ahead of time will play into which claims might be the most useful in a lawsuit, patent license negotiation, or other business/dispute-type situation.

The real point with these examples is that the claims should be drafted so that *as many legal options as is feasible* remain available for the time when the patent may be needed. Given this starting principle, it is recommended that the commercial motivation for filing a patent application be well understood, but not necessarily be employed to *strictly* limit the scope of the claims being pursued.

> The real point is that the claims should be drafted so that *as many legal options as is feasible* remain available for the time when the patent may be needed. Given this starting principle, it is recommended that the commercial motivation for the filing of a patent application be well understood, but not necessarily be employed to *strictly* limit the scope of the claims being pursued.

1.2 Business Strategy Drives Patent Strategy

A patent is a legal document; however, it has value in that it supports a business. Business strategy should and does drive patent strategy (and, more generally, intellectual property (IP) strategy).

For a company with a relatively large business involving several product lines, and perhaps even several divisions, there may be a different business strategy for each and, likewise, a different intellectual property/patent strategy for each. For example, in the previous hypothetical, a manufacturer may manufacture a product sold to consumers, such as a mobile device, as well as manufacture components for such a device sold to system integrators of mobile (as well as other types of) devices. One example of a company like this is Samsung, which manufactures components for cell phones and other electronic devices, like memory, and also manufactures cell phones. For example, with a consumer product (e.g., a mobile device), the business strategy may be to maximize consumer appeal; whereas for components, such as chips, the business strategy may be to maximize "wafer starts" (e.g., maximize production because chips are manufactured in wafers that are then subdivided into semiconductor chips).

Similarly, these products may have various forms of intellectual property associated with each, such as copyrights (e.g., for software and/or a graphical user interface (GUI)), trade secrets, and/or patents. Of course, a detailed discussion of other IP is beyond the scope of this work. However, this illustrates that issues may become complex for a large business with multiple products.

Our focus here is *patent* strategy and tactics. Nonetheless, patent strategy and tactics do not exist in isolation. Rather, a larger business strategy may involve various forms of IP with different strategies associated with each.

To be more specific, as an example, there may be trade secrets and know-how associated with semiconductor chip fabrication as well as patents. This is a typical occurrence. A manufacturing process that results in a product may have aspects of the process that are considered better protected as trade secrets, whereas other aspects of the process may be better protected with patents. Likewise, the result of the process may be protected with patents. The goal of trade secret protection may be to keep competitors from copying the details of a manufacturing process that provides a competitive advantage. This may also be a goal of patent protection, but patent protection may also provide other goals, as discussed in more detail in the next section.

IP, particularly patents, generally supports a business by creating a *legal* barrier to entry against competition. This permits a business to protect or increase its market share and protect its profit margin. The specifics of how this may play out generally defines the patent strategy and, at a more detailed level, may define associated tactics. The line between strategy and tactics is not always a clear one; however, one way to view the difference is that patent strategy usually concerns how to approach a portfolio of patents associated with a business. In contrast, claim-level decision-making for a specific patent may be thought of as more tactical in nature.

1.21 Identify the Patent Strategy Objective

The value in having a patent is that it provides a legal barrier to entry permitting a business to protect its competitive advantage. It may be thought of as protection to guard "the castle," so to speak (i.e., a core business). This relies on the exclusionary nature of a patent in that it provides exclusive rights to the subject matter protected by the patent (e.g., covered by the patent claims). It is helpful to understand that a patent does *not* give the owner a right to do something; rather, a patent gives the owner a right to *prevent others* from doing something.

Specifically, 35 USC section 154(a)(1) (2022) states:

> Every patent shall contain a short title of the invention and a grant to the patentee, his heirs or assigns, of **the right to exclude others** from making, using, offering for sale, or selling the invention throughout the United States or importing the invention into the United States, and, if the invention is a process, of **the right to exclude others** from using, offering for sale or selling throughout the United States, or importing into the United States, products made by that process, referring to the specification for the particulars thereof (emphasis supplied).

Thus, the owner of a patent may *prevent others* from making, using, selling, offering for sale, or importing the patented invention. The "invention" refers to subject matter that falls within the scope of the patent claims of the patent.

At a high level, how a patent may be used reduces to a few things. One may (1) choose to rely on the exclusive nature of a patent (i.e., it may be used to prevent others from practicing the invention). This, however, may entail enforcement, which may lead to litigation and a formal challenge to the validity of the patent. A patent may also (2) be licensed, for royalty income or other valuable consideration (such as equity, for example). Licensing a patent may advance the interests of a business by generating income, for example, while imposing a cost on a competitor who is paying the royalty income. Likewise, a license may provide information and/or partial control over your competitor in that the competitor is subject to audits and may be limited under the license to producing only a certain amount of product, for example. Consequently, this too may assist in protecting the castle. A third use of a patent may be to (3) consummate a patent cross-license. Some people refer to this as "design freedom," meaning the product designs are not limited by designing a product in such a manner as to avoid infringing patents of the other party to the cross-license. This protects the castle in that if the business is infringing a competitor's patent, rather than paying royalty income, which would reduce the after-tax bottom line income of a business, a trade of patent rights occurs.

Patent cross-licensing is considered procompetitive by the Department of Justice and the Federal Trade Commission in that it makes technology available to market participants.[30] There are many examples, but one particularly good example is the semiconductor chip manufacturing industry. To fabricate a semiconductor chip requires many complex technologies and no single company owns all the patents needed. Without patent cross-licensing, probably no one would be able to manufacture a semiconductor chip without infringing someone else's patents.

Finally, the fourth use of a patent, which has become more popular in recent years, is a sale or assignment of a patent. For example, large companies that have large numbers of patents may find that some of its patents cover technology that it is no longer using or was never using. The patents, however, are business assets. One way to realize the value of these assets that are otherwise not contributing to the business is via a sale to generate income.

1.211 Claim Drafting Tactical and Strategy Illustrations

A way to gain an appreciation for patent claim drafting tactics and strategy is to look at some typical examples of patent claims in various situations. However, as background, one should understand the elements of a cause of action for patent infringement. In general, two elements must be pled and proven to make out a prima facie case of patent infringement: (1) ownership of the patent and (2) that the accused product or service falls within the scope of at least one of the patent claims.[31]

Whether the accused product or service falls within the scope of a patent claim is judged under the "all elements rule." To find infringement under the all elements rule, an accused device (or service) must contain each and every element and limitation of a single patent claim in the manner recited in the patent claim, either literally or by an equivalent.[32]

A similar rule is used to determine whether a patent claim is not novel, referred to as anticipation. Under the all elements rule, for a claim to be anticipated (not novel), a single prior art reference must contain each and every

---

30. *See* U.S. Dep't of Just., Antitrust Guidelines for the Licensing of Intellectual Property (Jan. 12, 2017), https://www.justice.gov/atr/IPguidelines/download.

31. *See, e.g.*, Hall v. Bed Bath & Beyond, Inc., 705 F.3d 1357, 1362 (Fed. Cir. 2013) (citing Phonometrics, Inc. v. Hosp. Franchise Sys., Inc., 203 F.3d 790, 794 (Fed. Cir. 2000)).

32. *See, e.g.*, TIP Sys., LLC v. Phillips & Brooks/Gladwin, Inc., 529 F.3d 1364 (Fed. Cir. 2008).

element and limitation of a single patent claim in the manner recited in the patent claim. One maxim of patent law is "that which infringes if later in time, anticipates if earlier in time." The federal circuit has noted the maxim should really be "that which *literally* infringes if later, anticipates if earlier."[33] This brings out the difference that a patent claim may be infringed under the doctrine of equivalents,[34] which is not literally within the scope of the patent claim (hence, referred to as "non-literal infringement"), but that doctrine is not used to determine anticipation. Nonetheless, it is helpful to think of infringement and prior art with respect to patent claims as a sort of balanced equation. With few exceptions,[35] analysis of the scope of a patent claim is the same for direct, literal infringement as it is for anticipation of that claim.

The analysis undertaken is often referred to as "reading a claim" onto the accused device or "reading a claim" onto the prior art. That is, for purposes of literal, direct patent infringement, to determine if a patent claim is literally and directly infringed, each and every element and limitation of the claim is considered and must be found in the accused device in the manner recited in the claim. Likewise, for prior art to anticipate a patent claim, rendering it invalid, each and every element and limitation of the claim is considered and must be found in a single item of prior art in the manner recited in the claim.

Consider the following patent claim:

EXAMPLE 1.2

I claim:

1. An apparatus comprising:

   a substantially horizontally oriented, rectangularly shaped seat including four corners;

   wherein attached to a respective corner of the seat are four substantially vertically oriented legs such that the legs point in the same direction away from the seat, are oriented to be substantially mutually parallel, and are of substantially the same length.

---

33. *See* Marine, Inc. v. Barient, Inc. 827 F.2d 744 (Fed. Cir. 1987).

34. *See* section 3.23 and its subsections discussing the doctrine of equivalents (DOE).

35. One exception is product-by-process claims, introduced in a subsection of section 1.22, further discussed in Chapter 2 in connection with a discussion of method claims, and discussed in more detail in section 4.125 and its subsections.

Many will recognize that this simple claim covers a chair or a four-legged stool. The claim does not recite a chair back; nonetheless, due to the use of the word *comprising*, referred to as "open" form, as long as an accused product includes all the elements and limitations in the manner recited in the claim, the claim is infringed, even if the accused product includes other features not recited in the claim, such as a back. However, because of the choices made for the claimed features in Example 1.2, chairs or stools that have seats of a shape other than rectangular would not be covered by the claim. That is, the claim *cannot be read* on a circular seated stool or, similarly, a three-legged stool. That is, express features of the claim would be missing.

> Due to the use of the word *comprising*, referred to as "open" form, as long as an accused product includes all the elements and limitations in the manner recited in the claim, the claim is infringed, even if the accused product includes other features not recited in the claim.

Conducting a similar analysis regarding prior art, the claim, of course, would be invalid as anticipated under current law if it were an issued claim and such a chair meeting all the elements and limitations of claim 1 were in the prior art. However, the claim is not anticipated by a circular seated stool or a three-legged stool (although the claim might be rendered obvious by such prior art). To anticipate a claim, the prior art must include each and every element and limitation in the manner recited in the claim. A four-legged stool with a rectangular-shaped seat or a four-legged chair with a rectangular-shaped seat and meeting the other limitations of the claim would anticipate the claim, if it was in the prior art. Likewise, a similar analysis regarding "comprising" applies with respect to prior art. That is, the prior art may show additional features beyond those recited and still anticipate a patent claim.

Having considered the elements of a patent infringement cause of action and the process of reading a claim on an accused device or prior art, we next consider some more complex situations involving technology and patent claiming tactics and strategy.

1.2111 Component Manufacturer

Now that we have a basic understanding of a cause of action for patent infringement and the technique of "reading" a claim on an accused device and on the prior art, we take up some claiming issues that might confront someone drafting a patent claim for a component manufacturer versus those that might confront someone drafting a patent claim for a system integrator. *However, one should appreciate that the following examples and discussion provide only an introduction to common strategic and tactical issues involving component and system leveling claiming. If the reader has a feeling that there is more to understand, that is correct. These examples are provided as a tool to introduce some basic patent claim drafting concepts and help the reader gain some initial appreciation of a few strategic and tactical considerations in this area.*

Among other lessons, these examples illustrate the importance of understanding the technology being claimed, including aspects such as its technical value, its commercial value, how it might be distributed or sold, how use might be detected, how it might be used, how it might potentially change, and how it might be designed around.[36]

To make this more concrete, we consider a technical problem for a computer system involving transfers into or out of memory, usually to or from a peripheral device, such as a hard drive, a graphics card, a network interface card, and so on. These transfers may be thought of as transfers of *physical* signal values and/or *physical* state values.[37]

Typically, a central processing unit, abbreviated CPU (e.g., microprocessor), controls such transfers within a computer system. This approach has several disadvantages, however. It both ties up the resources of the CPU and it slows the transfer by adding latency due to overhead from having the CPU involved in the transfer.

A type of transfer into and out of memory was later invented, referred to as "burst mode." Although the CPU initiates such a transfer and provides a starting memory address and word count for the transfer, after initiation, the operation is controlled by a memory controller, which takes control of the system bus from the processor. After the transfer is complete, the CPU is notified and resumes control of the system bus.

Burst mode refers to a transfer of contents into or out of sequential memory cells in a "burst," rather than transfer of contents into and out of memory a single memory cell at a time. While the initial transfer (first memory cell) in burst mode may take as long as a transfer to or from a single memory cell, the subsequent memory transfers in burst mode each take a fraction of the time.

---

36. *See*, for example, Chapters 4, 5, and 6, which include sections directed to many of these topics.

37. This clarifies that these qualify as potentially patentable subject matter under 35 U.S.C. § 101 (2022).

For example, it might take a 100 MHz 32-bit bus about five bus cycles for a transfer of the contents of one cell that involves the CPU, whereas, in burst mode, after the initial transfer, it may take one bus cycle per memory cell. If substantial amounts of memory cells are involved, the savings in terms of time may be significant.

"Rewind" now to when burst mode was invented and assume it was sought to be patented. Claiming burst mode operation at the component level can be tricky. Burst mode operation involves the CPU, the memory cells, the memory controller, the system bus, and, perhaps, a peripheral. However, a claim that includes all these elements would be infringed by a system integrator or someone selling an end product, such as a mobile device, but not necessarily by someone manufacturing only a component, such as memory with a memory controller.

To capture a memory manufacturer, therefore, *burst mode should be claimed from the perspective of the memory component.* We start with an apparatus claim, since that covers rights to make, use, sell, offer for sale, and import the claimed invention. Based on the prior technical description, here is a possible patent claim:

EXAMPLE 1.3

I claim:

1. An apparatus comprising:

   random access memory (RAM) and a memory controller;

   wherein the memory controller is capable of initiating burst mode operation based, at least in part, on receipt of a request from a central processing unit (CPU);

   wherein the request is to include a memory address, a word count, and a read or a write control transfer designation; and

   wherein the memory controller is to process the request and take control of a system transfer bus.

To begin, please take note that we have previously described a technical problem that was present before the invention of burst mode and the claim is intended to cover a possible technical solution to the technical problem. This approach is more typical of patent prosecution in Europe, but it is a helpful way to think about technology and patent claims.[38] This approach becomes especially important in connection with software-related inventions, discussed later.[39]

Also, as a quick point, observe the language "initiating burst mode operation *based, at least in part, on* receipt of a request from a central processing unit (CPU)." The formulation "based, at least in part, on" is a handy one to make it clear that while a factor, such as a receipt of a request, may influence a feature, such as, here, initiating burst mode operation, there may be other factors as well. *Often, claim drafting amounts to making explicit what in layman's terms might be understood.* For example, if one merely stated "initiating burst mode operation based on receipt of a request from a central processing unit (CPU)," it might be understood that this is not meant to say it is based *only* on receipt of a request from a central processing unit. Because this language leaves no room for other influences, if used in a claim, an opponent may persuasively argue you are stuck with the exact language used since the burden should be on the drafter as the "least cost avoider" to make sure the language is clear regarding its scope.[40] Likewise, as another drafting point, "capable of initiating burst mode operation" is probably better than "capable of burst mode operation" since the former language is likely to be interpreted as broader than the latter language.

Although the claim mentions the CPU, it is from the perspective of receipt of a burst mode request. For example, the claim could omit the source of the request by stating "based, at least in part, on receipt of a request." Similarly, the claim mentions the system bus, but, again, from the perspective of assuming control. Thus, although the CPU and system bus are mentioned in the claim, it is drafted in a manner so that at least arguably these are not needed to be present for literal direct infringement, although the accused device should still be capable to meet these limitations.[41] That is, if a memory is made, used, or sold with the capability claimed, that memory should infringe the claim *without* necessarily having a CPU and system bus as part of the accused product.

These features are limitations of the claim but are intended to not be required elements for infringement. One way to view this is that the features

38. *See* Chris Konkol, *The 'Problem Solved' in In re Wright and In re Dillon*, IDEA J. Law & Tech. 131 (1990).

39. *See* section 5.44 and its subsections which discuss the issue of claiming software.

40. *See* Sage Products v. Devon, 126 F.3d 1420 (Fed. Cir. 1997).

41. *See* section 2.1411, which discusses the difference between a claim element and a claim limitation. *See also* section 2.1413.

are limitations of the claim, but not claim elements.[42] This might be made clearer through language added to claim 1 indicating that the CPU is external to the RAM and that the request is externally derived. An additional consideration to make such an intent even clearer might be to add a dependent claim that expressly adds the CPU and the system bus as claim elements, as follows.[43]

> 2. The apparatus of claim 1, comprising: the CPU and the system transfer bus, wherein the CPU is external to the RAM and memory controller, and the system transfer bus is external to the RAM and memory controller.

Such dependencies are suggested here to address infringement-type drafting considerations. That is, these dependencies are intended to increase the possibility that the claims (dependent and independent) will be interpreted in a manner that makes infringement more likely.

A more common use of dependent claims, however, relates to adding limitations that capture potential infringers while also providing a narrower dependent claim to reduce the risk of invalidity based on prior art, yet another tactical consideration.

At the time of filing, the patent drafter does not typically know the closest prior art.[44] Rather, it may take an inter partes review (IPR), a litigation, or even several litigations to locate such art, for example. Therefore, dependent claims are a type of hedge that narrow the base claim so that all is not lost if prior art is found that renders the base claim (called the "independent claim"[45]) invalid.

As an example, in that regard, perhaps one might consider this dependent claim:

> 2. The apparatus of claim 1, wherein the memory controller comprises an address register, a word count register, and a transfer mode register.

It is more likely that this claim will stand up against prior art by describing and claiming internal components of the memory controller. However, at the same time, the elements added are ones that almost any memory controller

---

42. *See* Dawn Equip. Co. v. Kentucky Farms, Inc., 140 F.3d 1009, 1014 n.1 (Fed. Cir. 1998). *See* discussion in sections 2.1411 and 2.1413 regarding the difference between a claim element and a claim limitation.

43. *See* section 6.4 and its subsections, discussing claiming higher levels of integration through dependent claims or separate independent claims.

44. *See* section 1.32, which discusses the advantages and disadvantages of searching.

45. *See* discussion of independent and dependent claims in Chapter 2.

implementing burst mode would likely include, which is desirable from an infringement perspective.

Previously, claim 1 recited "an apparatus." A perhaps simpler approach, however, might be to draft a claim to an integrated circuit chip (or module) that claims the memory controller specifically, such as:

I claim:

1. An integrated circuit comprising:

 random access memory (RAM) and a memory controller; . . .

One might then argue that the royalty base is an integrated circuit chip (or module), whereas previously an adversary might have argued that in light of the initially presented claim 1, the royalty base was potentially *only* that portion of a chip or module that includes the memory and memory controller, so that any damages are arguably less due to the smaller royalty base. One problem with the latter example, however, is that claim's "preamble" (e.g., in claim 1 as just presented, the part of the claim after the claim number and before the transition word *comprising*) is not necessarily limiting.[46] One might, therefore, to be conservative, move the integrated circuit (or module) limitation to the body of the claim (e.g., in claim 1, the part of the claim after the transition word *comprising* and the colon and before the period):

I claim:

1. An apparatus comprising:

 an integrated circuit including random access memory (RAM) and a memory controller; . . .

---

46. *See* Chapter 2 discussing the claim preamble and the claim body in detail.

This might, for example, potentially affect damages by making it clearer that an entire chip (or module) rather than just a part of a chip (or module) is the royalty base.[47] These are, of course, only a few options of many available to the drafter.

Likewise, another claim type to consider is an apparatus means plus function claim,[48] such as:

EXAMPLE 1.4

I claim:

1. An apparatus comprising:

   means for storing memory states and means for controlling the means for storing memory states;

   wherein the means for controlling comprises means for initiating burst mode operation based, at least in part, on receipt of a request from central means for processing memory states;

   wherein the request is to include a memory address, a word count, and a read or a write control transfer designation; and

   wherein the means for controlling comprises means for processing the request and means for taking control of a system transfer bus.

For most purposes, the term "means plus function claim" refers to a claim in which at least part of the claim recites a means for performing a specified function, which is permitted under 35 USC section 112(f).[49] These claims have many pitfalls, which are discussed in detail later[50] in this book.

Here, tactical and strategic differences between claims construed under section 112(f) and claims not construed under section 112(f) are highlighted. 35 USC section 112(f) specifically states:

47. *See* section 6.4 and its subsections, which discuss damages issues in connection with claim drafting.

48. *See* section 4.123 and its subsections, discussing drafting of means plus function claims.

49. Before the AIA, this was 35 U.S.C. § 112, ¶ 6; however, throughout this book it is referenced as 35 U.S.C. § 112(f) (2022).

50. *See* section 4.123 and its subsections, discussing drafting of means plus function claims.

(f) Element in Claim for a COMBINATION.—An element in a claim for a combination may be expressed as a means or step for performing a specified function without the recital of structure, material, or acts in support thereof, and such claim shall be construed to cover the corresponding structure, material, or acts described in the specification and equivalents thereof.

Therefore, rather than reciting so-called structural claim elements, the claim typically[51] recites "means for. . ." and a function to be performed. The difference between structure and function in an apparatus patent claim is described as reciting what the apparatus does (i.e., function) rather than what it is (i.e., structure).[52] As an example, rather than "memory," the claim recites "means for storing memory states."

The means plus function apparatus claim closely tracks the initially drafted apparatus claim. This is not required, but it is done here to make it clear that the drafter intends that the two claims have different scopes.[53] This topic is discussed more later.[54] In general, because of the language of section 112(f), means plus function claims (i.e., claims with clauses construed under section 112(f)) are usually narrower than similar claims without clauses construed under section 112(f). Sometimes one may want a broad construction (e.g., to capture a potential infringer); sometimes one may want a narrow construction (e.g., to avoid prior art). This latter point helps explain the use of this claim type.

Another claim to consider from a strategic and tactical perspective is a method of using claim. Many differences between apparatus and method claims exist that are relevant to patent claiming strategy and tactics. At one of the most basic levels, the set of rights granted is different. An apparatus claim provides the full set of statutory rights, which is: make, use, sell, and so on.[55] On the other hand, due to an inherent nature, a method claim essentially covers "use," as in a method of using, or "make," as in a method of making or manufacturing. At least partially for this reason, apparatus claims are usually perceived to be more valuable than method claims. However, do not read this to suggest that method claims are not valuable. In various situations, having a method claim may be important to have as an arrow in your quiver. It is

51. Law exists in which claims are construed under section 112(f) despite not reciting "means for." Generally, as discussed in later sections, claims are able to be drafted to reduce the risk of such an outcome. *See* section 4.123 and its subsections.

52. *See, e.g., In re* Swinehart, 439 F.2d 210 (C.C.P.A. 1971).

53. *But see* Mas-Hamilton Group v. La Gard, Inc., 156 F.3d 1206, 1214 (Fed. Cir. 1998). *See* section 4.123 and its subsections, discussing drafting of means plus function claims.

54. *See* section 4.123 and its subsections, discussing drafting of means plus function claims.

55. *See* 35 U.S.C. § 271(a) (2022).

recommended to nearly always include method claims with apparatus claims for claim diversity. Many patents are written that do not follow this simple principle.

> It is recommended to nearly always include method claims with apparatus claims for claim diversity.

Usually, an invention will more easily be claimed as one or the other, that is, as a method or as an apparatus. For example, software operation is usually more easily described as a method. Although not a requirement, it seems logical when beginning to draft claims for an invention, to begin with the claim type that is more easily drafted due to the inherent nature of the invention. In Example 1.3, the technology seems to more easily be described as an apparatus, hence, the rationale for starting with that claim type.

> Usually, an invention will more easily be claimed as one or the other, that is, as a method or as an apparatus. Although not a requirement, it seems logical when beginning to draft claims for an invention, to begin with the claim type that is more easily drafted due to the inherent nature of the invention.

Regardless, do not pass on the opportunity to claim the invention in method terms, in addition to apparatus terms. A litany of good reasons to do this exists. A method may stand up to prior art even in situations where an apparatus claim may not.[56] Depending on the limitations of the patent claim, a method claim may be infringed where an apparatus claim is not or it may be infringed in a different manner.[57] Further, a pure method claim generally is much less likely to be construed under section 112(f).[58] The failure to claim

---

56. *See* section 2.112 and its subsections which introduce method claims. *See also* sections 4.126, 4.127 and their subsections, which further discuss method claims and also include a discussion regarding claims directed to a new use of an old device.

57. *Id.*

58. *Id.*

a method also has the potential to dedicate to the public subject matter that might have otherwise been covered.[59] Other good reasons also exist to include method claims, but these reasons should be more than sufficient.

Here is a possible method of using claim related to the previous apparatus claim for burst mode.

EXAMPLE 1.5

I claim:

1. A method comprising: [60]

   receiving a request for burst mode operation;

   transmitting a request for control of a system bus in response to the received request;

   receiving a signal granting system bus control;

   transferring signals across the system bus into or out of a group of sequential memory cells after receiving the signal granting system bus control; and

   transmitting a signal indicating completion of the signal transfer.

One aspect to appreciate is the difference in drafting a method claim versus drafting an apparatus claim that flows from the preceding discussion about the set of rights for each. A method claim recites actions or operations. A method claim is infringed by performing an action or an operation, such as when using something or making something. Hence, the claim elements are actions like "receiving," "transmitting," and so on.

---

59. *See* Johnson & Johnston Assocs. v. R.E. Serv. Co., 285 F.3d 1046 (Fed. Cir. 2002) (en banc).

60. *See* Seal-Flex Inc. v. Athletic Track & Ct. Constr., 172 F.3d 836 (Fed. Cir. 1999). It used to be common to state "A method comprising the steps of:" However, it might be possible that the use of the word step might invoke section 112(f). *See* section 4.123, discussing means plus function and step plus function claims. A concurrence by Judge Rader in this case suggests that "comprising the steps of" would not be a problem, but best to avoid such questions by good drafting practice. Therefore, "comprising the steps of" is omitted, which has now become the common practice.

One way to think of a method claim is like a cooking recipe. It specifies the steps to follow. In contrast, an apparatus may often be capable of performing an action or an operation, but it is important to not claim an apparatus in a manner that suggests the apparatus is actually performing such actions or operations.[61] Thus, an apparatus claim either recites structural elements, such as a processor or memory, or it recites that such elements are able to perform an action, to make it clear that the action itself is not being claimed, the latter being the domain of method claims.

One way to think of a method claim is like a cooking recipe. It specifies the steps to follow.

The opportunity to claim a method of making even in situations where that is not necessarily the feature that is inventive should also not be overlooked.[62] Regarding Example 1.3, nothing about the invention appears to relate to fabrication or manufacture. Nonetheless, semiconductor chips shall be manufactured that are capable of burst mode operation. Why not include such a patent claim in one's arsenal? For example, it is becoming more common for companies, so-called fabless design houses, to outsource chip manufacturing to others. Coming up with the design does not generally by itself directly infringe a patent claim.[63] Yet, a claim directed to a company making the chip for someone else may have some value.[64]

Here is a possible method of making claim corresponding to Example 1.3:

---

61. *See, e.g.*, IPXL Holdings v. Amazon, 430 F.3d 1377, 1384 (Fed. Cir. 2005). *See* section 5.6 and its subsections, which discuss the problem of mixing statutory classes of patent claims in a single patent claim. *Cf.* INVT SPE LLC v. ITC, Appeal No. 20-1903 (Fed. Cir. August 31, 2022) (distinguishing between actual operation and capability of operating or performing for apparatus claims, particularly for software on a device, which tends to be functional, without discussing indefiniteness issue of mixing method and apparatus limitations), discussed in subsections 4.124 and 4.1272.

62. A similar observation applies to method of using claims. However, this observation about method of making claims is made here because while it is reasonably common to include method of using claims with apparatus claims, it is less common to include method of making claims unless the inventive concept is specifically related to fabrication, for example.

63. Although it might be a basis for a claim for indirect infringement; *see* section 3.22 and its subsections, discussing indirect infringement.

64. *See* section 4.127 and its sections, discussing method of making claims. *See also* section 2.112 and its sections, discussing method claims. This is also helpful because direct patent infringement is generally easier to prove than indirect patent infringement. *See* section 3.22 and its sections, discussing indirect infringement.

EXAMPLE 1.6

I claim:

1. A method of fabricating a memory controller and random access memory (RAM) comprising:

   fabricating an integrated circuit (IC) that includes a memory controller with random access memory (RAM) on the IC, wherein the memory controller and RAM are fabricated in an electrical configuration on a silicon substrate of the IC;

   wherein the fabricating includes forming transistors for the memory controller and RAM on the silicon substrate, wherein the transistors respectively include a source, a drain, and a gate;

   wherein the fabricating further includes fabricating the memory controller to be capable of initiating burst mode operation based, at least in part, on receipt of a request from a central processing unit (CPU) in which the request is to include a memory address, a word count, and a read or a write control transfer designation; and

   wherein the fabricating further includes fabricating the memory controller to be capable to process the request and take control of a system transfer bus.

Furthermore, the fabrication operations could be described more fully with dependent claims as follows, as examples:

---

2. The method of claim 1, wherein the fabricating that includes forming the transistors comprises:

   forming the gate from a conductive gate layer and an oxide layer over a silicon layer of the silicon substrate; and

   forming two N+ regions in the silicon layer via ion implantation or diffusion to form the source and the drain.

3. The method of claim 2, wherein the conductive gate layer comprises a polysilicon layer, and wherein the forming the gate from the conductive gate layer comprises forming the gate from the polysilicon gate layer.

Although claims 2 and 3 describe well-known fabrication operations as long as the base claim is patentable based on the burst mode limitations, that is not a problem regarding patentability of these claims.[65]

One limiting factor to consider is how easy or difficult would it be to discover or prove infringement of a method claim, particularly a manufacturing claim. For example, if there is little or no way to discover from the end product that a particular process was used to make the end product, this technology might be better protected as a trade secret.[66]

As one example, consider that in the aircraft manufacturing industry many holes are typically created in metal structures, such as for an engine, for a fuselage, and so on. The ability to create more precise holes, more quickly, and at a cheaper cost may, therefore, provide a competitive advantage. With the advent of laser technology, it seems likely that some type of laser was developed for such processes. However, it might be difficult or nearly impossible to determine how such a hole was generated during manufacture from looking at the end product. Consequently, assuming such laser technology was developed and even assuming it was patentable at the time of its creation, a patent on such technology may be difficult to enforce. Furthermore, by filing a patent application with 18-month publication, one would be educating one's competitors on how to perform such a process (again, a process performed behind closed doors and difficult to discover). Instead, as suggested, such technology may be better protected as a trade secret.

Another limiting factor for a fabless design house seeking a manufacturing claim may be that some so-called foundries that perform manufacturing for other fabless design houses are located outside the United States.[67] Such manufacture, therefore, may at times be beyond the territorial scope of U.S. patent law for a claim of infringement under 35 USC section 271(a). However, there are statutes directed to extraterritorial patent infringement.[68]

That was a relatively quick survey and introduction to various approaches to claiming an invention. We will return to this example in later sections as we explore the forgoing and other concepts in more detail.

---

65. *See* section 2.15 and its subsections, discussing dependent and independent claims.

66. Subject to other considerations, such as turnover in the industry and/or how easy it might be to limit knowledge of the technology to a few individuals within the company that developed it, as a few examples of considerations that may affect the desirability of trade secret protection.

67. One well-known example being Taiwan Semiconductor Manufacturing Company Limited (TSMC).

68. *See* 35 U.S.C. § 271(f), (g) (2022). *See* section 4.1252, discussing 35 U.S.C. § 271 (g) (2022).

1.2112 System Integrator

A system integrator is, in a sense, the flip side of a component manufacturer. The two frequently have a symbiotic relationship. A component manufacturer is a supplier to a system integrator. Similarly, a system integrator is a customer of a component manufacturer. It follows many of the considerations previously highlighted are similar or even the same. For convenience, following is a description of the previous technology example from the previous section.

As discussed, typically, a CPU (e.g., microprocessor) controls memory transfers within a computer system. This approach has several disadvantages, however. It both ties up the resources of the CPU and it slows the transfer by adding latency due to overhead from having the CPU involved in the transfer.

A type of transfer into and out of memory was invented, referred to as "burst mode." Although the CPU initiates such a transfer and provides a starting memory address and word count for the transfer, after initiation, the operation is controlled by a memory controller, which takes control of the system bus from the processor. After the transfer is complete, the CPU is notified and resumes control of the system bus.

Burst mode refers to transfer of contents "in a burst" into or out of sequential memory cells, rather than transfer of the contents a single memory cell at a time. While the initial transfer in burst mode (i.e., first memory cell transfer) may take as long as a transfer to or from a single memory cell, the subsequent memory cell transfers each take a fraction of the time. For example, it might take a 100 MHz 32-bit bus about five bus cycles for a transfer of the contents of one memory cell that involves the CPU, whereas, in burst mode, after the initial transfer to a first memory cell, it may take one bus cycle per memory cell. If a large amount of memory cells is involved, the savings in terms of time may be significant.

Previously, our example was to claim burst mode operation at the component level. However, from the technical description, burst mode operation involves the CPU, the memory cells, the memory controller, the system bus, and, perhaps, a peripheral. A claim that includes all these elements would be infringed by a system integrator or someone selling an end product, such as a mobile device, which includes a memory controller to implement burst mode, but not necessarily by someone manufacturing or selling only the memory controller. To capture a memory manufacturer, burst mode may be claimed from the perspective of the memory component, as demonstrated in the prior section.[69]

69. *See* section 1.2111, discussing claims for a component manufacturer.

As before, we start with an apparatus claim, since that covers rights to make, use, sell, offer for sale, and import the claimed invention. However, unlike previously, here, we claim a system of components (termed "a system claim").

EXAMPLE 1.7

I claim:

1. An apparatus comprising:

   random access memory (RAM), a memory controller, a central processing unit (CPU), and a system bus;

   wherein the memory controller is capable of initiating burst mode operation based, at least in part, on receipt of a request from the CPU;

   wherein the request is to include a memory address, a word count, and a read or a write control transfer designation; and

   wherein the memory controller is to process the request and take control of the system transfer bus.

Unlike previously in Example 1.3, in this example, the CPU and system bus are intended as claim elements. To infringe, these elements must specifically be present in an accused device. The claim recites an interaction of multiple components, all of which are required to be present for direct patent infringement; however, it is expected, here, that a single entity, a system integrator, such as a competitor of the patentee, will own or control all the elements of the claim so that direct infringement will be present.[70]

One may genuinely ask whether this approach of using a system level independent claim has advantages over an approach in which there is a component level independent claim, as in the previous section, with aspects of the overall system (e.g., CPU, system bus, etc.) being added via dependent claims, discussed and illustrated in the prior section (e.g., Example 1.3 and follow-on discussion). There are various considerations, but there is no clear answer to such a question.

70. *See* section 6.3 and its subsections, discussing the single infringer principle.

One consideration may be that the claim in Example 1.7 makes it clearer that specific end products infringe, which may be beneficial in some circumstances. If dealing with U.S. Customs, as one example, and trying to enforce an exclusion order[71] against importation of these consumer end products into the United States, this claim might be more likely to be enforced than the independent claim of Example 1.3. One would not expect U.S. Customs to tear apart end products to look for infringing memory components. Yet, in theory at least, using dependent claims to cover the system should have this same legal advantage. That is, the dependent claims may be asserted and result in an exclusion order, although the independent claim in Example 1.7 might be considered to more clearly be a system for purposes of enforcement.

One might also imagine that a system that is a combination of more elements may at least arguably be more likely to be patentable. In other words, the component interactions may provide patentability arguments. Yet, in theory at least, again, using dependent claims to cover the system, previously discussed, should have this same legal advantage. That is, those same arguments could be made with respect to the dependent claims. Still, a tangible benefit may relate to how patent prosecution typically proceeds.

Examiners usually focus on the independent claims. Here, the independent claim of Example 1.7 might potentially be slightly more likely to be allowed than a dependent claim that amounts to the same elements and limitations. With the prior claim of Example 1.3, the examiner may reject the independent claim and then, in passing, also reject the dependent claims, without much consideration,[72] even though usually there are additional technical arguments in favor of patentability. The patent prosecutor may, in our hypothetical, then, in a response, make an argument regarding the dependent claims separately from the independent claim, if this happens. At that point, however, the examiner may be reluctant to modify his decision, having previously rejected all the claims.

Both approaches have some merit, that is, an independent claim for the system and a separate independent claim for the component. In some cases, therefore, a drafter may employ both approaches.[73]

---

71. The International Trade Commission (ITC) is a quasi-judicial body in the executive branch that has the power to prevent foreign originating goods violating trade regulation U.S. laws from entering the U.S. by issuing exclusion orders. Thus, the ITC is one option in terms of enforcement of a U.S. patent.

72. Granted that this may not be legally appropriate, it does happen at times.

73. But *not* in a manner so that claim scope is identical in all respects between an independent claim of one claim set and a dependent claim of another set, which might otherwise produce a rejection.

Typically, a component claim is more valuable against a component manufacturer for asserting direct patent infringement and a system level claim is more valuable against a system integrator for asserting direct patent infringement. For example, a system integrator may have a contractual indemnity against patent infringement for components that it purchases. However, typically, such indemnities are limited to the part sold. One could certainly make a direct infringement claim against the system integrator with a memory component claim since the memory is part of the system and directly infringed. However, because of such contractual indemnities from component manufacturers, a component claim against a system integrator may be less valuable than a system level claim.[74]

Despite these latter potential considerations, if your client is a system integrator, they may generally profess to have no interest in covering a memory manufacturer and not want to incur the extra claim fees associated with employing both approaches (i.e., system claim approach and component claim approach), although employing both approaches would provide an ability to go after a memory manufacturer/supplier as well as a systems integrator. Specifically, a new application is permitted three independent claims and 20 total claims before incurring extra claim fees.[75]

Another consideration as to the two approaches might relate to damages, although this is also quite unclear to be sure. By claiming a system, one might try to argue for purposes of assessing damages that an entire market value effect occurs with sales of an entire system, justifying that damages be calculated using the entire system as a royalty base.[76] In essence, the notion is that the component may drive sales for the complete system due to the patented features it adds. This might be a reason to favor a system level claim as an independent claim, for example. However, this situation may be a challenge to establish legally.[77] Damages based on a reasonable royalty tend to more frequently use the "smallest saleable unit," rather than the entire market value, as a royalty base.[78] The smallest saleable unit might be argued to be an integrated circuit or module including the memory with memory controller.

---

74. *But see* section 6.4 and its subsections, discussing damage considerations in claim drafting.

75. *See* Manual of Patent Examining Procedure (MPEP) § 607 (2022).

76. *See* Finjan, Inc. v. Blue Coat Sys., Inc., 879 F.3d 1299 (Fed. Cir. 2018); Exmark Mfg. Co. v. Briggs & Stratton Power Prods. Grp., 879 F.3d 1332 (Fed. Cir. 2018). *See* section 6.4 and its subsections, discussing damage considerations in claim drafting.

77. *See* section 6.4 and its subsections, discussing damage considerations in claim drafting.

78. *Id.*

Consistent with the entire market value suggestion, however, one might attempt to draft a claim to potentially increase the royalty base by including language directed to an integrated circuit chip or module that claims the system specifically, assuming that the entire system is likely to be integrated on a single integrated chip or module, as previously illustrated in the prior section.[79]

As another example, an additional level of integration might be added with a dependent claim 2:

> 2. The apparatus of claim 1, wherein the RAM, memory controller, CPU, and system transfer bus are incorporated together in at least one of the following: a desktop computer, a laptop computer, a tablet, a smart phone, and/or a server.

Again, in some situations, a claim like this may be beneficial to assert against end products that use the system.

Typically, at the time of filing, the drafter does not know the closest prior art.[80] Rather, it may take an IPR, a litigation, or even several litigations to locate such art. Therefore, as previously illustrated in the prior section, dependent claims are a type of hedge that narrows the claim so that all is not lost if prior art is found that renders the independent claim invalid.

There are further issues to consider about the choice between an independent system claim (such as Example 1.7) and a component level independent claim (such as Example 1.3), in which the system may be covered via dependent claims. These issues include direct versus indirect infringement, patent exhaustion, implied patent licensing, and contractual indemnities against patent infringement. We introduce them next.

Direct versus indirect infringement is an important topic.[81] Basically, making, using, selling, importing, or offering to sell everything recited in a patent claim amounts to direct infringement;[82] making, using, selling, importing, or offering to sell a component of a patent claim that includes several components as elements or that is used in a method claiming amounts to indirect infringement if done with intent to infringe.[83] In general, both types of claims may be desirable, such as for reasons just discussed. More specifically, however, a

79. *See* Example 1.3 discussion in section 1.2111.
80. *See* section 1.32, discussing the advantages and disadvantages of searching.
81. These topics are discussed in detail in sections 3.21 and 3.22 and subsections thereof.
82. *See* 35 U.S.C. § 271(a) (2022).
83. *See* the discussion in sections 3.21 and 3.22. *See also* 35 U.S.C. § 271(b), (c) (2022).

claim of direct infringement is a much easier claim to assert. Indirect infringement requires intent, as indicated, and has additional requirements.[84]

Regarding patent exhaustion and implied patent licensing, one might think, with both types of independent claims, and because technically the component claim and the system claim are separate inventions,[85] a sale of memory covered by one claim, such as the independent component claim, should *not* impact enforcement of the other independent (e.g. system) claim. However, sale of the memory covered by the former claim likely either "exhausts" the system claim or may result in grant of an implied license to the system claim.[86] One may still benefit from including both types of claims; however, this is an issue to keep in mind.

Patent indemnity issues were previously discussed.[87]

For a situation like this, another claim to consider is an apparatus means plus function claim, discussed and illustrated in the prior section. Such claims have a long history and are statutorily permitted. For most purposes, a means plus function claim refers to a claim in which at least part of the claim recites a means for performing a specified function. These claims have lots of pitfalls, which are discussed in detail later.[88]

Here, tactical and strategic differences between claims construed under section 112(f) and claims not construed under section 112(f) are highlighted.[89] For example, an apparatus means plus function claim for Example 1.7 might be drafted as follows:

---

84. *See* discussion in section 3.22. Specifically, as later discussed, indirect infringement generally requires knowledge.

85. *See, e.g.*, Dollar Elec. Co. v. Syndevco, Inc., 205 USPQ 949, 959 (E.D. Mich. 1979), *aff'd*, 669 F.2d 1370, 214 USPQ 241 (6th Cir. 1982) ("[E]ach claim of a patent is treated as if it was a separate patent.").

86. Perhaps even both. See Quanta Computer v. LG Electronics 553 U.S. 617, 128 S. Ct. 2109 (2008); Met-Coil Systems Corp. v. Korners Unlimited 803 F.2d 684 (Fed. Cir. 1986). *See* discussion in section 6.10 and its subsections regarding drafting claims with patent exhaustion and implied patent licenses in mind.

87. *See* the discussion in the subsections of section 1.211.

88. *See* section 4.123 and its subsections for a detailed discussion of means plus function and step plus function claims.

89. *Id.*

EXAMPLE 1.8

I claim:

1. An apparatus comprising:

   random access memory (RAM), a memory controller, a central processing unit (CPU), and a system bus;

   wherein the memory controller comprises means for initiating burst mode operation based, at least in part, on receipt of a request from the CPU;

   wherein the request is to include a memory address, a word count, and a read or a write control transfer designation; and

   wherein the memory controller comprises means for processing the request and means for taking control of a system transfer bus.

The statute states that such claims are for combinations. Therefore, a so-called single means claim is not permitted; however, one might mix structural and means plus function clauses in a claim, as illustrated in the immediately preceding claim. For example, "memory," "memory controller," and "CPU" are likely structural features.

Note that this means plus function claim is somewhat different from Example 1.4 of the prior section, but does also track closely the apparatus claim of Example 1.7. This is not required, but it is done here, again, to make it clear that the drafter intended that the two claims have different scopes. This topic is discussed more later.[90]

Another claim to consider from a strategic and tactical perspective is a method of using claim, as discussed in the prior section. It is recommended to nearly always include method claims (e.g., method of using and/or method of making claims) with apparatus claims for claim diversity. Many patents are written that do not follow this simple principle.

---

90. *But see* Mas-Hamilton Grp. v. La Gard, Inc., 156 F.3d 1206, 1214 (Fed. Cir. 1998). *See* section 4.123 and its subsections for a detailed discussion of means plus function and step plus function claims.

> It is recommended to nearly always include method claims with apparatus claims for claim diversity.

Usually, an invention will more easily be claimed as one or the other, that is, as a method or as an apparatus. In Examples 1.3 and 1.7, the technology seems to more easily be described as an apparatus, hence, the rationale for starting with that claim type.

> When beginning to draft claims for an invention, begin with the claim type that is more easily drafted due to the inherent nature of the invention.

The opportunity to claim a method of making even in situations where that is not necessarily the feature that is inventive should not be overlooked, as discussed in the prior section.[91] Regarding Example 1.7, nothing about the invention appears to relate to fabrication or manufacture. However, it is becoming common for fabless design houses to generate designs and have another company manufacture the chip. Designing an infringing chip would not constitute direct infringement; however, it might constitute indirect infringement in which the company manufacturing might be the direct infringer.

One limiting factor to consider is how easy or difficult would it be to discover or prove infringement of a method of making claim. For example, if there is little or no way to discover from the end product that a particular process was used, this technology might be better protected as a trade secret.[92]

Another limiting factor for enforcing a claim against a fabless design house may be that typically so-called foundries that perform manufacturing

---

91. A similar observation applies to method of using claims. However, this observation about method of making claims is made here because while it is reasonably common to include method of using claims with apparatus claims, it is less common to include method of making claims unless the inventive concept relates to manufacturing.

92. Subject to other considerations, such as turnover in the industry and/or how easy it might be to limit knowledge of the technology to a few individuals within the company that developed it. These are a few examples of considerations that may affect the desirability of trade secret protection.

for fabless design houses are located outside the United States. Such manufacture, therefore, may at times be beyond the territorial scope of U.S. patent law for infringement under 35 USC section 271(a). However, there are statutes directed to extraterritorial patent infringement.[93]

As indicated, we will return to this example in later sections as we explore the forgoing and other concepts in more detail.

1.2113 Network Provider

The previous two sections illustrated hardware-related technology. More typically, however, today, in the predictable arts, technology involves some combination of hardware and software. In addition, quite typically innovative aspects of the technology are embedded in the software rather than the hardware (or in addition to the hardware). This situation may raise challenging issues related to patent eligibility that should be kept in mind.[94]

However, at a high level, the law that has developed appears to be primarily focused on assuring that the subject matter being claimed represents a *technical* solution to a *technical* problem.[95] By staying true to this, patent eligibility issues in many cases should be able to be addressed.[96] Networking provides an illustration of such a situation, that is, a mixture of hardware and software in which the innovation, at least today, is present primarily in the software.

Again, we consider a technical problem and then try to claim a possible technical solution. The problem, here, relates to linking or connecting otherwise physically separate private networks to operate like (e.g., mimic operation for) a single physically connected network.

For example, imagine an international business with offices in major cities, such as New York, London, Paris, Tokyo, and so on. It is desirable for the offices to be on a single network despite their physical separation. Each office represents a physically separate private network. That is, each network device on a local physical private network (e.g., for a particular office) is able to discover and communicate with every other network device on that local network without routing signal packets via a router. The devices on a network are referred to as "network devices," which means that they are able to send and receive communications over the network. Typically, a network device is implemented using a computing system (e.g., a CPU and memory coupled by a bus) executing software instructions.

---

93. *See* 35 U.S.C. § 271(f), (g) (2022). *See* section 4.1252, discussing 35 U.S.C. § 271(g) (2022).

94. *See* section 5.44 and its subsections, discussing patent eligibility issues and software, in particular.

95. *Id.*

96. *See* section 5.44 and its subsections, discussing patent eligibility issues regarding software.

The problem, then, relates to linking these otherwise physically separate private networks to operate as a single private network where, again, each network device on the "created" single private so-called virtual network formed by linking the independent and physically separate private networks is able to discovery and communicate with every other network device without using a router and without other sorts of technical processes that usually come into play with use of a routing table, for example.

Drawbacks of a router include use of network address translation (referred to as NAT), latency, and routing of extra network traffic that may "clog" the network, so to speak. In addition, a router treats as separate and independent the networks that are communicating via the router. Therefore, if separated by a router, a network device on one network is not able to discover the network devices on the other network. Specifically, signal packets communicated via a router appear as if they originate from the router.

Likewise, because of the physically separate offices, physically linking the separate networks so that they operate as one is not practical or even feasible. Nonetheless, virtual private networks (VPNs) do exist. These link a remote network device with a physical network, but do not link multiple network devices on separate and independent private physical networks, referred to as broadcast domains, in a manner to operate as a single physical network.

In an embodiment of the approach to be claimed, each physical, separate broadcast domain has a gateway device. The gateway devices communicate between the physically separate broadcast domains via one or more tunnel servers. A part of one solution (i.e., an embodiment of the technology) includes a master controller that "provisions" the tunnel server(s) to link the physically separate broadcast domains. That is, the tunnel server(s) may be generated and may be terminated based (at least partially) on instructions from the master controller. It is noted that the master controller is outside the "created" single "virtual" private network to be formed by the physically separate private networks (and, consequently, is outside the physically separate private networks).

For example, with two broadcast domains to be "virtually linked," the gateway device in the respective broadcast domains performs operations of discovery and emulation. A gateway device discovers the network devices on its local broadcast domain and transmits that to the master controller which then transmits that to the other gateway devices of the other broadcast domains along with the network address for one or more tunnel servers to which the gateway devices are instructed to direct signal packets from its local broadcast domain that are to be communicated to the other broadcast domains. The one or more tunnel servers are able to communicate signal packets between the gateway devices of the broadcast domains. Likewise, in this example, the respective gateway devices receiving the discovery of the network devices of the other broadcast domains are now able to locally emulate the other broadcast domains from receiving the discovered configuration of the network devices on the other broadcast domains.

So, imagine a physical network device 1 on a broadcast domain A in which domain A includes a gateway device B, and imagine a physical network device 2 on a broadcast domain C in which domain C includes a gateway device D. In this example, broadcast domains A and C are linked by at least one tunnel server.

If network device 1 desires to communicate with network device 2, it puts out a signal packet on its private local network for network device 2. From the normal operation of a network, that signal packet is directed to gateway device B, which, as described, is to emulate network device 2 so that it appears to device 1 as if device 2 is on its local network. Gateway device B then forwards the signal packet to the "at least one" tunnel server without modifying it, other than to encapsulate the signal packet. At the tunnel server, the encapsulation is removed to determine the intended destination of the signal packet. The tunnel server then re-encapsulates the packet in a manner so that it will be directed to gateway device D on domain C. The tunnel server is able to do so because the master controller provided the address location of gateway device D when provisioning the tunnel server. Gateway device D, after received the encapsulated signal packet, removes the encapsulation and puts the signal packet out on its local network, where it is directed to network device 2 through the normal operation of that local network. Thus, the signal packet is communicated as if the two domains are physically joined. That is, no routing or network address translation (which is typically performed by a router) is employed.

Observe that while the tunnel server does, in a sense, "forward" signal packets, as mentioned, it is not engaging in the technical act of *routing*, which involves use of a routing table and where the signal packet itself is modified to appear as if it originated from the router that routes it and which usually involves network address translation. The two physical broadcast domains in this example are able to communicate across a larger network of intermediate and transparent network devices (e.g., the internet or World Wide Web) without signal packet routing, as is performed by a router, and without performing NAT. Another advantage is that network traffic is reduced because a router would route all the local network traffic, whereas, here, only the signal packets to be communicated to the network devices of the other broadcast domain(s) are communicated through the gateway devices.

As we begin to draft a patent claim, again, notice the technique of identifying a technical problem and a possible technical solution. There are several features described here that might be patented; however, a significant one relates to permitting two (or more) physically separate broadcast domains to operate as one "virtual" broadcast domain without performing routing and without performing network address translation (a "negative" limitation). The following might be a method claim to cover this technology:

EXAMPLE 1.9

I claim:

1. A method of forming a virtual broadcast domain by virtually linking at least a first broadcast domain with at least a second broadcast domain in which the at least a first broadcast domain and the at least a second broadcast domain are physically separate, the method comprising:

   communicating one or more signal packets between respective physically separate broadcast domains via a gateway device included in the respective physically separate broadcast domains, wherein the communicating the one or more signal packets comprises:

      encapsulating the one or more signal packets in the respective physically separate broadcast domains to be communicated; and

      communicating the encapsulated signal packets between the respective gateway devices and at least one tunnel server so that the one or more signal packets are able to be communicated between the respective physically separate broadcast domains.

Several aspects are worth mentioning. Notice the claim is drafted so that it provides some symmetry. That is, it might have, instead, been drafted to describe first what happens at one broadcast domain and then at another. However, with appropriate drafting, it is made shorter and broader by referring to "respective" broadcast domains and "respective" gateway devices.

Also notice use of language such as "one or more" and "at least." Such language is used to make the intended scope of the claim clearer. That is, coverage includes one signal packet or multiple signal packets, one tunnel server or more than one tunnel server, and two physically separate broadcast domains or more than two physically separate broadcast domains.

Finally, notice the preamble (the part of the claim before "comprising:"): "A method of forming a virtual broadcast domain by virtually linking at least a first broadcast domain with at least a second broadcast domain in which the at least a first broadcast domain and the at least a second broadcast domain are physically separate." How much of that preamble is really needed? The claim could have just as easily stated,[97] more simply:

I claim:

1. A method of forming a virtual private network comprising:

   communicating one or more signal packets between respective physically separate broadcast domains via a gateway device included in the respective physically separate broadcast domains, wherein the communicating the one or more signal packets comprises:

      encapsulating the one or more signal packets in the respective physically separate broadcast domains to be communicated; and

      communicating the encapsulated signal packets between the respective gateway devices and at least one tunnel server so that the one or more signal packets are able to be communicated between the respective physically separate broadcast domains.

Of course, this is a very broad claim that may not stand up to scrutiny since encapsulation was known at the time of the invention, as were tunnel servers (but *not* for this purpose).

Establishing a reasonable fallback position using dependent claims would be prudent due to the *known* art. Dependent claims could, for example, recite features, such as a master controller, the discovery and emulation performed by the gateway devices, creating the virtual broadcast domain *without* performing routing and/or NAT, and so on. Each of these features provides a reasonable basis to potentially distinguish over prior art.

97. *See* Chapter 2, regarding discussion of claim preambles.

Care in drafting may be appropriate for any "negative" limitations,[98] for example, creating the virtual broadcast domain *without* performing routing and/or NAT, and so on. It is desirable to *expressly* have support for negative claim limitations in the written description. A prudent approach, if employing negative limitations in some claims, would be to include as "dependent claims" from the claims reciting negative limitations, affirmative or positive limitations that produce the result that is the basis for the negative limitation. Here, for example, one might try to draft the negative limitations more affirmatively, such as by claiming "bypassing" routing and/or NAT in a claim dependent from a claim having a negative limitation, such as dependent from an independent claim reciting "*without* NAT."

You may notice that previously we began with an apparatus claim, whereas here we began with a method claim. Generally, it is usually easier to start with a claim type that more naturally relates to the technology. For example, software operation is usually more naturally a method. Here, all the hardware involves standard off-the-shelf components. The innovative features all relate to software executing on the hardware devices. Here, then, a method claim is an easier initial claim to draft.

Previously, in Example 1.3, we deliberately drafted an initial claim from the perspective of only memory and a memory controller because the party that manufactures and provides the memory and memory controller may not be the same party that combines those parts with a CPU, and so on. Do we have a similar issue, here, since we have separate broadcast domains and a tunnel server? It does not appear so, because one party should be operating all these elements together; however, this is something to always consider or else perhaps run the risk that your claim is not infringed because it does not cover one single entity that owns and/or controls all the elements and limitations of the claim.[99]

Previously, we started with an apparatus claim and then drafted a method claim. Here, therefore, it would be prudent to include an apparatus claim for patent claim diversity, such as the following.

---

98. *See* section 5.413, discussing negative limitations. A recent case is *Novartis Pharm. Corp. v. Accord Healthcare, Inc.*, 38 F.4th 1013 (Fed. Cir. 2022). The case involves a negative limitation added to a drug treatment method claim during prosecution. The substantive question on appeal is whether the claim limitation lacks written description support. The initial federal circuit opinion by Judge O'Malley sided with the patentee; Chief Judge Moore wrote a dissent. Judge O'Malley subsequently retired and Judge Hughes was added to the panel to consider Accord's rehearing petition. The new panel flipped the outcome, with Judge Hughes joining the Chief Judge's position and, therefore, the new panel ruled that the claims are invalid.

99. *See* section 6.3 and its subsections, discussing the single infringer principle.

EXAMPLE 1.10

I claim:

1. An apparatus comprising:

   at least one gateway device of at least a first broadcast domain, wherein the at least one gateway device is to perform a network operation of discovery of any other network devices of the at least a first broadcast domain;

   wherein the at least one gateway device is to emulate one or more network devices of at least a second broadcast domain; and

   wherein the at least one gateway device is to encapsulate one or more signal packets of the at least a first broadcast domain to be directed to a network device of the at least a second broadcast domain and is to communicate the encapsulated one or more signal packets to at least one tunnel server.

2. The apparatus of claim 1, wherein the at least one tunnel server is to communicate the encapsulated one or more signal packets to the at least a second broadcast domain.

3. The apparatus of claim 1, wherein the at least one gateway device is to receive one or more encapsulated signal packets from the at least one tunnel server to be communicated to a network device of the at least a first broadcast domain.

Observe, here, we started from the perspective of only one broadcast domain. One advantage for this claim is that starting in this manner we are able to "construct" a local private network around the gateway device via dependent claims. Also, using a different approach provides claim diversity; although, we might have started from any number of perspectives. Consequently, the focus and scope of this claim is not precisely the same as the method claim, although there are overlapping features.

Notice that claim 1 of Example 1.10 recites in the first part of the claim body (the part of the claim after "comprising:"): "wherein the at least one gateway device is to perform a network operation of discovery of any other network devices of the at least a first broadcast domain." However, this is not used later in the claim. This relates to discovery information to be provided to the second broadcast domain. So, why include it here? It would broaden the claim without much downside to omit this language until dependent claims are included that are directed to using such discovery information so that a signal packet received from the "at least a second broadcast domain" is received at the gateway device of the "at least a first broadcast domain" to then be processed by the local network to be directed to a specific network device of the "at least a first broadcast domain."

One aspect to appreciate is the difference in drafting a method claim versus drafting an apparatus claim that flows from the discussion about the set of rights associated with the respective claims, highlighted previously, but repeated here for emphasis. A method claim recites actions or operations. As a consequence, a method claim is infringed by performing an action, such as *using* something or *making* something. The claim elements are actions like "communicating," "encapsulating," and so on. One way to think of a method claim is like a cooking recipe with step-by-step instructions. In contrast, an apparatus is usually capable of doing actions. It is important to not claim an apparatus in a manner that suggests that it is performing such actions or operations.[100] An apparatus claim either recites structural elements, such as a processor or memory, or it recites that such elements are able or capable to perform an action to make it clear that the action itself is not being claimed, the performance of actions being the domain of method claims.

> One way to think of a claim is like a cooking recipe with step-by-step instructions.

Observe that several dependent claims were included earlier. These features might have been included in the base claim; however, relegating these features to dependent claims accomplishes several things. It provides some fallback position while allowing the base claim to be broader. It also provides

100. *See, e.g.*, IPXL Holdings v. Amazon, 430 F.3d 1377, 1384 (Fed. Cir. 2005). *See* section 5.6 and its subsections, discussing the problems of mixing in a single patent claim different statutory claim types or classes. *Cf.* INVT SPE LLC v. ITC, Appeal No. 20-1903 (Fed. Cir. August 31, 2022) (distinguishing between actual operation and capability of operating or performing for apparatus claims, particularly for software on a device, which tends to be functional, without discussing indefiniteness issue of mixing method and apparatus limitations), discussed in subsections 4.124 and 4.1272.

a way to "test" the bounds of the prior art since the examiner typically focuses on the independent claims.

Some comments on subject matter and patent eligibility are appropriate with this technology example. It is not immediately apparent from these claims that the innovation resides in software; however, it will be apparent from the specification. Typically, therefore, one would not expect a patent eligibility rejection here, although such rejections are becoming more common.[101] However, if such a rejection were to be made, it should be easy to overcome based on legal argument. It is well-established that the innovation may reside entirely in the software of a platform that combines hardware and software.[102]

There are several advantages to this technology beyond the scope of this discussion, including signal packet traffic engineering, creating overlay networks, and managing a complex network simply by moving icons on a screen. These aspects would or could, of course, be claimed, assuming budget is available to pursue these related inventions. However, this technology also presents an example to consider where at times what is perceived to be most valuable may not always be correct, suggesting the desirability of claiming as many features as is feasible, as previously mentioned.

The aim of the technology at least in some respects was to join private and physically separate networks for separate offices, where each office includes many network devices. As mentioned, VPNs were known to be capable to connect a remote network device to a private network. However, imagine, here, a possible embodiment that was not an important focus of the claims in which a broadcast domain is linked with a remote device. Such an embodiment might be considered a sort of "corner" case, in that the remote device alone forms a second broadcast domain, and the remote device also operates as the gateway device for this broadcast domain of one network device. *However, notably this invention still has a technical advantage over a VPN by limiting the network traffic between broadcast domains, as one example.*

A close reading of the previous sample claims of Examples 1.9 and 1.10 will show that this type of embodiment *should* necessarily be covered. That this embodiment is covered, however, could be made clearer with one or more dependent claims, which could recite, for example, that the first or the second broadcast domain comprises a stand-alone network device.

---

101. *See* Yu v. Apple, 1 F.4th 1040 (Fed. Cir. 2021); Am. Axle v. Neapco Holdings, 977 F.3d 1379 (Fed. Cir. 2020). See section 5.44 and its subsections, discussing patent eligibility drafting issues for software.

102. *See* Enfish, LLC v. Microsoft Corp., 822 F.3d 1327 (Fed. Cir. 2016). *See also* section 5.44 and its subsections, discussing patent eligibility drafting issues for software.

The ability to cover such an embodiment is mentioned now, because imagine deployment, just before the worldwide pandemic. After the technology is deployed, one might imagine the most popular use of the technology with customers may be use in this manner involving a remote device. While this may not have been anticipated by the inventors, this embodiment might become so important such that additional dependent claims may be added or even perhaps a separate application with new claims claiming priority to the initial application filing may be filed.

Along similar lines, as the prior discussion illustrates, in drafting the claims, it can be important that the language used should, as much as is feasible, not foreclose situations that, while not typical, might be attempted to avoid infringement. Again, as an example, the claims are written to make it clear that the subject matter is not limited to only two broadcast domains. The claims are drafted so that only a single signal packet is covered, as well as multiple signal packets. The claims are also drafted so that a broadcast domain might consist of only a gateway device. Again, more dependent claims could also cement this latter understanding.

This is also a time to clarify good practice from what may be legally required. For example, the language used to suggest that the subject matter is not limited to only two broadcast domains may *not* be necessary, but it *is* good practice. The apparatus claim, as one example, used the language "of at least a first broadcast domain" and the language "of at least a second broadcast domain" to suggest that there may be more broadcast domains. This is also continued with the language "the at least a first broadcast domain" and the language "the at least a second broadcast domain." In other words, this may represent three or four broadcast domains or more, all of which would constitute "at least a first broadcast domain" and "at least a second broadcast domain."

On the other hand, if the claim had simply stated: "a first broadcast domain," "a second broadcast domain," "the first broadcast domain," and "the second broadcast domain," it could still be argued that the claim covers additional broadcast domains. This is due to the transition word "comprising."[103] In general, "comprising" is interpreted to mean "including."[104]

Consequently, without the language in the claim, mentioned previously, one might still make a case that the claim covers more than two broadcast domains. However, with that said, there have been cases in which courts have

103. *See* discussion of transition words or phrases in patent claims, in Chapter 2.

104. *See, e.g.*, Regents of Univ. of Cal. v. Eli Lilly & Co., 119 F.3d 1559 (Fed. Cir. 1997), *cert. denied*, 523 U.S. 1089 (1998) ("The word 'comprising,' . . . as is well-established, permits inclusion of other moieties."). *See also* discussion of transition words in patent claims, in Chapter 2.

limited claims to the exact language employed. A point to understand is that the principles or canons of claim construction, one example being as just stated regarding use of "comprising" as a transition word, represent a starting point for interpretation of the claim. Nonetheless, other factors, such as the specification, the file history, how those of ordinary skill would understand the technology, and so on, might cause a court to depart from a so-called canon of construction. With this knowledge, good practice suggests that other language (e.g., "at least," "one or more," and so on) be included so that the intent of what the claim is meant to cover is made much clearer, that is, as clear as possible.

Good practice suggests that other language (e.g., "at least," "one or more," and so on) be included so that the intent of what the claim is meant to cover is made much clearer, that is, as clear as possible.

As discussed in prior sections, it is also typical to include an apparatus means plus function claim (e.g., intended to be construed under section 112(f)) corresponding to the apparatus claim that is not intended to be construed under section 112(f), such as shown in the immediately following example. Note that the means plus function claim closely tracks the previous apparatus claim. This is not required, again, but it is done to make it clear the drafter intended the two claims have different scopes.[105] This topic is discussed more later.[106]

Section 112(f) states that such claims (i.e., claims with a means plus function clause) are used for combinations. A so-called single means claim is not permitted; however, one might mix structural and means plus function clauses in a claim. In general, because of the language of section 112(f), means plus function claims (i.e., claims with clauses construed under section 112(f)) are usually narrower than similar claims without clauses construed under section 112(f).

---

105. *See* section 4.123 and its subsections, discussing drafting means plus function and step plus function claims. *But see* Mas-Hamilton Grp. v. La Gard, Inc., 156 F.3d 1206, 1214 (Fed. Cir. 1998).

106. *See* section 4.123 and its subsections, discussing drafting means plus function and step plus function claims.

EXAMPLE 1.11

I claim:

1. An apparatus comprising:

   at least one gateway device of at least a first broadcast domain;

   wherein the at least one gateway device comprises means for emulating one or more network devices of at least a second broadcast domain; and

   wherein the at least one gateway device comprises means for encapsulating one or more network communication signal packets of the at least a first broadcast domain directed to a network device of the at least a second broadcast domain and means for transmitting the encapsulated one or more network communication signal packets to at least one tunnel server.

In Example 1.10 we recited a gateway device; however, in implementation, this is usually a network device in the form of a computing system with appropriate software. Therefore, we might draft the claim like this to imply broader scope, rather than as previously claimed:

I claim:

1. An apparatus comprising:

   at least one network device of at least a first broadcast domain;

   wherein the at least one network device is to emulate one or more network devices of at least a second broadcast domain; and

   wherein the at least one network device is to encapsulate one or more signal packets of the at least a first broadcast domain directed to a network device of the at least a second broadcast domain and is to communicate the encapsulated one or more signal packets to at least one tunnel server.

Of course, it would be important in the specification to clarify terms (e.g., network device, computing device, gateway device).

Also, because the technology is implemented in software, it would be typical, and prudent, to include a Beauregard claim.[107] A Beauregard claim refers to a claim that recites instructions (e.g., software instructions) stored on a "storage medium." A Beauregard claim may invite a patent eligibility rejection under section 101;[108] however, such claims can be powerful tools because they, in effect, cover the software as stored. They, in effect, may be asserted against anyone who uses, stores, sells, distributes, or generates the software. That is, anyone in the chain of distribution of the software may be sued, although they may not have created or used the software. In this regard, the form of the apparatus claim immediately preceding also provides guidance on drafting a Beauregard claim, such as the claim immediately following. Instead of reciting "apparatus," we are able to claim an "article" and, instead of a network device, we are able to claim "executable instructions," as follows:

EXAMPLE 1.12

I claim:

1. An article comprising: a non-transitory storage medium;

   wherein the storage medium includes stored thereon executable instructions;

   wherein the instructions are executable to: emulate one or more network devices of at least a second broadcast domain, encapsulate one or more signal packets from at least a first broadcast domain to be directed to a network device of the at least a second broadcast domain, and communicate the encapsulated one or more signal packets to at least one tunnel server.

This claim and the apparatus claim are quite similar in language, which reduces claim diversity in some respects (granted the apparatus claim and

107. *See* section 2.114 and its subsections as well as section 4.128 and its subsections, discussing Beauregard claims.

108. Because it makes it apparent that the invention is software related.

Beauregard claim are different claim types), but that may happen sometimes, especially if representing cost-conscious clients. Along similar lines from the Beauregard claim of the immediately preceding example, it is also quite easy to now formulate a method claim that is different from the previous method claim of Example 1.9, thereby adding some additional diversity.

EXAMPLE 1.13

I claim:

1. A method comprising:

   emulating one or more network devices of at least a second broadcast domain;

   encapsulating one or more signal packets from at least a first broadcast domain to be directed to a network device of the at least a second broadcast domain; and

   communicating the encapsulated one or more signal packets to at least one tunnel server.

Of course, we have now exceeded the three independent claims that are permitted with a standard filing fee and would incur extra claim fees. Five independent claims were just discussed and drafted (two method claims, an apparatus claim, a means plus function claim, and a Beauregard claim). One arrangement to reduce costs a bit might be to employ four independent claims (rather than the five discussed), in which we might either include two method claims, an apparatus claim, and a Beauregard claim or, instead, perhaps, a method claim, an apparatus claim, a Beauregard claim, and a means plus function claim. The advantage of the former is that it employs two different approaches for a method of using. It gives up a means plus function claim, but those tend to be construed narrowly and tend to be included if the technical field is crowded or as a fallback position, neither of which appears needed here. Later sections address advantages and disadvantages of several types of claims, especially Beauregard and means plus function claims.[109]

109. *See* sections 4.123 and 4.128 (and related subsections), respectively discussing advantages and disadvantages of means plus function claims and Beauregard claims.

As mentioned, this has been a quick survey and these examples may appear in later sections discussing in detail some aspects only touched upon here and/or raising new claim drafting considerations.

1.22 Anticipating Change in Patent Claim Drafting Strategy and/or Tactics

At a high level, there are two or three ways in which a patent may be employed strategically. These are, quite generally: enforcing the patent to protect one's competitive advantage; cross-licensing the patent (i.e., trading legal rights in protected technology for patent rights in another company's protected technology); or licensing the patent for other value (e.g., royalties, equity, etc.).[110]

Though a simple legal construct, in actual implementation, this may become more complex than it may seem, particular as it becomes translated into claim drafting strategy and tactics. For a company with multiple divisions, where each division may have multiple product lines (or services), there may be multiple combinations of these approaches employed for different divisions as well as for product lines or services. Furthermore, there may be other forms of intellectual property involved, also having various strategies.

If that were not enough potential complexity, translating high-level strategies into business objectives and then translating those business objectives into claim drafting strategy and tactics may not be simple. These issues unfortunately cannot satisfactorily be handled in the abstract. This is because specifics about the technology, the people involved, the corporate structure, manufacturing, distribution, sales, the underlying economics, the relevant markets, and so on, may and likely will affect the claiming strategy and tactics that may result.

Likewise, now consider that many of these things may change. Technology changes and creates new opportunities. Business strategy changes. Management changes. Consumer demand evolves. Court decisions, new legislation, and new regulations create legal changes. Consequently, how this all works to come together and result in meaningful claim drafting strategy and tactics by its nature is a bit vague, to say the least. For this reason, it is believed a discussion of some practical examples to illustrate some of the potential considerations may be the most productive way to at least gain some appreciation for this subject.

---

110. A fourth is simply an outright sale, but that seems more tactical than strategic, although in truth, it depends on the particulars.

However, several general statements are possible at this juncture, before discussing a few relatively simple illustrations. One point is that the drafter, when crafting patent claims, should anticipate change as much as is feasible and be ready to shift course if unanticipated change happens, as it surely will.[111] Patent claim drafting is not a "one size fits all activity"; to be even more pointed, it should not be treated as a "set and forget activity."

One should be mindful that various changes that may take place have the potential to impact approaches to how certain patent claims have been formulated. Second, as a corollary of this point, with each piece of PTO correspondence that arrives and/or with each correspondence sent to the PTO, it would be prudent to re-evaluate the strategy and tactics for the pending patent claims. Remember, within the bounds of the patent specification, the patent claims may be modified, and new claims may be added. Prosecution of patent claims is an ongoing, evolving process in which the initially filed claims are merely an opening bid, so to speak. Third, as another corollary, at each of these points (and, if appropriate, also points where there is not necessarily correspondence) one should make use of any new information that has been gained, such as knowledge about the prior art, deeper knowledge about the technical or commercial environment, any changes in client business strategy, product lines, management, and/or corporate organization, any changes in consumer demand, market economics, business conditions, and/or any legal changes. That is, one should be "on the lookout" for anything that might suggest changing the pending claims so as to generate more value for the client. For, if not, you may run the risk of missed opportunities, or even worse, having the claims you wrote, though issued, virtually have no value because something has changed so that, as formulated, no one is using the technology, but such claims might have been modified and resulted in meaningful, issued claims with suitable attention to these matters.

1.221 Illustrations

1.2211 Changes in Technology

Changes in technology have the potential to have a strategic and/or a tactical impact on claim formulation. Typically, the impact of technical changes tends to be more tactical, however, some changes do represent "strategic inflection points."[112] Consider two examples, the first being the shift from analog

---

111. To clarify, it is anticipated that change(s) will happen, what remains a mystery until it happens is the exact nature of such change(s).

112. *See generally* ANDREW GROVE, ONLY THE PARANOID SURVIVE: HOW TO EXPLOIT THE CRISIS POINTS THAT CHALLENGE EVERY COMPANY (1999).

communications to digital communications and the second being advances in memory technology, which, of course, involves Moore's law, in which the number of transistors on a semiconductor chip doubled about every year.[113] Both of these changes were on the horizon for quite some time. Not to have been aware of the potential impact of these technology changes on the drafting of patent claims might almost amount to being negligent.

> It is critical to anticipate change and be mindful that such changes have the potential to impact approaches to how certain patent claims have been formulated. Rather, with each piece of PTO correspondence that arrives and/or with each correspondence sent to the PTO, it would be prudent to re-evaluate the strategy and tactics of the pending patent claims.

As a concrete example, analog modems were with us for quite longer than expected before they became obsolete. Looking at this tactically, it would have been prudent for a drafter to prepare claims in such a manner that either digital or analog modem technology would result in infringement if modem technology was to be included in the subject matter to be claimed.

Imagine, for example, an early patent on downloading music to a computer for playback. If use of an analog modem was a feature of the claims, then the patent became virtually of no value once analog modems were no longer in use.

Remember patents have a potential 20-year life. Realize that today, at the current rate of technological development, many aspects of prevalent technical implementations may change. This sort of situation has in some cases resulted in wonderful noninfringement arguments for counsel for an accused infringer, such as the modem example, which is similar to an actual situation. Of course, one should likewise be mindful of a reverse situation. That is, in some situations, not limiting claims to digital signals in situations in

---

113. Moore's law is not really a law in the legal sense or even a proven theory in the scientific sense (such as $E=MC^2$). Rather, it was an observation by Gordon Moore in 1965 while he was working at Fairchild Semiconductor: that the number of transistors on a microchip (as they were called in 1965) doubled about every year. (There are several formulations of Moore's law, but this one is sufficient for this discussion.)

which mixed signaling is possible may also be deadly based on prior art.[114] One has to consider both extremes as potential possibilities and draft claims accordingly.[115]

In comparison, the general topic of advances in silicon memory is more strategic, than tactical. Over decades, the ability to store more content using digital technology has increased at a pace that is nearly unimaginable. Today, an external drive with several terabytes of storage is about $50 to $100. Not long ago several gigabytes of memory was considered large, although today this would be a small thumb drive. The advances may be due to many innovations, but the overall trend was predicted by Moore's law.

We have seen advances in static random access memory (SRAM), dynamic random access memory (DRAM), and flash memory. Furthermore, phase change and other types of newer memory are also being investigated. Not only might such technical changes affect one's claims but they may also open up opportunities for new features that previously may have been thought not feasible, not practical, or too costly to implement.

Consider how the computing platform has changed in only 15 years, about the current term of a patent, if one accounts for several years for the patent to issue. One can almost be sure that during the early days of computing, digital video processing was proposed as a possible application for a computer platform, but in those early days was likely rejected on such grounds as being at the time impossible, impractical, and/or too costly, only to be resurrected and implemented later. Many did not appreciate just how quickly the appropriate technical advances in processing power and in memory storage capability would develop to make such innovations feasible and economical.

1.2212 Changes in the Law

Anticipating and adapting to changes in the law might be easier than other topics because legal training usually prepares one for this. Nonetheless, in this era, the amount and degree of legal change in this area eclipses past generations. In the past 20 years or so, we have seen many decisions from the Supreme Court significantly alter the legal landscape for patent law.[116] Like-

---

114. *See* Personalized Media Commc'ns v. Apple, 952 F.3d 1336 (Fed. Cir. 2020) (claims avoided prior art because interpreted to mean only digital signals, rather than digital and analog signals).

115. Claim drafting is a good example of making a decision under uncertainty. The probabilities matter. We told you this was a challenging activity.

116. A few examples include Markman v. Westview, 517 U.S. 370 (1996); Pfaff v. Wells Electronics, 525 U.S. 55, 48 USPQ2d 1641 (1998); Festo Corp. v. Shoketsu Kinzoku Kogyo Kabushiki Co., 535 U.S. 722 (2002); eBay Inc. v. MercExchange, L.L.C., 547 U.S. 388 (2006); KSR

wise, a major statutory reform passed in 2011 and, of course, the regulatory framework promulgated to go with that statutory reform, have resulted in many changes. Even today, many years later, important legal questions with potential to affect patent claim drafting remain unanswered.[117]

Here are a few simple examples of major changes from federal court decisions: (1) clarification in the interpretation of product-by-process claims;[118] (2) clarification in the interpretation of means plus function clauses;[119] (3) clarification in the scope of the doctrine of equivalents;[120] and (4) clarification regarding the doctrine of patent exhaustion.[121] Again, many more examples exist. Whether the response to such changes is viewed as strategic or tactical may be a close call and might depend on the situation.

For many years it remained unclear how product-by-process claims should be interpreted.[122] This was due to two federal circuit panels that reached different outcomes. *Scripps Clinic & Research Foundation v. Genentech, Inc.*, a 1991 federal circuit decision, stated that a product-by-process claim was *not* limited to products prepared by the process recited in the claims.[123] However, in *Atlantic Thermoplastics Co., Inc. v. Faytex Corp.*, a 1992 federal circuit decision, a different three-judge panel ruled that "[P]rocess terms in product-by-process claims serve as limitations in determining infringement."[124]

These inconsistent rulings, however, did not foreclose use of such claims. Rather, the uncertainty provided a potential opportunity to argue for a desired interpretation, depending on issues related to invalidity or infringement. For a knowledgeable practitioner, product-by-process claims might be included, but with recognition of the interpretation risk. However, after nearly two decades, the federal circuit ultimately resolved the panel inconsistency, and

---

Int'l Co. v. Teleflex Inc., 550 U.S. 398 (2007); Impression Products v. Lexmark, 581 U.S. __; 137 S. Ct. 1523 (2017). There are many more.

117. *See* section 1.33 and its subsections, discussing post-AIA provisions regarding novelty and non-obviousness.

118. *See* section 4.125 and its subsections, discussing product-by-process claims.

119. *See* section 4.123 and its subsections, discussing means plus function claims.

120. *See* section 3.23 and its subsections, discussing the doctrine of equivalents.

121. *See* section 6.10 and its subsections, discussing drafting patent claims to reduce risk of patent exhaustion.

122. *See* Atlantic Thermoplastics Co., Inc. v. Faytex Corp., 970 F.2d 834, 23 USPQ2d 1481 (Fed. Cir. 1992), *suggestion for reh'g en banc declined*, 974 F.2d 1279, 23 USPQ2d 1801, 974 F.2d 1299, 24 USPQ2d 1138 (Fed. Cir. 1992).

123. *See* Scripps Clinic & Rsch. Found. v. Genentech, Inc., 927 F.2d 1565, 18 USPQ2d 1001 (Fed. Cir. 1991).

124. *See* Atlantic Thermoplastics Co., Inc. v. Faytex Corp., 970 F.2d 834, 23 USPQ2d 1481 (Fed. Cir. 1992).

the interpretation of such claims is now clear.[125] As a result of this interpretation, such claims are not generally advisable unless it is the only way to claim the subject matter at issue.[126] Part of the reason for this is that the process limitations *are not* considered for purposes of validity, but the process limitations *are* considered for purposes of infringement.[127]

Product-by-process claims represent one of the few situations where claims are *not* interpreted consistently regarding validity and infringement. As the court said in *Abbott Labs*:

> The impact of these different analyses is significant. For product-by-process claims, that which anticipates if earlier does not necessarily infringe if later. That is because a product in the prior art made by a different process can anticipate a product-by-process claim, but an accused product made by a different process cannot infringe a product-by-process claim.[128]

Thus, these claims get the worst of it, so to speak. That is, for such claims, process limitations do not help distinguish for validity purposes but may prevent a finding of infringement if not met.

Another legal change began in the early 1990s. The federal circuit began to clarify the interpretation of means plus function clauses. Some, if not most, patent attorneys had before that believed that section 112, paragraph 6 (which is today section 112(f)) was a claim broadening provision. However, the federal circuit explained that it was intended as a claim narrowing provision.[129] The current use of such claims is now quite different from if section 112(f) were a claim broadening provision, as had been thought previously.[130]

Likewise, in *Pennwalt v. Durand-Wayland, Inc.*, in an en banc decision resulting in clarification of the law, the federal circuit addressed application of the doctrine of equivalents (DOE) to the clauses of a patent claim.[131] This decision narrowed application of the DOE considerably. Essentially, it was determined that the DOE is to be applied on a limitation-by-limitation basis, rather than to a claim "as a whole." Before that, proper application of the DOE to claim language was not entirely clear permitting the doctrine of equivalents, in litigation, to "taken on a life of its own," so to speak. That is,

---

125. *See* Abbott Laboratories v. Sandoz, Inc., 566 F.3d 1282 (Fed. Cir. 2009) (en banc).
126. *See* section 4.125 and its subsections, discussing product-by-process claims.
127. *Id.*
128. *See* Abbott Laboratories v. Sandoz, Inc., 566 F.3d 1282 (Fed. Cir. 2009) (en banc).
129. *See* Johnston v. IVAC, 855 F.2d 1574, 1580 (Fed. Cir. 1989).
130. *See* section 4.123, discussing drafting means plus function claims.
131. *See* Pennwalt Corp. v. Durand-Wayland, Inc. 833 F.2d 931 (Fed. Cir. 1987) (en banc); *see* section 3.23 and its subsections, discussing the doctrine of equivalents.

even if one could *not* make out a case of literal infringement, one might still "get to the jury" under the doctrine of equivalents since how it was applied to claim language was unclear.

Because of the *Pennwalt* decision, the importance of quality claim drafting went up significantly, since, after *Pennwalt*, it became more difficult to rely on the doctrine of equivalents to enlarge what might be covered by a claim of limited literal scope. Under *Pennwalt*, one must establish an equivalent of *each* claim limitation not met literally.[132]

Clarification of the doctrine of patent exhaustion is yet another area that has impacted claim drafting. It has also affected patent licensing. The federal circuit created a body of law around patent exhaustion and implied patent licensing. Although the two concepts were similar, the differences as articulated by the federal circuit were important. Specifically, the legal tests suggested that it was easier to avoid creating an implied patent license than to avoid exhaustion, although both appeared to be avoidable with appropriate contractual language. However, in a decision, *Quanta v. LGE*, the Supreme Court, in effect, made differences between the two separate legal concepts much blurrier.[133] Then, in a subsequent decision, the Supreme Court clarified that exhaustion could not be avoided by contract, overruling a major, but heavily criticized, federal circuit decision.[134]

These decisions made it difficult to avoid exhaustion by agreement and by claim drafting.[135] These decisions also made it much less likely for a company to license its patents, because an unintended consequence of licensing might now be for a company licensing its patents to chosen companies to inadvertently exhaust its patent claims against a competitor it did not want to license.[136] Ironically, this result was the opposite of good policy, since patent cross-licensing is procompetitive and may result in creation of new technology. A good example is the semiconductor industry in which patent cross-licensing is widely adopted and has allowed the frontier of this technology

---

132. There are other limitations to applicability of the DOE, including prosecution history estoppel and the prior art. *See* section 3.23 and its subsections, discussing the DOE in detail.

133. *See* Quanta Computer, Inc. v. LG Electronics, Inc., 553 U.S. 617 (2008). *See also* section 6.10 and its subsections, discussing patent exhaustion and implied patent licenses.

134. *See* Mallinckrodt, Inc. v. Medipart, Inc., 976 F.2d 700 (Fed. Cir. 1992). *See also* section 6.10 and its subsections, discussing patent exhaustion and implied patent licenses.

135. Although a few tricks in claim drafting may remain in the right situation. *See* section 6.10 and its subsections.

136. *See* section 6.10 and its subsections, discussing patent exhaustion and implied patent licenses.

to continually move forward, at least partially, because of this industry-wide practice.

1.2213 Change in Business Strategy, Markets, Management, and/or Corporate Organization

The sorts of changes discussed in this section are grouped together because in many, if not most, cases, such changes may strategically alter a patent strategy. Aside from an express change in business strategy, which may genuinely happen, the other types of changes, such as a major shift in markets (e.g., changes in demand, supply, underlying economics, or simply creation of or growth in a new market), changes in top management, and/or changes in corporate organization, all have the potential to significantly impact business strategy and, consequently, patent strategy.

Again, concrete examples are helpful and illustrative. As many may know, Intel started as a memory company, but then reinvented itself into a microprocessor company. This change, of course, dramatically impacted its patent strategy. Although semiconductor manufacturing remained an emphasis in portfolio development, a movement from memory structures to microprocessor structures, of course, resulted. Furthermore, whereas Intel might have previously not been willing to license its memory technology, previously a core business, once it established itself as a successful microprocessor company, licensing of its memory technology either could be used to increase revenues to the company or could be used as a trading card with companies whose patents Intel may desire to license. Other changes much later in Intel's history included moves out of digital camera technology, which included movement out of CMOS sensor technology. As a seller of digital cameras, Intel was more than just a component supplier. Rather, it was providing an end product. With the move out of digital cameras, it became a pure component supplier, which, of course, impacted business and patent strategy. Furthermore, with a large portfolio of CMOS sensor and digital camera technology, Intel might now use these patents to protect its core business, microprocessors. One would expect that Intel would be reluctant to license its core microprocessor technology. Therefore, it was beneficial having other popular technologies available to license as trading cards, if needed, such as memory and CMOS sensor technology.

As other examples, consider companies like Qualcomm and Rambus, which started as manufacturing companies but evolved into companies that licensed their patented technology as a major source of revenue. In general, patent strategies around licensing rather than enforcement are likely to impact claim drafting.

Another example is Lenovo, which was primarily a computer company but then entered the cell phone market. Although there are similarities in the technology, for one thing, to compete, Lenovo needed to create or acquire patents focused on cell phone technology or else have its new business exposed to patents owned by other cell phone companies. Likewise, in addition to starting or increasing its patent filings related to cell phone technology, one would expect that changes to its approach to patent claim drafting resulted so that technologies potentially applicable to both cell phones and computers could be more effectively "leveraged."[137]

HP is a good example of management and corporate structure changes. HP acquired a competitor, Compaq. This surely affected its patent strategy having removed a major competitor and patent threat. Likewise, HP spun out Agilent. Thus, making the technologies that left HP less relevant to its now core business and altering its patent strategy for these technologies. Later, HP separated businesses again, creating HP Inc., focused on PCs and printing, and Hewlett Packard Enterprise, focused on enterprise products and business services. No doubt this changed the patent focus of both new companies in terms of technology and patent portfolio development.

As another example of changes in management and corporate structure, some may recall AT&T's divestiture in which it separated its communications services business, which retained the name AT&T, from its networking and hardware business, which became Lucent. In the process, it also spun-out NCR as a separate company, which it had previously acquired. This change affected not only its patent strategy but also its R&D. Furthermore, its goal with patents appears to have shifted. Previously, AT&T used to license its patents for revenue. It appears to have then switched to a strategy of selling off pieces of its portfolio that were no longer relevant to business strategy for revenue.

Again, the clear lesson here is that the business world of technology is a dynamic place. So, consequently, is the world of intellectual property and patents. It would be prudent to keep this in mind when drafting patent claims, so that changes that create opportunities are able to be exploited appropriately.

137. Although, one might expect that they were already doing so even before deciding to enter the cell phone market.

> The clear lesson here is that the business world of technology is a dynamic place. So, consequently, is the world of intellectual property and patents.

1.3 Claim Breadth—Is Being Broad Always the Goal?

When it comes to claim drafting, most people have in mind drafting to handle issues regarding prior art and creating claims that distinguish over such art. Of course, this certainly is desirable to accomplish; however, there are several other ways that a claim may fail to comply with title 35 of the United States Code (USC) despite *successfully* distinguishing from such prior art. Generally, in terms of prosecution of a patent application, these other ways are thought of as so-called non-art rejections during examination, in comparison with "art rejections." Likewise, these same non-art issues (as well as art issues, of course) may be raised in litigation after the patent has issued and various ones may also be raised in a post-issuance review of the patent, depending on the proceeding.[138]

The primary statutory sections of concern for patent claims in this regard are sections 101, 102, 103, and 112 of title 35. These might, similarly, be thought to capture the requirements to be met for an invention to be patentable. This follows logically since the patent claims define the invention.[139]

Section 101 is the statutory basis for requiring that an invention be new, useful, that it be "statutory subject matter"[140] and "patent eligible"[141] (which overlaps with statutory subject matter, but is a separate legal consideration), and that there not be "double patenting." Section 102 is the statutory basis

138. Although the patent claims are presumed to be valid in litigation. *See, e.g.*, Nautilus, Inc. v. Biosig Instruments, Inc., 134 S. Ct. 2120 (2014).

139. *See, e.g.*, Phillips v. AWH Corp., 415 F.2d 1303, 1312 (Fed. Cir. 2005) (en banc) ("It is a 'bedrock principle' of patent law that 'the claims of a patent define the invention to which the patentee is entitled the right to exclude.'"). *See also* Constant v. Advanced Micro-Devices, Inc., 848 F.2d 1560, 1571, 7 USPQ2d 1057, 1064 (Fed. Cir. 1988); Dollar Elec. Co. v. Syndevco, Inc., 205 USPQ 949, 959 (E.D. Mich. 1979), *aff'd*, 669 F.2d 1370, 214 USPQ 241 (6th Cir. 1982).

140. *See* section 5.44 and its subsections discussing statutory subject matter and patent eligibility.

141. *Id.*

for the principle that an invention must be novel[142] (i.e., new), providing conditions that negate novelty, and that it must be timely filed[143] (i.e., before the invention is commercialized). Section 103 is the statutory basis for the principle that the invention must be non-obvious.[144] Last, but not least, section 112 requires that the patent claims be definite[145] (i.e., not ambiguous) and is the statutory basis for means plus function claims.[146] These statutory sections have other specifics regarding claims (e.g., multi-dependent claims, for instance) and requirements for the specification that, if not present, may invalidate the claims (e.g., written description support, enablement).[147] Nonetheless, here, we are giving attention to claim drafting, as opposed to specification writing.

The foregoing claim drafting issues are addressed in depth in the sections of this book that follow and a few, such as means plus function claims, have been introduced quickly in previous sections and are also discussed in more detail later. Being broad, as should now be clear, while distinguishing from the prior art is *not* the *only* goal when drafting a claim. Nonetheless, here, we ask: should being as broad as possible *necessarily* be a goal at all and, if so, why?

Despite the legal issues that a properly drafted claim must address, such as those mentioned previously, in these next few sections, we focus on statutory sections 102 and 103, which relate to prior art.[148] Being able to draft a patent claim that legally distinguishes from prior art is one of the more basic skills required of someone who crafts patent claims. Furthermore, to be able to do so requires understanding what qualifies *legally* as prior art.

This latter point is important to fully grasp. Simply because something, such as a product, an article, an idea, and so on, exists before the date of creation of an invention and before the filing date of a patent application describing the invention at issue does not *necessarily* mean it qualifies as prior art, *at least legally*. Rather, to *legally* be prior art, it must fall under one of the subsections of 35 USC 102.[149] Consequently, it is important to understand how those

---

142. *See* sections 1.331 and 1.332, discussing pre-AIA and post-AIA novelty.

143. *See* sections 1.331 and 1.332, discussing pre- and post-AIA rights forfeiture considerations.

144. *See* sections 1.331 and 1.332, discussing pre-AIA and post-AIA non-obviousness.

145. *See* sections 5.43, 5.6, 5.8 (and subsections) and 6.13 (and subsections), which discuss indefiniteness along with other issues.

146. *See* section 4.123 and its subsections, discussing means plus function claims.

147. *See* section 5.4 and its subsections, discussing many of these issues.

148. As mentioned, the other issues raised are addressed in later sections, previously cited.

149. *See, e.g.*, Chisum, *supra* note 3, § 6.02[3](c) ("Federal Circuit decisions consistently confirm that Section 102(b) bar events constitute 'prior art' for purposes of obviousness."); Walterscheid, *Novelty in Historical Perspective (Part I)*, 75 J. Pat. & Trademark Off. Soc'y 689 (1993);

subsections operate to, in effect, define prior art. A complication is that on March 16, 2013, section 102 changed, the effective date of the portion of the America Invents Act (AIA) related to statutory sections 102 and 103.[150]

Once someone understands what qualifies as prior art, that knowledge allows the individual to then dissect available and relevant prior art before drafting a patent claim. Likewise, from interviewing the inventor and reading an invention disclosure prepared by the inventor, the individual should eventually understand enough to see how the invention is different from the prior art that has been dissected. These tasks are important basic skills for being able to draft a patent claim. These skills are like basic blocking and tackling in football, as an analogy.

Now, however, comes the *real challenge. The patent drafter must determine how similar or different the claim should be from the known prior art to protect the technology and still distinguish from that prior art (and must be able to formulate that difference in words).*

> The patent drafter must determine how similar or different the claim should be from the known prior art to adequately protect the technology and still distinguish from that prior art (and must be able to formulate that difference in words).

A claim that is overly narrow may easily distinguish from the art, but, likewise, may capture few if any potential infringers that might be using the technology and, consequently, be of little commercial value. Conversely, a claim that is overly broad may capture many infringers, but might not issue as being too broad relative to the prior art, or even if it does issue, may later be found invalid as being too "close" to the prior art. A trade-off between sweeping in less prior art versus capturing more infringers operates as a fundamental principle in this realm, not unlike the fundamental trade-off between bandwidth and signal-to-noise ratio in electrical engineering, as an example.

Walterscheid, *Novelty in Historical Perspective (Part II)*, 75 J. PAT. & TRADEMARK OFF. SOC'Y 777 (1993); Walterscheid, *The Ever Evolving Meaning of Prior Art (Part 9)*, 67 J. PAT. OFF. SOC'Y 33 (1985). Walterscheid, *The Ever Evolving Meaning of Prior Art (Part 5)*, 65 J. PAT. OFF. SOC'Y 477 (1983). Note, *Prior Art in Patent Law*, 73 HARV. L. REV. 369, 377 (1959). *See* section 1.331 and 1.332, discussing pre-AIA and post-AIA novelty and non-obviousness.

150. Although AIA became law on September 16, 2011, it went into effect in stages.

The drafter is seeking to achieve a "goldilocks" type claim that is neither too narrow nor too broad. However, that will usually depend quite a bit on the context and what may be known at the time of filing. According to one approach or theory, a broad claim should be presented such that it requires the examiner to ferret out all the close art. In this way, the prosecutor is able to craft a patent claim that leaves little or nothing "on the table" in terms of patent scope. That is, the ideal claim, for this context, is just close enough to "ferreted out" art from which the claim patentably distinguishes and still stand up as valid under scrutiny.

It might be helpful here to recall the discussion from section 1.1. What are the primary things that limit claim scope? One is self-imposed claim limitations and the other is the prior art. Given the prior discussion, it may now be clearer why it is that these two things typically limit claim scope. First, and foremost, the claim should not read on known prior art. Second, there should be enough difference from that art so that the claim is inventive over that art.[151] We, therefore, have come up against an area where judgment will be one's primary guide.

Also, there are a few schools of thought, here, rather than a single approach. One school of thought, as alluded to earlier, is to be as broad as possible and as close to the known prior art as possible without ensnaring it and with an inventive distinction. Again, this helps to "ferret out" the close art. Another school of thought is to only be as broad as needed for the commercial setting, lest your claims be held invalid and of no use at all.[152] Yet another is to be deliberately narrow so the patent will issue quickly (and perhaps follow up with a continuation seeking broader claim scope). One may well imagine even more complex approaches.

As a practical matter, you may end up using any one of these approaches, again, depending on circumstances and client desires. The real question, then, might be: absent unusual circumstances, what should your "default" approach be? Conventional wisdom suggests that one follow the first approach: be as broad as possible and as close to the known prior art as possible without ensnaring it and with an inventive distinction. However, rather than simply accepting this, we would like to investigate whether this wisdom should apply by considering its advantages and its disadvantages. This inquiry will provide other insights about the dynamics at work in this legal situation.

---

151. As suggested previously in section 1.1, relying *strictly* on commercial motivations for the patent filing may result in claims that are narrower than needed.

152. This is the approach alluded to in section 1.1 when suggesting that often commercial motivations are employed to limit claim scope.

1.31 Drafting the Broadest Claims Possible—Advantages and Disadvantages

A broad claim is only one of many aspects of a good claim. Rather, a good claim is an appropriate balance between breadth, vagueness, and precision. The claim is precise in some respects because the claim language should be specific enough to distinguish from the known prior art. This often involves some amount of detail in the language employed. For example, if the prior art shows red doorknobs, to be novel at least, the claim should recite a color other than red. For example, a recitation of "a blue doorknob," would be novel over such prior art (granted that it might be obvious, depending on other considerations). Patent claims are usually precise enough to show that the subject matter claimed is at least novel over the *known* prior art.

People sometimes confuse breadth and vagueness, the other features of a good claim. For example, "any and all electrical signals" is quite broad, but it is *not* vague. Rather, it is crystal clear. A good patent claim has breadth to cover those aspects not needed to distinguish from the known prior art. Breadth is desirable to protect the technology from those who might try to employ the technical idea in a manner that might otherwise not infringe a narrower claim. Vagueness may be appropriate, for example, when it may be unclear how certain technology may be implemented among various potential choices. That is, the future is uncertain. Being vague permits the claim to be infringed without spelling out in specific language how some aspects of the claim will be implemented.[153]

To understand vagueness better, consider, for example, a new type of razor blade for a handheld manual razor. Razor blades are a crowded art. Manufacturers are regularly coming out with designs that give a closer shave with less risk of being cut by the blade. How the blades for such razor blade cartridges are arranged is typically quite specific so the razor functions as intended.

---

153. However, appreciate that 35 U.S.C. § 112 (2022) has a requirement that a claim not be *too* vague, hence, making it indefinite. Understanding the line that amounts to being too vague depends on context and requires judgment. Various aspects of indefiniteness are discussed in later sections of this book. *See* sections 5.43, 5.6, 5.8 (and subsections) and 6.13 (and subsections), which discuss indefiniteness along with other issues. Notably, the federal circuit decided a number of indefiniteness cases in 2022, including these: Niazi Licensing Corp. v. St. Jude Med. S.C., Inc., 30 F.4th 1339 (Fed. Cir. 2022) (finding that claims to "resilient" and "pliable" catheters were indefinite); U. of Massachusetts v. L'Oreal S.A., 36 F.4th 1374 (Fed. Cir. 2022) (finding that claims to adenosine skin compositions were indefinite); ImmunoGen, Inc. v. Hirshfeld, 2021–1939, 2022 WL 885774, at *2 (Fed. Cir. Mar. 25, 2022) (vacating holding that "AIBW" is indefinite); ClearOne, Inc. v. Shure Acq. Holdings, Inc., 35 F.4th 1345 (Fed. Cir. 2022) (affirming PTAB determination that "self-similar" claim language was not indefinite); Dyfan, LLC v. Target Corp., 28 F.4th 1360, 1364 (Fed. Cir. 2022) ("code" was not in means plus function form and, therefore, not indefinite for lack of structural equivalents in the specification).

Specifics regarding number of blades, thicknesses, juxtapositions, relative or absolute distances between blades, materials of the blades, and so on, may all be important to achieve a certain function. Likewise, these specific and *precise* details, recited in the patent claim, should assist in distinguishing the subject matter to be patented from the prior art.

However, one may imagine, in a dependent claim, it may be desirable to recite a handheld razor along with the razor blade. For one thing, the two are frequently sold together, meaning potentially larger damages and with additional evidence, potentially having a basis for a charge of deliberate copying, which may result in up to treble damages being awarded.[154] Furthermore, this would help limit claim scope relative to prior art, such as blades in general and even relative to other types of razor blades perhaps.[155] Also, if the razor were to be sold by itself, this might result in the ability to make out a claim of contributory patent infringement or inducing patent infringement with respect to a "combination claim" of the blade and razor.[156]

To draft such a claim, however, may involve explaining how the cartridge and razor are joined. But there are a host of attachment mechanisms in use and many more may be possible. It might even be the case that a new attachment mechanism is created for this razor blade cartridge (and could be separately claimed). Each manufacturer likely has a favored attachment mechanism, so that the blades (or blade cartridges) are *not* interchangeable between different razors made by different manufacturers. One might, therefore, imagine a claim like this:

EXAMPLE 1.14

I claim:

1. An apparatus comprising: a razor blade cartridge comprising a multiplicity of razor blades; wherein the multiplicity of razor blades . . . [description and details of new razor blade arrangement that provides the intended function].

2. The apparatus of claim 1, comprising: a handheld razor blade cartridge holder; wherein the handheld razor blade cartridge holder and the razor blade cartridge are attachable to one another for use in shaving.

---

154. *See* 35 U.S.C. § 284 (2022).
155. Such as razor blades for electric razors, for example.
156. *See* 35 U.S.C. § 271(b), (c) (2022).

How the two attach is left vague; however, this amount of vagueness should not run afoul of section 112 for being indefinite.[157] Likewise, it would be prudent to do several additional things, such as, in the specification, define for this context the term "attachable" in a reasonably broad and in a reasonably clear manner, such as "to at least temporarily join and/or temporarily connect two physically separate items so that they are able to operate as a single functional unit, such as a handheld razor blade cartridge holder and a razor blade cartridge." Furthermore, it would also be appropriate to give details of a particular attachment mechanism to be used and claim that in further dependent claims, as a fallback position to address the risk of an indefiniteness rejection being made.

> A good claim is an appropriate balance between breadth, vagueness, and precision.

The point, of course, is that good claims are broad, vague, and precise in the appropriate balance for the situation. However, people often focus on obtaining broad claims *exclusively*. Here, then, we would like to consider the advantages and the disadvantages associated with broad claims. Doing so serves several purposes. It clarifies that claims are not required to be broad. It also clarifies that while broad claims are sometimes desirable, there are associated risks. So, it may be the case that it is not always best to "swing for the fences." This, of course, is a judgment call and may involve questioning the client about their desires and goals. In general, this book advocates for drafting broad claims; *however, claim drafting is not a one size fits all enterprise. Being able to adjust one's approach to the situation is the true mark of a claim drafting craftsman.*

> Being able to adjust one's approach to the situation is the true mark of a claim drafting craftsman.

157. *See* Shatterproof Glass Corp. v. Libbey-Owens Ford Co., 758 F.2d 613, 624, 225 USPQ 634, 641 (Fed. Cir. 1985), *cert. dismissed*, 474 U.S. 976 (1985) ("The amount of detail required to be included in claims depends on the particular invention and the prior art, and is not to be viewed in the abstract but in conjunction with whether the specification is in compliance with the first paragraph of Section 112. . . .").

Aside from the desire to ferret out prior art, a reason to draft broad claims is that it provides a good opening position in a negotiation. In fact, if possible, it would be prudent to draft claims broader than what may be desired or expected by the decision-maker (e.g., client, manager, overseeing attorney, etc.). Not all attorneys may agree with this latter suggestion, but most should. Technically, patent prosecution is ex parte litigation. However, as a practical matter, it is more like a negotiation. In an ideal setting, the attorney or agent presents something that is undoubtedly patent eligible and meets other "non-art" statutory requirements. In this case, the negotiation is primarily about the scope of the claims relative to the known prior art. As an advocate, the attorney desires broader claims for his client. As a type of protector of the public, the examiner desires narrower claims.

The situation, therefore, is like any business transaction. It is not unlike selling a house on the real estate market, for example. The two sides have their respective desires and somewhere in between is a "deal" to be made. In the house example, the market sets the backdrop for the negotiation. In the case of a patent application, the known prior art sets the backdrop. However, for the real estate example, consider this: having put your house on the market and then received your exact asking price, you may sense you have left "something on the table." Likewise, if you submit an initial set of patent claims that are allowed on the first action, similarly, you probably could have gotten broader claims allowed (which you might now seek via a continuation patent application claiming priority to your initial filing, but you might have gotten those broader claims allowed without a continuation patent application).

However, with all that said, there is a school of thought, and it does have some merit, that if you open with an overly broad set of patent claims, you may have trouble (or at least more trouble) getting *any* patent claims allowed. The thought process is that the examiner will focus on your broadest claim, which he may then reject. Likewise, he should quickly glance through the dependent claims and may not see how any added subject matter via dependent claims makes any presented claims allowable. Thus, he rejects all the claims.

On the next action, based on the prior art and reasoning to be provided, the attorney or agent may challenge the examiner's position, but the thought is that the examiner has given the case all the time he plans for now, and to get additional *serious* consideration from the examiner and/or further searching will require a continuation patent application, which will consume more resources, such as time and money.

Thus, advantages of broad claims include ferreting out the prior art and providing a good open position for a negotiation. However, disadvantages include biasing the examiner against allowance, potentially raising the cost of patent prosecution.

Another potential advantage of being broad is that one may get an issued claim that is broader "at the margin" than you would otherwise have obtained.[158] The idea here is that the examiner might only be willing to fight so hard, or even, one might expect, your articulate and incisive legal arguments may convince the examiner to issue the broader claim.

Although actual data on this point is not available to the author's knowledge, most of the time the examiner rejects the initially presented claims, regardless of breadth or narrowness, and regardless of known prior art. Another way to say this is: due to his *bias*, regardless of what you present, the examiner will *find* a reason to reject the claims. This is not intended as a statement about a conspiracy at the PTO or a statement about competence. Rather, this is a statement about human nature.

This, of course, is more anecdotal than it is scientific, but may be worth this consideration at least: if you are trying to draft a claim of only sufficient breadth so that it will be allowed more easily, are you not, in a sense, *simply negotiating against yourself*? Again, examiners like to reject claims. It's their job. That is most certainly true. In general, it is reasonably likely that the examiner will at least initially reject your claims even if you have written them to be allowable over the art you know of, and the examiner finds no better art. If you accept this latter proposition as true at least most of the time, then it seems logical, at least as an opening negotiating position, to file claims that are broader than you are truly seeking, just like no one puts their house on the market for the price they genuinely want. Rather, they always ask for more expecting to be negotiated down to the price they want. Negotiation is a requirement in this setting—not by law, but by human nature, just as in any business transaction. If you attempt to short circuit the negotiation process by deliberately sandbagging your initial set of claims, you will more likely end up with less than you had hoped or, even worse, less than you might have otherwise obtained.

Negotiation is a requirement in this setting—not by law, but by human nature, just as in any business transaction.

158. Further, it is entirely conceivable that you will get allowed claims that are broader than you "needed" or "expected." It generally depends on the quality of the prior art the examiner presents and the advocate's ability to distinguish that art.

Another potential advantage of this potentially broader "at the margin" claim is that it is presumed valid, if issued. The burden would fall on another to show it is invalid by *clear and convincing* evidence in a federal court litigation. Of course, other proceedings are also available, such as *ex parte* reexamination, an IPR, or a PGR.[159] A detailed discussion of these latter proceedings is beyond the scope of this book, but all have various trade-offs, including that the procedural law for IPRs and PGRs is still developing. Furthermore, it almost goes without saying that a broader claim opens one up to an attack from more prior art, a clear disadvantage; however, such is the fundamental trade-off in this discipline.

However, consider that, for a claim in which validity may be a close question, such as the broader "at the margin" claim you managed to convince an examiner to issue, it may still have significant value due to the procedural protections associated with being a claim of a patent. If a company's exposure to the claim is high (e.g., many $$$), they may prefer a more certain negotiated solution (e.g., a patent license or a covenant not to sue) to an uncertain litigation or other type of proceeding (e.g., IPR). After all, the claims after having their validity tested in one of these proceedings may emerge much stronger. A settled and reasonable solution may be better than rolling the dice.

This is typically how a rationale decision-maker should operate unless the amount being requested for a license/covenant not to sue is ridiculously out of line with the value to the target company of avoiding a lawsuit or similar proceeding. In addition, as the patent claim drafter, you may manage the risk of invalidity of the broadest claim by including a set of dependent claims in which one or more of these dependent claims may remain infringed, but also remains narrow enough to avoid problematic prior art. Thus, these are additional potential advantages associated with seeking the broader claims.

An experienced patent attorney once told me that if you are *persistent enough* you should be able to get a claim issued to meet your client's needs. Although this anecdotal statement is no guarantee, there still is at least an element of truth in this notion. However, this concept of persistence also implicitly points out a disadvantage of "swinging for the fences."

Your attempts at getting a broad claim issued will almost certainly result in additional cost, as mentioned, and perhaps, more importantly, it will likely create more prosecution history estoppel and "claim estoppel." In general, "estoppel" refers to being held to a position taken because another relied upon the position taken to their disadvantage. Under U.S. patent law, if you take

159. IPR stands for Inter Partes Review; PGR stands for Post-Grant Review.

a position before the PTO, you are held to that position, in theory at least, because it would disadvantage those who might rely on the written record. If, for example, you make an argument that your claim distinguishes from the prior art based on a particular interpretation of the claim language, you are not permitted to later advocate for another inconsistent interpretation. Patent law distinguishes between estoppel that affects literal claim scope (termed here "claim estoppel," but more typically is viewed as "claim interpretation in light of the prosecution history"[160]) and estoppel that affects nonliteral claim scope (termed generally "prosecution history estoppel").

Of course, part of the idea of such a process is that you may argue about or even amend your claims to address previously unknown prior art uncovered by the examiner. This is not necessarily bad; rather, it is expected. However, a claim amendment will likely create both types of estoppel and argument may also create both types of estoppel. Thus, an initial claim posture that does not require amendment and argument might provide a better end result than one that does.

To appreciate the consequence, one should compare a hypothetical situation in which broad claims are presented that result in a protracted prosecution to secure allowance with a scenario where narrower claims are presented and no change to the claim language and no argument is required to secure allowance. Also, one should also compare this former hypothetical situation with a scenario where at least some dependent claims of an initial set are allowed without amendment, likely creating less estoppel than may result from correspondence back and forth with the examiner that includes both various arguments and various amendments.

The point is that a greater amount of estoppel will likely result from a tortured prosecution involving several continuations, various pieces of art, and lots of attorney argument/amendment to secure allowance, than a simple "in and out" prosecution (e.g., no continuations needed). Of course, there is no way to predict which will result. This is where judgment, the specifics of the situation, client wishes, the technology, the art, the trade-offs just discussed, and so on, all bear on how best to draft the initial set of claims.

The bottom line is these types of considerations make patent claim drafting more than a commodity service. The issues are challenging and tend to vary by situation. Generally, experience is your guide, but the explanations provided in this book are intended to provide perspective to those with little to no experience. In general, as a "default" approach with no special or

160. That is, what you say in prosecution will affect how the claim will be interpreted by a court in part because the public should be entitled to rely on such representations.

unusual considerations, the conventional wisdom seems fairly good advice to follow while appreciating the potential consequences just discussed.

As one final comment, you would be surprised, if given the opportunity, to see how opposing counsel may be able to take the claim you thought was quite broad and come up with various arguable noninfringement arguments that you did not anticipate. Why create more opportunities for opposing counsel by not attempting to write the broadest claim possible at the time based on the *known* prior art?

1.32 Searching the Prior Art Prior to Drafting—Advantages and Disadvantages

Another question that comes up a lot in the context of drafting claims is whether to conduct a prior art search and/or how much to expend in terms of resources. This was touched upon in section 1.1. Searches are, in general, notoriously poor, and high-quality searches are notoriously expensive. A mediocre-quality search should be about $2,000 to $3,000, meaning that it may uncover some relevant prior art, but you cannot necessarily feel comfortable that, if prior art to invalidate the invention exists, it has necessarily been uncovered.[161] An extremely high-quality search, such as in anticipation of litigation, on the other hand, can cost $50,000 to $100,000, or more.[162]

Of course, more resources are coming online electronically, in general, to reduce searching costs so that for the same amount, a better search might be obtained. However, appreciate that searches are labor intensive, and the search quality depends significantly on the searcher. Giving a searcher a one- or two-page description of the technology and expecting thorough results is an expectation that may more often be disappointed than not. For a cost-conscious client that nonetheless demands a search or for a situation where a search appears appropriate, one might suggest that the inventor use the PTO patent- and published application- databases. This has an advantage of increasing quality (since the inventor knows the invention technology well) while not affecting out-of-pocket costs significantly. However, the client *must* also be made aware to keep careful records since forensic computer analysis has been used in the past to show that the inventor knew of prior art and did not disclose it.[163] In general, if conducting such a search, remind the client

161. This is only a ballpark estimate based on the author's experience, not a number derived from careful studies.

162. *Id.*

163. *See* Eolas Technologies v. Microsoft, 399 F.3d 1325 (Fed. Cir. 2005).

to error on the side of disclosing the art. If you submit the art in the manner specified in the PTO regulations,[164] the examiner should initial the submission, creating a presumption that it was considered and that the examiner did not find it to be material.[165]

Several advantages and disadvantages of searching have already been mentioned. Disadvantages include additional cost, marginal quality; however, advantages include: a search may at least uncover relevant art that is easy to locate, which may be used to draft the claims, and such art may be entered in the record, which supports validity if the claims issue. Some located prior art from a modestly priced search may potentially lead to including claims and description that you might have otherwise omitted. This latter point may be one of the better benefits/advantages.

The primary reason, however, most people search is to make sure the invention was not invented previously. Hence, these are typically referred to as "novelty searches." The chief benefit is to keep you from spending a lot of money to patent something that is unpatentable because it previously existed (e.g., getting a patent is expensive).

However, this reason to search may be slightly misleading. In truth, rarely does a search find the invention exactly (a plausible reason for this is discussed later). Instead, a bunch of similar technical art that may or may not bear on patentability is more typically located.

Now, keeping in mind the prior discussion, consider, for example, that an engineer who has worked in a particular technical field for 15 or 20 years comes to you with an invention. He comes to you at least believing that his invention is new because he has not seen anything like it in his 15 to 20 years of experience in the field. Plus, his visit to see you is not a mere whim. Rather, he must schedule an appointment, fit it into his busy schedule, and show up. Also, he may already know that to file a patent application will cost thousands and perhaps tens of thousands of dollars.

As a conditional probability, because he has never seen his invention during his 15 to 20 years working in the field at issue, there could be a 60 to 70 percent chance (perhaps higher) that the invention has not been done exactly as he envisions it. Given this, is it then worth another $2,000 to $3,000 to have someone with a two-page description perform a search? The client pays a PTO filing fee of around $1,000 to $2,000 and that fee primarily pays to have the examiner search the art. So, by conducting a search in advance (especially if it is unlikely to cause the patent application to not be filed), you

---

164. *See* 37 C.F.R. § 1.56 (2022).
165. *See, e.g.*, MPEP § 609.05(b) (2022).

have, roughly, at least doubled your client's filing fees. In addition, the prior art uncovered will need to be analyzed, also raising the cost of preparing the application. So, at this point, with these considerations, such an expenditure for searching might be on the "fringe" of what might be undertaken—some might do it and some might not.

Now, let us consider additional issues related to whether to search. For one thing, there is relevant prior art that cannot be located by searching. Under the pre-AIA version of section 102, discussed in the next section in detail, prior art under pre-AIA subsection 102(g), sometimes referred to as "secret prior art," would not be found by searching. This is material that qualifies as "prior art" by statute but is not easily accessible, such as research and development performed by others. However, this may be less of an issue due to the AIA, which removed that section and moved the United States from a first-to-invent patent system to essentially a first-to-file patent system.

However, assuming AIA has addressed the issue just described, other potential prior art may also be problematic to locate. Under subsections 102(e) (pre-AIA) and 102(a)(2) (post-AIA), for example, various U.S. patent application filings that are published applications or published as patents, once published, constitute prior art as of their patent application filing date (*not* their publication date). If they are to be published applications, they will be unable to be located for at least 18 months of pendency following application filing, since that is when they are to be published. If they are designated for non-publication in the United States, they will not be published until they are issued as patents. For example, it is *not* unknown for someone to sue on a patent, only to have it invalidated by a prior filed, but later issuing patent (that was not published as a patent application at 18 months) because the patent issued after suit was filed.

For another thing, and it absolutely does happen, a search may uncover patents that could be infringed by the product that would be sold if the invention being searched were put into practice.[166] Here is the problem. Once you know about prior art that might be material to patentability of the claims to be presented, you and your client *must* disclose it to the PTO if you file a patent application with those claims. In this hypothetical, it would be a matter of public record that you and your client knew about this patent, which your client's product may later be accused to infringe. Furthermore, under U.S. Patent law, if your client knows of a patent that it may infringe and does

166. This also could happen without invalidating the prior art patents or necessarily preventing patentability of the subject matter being searched. It just depends on timing, the technical description, and the scope of the issued claims.

not have a reasonable basis for a good faith belief that the allegedly infringed claims of the patent are invalid, unenforceable, or not infringed, your client could be liable for treble damages.[167] In other words, ignorance, quite literally, here, is bliss. That is, if a client, for example, does not know about a patent and infringes it, that client might be liable for lost profits and/or a reasonable royalty by statute.[168] If the client, however, knows about the patent, and infringes it anyway, the client may be liable for up to three times that amount.

Let us think about a rational decision-maker. If that decision-maker would change what it would do knowing about a patent it might infringe, it may very well want to know about that patent and the search may provide meaningful information beyond what was intended. However, if that decision-maker does not intend to alter its plans regardless of such a patent, which may sometimes be the situation, that decision-maker, if rational, would prefer *not* to know about that patent. A rational decision-maker would prefer not to know about that patent, on balance, because, at best, it may be of marginal use in deciding whether to seek patent protection on technology that may be commercialized. Realize that there is no duty to search. However, having performed a search, the inventor(s), the attorney, and the company, as the applicant, all *have* a duty to disclose information material to patentability that has been uncovered.[169] Here, again, ignorance is bliss.

One way to view searching in this context is as having a "risk-adjusted" cost to the information obtained *beyond* merely the out-of-pocket cost to do the search. The real question, in context, is whether the information sought is worth that risk-adjusted cost, such as the risk that an adverse patent may be uncovered. For this reason, different companies have different policies regarding whether it is appropriate to search and/or study prior art. This is an area where reasonable minds may differ. However, what is important is to understand the reason for looking at prior art before doing so. There may, for example, be a legitimate technical reason unrelated to seeking patent protection for studying prior art. One should at least be mindful of the cost/risk associated with seeking such information before beginning.

There is yet another risk-adjusted cost to the information obtained if a search is performed. Again, these are termed "novelty searches," but, in reality, the searches typically uncover what we call "103 art," meaning it could *not* be used in a novelty rejection under section 102, a topic discussed in some detail in the next few sections; however, uncovered prior art could perhaps be used

167. *See* 35 U.S.C. § 284 (2022).

168. *Id.*

169. *See, e.g.*, 37 C.F.R. § 1.56 (2022).

in an obviousness rejection under section 103, also touched upon in the next few sections. Thus, it is entirely possible that an examiner may refuse to issue submitted claims based on a 103 document that you provided from a search when you genuinely believe that the particular 103 document is not a barrier to patentability. Yet, if you had not performed the search, which, again, did not serve its main function of preventing filing of the application, then the examiner might have allowed the claims because he, you, and the inventor might not have known about the 103 document. Again, here, ignorance is bliss because there is nothing wrong with not conducting the search.

Appreciate that much of the previous discussion is about risk and probabilities. However, if you believe the risks just described could never happen, you would be mistaken. Granted it is anecdotal, but all the risks described have happened to the author, and, in some instances, have occurred more than once. That does not mean that it has a high probability of occurring; however, it means it is an *actual* risk.

There are a few more additional points to consider in the context of making a fully informed decision. By doing a search, you may uncover prior art that leads you to add more dependent claims and additional technical disclosure. If you chose not to search, the burden may fall on you to be reasonably thorough in preparing a patent application with a complete description and a set of claims having wide scope, lest you be undone by a document you might have been able to amend around with appropriate written description but are now unable to do so for want of written description.

It is also helpful to be aware that many and perhaps even most patent savvy technology companies and patent savvy intellectual property firms do *not* perform searches except in a few special circumstances. They likely believe the resources that would be used to search are better allocated to preparing a better-quality patent application. However, in contrast, also be aware that some companies in the business of getting patents and collecting significant royalties from those patents have a policy of *always* having a search performed. This may be speculative, but a plausible reason is that this, in general, provides prior art to disclose and may, therefore, like an inoculation, go far to undermining a charge of inequitable conduct for deliberately withholding known prior art if litigation ensues.[170] Companies in the business of filing, issuing, and asserting patents may do things in prosecution designed to undermine commonly used patent litigation tactics, which often may include a charge of inequitable conduct for withholding known, material prior art. The recommendation here is

170. *See* section 5.5, discussing inequitable conduct and how to avoid it.

to not perform a search except in special circumstances. Examples of unusual circumstances include: the inventors are not knowledgeable about the art, or it is too hard to believe the technology at issue has not been done previously given what is known, and so on.

Also, as previously discussed, this does not necessarily mean never look at prior art. Instead, it means understand the reasons for doing so and be mindful of the risks. There are legitimate technical reasons for studying prior art but be sure you have done the cost/benefit analysis ahead of time.

This does not necessarily mean never look at prior art. Instead, it means understand the reasons for doing so and be mindful of the risks. There are legitimate technical reasons for studying prior art but be sure you have done the cost/benefit analysis ahead of time.

1.33 What Is Considered to Be Prior Art?

Section 101 of the current statute requires that an invention be "new."

Section 102 then specifies conditions that result in anticipation, meaning that the invention is not new. To complicate matters, however, section 102 was changed on March 16, 2013. This situation requires contemplating the prior section 102 statute (pre-AIA) and the current section 102 statute (post-AIA).

Other related matters discussed later include issues in which an application filed after March 16, 2013 (i.e., post-AIA) claims priority to one filed before that date (pre-AIA), and admissions of prior art, which, of course, are best avoided if possible.

1.331 35 USC § 102/§ 103 PRE-AIA

102

We begin our discussion with the pre-AIA statute (i.e., sections 102 and 103 of title 35). We have several reasons for doing so. These statutes were in effect for many decades. So, many more cases have clarified the meaning of the language of these statutory sections. The part of the current statute that affected statutory sections 102 and 103 went into effect on March 16, 2013. In the time since then only a few cases have needed to clarify the post-AIA statutory language. In addition, the currently in effect statutory sections at issue either share identical language with the prior statutory sections or at least employ similar language. Consequently, interpretations of the currently in effect statutory sections have been and will in the future be made with reference to the prior statutory sections. Furthermore, these pre-AIA statutory sections apply to some pending applications: specifically, those patent applications filed pre-AIA that remain pending before the PTO, and those filed post-AIA, but which, under sections 120 and 121 are a continuation or a divisional patent application of a pre-AIA filed patent application may have what constitutes prior art construed under pre-AIA sections 102 and 103.

35 USC section 102 (pre-AIA) stated:

> A person shall be entitled to a patent unless:
>
> (a) the invention was known or used by others in this country, or patented or described in a printed publication in this or a foreign country, before the invention thereof by the applicant for patent, or
>
> (b) the invention was patented or described in a printed publication in this or a foreign country or in public use or on sale in this country, more than one year prior to the date of the application for patent in the United States, or
>
> (c) he has abandoned the invention, or
>
> (d) the invention was first patented or caused to be patented, or was the subject of an inventor's certificate, by the applicant or his legal representatives or assigns in a foreign country prior to the date of the application for patent in this country on an application for patent or inventor's certificate filed more than twelve months before the filing of the application in the United States, or
>
> (e) the invention was described in—(1) an application for patent, published under section 122(b), by another filed in the United States before the invention by the applicant for patent or (2) a patent granted on an application for patent by another filed in the United States before the invention by the applicant for patent, except that an international application filed under the treaty defined in section 351(a) shall have the effects for the purposes of this subsection of an application filed in the United States only if the international application designated the United States and was published under Article 21(2) of such treaty in the English language; or
>
> (f) he did not himself invent the subject matter sought to be patented, or
>
> (g) (1) during the course of an interference conducted under section 135 or section 291, another inventor involved therein establishes, to the extent permitted in section 104, that before such person's invention thereof the invention was made by such other inventor and not abandoned, suppressed, or concealed, or (2) before such person's invention thereof, the invention was

made in this country by another inventor who had not abandoned, suppressed, or concealed it. In determining priority of invention under this subsection, there shall be considered not only the respective dates of conception and reduction to practice of the invention, but also the reasonable diligence of one who was first to conceive and last to reduce to practice, from a time prior to conception by the other.

Pre-AIA 102 Generally

This pre-AIA statutory section begins by operating in the negative and stating "[a] person shall be **entitled** to a patent **unless** . . ." (emphasis supplied). Meeting the subsection conditions of the statute, in effect, negate novelty. Likewise, the subsections are separated by "or." Thus, meeting any one subsection would render the subject matter at issue unpatentable as being anticipated. In general, this section is thought of as defining the scope of what constitutes prior art, an important analytic concept with respect to drafting patent claims.[171]

Negating novelty is referred to as anticipation, which means that the invention at issue is contained in the prior art based on a strict identity test with the language of a claim.[172] In prosecution of the patent application, this would lead to a rejection of the claim at issue under section 102 as anticipated. Likewise, in federal court litigation, this would result in the patent claim being declared invalid under section 102. Strict identity under federal circuit law means that a single piece of prior art (such as a patent, for example, with a filing date before the filing date of the claim at issue) includes all the elements and limitations of the patent claim at issue arranged in the same way as recited in the patent claim.[173]

Notably, a single document *might* include all the elements and limitations of the claim and *still not* anticipate.[174] For example, a patent, again, with an earlier filing date, may describe various separate pieces of hardware but an examiner might try to combine those distinctive features of separate pieces of

171. *See, e.g.*, Chisum, *supra* note 3, § 6.02[3](c) ("Federal Circuit decisions consistently confirm that Section 102(b) bar events constitute 'prior art' for purposes of obviousness."); Walterscheid, *supra* note 149; *Prior Art in Patent Law*, *supra* note 149.

172. *See, e.g.*, U.S. Water Servs. v. Novozymes A/S, 843 F.3d 1345, 1350 (Fed. Cir. 2016) ("A reference is anticipatory under 35 U.S.C. §102(b) (2006) . . . if 'the prior art reference . . . disclose[s] each and every feature of the claimed invention, either explicitly or inherently.' Eli Lilly & Co. v. Zenith Goldline Pharms., Inc., 471 F.3d 1369, 1375 (Fed. Cir. 2006).").

173. *Id.*

174. *See* Linear Tech. Corp. v. Int'l Trade Comm'n., 566 F.3d 1049 (Fed. Cir. 2009); Boston Scientific Scimed, Inc. v. Cordis Corp., 554 F.3d 982 (Fed. Cir. 2009); Ecolochem, Inc. v. S. Cal. Edison Co., 227 F.3d 1361, 56 USPQ2d 1065 (Fed. Cir. 2000), *cert. denied*, 532 U.S. 974 (2001).

hardware and reject the claim as anticipated. This would be improper. At best, such a document would be a basis for a rejection of the claim as obvious under section 103, explained in more detail later. The point of having all the elements and limitations in a single document is so that the document contains a single description, either expressly or impliedly, that includes all the elements and limitations together arranged in the manner recited in the claim. If those elements and limitations, instead, are shown in different pieces of hardware throughout a document with different purposes and features regarding those different pieces of hardware, anticipation has not occurred.

We previously described the process of "reading" a claim on an accused device or on the prior art and discussed the axiom "that which anticipates, if later in time [literally] infringes."[175] This "reading" a claim onto prior art is the process used to determine if a claim is anticipated under section 102. It is worthy of a mention that just as claim construction is needed to determine infringement, likewise, it is needed to determine anticipation in a legal proceeding.[176] It almost goes without saying that as the claim drafter, you, through the words you chose and how you formulate the claims, have the ability to affect such a claim construction so that it is either straightforward, to benefit your client, or somewhat tortured, which may or may not win the day in a dispute.

Along these lines, a key point to understand is that, in general, *substantively* a claim is construed consistently in a later litigation as it was construed during examination.[177] However, the different procedural postures affect the procedural rules applied. That is, during litigation, the patent claims, being issued, are presumed valid;[178] however, during examination they are not. Likewise, during litigation, the file history is used to interpret the claims, whereas during normal examination, it is not. Finally, during examination, the claims may be modified, whereas during litigation they may not. Therefore, considering these *procedural* differences, examiners or the Patent Trial and Appeal Board (PTAB), if reviewing an examiner's rejection, are permitted to give claims their "broadest reasonable interpretation" (BRI), which is broader than the interpretation applied by a federal court in litigation. However, substantively, the claim language is to be construed consistently. That is, specific language

---

175. See section 1.211, discussing reading a patent claim on an accused product or on the prior art.

176. *See, e.g.*, Tate Access Floors, Inc. v. Interface Architectural Res., Inc., 279 F.3d 1357 (Fed. Cir. 2002).

177. *See, e.g.*, Traxcell Techs., LLC v. Sprint Commc'n. Co. LP, 15 F.4th 1121 (Fed. Cir. 2021); Traxcell Techs., LLC v. Nokia Sols. & Networks Oy, 15 F.4th 1136 (Fed. Cir. 2021).

178. *See, e.g.*, Microsoft v. i4i Ltd. P'ship, 564 U.S. 91, 131 S. Ct. 2238 (2011).

of a patent claim may not be construed one way in prosecution and then have that same language construed in a different manner in litigation. This relates to the estoppel previously discussed.[179] Notably, a key feature of the BRI standard is that the interpretation must be *reasonable* in light of the language of the claim and the specification.[180]

Two Types of Subsections—Novelty and Statutory Bars

The subsection conditions of pre-AIA section 102 are viewed as one of two types. The first type relates to lack of novelty (i.e., anticipation) of the invention and the second type relates to "statutory bars." The primary subsections related to novelty/anticipation are subsections 102(a), 102(e), and 102(g). More specifically, these subsections specify conditions that are followed by the phrase "before the invention thereof by the applicant for patent." For example, 102(a) states: "the invention was known or used by others in this country, or patented or described in a printed publication in this or a foreign country, **before the invention thereof by the applicant for patent**" (emphasis supplied). Thus, the invention is in the prior art if it was known or used by others in this country before it was invented by an applicant for a patent. Likewise, the invention is in the prior art if it was patented or described in a printed publication in this or a foreign country before it was invented by the applicant. Since the invention, in these examples, is in the prior art, the invention is not novel and, per the statute, the applicant "is not entitled to a patent."

Another important issue under the pre-AIA statute is how to interpret "before the invention thereof." To some extent, this is addressed by subsection 102(g), discussed in more detail later. Pre-AIA, the United States was a first-to-invent country.[181] Thus, rules existed, codified in subsection 102(g), to determined priority between two inventions involving the same or quite similar subject matter, invented close in time to one another. Priority is awarded to the party that demonstrates prior invention with evidence. Subsection 102(g)(2) states:

> In determining priority of invention under this subsection, there shall be considered not only the respective dates of conception and reduction to practice of the invention, but also the reasonable diligence of one who was first to conceive and last to reduce to practice, from a time prior to conception by the other.

---

179. *See* discussion of "claim estoppel" and "prosecution history estoppel" in section 1.31.

180. *See, e.g., In re* Suitco Surface, Inc., 603 F.3d 1255, 1260 (Fed. Cir. 2011).

181. Post-AIA, the United States is a first-to-file country with a few notable exceptions described in the next section.

Per subsection 102(g)(2), dates of "conception" and "reduction to practice" are used to determine the date of invention. However, for a filed patent application, unless evidence regarding earlier dates of conception and reduction to practice are introduced (for example, to prove the date of invention is before the date of a printed publication that is alleged to anticipate), it is presumed that *the filing date of the patent application* at issue is the date of the invention.[182]

Furthermore, unless an inventor's prior work operates under one of the statutory bars of pre-AIA section 102 (such as under subsection 102(b), discussed in detail later), an inventor *cannot*, under pre-AIA section 102, anticipate his own work.[183] This follows logically from the language "before the invention thereof by the applicant for patent" in the novelty provisions of section 102. That is, the inventor's prior work, to the extent it is related subject matter, is included as part of "the invention thereof."

The other subsections of pre-AIA 102, subsections 102(b), 102(c), and 102(d), are thought of as statutory "bars."[184] This refers to the idea that these subsections cover actions by the applicant that can result in the applicant's forfeiture of the right to seek a patent. However, here, too, if one of these subsections of 102 is met, analytically this means the invention is included in the prior art. However, the invention is barred, not because it was invented previously. Rather, the patentee/applicant engaged in conduct that resulted in forfeiture of the right to seek patent protection.

102(b)

For example, subsection 102(b), the most important of the statutory bars in pre-AIA 102, states "the invention was patented or described in a printed publication in this or a foreign country or in public use or on sale in this country, **more than one year prior to the date of the application for patent in the United States**" (emphasis supplied). By way of comparison, one may notice both the similarity and difference in language from subsection 102(a), for example.

Specifically, rather than "before the invention thereof," as in subsection 102(a), subsection 102(b) specifies: "more than one year prior to the date of the

---

182. Thinking in this manner will also be helpful to understand post-AIA section 102 in which the statutory language "before the invention thereof by the applicant for patent" is omitted and the relevant sections, instead, employ statutory language regarding "before the effective filing date of the claimed invention."

183. *See, e.g., In re* Costello, 717 F.2d 1346, 1349, 219 USPQ 389, 391 (Fed. Cir. 1983).

184. 35 U.S.C. § 102(f) is a condition that states the applicant or applicants must be inventors of the subject matter of the patent application. Notably, this provision was removed by the AIA; however, a definition of "inventor" was added that would have a similar effect.

application for patent in the United States." Thus, if the activities described in 102(b) (e.g., commercialization of the invention) take place one year and a day before the patent application filing date, then the invention would also be unpatentable as anticipated. This is often referred to as the "one-year grace" period because it gives the inventor up to a year to file a patent application, after having begun activities that could be considered to commercialize the invention, without forfeiting patent rights. Likewise, this forfeiture is interpreted as putting the invention in the public domain, hence, making the subject matter unpatentable as anticipated.

The language of subsection 102(b) that has been interpreted to address commercialization states: "the invention was . . . in public use or on sale in this country."[185] The language "in public use or on sale" has been interpreted by many Supreme Court and federal circuit cases and has special meaning in the patent context. It describes two categories of activities: putting the invention "on sale" or putting the invention in "public use."[186] Again, this language describes activities related to commercialization that may have taken place before the filing of a patent application.

The Supreme Court case, *Pfaff v. Wells Electronics*,[187] interpreted 102(b) and its "on sale" language. The decision concluded that an invention is "on sale" once subject to a commercial offer for sale under the principles of contract law if the invention is also "ready for patenting." Thus, once an inventor engaged in such conduct, under pre-AIA 102(b), the inventor had up to one year to file a patent application to prevent the forfeiture of patent-related rights.

Notably, under various federal circuit cases neither the offeror nor the offeree necessarily needs to be aware that an invention is involved in the offer for sale. For example, marketing personnel might be offering a chip or software for sale to customers and may be unaware of the specific technology and that it relates to a patentable invention. Similarly, the customer receiving the offer may likewise be unaware of this. Furthermore, the offer does not need to even be accepted. The fact that an offer that if accepted would constitute an enforceable contract is sufficient to indicate that commercialization of the invention has begun, triggering the one-year grace period. An invention being

185. It is worth noting that the post-AIA provision removed all "in this country" requirements.

186. Furthermore, recently, the Supreme Court determined that, because this language is carried forward in the post-AIA 102 statute, despite other changes in the language of 102 around it, Congress intended this language to retain its prior construed meaning. *See* Helsinn Healthcare S.A. v. Teva Pharm. USA, Inc.,139 S. Ct. 628 (2019).

187. *See* Pfaff v. Wells Electronics, Inc., 525 U.S. 55 (1998).

"on sale" (as well as being in "public use," explained later) is a pernicious trap for the unwary.

"Ready for patenting" is a phrase coined by the esteemed Judge Learned Hand and adopted by the Supreme Court in the *Pfaff* case. In general, it means that the inventor has a full and complete conception of the invention to such an extent that, if explained to "one of ordinary skill in the art" (such as might be a description as in the patent application as filed), the invention could be reduced to practice (i.e., implemented without requiring additional invention (e.g., without undue experimentation) for it to work as intended).[188]

A "public use" while different from being "on sale," has similar underlying policy considerations. It refers to a use that is public; however, it also refers to a "commercial use" that may occur in secret, such as a manufacturing process, if the process that would be the subject of a patent application is being used for its intended purpose.

To some extent, the law of "public use" for these purposes is derived based on a Supreme Court case from the 1800s, *Egbert v. Lippmann*.[189] The facts of that case demonstrate how difficult this law can be for the unwary. The invention in the case involved an improved corset. The inventor's girlfriend wore the improved corset in "public" (although no one knew it) under her outer clothing and was using it for its intended purpose (as opposed to an experimental purpose[190]), which was, therefore, held to constitute a public use. By analogy, then, *executing* software, as an example, through demonstration of a product at a trade show, will likely result in public use of an invention buried in the code, although no one is necessarily aware that the code being implemented contains a patentable invention "under the hood." That is, such an activity would trigger the one-year grace period under pre-AIA 102(b).

Similarity of 102(b) and 102(a)

It bears mention that 102(a) and 102(b) have language in common. Both state: "the invention was patented or described in a printed publication in this or a foreign country." It follows that this language is to be construed in the same manner, discussed in some detail in this section. The notable features include "patented," "described in a printed publication," and "in this or a foreign country." "Printed publication" appears to arise more frequently with respect

---

188. The term "one of ordinary skill in the art" comes from 35 U.S.C. § 103. It is used in both pre-AIA and post-AIA versions of section 103. *See* section 1.33 and its subsections, discussing pre- and post-AIA section 103.

189. *See* Egbert v. Lippmann, 104 U.S. (14 Otto) 333 (1881).

190. *See* Elizabeth v. Pavement Co., 97 U.S. 126, 24 L. Ed. 1000 (1878).

to anticipation than "patented" at least partially because in the United States when patents are granted, they are also published in full.

The "printed" portion of the term "printed publication" over the years has been read more expansively with the evolution of technology. In general, tangibility appears to be a feature of "printed."[191] A document appearing on a display of a device while being stored in memory to preserve the document would, therefore, seem to qualify as "printed." The term "publication" seems to be evolving as questions arise for the PTAB in Inter Partes Review (IPR) proceedings that are appealed to the federal circuit. Public accessibility appears to be key to that concept. The federal circuit has noted the "leading case on public accessibility" is *In re Hall*,[192] which involved a single *cataloged* thesis in a university library that constituted a "printed publication" because cataloging the thesis provided "sufficient accessibility to those interested in the art exercising reasonable diligence."[193]

The description provided by a printed publication must be adequate, meaning that it must enable one of ordinary skill in the relevant art (e.g., the art to which the claimed subject matter of the application pertains) to make and use the invention.[194] However, patents and even printed publications are presumed to be enabling, although that presumption may be rebutted with evidence.[195] The federal circuit employs a "four corners" rule for printed publications asserted to be anticipatory.[196] However, matters well-known to those of ordinary skill in the relevant art need not be described.[197]

"Patented" in subsections 102(a) and 102(b) does not usually arise for patents of the United States. A printed publication occurs at the same time that

191. *See In re* Enhanced Security Rsch., LLC, 739 F.3d 1347 (Fed. Cir. 2014).

192. *See In re* Hall, 781 F.2d 897 (Fed. Cir. 1986).

193. *See In re* Enhanced Security Rsch., LLC, 739 F.3d at 1354.

194. *See* Schering Corp. v. Geneva Pharmaceuticals, Inc., 339 F.3d 1373, 67 USPQ2d 1664 (Fed. Cir. 2003), *reh'g and reh'g en banc denied*, 348 F.3d 992, 68 USPQ2d 1760 (Fed. Cir. 2003).

195. *See* Amgen Inc. v. Hoechst Marion Roussel, Inc., 314 F.3d 1313, 65 USPQ2d 1385 (Fed. Cir. 2003), *on remand*, 339 F. Supp. 2d 202 (D. Mass. 2004), *vacated and remanded*, 457 F.3d 1293 (Fed. Cir. 2006), *reh'g and reh'g en banc denied*, 469 F.3d 1039 (Fed. Cir. 2006), *cert. denied*, 550 U.S. 953 (2007); *In re* Epstein, 32 F.3d 1559, 31 USPQ2d 1817 (Fed. Cir. 1994).

196. *See, e.g.*, Lindemann Maschinenfabrik GMBH v. Am. Hoist & Derrick Co., 730 F.2d 1452, 1459 (Fed. Cir. 1984). ("'[U]nless a reference discloses within the four corners of the document not only all of the limitations claimed but also all of the limitations arranged or combined in the same way as recited in the claim, it cannot be said to prove prior invention of the thing claimed and, thus, cannot anticipate under 35 U.S.C. §102.' Net MoneyIN, Inc. v. VeriSign, Inc., 545 F.3d 1359, 1371 (Fed. Cir. 2008)).").

197. *See, e.g.*, *In re* Wiggins, 488 F.2d 538, 179 USPQ 421 (CCPA 1973) ("a reference describing an oil refinery need not describe how to make bolts and rivets in order to be considered 'enabling.'").

something is patented. Thus, the entire document is available as prior art. For foreign patents, issues regarding timing as to when something is patented and/or the scope of the claims (versus a published disclosure that might, for example, be available later) may be issues to resolve, depending on the foreign country's patent procedures.

102(e)

Subsection 102(e) states:

> the invention was described in—(1) an application for patent, published under section 122(b), by another filed in the United States before the invention by the applicant for patent or (2) a patent granted on an application for patent by another filed in the United States before the invention by the applicant for patent, . . .[198]

Congress, via subsection 102(e), codified a Supreme Court decision written by Justice Holmes that made a patent effective as anticipatory prior art as of its filing date. The portion of the statute regarding published patent applications was added in 2000 because of 18-month publication of patent applications becoming part of patent law in the United States.

The language "by another" may raise tricky issues because it is interpreted to refer to a "so-called" inventive entity of the published application or patent.[199] Imagine a situation where A files a patent application and an examiner rejects A's patent application based on a published patent application by A, B, and C with an earlier filing date that has been published for less than a year.[200] This appears to be a different inventive entity than A alone and may qualify as "by another." However, recall that an inventor's own work cannot anticipate except under a statutory bar. If it can be shown that the material in the published patent application that is anticipatory was invented by A alone, then this published patent application may not anticipate under the principle that an inventor's own work cannot anticipate his later work.

Furthermore, subsection 103(c) (pre-AIA) was added to ameliorate situations like this, which may frequently arise at a company, university, and so on, where inventor teams may work on similar subject matter. That subsection of section 103 states:

198. It is noted that the substance of section 102(e) was retained in the post-AIA 102 provision under section 102(a)(2).

199. LSI Corp. v. Regents of Univ. of Minn., 43 F.4th 1349 (Fed. Cir. 2022).

200. This published application should have been disclosed by A to the PTO under 37 C.F.R. § 1.56, since it would have been known to A.

> Subject matter developed by another person, which qualifies as prior art only under one or more of subsections (e), (f), and (g) of section 102, shall not preclude patentability under this section [103] where the subject matter and the claimed invention were, at the time the claimed invention was made, owned by the same person or subject to an obligation of assignment to the same person.

The benefit of this subsection may be better understood with a later discussion of subsection 103(a) in this section; however, its effect is to remove prior art that qualifies under subsection 102(e) (or 102(f) or 102(g)) *from consideration under subsection 103(a)* if it is *not* anticipatory under the strict identity test. For example, assuming the published application in the prior example qualifies as prior art under 102(e), if the examiner were to cite the published application for most of the limitations of a claim of A's patent application being rejected, but the examiner needed to combine the published document with another prior art document to meet all the claim limitations, then under subsection 103(c) the published application does *not* qualify as prior art for purposes of subsection 103(a), assuming A's patent application and the published patent application are commonly owned, such as by a corporate entity that employs A, B, and C.[201]

Subsection 102(e) also captures published international applications, such as those published by the World Intellectual Property Organization (WIPO), which are filed in connection with the patent cooperation treaty (PCT), and that result in a published application or patent in the United States stating:

> except that an international application filed under the treaty defined in section 351(a) shall have the effects for the purposes of this subsection of an application filed in the United States only if the international application designated the United States and was published under Article 21(2) of such treaty in the English language; . . .

This, however, would not include a foreign filed patent application, such as filed in the patent office of another country, which was the basis for priority resulting in a U.S. patent. Rather, such a patent would only count as prior art as of its U.S. filing date under the *Hilmer* doctrine.[202]

A question arises regarding how subsection 102(e) is affected by provisional patent applications. Subsection 102(e), as mentioned, may result in a

201. It is noted that section 103 was modified post-AIA to remove this section; however, post-AIA section 102 has a section that has a similar effect. See the discussion in the next section, section 1.332.

202. *See In re* Hilmer, 359 F.2d 859, 149 USPQ 480 (CCPA 1966); however, be aware that the AIA abolished the Hilmer doctrine.

published patent application constituting prior art as of its publication date. A provisional patent application was added to section 119, permitting one to file a less than full patent application and then within 12 months of that date perfect (e.g., convert) it to a utility patent application by supplying missing elements of a full utility patent application and paying appropriate fees. That is, for example, for a published application that originated as a provisional patent application before becoming a utility patent application, what is the prior art effect of the provisional patent application under 102(e)? The material in the published application may be considered to be anticipatory as of the provisional filing date provided that the material relied upon is supported by the provisional application.[203]

102(g)

Subsection 102(g), as mentioned, relates to establishing priority in a first to invent system; under this subsection, therefore, similar rules are used to determine anticipatory prior art. Specifically, the subsection refers to invention by another before the invention for which a patent is sought. Subsection 102(g) is not present in the post-AIA statute, which establishes a first-to-file system in the United States, but this subsection has importance pre-AIA. Under subsection (2) of 102(g), it states:

> [A person shall be entitled to a patent unless…] before such person's invention thereof, the invention was made in this country by another inventor who had not abandoned, suppressed, or concealed it. In determining priority of invention under this subsection, there shall be considered not only the respective dates of conception and reduction to practice of the invention, but also the reasonable diligence of one who was first to conceive and last to reduce to practice, from a time prior to conception by the other.

Subsection 102(g)(2) involves notions of "conception" and "reduction to practice." Although the subsection now is gone from 102, these two notions will remain features of U.S. Patent law even post-AIA. For example, both are discussed in *Pfaff*.[204] Likewise, conception historically has had a role in determining the inventorship with respect to a patent application.[205] Under the "model" of inventing in subsection 102(g), two parts are involved—a mental part and a physical part. In theory, a conception of an invention, the mental

203. *See* Dynamic Drinkware, LLC v. Nat'l Graphics, Inc., 800 F.3d 1375 (Fed. Cir. 2015).

204. *See* Pfaff v. Wells Electronics, Inc., 525 U.S. 55 (1998).

205. *See* Sewall v. Walters, 21 F.3d 411, 415 (Fed. Cir. 1994); *In re* Land, 386 F.2d 866, 151 USPQ 621 (CCPA 1966); Mueller Brass Co. v. Reading Indus., 352 F. Supp. 1357 (E.D. Pa. 1972).

part, is "the formation in the mind of the inventor of a definite and permanent idea of the complete and operative invention as it is thereafter to be applied in practice."[206] The date on which this happens is the conception date of the invention.

Likewise, a reduction to practice is the physical, implementation part. Thus, it involves building the invention and proving that it works for its intended purpose.[207] The date on which this happens is the date of reduction to practice of the invention. Reduction to practice should involve no new inventing (e.g., not requiring undue experimentation) to get the invention to work for its intended purpose since conception is a "definite and permanent idea of the complete and operative invention as it is thereafter to be applied in practice." Thus, in theory, after having a conception, an inventor should be able to explain his conception to one of ordinary skill who then would be able to build it and prove it works for its intended purpose without requiring new inventing (e.g., without undue experimentation). It follows, therefore, that if an invention has not actually been reduced to practice when a patent application is filed, then the filing of the patent application is considered a *constructive* reduction to practice, since the specification of a valid patent enables one of ordinary skill regarding how to make and use the invention that is the subject matter of the patent application.

Of course, a conception occurs solely in the mind of the inventor. To establish a date on which the inventor had the conception, it must therefore be documented. Likewise, reduction to practice should also be documented, although there may also be other types of physical evidence for reduction to practice. Furthermore, some older Supreme Court cases recognized an inventor's bias in his desire to establish an early date of invention. Consequently, the evidence must be *independently* corroborated. That is, corroboration must be independent of the inventor. For example, if another person signs the inventor's documentation and indicates in written form that it was read and understood on a particular date by that other person, perhaps someone of ordinary skill in the art, for example, it seems that this would provide independent corroboration. Without some type of independent corroboration, as just described, based on case law, the evidence would be of little value in a federal litigation.

---

206. *See* Hybritech Inc. v. Monoclonal Antibodies, Inc., 802 F.2d 1367, 1376 (Fed. Cir. 1986) (quoting 1 Robinson on Patents 532 (1890)).

207. *See* Brunswick Corp. v. U.S., 34 Fed. Cl. 532, 584 (1995).

In addition to independent corroboration of conception and reduction to practice evidence, if an issue, independent corroboration of diligence evidence should also be available. Diligence relates to the part of 102(g)(2) that states:

> there shall be considered not only the respective dates of conception and reduction to practice of the invention, but also the **reasonable diligence** of one who was first to conceive and last to reduce to practice, from a time prior to conception by the other (emphasis supplied).

In terms of establishing priority, the statute operates as follows: The first to reduce to practice (based on corroborated evidence) wins the priority contest, with one exception. If the one who did *not* reduce to practice first had an earlier conception (based on corroborated evidence) and exercised reasonable diligence to reduce the invention to practice starting at a time *prior* to the conception by the one who reduced to practice first, then the one who had the later reduction to practice would win the priority contest. Also, appreciate that reduction to practice may be satisfied by filing a patent application. For some inventions, this may be the *only* reasonable approach to achieving a reduction to practice. Consider, for example, whether one could feasibly reduce to practice an invention that relates to a satellite system other than by filing a patent application.

As should now be clear, similar rules to the preceding apply regarding anticipation under subsection 102(g)(2). For example, depending on the nature of the alleged prior art, it may constitute a conception without a reduction to practice or it may constitute a conception with diligence to a reduction to practice, and so on. Affidavit practice[208] in the PTO may be employed during examination to overcome a prior art reference under these rules. Affidavit evidence in the PTO used during examination may not require independent corroboration; however, without independently corroborated evidence, someone may later challenge the patent in federal court, where independently corroborated evidence would be required, as previously explained.

Subsection 102(g)(2) specifies that the invention "was made . . . by another inventor who had not abandoned, suppressed, or concealed it." This language has a particular history and interpretation. In general, the three terms, "abandoned, suppressed, or concealed," are read together rather than as separate considerations. Furthermore, case law suggests that the scope of the language is not strictly defined, and, instead, several factors influence whether the invention has been "abandoned, suppressed, or concealed." Factors that

---

208. *See* 37 C.F.R. § 1.131 (2022); MPEP § 715 (2022).

are relevant include: length of a delay from reduction to practice to either an application for patent or commercialization; other activities during the delay; resumption of pursuit of the invention; and intent.

Subsection 102(g) also includes a subsection (1) related to interferences. This was added primarily so that subsection (2) could continue to be limited to activities "in this country" without patent interferences necessarily being similarly limited. Patent interferences were a proceeding in the PTO conducted under subsection 102(g) when there was a priority dispute over who "invented" an invention first. In a first-to-file system, as exists post-AIA, interferences have no place legally or logically.

102(a)

Subsection 102(a) is a bit complex to understand. One way to approach it is as a catchall for prior art not covered by the other major subsections of section 102, particularly 102(b) and 102(e). It is also helpful to keep in mind that a "first order analysis" is to treat the *filing date* of the subject application as the date of invention, recognizing that via subsection 102(g)(2), an earlier date of invention may be established.[209]

Pre-AIA subsection 102(a) states in part:

> the invention was known or used by others in this country, or patented or described in a printed publication in this or a foreign country, before . . . ,

One might, as an example, imagine a printed publication, such as a patent, and desire to evaluate whether it qualifies as prior art. If it is more than one year old, then it is prior art under subsection 102(b). Subsection 102(a) arises as a potential issue primarily for patents or printed publications from the United States or a foreign country, within a year or less of the patent application filing date. That is, these may be prior art under 102(a) (recognizing, again, that a potential issue remains under 102(g) if evidence is available to prove an earlier date of invention) for the subject matter to be claimed.

A similar analysis applies for "on sale" or "public use" activities, such as by a third party. If more than a year old, these are prior art under subsection 102(b). If less than a year, such activities may be prior art under 102(a) if they meet the requirements of 102(a) for "known or used by others," discussed next (again, recognizing the role of 102(g)).

---

209. This approach may simplify considerations when we move to post-AIA § 102 in which, practically speaking, the effective filing date of the claimed invention is the date of invention.

"Known or used by others" may include the description in a U.S. patent or a published U.S. patent application; however, this would, in general, be prior art under 102(e).

"Known or used by others" is, therefore, practically speaking, a catch-all for prior knowledge or prior use not arising under subsections 102(b) or 102(e).[210] However, there is not a large amount of case law around this language. Furthermore, the case law that exists is not always entirely consistent. For example, distinctions between knowledge and use are sometimes blurred. Although the statute does not expressly appear to require that the knowledge or use be public, some courts lean in that direction. This may be due to the language "by others," which suggests several individuals have prior knowledge or were engaged in prior use. In general, prior "use" or prior "knowledge" should be independently corroborated, although federal circuit case law is not fully consistent on this.

Federal circuit case law, although not fully consistent regarding prior "use," appears to suggest that to anticipate the prior use should have some amount of accessibility by members of the public.[211] Again, this may be based on the language "by others." A prior use that is deliberately concealed would then seem to not qualify as prior art under 102(a). The prior "use" must also be reduced to practice (meaning it worked for its intended purpose).

Prior "knowledge" is often difficult to distinguish from prior "use." However, it appears well-established that secret or private knowledge does not qualify as prior art under 102(a) and, therefore, cannot anticipate. Thus, it appears that prior "knowledge," like prior "use," implies at least some small amount of accessibility by members of the public.

103

Section 103 and obviousness has been the subject of entire books. Legal scholars, unsuccessfully, have tried to define what makes an invention "obvious." In Europe, they refer to this requirement as "inventive step." Obviousness is intended to be an objective standard rather than a subjective one.

The terminology "inventive step" may work better for several reasons. For one thing, it suggests more objectivity than the term "obvious." It also helps to clarify the difference from novelty as it relates to a potential invention. The

---

210. It is noted that this language is omitted from post-AIA § 102, but, instead, states: "or otherwise available to the public." It is believed that this language requires that the asserted prior art be adequate (e.g., fully enabling) and available to the public.

211. 35 U.S.C. § 102(g)(2) does not appear to have a similar requirement, so long as the invention has not been abandoned, suppressed, or concealed.

term "inventive step" clarifies that even an invention that is novel may still be unpatentable unless it demonstrates an "inventive step" over the known prior art. In other words, novel subject matter that is less than an inventive step from the closest known prior art is still unpatentable.

Given the complexity of obviousness, we will only cover a few basic points here. Previously, we discussed subsection 103(c), which created an exception under section 103(a) for certain prior art. This is notable, here, to understand the interaction between sections 102 and 103.

In general, section 102 defines anticipatory prior art. However, something may qualify as prior art without being anticipatory. For example, a patent that predates the filing date of a patent application by more than a year may be prior art, although it may not necessarily fully anticipate a patent claim. This type of prior art is sometimes referred to as 102(b)/103 prior art, for example. This means it qualifies as prior art under subsection 102(b) but does not include enough elements and limitations to anticipate the patent claim at issue. That is, under section 103, perhaps it may be combined, if done properly, with another piece of prior art under section 103 to render the invention unpatentable. Typically, then, it would be combined with another piece of prior art and the combination, if properly made, would be the basis for a rejection under subsection 103(a) during examination or, if raised in litigation, would potentially be a basis to hold a patent claim invalid.

Pre-AIA section 103 states, in full:

> (a) A patent may not be obtained though the invention is not identically disclosed or described as set forth in section 102, if the differences between the subject matter sought to be patented and the prior art are such that the subject matter as a whole would have been obvious at the time the invention was made to a person having ordinary skill in the art to which said subject matter pertains. Patentability shall not be negatived by the manner in which the invention was made.
>
> (b)
>
> (1) Notwithstanding subsection (a), and upon timely election by the applicant for patent to proceed under this subsection, a biotechnological process using or resulting in a composition of matter that is novel under section 102 and nonobvious under subsection (a) of this section shall be considered nonobvious if—
>
> > (A) claims to the process and the composition of matter are contained in either the same application for patent or in separate applications having the same effective filing date; and

(B) the composition of matter, and the process at the time it was invented, were owned by the same person or subject to an obligation of assignment to the same person.

(2) A patent issued on a process under paragraph (1)—

(A) shall also contain the claims to the composition of matter used in or made by that process, or

(B) shall, if such composition of matter is claimed in another patent, be set to expire on the same date as such other patent, notwithstanding section 154.

(3) For purposes of paragraph (1), the term "biotechnological process" means—

(A) a process of genetically altering or otherwise inducing a single- or multi-celled organism to—

(i) express an exogenous nucleotide sequence,

(ii) inhibit, eliminate, augment, or alter expression of an endogenous nucleotide sequence, or

(iii) express a specific physiological characteristic not naturally associated with said organism;

(B) cell fusion procedures yielding a cell line that expresses a specific protein, such as a monoclonal antibody; and

(C) a method of using a product produced by a process defined by subparagraph (A) or (B), or a combination of subparagraphs (A) and (B).

(c)

(1) Subject matter developed by another person, which qualifies as prior art only under one or more of subsections (e), (f), and (g) of section 102, shall not preclude patentability under this section where the subject matter and the claimed invention were, at the time the claimed invention was made, owned by the same person or subject to an obligation of assignment to the same person.

(2) For purposes of this subsection, subject matter developed by another person and a claimed invention shall be deemed to have been owned by the same person or subject to an obligation of assignment to the same person if—

(A) the claimed invention was made by or on behalf of parties to a joint research agreement that was in effect on or before the date the claimed invention was made;

> (B) the claimed invention was made as a result of activities undertaken within the scope of the joint research agreement; and
>
> (C) the application for patent for the claimed invention discloses or is amended to disclose the names of the parties to the joint research agreement.
>
> (3) For purposes of paragraph (2), the term "joint research agreement" means a written contract, grant, or cooperative agreement entered into by two or more persons or entities for the performance of experimental, developmental, or research work in the field of the claimed invention.

Here, we are concerned only with subsection 103(a).

Subsection 103(a) begins: "A patent may not be obtained though the invention is not identically disclosed or described as set forth in section 102. . . ." Sections 102 and 103 are separate hurdles. If a claim is anticipated under section 102, it may not be patented; however, even if not anticipated, the patent claim may still not be patented if the prior art meets the language of 103(a) with respect to the patent claim.

The subsection then states:

> [I]f the differences between the subject matter sought to be patented and the prior art are such that the subject matter as a whole would have been obvious at the time the invention was made to a person having ordinary skill in the art to which said subject matter pertains. Patentability shall not be negatived by the manner in which the invention was made.

The statute, therefore, focuses on "the differences between the subject matter sought to be patented," which refers to the patent claim at issue, and "the prior art." These differences, "as a whole" are considered "at the time the invention was made," this latter language referring to conception and reduction to practice, as previously discussed with respect to subsection 102(g).

The language "as a whole" is important because it means that for the purposes of 103(a), *the claim must be considered as a whole*. In other words, while the claim is a collection of elements and limitations, it is not proper under this subsection to simply dissect the claim into separate elements and limitations and see if the prior art has each recited element and limitation. Rather, the whole may be (and typically is) greater than the sum of the parts. This typically factors into what may make an invention unobvious. For example, there may be advantages that come from combining the elements and limitations together in the manner recited in the claim that would not be present if those elements and limitations were dissected and viewed in isolation from one another.[212] Those advantages that flow from "the whole" are relevant to determining whether the invention would have been obvious. Specifically, whether, at the time the invention was made, the invention would have been obvious to "a person having ordinary skill in the art to which said subject matter pertains."

This latter language also raises several relevant and important legal issues. What is the art to which "said subject matter pertains"? Then, for that art, what are characteristics of "a person having ordinary skill" in that art? Do they require a PhD? A master's degree? Do they require a certain amount of experience in a certain industry? And so on.

Of course, when preparing the claims, there is no way to know the answers to these questions. These issues are all subject to evidence and argument in a legal proceeding. A prudent approach may be to draft some patent claims narrower than the broadest claims to be presented such that the invention would have been unobvious at the time it was made when considering the closest known prior art to which the subject matter might pertain and even when considering someone who might have been a little *above* ordinary skill (i.e., at the time the invention was made). For the narrower claims, it may, therefore, be prudent to have arguments for patentability using the closest known prior art in the pertinent subjects that relate to the invention such that this "person" of ordinary skill would likely agree the invention would not have been obvious.

The latter may seem like a tall order; however, it is more of a way of thinking when drafting claims. That is, as discussed, while some claims are drafted to be relatively broad, you want to make sure you have a "fallback" position if the examiner comes up with closer prior art than you expected. Therefore, try to make sure that you also have claims that are sufficiently narrow so that you are able to provide persuasive arguments for patentability, even against reasonably close art.

---

212. *See, e.g.*, Panduit Corp. v. Dennison Mfg. Co., 810 F.2d 1561, 1567–68, 1 USPQ2d 1593, 1597 (Fed. Cir. 1987), *cert. denied*, 481 U.S. 1052 (1987) ("Analysis begins with a key legal question—what is the invention claimed? Courts are required to view the claimed invention as a whole. . . ."); *In re* Wright 848 F.2d 1216 (Fed. Cir. 1988) ("[I]t is the invention as a whole that must be considered in obviousness determinations. The invention as a whole embraces the structure, its properties, and the problem it solves . . .).

> For the narrower claims, it may be prudent to have arguments for patentability using the closest known prior art in the pertinent subjects that relate to the invention such that this "person" of ordinary skill would likely agree the invention would not have been obvious.

In this context, it is helpful to understand the nature of a rejection made under subsection 103(a) based on known prior art. As indicated, it is not sufficient for the examiner to take the elements and limitations of the claim and demonstrate that those are individually in the prior art.[213] Rather, the examiner must also demonstrate that the prior art contains the motivation for either combining those elements and limitations as recited in the claim or for modifying the elements and limitations from the prior art in a manner recited in the claim.[214] Specifically, such motivations *may not* come from the patent application. The latter is referred to as using "hindsight" and is legally improper. If the examiner is unable to demonstrate that such motivations are present in the prior art, then the examiner has not made a proper rejection under subsection 103(a).

Suppose an examiner has two pieces of prior art, A and B.[215] Typically, one, such as A, contains most of the features of the claim being rejected under subsection 103(a) as obvious. A, then, is the examiner's primary reference. However, there may be features of the claim not shown or described in A that are shown or described in B. B, then, is the examiner's secondary reference. The examiner will then formulate his rejection as being "based on reference A in light of reference B."

The examiner must also state on the record the basis for his assertion that there is motivation to combine references A and B. In some situations, however, be aware that even a combination of A and B does not provide the

---

213. Although examiners will, at times, do this. If so, they have not provided a legitimate (called prima facie) rejection under § 103. *See* MPEP § 2143 (2022).

214. For a recent case on lack of motivation to combine, *see* Tris Pharma Inc. v. Actavis Laboratories FL, Inc., No. 21-1495 (Fed. Cir. July 7, 2022) (non-precedential). *See also In re* Lee, 277 F.3d 1338 (Fed. Cir. 2002), ("[T]he agency tribunal must present a full and reasoned explanation of its decision. The agency tribunal must set forth its findings and the grounds thereof, as supported by the agency record, and explain its application of the law to the found facts.").

215. The examiner may also formulate a 103 rejection on a single prior art reference; however, a recent case has cast some doubt on such rejections. *See* Raytheon v. Gen. Elec., 993 F.3d 1374 (Fed. Cir. 2021).

elements and limitations from the patent claim in the manner recited in the patent claim, in which case the rejection is also improper.[216] That is, the examiner has overlooked something in formulating his rejection.

Under federal circuit law, unfortunately, the examiner may combine *any number* of prior art references in a 103 rejection. As an example, if the examiner also needs a reference C to meet the patent claim, the examiner will then formulate his rejection as "being based on reference A in light of reference B and further in light of reference C." However, as the examiner adds more pieces of prior art, some doubt may begin to increase as to whether the motivation for the proposed combination exists in the prior art. That is, while the examiner may combine any number of references, it is likely as he adds more references to make his 103 rejection that, in fact, the motivation needed to make such a combination is not present.

To summarize, the examiner must *do more than* show that the prior art he is relying upon to reject the claim meets all the elements and limitations of the claim and in the manner recited in the claim (much like in a 102 rejection for anticipation). If he cannot even accomplish the latter, his rejection is improper without evaluating "motivation to combine." However, even if he succeeds in accomplishing the latter, he must *also* show that the prior art contains the motivation to combine such prior art or to modify such prior art so that those elements and limitations are combined in the manner recited in the claim. If he fails to do this, the rejection is improper as well.

1.332 35 USC § 102/§ 103 POST-AIA

Post-AIA section 102 retains some language from pre-AIA section 102, but also has many important differences. Section 102 currently in force in the United States recites the following:

> (a) Novelty; Prior Art.—A person shall be entitled to a patent unless—
>
> (1) the claimed invention was patented, described in a printed publication, or in public use, on sale, or otherwise available to the public before the effective filing date of the claimed invention; or
>
> (2) the claimed invention was described in a patent issued under section 151, or in an application for patent published or deemed published under section 122(b), in which the patent or application, as the case may be, names another inventor and was effectively filed before the effective filing date of the claimed invention.

---

216. *See, e.g., In re* Stepan Co., 868 F.3d 1342, 1345–46 (Fed. Cir. 2017).

(b) EXCEPTIONS.—

(1) DISCLOSURES MADE 1 YEAR OR LESS BEFORE THE EFFECTIVE FILING DATE OF THE CLAIMED INVENTION.—A disclosure made 1 year or less before the effective filing date of a claimed invention shall not be prior art to the claimed invention under subsection (a)(1) if—

(A) the disclosure was made by the inventor or joint inventor or by another who obtained the subject matter disclosed directly or indirectly from the inventor or a joint inventor; or

(B) the subject matter disclosed had, before such disclosure, been publicly disclosed by the inventor or a joint inventor or another who obtained the subject matter disclosed directly or indirectly from the inventor or a joint inventor.

(2) DISCLOSURES APPEARING IN APPLICATIONS AND PATENTS.—A disclosure shall not be prior art to a claimed invention under subsection (a)(2) if—

(A) the subject matter disclosed was obtained directly or indirectly from the inventor or a joint inventor;

(B) the subject matter disclosed had, before such subject matter was effectively filed under subsection (a)(2), been publicly disclosed by the inventor or a joint inventor or another who obtained the subject matter disclosed directly or indirectly from the inventor or a joint inventor; or

(C) the subject matter disclosed and the claimed invention, not later than the effective filing date of the claimed invention, were owned by the same person or subject to an obligation of assignment to the same person.

(c) COMMON OWNERSHIP UNDER JOINT RESEARCH AGREEMENTS.—Subject matter disclosed and a claimed invention shall be deemed to have been owned by the same person or subject to an obligation of assignment to the same person in applying the provisions of subsection (b)(2)(C) if—

(1) the subject matter disclosed was developed and the claimed invention was made by, or on behalf of, 1 or more parties to a joint research agreement that was in effect on or before the effective filing date of the claimed invention;

(2) the claimed invention was made as a result of activities undertaken within the scope of the joint research agreement; and

(3) the application for patent for the claimed invention discloses or is amended to disclose the names of the parties to the joint research agreement.

(d) Patents and Published Applications Effective as Prior Art.—For purposes of determining whether a patent or application for patent is prior art to a claimed invention under subsection (a)(2), such patent or application shall be considered to have been effectively filed, with respect to any subject matter described in the patent or application—

(1) if paragraph (2) does not apply, as of the actual filing date of the patent or the application for patent; or

(2) if the patent or application for patent is entitled to claim a right of priority under section 119, 365(a), 365(b), 386(a), or 386(b), or to claim the benefit of an earlier filing date under section 120, 121, 365(c), or 386(c), based upon 1 or more prior filed applications for patent, as of the filing date of the earliest such application that describes the subject matter.

Furthermore, the AIA adds some definitions in section 100 of title 35 that were not previously codified. These include the meaning of the terms "claimed invention," "effective filing date," "inventor," and "joint inventor" (or "coinventor"). The AIA defines the term "claimed invention" as the subject matter defined by a claim in a patent or an application for a patent. This is consistent with our previous discussion of prior law. The AIA defines the term "effective filing date" for a claimed invention in a patent or application for patent (other than a reissue application or reissued patent) as meaning the earlier of (1) the actual filing date of the patent or the application for the patent containing the claimed invention; or (2) the filing date of the earliest provisional, nonprovisional, international (PCT), or foreign patent application to which the patent or application is entitled to benefit or priority as to such claimed invention. We have not previously emphasized this fine point regarding priority date, but this is consistent with prior law and assumptions made throughout this book. That is, under sections 119, 120, 121, and 365 of the statute, although a U.S. patent or patent application may have an actual filing date, it may be accorded an earlier priority date based on a previous domestic, foreign, or international patent application filing for purposes of determining prior art if properly handled. The AIA defines the term "inventor" as the individual or, if a joint invention, the individuals collectively who invented or discovered the subject matter of the invention, and defines the term "joint inventor" and "coinventor" to mean any one of the individuals who invented or discovered the subject matter of a joint invention. These are also in accordance with pre-AIA law.

Current section 102 (post-AIA) operates in a comparable manner to the previous statute by stating "A person shall be entitled to a patent unless. . . ." Thus, subsections (a)(1) and (a)(2) specify conditions that would render an invention unpatentable. Consequently, as under prior law, currently in force (post-AIA) section 102, in effect, defines prior art.

It is evident how different in structure post-AIA section 102 is from pre-AIA section 102. Subsection "a" defines prior art. Subsection "b" defines exceptions. Subsection "c" relates to common ownership and operates like subsection 103(c) of the prior statute regarding common ownership under a joint research agreement. Subsection "d" clarifies the date upon which a patent or published patent application becomes effective as prior art. This subsection, in effect, via section 365, abolishes the doctrine under *In re Hilmer*,[217] in which a U.S. patent that relied on a foreign filed application for priority was only effective as prior art as of its U.S. filing date.

In many respects, currently in force section 102 simplifies how the law now operates. As alluded to many times, the AIA moved the United States to a first-to-file system.[218] The distinction between subsections that operated as bars and those that operated based on "before the invention thereof by applicant" is no longer present. Instead, prior art is defined relative to the "effective filing date of the claimed invention," a statutorily defined term. Likewise, the ability to remove prior art from consideration because one is able to prove the invention "was made" before the date of the prior art is no longer available. This makes more prior art available to cite against a patent claim. Where possible, for this reason, one should seek to file a patent application in a manner so that the law as it was prior to March 16, 2013, applies to the patent claims, such as via a continuation patent application or a divisional patent application that claims priority to a domestic patent application filed pre-AIA.[219]

Under current law, prior art is defined concisely in subsection 102(a) by these subsections:

> A person shall be entitled to a patent unless—
>
> > (1) the claimed invention was patented, described in a printed publication, or in public use, on sale, or otherwise available to the public before the effective filing date of the claimed invention; or
> >
> > (2) the claimed invention was described in a patent issued under section 151, or in an application for patent published or deemed published under section 122(b), in which the patent or application, as the case may be, names another inventor and was effectively filed before the effective filing date of the claimed invention.

217. *See In re* Hilmer, 359 F.2d 859, 149 USPQ 480 (CCPA 1966).

218. With some exceptions, as described *infra*.

219. *See* section 1.3321, discussing how the transition provisions of the AIA operate for domestic patent applications filed on or after March 16, 2013, claiming priority to domestic patent applications filed before that date.

Subsection 102(a)(2) operates like 102(e) of the previous statute, although notably, all references to "in this country" are removed from current 102. Another notable difference is the handling of commonly owned patents and patent applications under subsection 102(a)(2). Under prior law, this was handled by subsection 103(c). Here, however, it is addressed by subsection 102(b)(2)(C). These documents are not prior art under either section 102 or 103 under current law; previously, the documents would remain prior art under pre-AIA 102(e), but were removed from consideration for the purposes of subsection 103(a). This exception also appears to be expanded in comparison to pre-AIA 102(e) based on the exception specified in post-AIA subsection 102(b)(2)(c). The current statute specifies "the subject matter disclosed and the claimed invention, not later than the effective filing date of the claimed invention, were owned by the same person or subject to an obligation of assignment to the same person," which is ostensibly later than was permitted under subsection 103(c).

Finally, there appears to be an expansion of the exception relative to "by another." Previously, this operated in accordance with inventive entity. However, under current law, an exception is provided under 102(b)(2)(A) that states: "the subject matter disclosed was obtained directly or indirectly from the inventor or a joint inventor." This suggests a broader exception because it appears to apply independent of inventive entity considerations.

Subsection 102(a)(1) of post-AIA section 102 handles everything else that was handled by the other subsections of pre-AIA 102. Specifically, subsections 102(c), 102(f), and 102(g) are removed, although the new codified definition of inventor implicitly addresses subsection 102(f) by specifying an inventor must have invented or discovered the subject matter of the invention. Pre-AIA subsection 102(g) is not needed in a first-to-file system.

As mentioned, geographical limitations on prior art have been removed. Subsection (a)(2) of section 102, however, retains "patented," "described in a printed publication," "on sale," and "public use." The language "known or used by others" is also omitted, but there is new additional language, "otherwise available to the public."

Generally, if Congress uses the same language in a new statute replacing a previous statute, courts usually interpret this to mean that Congress desires to retain the previous construction.

Furthermore, in *Helsinn*,[220] this was the result reached by the Supreme Court as to "on sale," despite the additional language "otherwise available to the public." It, therefore, is expected that all the common terms will be con-

220. *See* Helsinn Healthcare S.A. v. Teva Pharm. USA, Inc., 139 S. Ct. 628 (2019).

strued in the manner discussed previously with respect to pre-AIA section 102. It remains to be seen how "otherwise available to the public" will be construed; however, the similarity with the language used in the European Patent Convention, which states, "everything available to the public . . . ," and which has an absolute novelty standard, has not gone unnoticed.

The exceptions in subsection (b) of post-AIA section 102 raise issues that remain unsettled, even after the *Helsinn* decision, which many had hoped would clarify the status of the "grace period" under post-AIA section 102. Subsection (b)(1) specifies exceptions to (a)(1) for disclosures made one year or less before the effective filing date of the claimed invention. Subsection A of that subsection states that such a disclosure is not prior art under (a)(1) if: "the disclosure was made by the inventor or joint inventor or by another who obtained the subject matter disclosed directly or indirectly from the inventor or a joint inventor . . . ."

An ambiguity arises because the term "disclosure" is new in the statute and undefined. Its meaning in this context continues to be debated within the patent bar. Does the term refer to the elements of 102(a)(1), other than the element "otherwise available to the public," and thereby largely retaining the grace period under prior law?

A plain meaning interpretation, instead, would distinguish between activities that may or may not be accompanied by disclosure, such as the commercialization aspects under prior law regarding on sale and public use activities. Under this latter interpretation, current law has no grace period for on sale and public use activities. Rather, the grace period only applies to any accompanying disclosure. This latter interpretation, undesirable as it may be, appears more consistent with Supreme Court precedent, including *Helsinn*. For example, in that case, the Court drew a distinction between the commercial aspect of placing an invention on sale and the information made available to the public, which did not disclose details of the invention itself.

The language of subsection B of 102(b)(1) also raises questions as to its scope. It states that a disclosure one year or less before the effective filing of the claimed invention is not prior art under (a)(1) if "the subject matter disclosed had, before such disclosure, been publicly disclosed by the inventor or a joint inventor or another who obtained the subject matter disclosed directly or indirectly from the inventor or a joint inventor." The scope of "publicly disclosed" is not entirely clear. The language implies but does not expressly state that "the subject matter disclosed" is identically the same as what was "publicly disclosed." For example, what if "the subject matter disclosed" was not derived in any way from that which was "publicly disclosed"? The exception, in effect, under this interpretation would give the inventor(s) a right of priority for making the public disclosure, something that the law would like to encourage, but this is not fully consistent with what may be implied by the specific language.

Subsection (b)(2) specifies exceptions to (a)(2) regarding "DISCLOSURES APPEARING IN APPLICATIONS AND PATENTS." Subsections A and B are similar to the exceptions to (a)(1) provided under (b)(1) discussed previously. Subsection A is like 102(e), although, again, it may be slightly broader by appearing to not require an inventive entity analysis. Subsection B is similar to the corresponding exception under (b)(1) discussed earlier with similar questions as to scope. Subsection (b)(2) also includes a subsection C excluding from prior art under (a)(2) commonly owned patents and applications, similar to subsection 103(c) under the prior statute, although, again, a little broader.

103

Post-AIA section 103 is quite similar to pre-AIA subsection 103(a). Also, pre-AIA subsections (b) and (c) were eliminated in post-AIA 103, although subsection (c) under prior law is similar to post-AIA subsections 102(c) and 102(b)(2)(C).

Post-AIA section 103 states:

> A patent for a claimed invention may not be obtained, notwithstanding that the claimed invention is not identically disclosed as set forth in section 102, if the differences between the claimed invention and the prior art are such that the claimed invention as a whole would have been obvious before the effective filing date of the claimed invention to a person having ordinary skill in the art to which the claimed invention pertains. Patentability shall not be negated by the manner in which the invention was made.

Notably, it retains the reference to 102 and, therefore, operates with 102 in the manner previously described with respect to pre-AIA subsection 103(a).

The primary difference is the time at which obviousness is assessed because of the change from a first-to-invent patent system to a first-to-file patent system. Under the presently in force statute, obviousness is determined based on what would have been obvious to a person of ordinary skill in the art to which the claimed invention pertains "before the effective filing date of the claimed invention." Otherwise, current law appears to operate as the law operated under 103(a). Linguistically, the statute refers to "the claimed invention" rather than "the subject matter sought to be patented" and "negated" rather than "negatived," but these are not believed to result in any substantive interpretive difference.

1.3321 Claiming Priority to Pre-AIA Applications and Prior Art

As mentioned, the post-AIA section 102 and 103 provisions took effect on March 16, 2013. However, it is important to realize that not every patent application filed on that date and after is subject to these new provisions. Although previously we referred to "current law" when discussing post-AIA 102 and 103, since those are the statutes currently in force, to be more precise current law includes pre-AIA 102 and 103 and post-AIA 102 and 103 because of legacy filings and continuations or divisional thereof. For this reason, it is important to know which of these statutes applies to a particular application. Furthermore, if a patent application has the potential to be subject to pre-AIA 102 and 103, and that is the desire, it is important to be aware of what sorts of actions might jeopardize that status.

The AIA transition provisions (i.e., the provisions that determine the dates on which various portions of the modified statute become effective) are provided in subsection 3(n) of that AIA statute. The provisions are complex, and it takes some analysis to understand how these provisions operate.[221] Likewise, in this context, one should understand the difference between a divisional, a continuation and a continuation-in-part (CIP).[222] These are all types of patent applications having a priority date that relies on an earlier filed domestic patent application. This is permitted under sections 120 and 121 of title 35. These types of applications have an actual filing date later than their priority date, as we saw previously with respect to the definition of "effective filing date" in the AIA.

However, there is a distinction between these types of patent applications. In general, a continuation or divisional *should* not include new subject matter compared to the earlier filed application that is the basis for priority, whereas a CIP is permitted to include new subject matter compared to the earlier filed patent application that provides the basis for priority. New subject matter refers to content that was substantively not in the original filing. That is, it is subject matter not supported by the written description. For example, if you add a new patent claim, but it is supported by the written description, that is not new subject matter.

---

221. *See* Howard Skaist, *Patent Prosecution Across the AIA Divide: Warning to Patent Practitioners—Special Care Is Needed to Avoid Legal Malpractice*, IPWATCHDOG (Jan. 19, 2012, 7:30 AM), https://www.ipwatchdog.com/2012/01/19/patent-prosecution-across-the-aia-divide/id=21853/; Howard Skaist, *Traps for the Unwary Regarding Patent Claim Drafting and Definition of Prior Art Under Leahy Smith*, IPWATCHDOG (Sept. 21, 2011, 8 AM), https://www.ipwatchdog.com/2011/09/21/prior-art-under-leahy-smith/id=19290/.

222. *See* MPEP §§ 201.6, 201.7, 201.8 (2022).

These distinct types of patent applications may arise in different circumstances during patent examination. For example, a common situation for the filing of a continuation patent application is when the examiner has issued a final rejection. In this situation, patent examination may often be complete without obtaining any allowed claims. However, continuing prosecution may remain desirable because it may still be possible to convince the examiner to allow at least some of the pending claims. Filing a continuation patent application requires paying another filing fee, which entitles the owner of the patent application to an additional patent examination. Here, to be clear, new subject matter is not intended to be introduced.

There are many other situations where a continuation is desirable. As another example, during patent examination, suppose the initially filed claims have been allowed. Suppose it is desirable to let those allowed claims issue, but additional unclaimed subject matter remains in the initially filed patent application. Here, too, with the filing of a continuation patent application, new subject matter is not intended to be introduced. Remember this latter example because it is potentially relevant to our discussion regarding the AIA transition provisions and will be discussed further later.

A divisional patent application is a type of continuation patent application, but if filing a divisional patent application, *one must identify it as such* to properly claim priority.[223] In general, a divisional patent application refers to a continuation patent application where the intention is to separately prosecute a subset of the initially filed patent claims. This most frequently arises when the examiner has determined that he will only examine a subset of the initially filed patent claims because he believes multiple inventions are being claimed. He requires a divisional be filed by issuing a restriction requirement that requires splitting the claims into groupings reflecting the separate inventions he has identified. In general, one filing fee pays for examination of one invention. Thus, a divisional patent application is used to retain priority while requiring another payment of a filing fee to obtain examination for those claims the examiner will not examine in the initial patent application filing.[224]

The AIA transition provisions are written so that in the case of a continuation or divisional, pre-AIA sections 102 and 103 apply because new subject matter *should not* have been introduced in the continuation or the divisional, although these *filings take place after* March 16, 2013.

223. *Id.* § 201.6.

224. It is noted that a similar process exists in the EPO, referred to as unity of invention. See discussion thereof in Chapter 7.

The transition rules are different for a continuation-in-part (CIP). The typical situation for a CIP patent application is where the inventor has produced an extension or improvement to his initial invention, but it is not entirely clear if that extension or improvement would be patentable over the initial patent application filing. There are various legal advantages to filing a CIP patent application in this situation rather than as a separate patent application. However, a definite disadvantage, now, is that post-AIA sections 102 and 103 will apply to all the claims of the CIP, even any claims in the CIP patent application that rely entirely on the initial patent application filing for written description support.

These are the basics, but it is important to also point out a significant trap for the unwary. Recall our earlier continuation example in which the initially filed claims have been allowed. It is desirable to let those issue, although the initially filed patent application includes additional unclaimed subject matter.

In this situation, new claims need to be drafted for this continuation patent application. Suppose, in this example, in his zeal to draft valuable new patent claims the attorney or agent involved inadvertently includes a patent claim that is *clearly* new subject matter, that is, the patent claim is *not* supported by the written description of the previously filed patent application (i.e., filed before March 16, 2013). Suppose, further, that after filing the continuation patent application with the new claims, but before any action on the merits, the attorney or agent realizes what he has done and cancels the unsupported claim that constitutes new subject matter.

Under this scenario, does pre-AIA or post-AIA sections 102 and 103 apply? The wording of the transition provisions indicates that *post*-AIA sections 102 and 103 *would* apply to *all* the claims of the continuation patent application in the foregoing situation. At least partially for this reason, the PTO now requires one to certify, when filing a continuation patent application claiming priority to a pre-AIA patent application, in an application data sheet accompanying the continuation patent application filing, that the continuation contains no new subject matter.[225]

The upshot of the AIA transition provisions may be summarized as follows: if a patent claim is added at any time that does not have written description support in the original patent application filing, all the claims of the patent application filed on or after March 16, 2013, are subject to *post*-AIA section 102 and *post*-AIA section 103. Furthermore, once such a patent claim is added, this consequence cannot be undone. Once these statutory sections apply to all the

---

225. *See* PTO form PTO/AIA/14.

claims of a patent application, for example, as a result of adding new subject matter without written description support in the original pre-March 16, 2013, filing, such as by adding a patent claim, even if later the new subject matter is removed, such as cancelling the claim (because, for example, it constitutes new subject matter), those statutory sections will continue to apply to all the claims of the patent application filed on or after March 16, 2013. Furthermore, recent PTAB cases supports this interpretation.[226]

Now let us think for a moment about the potential consequences of the post-AIA provisions applying to a continuation application for the preceding scenario. For one thing, more prior art may now be citable against the patent claims. For example, if the date of invention under subsection 102(g)(2) (pre-AIA) is much earlier, one will be legally foreclosed from arguing that the invention predates prior art. However, potentially even more troubling, suppose the inventor had engaged in pre-filing commercialization activities with respect to his invention, but it took place within a year of the actual filing date, such as "on sale" or "public use" activities. Recall that the interpretation of post-AIA section 102 around these events is not settled, but *Helsinn* potentially implies that these events may bar an invention. Under these circumstances and this interpretation of post-AIA section 102, then, further prosecution, in theory, via the continuation patent application, potentially may be barred.

This is "in theory" because this all may happen inadvertently. For example, claims may be added that a judge in *later litigation* concludes do not have written description support in the original filing. At that time, then, the consequences of this on the validity of a patent that issued from the continuation patent application would need to be evaluated. This, of course, provides an excellent reason to make sure that drafted patent claims have written description support in any patent application to be filed.

> This, of course, provides an excellent reason to make sure that drafted patent claims have written description support in any patent application to be filed.

---

226. *See* Microsurgical Tech., Inc. v. Regents of the Univ. of Colo., PGR2021-00026, Paper 12 (PTAB, 2021); Rockwool Int'l A/S v. Knauf Insulation, Inc., PGR2022-00022, Paper 10 (P.T.A.B. July 6, 2022).

1.333 Avoid Prior Art Admissions

One of the riskier things to do when preparing a patent application is to either state or in any way imply that something is prior art to the patent application filing. The reason this is risky is because such a characterization, whether express or implied, may turn out to be incorrect. However, if one states or implies that something is prior art to a filed patent application, then, in certain circumstances, this is treated as an admission against interest that cannot be undone for that patent application, both during examination and even for later litigation, if it occurs.[227] Thus, any characterizations of prior art must be done with great care.

A simple rule would be to never make such a characterization, but sticking to such a rule is not so simple. For example, an examiner may require that you identify content or figures in the patent application as prior art. In addition, in explaining the benefits or advantages of an invention that would have been unobvious at the time it was made, it is often helpful to compare it with the prior art. Thus, the lesson is to be sure that something you characterize as prior art is, in fact, prior art legally, by statute, as we have discussed.

> Any characterizations of prior art must be done with great care. The lesson is to be sure that something you characterize as prior art is, in fact, prior art legally, by statute.

There are several ways to characterize something as prior art one should know. It may be done in the claims, as discussed next, using a Jepson-style claim or a claim format that is arguably Jepson-like. It may also be done by reciting that something is "prior art" in the specification, by labeling a figure as "prior art," or it may be implied by describing something in the background section of the patent application, which should *only* describe prior art and *nothing more*.[228] As a tip, the background should be written as if the invention has not yet even been invented.

---

227. *But see* Qualcomm, Inc. v. Apple Inc., 24 F.4th 1367 (Fed. Cir. 2022) (It was error to rely on applicant's admitted prior art to invalidate claims in an IPR in light of the controlling statute.).

228. *See* Moshe Wilensky, *The Past and Future of Admitted Prior Art*, 21 Tex. Intell. Prop. L.J. 237 (2013).

> As a tip, the background should be written as if the invention has not yet even been invented.

Regarding the claims, as mentioned, use of a Jepson-style claim has some risk. These claims are also discussed in more detail later.[229] 37 CFR section 1.75(e) (2022) defines the structure of a Jepson claim. It states:

> Where the nature of the case admits, as in the case of an improvement, any independent claim should contain in the following order:
>
> (1) A preamble comprising a general description of all the elements or steps of the claimed combination which are conventional or known,
>
> (2) A phrase such as "wherein the improvement comprises," and
>
> (3) Those elements, steps and/or relationships which constitute that portion of the claimed combination which the applicant considers as the new or improved portion.

Jepson claims are risky because the preamble has been held to be an admission of prior art.[230] The preamble is the initial part of the claims from the beginning up to a transition word, like "comprising." If what is recited in the preamble is without question in the prior art, use of these claims is fine. As discussed later in connection with drafting these claims, it is best to err on the side of being cautious when drafting the preamble of a Jepson claim.[231] That is, make sure that what you recite in the preamble is prior art.

Claims that are similar in structure to Jepson claims also have some risk, although the law is less settled on this. For example, it has been argued that the claim format used in the European Patent Convention (EPC) results in a prior art admission. That format uses a preamble of known or conventional elements, but then states "characterized in that" or something similar, followed by recitation of the new and improved subject matter. Similar caution should therefore be applied with this claiming style.

---

229. *See* section 2.1151, discussing Jepson claims.
230. *See In Re* Glatt Air Techniques, Inc., 630 F.3d 1026 (Fed. Cir. 2011).
231. *See* section 2.1151, discussing Jepson claims.

Jepson claims are risky because the preamble has been held to be an admission of prior art.

One reason that admissions of prior art may be inadvertently made in the background section is that some practitioners accord significance to advocacy in the background section. For example, some may describe the problem at issue in the background, believing this will aid in obtaining allowance. They wish to, in essence, "tell a story" that demonstrates the innovation. In general, such motivations are not misguided. However, doing this in the background section may be deadly. For example, there is law that states recognition of the problem, where it was not previously recognized, may render an invention unobvious, even if once the problem is recognized, the solution to the problem would be obvious to one of ordinary skill.[232] Thus, describing the problem in the background in a situation in which the problem was previously unrecognized would imply that it was recognized in the prior art, removing one of the most effective legal arguments for patentability of the invention. Again, to avoid this, draft the entire background as if the invention has not yet been invented.[233]

Another form of advocacy in the background is to state: "Therefore, a need for X exists." However, if that need is not recognized in the prior art, again, you have impliedly *or even expressly* admitted that the prior art recognizes such a need.

Again, as a rule, to be cautious, do not state *anything* in the background that you are not entirely sure is well-known and in the prior art. Any advocacy of the sort just illustrated may be done in the detailed description so that you have not inadvertently implied that what you describe predates the invention.

---

232. *See, e.g.*, Eibel Process Co. v. Minnesota & Ontario Paper Co., 261 U.S. 45 (1923).

233. *See* Wilensky, *supra* note 228. Instead, include that material in the detailed description rather than the background.

Chapter 2

Introduction to Patent Claim Drafting Mechanics and to Various Claim Types

---

High-Level Principles of This Chapter:[1]

- Understand the basic types of patent claims and what they are used to cover (via an initial introduction to this topic);
- Understand the constituent parts of a patent claim (preamble, transition phrase, and claim body) and how to draft a patent claim so that the separate parts are clearly identifiable;
- Understand the basic mechanics of how to formulate and draft a patent claim.

In this chapter we introduce the basic mechanics of patent claims and patent claim drafting, and introduce various types of claims. This introduction involves a discussion of the constituent parts of a patent claim as well as several basic patent claim drafting concepts. These concepts include the statutorily prescribed classes or categories of claims, dependent claims versus independent claims, structure versus function, method versus apparatus, and other features of patent claims.

2.1 What Is a Patent Claim?

A patent claim is a set of words that are formulated to define a set of legal rights. Of course, this describes many legal documents that affect or create legal rights. In a U.S. patent, the patent claims are the numbered "run-on sentences" at the end of the patent. The claims section is at the end of the patent

1. *See* List of Claim Drafting Principles, Appendix A.

and begins with "I claim," "We claim," "What is claimed is that," or similar language, followed by a colon, and then a sequence of numbered partial sentences to, in effect, complete a sentence that begins with "I claim:" and so on. Therefore, each patent claim ends with a period. Omitting the period may create interpretive problems that may even result in patent claim invalidity.[2] This latter format of a patent claim is largely historical.[3]

A reason claims tend to be so cumbersome is because the words are used in a reasonably precise manner to define the "metes and bounds" of the invention being patented without reference to other material. A patent is analogous to a real estate deed that provides notice to the public regarding the property boundaries. The patent claims serve to define the boundaries of the invention so that a member of the public is on notice regarding the scope of rights granted by the patent. In this manner, members of the public being on notice are able to avoid "trespassing" on legal rights owned by another.

With a deed, however, the object of the rights associated with the deed is real estate (termed the "res") and is tangible. For intellectual property, such as a patent, the res *itself* (as opposed to the legal rights) is not tangible. Hence, the term "intellectual" property.

Patent claims cover more than simply the embodiments described in the specification. Rather, what a patent claim covers is determined by the claim language used.[4] This is one reason why patents are so valuable and the language of a patent claim so important.

By custom, there are three parts to a patent claim: a preamble, a transition word or phrase, and a claim body. Previously, we have provided several claim examples that illustrate this basic structure. In general, a patent claim includes elements and limitations that, taken together, with their relationships, constitute the literal scope of rights granted if the patent claim is issued. To be more precise, the patent claim covers the right to (exclude others from) making, using, selling, offering for sale, and importing into the United States physical structures, processes, materials, and so on, that fall within the literal scope of the patent claim.

---

2. *See* Cultor Corp. v. A.E. Staley, 224 F.3d 1328 (Fed. Cir. 2000), in which the federal circuit construed a claim narrowly based on a comma. *See* Allen Eng'g Corp. v. Bartell Indus., 299 F.3d 1336 (Fed. Cir. 2002), where a claim did not contain any punctuation at all at the end of the limitation and the federal circuit found the claim indefinite under 35 U.S.C. § 112 due to a truncated limitation.

3. *See In re* Fressola, 22 USPQ2d 1828 (Comm'r Pat. & Trademarks 1992), in which Commissioner Manpack ruled that "[t]he single claim sentence requirement is within the PTO's statutory authority and is consistent with the statutory purpose of 35 U.S.C. § 112 ¶ 2."

4. *See, e.g.*, Vitronics Corp. v. Conceptronic, Inc., 90 F.3d 1576 (Fed. Cir. 1996) ("We look to the words of the claims themselves . . . to define the scope of the patented invention.").

Previously, we discussed the process of "reading a claim" on an accused product (or service). It is the patent claim words that are used in patent examination to determine whether the patent claim distinguishes sufficiently from known prior art to be patentable over that known prior art. The patent claim, in general, should be construed consistently in patent litigation as it is in patent examination. Consequently, a similar "reading on" process is used to determine literal, direct infringement of a patent claim.

Section 101 of title 35 enumerates the statutorily permitted classes or categories of patent claims. It states:

> Whoever invents or discovers any new and useful **process, machine, manufacture**, or **composition of matter**, or any new and useful improvement thereof, may obtain a patent therefor, subject to the conditions and requirements of this title (emphasis added).

The statutory classes or categories of claims are process claims (also called method claims), machine claims (also called apparatus claims), manufacture claims (also called article of manufacture claims), and composition of matter claims. MPEP section 2106.03, provided below in part, is instructive on these categories of patentable subject matter. In the sections that follow, we give examples of each category.

MPEP section 2106.03 (2022) states:

> 35 U.S.C. 101 enumerates four categories of subject matter that Congress deemed to be appropriate subject matter for a patent: processes, machines, manufactures and compositions of matter. As explained by the courts, these "four categories together describe the exclusive reach of patentable subject matter. If a claim covers material not found in any of the four statutory categories, that claim falls outside the plainly expressed scope of § 101 even if the subject matter is otherwise new and useful." *In re Nuijten*, 500 F.3d 1346, 1354, 84 USPQ2d 1495, 1500 (Fed. Cir. 2007).
>
> A process defines "actions," *i.e.*, an invention that is claimed as an act or step, or a series of acts or steps. As explained by the Supreme Court, a "process" is "a mode of treatment of certain materials to produce a given result. It is an *act, or a series of acts*, performed upon the subject-matter to be transformed and reduced to a different state or thing." *Gottschalk v. Benson*, 409 U.S. 63, 70, 175 USPQ 673, 676 (1972) (italics added) (quoting *Cochrane v. Deener*, 94 U.S. 780, 788, 24 L. Ed. 139, 141 (1876)). See also *Nuijten*, 500 F.3d at 1355, 84 USPQ2d at 1501 ("The Supreme Court and this court have consistently interpreted the statutory term 'process' to require action"); *NTP, Inc. v. Research in Motion, Ltd.*, 418 F.3d 1282, 1316, 75 USPQ2d 1763, 1791 (Fed. Cir. 2005) ("[A] process is a series of acts.") (quoting *Minton v. Natl. Ass'n. of Securities Dealers*, 336 F.3d 1373, 1378, 67 USPQ2d 1614, 1681 (Fed. Cir. 2003)). As defined in 35 U.S.C. 100(b), the term "process" is synonymous with "method."

The other three categories (machines, manufactures and compositions of matter) define the types of physical or tangible "things" or "products" that Congress deemed appropriate to patent. *Digitech Image Techs. v. Electronics for Imaging*, 758 F.3d 1344, 1348, 111 USPQ2d 1717, 1719 (Fed. Cir. 2014) ("For all categories except process claims, the eligible subject matter must exist in some physical or tangible form"). Thus, when determining whether a claimed invention falls within one of these three categories, examiners should verify that the invention is to at least one of the following categories and is claimed in a physical or tangible form.

- A machine is a "concrete thing, consisting of parts, or of certain devices and combination of devices." *Digitech*, 758 F.3d at 1348-49, 111 USPQ2d at 1719 (quoting *Burr v. Duryee*, 68 U.S. 531, 570, 17 L. Ed. 650, 657 (1863)). This category "includes every mechanical device or combination of mechanical powers and devices to perform some function and produce a certain effect or result." *Nuijten*, 500 F.3d at 1355, 84 USPQ2d at 1501 (quoting *Corning v. Burden*, 56 U.S. 252, 267, 14 L. Ed. 683, 690 (1854)).
- A manufacture is "a tangible article that is given a new form, quality, property, or combination through man-made or artificial means." *Digitech*, 758 F.3d at 1349, 111 USPQ2d at 1719-20 (citing *Diamond v. Chakrabarty*, 447 U.S. 303, 308, 206 USPQ 193, 197 (1980)). As the courts have explained, manufactures are articles that result from the process of manufacturing, *i.e.*, they were produced "from raw or prepared materials by giving to these materials new forms, qualities, properties, or combinations, whether by hand-labor or by machinery." *Samsung Electronics Co. v. Apple Inc.*, 580 U.S. __, 120 USPQ2d 1749, 1752-3 (2016) (quoting *Diamond v. Chakrabarty*, 447 U. S. 303, 308, 206 USPQ 193, 196-97 (1980)); *Nuijten*, 500 F.3d at 1356-57, 84 USPQ2d at 1502. Manufactures also include "the parts of a machine considered separately from the machine itself." *Samsung Electronics*, 137 S. Ct. at 435, 120 USPQ2d at 1753 (quoting 1 W. Robinson, The Law of Patents for Useful Inventions §183, p. 270 (1890)).
- A composition of matter is a "combination of two or more substances and includes all composite articles." *Digitech*, 758 F.3d at 1348-49, 111 USPQ2d at 1719 (citation omitted). This category includes all compositions of two or more substances and all composite articles, "'whether they be the results of chemical union or of mechanical mixture, or whether they be gases, fluids, powders or solids.'" *Chakrabarty*, 447 U.S. at 308, 206 USPQ at 197 (quoting *Shell Dev. Co. v. Watson*, 149 F. Supp. 279, 280 (D.D.C. 1957); *id.* at 310 holding genetically modified microorganism to be a manufacture or composition of matter).

It is not necessary to identify a single category into which a claim falls, so long as it is clear that the claim falls into at least one category. . . . It is also not necessary to identify a "correct" category into which the claim falls, because although in many instances it is clear within which category a claimed invention falls, a claim may satisfy the requirements of more than one category. For example, a bicycle satisfies both the machine and manufacture categories, because it is a tangible product that is concrete and consists of parts such as a frame and wheels (thus satisfying the machine category), and it is an article that was produced from raw materials such as aluminum ore and liquid rubber by giving them a new form (thus satisfying the manufacture category). Similarly, a genetically modified bacterium satisfies both the composition of matter and manufacture categories, because it is a tangible product that is a combination of two or more substances such as proteins, carbohydrates and other chemicals (thus satisfying the composition of matter category), and it is an article that was genetically modified by humans to have new properties such as the ability to digest multiple types of hydrocarbons (thus satisfying the manufacture category).

Non-limiting examples of claims that are not directed to any of the statutory categories include:

- Products that do not have a physical or tangible form, such as information (often referred to as "data per se") or a computer program per se (often referred to as "software per se") when claimed as a product without any structural recitations;
- Transitory forms of signal transmission (often referred to as "signals per se"), such as a propagating electrical or electromagnetic signal or carrier wave; and
- Subject matter that the statute expressly prohibits from being patented, such as humans per se, which are excluded under The Leahy-Smith America Invents Act (AIA), Public Law 112-29, sec. 33, 125 Stat. 284 (September 16, 2011).

As the courts' definitions of machines, manufactures and compositions of matter indicate, a product must have a physical or tangible form in order to fall within one of these statutory categories. *Digitech*, 758 F.3d at 1348, 111 USPQ2d at 1719. Thus, the Federal Circuit has held that a product claim to an intangible collection of information, even if created by human effort, does not fall within any statutory category. *Digitech*, 758 F.3d at 1350, 111 USPQ2d at 1720 (claimed "device profile" comprising two sets of data did not meet any of the categories because it was neither a process nor a tangible product). . . . Another example of an intangible product that does not fall within a statutory category is a paradigm or business model for a marketing company. *In re Ferguson*, 558 F.3d 1359, 1364, 90 USPQ2d 1035, 1039-40 (Fed. Cir. 2009).

Even when a product has a physical or tangible form, it may not fall within a statutory category. For instance, a transitory signal, while physical and real, does not possess concrete structure that would qualify as a device or part under the definition of a machine, is not a tangible article or commodity under the definition of a manufacture (even though it is man-made and physical in that it exists in the real world and has tangible causes and effects), and is not composed of matter such that it would qualify as a composition of matter. *Nuijten*, 500 F.3d at 1356-1357, 84 USPQ2d at 1501-03. As such, a transitory, propagating signal does not fall within any statutory category. *Mentor Graphics Corp. v. EVE-USA, Inc.*, 851 F.3d 1275, 1294, 112 USPQ2d 1120, 1133 (Fed. Cir. 2017); *Nuijten*, 500 F.3d at 1356-1357, 84 USPQ2d at 1501-03.

One aspect of a patent claim to keep in mind is that, in general, the whole is usually greater than the sum of the parts. In other words, it is the elements and limitations in combination, in the manner recited in the claim, that not only makes the claim unique but also unobvious. This aspect of a patent claim is expressly recognized by section 103, which states:

> A patent for a claimed invention may not be obtained, notwithstanding that the claimed invention is not identically disclosed as set forth in section 102, if the differences between the claimed invention and the prior art are such that the claimed invention as a whole would have been obvious before the effective filing date of the claimed invention to a person having ordinary skill in the art to which the claimed invention pertains. Patentability shall not be negated by the manner in which the invention was made.

The statute, therefore, focuses on "the differences between the claimed invention," which refers to the patent claim at issue, and "the prior art." These differences, "as a whole" are considered "before the effective filing date of the claimed invention" with respect to "a person having ordinary skill in the art to which the claimed invention pertains."

The language "as a whole" means that *the claim language must be considered as a whole for purposes of determining obviousness.* In other words, while the claim is a collection of elements and limitations, it is not proper, under this section, to simply dissect the claim into separate elements and limitations and see if the prior art has each recited element and limitation. Again, the whole may be (and typically is) greater than the sum of the parts. For example, *there may be advantages that come from combining the elements and limitations together in the manner recited in the claim that would not be present if those elements and limitations were dissected and viewed in isolation from one another. Those advantages that flow from "the whole" are relevant to determining whether the invention would have been non-obvious at the time the invention was made.*[5]

---

5. *See, e.g.*, Panduit Corp. v. Dennison Mfg. Co., 810 F.2d 1561, 1567–68, 1 USPQ2d 1593, 1597 (Fed. Cir. 1987), *cert. denied*, 481 U.S. 1052 (1987) ("Analysis begins with a key legal question—what is the invention claimed? Courts are required to view the claimed invention as a whole. . . ."); *In re* Wright 848 F.2d 1216 (Fed. Cir. 1988) ("[I]t is the invention as a whole

> There may be advantages that come from combining the elements and limitations together in the manner recited in the claim that would not be present if those elements and limitations were dissected and viewed in isolation from one another. Those advantages that flow from "the whole" are relevant to determining whether the invention would have been non-obvious at the time the invention was made.

2.11 Illustrative Claim Examples

2.111 Apparatus or Machine Claims[6]

Following are illustrative examples of apparatus or machine claims, as an introduction.

The following is an apparatus patent claim directed to an integrated circuit.

EXAMPLE 2.1

I claim:

1. An integrated circuit comprising: at least one metal conductor and at least one metal oxide semiconductor field effect transistor (MOSFET);

   wherein multiple contacts are coupled to the metal conductor along a major axis of the at least one metal conductor to conduct current to or from the at least one metal conductor and to or from drain or source regions of the MOSFET; and

   wherein the at least one metal conductor is tapered along the major axis so that during current flow the current density in the at least one metal conductor is substantially constant along the major axis.

---

that must be considered in obviousness determinations. The invention as a whole embraces the structure, its properties, and the problem it solves . . .").

6. *See also* Chapter 4 regarding additional discussion and examples of apparatus and machine claims.

The following is an example of an apparatus claim directed to a stool or chair.

EXAMPLE 2.2

I claim:

1. An apparatus comprising:

   a substantially horizontally oriented, rectangularly shaped seat including four corners;

   wherein attached to a respective corner of the seat is a substantially vertically oriented leg such that the legs point in the same direction away from the seat, are oriented to be substantially mutually parallel, and are of substantially the same length.

The following are examples of apparatus claims directed to memory and a memory controller.

EXAMPLE 2.3

I claim:

1. An apparatus comprising:

   random access memory (RAM) and a memory controller;

   wherein the memory controller is capable of initiating burst mode operation based, at least in part, on receipt of an externally derived request from an external central processing unit (CPU);

   wherein the request is to include a memory address, a word count, and a read or a write control transfer designation; and

   wherein the memory controller is to process the request and take control of a system transfer bus.

EXAMPLE 2.4

I claim:

1. An apparatus comprising:

random access memory (RAM), a memory controller, a central processing unit (CPU), and a system bus;

wherein the memory controller is capable of initiating burst mode operation based, at least in part, on receipt of a request from the CPU;

wherein the request is to include a memory address, a word count, and a read or a write control transfer designation; and

wherein the memory controller is to process the request and take control of the system transfer bus.

EXAMPLE 2.5

I claim:

1. An apparatus comprising:

random access memory (RAM), a memory controller, a central processing unit (CPU), and a system bus;

wherein the memory controller comprises means for initiating burst mode operation based, at least in part, on receipt of a request from the CPU;

wherein the request is to include a memory address, a word count, and a read or a write control transfer designation; and

wherein the memory controller comprises means for processing the request and means for taking control of a system transfer bus.

The following is an example of an apparatus claim directed to a network device for a broadcast domain of a network.

EXAMPLE 2.6

I claim:

1. An apparatus comprising:

   at least one network device of at least a first broadcast domain;

   wherein the at least one network device is to emulate one or more network devices of at least a second broadcast domain; and

   wherein the at least one network device is to encapsulate one or more signal packets of the at least a first broadcast domain directed to a network device of the at least a second broadcast domain and is to communicate the encapsulated one or more signal packets to at least one tunnel server.

One may notice several features by comparing these claim examples. Each example claim ends with a period, of course. Further, each begins with a preamble, usually stating "[a]n apparatus " or similar language. After the preamble is a transition word, in these examples "comprising," followed by a colon. After the colon, is the body of the claim, which contains the elements and limitations and associated relationships.

The structure of a patent claim that includes a preamble, transition word or phrase, and a claim body is largely by custom. However, courts use this structure to interpret the claims, so varying from it may be risky.

Instead, it is preferred to adhere to this structure and be quite clear what constitutes the preamble, the transition word or phrase, and the claim body. For example, it could be problematic if it were unclear where the preamble ends and the body begins. Likewise, it might be problematic if it were unclear which word is intended as the transition word. These issues might be problematic because, rather than receiving an interpretation as intended by the drafter, this may leave it to another decision-maker, such as an examiner or a judge, based on incorrect understandings, to decide how the claim should be interpreted. There may be times where a patent claim may be intended to be vague deliberately. However, the division between these basic components of a patent claim should be clear or one may risk an unintended interpretation with unknown consequences.

> It is preferred to adhere to this structure and be quite clear what constitutes the preamble, the transition word, and the claim body.

Another aspect to appreciate is that some claim features are described in "structural" terms and some are described in "functional" terms. It is well-recognized that both are permissible.[7] The distinction is that "structural" terms recite what the claim feature is, whereas "functional" terms recite what the claim feature does.[8] From the preceding examples, "memory," "CPU," "leg," "seat," and so on, are structural. "Means for storing," "means for processing," "to emulate," "to encapsulate," and "to communicate" are functional. Whether to use structural or functional terms is a tricky question, because it may affect claim scope in ways that are not always fully predictable. We explore this in the next few sections. Ideally, if only for claim diversity, using both approaches is usually recommended.

> If only for claim diversity, using both functional and structural approaches is usually recommended.

Another feature to appreciate is that these apparatus claims are written to make it clear the apparatus *as claimed* is *not* operating, but rather is *capable of* operation. If there is ambiguity on this point, the claim may be indefinite and, consequently, invalid.

> Another feature to appreciate is that these apparatus claims are written to make it clear the apparatus *as claimed* is *not* operating, but rather is *capable of* operation. If there is ambiguity on this point, the claim may be indefinite and, consequently, invalid.

7. *See, e.g.*, *In re* Schreiber, 128 F.3d 1473 (Fed. Cir. 1997); *In re* Swinehart, 439 F.2d 210 (C.C.P.A. 1971).
8. *See, e.g.*, *In re* Schreiber, 128 F.3d 1473 (Fed. Cir. 1997); *In re* Swinehart, 439 F.2d 210 (C.C.P.A. 1971).

In general, the world of machine claims is separate from the world of process claims. A claim that blends these worlds leaves unclear which was intended, which makes claim scope unclear and may make the claim invalid.[9] It is worth the time here to study the claims to see the linguistic approaches used to make this clear from the language of the claim itself.

Yet another feature is that the claims are written with the understanding that one party owns or controls all the features claimed. This is referred to as the single infringer principle or rule. If it takes multiple independent parties acting together to meet all the limitations of a single patent claim, it may be that no one infringes the claim.[10]

This difference may be understood with reference to Examples 2.3 and 2.4. Example 2.3 is specifically only intended to cover memory with a memory controller. The other limitations are directed to capabilities thereof only. In contrast, Example 2.4 is intended to cover a system that includes memory, memory controller, CPU, and system bus. Thus, this latter claim is formulated to clarify which features are intended as claim elements that must be present in an accused device, here, all the features mentioned in the preceding sentence. Suppose that one *independent* party provides memory and a memory controller and another *independent* party provides a CPU and system bus? Depending on other facts, it is a possibility that neither party infringes the claim of Example 2.4.

Still another aspect of these claim examples is more a matter of style than a requirement. The claims are written so that the primary claim elements are initially recited and then there is a series of "wherein" clauses that add further limitations. This is a nice style to use, but it is not required. One benefit is that it is similar to how dependent claims are written.[11] That is, it is easy to remove a wherein clause from a base claim, as with these examples, and move that limitation to a dependent claim as you draft.[12]

---

9. *See* section 5.6 and its subsections, discussing the problems of having the statutory class of a patent claim be unclear. *Cf.* INVT SPE LLC v. ITC, Appeal No. 20-1903 (Fed. Cir. August 31, 2022) (distinguishing between actual operation and capability of operating or performing for apparatus claims, particularly for software on a device, which tends to be functional, without discussing indefiniteness issue of mixing method and apparatus limitations), discussed in subsections 4.124 and 4.1272.

10. *See* section 6.3 and its subsections discussing the single infringer rule. One notable exception is 35 U.S.C. § 271(g). The federal circuit recently held that the single infringer rule does not apply. That is, as to a method of making claim implicated by that statutory section, there is liability without meeting the single infringer rule. *See* Syngenta v. Willowwood, 944 F.3d 1344 (Fed. Cir. 2019).

11. *See* section 2.15 and its subsections discussing independent and dependent claims.

12. *Id.*

In contrast, some like to write claims where claim elements and/or claim limitations may instead be inferred, rather than introduced by being separately and positively recited. These claims tend to have tighter language, but so-called inferential claiming may have more interpretive risk.[13] Example 2.2 partially illustrates this style. Example 2.2 begins:

---

1. An apparatus comprising:

   a substantially horizontally oriented, rectangularly shaped seat including four corners; . . .

The initial part of the claim body, instead, might have been written, to be more like the style using wherein clauses, to separately and positively recite specific claim features, as follows:

---

1. An apparatus comprising: a seat;

   wherein the seat is substantially horizontally oriented;

   wherein the substantially horizontally oriented seat is rectangularly shaped . . .

Many claims are a combination of both styles in which some features are first separately and positively recited and some features are first recited in connection with a particular, more detailed limitation.[14]

Related to the formalism of first separately and positively reciting a claim element, is a formalism in which a first recitation of a feature is introduced with an indefinite article (e.g., a or an)[15] and later references in the claim to that feature use either a definite article (e.g., the) or the word "said" before the feature. This clarifies that you are discussing a previously recited feature rather than a new and separate feature.

13. *See* subsection 2.1413, discussing inferential claiming.

14. *Id.*

15. There may be instances where grammatically an indefinite article may not be appropriate. For example, one may initially recite "four legs" but later recite either "the four legs" or "said four legs."

As may be clear, these formal conventions are to make the intended scope of the patent claim reasonably clear. Often, deviations from these conventions may introduce ambiguity into the claim, which in examination may lead to a rejection or, if issued, potentially may make the claim invalid or alter its intended scope. There are some situations where such formal conventions are not observed, perhaps to make a patent claim less cumbersome and easier to comprehend. However, it is generally good practice to start by adhering to these style conventions quite rigorously and avoid developing inadvertently sloppy drafting habits that may over time undermine the quality of the claims you draft.

> It is generally good practice to start by adhering to these style conventions quite rigorously and avoid developing inadvertently sloppy drafting habits that may over time undermine the quality of the claims you draft.

An issue that may divide patent practitioners is the use of "the" versus "said" when discussing a previously recited element or limitation. Use of "said" is an age-old practice that is frequently used primarily out of custom. In general, it is good to have the facility to draft claims either way, but a default approach in absence of client preference is recommended. Here is a simple example to show the difference.

EXAMPLE 2.7

I claim:

1. A bicycle comprising:

   a bicycle chassis and two bicycle wheels;

   wherein said wheels are able to attach to said chassis in a manner to be rotatable so that said bicycle is to be capable of being ridden with said wheels attached to said chassis.

Here is a formulation without "said."

EXAMPLE 2.8

I claim:

1. A bicycle comprising:

 a bicycle chassis and two bicycle wheels;

 wherein the bicycle wheels are able to attach to the bicycle chassis in a manner to be rotatable so that the bicycle is to be capable of being ridden with the bicycle wheels attached to the bicycle chassis.

Some practitioners profess to prefer using "the" so that a patent claim is easier to be understood by a lay person, such as members of a jury, for example. However, some prefer "said" due to its historical roots.

Here, however, "the" is recommended over "said" for a different reason. For a set of claims with dependencies, especially during a prosecution that may have many months between office action responses (or even longer), it becomes surprisingly easy to inadvertently intermix the use of "said" with "the" potentially raising difficult and undesired questions of interpretation.

For the claim of Example 2.7, consider a dependent claim as follows:

> 2. The bicycle of claim 1, wherein the wheels are respectively attached to the chassis via a bolt and nut.

This claim 2 may result in confusion. Are these the same wheels and chassis in claim 1 or different ones? Here, this ambiguity, while not ideal, may very well be resolvable. However, for complex claims with many dependencies, such ambiguities may be unresolvable with associated legally undesirable consequences.

2.1111 Structural Versus Functional Limitations[16]

It is well-established that claims may be structural and that claims may be functional.[17] However, which approach may be better is a matter of judgment. Furthermore, functional language, although potentially broader on the face of the claim, has several legal pitfalls. For this and other reasons, it is recommended that both approaches be employed.

---

16. *See also* Chapter 4 providing a deeper discussion on this topic.

17. *See, e.g., In re* Schreiber, 128 F.3d 1473 (Fed. Cir. 1997); *In re* Swinehart, 439 F.2d 210 (C.C.P.A. 1971).

For this and other reasons, it is recommended that both approaches, functional language and structural language, be employed.

Again, based on the face of the claim, functional limitations appear to be broader than structural limitations; however, it is not always easy to predict whether such limitations will be interpreted as the words appear in the claim. A related issue is whether a suitable structural term exists to claim the feature sought to be covered with claim language, suggesting that resort to functional language may more or less be necessary.

Some of the complex legal issues related to functional language in patent claims emanate from how the federal circuit has interpreted section 112(f). That section states:

> (f) Element in Claim for a Combination.—An element in a claim for a combination may be expressed as a means or step for performing a specified function without the recital of structure, material, or acts in support thereof, and such claim shall be construed to cover the corresponding structure, material, or acts described in the specification and equivalents thereof.

The provision, to be invoked for an element of a patent claim, appears to require the formulation "means for [function]." However, there is federal circuit case law in which section 112(f) is invoked to interpret an element of a claim, although the word "means" does not appear in the claim.[18] This may occur, for example, where the claim term or terms at issue do not recite sufficient structure.[19] There is a presumption that the absence of use of "means" in language of a patent claim should *not* be construed under section 112(f), but that presumption may be rebutted. The primary case is *Williamson v. Citrix Online*, decided *en banc*, which referred to use of "nonce words" for elements of a claim, such as the word "module," which in the context of the claim was not a recognized term of art. "Nonce words" refers to made up words that seek to make a functional limitation appear structural. The federal circuit stated (note that 112(f) has replace 112, Para. 6):

18. *See, e.g.*, Williams v. Citrix, 792 F.3d 1339 (Fed. Cir.) (en banc); Cole v. Kimberly–Clark Corp., 102 F.3d 524, 531 (Fed. Cir. 1996); *see also* Greenberg v. Ethicon Endo–Surgery, Inc., 91 F.3d 1580, 1584 (Fed. Cir. 1996).

19. *Id.*

The standard is whether the words of the claim are understood by persons of ordinary skill in the art to have a sufficiently definite meaning as the name for structure. *Greenberg*, 91 F.3d at 1583. When a claim term lacks the word "means," the presumption can be overcome and § 112, para. 6 will apply if the challenger demonstrates that the claim term fails to "recite sufficiently definite structure" or else recites "function without reciting sufficient structure for performing that function." *Watts*, 232 F.3d at 880. The converse presumption remains unaffected: "use of the word 'means' creates a presumption that § 112, ¶ 6 applies." *Personalized Media*, 161 F.3d at 703.

Some terms, as a result, appear to be sufficiently structural so as to not invoke section 112(f). A few example claim terms in which there have been court rulings indicating particular claim terms are structural rather than functional include processor; circuit or circuitry; and digital detector. There are many other case examples that could also be cited. More specifically, as an example of the reasoning used, the federal circuit case, *Personalized Media Communications v. Thomson*,[20] states:

'Detector' is not a generic structural term such as 'means,' 'element,' or 'device; nor is it a coined term lacking a clear meaning, such as 'widget' or 'ram-a-fram.' **Instead, as noted by the ALJ by reference to dictionary definitions, 'detector' had a well-known meaning to those of skill in the electrical arts connotative of structure**, . . . (emphasis supplied).

Further, in some other federal circuit cases, functional language was permissibly used and did *not* invoke 112(f).[21] That is, these cases suggest that

20. Personalized Media Commc'ns v. Thomson, 532 F.3d 1318, 1329 (Fed. Cir. 1998). It is noted that Personalized Media Commc'ns v. Thomson was decided before en banc decision Williams v. Citrix.

21. *See, e.g.*, K-2 Corp. v. Salomon S.A., 191 F.3d 1356, 1363 (Fed. Cir. 1999) (functional language "for substantially preventing movement" did not invoke 112(6)); BASF Corp. v. Johnson Matthey Inc., 875 F.3d 1360 (Fed. Cir. 2017) (functional phrase "effective to catalyze," did not involve 112(6)); *see also* Enzo Biochem, Inc. v. Applera Corp., 599 F.3d 1325, 1332–33 (Fed. Cir. 2010), *reh'g and reh'g en banc denied*, 605 F.3d 1347 (Fed. Cir. 2010) ("when a claim limitation is defined in 'purely functional terms,' a determination of whether the limitation is sufficiently definite is 'highly dependent on context (e.g., the disclosure in the specification and the knowledge of a person of ordinary skill in the relevant art area).'"; Miken Composites, L.L.C. v. Wilson Sporting Goods Co., 515 F.3d 1331 (Fed. Cir. 2008) (Court stated that while the term "insert" has "functional attributes," it was still a structural component); Plastic Container Corp. v. Cont'l Plastics of Oklahoma, Inc., 607 F.2d 885, 203 USPQ 27, 650, 651 (10th Cir. 1979), *cert. denied*, 444 U.S. 1018 (1980), *on remand*, 515 F. Supp. 834, 214 USPQ 530 (W.D. Okla. 1980), *aff'd in part, reversed in part*, 708 F.2d 1554, 219 USPQ 26 (10th Cir. 1983) ("the idea that functional language ipso facto cannot precisely define novelty in structure was laid to rest in In re Swinehart. . . ."); *In re* Swinehart, 439 F.2d 210, 212, 169 USPQ 226, 228 (CCPA 1971) ("[T]here is nothing intrinsically wrong with [employing functional limitations] in drafting patent claims.").

functional language may in some situations properly and appropriately be employed in claims without using the means-plus-function format of section 112(f) and without necessarily being interpreted under that section. Presumably, despite the functional language, the claim still recited sufficient structure to avoid invoking section 112(f). We recommend using both approaches to provide diversity and to signal a different intended scope for the separate claims.[22]

However, use of functional language may still be challenging.[23] In particular, the PTO has the authority to shift the burden to the applicant with respect to functional language.[24] The CCPA decision *In re Swinehart*[25] stated in this regard:

> Additionally, where the Patent Office has reason to believe that a functional limitation asserted to be critical for establishing novelty in the claimed subject matter may, in fact, be an inherent characteristic of the prior art, **it possesses the authority to require the applicant to prove that the subject matter shown to be in the prior art does not possess the characteristic relied on** (emphasis supplied).

If the PTO were to do this, it may require: (1) proof that the subject matter shown to be in the prior art does not possess the characteristic sought to be claimed (proving a negative proposition is usually a challenge to establish with evidence); (2) amending the claim; or (3) arguing that for some reason the PTO has inappropriately shifted the burden.

Some features, unfortunately, may not have a feasible way to be claimed structurally. In that situation, it is suggested a mix of structural and functional language be used so that at least the claim language at issue is not entirely devoid of structure. Consider Example 2.3 with claim language such as:

> wherein the memory controller is capable of initiating burst mode operation based, at least in part, on receipt of an externally derived request from an external central processing unit (CPU);
> wherein the request is to include a memory address, a word count, and a read or a write control transfer designation; and
> wherein the memory controller is to process the request and take control of a system transfer bus.

22. *But compare* Mas-Hamilton v. LaGard, 156 F.3d 1206 (Fed. Cir. 1998) (claim without "means" interpreted under 112, 6 despite a separate independent claim that employed "means.").

23. Note that 35 U.S.C. § 112(f) (2022) also refers to "materials" suggesting applicability to composition of matter claims as well.

24. *See In re* Swinehart, 439 F.2d 210, 212, 169 USPQ 226, 228 (CCPA 1971).

25. *In re* Swinehart, 439 F.2d 210, 212, 169 USPQ 226, 228 (CCPA 1971).

The claim, here, recites "the memory controller is capable of initiating burst mode operation" and "the memory controller is to process the request and take control of a system transfer bus." The term "memory controller" is likely structural, but the other recited limitations are more functional; however, a memory controller may be argued to support such functions.

Example 2.6 uses a similar approach reciting "network device," a potentially structural device, but adding functional limitations such as "to emulate," "to encapsulate," and "to communicate." Again, these could be argued to be operations a network device may support. With even more attention, these positions might be made even clearer through claim language and specification language. The point, here, is to pay attention to the use of structural versus function language in the claim and attempt to hedge your bets so that your claim is not construed to be limited to, essentially, your specification embodiment due to invocation of section 112(f).

The point, here, is to pay attention to the use of structural versus function language in the claim and attempt to hedge your bets so that your claim is not construed to be limited to, essentially, your specification embodiment due to invocation of section 112(f).

Along these lines, it is a good idea to be mindful of the consequences should, despite your best drafting efforts, your claim be construed under section 112(f) during examination or in litigation. In the event section 112(f) is invoked, the specification *must* provide sufficient *corresponding* structure for the recited function. That is, for the function or functions recited in the claim, the specification *must* describe *corresponding* structure able to perform the recited function or functions or the claim will be invalid if issued. Here, *corresponding* suggests that the specification is written to clearly associate the function and the structure in the description in a manner such that one of ordinary skill would comprehend the association.

If an element is construed under section 112(f) and the statutory requirements regarding corresponding structure are satisfied, then the claim covers, by express statutory direction:

> . . . the **corresponding** structure, material, or acts described in the specification **and equivalents** . . . (emphasis supplied).

Thus, the claim, by statute, under section 112(f), is *literally* construed to cover embodiments in your specification that *correspond* to the functional language or to *literally* cover a *112(f) equivalent* of what is shown in the specification; however, the *literal* scope of such *112(f) equivalents* is generally exceedingly narrow.[26] In other words, equivalents falling within the statutory language of section 112(f) are within the literal scope of the claim.

2.112 Method or Process Claims[27]

Many differences between apparatus and method claims exist that are relevant to patent claiming strategy and tactics. At one of the most basic levels, the set of rights granted by these different categories of patent claims is different. An apparatus claim provides the full set of statutory rights, that is, make, use, sell, and so on.[28] On the other hand, due to an inherent nature, a method claim essentially covers "use," as in a method of using, or "make," as in a method of making or manufacturing. At least partially for this reason, apparatus claims are usually perceived to be more valuable than method claims. However, do not read this to suggest that method claims are not valuable. In various situations, having a method claim may be important to have as an arrow in your quiver. It is recommended to nearly always include method claims with apparatus claims for claim diversity. Many patents are written that do not follow this simple principle.

> It is recommended to nearly always include method claims with apparatus claims for claim diversity.

Usually, an invention will more easily be claimed as one or the other, that is, as a method or as an apparatus. For example, software operation is usually more easily described as a method. Although not a requirement, it seems logical when beginning to draft claims for an invention, to begin with the claim type that is more easily drafted due to the inherent nature of the invention.

---

26. *See, e.g.*, Valmont v. Reinke, 983 F.2d 1039 (Fed. Cir. 1993).
27. *See also* Chapter 4 also discussing method claims with more examples.
28. *See* 35 U.S.C. § 271(a) (2022).

> When beginning to draft claims for an invention, begin with the claim type that is more easily drafted due to the inherent nature of the invention.

Regardless, do not pass on the opportunity to claim an invention in method terms (e.g., method of using and/or method of making in addition to apparatus terms). A litany of good reasons to do this exist. A method may stand up to prior art even in situations where an apparatus claim may not.[29] Depending on the limitations of the patent claim, a method claim may be infringed where an apparatus claim is not, it may be infringed in a different manner, or it may potentially result in greater damages.[30] Further, a pure method claim generally is much less likely to be construed under section 112(f).[31] The failure to claim a method described in the specification also has the potential to dedicate to the public subject matter that might have otherwise been covered by a method claim.[32] Other good reasons also exist to include method claims, but these reasons should be more than sufficient.

One aspect to appreciate is the difference in drafting a method claim versus drafting an apparatus claim that flows directly from the preceding discussion about the set of rights associated with each. A method claim recites actions or acts. A method claim is infringed by performing an action, an act, or an operation, such as when "using" something or "making" something. Hence, the claim elements of a method claim are actions like "receiving," "transmitting," and so on, that is, words ending in "ing."

One way to think of a method claim, for drafting purposes, is like a cooking recipe. It specifies the steps to follow. Usually, therefore, method claims are easier to draft than their apparatus counterparts. As has been stated, an apparatus may be capable of performing an action, an act, or an operation, but it is important to not claim an apparatus in a manner that suggests that it

---

29. *See* sections 4.126, 4.127 and subsections, including discussion regarding a new use of an old device.

30. *Id.*

31. *Id.*

32. *See* Johnson & Johnston Assoc. v. R.E. Serv. Co., 285 F.3d 1046 1054 (Fed. Cir. 2002) (en banc) ("As stated in *Maxwell*, when a patent drafter discloses but declines to claim subject matter, as in this case, this action dedicates that unclaimed subject matter to the public.").

is actually performing such actions or operations.[33] Thus, an apparatus claim either recites structural elements, such as a processor or memory, or it recites that such elements are able to perform an action to make it clear that the action itself is not being claimed. Claiming the action itself is the domain of method claims.

> One way to think of a method claim is like a cooking recipe. It specifies the steps to follow.

The opportunity to claim a method of making even in situations where that is *not necessarily* the feature that is inventive should also not be overlooked.[34] For example, consider an analog or digital circuit invention capable of being embedded in a silicon chip. Semiconductor or silicon chips, for example, shall be manufactured to implement such a circuit, if the inventive concept has value. If so, why not include a method of manufacturing patent claim in one's arsenal?

One may wonder how a method of making claim is patentable if the innovation relates to something else, such as how the circuit works or how the components are arranged. With appropriate drafting, however, the claim language that recites the manufacturing operations may include language to also capture the innovation.

Consider, as an example, the following example of a method of making claim for Example 2.3:

33. *See, e.g.*, IPXL Holdings v. Amazon, 430 F.3d 1377, 1384 (Fed. Cir. 2005). *See* section 5.6 and its subsections discussing indefiniteness from mixing statutory classes in a single claim. *Cf.* INVT SPE LLC v. ITC, Appeal No. 20-1903 (Fed. Cir. August 31, 2022) (distinguishing between actual operation and capability of operating or performing for apparatus claims, particularly for software on a device, which tends to be functional, without discussing indefiniteness issue of mixing method and apparatus limitations), discussed in subsections 4.124 and 4.1272.

34. This point also applies to method of using claims, but those are more conventionally written along with apparatus claims. Hence, the emphasis here on method of making claims, which are not typically included with apparatus claims.

EXAMPLE 2.9

I claim:

1. A method of fabricating a memory controller and random access memory (RAM) comprising

   fabricating an integrated circuit (IC) that includes a memory controller with random access memory (RAM) on the IC, wherein the memory controller and RAM are fabricated in an electrical configuration on a silicon substrate;

   wherein the fabricating includes forming transistors for the memory controller and RAM on the silicon substrate, wherein the transistors respectively have a source, a drain, a gate and a body;

   wherein the fabricating further includes fabricating the memory controller to be capable of initiating burst mode operation based, at least in part, on receipt of a request from a central processing unit (CPU) in which the request is to include a memory address, a word count, and a read or a write control transfer designation; and

   wherein the fabricating further includes fabricating the memory controller to be capable to process the request and take control of a system transfer bus.

As is shown, the claim employs language such as "wherein the fabricating further includes fabricating the memory controller to be capable of initiating burst mode operation." One may ask: at the time the invention was made, would this claim have been novel, non-obvious, and useful in light of such language? The answer seems to be yes.

The usefulness of this approach may matter more as it becomes more common for companies, so-called fabless design houses, to outsource chip manufacturing to others. Coming up with the design, however, does not generally by itself directly infringe a patent claim.[35] Yet, a claim directed to a

35. Although it might be a basis for a claim for indirect infringement; *see* section 3.22 and its subsections discussing indirect infringement.

company making the chip for someone else would be infringed and may have some value.[36]

One limiting factor to consider is how easy or difficult would it be to discover or prove infringement of a method of manufacture claim. For example, if there is little or no way to discover from the end-product that a particular process was used, this technology might be better protected as a trade secret.[37]

As one example, consider that in the aircraft manufacturing industry many holes are typically created in metal structures, such as for an engine, for a fuselage, and so on. The holes may be for nuts, screws, and other types of connectors to attach various mechanical components together. The ability to create more precise holes, more quickly, and at a cheaper cost in complex metal structures may, therefore, provide a competitive advantage. With the advent of laser technology, it seems likely that some type of laser was developed for just such processes. However, it might be very difficult or nearly impossible to determine how such a hole was generated during manufacture from looking at the end product itself. Consequently, assuming such laser technology was developed and even assuming it was patentable at the time of its creation, a patent on such technology may be difficult to enforce. Furthermore, by filing a patent, one would be educating one's competitors on how to perform such a process (again, a process performed behind closed doors and difficult to discover). Instead, as suggested, such technology may be better protected as a trade secret.

Another possible limiting factor, such as for a fabless design house seeking a manufacturing claim, may be that typically so-called foundries that perform manufacturing for other fabless design houses are located outside the United States. Such manufacturing activities, therefore, may at times be beyond the territorial scope of U.S. patent law for a claim of infringement under 35 USC section 271(a). However, there are statutes directed to extraterritorial patent infringement.[38]

2.1121 Method of Using Claims[39]

Following are several example method of using claims.

---

36. *See* section 4.127 and its subsections regarding method of making claims with examples. This is especially the case since direct infringement is generally easier to prove than indirect infringement. *See* discussion of indirect infringement in section 3.22 and its subsections.

37. For example, turnover in the industry and/or how easy it might be to limit trade secret knowledge of the technology within the company are a few examples of considerations that may affect the desirability of trade secret protection.

38. *See* 35 U.S.C. § 271(f), (g) (2022). *See* discussion of 35 U.S.C. § 271(g) (2022) in section 4.1252.

39. *See* Chapter 4, also discussing method of using claims with examples.

Here is a method of using claim directed to burst mode operation of a memory controller.

EXAMPLE 2.10

I claim:

1. A method comprising:

   receiving a request for burst mode operation;

   transmitting a request for control of a system bus in response to the received request;

   receiving a signal granting system bus control;

   transferring signals across the system bus into or out of a group of sequential memory cells after receiving the signal granting system bus control; and

   transmitting a signal indicating completion of the signal transfer.

Here are method of using claims directed to a virtual private network.

EXAMPLE 2.11

I claim:

1. A method of forming a virtual private network comprising:

   communicating one or more signal packets between respective physically separate broadcast domains via a gateway device included in the respective physically separate broadcast domains, wherein the communicating the one or more signal packets comprises:

      encapsulating the one or more signal packets in the respective physically separate broadcast domains to be communicated; and

      communicating the encapsulated signal packets between the respective gateway devices and at least one tunnel server so that the one or more signal packets are able to be communicated between the respective physically separate broadcast domains.

EXAMPLE 2.12

I claim:

1. A method comprising:

   emulating one or more network devices of at least a second broadcast domain;

   encapsulating one or more signal packets from at least a first broadcast domain to be directed to a network device of the at least a second broadcast domain; and

   communicating the encapsulated one or more signal packets to at least one tunnel server.

Observe that these patent claims, although not apparatus claims, follow some of the same principles discussed in the previous sections. For example, these patent claims employ a preamble, a transition word or phrase, and a claim body. Each also ends with a period.

Likewise, as for apparatus claims, method claims obey the single infringer rule. One party should control the set of acts, actions, or operations recited in the claim. If some are done by one party, and some are done by another party acting independently, then it may be that no one will infringe the patent claim.[40]

The principles previously discussed regarding structure versus function may also apply to ***tangible or physical components*** recited in the limitations of a method claim (to be distinguished from recited acts or actions). For example, the preceding claim examples recite "network device," broadcast domain," and "system bus." These should be interpreted as structural, but could, instead, be claimed using functional language. A system bus might be claimed as "means for transferring signals in a system." On the other hand, the language "system bus" seems broader and it is likely structural. Of course, these points relate to tangible aspects included in the limitations of a method claim, rather than to the elements involving actions, such as "transmitting," "communicating," and so on.

40. *See, e.g.*, Akamai v. Limelight, 572 U.S. 915, 921–22 (2014); Muniauction, Inc. v. Thompson Corp., 532 F.3d 1318 (Fed. Cir. 2008); BMC v. Paymentech, 489 F.3d 1373, 1379–81 (Fed. Cir. 2007).

One practice that used to be common was to recite in the claim "A method comprising the steps of:" This practice is less common today and, here, we also suggest avoiding it. At least one reason is to prevent someone from arguing that your method claim has a "step plus function" element recited that should properly be interpreted under section 112(f). There is not much case law on step plus function elements of combination claims, discussed later,[41] although they may be thought of as the method "analog" of a means plus function element[42] of an apparatus claim. In general, claim elements interpreted under section 112(f) tend to be construed more narrowly than claim elements not interpreted under section 112(f).

However, by their very nature, specifically regarding the action elements of a method claim, such as "transmitting," "encapsulating," and so on, these are less likely to be construed under section 112(f). This is based on an analysis of the language of 112(f) and the reasoning of *Seal-flex*.[43] Thus, invoking section 112(f) to interpret an act or action as a "step plus function" element is believed to not be particularly likely.

Section 112(f) states:

> (f) Element in Claim for a Combination.—An element in a claim for a combination may be expressed as a means or step for performing a specified function without the recital of structure, material, or acts in support thereof, and such claim shall be construed to cover the corresponding structure, material, or acts described in the specification and equivalents thereof.

In an apparatus claim, a means plus function element may recite function in place of structure via reciting "means for [function]." In a method claim, in light of the statute, a step plus function element may recite function in place of "acts" via the claim language "step for [function]." In the absence of the word *step*, like in the absence of "means," by analogy, an adversary trying to make this argument must *rebut a presumption against application* of 112(f) by arguing that the claim recites a "function" rather than "acts." That is, by analogy, the language would be argued to be devoid of "action," and assuming successful rebuttal of the presumption, would potentially be interpreted as

---

41. *See* Seal-Flex Inc. v. Athletic Track & Ct. Constr., 172 F.3d 836 (Fed. Cir. 1999). A concurrence by Judge Rader suggests that "comprising the steps of" would not be a problem, but best to avoid such questions by good drafting practice.

42. *See* section 4.123 and its subsections, discussing means plus function and step plus function claims.

43. *See* Seal-Flex Inc., 172 F.3d 836. A concurrence by Judge Rader suggests that "comprising the steps of" would not be a problem, but best to avoid such questions by good drafting practice.

functional and, hence, would also likely be interpreted narrowly in accordance with 112(f) jurisprudence.

What might be an example? Consider a method claim element such as: "generating a Fast Fourier Transform (FFT) signal from an audio signal." Is this a function or an act? That is a reasonably tricky question and may depend quite heavily on the specification description. Typically, generating an FFT involves many separate signal processing operations that individually could be "acts." Is this referring to all those acts together or is this more like a function by simply reciting a statement of a result? How would one of ordinary skill interpret this language? The point is that, in general, due at least partially to the inherent nature of language, it may be more challenging to argue that a function is recited versus an act, in comparison with arguing that a function is recited versus structure. That is, the difference between structure and function is usually more clear linguistically than the difference between action and function. Of course, good specification drafting may also make such an argument even more challenging.

Most method claims recite some tangible components as limitations, such as discussed in connection with the distinction between function and structure. However, care is warranted here. If a method claim recites a lot of tangible components, such as hardware, for example, and is sloppy, someone may argue it is not clear whether the claim is a method or an apparatus claim. There is not much, if any law, on this specific situation, but the argument follows from cases that have held claims invalid that were ostensibly apparatus claims but used too much language that typically appears in method claims.[44]

There are a few approaches to help ameliorate this risk. For one thing, attempt to recite only those tangible components needed to support the claimed acts or actions, particularly in the base claim. Example 2.10 illustrates this approach since it recites the system bus, but not the CPU, the memory, or the memory controller.

It also is a good idea to stick to the form of a method claim. Consider, for example, the independent claim of Example 2.12. The network device may be a gateway device. One way to write a dependent claim adding this feature might be:

---

44. *See, e.g.*, IPXL Holdings v. Amazon, 430 F.3d 1377, 1384 (Fed. Cir. 2005). *See also* section 5.6 and its subsections, discussing the issue of mixing statutory classes in a patent claim. *Cf.* INVT SPE LLC v. ITC, Appeal No. 20-1903 (Fed. Cir. August 31, 2022) (distinguishing between actual operation and capability of operating or performing for apparatus claims, particularly for software on a device, which tends to be functional, without discussing indefiniteness issue of mixing method and apparatus limitations), discussed in subsections 4.124 and 4.1272.

> 2. The method of claim 1, wherein the network device of the at least a second broadcast domain comprises a gateway device.

This claim is easy to write and clear; however, technically, it might *not* be interpreted as a method claim by not retaining the linguistic "ing" method claim structure of claim 1. Although it may be more cumbersome and perhaps less clear, it may be desirable to retain the method claim linguistic format and write this claim so there is no question that it is a method claim, such as:

> 2. The method of claim 1, wherein the encapsulating the one or more signal packets to be directed to the network device comprises: encapsulating the one or more signal packets to be directed to a gateway device.

Another approach that is used is to recite the tangible components, such as hardware, in the preamble first, rather than inferentially in the patent claim.[45] For example, consider the method claim in Example 2.12. It could be written as follows.

I claim:

1. A method of forming a virtual private network from at least a first and at least a second broadcast domain, respectively, including one or more network devices, and at least one tunnel server, the method comprising:

   emulating the one or more network devices of the at least a second broadcast domain;

   encapsulating one or more signal packets from the at least a first broadcast domain to be directed to a network device of the at least a second broadcast domain; and

   communicating the encapsulated one or more signal packets to the at least one tunnel server.

Since there is little meaningful law on this point, let good judgment be your guide. It is doubtful that a significant legal difference exists between the latter example claim and Example 2.12. That is, the difference appears primarily stylistic. What is most important is it be clear from the claim language that acts or actions are being claimed.

45. *See also* section 2.1413, discussing inferential claiming.

> What is most important is it be clear from the claim language that acts or actions are being claimed.

Another useful point about method claims is that the acts, actions, or operations (e.g., elements) may be done in any order unless the language expressly states an order or through its language implies an order. The claim of Example 2.10 illustrates an implied order written from the perspective of an operational memory controller:

I claim:

1. A method comprising:

   receiving a request for burst mode operation;

   transmitting a request for control of a system bus in response to the received request;

   receiving a signal granting system bus control;

   transferring signals across the system bus into or out of a group of sequential memory cells after receiving the signal granting system bus control; and

   transmitting a signal indicating completion of the signal transfer.

For example, "transmitting a request for control of the system bus in response to the received request;" is implied to come after "receiving a request for burst mode operation."

An express order used in a claim might be to recite "first," "second," and so on, with each respective act, action, or operation. Be aware of a practice in which the claim elements are recited with letter designations like "a," "b," "c" (or something similar) added merely for convenience to refer back to specific claim elements in various dependent claims. Someone may argue such designations specify order. The problem, here, may be that a specific order was not intended in the base claim. Thus, avoid such a practice unless a specific order is necessarily intended. Instead, use the dependent claiming approach discussed later in this book, which involves using language that might be called a "handle" for the particular feature.[46]

Because of this notion regarding no specific order to the particular operations unless stated or implied, it should be relatively easy to narrow a method claim with further dependent claims that might *intellectually* have been thought to come *before* the base claim's acts, actions, or operations (or in the middle of them or after them). For example, a dependent claim for Example 2.10 might be the following:

> 2. The method of claim 1, comprising: before the receiving the request for burst mode operation, at least partially directing transfer of signal values across the system bus into or out of a single, individual memory cell.

2.1122 Method of Making Claims[47]

Following are several example method of manufacture claims.

Here is an example claim directed to making a cake.

EXAMPLE 2.13

I claim:

1. A method comprising:

gathering constituent items in one place to make a cake, including: flour, eggs, butter, milk and sugar;

placing the constituent items in a mixing bowl;

mixing the constituent items thoroughly while in the mixing bowl;

transferring the thoroughly mixed constituent items to a cake mold;

placing the cake mold with the thoroughly mixed items in an oven set to an appropriate temperature to bake the cake; and

waiting an appropriate amount of time until the cake is suitably baked.

---

46. *See* discussion in section 2.152.
47. *See* Chapter 4, also discussing method of making claims.

Note that terminology like "appropriate temperature" and "appropriate amount of time" should be discussed in the specification to have a fall-back position in the event of an indefiniteness rejection. Likewise, dependent claims to flush these out would be a good idea as well. This is similar to the approach discussed regarding negative limitations.[48]

Here is an example claim directed to a manufacturing process for Example 2.3.

EXAMPLE 2.14

I claim:

1. A method of fabricating a memory controller and random access memory (RAM) comprising

   fabricating an integrated circuit (IC) that includes a memory controller with random access memory (RAM) on the IC, wherein the memory controller and RAM are fabricated in an electrical configuration on a silicon substrate;

   wherein the fabricating includes forming transistors for the memory controller and RAM on the silicon substrate, wherein the transistors respectively have a source, a drain, and a gate;

   wherein the fabricating further includes fabricating the memory controller to be capable of initiating burst mode operation based, at least in part, on receipt of a request from an external central processing unit (CPU) in which the request is to include a memory address, a word count, and a read or a write control transfer designation; and

   wherein the fabricating further includes fabricating the memory controller to be capable to process the request and take control of an external system transfer bus.

Furthermore, the fabrication operations could be described more fully with dependent claims as follows, as examples:

48. *See* section 1.2113, introducing negative limitations. *See also* section 5.413, discussing negative limitations in more detail.

---

2. The method of claim 1, wherein the fabricating that includes forming the transistors having the source, the drain, and the gate comprises:

   forming the gate from a conductive gate layer and an oxide layer over a silicon layer of the silicon substrate; and

   forming two N+ regions in the silicon layer via ion implantation or diffusion to form the source and the drain.

3. The method of claim 2, wherein the forming the gate from the conductive gate layer comprises forming the gate from a polysilicon gate layer.

Although claims 2 and 3 describe well-known fabrication operations, as long as the base claim is patentable based on the burst mode limitations, there is not a problem regarding patentability of these claims.[49] Note that the point raised earlier regarding following the method claim linguistic structure in dependent claims is illustrated here.

Method of making claims follow the same rules as method of using claims, although are directed to different substantive rights (i.e., the right to make). Thus, they employ a preamble, transition word or phrase, and body, and end with a period. They follow the single infringer rule, of course. They cover actual operations, acts, or actions, rather than the capability to perform an operation, act, or action. The elements consequently also use words ending in "ing." Similarly, there is no inherent order associated with the elements unless expressly stated or implied, as preceding Example 2.13, illustrated here for convenience.

I claim:

1. A method comprising:

   gathering constituent items in one place to make a cake, including: flour, eggs, butter, milk and sugar;

   placing the constituent items in a mixing bowl;

   mixing the constituent items thoroughly while in the mixing bowl;

49. *See In re* Fine, 837 F.2d 1071 (Fed. Cir. 1988) ("[d]ependent claims are nonobvious under section 103 if the independent claims from which they depend are nonobvious").

> transferring the thoroughly mixed constituent items to a cake mold;
>
> placing the cake mold with the thoroughly mixed items in an oven set to an appropriate temperature to bake the cake; and
>
> waiting an appropriate amount of time until the cake is suitably baked.

Thus, for example, "mixing the constituent items thoroughly" is followed by "transferring the thoroughly mixed constituent items."

One opportunity to be aware of in connection with method of manufacture claims is subsection 271(g). This subsection provides the ability to potentially get a type of product-by-process claim without the invalidity disadvantages.[50] The subsection states:

> (g) Whoever without authority imports into the United States or offers to sell, sells, or uses within the United States a product which is made by a process patented in the United States shall be liable as an infringer, if the importation, offer to sell, sale, or use of the product occurs during the term of such process patent. In an action for infringement of a process patent, no remedy may be granted for infringement on account of the noncommercial use or retail sale of a product unless there is no adequate remedy under this title for infringement on account of the importation or other use, offer to sell, or sale of that product. A product which is made by a patented process will, for purposes of this title, not be considered to be so made after—
>
> (1) it is materially changed by subsequent processes; or
>
> (2) it becomes a trivial and nonessential component of another product.

Note the specific language "a product which is *made* by a process patented in the United States" (emphasis supplied). This provision has been interpreted to be limited to manufacturing.[51] This provision as well as subsection 271(f) are directed to "extraterritorial activities" that may ultimately result in liability for patent infringement in the United States.

For example, it is becoming more common for companies, so-called fabless design houses, to outsource chip manufacturing to others. Coming up with the design does not generally by itself directly infringe a patent claim.[52] Yet,

50. *See* section 4.125 and its subsections discussing product-by-process claims.

51. *See* Bayer v. Houses Pharm., 340 F.3d 1367 (Fed. Cir. 2003).

52. Although it might be a basis for a claim for indirect infringement, *see* section 3.22 and its subsections, discussing indirect infringement.

a company making the chip for someone else could infringe a manufacturing claim absent extraterritorial considerations.[53]

Let's consider a situation in which a foundry *outside* the United States performs the claim of Example 2.14 for a U.S. company who then imports the IC with the memory controller into the United States. That U.S. company, while having not performed the process itself, is nonetheless liable for infringement in federal court, assuming (g)(1) and (g)(2) of 271(g) do not apply. Furthermore, those in the chain of distribution may similarly be sued in federal court as an infringer, subject to the defenses in the statute, such as a noncommercial use, a retail sale, or the conditions of subsections (1) or (2).

Thus, section, 271(g), in effect, gives one the equivalent of a product-by-process patent claim for this situation, but without the typical invalidity concerns that are generally present for a product-by-process claim.[54] That is, the claim is a process claim, but 271(g) involves "a *product* which is made by a process patented in the United States" (emphasis added). Furthermore, the federal circuit has ruled that the two defenses in (g)(1) and (g)(2) are not legally applicable in proceedings before the International Trade Commission (ITC), a quasi-judicial governmental body that hears and decides complaints regarding importations that may be in violation of certain U.S. trade regulation laws, including intellectual property laws.[55] Thus, one may potentially stop importation of the chips at the border of the United States without a concern regarding potential defenses under (g)(1) and (g)(2).[56]

2.1123 Method Versus Apparatus

As previously suggested, in one sense the difference between a method claim versus an apparatus claim may be a matter of linguistic form. On the other hand, the difference in the rights that flow from these differences of linguistic form are substantive. This relates to an important feature of U.S. patent law to remember: *in patent claim drafting, the linguistic form of the patent claim affects the substantive scope of the claim. That is, form becomes substance.* Although there

53. *See* section 4.127 with more discussion of method of manufacturing claims. Note that direct infringement is generally easier to prove than indirect infringement.

54. *See* section 1.2212, discussing product-by-process clams as a change in the law; *see also* section 4.125 and its subsections, discussing product-by-process claims. *See* Jennewein Biotechnologie GMBH v. ITC, 2021 U.S. App. LEXIS 28200 (Fed. Cir. Sept. 17, 2021); Kinik v. ITC, 362 F.3d 1359 (Fed. Cir. 2004).

55. *See* Jennewein Biotechnologie GMBH v. ITC, 2021 U.S. App. LEXIS 28200 (Fed. Cir. Sept. 17, 2021); Kinik v. ITC, 362 F.3d 1359 (Fed. Cir. 2004).

56. Another feature of 35 U.S.C. § 271(g) is that a single entity need not perform all the claim element. That is, as to the method claim, there is liability without meeting the single infringer rule. *See* Syngenta v. Willowwood, 944 F.3d 1344 (Fed. Cir. 2019).

are examples of this in other areas of law, it may be more true here than in other areas. The words used critically matter.

> This relates to an important feature of U.S. patent law to remember: in patent claim drafting, the linguistic form of the patent claim affects the substantive scope of the claim. That is, form becomes substance. . . . The words used critically matter.

It is in part for this reason that we recommend including both method and apparatus claims when claiming a particular underlying technical innovation.[57] To a technologist, the two may be largely directed to the same underlying technical subject matter. However, examination, the analysis of infringement, the proof required to make out a case of infringement, the damages calculation, and, of course, the rights granted may all be quite different as between an apparatus claim and a method claim.

For these reasons, one should also be aware of PTO policy regarding the examination of multiple inventions in a patent application. In general, one patent application filing fee pays for one examination of one invention[58] or, to state a related policy, the PTO intends one invention per patent. Of course, the notion of an invention in this context requires some clarification. It is well-established that for many purposes, each patent claim defines a separate invention.[59] However, that is not what is referred to here.

For the purpose of this policy, inventions are separate and independent in that you may perform one without involving the other.[60] Hence, you might, for example, have only one set of multiple claims (e.g., one independent claim

57. And in some cases, different types of methods, such as a method of using and a method of making.

58. *See* 37 C.F.R. § 1.142(a) (2022). Requirement for restriction, which states:

> (a) If two or more independent and distinct inventions are claimed in a single application, the examiner in an office action will require the applicant in the reply to that action to elect an invention to which the claims will be restricted, this official action being called a requirement for restriction (also known as a requirement for division). Such requirement will normally be made before any action on the merits; however, it may be made at any time before final action.

59. *See, e.g.*, Dollar Elec. Co. v. Syndevco, Inc., 205 USPQ 949, 959 (E.D. Mich. 1979), *aff'd*, 669 F.2d 1370, 214 USPQ 241 (6th Cir. 1982) ("[E]ach claim of a patent is treated as if it was a separate patent.").

60. *See* MPEP § 802 (2022).

with several dependent claims) that you may for these purposes believe to be one invention. On the other hand, the examiner may believe that you are claiming three separate and independent inventions, depending on the specifics. More commonly, however, if the examiner perceives separate and independent inventions, the inventions are usually perceived to align with different claim sets, such as where you claim a method with one independent claim and multiple dependent claims and a related apparatus with another independent claim and other multiple dependent claims.

This may be illustrated most readily in semiconductor chip manufacturing. A claim may be directed to the structure of a chip to be manufactured that would have been novel and unobvious at the time the invention was made. Consider, for example, so-called flip-chip technology, also known as controlled collapse chip connection technology or its abbreviation, C4. It provides a technique for interconnecting chips to external circuitry with solder bumps that have been deposited onto the *top* surface of a chip and connect to the chip pads through the chip packaging.

The solder bumps are deposited on the chip pads on the top side of the wafer at the end of wafer processing. To mount the chip to external circuitry, it is flipped over so that its top side faces down and is aligned so that its pads align with matching pads on the external circuit, and then the solder is reflowed to make an electrical connection. This technology has advantages over wire bonding, its predecessor technology, which is much more involved to make the electrical connections, requiring fine wires be bonded to chip leads and also connected to a lead frame.

One may, therefore, imagine an apparatus claim directed, for example, to the structure of a completed chip with solder bumps on the top of the chip. However, a method of manufacturing claim will likely be quite different, reciting the manufacturing operations, after manufacture of silicon circuitry, for example, to create the chip packaging that includes the solder bumps that connect to the chip pads.

To explain further, in a method claim, a number of process operations may be involved to designate the location and placement of the solder bumps relative to the silicon circuitry and processing so that the solder bumps are only in the desired locations with protective external packaging covering other areas of the chip surface. An apparatus claim might not need to recite such process operations.

The PTO may take the position that these claims represent separate and independent inventions. In a nutshell, the position may be that a chip as claimed by the apparatus claim may be manufactured using a process other than the claimed manufacturing process. Similarly, the PTO may take the position that the recited manufacturing process may be used to manufacture a chip having a structure that is other than the chip structure as recited in the apparatus claim. Thus, the PTO may assert that these are separate and independent inventions.

2.11231 Restriction and Double Patenting

In the situation of the latter section, the PTO may issue a restriction requirement, asking the applicant to elect which of the two (or more) inventions the applicant desires to have examined for the particular patent application, that is, either the method claims or the apparatus claims, in the hypothetical.[61] One may argue against restriction, but generally, for several reasons, this would not be advised. For one thing, such arguments rarely win. However, more importantly, arguments against restriction may be used by the examiner to make a 103 rejection or even in later litigation by an adversary to assert invalidity under section 103 with respect to the nonelected patent claims.[62]

This recommendation might not be immediately intuitive; however, consider, at a higher level of granularity, the examiner's ostensible position based on his decision to issue a restriction requirement. His position is that the two inventions are potentially independently patentable. When you argue against that, you would be arguing, on the written record, that the inventions are *not* independently patentable. Furthermore, to advance your argument, you may make factual assertions about the technology. For example, for the flip-chip claims, you might point to similar limitations in the method and apparatus claims and argue that, due to the similar limitations, the claimed process necessarily produces the claimed chip structure or vice versa, Therefore, after the examiner finds art he may use to reject the "first invention," that is, the one selected by you to be examined, he, or someone else reviewing the record, may then argue that such art, when combined with your stated positions (e.g., admissions against interest) on the record against restriction, suggest that your "second invention" is also unpatentable. This is a real, rather than a theoretical, risk.

Ultimately, appreciate that a restriction requirement primarily presents a cost issue. If not for the additional cost, generally, a restriction requirement might, in some situations, be viewed as a positive development. It means that there may be two patents for roughly the amount of attorney drafting work of one patent application. However, the cost issues usually are not irrelevant.

---

61. Under the Patent Cooperation Treaty (PCT) and European Patent Convention (EPC) a similar concept exists, referred to as "unity of invention," discussed in Chapter 7.

62. It is noted that after having searched the art, the examiner is permitted to withdraw the restriction, but this also rarely happens.

To preserve the claims that are not elected for immediate examination, a divisional patent application is filed.[63] In addition to another filing fee, this also means another, separate prosecution with associated costs, perhaps before a different examiner, another issue fee payment if successful, and additional maintenance fees after issuance.

On the one hand, if cost is not a significant issue, having two patents often appears better to outsiders than having one, especially for smaller to medium-sized companies interested in finding investors. For large companies, it may not matter as much that two rather than one patent might be obtained for a company with a sizable patent portfolio, but likewise cost may be less of an issue for such companies.

On the other hand, a significant legal benefit in this context, from a restriction requirement is that, by statute, if the appropriate rules and procedures are followed, then a restriction requirement provides a safe harbor against an attack on one of the patents based on obviousness-type double patenting, which might otherwise be used to invalidate a patent. Appreciating this legal benefit requires some explanation.

Obviousness-type double patenting is a judicially created doctrine.[64] It has become a legally complex topic at least partly due to various statutory changes over the years to the patent term that had to be reconciled by courts with the underlying policy behind the doctrine.

Obviousness-type double patenting came into existence to address potential patent system abuses. One potential abuse relates to a patentee attempting to extend patent coverage of an invention beyond its statutory term by later filing another patent application for an otherwise obvious variation of a patented innovation. For example, pharmaceutical companies have been accused of this with respect to blockbuster drugs in which, as an example, the follow-on patent application filing is directed to a straightforward extended-release version of the initial blockbuster drug.

This potential abuse was "solved" by requiring a "terminal disclaimer" be filed, meaning that the latter term of the second patent is terminally disclaimed so that the two patents expire at the same time.[65] Furthermore, later, the statutory term changed to 20 years from patent application filing (it had

63. *See* section 1.3321, discussing divisional patent applications in connection with a discussion of domestic priority.

64. *See, e.g.*, *In re* Longi, 759 F.2d 887, 893 (Fed. Cir. 1985).

65. *See* MPEP § 1490 (2022) ("35 U.S.C. 253(b) and 37 CFR 1.321(a) and (b) also provide for the filing by a patentee or applicant of a terminal disclaimer which disclaims or dedicates to the public the entire term or any terminal part of the term of a patent or patent to be granted").

been 17 years from issuance), more term-related changes to limit potential abuse. Patent term was changed so that patent applications claiming domestic priority to an earlier patent application have their term limited by the filing date (i.e., plus 20 years) of the originally filed patent application.

Although these principles seem simple, they may become more complex with system imperfections, such as PTO delay in issuing a patent, including situations in which the first filed patent issues later and/or other similar complications related to patent term extension or patent term adjustment.[66]

Another potential abuse was addressed by obviousness-type double patenting. As a matter of policy, members of the public should not be subject to the risk of liability to two separate parties over what may essentially be viewed as one invention. Here, again, one invention is understood to include its obvious variations.

For example, suppose a drug company has a blockbuster drug to reduce or remove stammering by an individual and the drug is covered by a patent. Suppose the company then seeks and has issued a patent for an obvious extended-release version of the drug.

The term extension issue may be addressed through the mechanism of using the filing date of the initial patent application filing to limit the term of the second patent (e.g., via a terminal disclaimer); however, what if both patents are in force at the same time and the drug company decides to sell the patent covering the extended released drug. In that scenario, a competitor might decide to obtain a license of the first patent from the drug company that developed the drug after the extended release patent has been sold. That license would not protect the competitor from potential liability to the company that purchased the patent that covers the extended-release drug if the competitor also manufactures such a drug.

This latter situation is also handled with a "terminal disclaimer." For the terminal disclaimer to be effective to prevent invalidity of the patent covering the extended-release drug, by the terms of the terminal disclaimer, the two patents must be commonly assigned.[67] To be clear, without the terminal disclaimer, the patent covering the extended-release drug, if an obvious varia-

---

66. *See* 35 U.S.C. §§ 154, 156 (2022). *See, e.g.*, Novartis AG v. Ezra Ventures LLC, 909 F.3d 1367 (Fed. Cir. 2018).

67. *See* 37 C.F.R. § 1.321(c)(3) (2022) ("A terminal disclaimer, when filed to obviate judicially created double patenting in a patent application . . . must: (3) Include a provision that any patent granted on that application or any patent subject to the reexamination proceeding shall be enforceable only for and during such period that said patent is commonly owned with the application or patent which formed the basis for the judicially created double patenting."); *see also* MPEP § 1490 (2022) ("35 U.S.C. 253(b) and 37 CFR § 1.321(a) and (b) also provide for the

tion, would be invalid.[68] Likewise, however, with the terminal disclaimer on file with the PTO, by express language in the terminal disclaimer, the two patents must be commonly assigned, and a violation of this restriction would render the terminal disclaimer ineffective to prevent invalidity such that the patent covering the extended-release drug would be invalid.[69]

One way to view the situation is that the description and claims to obvious variations should have been included in the originally filed patent application. A terminal disclaimer, with its term restrictions and common assignment requirements, in effect creates a functional equivalent. That is, an equivalent from a rights perspective to a single patent that includes the initial subject matter and the obvious variations.

Now, consider a reverse situation. The original application, as in our flip-chip situation, *does* include these *potentially* obvious variations, but suppose the PTO responds with a restriction requirement. Given this, it only seems appropriate (and is the case) that the applicant, now required by the PTO to separate into two patent applications subject matter that out of an abundance of caution the applicant filed as one patent application, should be given a safe harbor against invalidity based on double patenting. It is notable, however, that this safe harbor may be easily lost if care is not taken. For one thing, the nonelected claims must be filed as a divisional[70] patent application. Likewise, it must be done without having filed an intervening continuation patent application.[71] In addition, because claims may change during prosecution, the issued claims must be consonant with the original restriction requirement to fall within the safe harbor.[72]

2.113 Composition of Matter Claims

These are examples of composition of matter patent claims.

The following is a patent claim directed to a complex compound.

---

filing by a patentee or applicant of a terminal disclaimer which disclaims or dedicates to the public the entire term or any terminal part of the term of a patent or patent to be granted.").

68. Assuming obviousness-type patenting is present.

69. Assuming obviousness-type patenting is present.

70. *See* 35 U.S.C. § 121 (2022).

71. *See* G.D. Searle LLC v. Lupin Pharm. Inc., 790 F.3d 1349, 1354 (Fed. Cir. 2015) (citing Geneva Pharm., Inc. v. GlaxoSmithKline PLC, 349 F.3d 1373, 1382 (Fed. Cir. 2003); Amgen Inc. v. F. Hoffman-La-Roche Ltd., 580 F.3d 1340, 1353 (Fed. Cir. 2009)).

72. *See* G.D. Searle LLC v. Lupin Pharm. Inc., 790 F.3d 1349, 1354 (Fed. Cir. 2015) (citing Geneva Pharm., Inc. v. GlaxoSmithKline PLC, 349 F.3d 1373, 1382 (Fed. Cir. 2003); Amgen Inc. v. F. Hoffman-La-Roche Ltd., 580 F.3d 1340, 1353 (Fed. Cir. 2009)).

EXAMPLE 2.15

I claim:

1. A composition of matter consisting of: complex compounds of the formula $M(CO)_a H_b (NH_3)_c$, in which M is a metal of the actinide series of the Periodic Table of the Elements and each of a, b and c is a whole number ranging from 0 to 8, such that when a is 0, b is greater than 0 and otherwise a is equal to or greater than b and when c is greater than 0, both a and b are 0.
2. The composition of matter in accordance with claim 1, wherein M is uranium or thorium.
3. The composition of matter in accordance with claim 2, wherein M is uranium, a is 8, b is 2 and c is 0.
4. The composition of matter in accordance with claim 2, wherein M is uranium, a is 0, b is 0 and c is 8.

The following is a claim directed to a roofing underlaying garment material (and a dependent claim).

EXAMPLE 2.16

I claim:

1. A composition of matter comprising: a material comprising:

   a first composite layer consisting of:

   a first non-woven fabric layer;

   a second non-woven fabric layer; and

   a film layer between the first and second non-woven fabric layers;

   a second composite layer comprising:

   a third non-woven fabric layer;

   a glass-fiber net reinforcement layer to form a grid on the third non-woven fabric layer, wherein the glass-fiber net reinforcement layer comprises a glass-fiber fabric web;

   a second film layer on the glass-fiber net reinforcement layer; and a fourth non-woven fabric layer on the second film layer; and

an asphalt layer between the first composite layer and the second composite layer.

2. The composition of matter of claim 1, wherein the material comprises a roofing underlaying garment material.

The following is an independent claim, including dependent claims, directed to a door jamb that includes a composition of matter.

EXAMPLE 2.17

I claim:

1. A door jamb for a door frame comprising: a composite, the composite comprising:

   at least one first member comprising a composite material;

   at least one second member coupled to the first member, the second member comprising one or more materials; and

   an at least partially blended composite coating disposed over the first and the second members, the coating capable of providing structural support to the door frame.

2. The door jamb of claim 1, wherein the coating is further capable of facilitating bonding between the first and second members.
3. The door jamb of claim 1, wherein the coating is further capable of facilitating dimensional stability of the door frame.
4. The door jamb of claim 1, wherein the coating comprises any number or combination of the following: resin, substantially spherical structures, glass objects, polyvinyl acetate, a surfactant, glass micro spheres or a wetting agent.
5. The door jamb of claim 1, wherein the composite material further comprises any number or combination of the following: a metallic material, a mineral material, a ceramic material, a plastic material or a hard fibrous material.

The following is a patent claim directed to synthesized zinc oxide crystals.

EXAMPLE 2.18

I claim:

1. A composition of matter comprising: synthesized zinc oxide crystals, wherein the synthesized zinc oxide crystals include one or more synthesized zinc oxide crystals having fabricated intra-crystalline porosity, wherein the fabricated intra-crystalline porosity consists essentially of intra-crystalline porosity beyond incidental intra-crystalline porosity.
2. The composition of matter of claim 1, wherein pores in the fabricated intra-crystalline porosity comprise pores of substantially uniform size, shape and/or density.
3. The composition of matter of claim 1, wherein pores in the fabricated intra-crystalline porosity comprise pores of an average pore diameter approximately in the range from approximately 1 nm to approximately 100 nm.

Compositions of matter more frequently arise in the unpredictable arts, such as in chemistry or in biotechnology, although not necessarily. A composition of matter is not limited to chemistry or biotechnology. Also, some chemistry has become reasonably predictable from being well studied, such as silicon-related processing for the manufacture of silicon chips. In general, any type of composition of matter, so long as it would have been novel, non-obvious, and useful at the time it was made, would be appropriate to claim. These claims can be quite important.

We have discussed that apparatus claims cover make, use, sell, and so on, whereas method claims cover make or use. One might think of this as a type of claim domination. That is, anything that infringes the dominated claim infringes the dominant claim, but there are other things that also infringe the dominant claim. Apparatus claims, for example, may dominate related method claims, such as method of using claims because apparatus claims cover make, use, sell, and so on. In a similar manner, composition of matter claims may dominate related apparatus claims and method claims.

As an example, consider the continual search for new types of memory materials. In general, this amounts to seeking a substance able to be put in one of two states (e.g., writing to memory) and then being able to determine the state of the substance (e.g., reading from memory). Of course, silicon is an important substance used today for memory devices.

Suppose a substance is invented that is cheap to make and easy to create in which, if it is heated and then cooled in one way, it has a particular resistance; whereas, if it is heated and then cooled in another way, it has a different and distinct resistance. Further, suppose this heating and cooling can be done quickly (on the order of a picosecond) and it may be done to the substance hundreds of millions of times without degrading this property.[73] Also, the volume of material needed for a memory cell is small, such as a cubic nanometer. Likewise, suppose the substance is patented with a composition of matter claim in which the composition of matter is claimed as a type of "improved memory material."[74] Now, any apparatus or method that is made from or uses this "improved memory material" would constitute patent infringement of this composition of matter claim. Thus, the composition of matter claim, in a sense, dominates these other types of claims that may later be filed as the technology continues to develop.

The Supreme Court[75] has stated "composition of matter" means "all compositions of two or more substances and all composite articles, whether they be the results of chemical union, or of mechanical mixture, or whether they be gases, fluids, powders or solids." Composite articles may also be claimed as articles of manufacture—such as roofing, a bathtub or countertop, a door jamb, and so on.

Typically, the claim recites the constituent components and how they are to be combined, such as amounts and conditions (e.g., temperature, pressure, flow rates, catalysts, etc.). The purpose or use of the composition may or may not be stated. Likewise, a composition of matter claim may cover short-lived or intermediate compositions of an overall chemical process.

Composition of matter claims may at times use a transition word or phrase other than "comprising." The word *comprising* is understood to be open form. For some composition of matter claims, this may produce a rejection or result in invalidity either for undue breath in the unpredictable arts and/or for failing to enable or provide written description support for the full scope of the

73. This hypothetical is similar to how phase change memory (PCM) and other new types of memory materials operate.

74. This would not generally be sufficient, of course. This is just provided as a "handle" for discussion purposes.

75. *See* Diamond v. Deihr, 450 U.S. 175 (1981).

claim.[76] For example, it may require quite specific conditions to produce a particular composition of matter. Using "comprising," however, would imply the composition of matter could be produced with other conditions or substances, for example. Thus, the claim would on its face appear to cover many more inoperative embodiments than operative embodiments[77] or the claim could be said to fail to be enabled or described sufficiently as to its full scope,[78] rendering it invalid.

To address this, such claims often use "consisting of" or "consisting essentially" as the transition,[79] referred to as closed form and partially closed form, respectively. These transitions have a specific understood meaning that relates to canons of construction regarding patent claims, as explained in more detail later; however, there are federal circuit cases as well that have deviated from these canons when interpreting a claim. One may view these canons as a type of "first order" analysis or, perhaps, as a weak presumption. In the appropriate circumstances, depending on claim wording, the specification, the file history, the technology, and so on, a federal court may be willing to deviate from the applicable canon or canons.

With this in mind, "consisting of" is used to claim the elements and limitations as recited in the claim body (e.g., closed form).[80] "Consisting essentially of" is used to claim the elements and limitations as recited in the claim body including any additional unclaimed constituents that are of a nature

---

76. *See* Juno Therapeutics, Inc. v. Kite Pharma, Inc., 10 F.4th 1330 (Fed. Cir. 2021) (written description); Trustees of Boston v. Everlight, 896 F.3d 1357 (Fed. Cir. 2018) (enablement); Durel Corp. v. Osram Sylvania, 256 F.3d 1298, 1306–07 (Fed. Cir. 2001) (a significant number of inoperative embodiments within the scope of the claims might be sufficient to prove invalidity); *see* Atlas Powder v. DuPont, 750 F.2d 1569, 1576–77 (Fed. Cir. 1984). *See also* EMI Group North America, Inc. v. Cypress Semiconductor Corporation, 268 F. 3d 1342 (Fed. Cir. 2001) (claims reciting scientific process found to be impossible are invalid). *See* Sean Seymore, *Heightened Enablement in the Unpredictable Arts*, 56 UCLA L. Rev. 127 (2008).

77. *See* Durel Corp. v. Osram Sylvania, 256 F.3d 1298, 1306–07 (Fed. Cir. 2001) (a significant number of inoperative embodiments within the scope of the claims might be sufficient to prove invalidity); *see* Atlas Powder v. DuPont, 750 F.2d 1569, 1576–77 (Fed. Cir. 1984). *See also* EMI Group North America, Inc. v. Cypress Semiconductor Corporation, 268 F. 3d 1342 (Fed. Cir. 2001) (claims reciting scientific process found to be impossible are invalid).

78. *See* Juno Therapeutics, Inc. v. Kite Pharma, Inc., 10 F.4th 1330 (Fed. Cir. 2021) (written description); Trustees of Boston v. Everlight, 896 F3.d 1357 (Fed. Cir. 2018) (enablement); Durel Corp. v. Osram Sylvania, 256 F.3d 1298, 1306–07 (Fed. Cir. 2001) (a significant number of inoperative embodiments within the scope of the claims might be sufficient to prove invalidity); *see* Atlas Powder v. DuPont, 750 F.2d 1569, 1576–77 (Fed. Cir. 1984). *See also* EMI Group North America, Inc. v. Cypress Semiconductor Corporation, 268 F. 3d 1342 (Fed. Cir. 2001) (claims reciting scientific process found to be impossible are invalid). *See* Seymore, *supra* note 76.

79. *See* section 2.13 and its subsections, discussing transition words or phrases.

80. *See* AFG Indus. v. Cardinal, 239 F.3d 1236 (Fed. Cir. 2001); *cf.* Norian Corp. v. Stryker Corp., 363 F.3d 1321 (Fed. Cir. 2004) (claim includes ordinary impurities of recited elements).

or an amount to not alter the character of what is otherwise intended to be claimed as novel subject matter (e.g., partially closed form).[81] More discussion on the important topic of transition words or phrases is included later in this chapter.[82]

However, one important aspect to know about transition words, especially in connection with compositions of matter, is that different transition words may be used *within the claim body* to limit or enlarge scope as well. For example, suppose our "improved memory material" easily integrates into a silicon chip. One may want to claim an integrated device using "comprising," but within the claim body, employ "consisting of" to claim the portion of the integrated device made from the constituents for our "improved memory material." This approach is illustrated earlier with Example 2.16 and immediately following is another example to illustrate the concept, although technically the following is an apparatus claim with composition of matter clauses.

EXAMPLE 2.19

I claim:

1. A semiconductor device comprising:

   a substrate, the substrate consisting of a material selected from the group consisting of silicon, sapphire, gallium arsenide, magnesium oxide, zinc oxide, and silicon carbide;

   a crystalline buffer layer on the substrate consisting essentially of gallium nitride; and

   a growth layer on the buffer layer, the growth layer comprising gallium nitride and a first dopant material.

For this claim, "comprising" is used to join three elements, which respectively include a clause using closed form, partially closed form, and open form. Also, the clause of the substrate element uses a format referred to as a Markush group, discussed in more detail later.[83]

81. *See* PPG Indus. v. Guardian Indus., 156 F.3d 1351 (Fed. Cir. 1998); *see also* section 2.13 and its subsections, discussing transition words or phrases.

82. *See* section 2.13 and its subsections, discussing transition words or phrases.

83. *See* section 4.129 and its subsections, discussing Markush groups.

Composition of matter claims are frequently used for alloy or other types of mixtures having specific properties. Likewise, as examples, aspects about the crystal structure or about the microstructure might be claimed. Usually, however, for patentability, an improved, unexpected property should be shown, such as with respect to mechanical, thermal, electrical, optical, or other properties.

One issue to be aware of in this context is inadvertent use of "product-by-process" limitations.[84] Words that may be the past tense of a verb that suggests a process, as illustrated in Example 2.17, may have some risk. There, "coating," "blended," or "disposed over" are illustrative examples. A common word used that may be another example is "formed." The nature of materials technology may often lend itself to this sort of description. This sort of language is highlighted here because, if interpreted to be a product-by-process limitation, the language would be subject to the rules governing product-by-process claims, which increases risk of invalidity.[85]

However, the federal circuit has ruled that this language is not "product-by-process," but "structural" if used in a non-process sense. An example might be as for an apparatus claim.[86] Still, some may challenge that. Care is called for to draft the claims and the specification to support the argument that the language is structural, rather than "product-by-process."

For a composition of matter claim, use of functional language may also be challenging.[87] The PTO has the authority to shift the burden to the applicant with respect to functional language.[88] The CCPA decision *In re Swinehart*[89] stated in this regard:

> Additionally, where the Patent Office has reason to believe that a functional limitation asserted to be critical for establishing novelty in the claimed subject matter may, in fact, be an inherent characteristic of the prior art, **it possesses the authority to require the applicant to prove that the subject**

84. *See* section 1.2122 discussing product-by-process claims as an example of a legal change that may impact patent strategy and tactics.

85. *See* section 1.2122 and section 4.125 and its subsections, discussing validity issues regarding product-by-process claims. For a recent case, *see* Kamstrup A/S v. Axioma Metering UAB, 43 F.4th 1374 (Fed. Cir. 2022). The Federal Circuit found that the PTAB properly construed a product-by-process claim element as not entitled to patentable weight.

86. *See* Fromson v. Advance Offset Plate, Inc., 720 F.2d 1565, 1570, 219 USPQ 1137, 1140 (Fed. Cir. 1983) ("That a process limitation appears in a claim does not convert it to a product by process claim.").

87. Note that 35 U.S.C. § 112(f) (2022) also refers to "materials" suggesting applicability to compositions of matter.

88. *See In re* Swinehart, 439 F.2d 210 (C.C.P.A. 1971).

89. *In re* Swinehart, 439 F.2d 210 (C.C.P.A. 1971).

matter shown to be in the prior art does not possess the characteristic relied on (emphasis supplied).

If the PTO were to do this it may require seeking to prove the characteristic is not in the prior art (e.g., proving a negative proposition with evidence is usually a challenge), amending the claim, or arguing that for some reason the PTO has inappropriately shifted the burden.

2.114 Article of Manufacture Claims[90]

Article of manufacture claims are quite similar to apparatus claims. In fact, one may wonder what the difference might be to recite, for the same claim body:

"An apparatus comprising:" versus

"An article comprising:"

The answer may be more an issue of style.[91] However, although the preamble is not usually limiting,[92] it is good practice to ensure that the words you use in the preamble are broad enough to encompass all potential infringements. Hence, out of caution, "apparatus" may often be favored, as arguably broader.

With that said, there are times when "article" is more descriptive and consequently more appropriate than "apparatus." An article is thought of more as a physical object without moving parts, in comparison with an apparatus.[93]

The rules discussed for an "apparatus " or "machine" claim are the same for an article of manufacture. That is, obey the single infringer rule; include a preamble, transition word, and body; include a period at the end; and be mindful of the difference between function and structure.

2.1141 Beauregard Claims[94]

An important and frequently used type of article claim is referred to as a Beauregard claim, after the case *In re Beauregard*.[95] This type of claim may also be referred to as a CRM claim for "computer readable medium." IBM is credited with devising this type of claim, which was the assignee of the patent application in the *Beauregard* case. In that case, the PTO rejected the claim as nonstatutory and this rejection was appealed to the federal circuit; however, before the federal circuit ruled, the parties agreed to withdraw the appeal and

90. *See also* Chapter 4, also discussing article and Beauregard claims.
91. *See* MPEP § 2106.03 (2022).
92. *See, e.g.*, Catalina Mktg. Int'l v. Coolsavings.com, Inc., 289 F.3d 801 (2002).
93. *See* MPEP § 2106.03 (2022).
94. *See* Chapter 4, also discussing Beauregard claims.
95. *See In re* Beauregard, 53 F.3d 1583 (Fed. Cir. 1995).

the PTO permitted the use of such claims. These claims have a few formats that are similar, but some formats have potential for more problematic legal issues than others.

The general idea is to claim software stored on a "storage medium," such as on a flash drive, a head disk drive, and so on. However, the claim recites features of the software in a manner so that it is clear the software is *not* operating, similar to the approach previously discussed for apparatus claims. These claims have become quite commonly used most likely because anyone in the chain of distribution of the software can be sued. Software is always stored on some type of storage medium.

Although most of these claims refer to a "machine readable storage medium" or "computer readable storage medium," a question may be whether this is narrower than needed. Why not just recite "storage medium"?

Similarly, a lot of examples do not clearly distinguish the claim preamble from the claim body. Some Beauregard claims, for example, recite "A computer readable storage medium *having* stored thereon executable computer instructions *comprising*."

Is the transition word "having" or is it "comprising"? If it is "having," then the claim is subject to the argument that it is not an "open format claim." Furthermore, is this format nonstatutory because "computer readable storage medium" is the preamble and, consequently, not necessarily limiting? Recall that the federal circuit never resolved the issue regarding whether the claim in the *Beauregard* case was necessarily statutory.

Consider this imaginary claim example:

A storage medium having stored thereon computer readable software instructions that, when executed by a computer, cause to be performed a method of transmitting signals over a network comprising:

Action A;
Action B;
Action C.

From the face of this claim, it is not entirely clear whether the entire preamble is "a storage medium" or whether it is everything that precedes the word "comprising." One problem with this ambiguity is that it permits an opponent to take the position that best suits his or her case and it permits a court to go along with that position. As previously indicated, preambles are not always limiting, whereas the words in the body of the claim are.[96] Thus, in

96. *See* sections 2.12, 2.14 and their subsections, discussing the claim preamble and the claim body, respectively.

this example, it is not entirely clear whether the words between "having" and "comprising" necessarily limit the scope of the claim or not.

A clearer approach would be to recite:

An article comprising:
a storage medium including stored thereon . . .

Here, it is arguably much clearer that "comprising" is the transition word and that "storage medium" is within the claim body.

Another issue that may arise with this claim type is whether it might cover "signals per se."[97] By court ruling, such claims are not statutory. So, if a claim is presented that might read on "signals per se" it will be rejected. To address this, an examiner may require one recite a "non-transitory" storage medium. This concern is based in part on the notion that the PTO is permitted to apply the broadest reasonable interpretation to a claim. In theory, perhaps a wire transmitting an electrical signal along it would constitute a "transitory" storage medium for the signal, hence arguably meeting the claim language "storage medium." Whether this is a real concern or not, it has become clear that some examiners will *not* issue a Beauregard claim unless it recites "non-transitory" before "storage medium" so that it is clear that it does not cover signals per se. For this reason, it is a good idea to describe a "non-transitory storage medium" in your specification so that there is clear written description support for the following:

An article comprising:

a non-transitory storage medium including stored thereon executable instructions to . . .

Appreciate that "non-transitory" does not exclude memory states stored on a "temporary" (as opposed to "transitory") basis, as is done with random access memory, for example. However, clarifying this in the specification would be prudent.

Another issue to appreciate is that the language of the claim reciting features of the software may be functional, raising issues regarding structural and functional language.

Consider, for example, the Beauregard claim associated with Example 1.12 from Chapter 1, reproduced here for convenience.

97. *See In re* Nuijten, 500 F.3d 1346 (Fed. Cir. 2007).

EXAMPLE 2.20

I claim:

1. An article comprising: a non-transitory storage medium;

   wherein the storage medium includes stored thereon executable instructions; and

   wherein the instructions are executable to: emulate one or more network devices of at least a second broadcast domain, encapsulate one or more signal packets from at least a first broadcast domain to be directed to a network device of the at least a second broadcast domain, and communicate the encapsulated one or more signal packets to at least one tunnel server.

The language used is highly functional. On the other hand, it does not seem that the claim is *entirely* devoid of structure. This is consistent with how we previously recommended drafting functional limitations to reduce the risk of invoking section 112(f). Nonetheless, it may be a challenge to know with a reasonable degree of certainty how the claim might be construed with respect to section 112(f), if tested.

Fortunately, there is another formulation for a Beauregard claim that may address this concern. It uses the concept explained previously with respect to method claims that they are more difficult to attack as being functional because they recite "acts" or "actions."[98] Hence, a Beauregard claim might, instead, have the following form:

An article comprising: a non-transitory storage medium;

wherein the storage medium includes stored thereon executable instructions; and

wherein the instructions are executable to perform a method comprising the following:

98. *See* section 2.112, discussing method or process claims.

Action A;

Action B; and

Action C.

This may to a large extent address the functionality issue, although one may wonder if the claim could be attacked as having unclear scope for mixing method claim terminology with apparatus claim terminology, potentially making it indefinite, an issue previously raised.[99] However, federal circuit cases have addressed a similar issue where the apparatus function was described using terms ending in "ing" and determined that such claim was not indefinite because it was clear that a method was *not* being claimed, providing a strong reasoned basis for concluding that such a claim would not be indefinite for mixing statutory classes if carefully drafted.[100]

To demonstrate this, recall Example 2.12, providing this method claim as an illustration:

I claim:

1. A method comprising:

   emulating one or more network devices of at least a second broadcast domain;

   encapsulating one or more signal packets from at least a first broadcast domain to be directed to a network device of the at least a second broadcast domain; and

   communicating the encapsulated one or more signal packets to at least one tunnel server.

---

99. *See, e.g.*, IPXL Holdings v. Amazon, 430 F.3d 1377, 1384 (Fed. Cir. 2005). *See also* section 5.6 and its subsections regarding mixing statutory classes in a claim. Cf. INVT SPE LLC v. ITC, Appeal No. 20-1903 (Fed. Cir. August 31, 2022) (distinguishing between actual operation and capability of operating or performing for apparatus claims, particularly for software on a device, which tends to be functional, without discussing indefiniteness issue of mixing method and apparatus limitations), discussed in subsections 4.124 and 4.1272.

100. *See* Microprocessor Enhancement Corp. v. Texas Instruments Inc. 520 F.3d 1367 (Fed. Cir. 2008); HTC Corp. v. IPCom GmbH & Co., 667 F.3d 1270, 101 U.S.P.Q.2d 1518 (Fed. Cir. 2012).

Using the alternate Beauregard claim format, a Beauregard claim might be:

I claim:

1. An article comprising: a non-transitory storage medium:

   wherein the storage medium includes stored thereon executable instructions; and

   wherein the instructions are executable to perform a method comprising the following:

      emulating one or more network devices of at least a second broadcast domain;

      encapsulating one or more signal packets from at least a first broadcast domain to be directed to a network device of the at least a second broadcast domain; and

      communicating the encapsulated one or more signal packets to at least one tunnel server.

2.115 Improvement Claims

Improvement claims are included as a separate type of claim; however, most, if not all, patent claims represent an improvement. The language of section 101 specifically states:

> Whoever invents or discovers any new and useful process, machine, manufacture, or composition of matter, **or any new and useful improvement thereof**, may obtain a patent therefor, subject to the conditions and requirements of this title (emphasis added).

Here, therefore, by improvement claim, we mean a very specific type of claim in which the improvement is *specifically identified*. In the United States, these are referred to as Jepson claims. Europe also employs a similar claim format in which the improvement is introduced with the phase "characterized in that."[101] An example is included at the end of the next section.

---

101. *See* Chapter 7 and its subsections, discussing various aspects of patent claim drafting practice in the EPC.

The key feature of these claim types is that the preamble recites known prior art. Normally, under U.S. law, a question exists whether the preamble is limiting. However, because there is a reasonable, if not likely, risk that the preamble would constitute an admission of prior art,[102] a prudent approach would *assume* the preamble *is* limiting.

2.1151 Jepson Claims

We discuss Jepson claims here. European-style claims are discussed in Chapter 7, which quickly addresses a set of special topics regarding claim drafting issues in the EPC. However, we mention improvement style claims as used in Europe (i.e., the European Patent Convention (EPC)) at the end of this section for completeness.

37 CFR section 1.75(e) defines the structure of a Jepson claim. It states:

> Where the nature of the case admits, as in the case of an improvement, any independent claim should contain in the following order:
>
> (1) A preamble comprising a general description of all the elements or steps of the claimed combination which are conventional or known,
> (2) A phrase such as "wherein the improvement comprises," and
> (3) Those elements, steps and/or relationships which constitute that portion of the claimed combination which the applicant considers as the new or improved portion.

The PTO for years has encouraged the use of Jepson claims, although practitioners are less enamored with this type of claim. The PTO likes this claim format because it identifies in language what is considered to be prior art, as stated in part (1) of section 1.75(e). Practitioners, on the other hand, are wary because cases have held the preamble constitutes an admission of prior art.[103]

Two considerations, therefore, apply here. First, it is essential to confirm that what you believe to be prior art is, in fact, prior art. Second, it is equally essential to draft the preamble with care to ensure it *correctly* characterizes what you have confirmed to be prior art.

Consider Example 2.4. Per regulation 1.75, a Jepson claim for that example claim might look like:

---

102. *See* Kegel, 127 F.3d 1420, 1426 (Fed. Cir. 1997) ("To the extent [a phrase] is the preamble of a Jepson claim, it is admittedly prior art.").

103. *Id.*

I claim:

1. An apparatus including a central processing unit (CPU) coupled to random access memory (RAM) via a system transfer bus, wherein the improvement comprises: a memory controller coupled to the RAM;

   wherein the memory controller is capable of initiating burst mode operation based, at least in part, on receipt of a request from the CPU;

   wherein the request is to include a memory address, a word count, and a read or a write control transfer designation; and

   wherein the memory controller is to process the request and take control of the system transfer bus.

A comparison of Example 2.4 with the previously drafted claim illustrates that the primary change was to move elements from the body to the preamble. Also, appreciate the conservative nature of this claim. It, in effect, admits that a computing system including a central processing unit (CPU) coupled to random access memory (RAM) via a system transfer bus is known prior art. While this preamble is reasonably broad, it also appears to be factually correct. Furthermore, although memory controllers were known, the claim does not recite "memory controller" in the preamble; however, this stance is defensible because of the additional limitations also included in the claim body.

Recall that while Example 2.4 dealt with a system, Example 2.3 dealt with a component of a system. A tricky aspect of Example 2.3 was to draft the claim so that it was clearly directed to a component, rather than a system, although the claim, Example 2.3, also recited the CPU and system bus to properly claim the invention. Here, interestingly, a Jepson claim might make distinguishing Examples 2.3 and 2.4 easier to accomplish, such as follows, for Example 2.3, for example:

I claim:

1. An apparatus including random access memory (RAM), wherein the improvement comprises: a memory controller coupled to the RAM;

wherein the memory controller is capable of initiating burst mode operation based, at least in part, on receipt of an externally derived request from an external central processing unit (CPU);

wherein the request is to include a memory address, a word count, and a read or a write control transfer designation; and

wherein the memory controller is to process the request and take control of an external system transfer bus.

With this claim structure or format, it seems clearer that the claim is specifically directed to RAM and a memory controller. However, again, it is also easy to see by inspection that the primary difference is moving RAM into the claim preamble. Likewise, the risk of an inadvertently incorrect admission here is not great since the preamble seems to at most admit that RAM is known.

For completeness, here, these claims could be made to conform to EPC practice by replacing "wherein the improvement comprises" with "characterized in that" as follows, for the claim immediately preceding:

---

1. An apparatus including random access memory (RAM), wherein the RAM is characterized in that it includes: a memory controller;

   wherein the memory controller is capable of initiating burst mode operation based, at least in part, on receipt of an externally derived request from an external central processing unit (CPU);

   wherein the request is to include a memory address, a word count, and a read or a write control transfer designation; and

   wherein the memory controller is to process the request and take control of an external system transfer bus.

2.12 The Patent Claim Preamble

Previously, the basic structure of a claim was discussed as including a preamble, transition word or phrase, and claim body. This structure is primarily based on custom, but because federal courts expect this basic structure and some canons of construction revolve around this approach, it is highly recommended that it be used. Adhering to this basic approach and, furthermore, making it clear your intention regarding how the language of a claim you draft clearly divides among these separate components promotes certainty regarding how the claim should be interpreted. On the other hand, major deviations from it raise the risk that the intended meaning of the claim will be more likely to be challenged with the ultimate decision as to claim scope being put in the hands of another, who may interpret the claim differently from what you, the drafter, intended.

The preamble for these purposes is everything from the beginning of the claim up to but not including the transition word or phrase. How do you know which word is the transition word? Again, we recommend a structure that clearly signals your intention. Thus, we suggest you always use a colon immediately after the transition word or phrase.

Hence, here is a simple diagram of the basic structure:

[claim number]. [claim preamble] [claim transition word or words]:
[claim body].

The punctuation shown is believed important here to signal how the claim is divided into the basic components of a patent claim. Without these "signals," an opportunity exists for someone to more easily argue that part of the intended preamble is in the claim body or part of the intended claim body is in the preamble, for example. Since preambles are not necessarily limiting, this might create problems relative to a desired interpretation.

Likewise, with uncertainty where the preamble ends and the claim body begins, someone may argue that another word may be the transition word of the claim, such as "having." The issue with a transition other than "comprising" is that it may be found to be something other than open, depending on other factors.[104] If "comprising" is not employed (or one of the other well-established transitional phrases), a court will endeavor to determine what might have otherwise been intended, based on the specification, file history, and so on. That is, the claim may not be determined to be "open." The outcome, hence, may potentially turn out other than as intended.

104. *See* Crystal v. Tritech, 246 F.3d 1336, 1338 (Fed. Cir. 2001); *cf.* Moleculon Rsch. v. CBS, 793 F.2d 1261, 1271 n.8 (Fed. Cir.), *cert. denied*, 479 U.S. 1030 (1987).

2.121 Theory of the Preamble

Patents, or more precisely, patent claims, are often compared with contracts and with statutes. Patent claims have similarities with both and differences from both. A contract is a private document defining legal rights between at least two parties. A statute is a public document and, in general, often defines rights with respect to members of the public that may be the object of the language of the statute.

A patent claim is neither of these, but similar to each. A patent claim is like a statute in that it may restrict actions of the members of the public. Courts often refer to the "public notice function" of patent claims. However, similar to a contract and less like a statute, a patent claim creates legal rights for the owner. Yet, unlike a contract and more like a statute, those rights are with respect to members of the public, whose actions (make, use, sell, etc.), again, may be circumscribed by a patent claim or claims. Furthermore, more like a contract and less like a statute, the words of a patent claim are often the result of drafting and negotiation between two parties.[105]

For such reasons, while there is some similarity in the rules used to interpret these respective documents, there are also significant differences in the rules of interpretation that govern the three situations.

With this as background, it is worthy of mention that all three, statute, contract, and patent claim, typically include a preamble. For a contract and a statute, a preamble often states the background and/or purpose of the statute or contract, but, generally, these preambles precede the portion of these documents that are employed to define the legal rights that are being created. Consequently, for contracts and statutes, the preamble is to set the stage, so to speak, for the creation of legal rights, but does not itself, in general, affect those rights.

However, if there is ambiguity in the portion of the document that is employed to create such legal rights, courts often rely on the preamble to help resolve the ambiguity. Thus, the preamble, for contracts and statutes, may in some cases affect the legal rights created by the document, although that was not the purpose of the preamble when written.

So, it may also be said to be the case for preambles of patent claims. Generally, such language is simply a statement of intention that was not, in

---

105. For a patent claim, it is typically an examiner and legal representative of the applicant; for a contract, it is usually the parties to the contract or their legal representatives.

general, necessarily intended to affect the scope of the patent claim.[106] However, despite that general rule, there are situations identified by courts where a patent preamble may be used to limit the scope of a patent claim. In *Catalina Marketing v. Coolsavings.com*,[107] the federal circuit noted that no litmus test defines when a preamble limits claim scope. Thus, whether a preamble is limiting may be challenging to predict.

Claim preambles, therefore, present a variety of risks. One risk is that the preamble will inadvertently introduce an unintended limitation into the claims. This is what most commonly occurs. However, another risk is that you may, in fact, expect the preamble to introduce a limitation to a patent claim to distinguish from the prior art (a risky approach); but a court may, instead, conclude that the preamble is not a limitation and, therefore, hold the claim invalid. Likewise, if a court construes the preamble to be a limitation, then there is always the risk that the court will conclude that the limitation is not adequately supported by the specification, is not enabled by the specification, is indefinite, and so on, perhaps because at the time of drafting the claim preamble language was not given sufficiently close attention in comparison with the language of the claim body.

2.122 Examples of Preambles

One possible approach to drafting preambles is to limit the preamble to recite *only* the statutory class or category of the invention such as "A method comprising:"[108] and so on. Although such a restrictive approach is not absolutely necessary, it is recommended that care be used to draft the preamble and ensure that the preamble is short and to the point.[109] Some simple examples are provided here.[110]

Examples:

A system	A subsystem
An apparatus	An integrated circuit

---

106. *See* Catalina Mktg. v. Coolsavings, 289 F.3d 801, 808 (Fed. Cir. 2002). The court also discusses that a limiting preamble "breathes life and meaning" into the claim.

107. 289 F.3d 801, 808 (Fed. Cir. 2002).

108. Note that "comprising" is actually not part of the preamble, but is the transition word, as explained in more detail *infra*.

109. This is discussed in more detail in section 5.1 and its subsections.

110. *See* Robert Kahrl & Stuart Soffer, Thesaurus of Claim Construction (2011) for additional examples of terms for use in a preamble.

A module
A composition of matter
A machine
An article
A component
A process
A circuit
A device
A method
A composite
A material

A method of communicating [anything, e.g., an electronic message]
A method of operating [anything, e.g., a system]
A method of processing [anything, e.g., signals]
A method of manufacturing [anything, e.g., a component]
A method of using [anything, e.g., a device]
A method of coding
A method of decoding
A method of synthesizing
A set of [anything, e.g., components]

Method claims deserve special mention in the context of preambles. It is common practice when drafting method claims to use the preamble to provide antecedent basis for words, usually tangible elements, that are then used later in the body of the claim. Consider the following example.

EXAMPLE 2.21

I claim:

1. A method of cooking pasta comprising:

   placing the pasta in boiling water; and

   waiting until the pasta becomes at least slightly tender.

As is clear in this example, the preamble provides antecedent basis for the word *pasta*. In this case, the preamble will likely be construed to be limiting, although perhaps, in this example, with little consequence. However, because the words of the preamble provide antecedent basis for terms used in the body of the claim, for this situation, courts usually find preambles to be limiting.[111] Of course, in this simple example, the claim could have been drafted so that the preamble did not provide antecedent basis, as follows:

111. *See* Catalina Mktg. v. Coolsavings, 289 F.3d 801, 808 (Fed. Cir. 2002).

I claim:

1. A method comprising:

placing pasta in boiling water; and

waiting until the pasta becomes at least slightly tender.

However, for more complex method claims, drafting the claim so that the preamble does not serve this function and consequently is not limiting can be much trickier, depending upon the situation.

There is also a legitimate question whether one should use the preamble for antecedent basis, employ express recitation in the body for antecedent basis, or employ inferential claiming.[112] This is an area where reasonable minds may differ and different situations may suggest different approaches.

The trade-offs may be complex and require use of judgment. Generally, we recommend preambles be short and to the point to reduce uncertainty as to what may or may not be limiting.[113] However, this suggests that antecedent basis for any hardware or tangible elements of the claim, for example, would be in the claim body. This may subject a method claim to the risk of a challenge that it is indefinite by making it unclear whether the patent claim is an apparatus claim or a method claim.[114] If the method claim is carefully drafted, however, we believe this is an acceptable risk, but it is something to consider. Following is another, more complex, example method claim in which the tangible elements are included in the preamble to provide antecedent basis rather than relying on the patent claim body, which is a legitimate alternate approach.

I claim:

1. A method of operating a module, the module including at least one integrated circuit chip comprising a plurality of series N-type metal oxide semiconductor (NMOS) field effect transistors in a series connected stack

112. Inferential claiming is discussed in more detail later in this chapter. *See* section 2.1413.

113. This is discussed in more detail in section 5.1 and its subsections.

114. *See* section 5.6 and its subsections, discussing mixing statutory classes in a single patent claim.

configuration that comprises at least one series NMOS field effect transistor including a body, the at least one series NMOS field effect transistor either to pass an RF signal in a series enable state or to not pass the RF signal in a series disable state, the method comprising:

electrically biasing the body of the at least one series NMOS field effect transistor of the module in the series disable state to have a voltage level substantially more negative than the lowest voltage level of the following: ground, a DC voltage level of a source of the at least one series NMOS field effect transistor of the module, and a DC voltage level of a drain of the at least one series NMOS field effect transistor of the module.

It is noted that this claim is a one act or action method claim.

Also, as a separate point regarding preambles, recall from the prior section that the preamble may take on added importance for an improvement claim, such as a Jepson claim.

2.13 The Patent Claim Transition Word

We often speak of the transition word, however, truly we should refer to the transition phrase, because in many cases a transition may involve more than one word. The most common transition word is "comprising," however, two other commonly used transition phrases are "consisting of" or "consisting essentially of." It is quite likely that this word choice for the transition may be the most important of all the words chosen for a patent claim, granted that this choice is highly circumscribed (e.g., to a limited number of possibilities).

This choice has significant importance because, more than any other words, the transition word or phrase fundamentally affects claim scope. For this reason, it is critically important that through your claim format and claim language you make it absolutely clear which word or words you intend to be the transition word or phrase.

> It is critically important that through your claim format and claim language you make it absolutely clear which word or words you intend to be the transition word or phrase.

2.131 Theory of the Transition Word

The theory of the transition word (or phrase) follows directly from the theory of a patent claim. A patent claim is a set of elements and limitations that in combination defines the metes and bounds of an invention.[115] However, one fine point about claim types relates to differences in technology. As a formal, legal matter, the patent statutes that govern U.S. patent law are neutral with respect to technology.[116]

As a patentee, one would like a claim to define, via the language used, the elements, limitations, and relationships considered to be the invention. However, likewise, from the perspective of scope of rights, if someone makes, uses, or sells a product that is exactly as you have recited with claim language, generally, a patentee would not want them to escape liability by simply adding something else to the product. Otherwise, it would take little effort to design around a patent claim. Such a patent system would not provide much legal protection. Hence, the use of the word "comprising."

There is also a good policy reason for this approach. In general, the idea of a patent system is for others to build on the work of the patentee. Thus, if someone, for example, builds a better mousetrap, it stands to reason that if the patent on the original mousetrap has not expired, the owner of the mousetrap patent should have rights as to the improved mousetrap (assuming the claims are properly drafted to accomplish such a result).

This point relates to the notion that, in general, most patents represent *improvements* on something that preceded the patent, often, but not necessarily, another patented technology. The system is designed with this in mind and supports the use of "comprising." A stylized example relates to the steam engine versus the combustion engine.

Suppose the steam engine is invented[117] by A. The notion of an engine, being new, is broadly defined as a machine or apparatus that converts up and down motion (i.e., motion by pistons) to rotary motion (i.e., motion by wheels

---

115. *See, e.g.*, Phillips v. AWH Corp., 415 F.2d 1303, 1312 (Fed. Cir. 2005) (en banc) ("It is a 'bedrock principle' of patent law that 'the claims of a patent define the invention to which the patentee is entitled the right to exclude.'"). *See also* Constant v. Advanced Micro-Devices, Inc., 848 F.2d 1560, 1571, 7 USPQ2d 1057, 1064 (Fed. Cir. 1988); Dollar Elec. Co. v. Syndevco, Inc., 205 USPQ 949, 959 (E.D. Mich. 1979), *aff'd*, 669 F.2d 1370, 214 USPQ 241 (6th Cir. 1982).

116. See Dan L. Burk & Mark A. Lemley, Policy Levers in Patent Law, 89 Va. L. Rev. 1575, 1654–55 (2003); William A. Drennan, The Patented Loophole: How Should Congress Respond to This Judicial Invention?, 59 Ra. L. Rev. 229, 323–28 (2007).

117. This is a made-up example, so please, as to technical details, permit so-called literary allowances.

or a rotary rod, etc.). Thus, a skilled practitioner may, if extremely successful, obtain an issued claim 1 reciting:

1. A machine comprising: an engine.[118]

This claim would have been novel, non-obvious, useful, and so on at the time the invention was made. Now, we note, that the embodiment in the technical specification is a steam engine. However, it is well established that the patent claims are not limited to the description in the specification. Furthermore, an issued claim 2 of the same patent might recite:

2. The machine of claim 1, wherein the engine comprises a steam engine.

This suggests, via claim differentiation,[119] that claim 1 has scope beyond the literal embodiment described, specifically the steam engine, a not unusual circumstance regarding patent claims and specification embodiments.

In this highly stylized hypothetical, suppose after the patent has issued to A, someone, B, quite knowledgeable in combustion technology, reads it and realizes that, while it is a wonderful invention, an engine could be made to output much more "work" in terms of power or energy, by using a combustion mechanism inside the engine to toggle the pistons, rather than using steam. This person, B, realizing the potential for such an invention, obtains skilled patent counsel who manages to obtain issuance of a patent with the claim (note that the steam engine patent with its claim 1 is still in force during this time):

1. A machine comprising: a combustion engine.

Again, this claim would have been novel, non-obvious and useful at the time the invention was made. It, therefore, patentably distinguishes from the disclosure and the claims of the steam engine patent.

Now, in this made-up world, the question is this: who has the legal right to manufacture a combustion engine? A bit surprisingly, *no one does*. A patent claim gives you the right *to prevent others* from practicing the claim but does not grant an owner an affirmative right for the owner to practice it himself.[120]

---

118. Remember to permit literary allowances for the purpose of the overall point to be made.

119. *See* section 2.15 and its subsections discussing claim differentiation.

120. *See* 24 U.S.C. § 154(a)(1) (2022) ("Every patent shall contain a short title of the invention and a grant to the patentee, his heirs or assigns, of the right to **exclude** others from making, using, offering for sale, or selling the invention throughout the United States or importing the invention into the United States, and, if the invention is a process, of the right to exclude others from using, offering for sale or selling throughout the United States, or importing into the United States, products made by that process, referring to the specification for the particulars thereof.") (emphasis supplied).

This becomes particularly relevant, here, in connection with improvements and building on the patented work of others.

Thus, if B were to manufacture a combustion engine because he has the patent claim to a combustion engine, his engine would infringe A's more general claim to an engine. Likewise, if A were to attempt to manufacture a combustion engine because he has a patent claim to engines generally and combustion engines are desirable to introduce to the market, A's combustion engine would infringe B's combustion engine claim. In a world with rational decision-makers driven by the profit motive, A and B should consummate a cross-license so one or both might supply combustion engines to the market.

However, in the balance of value between the two patents, does A pay B because B has the hot, new technology or does B pay A because A has a foundational lock on all engines generally? Of course, this is a matter of negotiation, and so on. Thus, this next point is a little speculative; however, we see today that combustion engines appear to have significantly greater demand than steam engines. It seems probable that A will pay B, assuming A wants to produce combustion engines.

Hence, the nature of technological improvements, which the patent system is designed to advance, is illustrated. It is often the latest and greatest technology that drives market demand, rather than the foundational technology, though the foundational technology, of course, is important to move the technology frontier forward.

It is often the latest and greatest technology that drives market demand, rather than the foundational technology, though the foundational technology, of course, is important to move the technology frontier forward.

How does this lengthy, perhaps interesting (and certainly educational) detour relate to transition words or phrases? As noted, the U.S. patent system is built upon improvements.[121] This helps explain why "comprising" is the much more common and more favored transition word. That is, it has an open format with respect to the scope of the claim.

121. Some might say incrementally small improvements; others might say incrementally sizable improvements. However, either way, improvements.

> This helps explain why "comprising" is the much more common and more favored transition word. That is, it has an open format with respect to the scope of the claim.

Knowing this, then, why ever use a different transition word or phrase? This is where inherent differences in technology potentially impact the choice of a transitional phrase. Let us consider some major technological and scientific areas: mechanical devices, electrical or electronic devices, software, materials science, chemistry, and biotechnology. In this order, these technologies represent a spectrum in which moving from left to right, the technologies become less predictable. By predictable, we mean that given an invention or innovation, it becomes more difficult to extrapolate from that invention or innovation to additional possible related technology that would be enabled from knowing the invention in light of the state of the art.

Chemistry and biotechnology tend to be highly experimental sciences in which the properties of various combinations of known technical components are more unexpected than for mechanical devices, electronic devices, and software.[122] Hence, in patent law, the latter technologies are characterized more generally as being in the predictable arts and the former technologies are characterized as being in the unpredictable arts.[123]

Imagine, for example, a chemical invention (e.g., composition of matter) such that the properties of the constituents are nothing like the properties of

---

122. *See* Seymore, *supra* note 76. *See In re* Rainer, 377 F.2d 1006, 1012 (C.C.P.A. 1967) (Important considerations include "the type[s] of reactions, the state of the art, the representative nature of the examples, and the breadth of the claims."). *See also* PPG Indus., Inc. v. Guardian Indus. Corp., 75 F.3d 1558, 1564 (Fed. Cir. 1996) (explaining that "enablement is lacking. . . , because the undescribed embodiments cannot be made, based on the disclosure . . . without undue experimentation"); *In re* Prutton, 200 F.2d 706 (C.C.P.A. 1952) (holding that claims to a class of chemical compounds that were sufficiently broad to involve some speculation lack enablement notwithstanding the presence of the operative specific examples within the class); *In re* Fisher, 427 F.2d 833 (C.C.P.A. 1970).

123. *Compare In re* Vaeck, 947 F.2d 488, 496 (Fed. Cir. 1991) (noting that the requisite level of disclosure for an invention involving predictable mechanical or electrical elements is less than that required for the unpredictable arts) *with* PPG Indus., Inc. v. Guardian Indus. Corp., 75 F.3d 1558, 1564 (Fed. Cir. 1996) (explaining that "enablement is lacking . . . , because the undescribed embodiments cannot be made, based on the disclosure . . . without undue experimentation"); *In re* Prutton, 200 F.2d 706 (C.C.P.A. 1952) (holding that claims to a class of chemical compounds that were sufficiently broad to involve some speculation lack enablement notwithstanding the presence of the operative specific examples within the class).

the result, as is usually the case in the chemical arts. Furthermore, for patentability under section 103, often the compounds or compositions of matter that result should have improved and unexpected properties relative to similar, previously known formulations.

Typically, formation of such compounds requires precise conditions. Important considerations with a composition of matter claim may include "the type[s] of reactions, the state of the art, the representative nature of the examples, and the breadth of the claims."[124] If one were to use the word "comprising" in a patent claim for a compound formulation, the patent claim could sweep in a host of other possible constituents, conditions, chemical catalysts, and so on, that may not produce the desired result being described and sought to be claimed and patented. In this case, then, the claim may be invalid because its full scope would not and possibly could not be enabled or may not be sufficiently described, as is legally required.[125] That is, the specification may describe precise conditions to produce a chemical compound, as a working example, perhaps; however, the claim language with "comprising" as the transition word may sweep in other subject matter that has not been enabled or even described because the described conditions will not produce compounds literally covered by the claim or, perhaps even, compounds literally covered by the claim may not even be possible to produce.[126]

Consider Example 2.15 again.

I claim:

1. A composition of matter consisting of: complex compounds of the formula $M(CO)_a H_b (NH_3)_c$, in which M is a metal of the actinide series of the Periodic Table of the Elements and each of a, b and c is a whole number

124. *See In re* Rainer, 377 F.2d 1006, 1012 (C.C.P.A. 1967).

125. *See* Juno Therapeutics, Inc. v. Kite Pharma, Inc. 10 F.4th 1330 (Fed. Cir. 2021) (written description); Trustees of Boston v. Everlight, 896 F3.d 1357 (Fed. Cir. 2018) (enablement); Durel Corp. v. Osram Sylvania, 256 F.3d 1298, 1306–07 (Fed. Cir. 2001) (a significant number of inoperative embodiments within the scope of the claims might be sufficient to prove invalidity); *see also* Atlas Powder v. DuPont, 750 F.2d 1569, 1576–77 (Fed. Cir. 1984).

126. For example, this would require undue experimentation. *See* Trustees of Boston v. Everlight, 896 F3.d 1357 (Fed. Cir. 2018) (enablement); Durel Corp. v. Osram Sylvania, 256 F.3d 1298, 1306–07 (Fed. Cir. 2001) (a significant number of inoperative embodiments within the scope of the claims might be sufficient to prove invalidity); *see* Atlas Powder v. DuPont, 750 F.2d 1569, 1576–77 (Fed. Cir. 1984). *See also* EMI Grp. North America, Inc. v. Cypress Semiconductor Corp., 268 F. 3d 1342 (Fed. Cir. 2001) (claims reciting scientific process found to be impossible are invalid).

ranging from 0 to 8, such that when a is 0, b is greater than 0 and otherwise a is equal to or greater than b and when c is greater than 0, both a and b are 0.

2. The composition of matter in accordance with claim 1, wherein M is uranium or thorium.

3. The composition of matter in accordance with claim 2, wherein M is uranium, a is 8, b is 2 and c is 0.

4. The composition of matter in accordance with claim 2, wherein M is uranium, a is 0, b is 0 and c is 8.

For this claim, in the so-called unpredictable arts, a transition phrase is called for to limit scope and thereby avoid invalidity for lack of enablement or lack of written description that might result from use of an open form transition word. Claim drafters may, instead, with other types of transitional phrases, vary claim scope linguistically to capture more than the working examples described in the specification *without* use of an open form transition word. As one example, for the one just preceding, precisely varying specified parameters defined by the specification and claim permits one to achieve a desired claim scope.

Again, this difference in transition phrases is a result of the inherent nature of the technology involved. In the predictable arts, a broad claim that uses the open form "comprising" may still be enabled and potentially be sufficiently described to its full scope from only one embodiment due the nature of the technology and the state of the art.[127]

To address this issue for the unpredictable arts, patent claims in the unpredictable arts often use "consisting of" or "consisting essentially" as the transition, referred to as closed form and partially closed form, respectively. These transitions have a specific meaning based on canons of construction regarding patent claims, as explained; however, there are federal circuit cases as well

127. *See, e.g.*, Leibel-Flarsheim v. Medrad, 358 F.3d 898, 905 (Fed. Cir. 2004); Spectra-Physics, Inc. v. Coherent, Inc., 827 F.2d 1524, 1533 (Fed. Cir. 1987) ("[i]f an invention pertains to an art where the results are predictable, e.g., mechanical as opposed to chemical arts, a broad claim can be enabled by disclosure of a single embodiment, and is not invalid for lack of enablement simply because it reads on another embodiment of the invention which is inadequately disclosed."). However, there are cases where the federal circuit concluded a claim was not enabled by a single embodiment. Thus, it is best to provide multiple embodiments. *See* section 4.11 and its subsections.

that have deviated from these canons when interpreting a claim. One may view these canons as a type of "first order" analysis or, perhaps, as a weak presumption. In the appropriate circumstances, depending on claim wording, the specification, the file history, the technology, and so on, a federal court may be willing to deviate from the canon.

With this in mind, "consisting of" is used to claim the elements and limitations as recited in the claim body (i.e., closed form).[128] "Consisting essentially of" is used to claim the elements and limitations as recited in the claim body, including any additional unclaimed constituents that are of a nature or an amount to not alter the character of what is otherwise intended to be claimed as novel subject matter (i.e., partially closed form).[129]

However, one feature to know about transition words, especially in connection with compositions of matter, is that different transition words may be used within the claim to limit or enlarge scope as well. For example, suppose our "improved memory material" from earlier[130] easily integrates into a silicon chip. One may, as an example, want to claim an integrated device with "comprising," but within the claim body, employ "consisting of" to claim the portion of the integrated device made from the constituents for our "improved memory material." This sort of approach is illustrated with Example 2.16 and with Example 2.18, provided here for convenience.

I claim:

1. A semiconductor device comprising:

   a substrate, the substrate consisting of a material selected from the group consisting of silicon, sapphire, gallium arsenide, magnesium oxide, zinc oxide, and silicon carbide;

128. *See* AFG Indus. v. Cardinal, 239 F.3d 1236 (Fed. Cir. 2001); *cf.* Norian Corp. v. Stryker Corp., 363 F.3d 1321 (Fed. Cir. 2004) (claim includes ordinary impurities of recited elements). *See* section 2.113, regarding composition of matter claims.

129. *See* PPG Indus. v. Guardian Indus., 156 F.3d 1351 (Fed. Cir. 1998). *See* section 2.113, regarding composition of matter claims. Note that use of "consisting essentially of" was recently held to raise an indefiniteness issue in HZNP Medicines LLC v. Actavis Laboratories UT, Inc., 940 F.3d 680 (Fed. Cir. 2019). This was because a basic and novel property was indefinite. However, with this transition phrase, unclaimed constituents are to be of a nature or an amount to not alter the character of what is otherwise intended to be claimed as novel subject matter. Hence, claim scope was unclear.

130. *See* section 2.113, regarding composition of matter claims.

a crystalline buffer layer on the substrate consisting essentially of gallium nitride; and

a growth layer on the buffer layer, the growth layer comprising gallium nitride and a first dopant material.

For the preceding claim, "comprising" is used to join three elements, which respectively include a clause using closed form, partially closed form, and open form. The clause of the substrate element uses a format referred to as a Markush group, discussed in more detail later.[131]

2.132 Examples of Transition Words

Earlier we discussed the three basic types of transition words or phrases used in patent claims and their understood meaning in accordance with basic patent law canons. We recommend these be used without deviation of language.

> We recommend the three basic types of transition words or phrases discussed earlier (and later) be used in patent claims without deviation of language.

A long line of patent cases has construed claims so that when the word "comprising" is employed as the transition word, the claim is interpreted as open. One statement of this basic proposition is contained in the federal circuit case *Invitrogen v. Biocrest*.[132] This means the claim is construed to cover *more than* simply all the elements and limitations provided in the body of the claim. The claim is interpreted so that, as long as all the listed elements and limitations are present in the relationship recited in the claim, then the claim is met, even if other aspects of the so-called accused product or accused process are not explicitly listed in the claim.

In virtually all cases in the predictable arts, "comprising" should be used as the transition word. This is because it would be unusual in the predictable arts to find all the elements and limitations of a claim present in the accused product or process, but still find that the inventive concept was not being

131. *See* section 4.129 and its subsections.
132. 327 F.3d 1364 (Fed. Cir. 2003).

employed, regardless of what else might also be present in the accused product or process.

It is also a good idea to follow the word "comprising" with a colon. This will make it clear that "comprising" is intended to be the transition word and that everything that follows the colon is intended to be the body of the claim. Again, it is best to have it be clear which portion of the claim is the preamble, which portion is the transition word, and which portion is the claim body. This will make it more clear which words of the claim are necessarily intended as limitations.

> In virtually all cases in the predictable arts, "comprising" should be used as the transition word. It is also a good idea to follow the word "comprising" with a colon. This will make it clear that "comprising" is intended to be the transition word and that everything that follows the colon is intended to be the body of the claim.

Sometimes in patent claims "comprised of" is used in place of "comprising." Comprising is the much more common term and, consequently, the one recommended for use. However, case law indicates that "comprised of" will be interpreted in the same manner as "comprising."[133]

However, other less-traditional terms have been employed. One example is "having." Another is "composed of."[134] It is strongly recommended that these terms *not* be employed *as a claim transition word or phrase*. Using "having" as the transition word for a patent claim, for example, is not recommended because there is some risk that the claim might otherwise not be interpreted to be "open." For example, in *Crystal v. Tritech*,[135] the federal circuit stated that if the transition word employed is "having," the claim may be interpreted to be open or closed, depending on the context. Here, context refers to the claim language itself, the other claims, the specification, and the file history.[136]

---

133. *See* CIAS, Inc. v. Alliance Gaming Corp., 504 F.3d 1356–60 (Fed. Cir. 2007).

134. *See* AFG Industries, Inc. v. Cardinal IG Company, Inc., 239 F.3d 1239 (Fed. Cir. 2001).

135. *See* Crystal v. Tritech, 246 F.3d 1336, 1338 (Fed. Cir. 2001).

136. Likewise, note that use of the word "comprising" elsewhere in the claim other than as the transition word is subject to interpretation. *See* Moleculon Rsch. v. CBS, 793 F.2d 1261, 1271 n.8 (Fed. Cir.), *cert. denied*, 479 U.S. 1030 (1987).

2.14 The Patent Claim Body

Of course, the body of the claim is crucial to a patentability determination and to an infringement determination. The body is made up of claim elements and claim limitations recited in a particular relationship.

Previously, we provided various claim examples of various claim types, each of which included a claim body.

2.141 Theory of the Claim Body

The ultimate goal of the body is to capture in words the patentable innovation. Of course, this is easier said than done. This idea may relate more, as a drafting exercise, to section 103, than to section 102.

In general, if an examiner comes up with a piece of anticipatory art, per section 102, an element or limitation may be added to the claim, as long as the specification provides written description support for that element or limitation, to obviate the rejection. Thus, "the game," so to speak, is to capture the innovation so that the claim may be said to exhibit to "an inventive step" over the closest known prior art, as discussed previously.[137]

In this regard, the language of section 103 directs a court or other decision-maker to compare differences between the prior art and the "subject matter sought to be patented" (pre-AIA) or "the claimed invention" (post-AIA) (i.e., the patent claim) "as a whole." This is important because it means that for the purposes of determining obviousness, *the claim must be considered as a whole.*

In other words, the claim is a collection of elements and limitations and associated relationships. It is not proper under section 103 to simply dissect the claim into separate elements and limitations and see if the prior art has each recited element and limitation. Rather, the whole may be (and typically is) greater than the sum of the parts. This typically factors into what would have made an invention unobvious. For example, there may be advantages that come from combining the elements and limitations together in the manner recited in the claim that would *not* be present if those elements and limitations were dissected and viewed in isolation from one another. Those advantages that flow from "the whole" are relevant to determining whether the invention would have been obvious at the time the invention was made. Specifically, such advantages may be relevant to whether, at the time the invention was made, the invention would have been obvious to "a person having ordinary skill in the art to which said subject matter pertains."

It is this aspect of the innovation that the claim body should seek to capture in language.

---

137. *See* sections 1.331 and 1.332, discussing section 103 pre- and post-AIA.

Specifically, advantages that flow from the claim language viewed "as a whole" may be relevant to whether, at the time the invention was made, the invention would have been obvious to "a person having ordinary skill in the art to which said subject matter pertains."

It is this aspect of the innovation that the claim body should seek to capture in language.

Furthermore, a good claim, primarily referring to the claim body, is an appropriate balance between breadth, vagueness, and precision. The claim body is precise in some respects because the claim language should be specific enough to distinguish from the known prior art. This often involves some amount of detail in the language employed for the claim body. For example, if the prior art shows red doorknobs, to be novel at least, the claim body should recite a color other than red. For example, a recitation in the claim body of "a blue doorknob," would be novel over such prior art (granted that it might have been obvious at the time the invention was made, depending on other considerations). Patent claim bodies are usually precise enough to show that the subject matter claimed is at least novel over the known prior art.

People sometimes confuse breadth and vagueness, the other features of a good claim body. For example, "any and all electrical signals" is quite broad, but it is *not* vague. Rather, it is crystal clear. A good patent claim body has breadth to cover those aspects not needed to distinguish from the known prior art. Breadth is desirable to protect the technology from those who might try to employ the technical idea in a manner that might otherwise not infringe a narrower claim.

Vagueness, however, may be appropriate, for example, when it may at the time of patenting remain unclear how certain technology may be implemented among various potential choices. That is, the future is uncertain. Being vague permits the claim, primarily the body, to be infringed without necessarily spelling out in specific language how some aspects of the claim body will be implemented.

The point, of course, is that good claim bodies are broad, vague, and precise in the appropriate balance for the situation. Thus, the claim body should capture the innovation and employ an appropriate balance regarding precision, breadth, and ambiguity (i.e., vagueness).

> The claim body should capture the innovation and employ an appropriate balance regarding precision, breadth and ambiguity (i.e., vagueness).

Consider, again, for example, Example 2.2.

I claim:

1. An apparatus comprising:

   a substantially horizontally oriented, rectangularly shaped seat including four corners;

   wherein attached to a respective corner of the seat is a substantially vertically oriented leg such that the legs point in the same direction away from the seat, are oriented to be substantially mutually parallel, and are of substantially the same length.

This sample claim has precision and some breadth. More to the point, however, what is the innovation sought to be captured? It is not clear from the claim body. By focusing on the innovation, using claim language in the body to capture it, the aspects involving breadth and vagueness, which are to be balanced along with precision, may be better developed.

It is important, however, in performing such an evaluation, to consider the closest *known* prior art. This is a hypothetical situation. In this hypothetical world, chairs have not been invented yet. So, what did people use to sit in groups or to sit upon after becoming tired from a lot of walking, and so on? Perhaps, they used very large rock formations, the ground, or trees that had fallen due to windstorms and the like. Of course, these "prior art" approaches are not convenient. To sit in groups, for example, you would need a bunch of fallen trees or boulders close together.

So, in light of this background, what might one conclude is innovative about a chair? It appears to be that it is portable. That is, it provides a place to sit that is easily and conveniently portable. What would that look like in a patent claim body?

EXAMPLE 2.22

I claim:

1. An apparatus comprising: a portable seat.

Of course, this is a stylized example and, hence, here, results in a possibly overly broad claim, but it *does* begin the process of formulating the claim body. A portable seat seems like it would have been novel and unobvious at the time it was made in light of prior art, such as the ground or fallen trees. Also, it is useful.

Appreciate, however, if allowable, what this potentially captures compared with the previous claim: many potential follow-on improvements—wheel chairs, swivel chairs, ergonomic chairs, and so on. Many things that the previous claim would not have captured. Patents have a 20-year term. With the pace of technical change, it might be surprising how quickly products built on a fundamental concept, such as this example, may develop.

Someone, a lawyer most likely, may argue that a small boulder could be a portable seat. That may be a good point; again, Example 2.22 was a starting point. Perhaps, to distinguish from the known art, the claim should be:

EXAMPLE 2.23

I claim:

1. An apparatus comprising: a portable seat;

   wherein the portable seat includes a back oriented to be roughly perpendicular to the portable seat.

So, the claim body now includes elements (seat and back) and limitations (portable, oriented to be roughly perpendicular) that provide relationships between the elements.[138]

138. Alternatively, perhaps, Example 2.22 is claim 1, and a claim 2 that is dependent provides the additional features of Example 2.23.

2.1411 *Claim Elements/Limitations and their Relatonship*

One issue that may be confusing relates to the difference between an element and a limitation of a patent claim.[139] Likewise, if the patent claim includes elements *and* limitations, what part of the claim constitutes the relationships among claim components?

These are good questions, and the case law may not be fully consistent regarding the answers to such questions. There may be multiple ways to view the situation, although, here, we provide an internally consistent view.

The federal circuit has used both terms, "elements" and "limitations," to describe the words of a claim.[140] However, the federal circuit has expressed a preference for "limitation" over "element." In *Dawn*, as one example, the court indicates that "limitation" applies to the claim, whereas "element" applies to the accused device.[141]

It might be more helpful to consider elements, limitations, and the relationship thereof, as on a spectrum. An analogy with other areas of law might also be helpful. In criminal law and in tort law, there is a notion of an "act" that is committed and also of "attendant circumstances" that must be present. Perhaps, one way to think of a claim is that the elements are like "the act or acts" of a tort or crime and the limitations are like "the attendant circumstances."[142]

In this construct, the elements are components recited in the claim that necessarily are present in the accused product and limitations are further clarifications about those elements that also must be met. What then of "the relationship among elements and/or limitations?" "The relationship" may refer

---

139. It is noted that 37 C.F.R. § 1.75(i) (2022) states: "(i) Where a claim sets forth a plurality of elements or steps, each element or step of the claim should be separated by a line indentation." However, it appears that examiner's rarely invoke this rule. If they were to do so, it would be as an informality objection that could easily be addressed.

140. *See, e.g.*, Festo Corp. v. Shoketsu Kinzoku Kogyo Kabushiki Co., 234 F.3d 558, 56 USPQ2d 1865 (Fed. Cir. 2000) (en banc), rev'd and remanded, 535 U.S. 722 (2002), on remand, 344 F.3d 1359 (Fed. Cir. 2003), cert. denied, 541 U.S. 988 (2004) stating: "In our prior cases, we have used both the term 'element' and the term 'limitation' to refer to words in a claim." See, e.g., Lemelson v. United States, 752 F.2d 1538, 1551, 224 USPQ 526, 533 (Fed. Cir. 1985) (using the term "element"); Sextant Avionique, S.A. v. Analog Devices, Inc., 172 F.3d 817, 826–27, 49 USPQ2d 1865, 1870–71 (Fed. Cir. 1999) (using the term "limitation"). It is preferable to use the term "limitation" when referring to claim language and the term "element" when referring to the accused device. See Dawn Equip. Co. v. Kentucky Farms, Inc., 140 F.3d 1009, 1014 n.1, 46 USPQ2d 1109, 1112 n.1 (Fed. Cir. 1998).

141. See Dawn Equip. Co. v. Kentucky Farms, Inc., 140 F.3d 1009, 1014 n.1, 46 USPQ2d 1109, 1112 n.1 (Fed. Cir. 1998).

142. *Cf.* INVT SPE LLC v. ITC, Appeal No. 20-1903 (Fed. Cir. August 31, 2022) (distinguishing in analysis of claim, whether base station was part of the environment of the claims and whether to infinge one would need to make, use or sell the base station).

the relationship among the elements and may comprise all the limitations of the claim as a whole. Consider preceding Examples 2.3 and 2.4, repeated here:

EXAMPLE 2.3

I claim:

1. An apparatus comprising:

    random access memory (RAM) and a memory controller;

    wherein the memory controller is capable of initiating burst mode operation based, at least in part, on receipt of an externally derived request from an external central processing unit (CPU);

    wherein the request is to include a memory address, a word count, and a read or a write control transfer designation; and

    wherein the memory controller is to process the request and take control of an external system transfer bus.

In Example 2.3, random access memory and the memory controller are claim elements in that they must be present in the accused product. In this claim, the CPU and system bus, though recited, are part of the claim with respect to the limitations. The recited limitations must be met but, under the view presented here, the CPU and system bus are not required to be present for infringement of claim 1 of Example 2.3.[143] That is, while the system bus need not be present, nonetheless "the memory controller must be able to process the request and take control of a system transfer bus" as a limitation that must be met, as an example.

EXAMPLE 2.4

I claim:

1. An apparatus comprising:

143. *Id. Cf.* INVT SPE LLC v. ITC, Appeal No. 20-1903 (Fed. Cir. August 31, 2022) (distinguishing in analysis of claim, whether base station was part of the environment of the claims and whether to infinge one would need to make, use or sell the base station).

random access memory (RAM), a memory controller, a central processing unit (CPU), and a system bus;

wherein the memory controller is capable of initiating burst mode operation based, at least in part, on receipt of a request from the CPU;

wherein the request is to include a memory address, a word count, and a read or a write control transfer designation; and

wherein the memory controller is to process the request and take control of the system transfer bus.

In Example 2.4, random access memory and the memory controller are claim elements, *as are the CPU and system bus. These must all be present in the accused product to infringe.* In this claim, the CPU and system bus are also part of the claim with respect to the limitations. The recited limitations must also be met, as before. However, here, as recited elements, the CPU and system bus are required to be present for infringement of claim 1 of Example 2.4, but not because of being recited in the limitations. Rather, in claim 1 of Example 2.4, these are recited to be (and are intended to be) claim elements.

Cases talk of an "all elements rule" for patent infringement; however, sometimes this is called an "all limitations rule."[144]

2.1412 Structure Versus Function Versus Process

In a previous section, structure versus function was discussed.[145] Similarly, previously, we discussed limitations that, though potentially interpreted as product-by-process limitations, may nonetheless be interpreted as structural if used in a non-process sense.[146] These discussions raise the point that some claim terms have potential to suggest a particular type of limitation, such as a functional limitation, a structural limitation, or a process-type limitation. To avoid repetition, those sections that discuss this more fully and provide examples are referenced.[147]

---

144. *See* Ethicon Endo-Surgery, Inc. v. United States Surgical Corp., 149 F.3d 1309, 1317, 47 USPQ2d 1272 (Fed. Cir. 1998) ("[T]he All Elements rule might better be called the All Limitations rule. It will be referred to as such throughout the remainder of this opinion."). *See* section 3.23 and its subsections, discussing the "All Elements" rule.

145. *See* section 2.1111, discussing structural versus functional limitations.

146. *See* section 4.125 and its subsections, discussing product-by-process limitations; *see also* section 2.112 and its subsections, discussing method or process claims.

147. *Id.*

It is a good idea also to be mindful that claim terms have the potential to cross boundaries, such as function, structure, or process, and might be construed in more than one manner. It may, in some cases, be important to make it clear via claim language and/or specification language, which is intended, especially if a lot rides on a particular interpretation.

It is a good idea also to be mindful that claim terms have the potential to cross boundaries, such as function, structure, or process, and might be construed in more than one manner. It may, in some cases, be important to make it clear via claim language and/or specification language, which is intended, especially if a lot rides on a particular interpretation.

2.1413 Inferential Claiming

Generally, inferential claiming has a bad "reputation" in U.S. patent law as leading to indefiniteness. It is certainly true that unintentional inferential claiming may lead to indefiniteness; however, inferential claiming, if done intentionally and appropriately, is a powerful drafting tool and should not always be cast aside. As with all claim drafting, care and thought are required, however.

Inferential claiming, in general, means to claim something without having first provided a positive recitation thereof.[148] However, there are varying definitions, which may be termed, here, the antecedent basis view of inferential claiming and the positive recitation view of inferential claiming. This may be more easily understood by first considering a standardly used claim format, such as for an apparatus claim:

I claim:

1. An apparatus comprising:

148. Perhaps, this approach is better described as implication claiming rather than inferential claiming since the language may be said to *imply* a feature, rather than to *infer* a feature, without first having positively recited the feature.

an element A, an element B, and an element C;[149]

wherein [relationships among the element A, the element B and the element C].

Employing an antecedent basis view of inferential patent claiming means to introduce an element without first employing an indefinite article, in contradiction of the format just shown.

Consider, for example, the following claim:

EXAMPLE 2.24

I claim:

1. An apparatus comprising:

 a hip prosthesis;

 wherein the hip prosthesis includes: a ball and a socket;

 wherein the ball has an elliptical shape and the socket has a corresponding elliptical shape to receive the ball within the socket for mutual engagement;

 wherein the elliptical shape of the ball has a major axis; and

 wherein during the mutual engagement of the ball and the socket, the ball is at least able to rotate within the socket substantially perpendicular to the minor axis of the ball.

In this claim, we see that, in general, the claim elements are introduced first positively with an indefinite article. These include hip prosthesis, ball, socket, elliptical shape, corresponding elliptical shape, and major axis. However, we see that the term "minor axis" is ***not*** first introduced with an indefinite article. Nonetheless, because elliptical shape and major axis are introduced through positive recitation, we are able to ***infer*** that the elliptical shape also has a minor axis. Thus, indefiniteness is not a significant risk here.

149. May be on separate lines per rule 37 C.F.R. § 1.75 (2022).

With this understanding, it is easy to see how, if taken too far, this drafting approach might lead to indefiniteness. However, it is noted that the federal circuit has stated that recitation of a claim term without having antecedent basis does not necessarily make a claim indefinite.[150]

The positive recitation view of inferential claiming, instead, refers to not separately calling out a feature as a claim element before introducing it. This may also create potential ambiguity or at least potentially raise a question as to intended scope. As an illustration, consider the following claim similar to claim 1 of Example 2.3:

EXAMPLE 2.25

I claim:

1. An apparatus comprising:

   random access memory (RAM) and a memory controller;

   wherein the memory controller is capable of initiating burst mode operation based, at least in part, on receipt of a request from a central processing unit (CPU);

   wherein the request is to include a memory address, a word count, and a read or a write control transfer designation; and

   wherein the memory controller is to process the request and take control of a system transfer bus.

The CPU and the system bus, as examples, *are* introduced with an indefinite article, but *are not* first positively recited (in comparison with "random access memory" and "memory controller"). Under a positive recitation view of inferential claiming, the CPU and the system bus are claimed inferentially.

As suggested in the previous section, a way to understand the latter claiming approach is that random access memory and memory controller are elements and are required to be present in the accused device. The CPU and the system bus are *not* claim elements and are *not* required to be present in the accused device. The language of the claim around CPU and system bus,

150. *See, e.g.*, Bose Corp. v. JBL, Inc., 274 F.3d 1354, 1359 (Fed. Cir. 2001); Slimfold Mfg. Co. v. Kinkead Indus., Inc., 810 F.2d 1113, 1117 (Fed. Cir. 1987).

instead, constitutes claim limitations that clarify how the accused device is to operate when combined with a CPU and system bus. Thus, this view of inferential claiming might be thought of as related to the previous discussion[151] regarding claim elements and claim limitations. A potential ambiguity in situations such as this might be, however, what terms are specifically intended as claim elements and what terms are not intended specifically as claim elements, hence, creating risk of indefiniteness or improper interpretation.

With the foregoing understanding, are the following examples of inferential claiming?

EXAMPLE 2.26

I claim:

1. A method comprising:

   receiving a request for burst mode operation;

   transmitting a request for control of a system bus in response to the received request;

   receiving a signal granting system bus control;

   transferring signals across the system bus into or out of a group of sequential memory cells after receiving the signal granting system bus control; and

   transmitting a signal indicating completion of the signal transfer.

I claim:

1. An apparatus comprising:

   a substantially horizontally oriented, rectangularly shaped seat including four corners;

   wherein attached to a respective corner of the seat is a substantially vertically oriented leg such that the legs point in the same direction away from the seat, are oriented to be substantially mutually parallel, and are of substantially the same length.

151. *See* section 2.1411.

Under the antecedent basis view, probably not, but under the positive recitation view, probably so. For example, for the latter claim, it might have been more formally formulated as:

I claim:

1. An apparatus comprising:

   a seat;

   wherein the seat comprises a rectangularly shaped seat;

   wherein the rectangularly shaped seat comprises a horizontally oriented, rectangularly shaped seat;

   wherein the horizontally oriented, rectangularly shaped seat has four corners; . . .

---

and so on. One should recognize that the rules that discourage inferential claiming are designed to reduce claim ambiguity, which is a desirable goal because indefiniteness may invalidate a claim. On the other hand, employing a non-inferential claiming approach quite strictly may also lead to a more cumbersome patent claim in terms of language, which may be a barrier to comprehension. This, of course, would be a disadvantage, as well, such as if the judge or jury is not able to comprehend the claim due to overly formalistic and exceedingly cumbersome wording. In dealing with method claims, for example, we have discussed the alternative approaches of first positively reciting tangible components, such as hardware, in the preamble versus reciting such tangible components "inferentially" as part of an action or action element, and the potentially associated legal issues.[152]

The risk arises, again, where the possible inference (or implication, depending on your preference) creates a genuine ambiguity as to intention with respect to claim coverage. The guidance is to use approaches that lead to tighter claims if it may be done without creating an ambiguity.

---

152. *See* section 2.112 and its subsections, discussing method or process claims.

> Use approaches that lead to tighter claims if it may be done without creating an ambiguity.

Here is one simple example of what not to do:

EXAMPLE 2.27

I claim:

1. An apparatus comprising:

   a portable seat.

2. The apparatus of claim 1, wherein the horizontally oriented seat has four corners.

In this example, does claim 1 have a horizontally oriented seat? One could argue that it does and one could argue that it does not. Thus, if not indefinite, at a minimum, scope is unclear. However, likewise, scope being unclear supports the position that the claim is indefinite.

2.1414 Interpreting Claims in Light of the Specification Versus Importing Limitations; Redefining Claim Terms Versus Importing Limitations

The canons of claim construction have several important principles, but tension may exist between some principles. This topic is introduced here to demonstrate it may at times be possible to rely on specification detail to supplement the claim limitation language, although this may be a risky approach. This is due at least in part to the difficulty of predicting with confidence how a court may apply the appropriate canon in a given situation. Instead, it is believed to be better to include a spectrum of patent claims that cover the subject matter at a broad level of specificity, at an intermediate level of specificity of detail, and at a narrow level of specificity.[153] Also, in this manner, one may be reasonably assured that such claims are supported by the written description, because the written patent claims are part of the written description.

153. *See* section 4.11, discussing claiming multiple embodiments, from broadest to narrowest.

One canon is that claims are to be interpreted in light of the specification of which they are a part.[154] Another canon is that it is improper under the guise of claim interpretation to import a limitation from the specification into the claims.[155] The latter principle even applies where a specification provides a single embodiment unless the specification evidences a clear intention to limit the claims to that single embodiment. That is, the claims are not to be limited to that single embodiment.[156]

However, navigating between these two canons is not quite so easy as stating them. The federal circuit itself has recognized the difficulty.[157] An early case that clearly illustrates this challenge is *Renishaw v. Marposs*.[158]

The invention concerned a touch probe used to measure very fine distances (e.g., dimensions) of machined parts. It appears that the accused product met every limitation of the claim at issue but one, whose interpretation was in dispute. The patent claim at issue recited: "the probe generat[e] a trigger signal *when* said sensing tip contacts an object and said stylus holder is thereby deflected relative to said housing" (emphasis supplied).

The ultimate question was the meaning of "when." The specification described the invention in a manner that suggested there was virtually no appreciable delay between contacting an object and generating a trigger signal. However, the accused product had an appreciable delay due to its method of operation. Despite this contrast, the term "when" more generally may be understood to not mean simply "at the time of." Rather, it may be understood to also include within a short time thereafter. Claim terms are heavily presumed to be interpreted in accordance with their ordinary and customary meaning,[159] unless clearly redefined in the specification to have a different meaning.

The federal circuit discussed the tension between the two canons in the opinion:

---

154. *See, e.g.*, SimpleAir v. Sony Ericsson 820 F.3d 419, 429–38 (Fed. Cir. 2016); Phillips v. AWH, 415 F.3d 1303, 1315 (Fed. Cir. 2005) (en banc).

155. *See, e.g.*, Phillips v. AWH, 415 F.3d 1303, 1313 (Fed. Cir. 2005) (en banc); Leibel-Flarsheim v. Medrad, 358 F.3d 898, 913 (Fed. Cir. 2004). For a recent example, *see* Lowe v. ShieldMark, Inc., No. 2021-2164, 2022 WL 636100 (Fed. Cir. Mar. 4, 2022), in which the federal circuit held that the lower court erred by importing terms from the specification into the claims.

156. *See, e.g.*, Leibel-Flarsheim v. Medrad, 358 F.3d 898, 905 (Fed. Cir. 2004).

157. *See, e.g.*, Phillips v. AWH, 415 F.3d 1303, 1323 (Fed. Cir. 2005) (en banc); Comark Commc'ns v. Harris Corp. 156 F.3d 1182, 1186–87 (Fed. Cir. 1998).

158. Renishaw v. Marposs, 1580 F.3d 1243 (Fed. Cir. 1998).

159. *See, e.g.*, Azure Neyworks v. CSR, 771 F.3d 1336, 1347–48 (Fed. Cir. 2014); Aventis Pharm. v. Amino Chem., 715 F.3d 1363, 1373 (Fed. Cir. 2013).

> Renishaw, of course, alludes to a familiar pair of claim construction canons: (a) one may not read a limitation into a claim from the written description, but (b) one may look to the written description to define a term already in a claim limitation, for a claim must be read in view of the specification of which it is a part. These two rules lay out the general relationship between the claims and the written description. *See Vitronics Corp. v. Conceptronic*, Inc., 90 F.3d 1576, 1582, 39 USPQ2d 1573, 1576 (Fed.Cir.1996); *Markman v. Westview Instruments, Inc.*, 52 F.3d 967, 979-80, 34 USPQ2d 1321, 1329-30 (Fed. Cir. 1995) (in banc), *aff'd*, 517 U.S. 370, 116 S.Ct. 1384, 134 L.Ed.2d 577, 38 USPQ2d 1461 (1996).
>
> As rules at the core of claim construction methodology, they provide guideposts for a spectrum of claim construction problems.
>
> Thus, where there are several common meanings for a claim term, the patent disclosure serves to point away from the improper meanings and toward the proper meaning. Ultimately, the interpretation to be given a term can only be determined and confirmed with a full understanding of what the inventors actually invented and intended to envelop with the claim. *See Markman v. Westview Instruments, Inc.*, 517 U.S. 370, 389, 116 S. Ct. 1384, 134 L.Ed.2d 577, 38 USPQ2d 1461, 1470 (1996). The construction that stays true to the claim language and most naturally aligns with the patent's description of the invention will be, in the end, the correct construction.[160]

The court, hence, resolves the question by looking at how the term "when" is used in the description. The court, for example, states:[161]

> For example, in describing the invention's place within the prior art, the '904 patent notes: "When the stylus contacts a workpiece surface, a trigger signal is generated by the probe, which is used to trigger the taking of a reading of the instantaneous position of the movable spindle, quill or arm." Col. 1, ll. 36-42. Likewise, the Summary of the Invention states that the preferred embodiment of the probe "includes means for providing a signal when said stylus contacts a workpiece," col. 3, ll. 28-29, and that the movable elements are displaced "out of said rest position when said stylus contacts a workpiece," col. 3, ll. 21-22.
>
> Statements in the "Description of Preferred Embodiments" also use the term "when" to describe a time very close to the precise instant that the stylus contacts the object to be measured and not some appreciable time thereafter. . . .

Thus, concluding that "when" means "at the time of," the Federal Circuit stated:

---

160. *See* Renishaw v. Marposs, 1580 F.3d at 1248.
161. *See id.* at 1252–53.

> "These passages make abundantly clear that 'when' in the patent means at the time of, and not some appreciable time thereafter." *See Autogiro Co.*, 384 F.2d at 397, 155 USPQ at 702-03 ("[W]ords must be used in the same way in both the claims and the specification.").
>
> To the extent that these passages refer to the preferred embodiment, they cannot be read into the claims without some hook. The claim term "when" is that hook. Each of the preceding passages above show that the patentee wanted "when" to mean as soon as possible after contact. In contrast, Renishaw's preferred construction of "when," which would sweep in any time whatsoever after contact, is so broad that it would require us to ignore the abounding statements in the written description that point decidedly the other way.[162]

The court is trying to be helpful with its "hook" analogy. However, this approach logically pushes the question back to how specifically or generally a claim term is to be understood from the usage of that term in the specification. It seems a court will not have difficulty locating such "a hook" for those cases in which it wants to import a limitation from the specification.

Renishaw did not deliberately limit its claim in this manner. How clear and unmistakable is it that the drafter intended to "redefine" the term "when" from its ordinary and customary meaning? If the patent draftsman had perceived the precise issue that might later be raised, there is little doubt the specification would have clarified the point and even the claim language itself. Thus, concluding noninfringement from such a general term in the claim, while demonstrating good lawyering by those representing the defendant, does not give sufficiently clear guidance regarding the difference between construing claims in light of the specification and importing limitations. Yet, *Renishaw* is heavily cited and held out as an example of a case that clarifies the difference.

A drafting lesson, here, might be to be circumspect in the use of everyday language and endeavor to uncover potential interpretations that might lead to noninfringement, and revise claim and specification language accordingly. In this regard, later sections of this book discuss reviewing claims with an eye toward possible design around opportunities so that claims may be redrafted before filing so as to cover such noninfringement opportunities.[163]

162. *See Renishaw*, 1580 F.3d at 1252–53.

163. *See* section 6.5, discussing making designing around patent claims more difficult.

> A drafting lesson, here, might be to be circumspect in the use of everyday language and endeavor to uncover potential interpretations that might lead to noninfringement, and revise claim and specification language accordingly.

A similar tension also exists between impliedly redefining a claim term and importing limitations from the written description. For example, a specification may employ terms in an idiosyncratic manner, terms may be highly technical or terms may be coined by an inventor.[164] Generally, it has been recognized that the specification is reviewed to resolve such ambiguities.[165] While a specification may *expressly* redefine a claim term, the federal circuit has also recognized that this may occur *by implication* without express definition *if it is clear*.[166] Again, as a result, a tension exists between the occurrence of a redefinition by implication and importing a limitation from the written description into the claims. That is, the difference may be a fine one.

One example case is *Sony v. Thorner*,[167] which, like *Renishaw*, involved an issue of claim construction. The district court had construed "attached to said pad" in a manner so that the defendant, Sony, did not infringe. The district court held that "the specification redefines 'attached' by implication." The district court reasoned that the word "attached" was limited to attached to the outside of an object because the embodiments in the specification consistently use the term "attached" to indicate affixing an actuator to the outer surface of an object and used the word "embedded" when referring to an actuator inside an object. For additional support for the notion that "attached" and "embedded" have different meanings, the district court pointed to claim 1 which used the word "attached" and dependent claim 10 which used the word "embedded."

Following claim construction by the district court, the parties stipulated to noninfringement by the accused products so that the construction by the district court could be appealed to the federal circuit.

---

164. *See, e.g.*, Phillips v. AWH, 415 F.3d 1303, 1313 (Fed. Cir. 2005) (en banc).
165. *See, e.g.*, Straight Path IP Grp. v. Snipet, 806 F.3d 1356, 1361 (Fed. Cir. 2015).
166. *See* Irdeto Access v. EchoStar, 383 F.3d 1295, 1300 (Fed. Cir. 2004); Bell Atlantic v. Covad, 262 F.3d 1258, 1268 (Fed. Cir. 2001).
167. *See* Thorner v. Sony, 669 F.3d 1362 (Fed. Cir. 2012).

In *Thorner*, the appellate court stated, regarding claim construction:

Our case law is clear, claim terms must be given their plain and ordinary meaning to one of skill in the art. *Phillips*, 415 F.3d at 1316. The plain meaning of the term "attached" encompasses either an external or internal attachment. We must decide whether the patentee has redefined this term to mean only attachment to an external surface. As Sony argues, the specification repeatedly uses the term "attached" in reference to embodiments where the actuators are "attached to [an] outer side." '941 patent col.33 ll.40–41. In fact, the specification never uses the word "attached" when referring to an actuator located on the interior of a controller. We hold that this does not rise to the level of either lexicography or disavowal. Both exceptions require a clear and explicit statement by the patentee. *CCS Fitness*, 288 F.3d at 1366; *Teleflex*, 299 F.3d at 1325. It is not enough that the patentee used the term when referencing an attachment to an outer surface in each embodiment. *See Kara Tech.*, 582 F.3d at 1347–48. In fact, the specification explains that an actuator was "attached to [an] outer surface." *See* '941 patent col.33 ll.40–41. If the applicant had redefined the term "attached" to mean only "attached to an outer surface," then it would have been unnecessary to specify that the attachment was "to [an] outer surface" in the specification. We conclude that the term attached should be given its plain and ordinary meaning. The specification does not redefine attached nor is there any disavowal.[168]

The appellate court further stated:

The fact that the specification uses the two terms "attached" and "embedded" as alternatives does not require a different result. *See, e.g., id.* col.32 l.66. There is nothing inconsistent about the applicant's use of the narrower term, "embedded," to describe embodiments affixed to an internal surface. The plain and ordinary meaning of embedded, "attached within," is narrower than "attached." Hence it makes sense that the applicant would want to use embedded when it meant to explicitly claim attached to the inside only. That does not mean the word attached automatically means attached to the external surface, as opposed to the broader plain meaning—attached to either the interior or exterior.

It is true that in certain pre-*Phillips* cases, we held that use of two terms as alternatives could amount to an implicit redefinition of the terms. *See Bell Atl. Network Servs., Inc. v. Covad Commc'ns Grp., Inc.*, 262 F.3d 1258, 1271 (Fed. Cir.2001). But the "implied" redefinition must be so clear that it equates to an explicit one. In other words, a person of ordinary skill in the art would have to read the specification and conclude that the applicant has clearly

168. *See id.* at 1367–68.

> disavowed claim scope or has acted as its own lexicographer. Simply referring to two terms as alternatives or disclosing embodiments that all use the term the same way is not sufficient to redefine a claim term.
>
> Other parts of the claim and specification also support this construction. The claim at issue requires a "flexible pad." The only embodiment in the specification that includes flexible material is the seat cushion 510 shown in Figure 2. The specification states that "the tactile feedback seating unit 510 is a semi-rigid flexible foam structure . . . with a plurality of actuators embedded within the foam structure." '941 patent col.37 ll.6–10. Thus, the only flexible embodiment in the specification has embedded actuators. If we agreed with Sony that "attached" must mean attached to an outer surface, then the claim would exclude the only flexible embodiment disclosed in the specification. This is further evidence that the term "attached" should have its plain and ordinary meaning which includes either internal or external attachments.
>
> We hold that the term "attached to said pad" should be given its plain and ordinary meaning which encompasses either internal or external attachment. Because the parties based the stipulation of noninfringement on the district court's erroneous construction of this claim term, we vacate and remand.[169]

It is helpful to compare the approach of the panel in *Renishaw* with the approach of the panel in *Thorner v. Sony*. It is true that *Renishaw* is an earlier case compared with *Thorner*; however, *Renishaw* is repeatedly cited throughout federal circuit claim construction jurisprudence. Furthermore, many other examples along the lines of *Renishaw* continued to be decided in the years following that decision.[170] The point, then, is to show, by contrast, that various outcomes are possible, depending on the context, which may even include the panel of judges deciding the case. The best way to hedge one's bets is to make sure the desired interpretation follows both from the clear language of the claims as well as the clear description in the specification.

The point, then, is to show, by contrast, that various outcomes are possible, depending on the context, which may even include the panel of judges deciding the case. The best way to hedge one's bets is to make sure the desired interpretation follows both from the clear language of the claims as well as the clear description in the specification.

---

169. *Id.*

170. *See* Chapter 3, discussing claim construction, such as section 3.212.

Throughout the post-Markman era in which claim construction was determined to be a court function, a tension is evident on the federal circuit illustrated by the comparison between *Renishaw* and *Thorner*. On the one hand, the court would like a consistent set of rules that gives predictability. These principles include the presumption of ordinary meaning and that any deviation requires a clear and unmistakable redefinition in the specification. On the other hand, principles also exist that the specification should be used to point the way to a proper claim construction. Thus, a construction may be sought that aligns with specification usage. However, this latter principle appears to be applied in a manner that is not as exacting or is without the same high evidentiary showing as suggested by principles that apply the presumption of ordinary meaning and that require a clear and unmistakable redefinition in the specification. Hence, close cases are harder to resolve.

For the drafter, the "game," so to speak, is to ensure either approach leads to the same construction. This is discussed more in the next chapter, but it would be best that a definition of a key claim term provided in the specification align as much as possible with the known and understood ordinary meaning in accordance with the presumption of ordinary meaning and while also abiding by the principle that definitions of claim terms in the specification are clear and unmistakable.

2.15 Independent Versus Dependent Claims

Understanding the legal relationship between independent and dependent claims and how that relationship may affect validity and infringement determinations is an important part of the basic principles of claim drafting. Dependent claims may also influence the interpretation of the independent claim. Hence, although the tendency in claim drafting is to focus most attention on the independent claim, the dependent claims may enhance (or unintentionally undermine) the scope of the independent claim depending on execution. Drafting a full set of claims, including one or more independent claims and many dependent claims, therefore, is usually desirable for a patent application.

2.151 Theory of Dependent Claims

In general, the relationship between an independent claim and a dependent claim is logical. 35 USC subsection 112(d) discusses dependent claims.[171] It states:

171. Section (e) of 112 addresses multiply dependent claims, not specifically discussed here in detail. These are more commonly used in Europe, discussed in Chapter 7. The PTO

> (d) Reference in dependent forms.—Subject to subsection (e), a claim in dependent form shall contain a reference to a claim previously set forth and then specify a further limitation of the subject matter claimed. A claim in dependent form shall be construed to incorporate by reference all the limitations of the claim to which it refers.

Dependent claims may only narrow independent claims. That is, dependent claims add additional limitations to the independent claim and must by construction always be narrower. Therefore, the independent claim is always the broadest claim of a set of claims.[172]

Consider claims 1 and 2:

> 1. An apparatus comprising:
>
> element A, element B, and element C.
>
> 2. The apparatus of claim 1, comprising: element D.

In this example, an apparatus with A, B, and C infringes claim 1, but not claim 2. However, an apparatus with A, B, C, and D infringes claim 1 *and* claim 2.

Consider, now, this example[173]

EXAMPLE 2.28

I claim:

1. An automobile comprising: an engine, four wheels, and a drive train;

   wherein the drive train is to transmit drive power to at least one opposing pair of the wheels.

2. The automobile of claim 1, wherein the drive train includes both forward and reverse gears and means for shifting between the gears so that the opposing pair of wheels are to be driven in either the forward or the reverse direction.

---

charges an extra fee for such a claim beyond fees for the dependency claim equivalent, so most applicants avoid them. See https://www.uspto.gov/learning-and-resources/fees-and-payment/uspto-fee-schedule. *See also* MPEP § 608.01(n) (2022).

172. Here, in this context, a set of claims specifically refers to one independent claim followed by a series of dependent claims.

173. Adopted from district court case, TM Patents v. IBM, 107 F. Supp. 2d 352 (S.D.N.Y. 2000).

Claim 2 is narrower, clearly. However, one might think that an automobile with more capabilities infringes claim 2 rather than claim 1. Logically and legally, however, that would not be correct. Rather, it only *appears* that a car drivable *only* in the forward direction infringes claim 1 and a car drivable in both directions infringes claim 2. A car drivable in *both* directions would infringe *both* claim 1 and claim 2.

Consequently, there may be situations where a dependent claim might "appear" to broaden the independent claim, but that would be legally improper. Usually, those situations only superficially appear to broaden, but in terms of legal rights, actually narrow. For example, a dependent claim may seem to expand the capabilities of the subject matter of the independent claim, as shown by the preceding example. In truth, the dependent claim specifically "recites" an additional feature that may or may not be present in an actual infringement of the independent claim. Whereas, for the dependent claim, the feature *must necessarily* be present for infringement.

Dependent claims also illustrate the fundamental trade-off between infringement and validity.[174] That is, although a broader claim may capture more infringers, it also is open to attack based on a broader set of prior art.

One of the most common reasons for adding dependent claims, therefore, is as a sort of hedge vis-à-vis prior art. After filing, during prosecution, and even after issuance, and, perhaps, after multiple litigations, more and more prior art may be discovered. That is, one never knows exactly what the prior art contains until discovered. With dependent claims, limitations may be added so that, while discovered prior art may render broader claims invalid, other narrower, dependent claims, may stand up to such art and still capture some potential infringers. In this context, it is worth noting that as a technical legal matter, a court does *not* hold a patent claim *valid*. A patent claim is presumed valid. Rather, a court holds a patent claim *not* invalid, because, at a later time, in another suit, for example, it is still possible that it may be found to be invalid in light of newly discovered prior art, for example.

The doctrine of claim differentiation also relates to the logical structure of dependent claims. Essentially, the doctrine is a presumption that because different words are used in different claims, the claims are presumed to cover different subject matter.[175] Of course, because it is a presumption, it may be

174. *Cf.* Unique Concepts, Inc. v. Brown, 939 F.2d 1558 (Fed. Cir. 1991) (infringement and validity are separate issues so that a claim may be infringed and invalid, although there may be no liability for that infringement) (dissent by J. Rich).

175. *See, e.g.*, Wi-LAN USA, Inc. v. Apple Inc., 830 F.3d 1347 (Fed. Cir. 2016).

overcome based on other factors.[176] However, the doctrine may be helpful in claim drafting to suggest, via a dependent claim structure, that particular claims have a certain scope. For example, if the *dependent claims* in your claim set recite *specific features* in the specification with respect to an embodiment, the logical implication is that the claims from which those claims depend *cover broader subject matter than the embodiment.*[177]

Here Example 2.3 is repeated.

I claim:

1. An apparatus comprising:

   random access memory (RAM) and a memory controller;

   wherein the memory controller is capable of initiating burst mode operation based, at least in part, on receipt of an externally derived request from an external central processing unit (CPU);

   wherein the request is to include a memory address, a word count, and a read or a write control transfer designation; and

   wherein the memory controller is to process the request and take control of an external system transfer bus.

In section 1.2111, we previously provided an illustrative dependent claim:

> 2. The apparatus of claim 1, wherein the memory controller comprises an address register, a word count register, and a transfer mode register.

The implication is that if a memory controller is able to implement burst mode operation without the specific registers of claim 2, it infringes claim 1.

176. *Id.*

177. *See, e.g.*, Interdigital Commons v. ITC, 690 F.3d 1315, 1324 (Fed. Cir. 2012) (The doctrine of claim differentiation disfavors reading a limitation from a dependent claim into an independent claim.) For a recent example of claim differentiation, *see* Littelfuse, Inc. v. Mersen USA EP Corp., 29 F.4th 1376 (Fed. Cir. 2022), in which the federal circuit vacated and remanded the district court's ruling of noninfringement and emphasized that by definition, an independent claim is broader in scope than a dependent claim, and, hence, an embodiment recited in a dependent claim should also be covered by the corresponding independent claim.

Using dependent claims, in light of claim differentiation, therefore, has a boot strapping effect with respect to the base claim.

It is also noted that claim differentiation is stronger if the dependent claim adds one new feature as opposed to many new features.[178]

It is also helpful to consider the validity and infringement considerations that follow from a dependent claim structure, particularly in which the transition word is "comprising." The relationships might be thought of as being the inverse of each other. In particular, something that *literally* infringes a dependent claim should by construction *literally* infringe the independent claim.[179] This is based on the additional limitation introduced by the dependent claim that is not present in the independent claim. By contrast, a piece of prior art that invalidates an independent claim may not necessarily invalidate a dependent claim.[180] This is also based on the additional limitation introduced by the dependent claim.

Using similar reasoning, something that does not literally infringe the independent claim should not literally infringe the dependent claim, again, particularly for the transition word "comprising." The independent claim is the broadest claim of a set of claims, by construction. On the other hand, a piece of prior art that invalidates a dependent claim should invalidate the independent claim.

As to issues other than prior art, the relationship of invalidity may be dependent on the claims themselves. For example, an independent claim may be indefinite, but a dependent claim may potentially cure that indefiniteness. Alternatively, an independent claim may be definite, but a related dependent claim may be indefinite.

---

178. *See* Anderson v. Fiber Composites, 474 F.3d 1361, 169–70 (Fed. Cir. 2007); Acumed v. Stryker, 483 F.3d 800, 806 (Fed. Cir. 2007).

179. The statement is qualified by "should" because there might be unusual claim formulations in which although the dependent claim is necessarily narrower, it may be that something which infringes the dependent claim does not necessarily infringe the independent claim. For example, claim 1 may recite "consisting of A and B." Claim 2 may recite, and further "consisting of C." A product A, B, and C would literally infringe claim 2 but not claim 1.

The statement is also limited to literal infringement because there is a possible, but unusual, situation in which a product may infringe a dependent claim under the doctrine of equivalents and not infringe the independent claim under the doctrine of equivalents. This situation was first articulated by Judge Rich in the Wilson Sporting Goods decision. *See* Wilson Sporting Goods v. David Geoffrey, 904 F.2d 677 (Fed. Cir. 1990). *See also* section 3.2314, discussing the Wilson Sporting Goods Case.

180. *See, e.g.*, Innova/Pure Water, Inc. v. Safari Water Filtration Sys., Inc., 381 F.3d 1111, 1123 (Fed. Cir. 2004) ("dependent claims are typically narrower and, by so being, are more likely to clearly distinguish the prior art. Generally speaking, this is, in part, their function.").

In general, dependency is a matter of substance rather than form. However, there are preferred forms for dependent claims discussed in the next section. It is not a requirement that a dependent claim be in the same statutory class as the independent claim (although it is recommended);[181] however, it must narrow the independent claim.[182] Here is an example:

I claim:

1. A method comprising:

   emulating one or more network devices of at least a second broadcast domain;

   encapsulating one or more signal packets from at least a first broadcast domain to be directed to a network device of the at least a second broadcast domain; and

   communicating the encapsulated one or more signal packets to at least one tunnel server.

2. An article comprising: a non-transitory storage medium;

   wherein the storage medium has stored thereon executable instructions;

   wherein the instructions are executable to perform the method of claim 1;

   wherein the at least one tunnel server comprises at least two tunnel servers.

---

37 CFR section 1.75 (2022) addresses some aspects relevant to dependent claims. For example, subsection (b) states:

> (b) More than one claim may be presented provided they differ substantially from each other and are not unduly multiplied.

181. *See* section 5.6 and its subsection.

182. *See* MPEP § 608.01(n) (2022) ("The fact that the independent and dependent claims are in different statutory classes does not, in itself, render the latter improper.").

The number of permissible dependent claims is generally subject to applicant discretion; however, in litigation, it may be within a court's inherent power to limit the number of dependent claims to be considered in that case.[183]

2.152 Adding a New Element Versus Further Clarifying an Existing Element or Limitation

As mentioned, although dependency is a substantive requirement,[184] there are claim drafting conventions that have become used as a matter of custom. It is highly recommended that these be followed for similar reasons discussed with respect to employing the format of a preamble, transition word or phrase, and claim body. These conventions are expected, and an unexplained departure might potentially suggest another meaning is intended other than the generally understood meaning.

If writing a dependent claim, logically, there are two ways to narrow the claim from which the dependent claim will depend. One way is to add a new element to the claim that is being narrowed. This example from earlier is illustrative.

---

1. An apparatus comprising:

   element A, element B, and element C.[185]

2. The apparatus of claim 1, comprising: element D.

Observe that in claim 2 (the dependent claim), the claim that is being depended from, here, claim 1, must be referenced. Hence, claim 2 necessarily includes elements A, B, and C. Note also that the additional element, here, D, was added using "comprising:" Some prefer "and further comprising:" Likewise, a colon is used after "comprising" to highlight separation between the transition word and new element. Whichever form is employed, one should

183. *See In re* Katz Interactive Call Processing Patent Litig., 639 F.3d 1303 (Fed. Cir. 2011).

184. *See* Monsanto Co. v. Syngenta Seeds, Inc., 503 F.3d 1352, 1357–58 (Fed. Cir. 2007) ("To establish whether a claim is dependent upon another, this court examines if the new claim both refers to an earlier claim and further limits that referent. *See* 35 U.S.C. § 112, ¶ 4 (2000) ('[A] claim in dependent form shall contain a reference to a claim previously set forth and then specify a further limitation of the subject matter claimed. A claim in dependent form shall be construed to incorporate by reference all the limitations of the claim to which it refers.').")

185. *See* 37 C.F.R. § 1.75(i) (2022).

do so consistently throughout the claims, again, so as not to suggest a departure is intended to convey a different meaning. The form illustrated seems the simplest to implement.

The other way to logically narrow a dependent claim is to further clarify an existing element or limitation. Here is a simple example.

---

1. An apparatus comprising: a portable seat.
2. The apparatus of claim 1, wherein the portable seat includes a back that is attached to the portable seat and oriented to be in a plane substantially perpendicular to a plane that includes the portable seat.

As before, the claim being "depended from" is referenced in the dependent claim. Some may ponder why this is clarifying an existing element or limitation since a (new) back element is added. This would be an astute query.

In some situations, you may employ both approaches or have a choice as to which approach is employed because, logically, the element that may be added may also result in clarifying a prior element or limitation.

For example, claim 2 might have been written as follows:

---

2. The apparatus of claim 1, comprising: a back;

   wherein the back is attached to the portable seat and oriented to be in a plane substantially perpendicular to a plane that includes the portable seat.

Here, both "comprising" and "wherein" are employed because a new element is added *and* an existing element or limitation, the portable seat, is further clarified.

The latter approach is more formalistic in terms of positively reciting a new element; the former approach is a little tighter in terms of language, not unlike positive recitation inferential claiming.[186]

186. *See* section 2.1413, discussing inferential claiming.

37 CFR section 1.75 (2020) addresses some notable aspects relevant to dependent claims. For example, it addresses numbering and grouping in subsections (f) and (g):

> (f) If there are several claims, they shall be numbered consecutively in Arabic numerals.
>
> (g) The least restrictive claim should be presented as claim number 1, and all dependent claims should be grouped together with the claim or claims to which they refer to the extent practicable.

It is accepted practice that your first claim should be your broadest claim, reflected in subsection (g). If there is more than one independent claim, to the extent possible, claim 1 should be the broadest one, although there may be times where it may be unclear which independent claim is necessarily the broadest one.

Because claim numbering is consecutive, all the dependent claims for the first independent claim should be numbered consecutively after claim 1 before presenting the second independent claim. Because there are 20 claims permitted without incurring extra claim fees,[187] typically one might have a first independent claim, numbered claim 1, followed by nine dependent claims, numbered 2 to 10, and then a claim numbered 11 may be the second independent claim, also then followed by nine dependent claims, numbered 12 to 20.

Because dependent claims may skip over intervening claims, it is best to employ a form of nesting to group related claims, per subsection (g) of 1.75. For example, the following would probably not be proper in light of subsection (g):

Claim 1: Element A—Independent claim.
An apparatus comprising: element A.

Claim 2: Element B—Depends from 1 and adds B.
The apparatus of claim 1, comprising: element B.

Claim 3: Element C—Depends from 2 and adds C.
The apparatus of claim 2, comprising: element C.

Claim 4: Element E—Depends from 2 and adds E.
The apparatus of claim 2, comprising: element E.

Claim 5: Element D—Depends from 3 and adds D.
The apparatus of claim 3, comprising element D.

---

187. *See* Manual of Patent Examining Procedure (MPEP) § 607 (2022).

That is, claim 5 is not properly nested. For proper nesting in a complete group, the claiming content of claim 5, D, should come after claim 3. That is, claim 4 and 5 may be interchanged to achieve proper nesting. You may wonder why this is proper since new claim 5 would depend from claim 2; however, new claims may be the start of another claim grouping that depends from claim 2, which is illustrated by the new claim 5 that recites E. For example, a claim 6 may now depend from new claim 5, reciting F (hence, claim 5 begins another grouping of claims). Thus, dependent claims may be thought of as groupings. With such a(n) (inter)change between claims 4 and 5 as just suggested, it should be clear that claim 4 in substance includes the elements and limitations of claim 1, claim 2, claim 3, and claim 4, that is, A, B, C, and D. After claim 4 and 5 are interchanged for proper nesting, claim 5 in substance includes the limitations of claim 1, claim 2, and claim 5, that is, A, B, and E.

Dependency relationships may be varied or change among the dependent claims to alter claim scope, particularly during examination. It is not uncommon for this reason to diagram the relationships between the independent and dependent claims for a claim set. Often this is done as a tree with the independent claim as a root node and with other nodes connected to the root node via an edge to depict a direct dependency relationship and so forth. For example, with claims 4 and 5 interchanged, a claim tree diagram (Figure 2.1) would be:

Figure 2.1 Tree Showing Claim Dependency Relationships

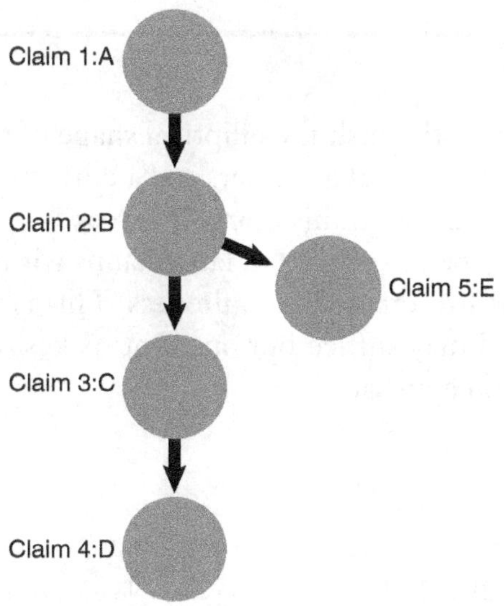

Another claim drafting fine point relates to how, in a dependent claim, to distinguish between similar, but different, elements of the independent claim. This was mentioned quickly in connection with method claims,[188] because it was noted that some practitioners have used alphabetic designations in an independent method claim with the risk that someone might argue the letters imply an order to the method acts recited.

This issue of how to reference similar but different terms of an independent claim applies generally in drafting dependent claims. Consider the claim from Example 2.22.

I claim:

1. An apparatus comprising:

   a hip prosthesis;

   wherein the hip prosthesis includes: a ball and a socket;

   wherein the ball has an elliptical shape and the socket has a corresponding elliptical shape to receive the ball within the socket for mutual engagement;

   wherein the elliptical shape of the ball has a major axis; and

   wherein during the mutual engagement of the ball and the socket, the ball is at least able to rotate within the socket substantially perpendicular to the minor axis of the ball.

For example, to distinguish the elliptical shape of the ball from the elliptical shape of the socket, the claim refers to "a corresponding elliptical shape." The word "corresponding" in this example serves as a "handle" so that the two elliptical shapes may be referenced in later claims without a misunderstanding that might be argued to create indefiniteness. This is a commonly used technique, and any word may suffice but one that makes sense within the context of the claim is a good approach.

188. *See* sections 2.1121 and 2.1122, providing example method claims.

3

Introduction to Claim Construction and to Related Claim Drafting Principles

High-Level Principles of This Chapter:[1]

- Understand the differences between direct patent infringement and indirect patent infringement as well as the differences between literal patent infringement and nonliteral patent infringement;
- At the start of drafting, consider the types of direct infringement and the business and economic considerations surrounding the invention;
- Draft short claims;
- Make claim coverage clear from the face of the claim (i.e., based on the language used for the claim);
- Use words in the claims consistent with their understood meaning;
- Use words in the claims with broadly understood meanings where appropriate;
- Employ a hierarchy of claim terms for the independent and dependent claims;
- Avoid overly specific modifiers in the independent claims;
- Draft claims that will be directly infringed (rather than indirectly infringed);
- Draft claims that will be literally infringed (rather than nonliterally infringed);
- Avoid drafting claims clearly narrower than needed and easily designed around.

1. *See* List of Claim Drafting Principles, Appendix A.

In this chapter, we discuss the *Markman v. Westview Instruments, Inc.*[2] case, a Supreme Court decision, and the *Phillips v. AWH Corp.*[3] case, an *en banc* federal circuit decision. These decisions continue to have a major impact on the interpretation of patent claims. One may, in fact, think in terms of a post-*Markman* era of claim construction in patent law due to the significance of how claim language interpretation changed after the *Markman* decision.

Understanding how federal courts interpret patent claims assists in drafting patent claims and leads to some basic claim drafting principles, as discussed later. Direct patent infringement, literal patent infringement, indirect patent infringement, and patent infringement under the doctrine of equivalents (DOE) are discussed in this chapter.

3.1 Legal Framework for Claim Construction

Following the Supreme Court's decision in *Markman*, a host of substantive and procedural questions emerged that were not resolved by that decision and required lower courts to fill in the blanks, so to speak. In the time since then, many issues, procedural and substantive, have become reasonably well settled. This body of law represents the existing legal framework for claim construction. Our primary focus relates to understanding the substantive legal issues that could be of use in claim drafting.

3.11 *Markman* Decision and *Markman* Hearings

The Supreme Court's *Markman v. Westview Instruments* decision fundamentally changed how patent claims are interpreted under U.S. patent law. Before that decision, interpretation of patent claims was usually relegated to the jury along with the determination whether patent infringement had occurred. However, in the *Markman* decision, the Supreme Court determined that how claims are construed should be performed by the judge rather than the jury for federal court patent litigation. This was a policy-based decision emanating from the view that construing claims is more legal (province of the judge) than it is factual (province of the jury). The Court believed having the

2. 517 U.S. 370 (1996).
3. 415 F.3d 1303 (Fed. Cir. 2005) (en banc).

judge construe the claims would lead to greater consistency in how claims are construed.[4]

Nonetheless, the Seventh Amendment provides a right to jury trial in patent cases. Thus, the jury makes the factual determination of whether the accused product or accused service falls within the scope of the patent claims, once properly construed. Hence, determination of patent infringement is a two-step process: (1) construing the claims and (2) determining whether the accused product or accused service falls within the construed claim scope.

Interestingly, despite the rationale provided for the decision, studies of federal circuit decisions before and after *Markman* suggest that having a judge construe the claims has had little impact on appellate court reversal rates, which is typically around 50 percent, depending on the study.[5]

Thus, as a result of *Markman*, the judge interprets the patent claims and instructs the jury as to the meaning thereof. The jury then determines whether patent infringement has occurred in light of the evidence presented and the court's claim construction. This division should generally be kept in mind, because it is important to have a federal court in a given case, under the guise of claim construction, *not* inadvertently invade the domain left for jury decision.[6]

Soon after the decision, a procedural mechanism, referred to as a "Markman hearing," came into existence, in which parties present respective positions to a federal judge regarding how the patent claims should be interpreted. The Supreme Court case did not address the procedural issue of holding a hearing. Thus, it was left to lower courts to figure out how and when to conduct such hearings.

---

4. The Markman decision did not resolve the standard of review an appellate court should apply to lower court determinations regarding claim construction. That issue was resolved by the en banc decision, *Cybor Corp. v. FAS Technologies, Inc.*, 138 F.3d 1448 (Fed. Cir. 1998) (en banc), to be de novo review. However, a later Supreme Court decision clarified that for subsidiary factual issues related to extrinsic evidence (as opposed to intrinsic evidence) a clear error standard should be applied on appeal; *see* Teva Pharmaceuticals v. Sandoz, 574 U.S. 318 (2015).

5. *See* Christian A. Chu, *Empirical Analysis of the Federal Circuit's Claim Construction Trends*, 16 Berkeley Tech. L.J. 1075, 1143 (2001); Kimberly A. Moore, *Markman Eight Years Later: Is Claim Construction More Predictable?*, 9 Lewis & Clark L. Rev. 231, 232–34 (2005); Michael Saunders, *A Survey of Post-Phillips Claim Construction Cases*, 22 Berkeley Tech. L.J. 215, 233 (2007); Andrew T. Zidel, *Patent Claim Construction in the Trial Courts: A Study Showing the Need for Clear Guidance from the Federal Circuit*, 33 Seton Hall L. Rev. 711, 743 (2003).

6. *Cf.* Acumed LLC v. Stryker Corp., 483 F.3d 800, 806 (Fed. Cir. 2007) ("[A] sound claim construction need not always purge every shred of ambiguity. The resolution of some line-drawing problems—especially easy ones like this one—is properly left to the trier of fact.").

It bears mention that how the patent claims are construed touches every important issue in a patent infringement case. Consequently, the rules surrounding such hearings were and are quite important. Some federal jurisdictions that frequently hear patent cases, such as the Northern District of California,[7] have fashioned local rules to govern such proceedings.

It bears mention that how the patent claims are construed touches every important issue in a patent infringement case.

Typically, Markman hearings are held reasonably early in a patent case, after a certain amount of discovery has taken place. Of course, this is not required, but it is a common practice. The claim construction found early in the case may be revisited later; however, it is more desirable to time the hearing in a manner so that revisiting claim construction is not needed. Likewise, it is not unusual for a Markman hearing to be combined with a hearing regarding a motion for summary judgment. This often aids court efficiency because claim interpretation may resolve the case, allowing an immediate appeal to the federal circuit regarding the claim construction found by the district court.

Table 3.1 provides a typical example of how filings leading up to a Markman hearing may be docketed in federal court. This is simply provided as an illustration. Other courts may docket these and other items differently.

Table 3.1[8]

1. Case Management Conference
2. Disclosure of Asserted Claims and Infringement Contentions
3. Invalidity Contentions
4. Identify Claim Terms to Be Construed
5. Preliminary Claim Constructions
6. Joint Claim Construction Statement
7. Close of Claim Construction Discovery
8. Opening Claim Construction Brief
9. Responsive Claim Construction Brief
10. Reply Claim Construction Brief
11. Markman Hearing
12. Claim Construction Order

7. *See* https://www.cand.uscourts.gov/rules/patent-local-rules/, providing patent local rules for Northern District of California.

8. *Id.*

As shown, there is usually an initial conference to set timelines, and so on. Then asserted claims are identified and infringement and invalidity contentions are exchanged. Following that, claims to be construed are identified by respective sides, initial claim constructions are exchanged, and a joint claim construction statement is produced. After close of claim construction discovery, an initial or opening claim construction brief is filed, followed by a responsive brief and a reply brief. This all leads up to the Markman hearing itself, which typically results in a claim construction order.

ITC Investigation—Another Option

The most common form of enforcement of Intellectual Property (IP) rights, particularly patent rights, occurs by bringing a lawsuit in federal district court. Unfortunately, federal court litigation may not fully address the needs of an IP holder, such as a patent holder, whose products are copied and sold in the United States (US) by a foreign entity *without the authority to do so*. Seeking redress against a foreign entity importing so-called knockoffs into the United States may be especially challenging. That is, federal court remedies and procedures appear or at least may, at times, permit a foreign entity to infringe on patent rights without full redress of those rights. Examples include that federal courts have jurisdiction and venue requirements that may be limited to specific locales,[9] and that federal court legal remedies may be limited because, as an example, the requirements for an injunction against an infringer are quite stringent.[10] In essence, to obtain a federal court injunction, one must show that the patent holder cannot be made whole with monetary damages.[11] Consequently, the International Trade Commission (ITC), a federal agency with quasi-judicial power, is becoming a more popular choice for patent enforcement.[12] While having some advantages relative to federal court, the ITC may also have some disadvantages relative to federal court. Consequently, one of the more effective strategies for redress against foreign entities importing goods into the United States that infringe on an entity's patents is a parallel strategy of enforcement in federal court *and* in the ITC.[13]

9. *See* Tom Schaumberg, *Advantages of International Trade Commission Practice: Gaining an Edge over Infringing Imports*, 25(2) Comput. & Internet Law. 19–24 (Feb. 2008).
10. *Id.*
11. *Id.*
12. *Id.*; Mark J. Abate & Calvin E. Wingfield Jr., *Pleading Requirements in the ITC and Tips to Starting an Investigation on the Right Foot*, IP Litigator 8–13 (Mar./Apr. 2009).
13. *See* Schaumberg, *supra* note 9.

Some important differences between federal court litigation and an ITC investigation suggest several advantages for ITC enforcement. For example, while a lawsuit is typically limited to a particular locale based on principles of jurisdiction and venue, an ITC investigation is not limited in this respect.[14] The investigation and resulting exclusion order from the ITC are directed to the goods at issue, rather than to the parties involved or to a particular location.[15] Thus, the ITC with its broad powers may be more effective against goods sold throughout the United States.[16] One potential disadvantage, on the other hand, is that a broad ITC exclusion order intended to sweep in goods sold by a foreign entity and prevent those goods from entering the United States may affect sales by the foreign entity to an existing customer of the patent holder. This may detrimentally affect the patent holder's relationship with that customer. As to remedies, exclusion orders capable of issuing from the ITC may provide the functional equivalent of a federal court–issued injunction because such an order prevents foreign goods, if infringing on patent rights, from entering the country. Obtaining an injunction in a federal lawsuit, however, may often be more challenging than obtaining an exclusion order from the ITC due to stringent requirements applied by federal courts to issue an injunction.[17] The ITC also offers an advantage from a discovery perspective.[18] Discovery orders issued by a U.S. court are typically limited to the United States; however, a discovery order to a foreign entity issued by the ITC, even if seeking evidence from outside the United States, usually receives compliance because noncompliance may lead to exclusion of the entity's goods from the United States.[19] The different decision-makers for the two proceedings also suggests an advantage in the ITC. The administrative law judges (ALJs) and Commission members of the ITC are well versed in patent law and technology, while district court judges and juries often are not.[20] This difference may also explain the significantly higher affirmance rate for ITC decisions taken on appeal relative to district court decisions.[21] Furthermore, there are no juries in the ITC, which is typically an advantage for the patent holder, primarily because, again, ITC judges are well versed in patent law.[22]

14. *Id.*; Abate & Wingfield, *supra* note 12.
15. *See* Schaumberg, *supra* note 9; Abate & Wingfield, *supra* note 12.
16. *Id.*
17. *See* Schaumberg, *supra* note 9.
18. *Id.*
19. *Id.*
20. *Id.*
21. *Id.*
22. *Id.*

Because an action in the ITC is an investigation and not a lawsuit, counterclaims by the importer are not permitted, another advantage for the patent holder. From an enforcement perspective, the ITC also provides an advantage in terms of time frame to completion. ITC investigations are usually completed in 12–15 months, which puts pressure on the entity whose goods are being imported.[23] In contrast, a federal district court case may last two to five years or longer before a final decision is issued, often due to many procedural opportunities by the defendant to drag it out. Another advantage associated with an ITC investigation is that a district court will stay (i.e., hold in abeyance) a lawsuit pending outcome of a Commission investigation.[24] A further advantage is that the ITC will rarely stay its investigation for a parallel Patent and Trademark Office (PTO) proceeding involving the patents at issue, such as a patent reexamination, for example.[25] This is in direct contrast to a district court that often might stay the lawsuit in favor of the parallel PTO proceeding.[26] This strategic situation gives the patent holder an opportunity to secure a win in the ITC before battling things out in federal court.

There are a few areas, however, where a federal district court lawsuit may be more advantageous. For one thing, damages are available in federal district court, but not in the ITC. The complaint process for an ITC investigation is much more complex and document intensive.[27] One must establish with evidence the presence of "importation" and an affected "domestic industry" for investigation in the ITC to proceed, *in addition to* proving the typical elements of a patent infringement case.[28] Federal district courts, by contrast, employ a pleading standard where the basis for the lawsuit needs to be explained in the complaint with sufficient facts pled to show that it is plausible that the asserted claim can be established.[29] Detailed and more specific allegations come later in the suit. Furthermore, once a complaint is filed in federal court, it is relatively easy to amend if the amendment is timely and with good cause. A complaint in an ITC investigation, after having been filed, is relatively difficult to amend.[30] Federal courts also typically use Markman hearings early in the lawsuit to interpret the patent claims, which tends to focus the issues for

23. *Id.*
24. *Id.*
25. *See* Abate & Wingfield, *supra* note 12.
26. *Id.*
27. *See* Schaumberg, *supra* note 9; Abate & Wingfield, *supra* note 12.
28. *Id.*
29. *See* Abate & Wingfield, *supra* note 12.
30. *Id.*

the case and may even resolve the dispute without trial.[31] As previously noted, a Markman hearing is a special proceeding in federal court patent litigation in which each side presents its position on the correct interpretation of the patent claims to a federal district judge.[32] Ultimately, this important question is then decided *exclusively* by the district court judge in a Markman order.[33] Also, federal district court rulings, such as a Markman order, may have a res judicata effect (e.g., be binding on future litigation between the parties).[34] ITC investigations rarely conduct Markman hearings and the orders from the ITC are not binding on federal courts and, consequently, have no res judicata effect.[35] Federal courts, in general, have an inherent contempt power with respect to the parties to obtain compliance with orders and rulings. The ITC does not have a contempt power, but the threat of exclusion of an entity's goods for noncompliance is a powerful incentive.[36] Furthermore, decisions by the Commission may become political (e.g., requiring the approval of the President),[37] while the constitutional separation of powers between the Judicial Branch and the Executive Branch generally tends to keep courts isolated from political pressures. Also, there is some enforcement risk of an ITC exclusion order, not present for a district court ruling due a federal court's inherent contempt power, depending on the nature of the product at issue. U.S. customs may not be able to identify infringing product by simple product inspection (e.g., infringing software or an infringing chip may be buried deep in a system level product being imported). If U.S. customs is not able to verify infringement by inspection, the goods are permitted to enter the United States.

Given the trade-offs between a federal court lawsuit and an ITC investigation, one strategy to get the benefits of both may be to engage in parallel proceedings.[38] One benefit might be timing because both may be filed concurrently, but the federal suit is likely to be stayed until the conclusion of the ITC investigation.[39] Filing the suit in federal court with a stay is a type of preemptive strike preventing the potential defendant from "shopping" for a more

31. *See* Peter S. Menell, Matthew D. Powers & Steven C. Carlson, *Patent Claim Construction: A Modern Synthesis and Structured Framework*, 25(2) Berkeley Tech. L.J. 713–831 (July 2010).

32. *Id.*

33. *Id.*

34. *See* Schaumberg, *supra* note 9.

35. *Id.*

36. *Id.*

37. For example, during the Obama administration, President Obama, largely on political grounds, did not approve an ITC exclusion order that resulted from a complaint by a foreign entity against a U.S. company.

38. *See* Schaumberg, *supra* note 9.

39. *Id.*

sympathetic court by attempting to file in federal court first.[40] Meanwhile, the ITC investigation may proceed at its accelerated pace. If there is a decision to ultimately go forward with a federal court litigation after the ITC investigation, this may draw the process out considerably, but an ongoing ITC investigation with the threat that a pending federal suit that has been stayed may proceed later might be a sufficient legal threat to get early resolution with an adverse party. A key benefit of a parallel strategy is the potential to stop future importation (e.g., via the ITC) *and* recover damages for past infringement (via federal court).[41] Likewise, proceeding with the ITC investigation first should benefit a stayed lawsuit for the patent holder. For example, the ITC discovery may be transferred to the lawsuit.[42] In addition, the analysis at the ITC, in which the ALJs are well versed in patent law, may influence a federal court judge in a district court case. Likewise, by proceeding with a federal district court case, the binding res judicata effect of a federal court decision will ultimately be obtained.

Nonetheless, there are also challenges with a parallel enforcement strategy. For one thing, both parties experience a "war on two fronts," so to speak. This suggests greater costs related to the dispute and a greater distraction for management, whose main occupation should be running the business of the particular entity. Likewise, potentially, there may be a longer time to full resolution for a parallel enforcement strategy. In general, these issues may affect both the importer and the patent holder. The advantage, here, may, thus, be to the larger entity of the two having greater resources to handle such burdens. Of course, a loss in the ITC for either entity would have a potentially negative impact overall and certainly may affect the district court litigation.

Unfortunately, in today's international economy, the fact that IP rights, particularly patents rights, are country-based may be a barrier to extracting full value from owning such rights. A foreign entity importing so-called knockoffs into the United States may fall outside the powers of a federal court in some situations. That is, federal court remedies and procedures, based on principles of fairness and governmental authority, are not entirely equipped to handle situations that typically may arise in a worldwide economy. The ITC, a federal agency with quasi-judicial power, is becoming a more popular venue for patent enforcement, but while having some advantages over federal court, it may also have some disadvantages relative to federal court in part due to its federal agency status. However, notably, it is not hampered by some

40. *Id.*
41. *Id.*
42. *Id.*

of the procedural limits imposed on federal courts. Thus, it appears the most effective strategy for redress against foreign entities importing goods into the United States that infringe on an entity's patents is a parallel strategy that pursues enforcement in federal court and in the ITC; however, this assumes adequate resources by the patent holder to pursue such a strategy.

3.12 Intrinsic Evidence Versus Extrinsic Evidence

The *Markman* decision was handed down by the Supreme Court in 1996. Not long after, that same year, the federal circuit decided the *Vitronics Corp. v. Conceptronic, Inc.*[43] case. That case reads like a "how to" guide on claim construction. One of the more fundamental aspects of the decision was the distinction between intrinsic and extrinsic evidence for purposes of claim construction. Furthermore, within each of these respective categories, there was a pecking order to the evidence regarding greater preference/reliance and lesser preference/reliance.

In general, intrinsic evidence was and is preferred over extrinsic evidence. Part of the rationale in *Vitronics* was the public notice aspect associated with patent claims. Typically, someone reviewing a patent record would be unaware of what extrinsic evidence might be used to interpret the patent claims for a given patent.

Intrinsic evidence was and is: the patent claims, the patent specification, and the prosecution history, generally in that order of preference.[44] Extrinsic evidence technically is any evidence that is not intrinsic. A typical order of preference is: technical dictionaries and treatises, technical publications, general dictionaries, and expert witness (typically other than attorney or inventor) testimony.[45]

Essentially, the job of the court is to figure out what the claims *truly* mean as best as possible using the intrinsic and extrinsic evidence. One tricky aspect relates to the ordinary and customary meaning of a claim term, which has a role in patent claim interpretation. There is a heavy presumption that claims

---

43. 90 F.3d 1576 (Fed. Cir. 1996).

44. Intrinsic evidence also includes cited prior art and foreign counterpart patent applications. *See, e.g.*, Vitronics Corp. v. Conceptronic, Inc., 90 F.3d 1576 (Fed. Cir. 1996). *See also* Apple v. Motorola, 757 F.3d 1286 (Fed. Cir. 2014); Glaxo Group Ltd. v. Ranbaxy Pharms., Inc., 262 F.3d 1333, 1337 (Fed. Cir. 2001); Tanabe Seiyaku Co., Ltd. v. U.S. Int'l Trade Comm'n, 109 F.3d 726, 733 (Fed. Cir. 1997).

45. *See, e.g.*, Sandra Solomon v. Kimberly-Clark Corp., 216 F.3d 1372 (Fed. Cir. 2000) (testimony of inventor and his attorney concerning claim construction entitled to little or no consideration).

terms are used in a manner that is consistent with their ordinary and customary meaning at the time of filing the patent application.[46] This presumption may be overcome expressly or by implication based on the intrinsic evidence. Yet, to make such determinations often involves looking to extrinsic evidence as well. Thus, in the period up to 2005, there were lines of cases and divisions on the federal circuit regarding the appropriate weight to accord the intrinsic evidence, often in the form of the specification, relative to extrinsic evidence, often in the form of technical dictionaries. One of the primary concerns that lead to this division was the concern to *not* read limitations from the specification into the claims.[47]

To resolve the lines of cases and unify these divisions, the federal circuit decided the *Phillips* case en banc in 2005. Today, that decision represents the most comprehensive statement regarding the use of intrinsic and extrinsic evidence to interpret patent claims. *Phillips* reaffirms the principles of *Vitronics*. However, it clarifies that *Vitronics*, in the search for the ordinary and customary meaning of claim terms, did not create rigid rules regarding (1) use of dictionaries, technical treatises, and so on; (2) preventing consultation of extrinsic evidence to supplement the court's understanding of such terms and technology; and (3) a particular temporal order in which evidence is to be consulted by a federal judge (this is not the same as preference order, which remains a feature of claim construction). Thus, while there is a pecking order as to the intrinsic and extrinsic evidence as a guide, the real goal is to determine what the claims *truly* mean, which is not subject to rigid rules and, per *Phillips*, it may be appropriate in some circumstances to depart from the general guidelines *so long as a court does not use extrinsic evidence to modify or contradict the intrinsic evidence.*

The court's job, consequently, is to determine whether claim terms are used in a manner consistent with the ordinary and customary meaning of those terms at the time of filing. If so, the court is to determine the ordinary and customary meaning of such claim terms. If not, the court is to determine the special meaning accorded such terms, generally, in light of the intrinsic evidence.

3.121 Pecking Order of Intrinsic Evidence

As suggested, *Vitronics* established a pecking order of intrinsic evidence as follows: patent claims, patent specification, patent file history. Again, *Phillips*

---

46. *See, e.g.*, Johnson Worldwide v. Zebo, 175 F.3d 985, 989 (Fed. Cir. 1999).

47. *See* sections 3.1211, 3.1212, and 3.1221 and discussion of the Texas Digital case. *See also* section 2.1414, discussing importing limitations from the specification into the claims.

reaffirmed the importance of intrinsic evidence and this pecking order, but with some clarifications.

3.1211 Vitronics *Decision*

It is now well-established patent law that the starting point for claim construction is always the words of the claims themselves. Although this principle, by itself, should not be particularly surprising to patent attorneys, one of the clearer statements of the principle is found in *Vitronics Corp. v. Conceptronic, Inc. Markman v. Westview Instruments, Inc.* made it clear that, for policy reasons, patent claim construction is a function that should always be performed by judges, rather than juries. Therefore, relatively soon after that watershed Supreme Court decision, the federal circuit handed down the *Vitronics* decision, which, even today, provides as an excellent "how to" guide for claim construction. It is further noted that the principles of *Vitronics* were reaffirmed in an en banc decision by the federal circuit, *Phillips v. AWH*,[48] discussed in more detail in the next section.

The invention in *Vitronics* related to a technique for using solder to surface mount components or circuit devices to circuit boards. The components passed through various ovens providing a variety of heat zones. The zones, including the last zone, in particular, were set at temperatures to heat the solder to a higher temperature than the component itself, thereby making the solder adhere more solidly. This heating process apparently caused the solder to reflow in a way that formed a more solid connection. The claims specifically indicated that the solder needed to be heated to its "solder reflow temperature," which was intended to be higher than the temperature of the components. However, as one might expect, a dispute ensued over the meaning of "solder reflow temperature," the language used in the patent claims.

It appears from the case that if the term were to be construed in a manner consistent with the relevant art, rather than the manner in which it was used in the specification, then the defendant would *not* be infringing. Vitronics, of course, asserted that it had clearly imparted a special meaning to this particular claim terminology in the patent application, acting as its own lexicographer. The lower court, however, sided with the defendant, relying principally on extrinsic evidence regarding the meaning in the art.

On appeal, the federal circuit reversed and remanded and, in a well-formulated opinion written by the scholarly Judge Michel, provided a relatively clear set of guidelines for district court judges to follow when construing

48. 415 F.3d 1303 (Fed. Cir. 2005) (en banc).

patent claims. The federal circuit went out of its way to specify a particular pecking order with respect to the intrinsic evidence that a court should follow when attempting to construe a claim, namely, the claims, specification, and prosecution history. The federal circuit stated (emphasis supplied):

> First, we look to the words of the claims themselves. . . .
>
> Although words in a claim are generally given their ordinary and customary meaning, **a patentee may choose to be his own lexicographer and use terms in a manner other than their ordinary meaning, as long as the special definition of the term is clearly stated in the patent specification or file history. . . .**
>
> Second, it is always necessary to review the specification to determine whether the inventor used any terms in a manner inconsistent with their ordinary meaning. . . . **Usually, it [the spec] is dispositive; it is the single best guide to the meaning of a disputed term.**
>
> Third, the court may also consider the prosecution history of the patent, if in evidence. . . . [T]he record before the Patent and Trademark Office is often of critical significance in determining the meaning of claims[49] (emphasis supplied).

For our purposes, then, one important pronouncement from *Vitronics*, as indicated by the preceding quote, is that claim construction *always* begins with the claim language itself.

This recognition is critical to providing good representation before the PTO and to obtaining patents of value that will likely be enforceable in federal court. *Vitronics* suggests, and other cases have also suggested, if the intrinsic evidence is clear, then claim construction should, for all practical purposes, be complete. *Phillips* loosened this a bit by clarifying that a court is always free to consult extrinsic evidence, so long as the intrinsic evidence is not modified or contradicted. However, federal circuit cases that came after *Vitronics* also included a similar point regarding reliance on intrinsic evidence.[50] There is no doubt regarding the preference for intrinsic evidence and no doubt that among the intrinsic evidence the importance of the claims is paramount.

To be clear, the claim language defines the grant of rights. The other intrinsic evidence aids interpretation. The patent drafter, then, may provide

---

49. 90 F.3d at 1582–83.

50. *See, e.g.*, Mantech v. Hudson, 152 F.3d 1368 (Fed. Cir. 1998); Comark Comm'ns, Inc. v. Harris Corp., 156 F.3d 1182, 1186–87 (Fed. Cir. 1998).

the best representation by preparing simple, straightforward claims that are as clear as possible as to their intended meaning from the very face of the claim.[51]

> To be clear, the claim language defines the grant of rights. The other intrinsic evidence aids interpretation.

Vitronics also clearly states that the specification *must* be consulted as part of the claim construction process, as confirmed by the preceding quote. However, *Vitronics* further clearly states that the specification is consulted primarily to determine whether the claim terms are used in the specification in a manner consistent with their ordinary meaning. Therefore, if the claims terms are used consistently in the specification, then, at least in principle, there may be little need for further consultation of the specification to interpret the claims.[52] To restate this, for claim construction, the words of the claims are of paramount importance, and the claim language in some cases may virtually alone determine the scope of claim coverage. This is an ideal, of course. More frequently, resorting to the specification to establish context, and so on, may be needed; however, there is little harm in shooting for the ideal when drafting claims since achieving it has occurred in previous examples of patent litigation.[53]

> For claim construction, the words of the claims are of paramount importance.

---

51. This preference for being clear on the face of the claim has also risen to be of importance in another area, the jurisprudence surrounding section 101. *See* section 5.44 and its subsections, discussing patent eligibility.

52. *See* Straight Path IP Group, Inc. v. Sipnet EU S.R.O., 806 F.3d 1356 (Fed. Cir. 2015), which stated the specification played a "more limited role" when the claim term had an especially "plain" meaning.

53. *See, e.g.*, Mantech v. Hudson, 152 F.3d 1368 (Fed. Cir. 1998); Comark Comm'ns, Inc. v. Harris Corp., 156 F.3d 1182, 1186–87 (Fed. Cir. 1998); *cf.* McGill Inc. v. John Zink Co., 736 F. 2d 666 (Fed. Cir. 1984) (consulting specification and prosecution history to determine the proper interpretation of "recovered liquid hydrocarbon absorbent").

3.1212 Phillips *Decision*

After *Vitronics*, there were still questions about substantive claim construction. Again, the period up to 2005 resulted in some splintering in approach among judges on the federal circuit. This appeared to become more pronounced particularly in the period 2002–2005.

More specifically, how to appropriately treat dictionaries appeared to vary at times, from being important as an unbiased source for ordinary and customary meaning to not being quite so important relative to intrinsic evidence since dictionaries are extrinsic evidence. Thus, the proper process for claim construction was unclear at times.

Furthermore, how to treat extrinsic evidence in general was in question. *Vitronics* appeared to suggest that it required a claim language ambiguity *before* resort to such evidence was appropriate.[54] However, other federal circuit decisions suggested otherwise, in that claim language should not be divorced from the context of usage.[55]

This division in approach became pronounced in the *Texas Digital*[56] case, which suggested that, so as not to import limitations from the specification into the claims, an unbiased dictionary definition took on greater importance than was suggested under *Vitronics*. Likewise, the case suggested a particular temporal order in which a court was to consider (not simply a precedence order, but the order of consideration) evidentiary sources, such as the specification (intrinsic) versus dictionaries or technical treatises (extrinsic). The approach suggested greater importance for extrinsic sources than articulated in *Vitronics*.

To resolve these separate lines of cases, the federal circuit took a panel decision, *Phillips v. AWH*, en banc. The principles articulated in *Phillips* remain true today, although disagreement at the margins on some fine points appears to affect decisions by the appellate court.

The invention in the case concerned modular, steel-shell panels that can be welded together to form vandalism-resistant walls. The panels were especially useful in building prisons because they were load bearing and impact

---

54. *See* Vitronics Corp. v. Conceptronic, Inc., 90 F.3d 1576, 1583 (Fed. Cir. 1996) ("In most situations, an analysis of the intrinsic evidence alone will resolve any ambiguity in a disputed claim term. In such circumstances, it is improper to rely on extrinsic evidence.").

55. *See, e.g.*, Home Diagnostics, Inc. v. Lifescan, Inc., 381 F.3d 1352, 1355 (Fed. Cir. 2004) ("This court construes the meaning of claim language according to its usage and context"); Metabolite Laboratories, Inc. v. Lab'y Corp. of Am. Holdings, 370 F.3d 1354, 1360, 71 USPQ2d 1081 (Fed. Cir. 2004), *cert. dismissed*, 126 S. Ct. 2921 (2006) ("[t]his court sets the meaning of claim terms by ascertaining their technological and temporal context").

56. *See* Texas Digital Sys., Inc. v. Telegenix, 308 F.3d 1193 (Fed. Cir. 2002).

resistant, while also insulating against fire and noise. There had been an arrangement with a company, AWH, made under a patent (the '798 patent) to Phillips to market and sell the panels; however, after the arrangement ended, Phillips found evidence that AWH continued to sell the panels and instituted a lawsuit in federal district court.

In the district court case, regarding patent infringement, the district court focused on the language of claim 1, which recited "further means disposed inside the shell for increasing its load bearing capacity comprising internal steel baffles extending inwardly from the steel shell walls." The district court interpreted this language as "a means . . . for performing a specified function," subject to 35 U.S.C. § 112, paragraph 6,[57] which provides that such a claim "shall be construed to cover the corresponding structure, material, or acts described in the specification and equivalents thereof." Looking to the specification of the '798 patent, the court noted that "every textual reference in the specification and its diagrams show baffle deployment at an angle other than 90 to the wall faces" and that "placement of the baffles at such angles creates an intermediate interlocking, but not solid, internal barrier." The district court therefore ruled that, for purposes of the '798 patent, a baffle must "extend inward from the steel shell walls at an oblique or acute angle to the wall face" and must form part of an interlocking barrier in the interior of the wall module. Because Phillips could not prove infringement under that claim construction, the district court granted summary judgment of noninfringement, and an appeal by Phillips followed.

In the appeal to a panel of appellate judges, the majority sustained the district court's summary judgment of noninfringement, although on different grounds. A dissenting judge, however, would have reversed the summary judgment of noninfringement.

The appellate panel first determined that because the asserted claims of the '798 patent contained a sufficient recitation of structure, the district court erred by construing the term "baffles" to invoke the "means-plus-function" claim format authorized by section 112, paragraph 6. Nonetheless, the panel concluded that the patent used the term "baffles" in a restrictive manner. Based on the patent's written description, the panel held that the claim term "baffles" excluded structures that extend at a 90-degree angle from the walls. The panel noted that the specification repeatedly referred to the ability of the claimed baffles to deflect projectiles and that it described the baffles as being

57. Currently, 35 U.S.C. § 112(f) (2022).

"disposed at such angles that bullets which might penetrate the outer steel panels are deflected."

In addition, the panel observed that nowhere in the patent was there any disclosure of a baffle projecting from the wall at a right angle and that baffles oriented at 90 degrees to the wall were found in the prior art. Based on "the specification's explicit descriptions," the panel concluded "that the patentee regarded his invention as panels providing impact or projectile resistance and that the baffles must be oriented at angles other than 90." The panel added that the patent specification "is intended to support and inform the claims, and here it makes it unmistakably clear that the invention involves baffles angled at other than 90." The panel therefore upheld the district court's summary judgment of noninfringement.

The federal circuit court agreed to rehear the *Phillips* appeal en banc, largely based on the points made by the dissent regarding how the approach of the decision deviated from federal circuit precedent. Ultimately, the portion of the panel's decision addressed to the issue of infringement was reversed.

The en banc court decision begins (emphasis supplied):

> **. . . The principal question that this case presents to us is the extent to which we should resort to and rely on a patent's specification in seeking to ascertain the proper scope of its claims.**
>
> This is hardly a new question. The role of the specification in claim construction has been an issue in patent law decisions in this country for nearly two centuries. We addressed the relationship between the specification and the claims at some length in our en banc opinion in *Markman v. Westview Instruments, Inc.*, 52 F.3d 967, 979-81 (Fed. Cir. 1995) *(en banc), aff'd*, 517 U.S. 370, 116 S.Ct. 1384, 134 L.Ed.2d 577 (1996). We again summarized the applicable principles in *Vitronics Corp. v. Conceptronic, Inc.*, 90 F.3d 1576 (Fed. Cir. 1996), and more recently in *Innova/Pure Water, Inc. v. Safari Water Filtration Systems, Inc.*, 381 F.3d 1111 (Fed. Cir. 2004). **What we said in those cases bears restating, for the basic principles of claim construction outlined there are still applicable, and we reaffirm them today. We have also previously considered the use of dictionaries in claim construction. What we have said in that regard requires clarification.**

The appellate court continues (emphasis supplied):

> It is a "bedrock principle" of patent law that "the claims of a patent define the invention to which the patentee is entitled the right to exclude." *Innova*, 381 F.3d at 1115; *see also Vitronics*, 90 F.3d at 1582 ("we look to the words of the claims themselves . . . to define the scope of the patented invention"); *Markman*, 52 F.3d at 980 ("The written description part of the specification itself

does not delimit the right to exclude. That is the function and purpose of claims.")....

We have frequently stated that the words of a claim "are generally given their ordinary and customary meaning." *Vitronics*, 90 F.3d at 1582; *see also Toro Co. v. White Consol. Indus., Inc.*, 199 F.3d 1295, 1299 (Fed. Cir. 1999); *Renishaw PLC v. Marposs Societa' per Azioni*, 158 F.3d 1243, 1249 (Fed. Cir. 1998). **We have made clear, moreover, that the ordinary and customary meaning of a claim term is the meaning that the term would have to a person of ordinary skill in the art in question at the time of the invention, i.e., as of the effective filing date of the patent application.** *See Innova*, 381 F.3d at 1116 ("A court construing a patent claim seeks to accord a claim the meaning it would have to a person of ordinary skill in the art at the time of the invention."); *Home Diagnostics, Inc. v. LifeScan, Inc.*, 381 F.3d 1352, 1358 (Fed. Cir. 2004) ("customary meaning" refers to the "customary meaning in [the] art field"); *Ferguson Beauregard/Logic Controls v. Mega Sys., LLC*, 350 F.3d 1327, 1338 (Fed. Cir. 2003) (claim terms "are examined through the viewing glass of a person skilled in the art"); *see also PC Connector Solutions LLC v. SmartDisk Corp.*, 406 F.3d 1359, 1363 (Fed. Cir. 2005) (meaning of claim "must be interpreted as of [the] effective filing date" of the patent application); *Schering Corp. v. Amgen Inc.*, 222 F.3d 1347, 1353 (Fed. Cir. 2000) (same).

The inquiry into how a person of ordinary skill in the art understands a claim term provides an objective baseline from which to begin claim interpretation. *See Innova*, 381 F.3d at 1116. That starting point is based on the well-settled understanding that inventors are typically persons skilled in the field of the invention....

The appellate court provides five strong rationales as to why extrinsic evidence is less reliable than intrinsic evidence (emphasis supplied):

We have viewed extrinsic evidence in general as less reliable than the patent and its prosecution history in determining how to read claim terms, for several reasons. First, extrinsic evidence by definition is not part of the patent and does not have the specification's virtue of being created at the time of patent prosecution for the purpose of explaining the patent's scope and meaning. Second, while claims are construed as they would be understood by a hypothetical person of skill in the art, extrinsic publications may not be written by or for skilled artisans and therefore may not reflect the understanding of a skilled artisan in the field of the patent. Third, extrinsic evidence consisting of expert reports and testimony is generated at the time of and for the purpose of litigation and thus can suffer from bias that is not present in intrinsic evidence. The effect of that bias can be exacerbated if the expert is not one of skill in the relevant art or if the expert's opinion

> is offered in a form that is not subject to cross-examination. *See Senmed, Inc. v. Richard-Allan Med. Indus., Inc.*, 888 F.2d 815, 819 n. 8 (Fed. Cir. 1989). Fourth, there is a virtually unbounded universe of potential extrinsic evidence of some marginal relevance that could be brought to bear on any claim construction question. In the course of litigation, each party will naturally choose the pieces of extrinsic evidence most favorable to its cause, leaving the court with the considerable task of filtering the useful extrinsic evidence from the fluff. *See Daubert v. Merrell Dow Pharms., Inc.*, 509 U.S. 579, 595, 113 S.Ct. 2786, 125 L.Ed.2d 469 (1993) ("Expert evidence can be both powerful and quite misleading because of the difficulty in evaluating it."). Finally, undue reliance on extrinsic evidence poses the risk that it will be used to change the meaning of claims in derogation of the "indisputable public records consisting of the claims, the specification and the prosecution history," thereby undermining the public notice function of patents. *Southwall Techs.*, 54 F.3d at 1578.

The appellate court summarizes as follows (emphasis supplied):

> **In sum, extrinsic evidence may be useful to the court, but it is unlikely to result in a reliable interpretation of patent claim scope unless considered in the context of the intrinsic evidence.** Nonetheless, because extrinsic evidence can help educate the court regarding the field of the invention and can help the court determine what a person of ordinary skill in the art would understand claim terms to mean, it is permissible for the district court in its sound discretion to admit and use such evidence. **In exercising that discretion, and in weighing all the evidence bearing on claim construction, the court should keep in mind the flaws inherent in each type of evidence and assess that evidence accordingly.**

Finally, the appellate court, for a second time in the opinion, reaffirmed *Vitronics* and other similar cases, stating (emphasis supplied):

> In *Vitronics*, this court grappled with the same problem and set forth guidelines for reaching the correct claim construction and not imposing improper limitations on claims. 90 F.3d at 1582. **The underlying goal of our decision in *Vitronics* was to increase the likelihood that a court will comprehend how a person of ordinary skill in the art would understand the claim terms.** *See id.* at 1584. **In that process, we recognized that there is no magic formula or catechism for conducting claim construction. Nor is the court barred from considering any particular sources or required to analyze sources in any specific sequence, as long as those sources are not used to contradict claim meaning that is unambiguous in light of the intrinsic evidence.** *See id.* at 1583-84; *Intel Corp. v. VIA Techs., Inc.*, 319 F.3d 1357, 1367 (Fed. Cir. 2003). For example, a judge who encounters

a claim term while reading a patent might consult a general purpose or specialized dictionary to begin to understand the meaning of the term, before reviewing the remainder of the patent to determine how the patentee has used the term. **The sequence of steps used by the judge in consulting various sources is not important; what matters is for the court to attach the appropriate weight to be assigned to those sources in light of the statutes and policies that inform patent law.** *Vitronics*, 90 F.3d at 1582. **In *Vitronics*, we did not attempt to provide a rigid algorithm for claim construction, but simply attempted to explain why, in general, certain types of evidence are more valuable than others. *Today, we adhere to that approach and reaffirm the approach to claim construction outlined in that case*,** in *Markman*, and in *Innova*. . . .

3.122 Ordinary and Customary Meaning

An important job for the court is to determine whether terms are used in the claims in accordance with the ordinary and customary meaning of those terms as of the filing date of the patent application.[58] There is a presumption in favor of ordinary and customary meaning rather than a specialized meaning,[59] although this presumption may be overcome. As made clear by *Vitronics* and *Phillips*, a court reviews multiple sources, intrinsic and extrinsic, to arrive at the ordinary and customary meaning.

Although there is a presumption of ordinary meaning, the actual goal of the court is to determine what the patent claims truly mean, not simply the ordinary meaning of such terms. Ordinary meaning is simply a baseline used to assist in reaching the goal of what the claims mean.[60] Thus, determining ordinary meaning may exhibit some amount of fluidity as a court reviews and compares the various sources available to it.

The language of the patent claims takes a paramount role; however, patent claims in the abstract may not always provide clear guidance.[61] In accordance with federal circuit jurisprudence, the next most important source is the specification. According to the court, it is "the single best guide."[62] Furthermore, with true meaning as the goal, various doctrines of claim interpretation may push or pull on ordinary meaning so that a court may find the true meaning.[63]

58. *See, e.g.*, Phillips v. AWH, 415 F.3d 1303 (Fed. Cir. 2005) (en banc).
59. *Id.*
60. *Id.*
61. *Id.*
62. *Id.*; Vitronics Corp. v. Conceptronic, 90 F.3d 1576 (Fed. Cir. 1996).
63. *See* Menell, Powers & Carlson, *supra* note 31, Appendix, Narrowing or Broadening "Ordinary Meaning."

A number of principles have been discussed in this book so far. Many of them are used to guide a court to determine ordinary meaning and/or to guide a court to determine what the claim terms mean. Some basic principles, as discussed, include construing the claims and specification and the file history as a single package from the perspective of one of ordinary skill in the art and reviewing this package in its entirety with respect to the time period of the invention at issue, that is, the *effective* filing date. Again, while extrinsic evidence may be considered, it may not modify or contradict the intrinsic evidence. Furthermore, as stated, there is a presumption that the claim terms are used consistent with ordinary and customary meaning.

Doctrines that push or pull on ordinary meaning relate to various aspects of the claims, specification, and file history, including the following: how what is believed to be inventive is specifically described; whether the specification contains multiple embodiments; whether some embodiments are described as preferred over others; whether terms are used in a slavishly consistent manner or are used in a manner that is varied and demonstrates breadth; how the prior art is characterized relative to subject matter sought to be patented; what advantages are described regarding the subject matter sought to be patented; whether any scope regarding the subject matter is disavowed in the specification or during prosecution, including claim amendments in response to art; whether terms are defined in the specification or file history; and whether terms are used in a manner that creates ambiguity as to meaning or scope.[64]

Thus, the court's job is a complex one in terms of balancing many considerations as it reviews intrinsic and extrinsic evidence. As claim drafters that appreciate the process of claim construction and the doctrines that govern, our job is to adopt approaches that are more likely to lead to a broader interpretation of the claims, other things being equal, while also making it reasonably clear from the words used the claim scope actually intended.

As claim drafters that appreciate the process of claim construction and the doctrines that govern, our job is to adopt approaches that are more likely to lead to a broader interpretation of the claims, other things being equal, while also making it reasonably clear from the words used the claim scope actually intended.

64. *See id.*

3.1221 Use of Dictionaries

After *Vitronics*, although dictionaries and technical treatises were deemed extrinsic evidence, the federal circuit appeared to treat those sources differently from other types of extrinsic evidence, seeing such sources as unbiased, relative to expert testimony. In general, it seemed federal courts were permitted to consult such sources at any time during claim construction.[65] However, *Vitronics* appeared to suggest that extrinsic evidence should not generally be consulted unless there was a genuine claim ambiguity.[66]

It is fair to say that a perception was created that dictionaries and the like had a special status in claim construction relative to other types of extrinsic evidence. However, federal circuit cases were not entirely consistent and different panels of judges seemed to take different stances. The special status treatment of dictionaries reached a pinnacle in the *Texas Digital* case.[67]

This issue at least in part led to the en banc decision in *Phillips*. The *Phillips* case, therefore, addressed the line of cases, epitomized by *Texas Digital*, and clarified the appropriate status of dictionaries and the like, stating (emphasis supplied):

> . . . some of this court's cases have suggested a somewhat different approach to claim construction, in which the court has given greater emphasis to dictionary definitions of claim terms and has assigned a less prominent role to the specification and the prosecution history . . .
>
> . . .
>
> Although the concern expressed by the court in *Texas Digital* was valid [to avoid reading limitations from the specification into the claims], the methodology it adopted placed too much reliance on extrinsic sources such as dictionaries, treatises, and encyclopedias and too little on intrinsic sources, in particular the specification and prosecution history . . .
>
> . . .
>
> The main problem with elevating the dictionary to such prominence is that it focuses the inquiry on the abstract meaning of words rather than on the meaning of claim terms within the context of the patent. **Properly viewed, the "ordinary meaning" of a claim term is its meaning to the**

---

65. *See, e.g.*, Home Diagnostics, Inc. v. Lifescan, Inc., 381 F.3d 1352, 1355 (Fed. Cir. 2004) ("This court construes the meaning of claim language according to its usage and context."); Metabolite Laboratories, Inc. v. Lab'y Corp. of Am. Holdings, 370 F.3d 1354, 1360, 71 USPQ2d 1081 (Fed. Cir. 2004), *cert. dismissed*, 126 S. Ct. 2921 (2006) ("[t]his court sets the meaning of claim terms by ascertaining their technological and temporal context").

66. *See* Vitronics Corp. v. Conceptronic, Inc., 90 F.3d 1576, 1583 (Fed. Cir. 1996) ("In most situations, an analysis of the intrinsic evidence alone will resolve any ambiguity in a disputed claim term. In such circumstances, it is improper to rely on extrinsic evidence.").

67. *See* discussion in immediately preceding sections.

ordinary artisan after reading the entire patent. Yet heavy reliance on the dictionary divorced from the intrinsic evidence risks transforming the meaning of the claim term to the artisan into the meaning of the term in the abstract, out of its particular context, which is the specification. **The patent system is based on the proposition that claims cover only the invented subject matter.** . . .

. . . The problem is that if the district court starts with the broad dictionary definition in every case and fails to fully appreciate how the specification implicitly limits that definition, the error will systematically cause the construction of the claim to be unduly expansive. The risk of systematic overbreadth is greatly reduced if the court instead focuses at the outset on how the patentee used the claim term in the claims, specification, and prosecution history, rather than starting with a broad definition and whittling it down.

Dictionaries, by their nature, provide an expansive array of definitions. General dictionaries, in particular, strive to collect all uses of particular words, from the common to the obscure. By design, general dictionaries collect the definitions of a term as used not only in a particular art field, but in many different settings. In such circumstances, it is inevitable that the multiple dictionary definitions for a term will extend beyond the "construction of the patent [that] is confirmed by the avowed understanding of the patentee, expressed by him, or on his behalf, when his application for the original patent was pending." *Goodyear Dental Vulcanite Co. v. Davis*, 102 U.S. 222, 227, 26 L.Ed. 149 (1880). Thus, the use of the dictionary may extend patent protection beyond what should properly be afforded by the inventor's patent. *See Smith v. Snow*, 294 U.S. 1, 14, 55 S.Ct. 279, 79 L. Ed. 721 (1935) ("if the claim were fairly susceptible of two constructions, that should be adopted which will secure to the patentee his actual invention") (emphasis added). For that reason, we have stated that "a general-usage dictionary cannot overcome art-specific evidence of the meaning" of a claim term. *Vanderlande Indus. Nederland*, 366 F.3d at 1321; *see also Renishaw*, 158 F.3d at 1250, *quoting Liebscher v. Boothroyd*, 46 C.C.P.A. 701, 258 F.2d 948, 951 (CCPA 1958) ("Indiscriminate reliance on definitions found in dictionaries can often produce absurd results. . . . One need not arbitrarily pick and choose from the various accepted definitions of a word to decide which meaning was intended as the word is used in a given claim. The subject matter, the context, etc., will more often than not lead to the correct conclusion.").

Even technical dictionaries or treatises, under certain circumstances, may suffer from some of these deficiencies. There is no guarantee that a term is used in the same way in a treatise as it would be by the patentee. In fact, discrepancies between the patent and treatises are apt to be common because the patent by its nature describes something novel. *See Autogiro*, 384 F.2d at 397 ("Often the invention is novel and words do not exist to describe it. The dictionary does not always keep abreast of the inventor. It cannot.").

Moreover, different dictionaries may contain somewhat different sets of definitions for the same words. A claim should not rise or fall based upon the preferences of a particular dictionary editor, or the court's independent decision, uninformed by the specification, to rely on one dictionary rather than another. Finally, the authors of dictionaries or treatises may simplify ideas to communicate them most effectively to the public and may thus choose a meaning that is not pertinent to the understanding of particular claim language. *See generally* Ellen P. Aprill, The Law of the Word: Dictionary Shopping in the Supreme Court, 30 Ariz. St. L.J. 275, 293-314 (1998). The resulting definitions therefore do not necessarily reflect the inventor's goal of distinctly setting forth his invention as a person of ordinary skill in that particular art would understand it.

As we have noted above, however, we do not intend to preclude the appropriate use of dictionaries. Dictionaries or comparable sources are often useful to assist in understanding the commonly understood meaning of words and have been used both by our court and the Supreme Court in claim interpretation. *See Exhibit Supply Co. v. Ace Patents Corp.*, 315 U.S. 126, 134, 62 S.Ct. 513, 86 L.Ed. 736 (1942) (relying on dictionaries to construe the claim term "embedded"); *Weber Elec. Co. v. E.H. Freeman Elec. Co.*, 256 U.S. 668, 678, 41 S.Ct. 600, 65 L.Ed. 1162 (1921) (approving circuit court's use of dictionary definitions to define claim terms); *Renishaw*, 158 F.3d at 1247-53 (approving the use of dictionaries with proper respect for the role of intrinsic evidence). **A dictionary definition has the value of being an unbiased source "accessible to the public in advance of litigation."** ***Vitronics*, 90 F.3d at 1585. As we said in *Vitronics*, judges are free to consult dictionaries and technical treatises at any time in order to better understand the underlying technology and may also rely on dictionary definitions when construing claim terms, so long as the dictionary definition does not contradict any definition found in or ascertained by a reading of the patent documents.**

The federal circuit in *Phillips* then addressed the issue of reading limitations from the specification into the claims[68] (emphasis supplied):

[W]e recognize that the distinction between using the specification to interpret the meaning of a claim and importing limitations from the specification into the claim can be a difficult one to apply in practice. *See Comark Communications, Inc. v. Harris Corp.*, 156 F.3d 1182, 1186-87 (Fed. Cir. 1998) ("there is sometimes a fine line between reading a claim in light of the specification, and reading a limitation into the claim from the specification"). **However, the line between construing terms and importing limitations can be discerned with reasonable certainty and predictability if**

68. *See* discussion in immediately preceding sections.

the court's focus remains on understanding how a person of ordinary skill in the art would understand the claim terms. For instance, although the specification often describes very specific embodiments of the invention, we have repeatedly warned against confining the claims to those embodiments. *See, e.g., Nazomi Communications, Inc. v. ARM Holdings, PLC,* 403 F.3d 1364, 1369 (Fed. Cir. 2005) (claims may embrace "different subject matter than is illustrated in the specific embodiments in the specification"); Liebel-Flarsheim, 358 F.3d at 906-08; *Teleflex,* 299 F.3d at 1327; *SRI Int'l v. Matsushita Elec. Corp. of Am.,* 775 F.2d 1107, 1121 (Fed. Cir. 1985). **In particular, we have expressly rejected the contention that if a patent describes only a single embodiment, the claims of the patent must be construed as being limited to that embodiment.** *Gemstar-TV Guide,* 383 F.3d at 1366. That is not just because section 112 of the Patent Act requires that the claims themselves set forth the limits of the patent grant, but also because persons of ordinary skill in the art rarely would confine their definitions of terms to the exact representations depicted in the embodiments.

To avoid importing limitations from the specification into the claims, it is important to keep in mind that the purposes of the specification are to teach and enable those of skill in the art to make and use the invention and to provide a best mode for doing so. *See Spectra-Physics, Inc. v. Coherent, Inc.,* 827 F.2d 1524, 1533 (Fed. Cir. 1987). One of the best ways to teach a person of ordinary skill in the art how to make and use the invention is to provide an example of how to practice the invention in a particular case. **Much of the time, upon reading the specification in that context, it will become clear whether the patentee is setting out specific examples of the invention to accomplish those goals, or whether the patentee instead intends for the claims and the embodiments in the specification to be strictly coextensive.** *See SciMed Life Sys.,* 242 F.3d at 1341. *See Snow v. Lake Shore M.S. Ry. Co.,* 121 U.S. 617, 630, 7 S.Ct. 1343, 30 L.Ed. 1004 (1887) (it was clear from the specification that there was "nothing in the context to indicate that the patentee contemplated any alternative" embodiment to the one presented).

In the end, there will still remain some cases in which it will be hard to determine whether a person of skill in the art would understand the embodiments to define the outer limits of the claim term or merely to be exemplary in nature. **While that task may present difficulties in some cases, we nonetheless believe that attempting to resolve that problem in the context of the particular patent is likely to capture the scope of the actual invention more accurately than either strictly limiting the scope of the claims to the embodiments disclosed in the specification or divorcing the claim language from the specification.**

Thus, a federal court may consult dictionaries and the like at any time so long it does not modify or contradict the intrinsic evidence. However, it is noted that the tension between the intrinsic (e.g., importance of specification) and extrinsic evidence (e.g., importance of ordinary meaning) that led to the federal circuit's en banc decision in *Phillips* remains. For example, in *MySpace, Inc. v. GraphOn Corp.*,[69] a federal circuit panel, per Judge Plager, stated:

> One approach is to focus on the invention disclosed in the patent: '[t]ry to understand what the inventor has invented (what he says is his contribution in the art) and then choose the claim meaning that best fits the invention.' . . . The other is to focus on the words that the prosecuting lawyer used to craft the claims and 'then apply legal rules of construction to divine the meaning of the claim.' . . . While this is insightful regarding the approaches highlighted in one or another of our cases, it is an oversimplification to suggest that these are competing theories; rather, they are complementary. An inventor is entitled to claim in a patent what he has invented, but no more. . . . He can, however, claim less, to avoid prior art or for any other reason. Therefore, in construing a claim there are two limiting factors—what was invented, and what exactly was claimed. To determine the former—what was invented—we look at the entire patent, with particular attention to the specification (the written description of the invention and the several claims made). To determine the latter—what exactly was claimed—the focus is on the precise words of the particular claim or claims at issue; the written description and preferred embodiments are aids in understanding those words. In the case before us, proper claim construction requires that we understand what the invention encompasses as well as how the claims are stated.

Hence, the appellate court clarified that consulting dictionaries or technical treatises is clearly permissible at any time; however, such extrinsic evidence may never be used to contradict or modify the intrinsic evidence. The court pointed out the benefits and disadvantages of such sources, which a district court should consider when reviewing such sources. The court also recognized the tension previously expressed[70] between interpreting claims in light of the specification and importing limitations from the specification into the claims. Some cases from the federal circuit are strict regarding the presumption of ordinary and customary meaning, such as *Sony v. Thorner*, whereas other cases use the specification "to point the way," such as *Renishaw*, employing what appears to be a lesser standard than a clear and unambiguous redefinition or disavowal. We recommend a spectrum of patent claims from quite broad to quite narrow to address these uncertainties.[71]

69. *See* 672 F.3d 1250 (Fed. Cir. 2012).
70. *See* section 2.1414.
71. *Id. See also* section 4.11 and related sections, discussing using a spectrum of claims.

Some cases from the federal circuit are strict regarding the presumption of ordinary and customary meaning, such as *Sony v. Thorner*, whereas other cases use the specification "to point the way," such as *Renishaw*, employing what appears to be a lesser standard than a clear and unambiguous redefinition or disavowal. We recommend a spectrum of patent claims from quite broad to quite narrow to address these uncertainties.

3.123 Patentee as Lexicographer

That a patentee may act as his own lexicographer has a long pedigree in patent law, both at the Supreme Court[72] and the federal circuit.[73] However, it is not necessarily easy to establish that a special meaning is being used, rather than the ordinary and customary meaning. Several cases state that redefinition by the patentee may be done expressly or by implication. However, whether express or implied, it must be clear.[74]

In this regard, the *Phillips* decision states (emphasis supplied):

> The importance of the specification in claim construction derives from its statutory role. The close kinship between the written description and the claims is enforced by the statutory requirement that the specification describe the claimed invention in "full, clear, concise, and exact terms." 35 U.S.C. § 112, para. 1; *see Netword, LLC v. Centraal Corp.*, 242 F.3d 1347, 1352 (Fed. Cir. 2001) ("The claims are directed to the invention that is described in the specification; they do not have meaning removed from the context from which they arose."); *see also Markman v. Westview Instruments, Inc.*, 517 U.S. 370, 389, 116 S.Ct. 1384, 134 L.Ed.2d 577 (1996) ("[A claim] term can be defined only in a way that comports with the instrument as a whole."). In light of the statutory directive that the inventor provide a "full" and "exact" description of the claimed invention, the specification necessarily informs the proper construction of the claims. *See Merck Co. v. Teva Pharms. USA, Inc.*, 347 F.3d 1367, 1371 (Fed. Cir. 2003) ("A fundamental rule of claim construction is that terms in a patent document are construed with the meaning with which they are presented in the patent document. Thus claims must be

72. *See, e.g.*, United States v. Adams, 383 U.S. 39 (1966).
73. *See, e.g.*, CCS Fitness v. Brunswick Corp., 288 F.3d 1359 (Fed. Cir. 2002).
74. *See, e.g.*, Thorner v. Sony, 669 F.3d 1362 (Fed. Cir. 2012).

construed so as to be consistent with the specification, of which they are a part.") (citations omitted).

In *Renishaw*, this court summarized that point succinctly:

> Ultimately, the interpretation to be given a term can only be determined and confirmed with a full understanding of what the inventors actually invented and intended to envelop with the claim. The construction that stays true to the claim language and most naturally aligns with the patent's description of the invention will be, in the end, the correct construction.
>
> **Consistent with that general principle, our cases recognize that the specification may reveal a special definition given to a claim term by the patentee that differs from the meaning it would otherwise possess. In such cases, the inventor's lexicography governs. *See CCS Fitness, Inc. v. Brunswick Corp.*, 288 F.3d 1359, 1366 (Fed. Cir. 2002). In other cases, the specification may reveal an intentional disclaimer, or disavowal, of claim scope by the inventor. In that instance as well, the inventor has dictated the correct claim scope, and the inventor's intention, as expressed in the specification, is regarded as dispositive. *See SciMed Life Sys., Inc. v. Advanced Cardiovascular Sys., Inc.*, 242 F.3d 1337, 1343-44 (Fed. Cir. 2001).**

In general, in light of this law, we recommend that claim terms be broadly and expressly defined in the specification, but in a manner consistent with ordinary and customary meaning.[75] In this manner, one need not necessarily take a position during prosecution whether the ordinary meaning applies or whether the term has a special meaning. Rather, one may argue that under either approach, the same conclusion is reached with respect to claim scope relative to cited art, and so on.

> In general, in light of this law, we recommend that claim terms be broadly and expressly defined in the specification, but in a manner consistent with ordinary and customary meaning. In this manner, one need not necessarily take a position during prosecution whether the ordinary meaning applies or whether the term has been redefined. Rather, one may argue that under either approach the same conclusion is reached with respect to scope, cited art, and so on.

75. *See also* section 2.1414.

This book is primarily focused on drafting claims, rather than specification drafting; however, to illustrate the proposed approach, suppose the term "computing device" is used in the claims. In the specification, an example of an appropriate statement may be the following:

> For purposes of this patent application, the term "computing device" refers to a central processing unit (CPU), a microprocessor, or the like coupled by a bus to random access memory (RAM), such as, for example, static RAM (SRAM). Examples of a computing device include, not intending to imply any particular limits on scope by these examples, a set-top box, a mobile device (such as a laptop computer, a tablet or a smartphone), a server computer, a desktop computer, or any combination thereof.

3.1231 Express Versus Implied Meaning of Claim Terms

Federal circuit jurisprudence has held that claim terms may be defined in the specification expressly or by implication. We generally recommend that all important claim terms be expressly defined in the specification similar to the manner illustrated earlier.[76] Of course, once this has been done, the claims must be properly drafted to implement the definition provided, an important and still challenging claim drafting exercise.

One problem with defining claim terms by implication is that whether this has occurred may be arguable, and the ultimate decision is usually left to someone else, such as a judge in a suit, a competitor in a negotiation, and so on. Furthermore, what is required to define a claim term by implication is not entirely clear.

Cases in which claim terms were found to be defined in the specification by implication include *Covad Communications*[77] and *Scimed.*[78] On the other hand, *Sony v. Thorner*[79] suggests that the federal circuit may, instead, be reluctant to conclude a claim term has been defined by implication. As suggested previously,[80] the line may be a fine one between reading limitations from the specification into the claims, highlighted in *Phillips* as something to avoid, and providing a special meaning to a claim term. It also appears that different panels of judges may reach different conclusions, further confounding the issue.

---

76. *See* previous section.

77. 262 F.3d 1258 (Fed. Cir. 2001).

78. 242 F.3d 1337 (Fed. Cir. 2001). *See also* Microsoft Corp. v. Multi-Tech Sys., Inc., 357 F.3d 1340, 1347 (Fed. Cir. 2004), *cert. denied*, 543 U.S. 821 (2004) (citing and applying SciMed.); Alloc, Inc. v. U.S. Int'l Trade Comm'n, 342 F.3d 1361, 1370, 68 USPQ2d 1161 (Fed. Cir. 2003), *cert. denied*, 541 U.S. 1063 (2004) (citing and applying SciMed.).

79. 669 F.3d 1362 (Fed. Cir. 2012); *see* discussion in section 2.1414.

80. *See* discussion in section 2.1414.

Thus, it is recommended that important claim terms be expressly defined; however, in a manner consistent with ordinary and customary meaning. In this way, two risks are addressed. One risk relates to whether the patentee has imparted a special meaning to the claim term. The other risk relates to whether the ordinary meaning includes the intended meaning. Again, by following this approach, either position may be argued. It may turn out, depending on the circumstances, that one position is preferred. However, by an approach that supports either position, the opportunity is preserved to take a preferred position later.

> It is recommended that important claim terms be expressly defined; however, in a manner consistent with ordinary and customary meaning. In this way, two risks are addressed. One risk relates to whether the patentee has imparted a special meaning to the claim term. The other risk relates to whether the ordinary meaning includes the intended meaning.

3.1232 Categories of Claim Terminology

Terminology finding its way into claims may be viewed in different categories. A reason for viewing claim terms in this manner is that the particular category may affect the likelihood that the claim term meaning will be disputed and, therefore, potentially construed by a court if a litigation were to ensue. The category may also suggest how a court is likely to treat the term. For example, claim terms may be divided into four categories. These are: lay terms, technical terms, patent law terms of art, and terms of degree.[81] A close variation of this approach was suggested by individuals who have studied and engaged in patent litigation.[82]

Of course, it may not always be clear which category a claim term may fall into; however, perceiving claim terms in this manner may aid claim drafting (as well as specification drafting) by focusing attention on the terms used and the likelihood of a dispute as to meaning so that one may take care regarding use in drafting.

---

81. Terms of degree may be thought of as a subcategory of patent law terms of art but require special attention due to the risk of indefiniteness associated with this category of terms.

82. *See* Menell, Powers & Carlson, *supra* note 31.

For example, as to patent law terms of art, these typically have an adjudicated meaning and should, therefore, be used in a manner consistent with that meaning. Clear examples include "comprising" and other transition phrases, previously discussed.[83] These are the primary examples for this category. Another example might be "plurality." However, there are other terms commonly used in claims that might be considered a patent law term of art but may also be viewed as in another category.[84] A good example is "substantially," discussed here as a term of degree.

For all these examples, appreciate that particular adjudicated meaning may be affected by the facts in a particular situation, so that the meaning of these terms may change in a given situation.[85] A good example is the indefinite article "a" or "an." Although in patent law, this should mean one or more as a term of art, cases exist that have held otherwise based on unusual facts.[86] Thus, it is suggested that such terms be used in the specification in a manner so that intended meaning is clear and, if appropriate, expressly defined. Patent applications often employ boilerplate language[87] near the beginning or end of the specification for such purposes.[88]

---

83. *See* subsections of section 2.13, discussing patent claim transition words or phrases.

84. *See* Menell, Powers & Carlson, *supra* note 31, Table B, listing terms commonly construed by the federal circuit.

85. *See* In Medrad, Inc. v. MRI Devices Corp. (Fed. Cir. 2005) (Interpretations of the same word or phrase in separate patents may diverge because (1) "[a] patentee may define a particular term in a particular way, and in that event the term will be defined in that fashion for purposes of that particular patent, no matter what its meaning in other contexts"; (2) "claim terms are typically given their ordinary and accustomed meaning as understood by one of ordinary skill in the pertinent art, and the generally understood meaning of particular terms may vary from art to art"; and (3) "[e]ven absent an express definition of a term in the specification or prosecution history, or a clearly established understanding of the meaning of the term in the art, the manner in which the term is used in the patent may dictate a definition that differs from the definition that would be given to the same term in a different patent with a different specification or prosecution history.").

86. *See* Tivo, Inc. v. Echostar Comm'ns Corp. 516 F.3d 1290, 1303 (Fed. Cir. 2008) (Term "a" or "an" interpreted to be singular.); Aug. Tech. Corp. v. Camtek, Ltd., 655 F.3d 1278, 1282 (Fed. Cir. 2011) (Term "a wafer" interpreted to mean one and only one wafer.).

87. *See* Appendix B, providing sample patent application boilerplate.

88. *See* In Medrad, Inc. v. MRI Devices Corp. (Fed. Cir 2005) (Interpretations of the same word or phrase in separate patents may diverge because (1) "[a] patentee may define a particular term in a particular way, and in that event the term will be defined in that fashion for purposes of that particular patent, no matter what its meaning in other contexts"; (2) "claim terms are typically given their ordinary and accustomed meaning as understood by one of ordinary skill in the pertinent art, and the generally understood meaning of particular terms may vary from art to art"; and (3) "[e]ven absent an express definition of a term in the specification or prosecution history, or a clearly established understanding of the meaning of the term in the art, the manner in which the term is used in the patent may dictate a definition that differs from the

For terms of degree, use and meaning may be able to be significantly affected via drafting. Terms of degree often include words that might be viewed as a patent law term of art (e.g., substantially) or as lay terminology (e.g., about). However, terms of degree are identified as a separate term category because without some clarity as to meaning, there is a risk of a claim using the term being held indefinite.

The legal standard for indefiniteness is different for examination than it is for litigation. The rationale for the difference is that a patent claim has a presumption of validity. A court will not find a patented claim indefinite unless the claim interpreted in light of the specification and the prosecution history fails to "inform those skilled in the art about the scope of the invention with reasonable certainty."[89] In contrast, during examination, examiners apply the broadest reasonable interpretation. In this regard, MPEP section 2173.02(I) (2022) states:

> Patented claims are not given the broadest reasonable interpretation during court proceedings involving infringement and validity, and can be interpreted based on a fully developed prosecution record. While "absolute precision is unattainable" in patented claims, the definiteness requirement "mandates clarity." *Nautilus, Inc. v. Biosig Instruments, Inc.*, 527 U.S. ___, 110 USPQ2d 1688, 1693 (2014). A court will not find a patented claim indefinite unless the claim interpreted in light of the specification and the prosecution history fails to "inform those skilled in the art about the scope of the invention with reasonable certainty." *Id.* at 1689.
>
> The Office does not interpret claims when examining patent applications in the same manner as the courts. *In re Packard*, 751 F.3d 1307, 1312, 110 USPQ2d 1785, 1788 (Fed. Cir. 2014); *In re Morris*, 127 F.3d 1048, 1054, 44 USPQ2d 1023, 1028 (Fed. Cir. 1997); *In re Zletz*, 893 F.2d 319, 321-22, 13 USPQ2d 1320, 1321-22 (Fed. Cir. 1989). The Office construes claims by giving them their broadest reasonable interpretation during prosecution in an effort to establish a clear record of what the applicant intends to claim. Such claim construction during prosecution may effectively result in a lower threshold for ambiguity than a court's determination. *Packard*, 751 F.3d at 1323-24, 110 USPQ2d at 1796-97 (Plager, J., concurring). However, applicant has the ability to amend the claims during prosecution to ensure that the meaning of the language is clear and definite prior to issuance or provide a persuasive explanation (with evidence as necessary) that a person of ordinary skill in the art would not consider the claim language unclear. *In re Buszard*,

---

definition that would be given to the same term in a different patent with a different specification or prosecution history.").

89. *See* Nautilus v. Biosig, 572 U.S. 898 (2014).

504 F.3d 1364, 1366, 84 USPQ2d 1749, 1750 (Fed. Cir. 2007) (claims are given their broadest reasonable interpretation during prosecution "to facilitate sharpening and clarifying the claims at the application stage"); *see also In re Yamamoto*, 740 F.2d 1569, 1571, 222 USPQ 934, 936 (Fed. Cir. 1984); *In re Zletz*, 893 F.2d 319, 322, 13 USPQ2d 1320, 1322 (Fed. Cir. 1989); *Ex parte McAward*, Appeal 2015-006416 (PTAB Aug. 25, 2017) (precedential).

As suggested, one example of a term of degree may be "substantially." Although often seen as a patent law term of art, its meaning could be clarified in the specification, and/or perhaps the term may be given a technical meaning in the particular context so that it may then be construed as a technical term by a court in an appropriate situation. For example, if "substantially" were defined using a reasonably objective technical standard, that term would then likely be understood by one of ordinary skill and, similarly, be interpreted in a manner that one of ordinary skill would likely employ.

Consider this claim as an example:

EXAMPLE 3.1

I claim:

1. A method of operating a module, the module including at least one integrated circuit chip comprising a plurality of series N-type metal oxide semiconductor (NMOS) field effect transistors configured in a series connected stack configuration that comprises at least one series NMOS field effect transistor including a body, the at least one series NMOS field effect transistor either to pass an RF signal in a series enable state or to not pass the RF signal in a series disable state, the method comprising:

   electrically biasing the body of the at least one series NMOS field effect transistor of the module in the series disable state to have a voltage level substantially more negative than the lowest voltage level of the following: ground, a DC voltage level of a source of the at least one series NMOS field effect transistor of the module, and a DC voltage level of a drain of the at least one series NMOS field effect transistor of the module.

The claim refers to "a voltage level **substantially** more negative than the lowest voltage level of the following." The specification may assign a value, such as more than 1 volt, or perhaps clarify in the context the intended meaning of "substantially." Here, for example, since the transistor is biased to be in a "disable state," "substantially more negative" could mean a voltage level more negative so that the "at least one series NMOS field effect transistor" is clearly electrically off.

Even without some language in the specification, if issued, a claim using the term "substantially" might not necessarily be held indefinite. A court may be able to clarify meaning from the particular context, for example; however, depending on importance, this may become a term whose meaning is disputed, increasing uncertainty as to what the claims cover. Thus, aside from the risk of being indefinite, another good reason to clarify meaning is to reduce uncertainty as to claim scope. Other examples of terms of degree include "approximately" and "about."[90]

Another category of terms are technical terms. To illustrate, for the claims discussed in Examples 1.3 and 1.4 of Chapter 1, the technical terms include "burst mode," "memory controller," "CPU," "system bus," and so on. Claim scope will necessarily turn on how these terms are interpreted. *It is, therefore, important that these terms have express definitions but as indicated definitions also that are consistent with ordinary meaning.* The law is well established that if these types of terms are disputed then the court must construe these terms for the jury.[91]

A final category of terms are lay terms, which basically includes terms not in one of the preceding categories. Recognizing these terms may be useful when drafting because these terms are less likely to be construed by a court. The court construes terms for the jury, but, for some terms, it may not aid the jury in its deliberations to have the court provide a construction. The jury will understand these words without an interpretation.[92] These are common, everyday words. However, care is justified to make sure words that may seem like lay terms are not technical terms, terms of degree, or even patent law terms of art. A good example of the latter is "a" or "an," discussed earlier. This seems like a lay term, but it would probably be better viewed as a patent law term of art.

90. *See* Menell, Powers & Carlson, *supra* note 31, Table B, listing terms commonly construed by the federal circuit.

91. *See* O2 Micro Int'l Ltd. v. Beyond Innovation Tech. Co., 521 F.3d 1351, 1362 (Fed. Cir. 2008) (holding that failure to construe the term "only if" was error where parties engaged in technical dispute over its scope).

92. *See* Acumed LLC v. Stryker Corp., 483 F.3d 800, 806 (Fed. Cir. 2007)) ("[A] sound claim construction need not always purge every shred of ambiguity. The resolution of some line-drawing problems—especially easy ones like this one—is properly left to the trier of fact.").

One source for possible terms of art is the article, "Patent Claim Construction: A Modern Synthesis and Structured Framework," by Peter S. Menell, Matthew D. Powers, and Steven C. Carlson, appearing in *Berkeley Technology Law Journal*, Vol. 25, No. 2 (Spring 2010). The article contains a table of terms that courts have commonly construed.[93] Another source is *The Thesaurus of Claim Construction*.[94]

One should appreciate that viewing terms in this manner is not a science, so to speak, and involves significant use of judgment. This approach is introduced simply to assist in understanding which claim terms are more likely to raise legal issues in litigation and should perhaps receive special drafting attention.

One should appreciate that viewing terms in this manner is not a science, so to speak, and involves significant use of judgment. This approach is introduced simply to assist in understanding which claim terms are more likely to raise legal issues in litigation and should perhaps receive special drafting attention.

3.2 Claim Drafting Principles Based on *Markman* Framework and Type of Infringement

Having discussed *Markman* and claim construction principles in some detail, we may now discuss a set of basic claim drafting principles that follow logically from these principles of claim construction. One or two we have stated or implied previously, but, here, we discuss these as principles derived from an understanding of claim construction and, if appropriate, provide examples for purposes of illustration.

3.21 Direct, Literal Infringement

One thing to appreciate, which will be developed throughout this chapter, is that there are several types of patent infringement, and each has associated

93. *See* Menell, Powers & Carlson, *supra* note 31, Table B, listing terms commonly construed by the federal circuit.

94. *See* Robert Kahrl & Stuart Soffer, Thesaurus of Claim Construction (2011).

legal rules. Much is based on section 271 of the statute, but court development is also a basis for these types of patent infringement and the differences.

The most straightforward patent infringement is direct, literal infringement, which derives from section 271(a). That section states:

> Except as otherwise provided in this title, whoever without authority makes, uses, offers to sell, or sells any patented invention, within the United States or imports into the United States any patented invention during the term of the patent therefor, infringes the patent.

Thus, the acts that result in infringement are: making, using, offering for sale, selling, or importing into the United States, the patented invention. As has been noted, the patented invention is quite literally defined by the claims.[95] Thus, an accused product must meet the "all elements" rule that applies for a claim. That is, the accused product must meet each and every element and limitation of the particular claim literally for literal patent infringement.

If each and every element and limitation is met literally, then this constitutes direct, literal infringement of the patent claim at issue. Another way to infringe a patent claim directly, is to infringe it nonliterally. This relates to the doctrine of equivalents (DOE), which is a type of infringement created by federal courts in light of the policies behind patent law. We discuss the principles related to the DOE later in this chapter.[96] It is often said that to infringe a patent claim requires that each element and limitation of the patent claim be met by the accused device either *literally* or *equivalently*. This statement is referring to direct patent infringement but includes both literal and nonliteral infringement.

Another type of patent infringement is indirect patent infringement. This topic was introduced in Chapter 1. The basis for indirect patent infringement is statutory sections 271(b) and (c), which state:

> (b) Whoever actively induces infringement of a patent shall be liable as an infringer;
>
> (c) Whoever offers to sell or sells within the United States or imports into the United States a component of a patented machine, manufacture, combination or composition, or a material or apparatus for use in practicing a patented process, constituting a material part of the invention, knowing the same to be especially made or especially adapted for use in an infringement

95. *See, e.g.*, Phillips v. AWH, 415 F.3d 1303 (Fed. Cir. 2005) (en banc).

96. *See* the subsections of section 3.23, discussing patent infringement under the doctrine of equivalents.

> of such patent, and not a staple article or commodity of commerce suitable for substantial noninfringing use, shall be liable as a contributory infringer.

These sections are discussed in much more detail later in this chapter.[97] In general, these sections are directed to someone who in some manner aids and abets a direct infringer but does not otherwise directly infringe the patent claim at issue. Hence, the name "indirect infringement." As with direct infringement, this infringement may occur literally or nonliterally.

3.211 At the Start of Drafting, Consider the Types of Direct Infringement and the Business and Economic Considerations Surrounding the Invention

When beginning to draft patent claims, it is helpful to have in mind a type of patent infringement. Typically, one begins with direct, literal patent infringement since it is the easiest to make out legally. As discussed later, for indirect infringement or nonliteral infringement, more things must generally be proven to establish in federal court that these types of patent infringement have occurred.

Not unlike our discussion in Chapter 2 regarding claim types, such as apparatus claims, method of making claims, and method of using claims, it is helpful when beginning to draft claims to think about the types of acts that might constitute direct, literal infringement for a patent claim you are beginning to draft. The goal is to create an asset that has commercial value and aids the business and patent strategy of a client/patentee. The more the claims cover potential acts of direct infringement, the more valuable the patent that issues will be and the more the asset will support such strategies.

As discussed previously, the acts of patent infringement protected by a patent claim are: making, using, selling, offering for sale, and importing the claimed invention. There are a number of possible and related questions to ponder that will aid in drafting a patent claim. For example, how is the invention likely to be infringed by another? Will it be copied? Will it be infringed via a technical specification that companies voluntarily meet, such as USB, PCI, or Bluetooth? Will others develop technology along the lines of the invention because it provides performance or cost advantages? Will an infringer *sell* a competitive product or *offer* a competitive service? Will an infringer *manufacture* abroad and *import* onto this country? Will they have someone else *manufacture* for them? Will there be multiple *manufacturers* for different components and then integration by a system integrator? How easy

97. *See* subsections of section 3.22, discussing indirect infringement.

is it to avoid infringing by using a different approach? How easy is it to know whether someone else is infringing? Chapter 1 discusses various scenarios to see how the possibilities may be varied and may impact desired claim scope. Some of these issues are also discussed in more detail in later sections.[98]

You may not have all the answers to all the possible questions, but it is still important to think about them to begin the process of drafting a patent claim of appropriate scope. As demonstrated in Chapter 1, the economics and the business details matter if the claims are to be valuable. Likewise, the business and intellectual property strategies of the client/patentee matter. This section is to highlight that initially understanding these issues or initially thinking about them may be a good way to start, as it relates to literal, direct claim scope.

3.212 Make Claim Coverage Clear from the Face of the Claims

It is now well-established patent law that the starting point for claim construction is always the words of the claims themselves. Although this principle, by itself, should not be particularly surprising to patent attorneys, the clearest statement of the principle is found in *Vitronics Corp. v. Conceptronic, Inc.*,[99] discussed previously. In *Markman v. Westview Instruments, Inc.*,[100] the U.S. Supreme Court made it clear that, for policy reasons, patent claim construction is a function that should always be performed by judges, rather than juries. Therefore, relatively soon after that watershed Supreme Court decision, the federal circuit handed down the *Vitronics* decision, which, even today, provides an excellent "how to" guide for claim construction. As discussed previously, the principles of *Vitronics* were reaffirmed in the en banc decision by the federal circuit, *Phillips v. AWH*.[101]

In *Vitronics*, the federal circuit went out of its way to specify a particular pecking order with respect to the intrinsic evidence that a court should follow, namely, the claims, specification, and prosecution history, when attempting to construe a claim (emphasis supplied):

> **First, we look to the words of the claims themselves . . . .**
>
> Although words in a claim are generally given their ordinary and customary meaning, a patentee may choose to be his own lexicographer and use terms in a manner other than their ordinary meaning, as long as the special

98. *See* sections 6.5 and 6.6 and their subsections, discussing reducing opportunities for designing around patent claims, and increasing the likelihood of detecting patent infringement.

99. 90 F.3d 1576, 1582 (Fed. Cir. 1996).

100. 517 U.S. 370, 372 (1996).

101. 415 F.3d 1303 (Fed. Cir. 2005) (en banc).

> definition of the term is clearly stated in the patent specification or file history. . . .
>
> Second, it is always necessary to review the specification to determine whether the inventor used any terms in a manner inconsistent with their ordinary meaning. . . . Usually, it [the spec] is dispositive; it is the single best guide to the meaning of a disputed term.
>
> Third, the court may also consider the prosecution history of the patent, if in evidence. . . . The record before the Patent and Trademark Office is often of critical significance in determining the meaning of claims.[102]

For our purposes, then, one important pronouncement from *Vitronics*, as indicated by the preceding quote, is that claim construction begins with the claim language itself.

To a patent claim drafter, this recognition is critical to providing good representation before the PTO and to obtaining enforceable patents of value. What it means, in essence, is that if the claims are clear on their face, then claim construction may in some cases be complete.[103] The patent drafter, then, may provide the best representation by preparing simple, straightforward claims that are clear as to their intended meaning.

Vitronics does state that the specification *must* be consulted as part of the claim construction process, as confirmed by the preceding quote. However, the specification is often consulted primarily to determine whether the claim terms are used in the specification in a manner consistent with their ordinary meaning. Therefore, if the claims terms are used consistently in the specification in this manner, then, at least in principle, there is no need for further consultation of the specification to further interpret the claims. To restate this, for claim construction, it is the words of the claims that are paramount.

> For claim construction, it is the words of the claims that are paramount.

Many federal circuit cases have clearly established that if the claims are clear on their face and the specification is entirely consistent, then the specification need not be used to further limit the claims.[104] In such circumstances,

---

102. 90 F.3d at 1582–83.

103. *See, e.g.*, Straight Path IP Grp., Inc. v. Sipnet EU S.R.O., 806 F.3d 1356 (Fed. Cir. 2015), which stated the specification played a "more limited role" when the claim term had an especially "plain" meaning.

104. *See id.*

claim construction should be based on the claim language itself. For example, in *Mantech Environmental v. Hudson Environmental*,[105] at issue was the meaning of the disputed claim term "well" in a groundwater monitoring system for reducing the levels of hydrocarbon contaminants.

Mantech argued that the term "well" referred to a structure able to perform either the function of monitoring or the function of injecting test fluid into the groundwater, or both. Hudson's experts, not surprisingly, testified that the term "well" was limited to a structure that performed both monitoring and injecting. In the accused systems, not all the wells performed both functions. It is worth noting, in this context, that the preferred embodiment in the application showed *only a well capable of performing both*.

The court determined that the specification was entirely consistent with the claims. The court's claim construction was based strictly on the claim language, which recited a series of wells, at least one of which had to be used for injecting test fluid, and at least one of which had to be used for monitoring. In other words, the claim was written so that it was not required, either expressly or impliedly, that a well perform both functions.

The federal circuit specifically stated: "If the written description supports the definition of the term that is apparent from the claim limitation, then reading in a further limiting definition [based upon the specification] would be improper."[106] Therefore, while a well could perform both functions, *and* the preferred embodiment showed a well capable of performing both functions, the claims and specification did not require this narrow construction. According to the court, the term "well" *as used in the claims* was not and should not have been limited in such a manner. The appellate court further stated: "The district court erred because it, in essence, incorporated from the preferred embodiment into the claims a narrow definition for the term 'well.'"[107]

A similar result occurred in *Comark Communications v. Harris Corp.*[108] The key language of the claim in dispute related to a "video delay circuit." The invention related to UHF television transmission equipment. Comark had developed a common amplification system that allowed audio and video signals to be amplified together, thereby saving hardware. However, this also created cross-modulation, and so Comark also devised an invention to reduce the cross-modulation distortions. It is the latter invention that was the subject of the suit.

105. 152 F.3d 1368 (Fed. Cir. 1998).
106. *Id.* at 1374.
107. *Id.* at 1375.
108. 156 F.3d 1182 (Fed. Cir. 1998).

The defendant attempted to limit the claims to the specific embodiment shown in the specification; however, the court reasoned that because the specification was entirely consistent with the claims, there was no need to consult the specification for claim construction or to limit the claims in the manner proposed. The federal circuit stated (emphasis supplied):

> Despite our repeated statements that limitations from the specification are not to be read into the claims [citations omitted], Harris nonetheless argues that the term "video delay circuit" should be read "in light of the specification" to include a limitation that the video delay circuit must also function to compensate for delay introduced to the video signal by the IF vision modulator. We have previously stated that "while . . . claims are to be interpreted in light of the specification and with a view to ascertaining the invention, it does not follow that limitations from the specification may be read into the claims." [citations omitted] We recognize that there is sometimes a fine line between reading a claim in light of the specification and reading a limitation into the claim from the specification. [citations omitted] However, we believe that Harris advocates the latter rather than the former.
>
> **In this case, the term "video delay circuit" has a clear and well-defined meaning. This term is not so amorphous that one of skill in the art can only reconcile the claim language with the inventor's disclosure by recourse to the specification.** . . . Harris is indeed correct that the specification clearly discloses that the video delay circuit functions to compensate for delay introduced to the video signal being processed by the IF vision modulator by introducing a similar delay to the same video signal in the correct path. However, **the language of the specification does not at all aid in our interpretation of the phrase "video delay circuit." It simply details how the video delay circuit is to be used in a single embodiment of the invention. It in no way sheds light on either the meaning of the term to the inventor, or the common meaning of the term to one of skill in the art.**[109]

The court, thus, appears to recognize it will be true that the specification, out of necessity, provides an embodiment that is likely narrower than the language of the claims. This is necessitated in some measure from the requirements of enablement and best mode, which require a relatively detailed description of operation directed to one of ordinary skill in the art. The claims, however, have no such requirements of enablement or best mode, independent of the specification itself. Therefore, if the specification uses the terms of the claim consistently, then, the fact that the specification may

109. *Id.* at 1186–87.

contain an embodiment narrower than the claims should not, by itself, be a valid justification for limiting those claims terms to that narrow embodiment. It is further noted that in addition to *Vitronics*, both *Mantech* and *Comark* are regularly cited by the federal circuit as good law.

A more recent case is *Evolusion v. HOC.*[110] Based on the specification, the district court had ruled that the term "magazine catch bar" *excluded* a factory installed magazine catch bar. The federal circuit reversed and stated:

> The specification supports the ordinary-meaning interpretation of "magazine catch bar." *Phillips*, 415 F.3d at 1315 ("[C]laims must be read in view of the specification, of which they are part." (internal quotation marks and citation omitted)). The specification nowhere limits the scope of a "magazine catch bar" to exclude factory-installed ones from the assembly that achieves the fixed-magazine goal. Nor, contrary to a suggestion made by Juggernaut, does it explain that only a customized or modified magazine catch bar, one necessarily different from what was factory installed, may be used on the firearm. It simply explains that the described embodiments of the invention all include a "magazine catch bar" that can be securely attached to the lower receiver of the firearm, and consistently describes the component in generic terms. *Id.*, col. 2, line 65, through col. 3, line 2; *see also id.*, col. 5, lines 5-7. Juggernaut argues, and Evolusion concedes, that the disclosed embodiments do not illustrate OEM magazine catch bars. *See id.*, figs. 3 & 4.
>
> But that cannot make a difference in this case. We have repeatedly held that "it is not enough that the only embodiments, or all of the embodiments, contain a particular limitation to limit claims beyond their plain meaning." *Unwired Planet, LLC v. Apple, Inc.*, 829 F.3d 1353, 1359 (Fed. Cir. 2016) (internal quotation marks and citation omitted). Here, nothing in the specification suggests that factory (or OEM) provenance of a bar disqualifies it from being part of the invention if, as a structural matter, it is a magazine catch bar under the ordinary meaning. And nothing in the specification suggests that factory (or OEM) installation precludes the possession of the structural features required by the invention. The specification reiterates the background principle that the claims are not limited to the illustrated embodiments. '845 patent, col. 4, lines 46-53. And it describes and illustrates at least one embodiment in which the magazine catch bar is a separate element from the upper tension bar, *id.*, col. 5, lines 5-10, 17-20; *id.*, fig. 3, reinforcing the idea that there is no requirement to replace each individual component in the assembly in order to replace the assembly as a whole.

Of course, there are federal circuit cases that have introduced limitations from the specification into the claims. As the previous quote from *Comark*

110. 2022 U.S. App. LEXIS 1126 (Fed. Cir. 2022).

makes clear, the line between interpreting the claims in light of the specification, which is permissible, and reading limitations from the specification into the claims, which is impermissible, is a fine one indeed.[111] For example, in *Medegen MMS, Inc. v. ICU Medical, Inc.*,[112] Judge Walker, a district court judge sitting by designation, dissented from the decision and asserted that the issues before the federal circuit present "a conundrum often faced by district courts when construing" claim terms. He cited the "twin axioms" of claim construction that produced the conundrum: "[o]n the one hand, claims 'must be read in view of the specification,'" while "[o]n the other hand, it is improper to read a limitation from the specification into the claims." The problem with these axioms, according to Judge Walker, is that "the axioms themselves seldom provide an answer, but instead merely frame the question to be resolved."

Thus, it may be difficult to predict in advance which way a court may lean, for example, toward a broader construction employing ordinary and customary meaning or toward a narrower construction relying on the specification to impart a narrow meaning.[113] In *Medegen*, the federal circuit determined that the district court had read limitations from the specification into the claims.

By contrast, however, in *Bell Atlantic v. Covad*,[114] despite the claims including a relatively broad term "mode," the federal circuit, in a case involving digital subscriber loop (DSL) communications technology, interpreted the terminology "different modes" narrowly. The patent claims required transceiver modems to selectively operate in one of a plurality of "different modes" over a network. Thus, the claim reciting "different modes," which was interpreted by the federal circuit to refer to only one of the *three* specific modes described in the specification. According to the federal circuit, the patentee had redefined the term "mode" *by implication*. To help reduce the risk of this eventuality, it is strongly recommended to both describe and claim multiple embodiments of varying scope.[115]

To recap, when drafting patent claims, the best claims are those where the drafter's intent is clear on the face of the claims themselves. This should

111. *See* CCS Fitness v. Brunswick Corp., 288 F.3d 1359 (Fed. Cir. 2002), also written by Judge Michel, as simply one example, provides a logical framework for analyzing when it is appropriate to depart from the ordinary and customary meaning of a claim term and when such a departure is not appropriate. The typical reason is because the drafter has demonstrated an intent to depart from the ordinary and customary meaning in either the specification or the file history of the patent.

112. 317 F. App'x 982 (Fed. Cir. 2009).

113. *See* section 2.1414.

114. 262 F.3d 1258 (Fed. Cir. 2001).

115. As discussed in other sections of this book, such as section 4.11.

be a guiding principle in claim drafting. It is, of course, possible that you may come in contact with a judge who prefers the line of authority in which limitations are read into the claims from the specification over the line of authority in which the claims are given their ordinary and customary meaning, broad though it may be. In fact, in high-quality Patent Claim Drafting Practice (PCDP), it is largely assumed that this may happen, and you are encouraged to draft the patent application, that is, both the claims *and the specification*, in a manner that reduces the risk that broad terms will be construed narrowly. As has been alluded, ways to do this include employing claims of varying scope,[116] defining the key terms used in the claims,[117] and covering multiple embodiments (fully described in the specification) with an array of verbal formulations that are logically consistent and employ a hierarchy of terms.[118] For those situations, therefore, the sections of this book will guide you regarding how to draft the patent claims (and provide appropriate support in the specification) to provide the best protection for your client. However, if you meet the criteria just set out when drafting the patent claims; you are ahead of the game, by far, regardless of the precedent the court chooses to follow.

> To recap, when drafting patent claims, the best claims are those where the drafter's intent is clear on the face of the claims themselves.

3.213 Use Words in the Claims Consistent with Their Understood Meaning

A reason to use words consistent with their understood meaning, quite simply, is because that is precisely how those words are likely to be construed. A relatively impressive body of federal circuit law has developed, as suggested, to the effect that words of a claim are to be given their ordinary and customary meaning, unless it is relatively clear that the words are not intended to have that meaning. This principle is stated in *Phillips*[119] and *Vitronics*.[120] Furthermore, after *Vitronics*, a number of cases, beginning with *Johnson Worldwide v.*

116. *See* section 4.11, discussing claims of varying scope.
117. *See* section 6.11 and subsection 5.411, discussing defining key claim terms.
118. *See* section 5.3 and its subsections, discussing using multiple but consistent verbal formulations to capture the inventive subject matter.
119. *See* section 3.1212, discussing *Phillips*.
120. *See* section 3.1211, discussing *Vitronics*.

Zebco,[121] recite that this is not simply a presumption but rather a *heavy* presumption. The federal circuit has never recanted this principle, although they cite it much less frequently after *Phillips*. A helpful case, cited in *Phillips*, is *CCS Fitness v. Brunswick Corp.*[122] Thus, ordinary and customary meaning is a presumption and according to case law that has not been rejected or overturned, it is a heavy one.

Of course, it is not absolutely guaranteed that claim terms will receive their ordinary and customary meaning. However, good practice suggests that you would do far better to *use terms in a manner consistent* with their ordinary and customary meaning, rather *than in a manner inconsistent* with or that departs from that meaning.

> Good practice suggests that you would do far better to use terms in a manner consistent with their ordinary and customary meaning, rather than in a manner inconsistent with or that departs from that meaning.

Although few probably view the case this way, *Vitronics* itself is a wonderful example of what might happen if you fail to follow this simple principle. As it now well-known,[123] in *Vitronics*, the patent drafter employed the terminology "solder reflow temperature" in the specification and claims in a manner not consistent with the art. While it is true that the drafter made it clear in the specification the special meaning he intended these words to have, the meaning he intended was not consistent with the established meaning in the relevant art. This gave opposing counsel a basis to dispute the meaning of these terms.

Therefore, while the specification, clearly, intended that these words mean the peak reflow temperature, that is, the peak temperature the solder may reach as a liquid, this was not the generally accepted meaning of solder reflow temperature. Instead, the generally accepted meaning of solder reflow temperature is liquidus temperature, that is, the temperature at which the solder first begins

121. 175 F.3d 985, 989 (Fed. Cir. 1999).

122. 288 F.3d 1359 (Fed. Cir. 2002). This case provides a logical framework for analyzing when it is appropriate to depart from the ordinary and customary meaning of a claim term and when such a departure is not appropriate. The typical reason is because the drafter has demonstrated an intent to depart from the ordinary and customary meaning in either the specification or the file history of the patent.

123. *See* section 3.1211, discussing *Vitronics*.

to become liquid, something quite different. It is worth noting that the patentee eventually did prevail and convinced the federal circuit that the meaning demonstrated by the specification was the meaning intended in the claims; however, perhaps what practitioners should take from the case is the observation that Vitronics lost at the trial level, and it took an appeal to the federal circuit to obtain the proper construction under the law. Therefore, it took significantly more time and expense for Vitronics to obtain the proper claim interpretation, the claim interpretation that was intended by the drafter.

3.214 Use Words in the Claims with Broadly Understood Meanings where Appropriate

In addition to the principle that words of a claim are presumed to have their ordinary and customary meaning, those words are entitled to a full scope of meaning.[124] That is, the meanings associated with the term that are consistent with the use in the claims, unless it's clear that this is not what is intended (or if it leads to a ridiculous interpretation, which would not be a meaning consistent with the usage in the claims).[125]

To the patent drafter, this suggests that the best words to use for claim terms are those that generally encompass a broad understanding for the particular context.

> The best words to use for claim terms are those that generally encompass a broad understanding for the particular context.

In many ways, this is nothing new to the seasoned patent practitioner. The federal circuit has made part of the black letter law what patent drafters have known for years. Therefore, it should come as no surprise that some of the best words to employ in claims are *already an established part of the parlance of patent claim drafting, not unlike patent terms of art.*[126] A few examples are provided here, although, of course, many more such terms exist:[127]

124. *See, e.g.*, Liebel-Flarsheim Co. v. Medrad, Inc., 358 F.3d 898, 905–09 (Fed. Cir. 2004), *cert. denied*, 543 U.S. 925 (2004) (holding that claim terms are given the full breadth of their ordinary meaning unless a clear disavowal of scope is stated in the specification).

125. *See, e.g.*, Phillips v. AWH, 415 F.3d 1303 (Fed. Cir. 2005) (en banc).

126. *See* section 3.1232, discussing categories and examples of claim terminology.

127. *See* KAHRL & SOFFER, *supra* note 94; *see also* section 3.1232, discussing categories and examples of claim terminology.

Actuator
Adjust
Analog
Application
Arrangement
Assembly
Associate
Attachment
Base
Branch
Buffer
Card
Cell
Change
Channel
Chassis
Circuit
Code
Component
Conductor
Conduit
Configuration
Connection
Contact
Control
Converter
Corresponding
Coupled
Cycle
Decode
Derivative
Detector
Device
Digital
Direct
Discrete
Division
Encode
Feedback
Feed Forward
Gate
Grouping
Hold
If (instead of "when")
Indirect
Initial
Insulator
Interface
Layer
Limit
Link
Location
Magnitude
Measurement
Medium
Member
Memory
Mode
Modulate
Module
Movement
Network
Node
Operation
Operative
Overlap
Part
Pass
Path
Peripheral
Physical
Port
Portion
Position
Processing
Processor
Product
Receive
Register
Regulator
Relation
Sensor
Separate
Shunt
Signal
Sink
Sort
Source
Spectrum
State
Store
Switch
System
Terminal
Terminate
Timing
Transform
Translate
Transmit
Unit
Update
Using
Value
Work piece

As should be clear, although these words have discernible meanings, suggesting that they are not ambiguous; nonetheless, the full scope of their meaning may include a broad array of possibilities. Consider, for example, the word "interface." One may imagine a myriad of possibilities that such a word may conjure up across a broad array of technologies. It may likewise be appropriate to bolster this understanding with a consistent and broad (but not vague) definition in the specification, so that one may legitimately take the position that whether one applies the ordinary and customary meaning or one employs the meaning imparted by the specification, in either case, the accused product would be covered.

It is worth noting that even in particular technologies, although certain words have acquired a particularized meaning related to that technology, nonetheless, within that particular technology, the understanding of the word may still be somewhat broad and flexible, depending upon the circumstances. It is, therefore, helpful to be cognizant of such words and use them when working in such technologies. The key point is to think carefully when choosing words of the claim and use those words that have an inherent breadth and potentially wide scope, even where the word may, in some instances, have some particularized technological associations with it. For example, some of the preceding words illustrate this point—*signal*, *medium*, *layer*, *interface*, *detector*, *sensor*, *converter*, and so on. However, again, it will also be important to make sure that these terms are adequately supported in the specification through use in the description of multiple embodiments of varying scope to support the intended breadth and meaning.

> The key point is to think carefully when choosing words of the claim and use those words that have an inherent breadth and potentially wide scope, even where the word may, in some instances, have some particularized technological associations with it.

3.2141 Employ a Hierarchy of Claim Terms

For purposes of claim drafting and for specification drafting, it is desirable to create and employ a hierarchy of terms that relate to the subject matter of the invention. The point of doing so is to make clear the scope intended for certain terms and then support that with specification description. This is at least one reason that it usually makes sense to draft a set of claims before drafting the specification. That set of claims may be updated, modified, and grow as you draft the specification, but it crystallizes your thinking initially and creates a list of terms.

> This is at least one reason that it usually makes sense to draft a set of claims before drafting the specification. That set of claims may be updated, modified, and grow as you draft the specification, but it crystallizes your thinking initially and creates a list of terms.

As should now be clear, how terms are used in the specification and claims is legally significant. Thus, creating an initial set of claims that may be viewed as hierarchical would be prudent. The hierarchy relates to narrower or more specific embodiments, that is, differing scope. In this manner, terms are able to be used consistently so as not to create ambiguity while still being clear regarding intended scope.

3.21411 Illustrative Claim Examples

Let's begin with some simple examples.

Suppose an invention may be implemented with the following: an analog circuit, a digital circuit, a microprocessor, and so on. This is not such an unusual situation because for most types of electrical filters this is the case. Imagine, for example, a filter related to a medical application in which this is the case. For example, in medical imaging, filters are needed. Filters are also used for test equipment. So, as another example, imagine a filter uniquely designed for equipment that tests an optical waveguide. These are just two illustrative technical examples.

At a high level, the filter for an optical waveguide operates on signals. The signals may be optical or electrical, both of which are electromagnetic in nature. Likewise, the signals may be analog or digital. In addition, the signals may be binary, such as in a microprocessor, for example. Thus, one may imagine a hierarchy of terms such as shown in Figure 3.1 used to draft the following claims:

1. An apparatus comprising: a filter to process signal measurements for a waveguide, the signal measurements to be taken at angular focal positions of the waveguide relative to a transverse directional path of light to illuminate an object, wherein sum and difference patterns are to be formed from the signal measurements for the respective focal angular positions taken two at a time.
2. The apparatus of claim 1, wherein the signal measurements are to comprise optical signal measurements to form one or more spectra.

3. The apparatus of claim 2, wherein the optical signal measurements are to be converted to analog electrical signals and the filter to process the signal measurements comprises an analog filter to process the analog electrical signals.
4. The apparatus of claim 2, wherein the optical signal measurements are to be converted to digital electrical signals and the filter to process the signal measurements comprises a digital filter to process the digital electrical signals.
5. The apparatus of claim 4, wherein the optical signal measurements are to be converted to binary digital electrical signals and the filter to process the signal measurements comprises a microprocessor programmed to process the binary digital electrical signals.

Figure 3.1 An Example Hierarchy of Claim Terms

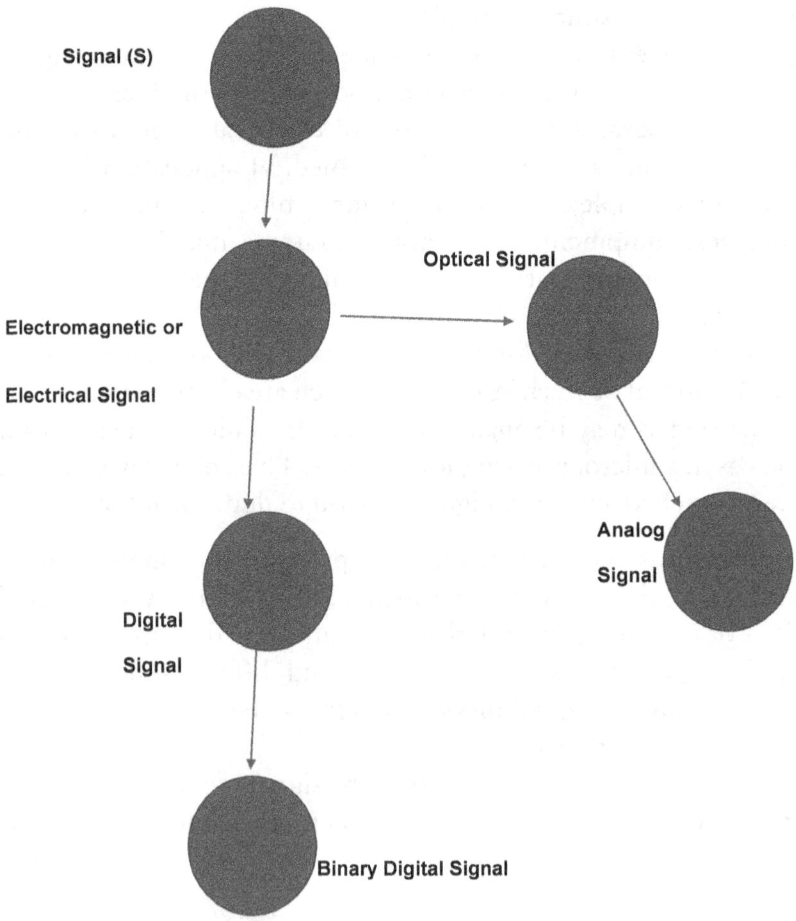

In another example, a metal oxide semiconductor (MOS) transistor body made from silicon may be biased in a manner to reduce noise for analog signals being transmitted, as in an electrical or electronic switch. MOS transistors may be P-channel (also called P-type) MOS (PMOS) transistors or N-channel (also called N-type) MOS (NMOS) transistors. For example, an electronic switch may comprise a radio frequency (RF) switch, which is used, for example, in cell phones. A similar body biasing mechanism may be used in the MOS transistor of a modulator, as may be employed in radio communications, for example. The switch or modulator may be implemented in an integrated circuit (IC) and the IC may be part of a module. In addition to silicon, a transistor made from Gallium Arsenide (GaAs) may include body biasing to reduce noise as well for similar applications. Typically, an electronic switch has multiple signal paths, such as a path to pass an analog signal, which may be implemented as a pass gate, and a path to not pass the analog signal, which may be implemented as a shunt gate. It is a transistor in the shunt gate that is electrically body biased when OFF while the pass gate is ON to pass an analog signal. This electrical body biasing of the transistor in the shunt gate reduces noise that might otherwise corrupt the analog signal passing through the pass gate of the switch.

These terms may be used in claims such as those illustrated here.

---

1. An apparatus comprising: a module; wherein the module comprises an integrated circuit chip;

   wherein a component of the integrated circuit chip comprises at least one field effect transistor, the at least one field effect transistor including a gate, a drain, a source, and a body;

   wherein, during at least a portion of an off state, the body of the at least one field effect transistor is to be electrically biased to have a voltage level substantially more negative than the lowest voltage level of the following: ground, the DC voltage level of the source of the at least one field effect transistor, and the DC voltage level of the drain of the at least one field effect transistor.

2. The apparatus of claim 2, wherein the component comprises at least one of the following: an electrical switch or a modulator.

3. The apparatus of claim 2, wherein the electrical switch comprises an RF switch including a pass gate and a shunt gate, wherein the shunt gate comprises the at least one field effect transistor.
4. The apparatus of claim 3, wherein the at least one field effect transistor comprises at least one of the following: a Silicon metal oxide semiconductor (MOS) field effect transistor or a Gallium Arsenide (GaAs) field effect transistor.
5. The apparatus of claim 4, wherein the Silicon metal oxide semiconductor (MOS) field effect transistor comprises an N-channel metal oxide semiconductor transistor (NMOS).
6. The apparatus of claim 4, wherein the Silicon metal oxide semiconductor (MOS) field effect transistor comprises a P-channel metal oxide semiconductor transistor (PMOS).

Figure 3.2 is a hierarchical diagram of the terms.

These terms should be used in a manner in the specification to clarify the subject matter intended to be included (as opposed to excluding subject matter, unless a logical necessity). In some, if not all, cases, express definitions may be appropriate. In patent law, the terms "genus" and "species" are often used to explain relationships. For example, "silicon" is the genus for the species "PMOS" and "NMOS" in Figure 3.2. The terms "genus" and "species" are also used to describe claims, such as a genus claim or a species claim.

At times, it may be appropriate for certain terms to be used interchangeably. If so, it is recommended that this be made clear in the specification so as not to create a claim construction issue, since the use of different terms may suggest different scope. This is usually a matter of convenience and judgment that may vary with the particular technical subject matter, and so on. Varying terms may be fine as long as it does not create ambiguity; thus, it may be desirable to clarify whether a change in terminology means a change in scope or is merely an interchangeable term. For example, in the second hierarchy, a term is "component." At times, it may be convenient to refer to a "component" as a "part" without a change in meaning or loss of generality. Likewise, rather than "electrical switch," the term "electronic switch" may be used without a change in meaning or loss in generality. If this takes place in the claims, in particular, it would be highly desirable to clarify in the specification that these terms are used interchangeably and are intended to have corresponding scope. That is, some extra care is required if using terms interchangeably.

Figure 3.2 Another Example Hierarchy of Claim Terms

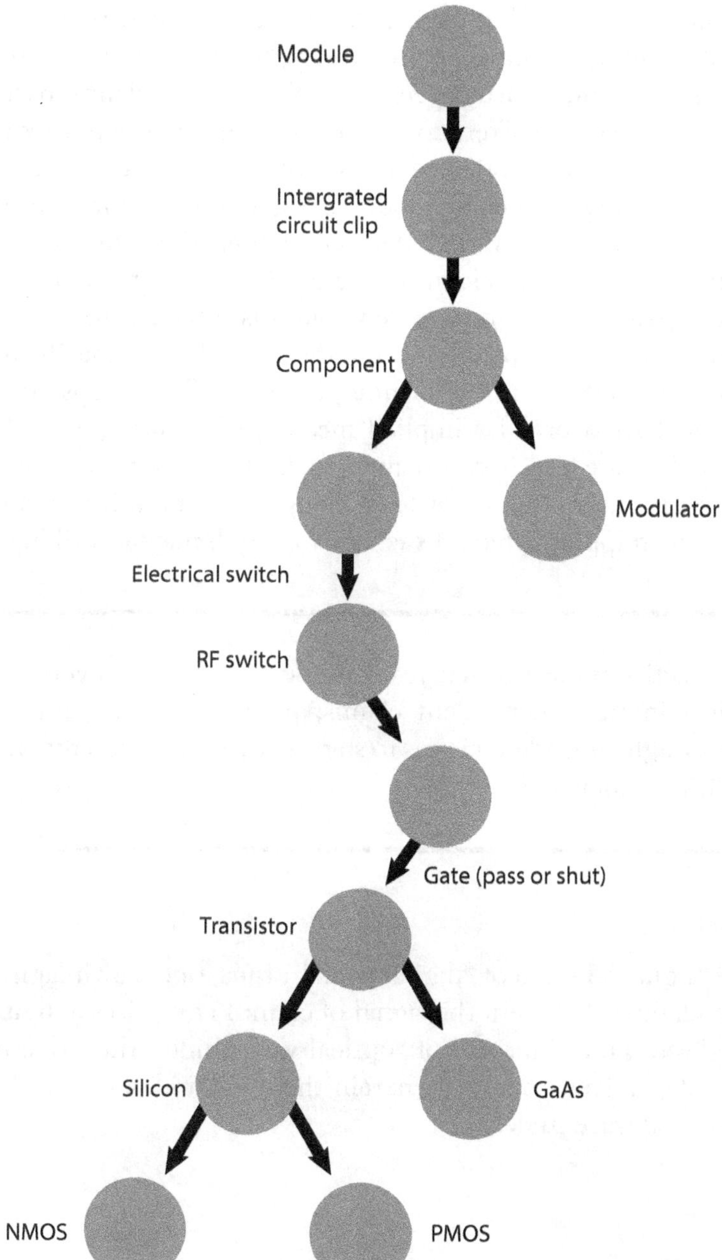

3.215 Avoid Overly Specific Term Modifiers in the Independent Claims

One tendency when drafting claims that is best avoided is the use of relatively specific and often unneeded modifiers, particularly in the independent claims. Using an unnecessarily specific modifier in the claims, particularly in the independent claim, is likely to be construed as an attempt by the drafter to limit claim scope. Good practice, therefore, would indicate that it would be best to omit such highly specific modifiers or, at a minimum, introduce them through dependent claims rather than employing them in the independent claims to take advantage of claim differentiation.[128] In this way, claim differentiation suggests that the independent claim is intended to have a meaning that is broader than the dependent claim that includes the specific modifier.[129] Thus, structuring claims in this manner, in effect, "bootstraps" the independent claim to have a broader implied meaning. Following are a few simple examples to illustrate how easy it may be to limit a claim term unintentionally. Furthermore, if one considers, instead, using those modifiers in a dependent claim, the bootstrapping effect of such an approach may be striking.

> Good practice indicates that it would be best to omit overly specific modifiers in the independent claims; perhaps, instead, introducing them through dependent claims to suggest by implication that the base claim has broader scope.

Examples:

- Use "signal" instead of "digital signal"; thus, one may imagine a dependent claim 2: "wherein the signal of claim 1 comprises a digital signal."
- Use "waveguide" instead of "optical waveguide"; thus, one may imagine a dependent claim 2: "wherein the waveguide of claim 1 comprises an optical waveguide."

---

128. *See* section 2.151, discussing claim differentiation in the context of dependent claims.

129. *See, e.g.*, Interdigital Commons v. ITC, 690 F.3d 1315, 1324 (Fed. Cir. 2012) (The doctrine of claim differentiation disfavors reading a limitation from a dependent claim into an independent claim.).

- Use "frequency" instead of "radio frequency"; thus, one may imagine a dependent claim 2: "wherein the frequency of claim 1, comprises a radio frequency."
- Use "conductive material" instead of "electrically conductive"; thus, one may imagine a dependent claim 2: "wherein the conductive material of claim 1, comprises an electrically conductive material."
- Use "radiation" instead of "electromagnetic radiation"; thus, one may imagine a dependent claim 2: "wherein the radiation of claim 1, comprises electromagnetic radiation."

These are simply a few examples; however, they are sufficient to illustrate this basic principle of claim drafting.

3.216 Draft Short Claims

It may seem deceptively simple; however, the best claims are almost always the shortest ones. Of course, there are many examples of valuable claims that are not short; nonetheless, this does not mean that, even for those valuable claims, a better claim could not have been drafted that would have been shorter. On the contrary, to be quite blunt, more words provide a greater opportunity for a clever opponent to argue that additional limitations are present, or for an unfavorably disposed judge to interpret the claim or claims more narrowly.[130] It is quite simple. Short claims are broad claims.[131] Use dependent claims to narrow scope.

Always endeavor to reduce the number of words in your claims, particularly the independent ones. It is probably a good practice to review each word of a claim to make sure that each and every word is absolutely necessary. In fact, review each word of the claim with the inventors themselves to see if they consider each word to be necessary. This is an excellent practice that is often overlooked or skipped.

---

130. It may also give someone an opportunity to argue that the claim is not properly supported for want of written description.

131. Of course, this approach assumes that prior art is not a problem and, thus, narrower claims are not as desirable. This is an issue that will certainly be flushed out in patent prosecution and, as explained in more detail later in this book, such as sections 4.11 and 4.12, good PCDP strongly recommends claims of varying scope, from broad to intermediate to narrow. In the absence of any particular knowledge about troubling prior art, broad claims are generally accepted to be preferred over narrow claims; however, this issue, as well, is explored in greater depth in section 1.31 of this book.

> It is a good practice to review each word of a claim to make sure that each and every word is absolutely necessary. In fact, review each word of the claim with the inventors themselves to see if they consider each word to be necessary. This is an excellent practice that is often overlooked or skipped.

As most patent attorneys are aware, shorter claims also typically bring more heartache from the PTO. This, of course, is not a reason to write longer claims. To the contrary, where is the challenge as a practitioner in writing long, narrow claims that you know will sail through the PTO because the examiner has not even bothered to read the entire claim? Ultimately, an examiner is usually more than willing to allow an overly narrow claim since he knows that such a claim will not bother anyone (meaning it is unlikely to be infringed).[132]

The goal, of course, is not to get claims allowed that are so broad that the issued claims will generate snickering from an opponent when presented (because the opponent knows that claim is so broad that it is probably invalid). Rather, the goal is to get claims allowed that generate value for your client. However, be aware that patent examiners apply the "broadest reasonable interpretation" (BRI) to patent claims during prosecution.[133] The "broadest reasonable interpretation," even when properly applied, by design is necessarily broader than the interpretation that a federal court will apply to the claim. It is not unusual for what an examiner considers to be the "broadest reasonable interpretation" to actually be an *unreasonably* broad interpretation, since even the broadest reasonable interpretation is supposed to be an interpretation that is in light of the specification.[134] The point simply is this: expect that examiners will be pushing for claims that are narrower than may be appropriate in light of the prior art. Thus, as an advocate, it is important for you to push for claims having a scope *that is appropriate* in light of the prior art.

Ultimately, patent prosecution is a type of negotiation. In any negotiation, strategically you should at least initially be asking for more than you are willing to take. (Assuming you can do so ethically—that is, without reading on the

132. Such narrow claims may also undermine patent infringement under the doctrine of equivalents. *See* subsections of section 3.23, discussing this point.

133. *See* section 6.111, discussing broadest reasonable interpretation (BRI).

134. *See In re* Smith, 872 F.3d 1374 (Fed. Cir. 2017).

known prior art).[135] That is simply good negotiating. If you initially ask for *only* what you are seeking *and no more*, it will almost certainly be the case that *you will end up with less than that.* Thus, one way you can help your client's position in this "negotiation" with the PTO is by making sure that the claims you initially present are short.

It is correct conventional wisdom that a short claim is more likely to be rejected by the PTO than a long claim. That is just the way the PTO works. Still, if the examiner does not have the prior art to support his rejection (and you know of none), does it matter that he has a visceral reaction because your claim is short? Part of the point of the process, in fact, is to ferret out the closest prior art. You do that by presenting short claims and seeing what art the examiner is then able to apply to reject them. Under the law, at least in theory, you should prevail in getting your claim allowed, unless he has the evidence, in the form of prior art, to support the position that the claim is unpatentable. The prior point says "in theory" because, unfortunately, examiners do not always follow the law or do not always fully grasp the technology. In addition, they have limited time and they usually have to get their boss to approve their recommendations. So, yes, in some situations, it may be prudent to give in to an examiner who does not have the art to make his case. Yet another negotiation advantage of short claims, however, is that you may add language to address the examiner's desire for a longer claim without necessarily introducing significant limitations to overall claim scope. Furthermore, if you do believe it is appropriate to concede despite an examiner not providing prior art to support his position, this should be done only if your client approves and only if by doing so you are still able to get claims of a sufficient scope to meet your client's needs.[136] Again, this is a negotiation and you are entitled to present claims that you believe are patentable over the known art. Years of experience have shown that you are better off starting with short claims, even if you ultimately give in to the examiner and add some language. If you start with overly narrow claims, it is more likely than not that the examiner will still want you to narrow those claims further.

It is a bit of PTO lore that if a claim can be covered by two or three outstretched fingers of one hand, then it receives an automatic rejection from the examiner, whether he or she has the prior art to support the rejection or not.

---

135. Knowingly submitting a claim that reads on prior art may result in an ethical violation. *See* 37 C.F.R. § 1.56. That is, for each claim, there should be a good faith argument for patentably distinguishing from the known prior art. *See* section 5.5 and its subsections.

136. In addition, you may want to file a continuation, once you have allowed claims, so you are still able to seek broader claims since the prior art suggests such claims should be patentable.

No official confirmation of this bit of "wisdom" exists; however, it is true that exceedingly short claims are nearly always rejected. However, those rejections also are usually quite weak on substantive grounds. Thus, instead, a countervailing tenet for claim drafting may be adopted as a sort of drafting challenge. If the independent claim you draft cannot be covered by two or three outstretched fingers, then consider that there probably exists a way to rewrite the claim that will protect the invention, avoid the prior art you are aware of, and put the claim below the two- or three-finger maximum. One reason to do this is because the rewritten claim will likely be broader. Again, the shorter the claim is, the broader it is. Likewise, of course, such broad claims must be adequately supported with multiple embodiments of varying scope to reduce the risk of a court reading limitations into the claims or finding the claim invalid for want of written description, although, again, this will be discussed in later sections of this book.

> If the independent claim you draft cannot be covered by two or three outstretched fingers, then there probably exists a way to rewrite the claim that will protect the invention, avoid the prior art you are aware of, and put the claim below the two- or three-finger maximum.

3.22 Indirect Infringement

Direct versus indirect infringement was previously touched upon.[137] Basically, making, using, selling, importing or offering to sell a product that literally meets all the elements and limitations recited in a patent claim amounts to literal, direct infringement; making, using, selling, importing or offering to sell a component of a patent claim in which the patent claim recites several components, as an example, may result in indirect infringement, if other requirements, as discussed later, are met.

As mentioned, a claim of direct infringement is a much easier claim to assert. Indirect infringement requires intent and has additional requirements. Thus, a component claim is generally more valuable against a component manufacturer, as a direct patent infringement claim, and a system level

137. *See* Chapter 1, particularly section 1.211 and its subsections.

claim is generally more valuable against a system integrator, as a direct patent infringement claim.[138]

The basis for indirect patent infringement is statutory sections 271(b) and (c), which state:

> (b) Whoever actively induces infringement of a patent shall be liable as an infringer;
>
> (c) Whoever offers to sell or sells within the United States or imports into the United States a component of a patented machine, manufacture, combination or composition, or a material or apparatus for use in practicing a patented process, constituting a material part of the invention, knowing the same to be especially made or especially adapted for use in an infringement of such patent, and not a staple article or commodity of commerce suitable for substantial noninfringing use, shall be liable as a contributory infringer.

In general, these sections are directed to someone who in some manner aids and abets a direct infringer but does not otherwise directly infringe the patent claim at issue. Hence, the name "indirect infringement." As with direct infringement, this infringement may occur literally or nonliterally.

The rationale for liability for indirect infringement is that an indirect infringer furthers direct infringement and should be jointly and severally liable as a joint tortfeasor. Hence, unlike direct infringement, which has no intent requirement, indirect infringement does have an intent requirement. That is, to be liable, one has to at least knowingly aid and abet direct infringement by a direct infringer. The logical basis for this comes from the basic principles of tort law.

In general, there are two types of indirect patent infringement:[139] contributory patent infringement and inducing patent infringement. The latter is governed by 271(b) and the former is governed by 271(c), both were introduced in the 1952 patent statute, a major milestone in terms of the statutory origins of U.S. Patent Law. The legislative history of these provisions indicates that they are a codification of previous case law.[140]

---

138. *Id.*

139. This is distinguished from imputed patent infringement, which is yet another type of patent infringement. For example, if an employee infringes a patent, that infringement may be imputed to the employer. Likewise, acts of a subsidiary company may be imputed to the parent company. *See* Emma Tracy, *Imputed Liability: How to Determine When Parent Companies Should Be Held Liable for the Patent Infringements of Their Subsidiary Companies*, 82 Mo. L. Rev. (2017), https://scholarship.law.missouri.edu/mlr/vol82/iss2/13.

140. *See, e.g.*, Hewlett-Packard Co. v. Bausch Lomb Inc., 909 F.2d 1464 (Fed. Cir. 1990).

3.221 A Claim for Indirect Infringement Is Harder to Prove Because It Requires Knowledge of the Patent and Knowledge That the Acts Contributed to or Induced Would Be Infringing; thus, Attempt to Draft Claims That Will Be Directly Infringed

If possible, it is best to draft claims that are directly infringed rather than indirectly infringed. Cases for indirect infringement are much harder to establish in federal court. In general, for a claim of indirect infringement, you must prove the same case elements as direct infringement *and* also additional case elements. It is well established that direct infringement must *necessarily* be present to have a claim for indirect infringement.[141]

Appreciate that without direct infringement, there would be no patent infringement that the indirect infringer induced or contributed to; hence, it is fundamental that direct infringement must necessarily be shown to make out a case for indirect infringement.[142] However, direct infringement may be proven with circumstantial evidence.[143] Due to these additional case elements to establish a claim, there is much less case law regarding indirect patent infringement than direct patent infringement.

In addition, proving indirect infringement requires proving that the indirect infringer at least knowingly engaged in the acts that constituted the indirect infringement and knew that direct infringement would result.[144] Although, again, this may be proven by circumstantial evidence.[145]

Thus, it must be proven that the indirect infringer knew of the patent, and, further, that the acts being induced or contributed to would have resulted in infringement. Generally, contributory infringement requires knowledge. The statute, 271(c), expressly states (emphasis supplied):

> Whoever offers to sell or sells within the United States or imports into the United States a component of a patented machine, manufacture, combination

---

141. *Id.* However, it remains somewhat unclear whether the direct infringement must precede the indirect infringement. *See* Fina Rsch., S.A. v. Baroid Ltd., 141 F.3d 1479, 1485, 46 USPQ2d 1461, 1467 (Fed. Cir. 1998) ("[W]e decline . . . to create a per se rule that an actual controversy predicated only on induced infringement may exist only if direct infringement has already occurred."). *Cf.* Waymark Corp. v. Porta Sys. Corp., 245 F.3d 1364 (Fed. Cir. 2001) regarding liability under section 271(f)(2) for exportation of a component, in which the court noted that "infringement without a completed infringing embodiment is not the norm in patent law, but it is reasonable in the context of 271(f)(2)."

142. *See, e.g.,* Aro Mfg. Co. v. Convertible Top Replacement Co., 377 U.S. 476 (1964).

143. Cases involving indirect infringement have permitted circumstantial evidence of direct infringement. *See, e.g.,* R&L Carriers, Inc. v. Pitt Ohio Express, Inc., 681 F.3d 1323 (Fed. Cir. 2012).

144. *See* Commil USA, LLC v. Cisco Sys. 575 U.S. 632, 135 S. Ct. 1920 (2015).

145. *See* Water Technologies Corp. v. Calco, Ltd., 850 F.2d 660 (Fed. Cir. 1988).

> or composition, or a material or apparatus for use in practicing a patented process, constituting a material part of the invention, **knowing** the same to be especially made or especially adapted for use in an infringement of such patent, and not a staple article or commodity of commerce suitable for substantial noninfringing use, shall be liable as a contributory infringer.

In contrast, 271(b) does not specify a level intent. It states:

> Whoever actively induces infringement of a patent shall be liable as an infringer.

Over the years federal circuit law has not been entirely consistent as to the level of intent needed for inducement; however, the Supreme Court appears to have resolved that contributory infringement and inducing infringement require the same level of intent, that is, knowledge rather than purposeful conduct.[146]

3.2211 Contributory Infringement

As mentioned, contributory patent infringement is defined by statute. Typically, it involves sale of a component especially designed for use in a patented combination or process. The statute specifies the elements for a claim of such infringement:

> [1] a component of a patented machine, manufacture, combination or composition, or a material or apparatus for use in practicing a patented process, [2] constituting a material part of the invention, [3] knowing the same to be especially made or especially adapted for use in an infringement of such patent, and [4] not a staple article or commodity of commerce suitable for substantial noninfringing use . . .

As mentioned, direct infringement is a perquisite for indirect infringement. If this is not capable of being proven, then there is no claim for indirect infringement, although, as mentioned, direct infringement may be proven with circumstantial evidence.[147]

As the statute makes clear, contributory infringement relates to supplying a component of a patented invention (i.e., a component of a patent

146. *See* Life Technologies Corp. v. Promega Corp., 137 S. Ct. 734 (2017), in which the Supreme Court stated in a footnote that, in the Global-Tech case, it had "substantially equat[ed] the intent requirements for §§ 271(b) and 271(c)."

147. *See, e.g.*, Refac Int'l, Ltd. v. IBM, 798 F.2d 459, 460, 230 USPQ 537 (Fed. Cir. 1986). *Cf.* Waymark Corp. v. Porta Sys. Corp., 245 F.3d 1364 (Fed. Cir. 2001) regarding liability under section 271(f)(2) for exportation of a component, in which the court noted that "infringement without a completed infringing embodiment is not the norm in patent law, but it is reasonable in the context of 271(f)(2)."

claim), typically as a sale, although the statute also recites offer for sale and importation. Likewise, the intent element requires that the party supplying the component for a patented combination, for example, know both that the combination is patented and infringing.[148] Intent, however, may be proven by circumstantial evidence, as mentioned.[149]

The component must also (1) be specially made so as to result in infringement in the combination, (2) *not* be capable of substantial noninfringing use (i.e., not be a staple article of commerce), and (3) be a material part of the invention. Very few cases construe the material part requirement. Generally, if a component meets the requirements of being specially made to infringe and being not capable of substantial noninfringing use, it will likely constitute a material part.[150]

3.22111 Non-Staple Articles of Commerce

If the component is capable of substantial noninfringing use, there would be no liability for contributory infringement; however, there may be liability for inducing infringement in that instance.[151] A use that is not unusual, far-fetched, illusory, impractical, occasional, aberrant, or experimental is a substantial noninfringing use.[152] The statutory language indicates that if an article is not suitable for substantial noninfringing use, then the article is not a staple article or commodity of commerce.

A tricky issue relates to how to apply this test to a complex product that has several components, one of which is specially adapted to infringe, but in which other components are not. This issue, however, appears to have been resolved by the federal circuit. For example, in *Lucent Technologies, Inc. v. Gateway*,[153] the federal circuit indicated that the issue is "whether the 'material or apparatus' is the entire software package or just the particular tool (e.g., the calendar date-picker [the accused product in the case]) that performs the claimed method." The federal circuit stated:

---

148. *See, e.g.*, Aro Mfg. Co. v. Convertible Top Replacement Co., 377 U.S. 476 (1964).

149. *See* Metabolite Laboratories, Inc. v. Lab'y Corp. of Am. Holdings, 370 F.3d 1354, 71 USPQ2d 1081 (Fed. Cir. 2004) (A "patentee may prove such intent through circumstantial evidence.").

150. *But see* Fujitsu Ltd. v. Netgear Inc., 620 F.3d 1321 (Fed. Cir. 2010), in which an accused infringer's software product was not a material part of a patented invention, although the product was for use in a system that carried out the invention.

151. *See* subsections of section 3.2212, discussing inducing patent infringement; *see, e.g.*, Toshiba Corp. v. Imation Corp., 681 F.3d 1358 (Fed. Cir. 2012).

152. *See, e.g.*, Nalco Co. v. Chem-Mod, LLC, 883 F.3d 1337, 1357 (Fed. Cir. 2018) ("A substantial noninfringing use is any use that is 'not unusual, far-fetched, illusory, impractical, occasional, aberrant, or experimental.'").

153. 580 F.3d 1301, 1320 (Fed. Cir. 2009), *cert. denied*, 560 U.S. 935 (2010).

> One example illustrates the problem with Microsoft's approach. Consider a software program comprising five—and only five—features. Each of the five features is separately and distinctly patented using a method claim. That is, the first feature infringes a method claim in a first patent, the second feature infringes a method claim in a second patent, and so forth. Assume also that the company selling the software doesn't provide specific instructions on how to use the five features, thus taking potential liability outside the realm of § 271(b). In this scenario, under Microsoft's position, the software seller can never be liable for contributory infringement of any one of the method patents because the entire software program is capable of substantial noninfringing use. This seems both untenable as a practical outcome and inconsistent with both the statute and governing precedent.

Thus, such a situation will generally not prevent contributory infringement from being applicable, that is, for this particular case, the test was applied to the particular accused tool rather than the entire software program.[154]

3.22112 Component of a Claim

To illustrate more clearly the benefits of direct infringement over indirect infringement, we will work through a few examples. As stated, one who knowingly sells a component of a claim that is a non-staple article of commerce (i.e., not capable of substantial noninfringing use) may be liable for contributory infringement. Typically, this may involve selling a component of an apparatus claim or selling an apparatus or component capable of performing a method claim.

3.221121 Component of a Method Claim

Consider a situation involving method claim 1 from Example 3.2. This claim was introduced in Chapter 1.[155]

EXAMPLE 3.2

I claim:

1. A method of forming a virtual broadcast domain by virtually linking at least a first broadcast domain with at least a second broadcast domain in which the at least a first broadcast domain and the at least a second broadcast domain are physically separate, the method comprising:

---

154. *Cf.* Vita-Mix Corp. v. Basic Holding, Inc., 581 F.3d 1317 (Fed. Cir. 2009) (regarding contributory infringement, use was in a noninfringing manner because the claim recited "not merely additional separable features" but, instead, "defining features of the device").

155. *See* section 1.2113, discussing a network provider example.

communicating one or more signal packets between respective physically separate broadcast domains *via a gateway device* included in the respective physically separate broadcast domains, wherein the communicating the one or more signal packets comprises:

encapsulating the one or more signal packets in the respective physically separate broadcast domains to be communicated; and

communicating the encapsulated signal packets between the respective gateway devices and at least one tunnel server so that the one or more signal packets are communicated between the respective physically separate broadcast domains.

3.2211211 Illustrative Claim Example

Suppose a networking competitor to the patentee who owns the patent that includes claim 1 sells a gateway device in accordance with claim 1. For example, the competitor may establish a network for a business customer. A gateway device is really a computer loaded with software that in operation results in infringement of claim 1. Thus, in this hypothetical, the competitor sells the computers and software to establish the virtual broadcast domain recited in claim 1.

The business customer for whom the network was established is a direct infringer such that the aspect of a claim to contributory infringement requiring direct infringement is met. The patentee may sue both the business customer and the competitor. However, the patentee may be more interested in suing or stopping the competitor than the competitor's customer. Perhaps, the patentee only sues the competitor, for example. Note that the competitor is fully liable for the customer's direct infringement. That is, as joint tortfeasors, the customer and competitor are joint and severally liable.

The patentee must also establish that the competitor knew of the patent and knew that use of the component would result in infringement of the method claim. Unless the patentee specifically provided notice to the competitor previously, the patentee may be out of luck. It may be that the competitor did not know of the patent at the time it sold the gateway device and, perhaps, assembled the network. For example, the patentee may have found out about the network after it was created and then put the competitor on notice. *Of course, the direct infringement likely continues through use of the network. However, direct patent infringement alone, of course, does not establish contributory infringement.* Unless the competitor sets up another network resulting in use *after* being put on notice or there is a basis to believe the competitor will continue sales of such networks/gateway devices that result in use *after* being put on notice, the intent needed would not be present. Thus, intent or knowledge is a significant hurdle to establish a claim for contributory infringement.

It, however, is pretty clear that the gateway device is a material part of the invention since it implements much of the functionality claimed.

Even assuming "knowledge" could be established, there remains the issue of substantial noninfringing use. There is little doubt that a computer loaded with networking software is capable of doing things other than infringe claim 1. Thus, the competitor will argue that the product sold, the gateway device, is a staple article of commerce.

Fortunately, *Lucent v. Gateway*[156] supports the argument for contributory infringement despite the potential for these other capabilities. Likewise, one could simply take the position that the networking software, rather than the gateway device, meets the elements for contributory infringement. However, it may be that the networking software itself has substantial noninfringing uses. This is clearly an issue needing resolution. Thus, contributory infringement here is not necessarily a slam dunk. There are significant factual issues that impact the legal analysis requiring investigation and resolution.

Now, compare the preceding situation, with asserting a claim directed only to the gateway device or only to the software. Here, for example, is a claim from Chapter 1[157] directed to the gateway device.

I claim:

1. An apparatus comprising:

   at least one gateway device of at least a first broadcast domain, wherein the at least one gateway device is to perform a network operation of discovery of any other network devices of the at least a first broadcast domain;

   wherein the at least one gateway device is to emulate one or more network devices of at least a second broadcast domain; and

156. *See* discussion of this case in the immediately preceding section.
157. *See* section 1.2113, discussing a network provider example.

> wherein the at least one gateway device is to encapsulate one or more signal packets within the at least a first broadcast domain to be directed to a network device of the at least a second broadcast domain and is to communicate the encapsulated one or more signal packets to at least one tunnel server.

Here, there is no requirement of intent or of no substantial noninfringing use.

Likewise, here is a claim from Chapter 1 directed to the networking software.[158]

I claim:

An article comprising: a non-transitory storage medium;

> wherein the storage medium includes stored thereon executable instructions; and
>
> wherein the instructions are executable to: emulate one or more network devices of at least a second broadcast domain, encapsulate one or more signal packets from at least a first broadcast domain to be directed to a network device of the at least a second broadcast domain, and communicate the encapsulated one or more signal packets to at least one tunnel server.

These example claims are much easier to assert and prove regarding direct infringement than the method claim at the beginning of Example 3.2 regarding contributory infringement. While claims for indirect infringement certainly have value, it should be apparent that to provide good representation one should try to craft claims, assuming the client approves and has available budget, of course, that would be directly infringed, even if those claims are directed to a component, rather than to the ultimate end product.

3.221122 Component of an Apparatus Claim

Now consider a situation involving apparatus claim 1 from Example 3.3.[159]

---

158. *See* section 1.2113, discussing a network provider example.

159. This was another example from Chapter 1.

EXAMPLE 3.3

I claim:

1. An apparatus comprising:

random access memory (RAM), a memory controller, a central processing unit (CPU), and a system bus;

wherein the memory controller is capable of initiating burst mode operation based, at least in part, on receipt of a request from the CPU;

wherein the request is to include a memory address, a word count, and a read or a write control transfer designation; and

wherein the memory controller is to process the request and take control of the system transfer bus.

3.2211221 Illustrative Claim Example

For this situation, consider a competitor who is selling memory with a memory controller[160] that would infringe claim 1 of Example 3.3 if combined with the other claim elements in the manner recited in that claim. The analysis may be quite similar to the last example, although the facts may, of course, affect the analysis. First, imagine that a memory manufacturer who competes with a patentee memory manufacturer supplies the memory and memory controller to a company that integrates this into a computing system with a CPU, system bus, and so on. Again, direct infringement is established by the activities of the company that performs the integration. However, the patentee may not want to sue that party, who may even be a current customer. Rather, the patentee would prefer to sue its competitor, another memory manufacturer.

Now, a much trickier situation might be if the company performing integration is a foreign entity performing the integration outside the United States. Technically, there is no infringement under section 271(a) by virtue of the assembly abroad, thus, meaning no indirect infringement under 271(c).[161]

160. The claim might have been limited to the memory controller, but it would be unusual to sell a memory controller without the memory it is intended to operate on the same integrated circuit.

161. *See* Deepsouth Packing Co. v. Laitram Corp., 406 U.S. 518, 528 (1972).

However, fortunately, there are other subsections of section 271 to address this.[162]

Assuming this is not a foreign entity situation, much like the analysis regarding the component of the method claim, the patentee must establish that the competitor knew of the patent and knew that using the component in the recited combination would result in infringement of the apparatus claim in this example. Unless the patentee specifically previously provided notice to the competitor, again, the patentee may be challenged here. It may be that the competitor did not know of the patent. For example, the patentee may have found out about a system to implement burst mode using memory and a memory controller manufactured by someone else *after* the sale. However, in this situation, in comparison with the preceding method example, *if direct infringement continues after notice is provided, then it may be possible to establish intent for contributory infringement.* That is, the competitor may provide the memory and controller for an infringing system *again to another customer after* being put on notice. The difference here from the previous example is that the claim directly infringed here is an apparatus claim rather than a method claim, in the previous example. Thus, continued direct infringement, here, that is additional sales of infringing systems, after notice, necessarily results in the intent needed for contributory infringement. On the other hand, in the previous example, continued direct infringement of a method claim after notice does not necessarily implicate intent for contributory infringement, because the competitor does not necessarily engage in another sale resulting

---

162. 35 U.S.C. § 271(f) (2022) states:

> (1) Whoever without authority supplies or causes to be supplied in or from the United States all or a substantial portion of the components of a patented invention, where such components are uncombined in whole or in part, in such manner as to actively induce the combination of such components outside of the United States in a manner that would infringe the patent if such combination occurred within the United States, shall be liable as an infringer.
>
> (2) Whoever without authority supplies or causes to be supplied in or from the United States any component of a patented invention that is especially made or especially adapted for use in the invention and not a staple article or commodity of commerce suitable for substantial noninfringing use, where such component is uncombined in whole or in part, knowing that such component is so made or adapted and intending that such component will be combined outside of the United States in a manner that would infringe the patent if such combination occurred within the United States, shall be liable as an infringer.

Section (1) is similar to inducement and section (2) is similar to contributory infringement. *See also* Waymark Corp. v. Porta Sys. Corp., 245 F.3d 1364 (Fed. Cir. 2001) regarding liability under section 271(f)(2) for exportation of a component, in which the court noted that "infringement without a completed infringing embodiment is not the norm in patent law, but it is reasonable in the context of 271(f)(2)."

in infringing use of the method claim, producing direct infringement for which notice to result in the knowledge needed for contributory infringement has been provided.

The memory and memory controller likely constitute a material part of the invention since they implement much of the functionality claimed.

Assuming knowledge could be established, as suggested, there remains the issue of substantial noninfringing use. For this situation, this issue may present a greater challenge than establishing "knowledge," discussed earlier, although it really depends on details regarding the memory controller. For example, could the memory and memory controller work with a system that does *not* implement burst mode? Have there been examples of such sales? Is it possible to turn burst mode operation *off*? These are all important questions for resolution. If the answers are yes, it may be that the memory and memory controller together are capable of substantial noninfringing use. Of course, all is not lost, because there may still be a basis for asserting a claim of inducing infringement.[163]

Now, compare the preceding situation, with asserting a claim directed only to the memory and memory controller. Following is the claim from Chapter 1 directed to memory and a memory controller.[164]

I claim:

1. An apparatus comprising:

   random access memory (RAM) and a memory controller;

   wherein the memory controller is capable of initiating burst mode operation based, at least in part, on receipt of a request from a central processing unit (CPU);

   wherein the request is to include a memory address, a word count, and a read or a write control transfer designation; and

   wherein the memory controller is to process the request and take control of a system transfer bus.

---

163. *See* section 3.2212, discussing inducing patent infringement.

164. If the memory controller is sold stand alone, then we would not have direct infringement, but, again, an indirect infringement claim. However, since memory is almost always sold with an *embedded* controller, this should not be an issue. Nonetheless, someone very conservative might prefer a claim only to the memory controller.

As suggested with the prior example, this claim avoids the potential issues associated with asserting contributory infringement. There is no need to show knowledge or that there is no substantial noninfringing use. It should be much clearer now why there is less case law on indirect infringement than direct infringement. It may be a challenge to establish indirect infringement. If one has a claim of direct infringement, that claim is more likely to be pursued. Typically, of course, both are asserted in a lawsuit if the facts for both are present.

One should also appreciate that with respect to the initial apparatus claim 1 of Example 3.3, the component sold, even assuming it is a *non*-staple article of commerce *not* capable of substantial noninfringing use (that is, it is a product that sale thereof may amount to contributory infringement) is technically an *unpatented* product, if sold by itself. As such, before the 1952 act, attempting to assert a patent claim against such a product, such as a component of a claim, in some courts, amounted to patent misuse. However, section 271(d) of the 1952 act (which remains in the current statute) clarified that bringing such a claim is no longer patent misuse.[165]

3.2212 Inducing Infringement

Section 271(b) states: "[w]hoever actively induces infringement of a patent shall be liable as an infringer." Thus, inducing patent infringement is actively and knowingly aiding and abetting the direct patent infringement of another.[166] As with contributory infringement, direct patent infringement is required for a claim of inducing patent infringement, but direct infringement may be established by circumstantial evidence.[167]

The intent requirement for inducing patent infringement has not been entirely consistent over the years but appears to have been resolved to be knowledge of the patent and knowledge that the acts induced would result in direct patent infringement.[168] Intent for indirect infringement may also be proven by circumstantial evidence.[169]

---

165. *See* Dawson Chem. Co. v. Rohm & Haas Co., 448 U.S. 176 (1980).

166. *See* Nat'l Presto Industries, Inc. v. West Bend Co., 76 F.3d 1185, 1194, 37 USPQ2d 1685, 1691 (Fed. Cir. 1996) ("The statutory liability for inducement of infringement derives from the common law, wherein acts that the actor knows will lead to the commission of a wrong by another, place shared liability for the wrong on the actor.").

167. *See* Limelight Networks, Inc. v. Akamai Technologies, Inc., 572 U.S. 915 (2014). Note that an act of indirect infringement by inducement could occur *outside* the United States and still result in liability if the induced activity was a direct infringement in the United States.

168. *See* Life Technologies Corp. v. Promega Corp., 137 S. Ct. 734 (2017), in which the Supreme Court stated in a footnote that, in Global-Tech, it had "substantially equat[ed] the intent requirements for §§271(b) and 271(c)."

169. Metabolite Laboratories, Inc. v. Lab'y Corp. of Am. Holdings, 370 F.3d 1354, 71 USPQ2d 1081 (Fed. Cir. 2004) (A "patentee may prove such intent through circumstantial evidence.").

Legislative history suggests that inducement and contributory infringement should be seen as complementary causes of action.[170] Thus, while sale of a staple article of commerce will not result in liability under section 271(c), it may, in appropriate circumstances, result in liability under section 271(b).[171]

Section 271(b) sweeps in a broad range of acts. One court articulated it as follows:

> [C]ivil culpability need not stop with the dealer who does the final act of making using, or selling. The prohibition of the law, now codified in §271(b), extends to those who induce that infringement. Of course inducement has connotations of active steps knowingly taken—knowingly at least in the sense of purposeful, intentional, as distinguished from accidental or inadvertent. But with that qualifying approach, the term is as broad as the range of actions by which one in fact causes, or urges, or encourage[s], or aids another to infringe a patent.[172]

Examples include advertising, such as advertising compliance with an infringing communications standard covered by the patent claims; providing instructions, such as distributing sales literature and manuals that instruct how to use a product in an infringing manner;[173] certain types of repair of an otherwise infringing product;[174] design of an infringing product;[175] and so on.

3.22121 Staple Articles of Commerce

If the component is capable of substantial noninfringing use there would be no liability for contributory infringement; however, there may be liability for inducing infringement.[176] Rather than a non-staple article, the component would be a staple article of commerce. That is, an article capable of substantial noninfringing uses is a staple article of commerce.

---

170. *See, e.g.*, Hewlett-Packard Co. v. Bausch Lomb Inc., 909 F.2d 1464 (Fed. Cir. 1990).

171. *Compare* Warner-Lambert Co. v. Apotex Corp., 316 F.3d 1348 (2003) ("Especially where a product has substantial noninfringing uses, intent to induce infringement cannot be inferred even when the defendant has actual knowledge that some users of its product may be infringing the patent."), *with* Toshiba Corp. v. Imation Corp., 681 F.3d 1358 (2012) ("existence of a substantial non-infringing use does not preclude liability for active inducement.").

172. *See* Fromberg, Inc. v. Thornhill, 315 F.2d 407, 411, 137 USPQ 84 (5th Cir. 1963).

173. *See* Ericsson, Inc. v. D-Link Sys., Inc. 773 F.3d 1201 (2014) (affirming a "jury's induced infringement verdict where defendant advertised compliance with an infringing standard"); Arthrocare Corp. v. Smith & Nephew, Inc. 406 F.3d 1465 (2005) (affirming a "jury's induced infringement verdict where defendant distributed 'sales literature' and 'manuals' that instructed how to use product in infringing manner").

174. *See, e.g.*, Aro Mfg. Co. v. Convertible Top Replacement Co., 377 U.S. 476 (1964).

175. *See* Ricoh Comp., Ltd. v. Quanta Comput. Inc., 550 F.3d 1325, 1342–43 (Fed. Cir. 2008), *cert. denied*, 129 S. Ct. 2864 (2009).

176. *See, e.g.*, Toshiba Corp. v. Imation Corp., 681 F.3d 1358 (Fed. Cir. 2012).

Sale of a staple article by itself, even with knowledge that it will be used in a manner that will directly infringe a patent claim, is not sufficient to establish liability for inducing infringement.[177] However, additional activities may be sufficient, such as the previous examples. For example, encouraging use in a manner that will directly infringe with the appropriate knowledge, such as via instructions, as one example, is sufficient.[178]

Thus, it is not required that a *non*-staple article of commerce be sold in order to make out a claim for indirect infringement.

3.22122 Inducing Infringement of a Method Claim

Consider a situation involving method claim 1 from Example 3.4.

EXAMPLE 3.4

I claim:

1. A method of forming a virtual private network comprising:

   communicating one or more signal packets between respective physically separate broadcast domains via a gateway device included in the respective physically separate broadcast domains, wherein the communicating the one or more signal packets comprises:

   encapsulating the one or more signal packets in the respective physically separate broadcast domains to be communicated; and

   communicating the encapsulated signal packets between the respective gateway devices and at least one tunnel server so that the one or more signal packets are communicated between the respective physically separate broadcast domains.

---

177. *See* Takeda Pharma. U.S.A., Inc. v. West-Ward Pharma. Corp., 785 F.3d 625 (Fed. Cir. 2015); Tegal Corp. v. Tokyo Electron Co., Ltd., 248 F.3d 1376, 58 USPQ2d 1791 (Fed. Cir. 2001) ("Facilitation . . . In the absence of a showing of control over another party, merely permitting that party to commit infringing acts does not constitute infringement, and it likewise cannot constitute 'facilitating infringing acts.'").

178. *See, e.g.*, Arthrocare Corp. v. Smith & Nephew, Inc. 406 F.3d 1465 (2005) (affirming a "jury's induced infringement verdict where defendant distributed 'sales literature' and 'manuals' that instructed how to use product in infringing manner").

3.221221 Illustrative Claim Example

Again, suppose a networking competitor to the patentee who owns the patent, that is, that includes claim 1, provides instructions to a business customer on implementation of a gateway device in accordance with claim 1. Again, a gateway device is really a computer loaded with software that in operation results in infringement of claim 1. The competitor may not necessarily sell the computers and software to establish the virtual broadcast domain recited in claim 1 but may direct a customer to a source along with implementation instructions or may perform the assembly once the appropriate components are purchased.

Now, the business customer for whom this network is established is a direct infringer such that the aspect of a claim to inducing infringement requiring direct infringement is met. Thus, the patentee may sue various parties, including the business customer, the networking competitor, and the party supplying the hardware and software. Note that all these parties, some with requisite intent,[179] are fully liable, that is, as joint tortfeasors, the parties are joint and severally liable, but the patentee gets to choose whether to sue one, some, or all.

The patentee must establish that the parties (other than the direct infringer) being sued knew of the patent and that assembly or implementing the instructions would result in infringement of the method claim. However, it may be that no one involved knew of the patent initially. If the patentee found out about the network after it was established and then put the parties on notice, the direct infringement may continue, as in prior examples.

However, this does not address the issue regarding intent or knowledge regarding the inducement claim. This element would not be met unless another network is set up and sold by the parties resulting in infringing use *after* being put on notice or if there is a basis to believe the parties will continue to perform assembly or distribute instructions resulting in infringing use *after* being put on notice. Thus, as with contributory patent infringement, intent or knowledge is a significant hurdle to establish a claim for inducing patent infringement.

However, unlike contributory infringement, there is no need to establish the lack of substantial noninfringing uses. This is helpful here because factual issues remain, as previously described, regarding whether this could be satisfied to meet contributory infringement.

179. No intent is required for the direct infringer.

Now, again, compare the preceding situation, with asserting a claim directed only to the gateway device or only to the software. Following is a claim directed to the gateway device from Chapter 1.

I claim:

1. An apparatus comprising:

   at least one gateway device of at least a first broadcast domain, wherein the at least one gateway device is to perform a network operation of discovery of any other network devices of the at least a first broadcast domain;

   wherein the at least one gateway device is to emulate one or more network devices of at least a second broadcast domain; and

   wherein the at least one gateway device is to encapsulate one or more signal packets within the at least a first broadcast domain to be directed to a network device of the at least a second broadcast domain and is to communicate the encapsulated one or more signal packets to at least one tunnel server.

Here, there is no requirement of intent to establish.

Likewise, following is a claim directed to the networking software from Chapter 1.

I claim:

1. An article comprising: a non-transitory storage medium;

   wherein the storage medium includes stored thereon executable instructions; and

   wherein the instructions are executable to: emulate one or more network devices of at least a second broadcast domain, encapsulate one or more signal packets from at least a first broadcast domain to be directed to a network device of the at least a second broadcast domain, and communicate the encapsulated one or more signal packets to at least one tunnel server.

These claims are much easier to assert and prove, again, relative to proving inducing infringement for the initial claim 1 of Example 3.4. While claims for indirect infringement, again, have value, it should be apparent that to provide good representation one should try to craft claims, with client approval and available budget, that would be directly infringed, even if those claims are directed to a component, rather than the ultimate end product.

3.22123 Inducing Infringement of an Apparatus Claim

Now consider another situation involving apparatus claim 1 from Example 3.3.

EXAMPLE 3.3

I claim:

1. An apparatus comprising:

   random access memory (RAM), a memory controller, a central processing unit (CPU), and a system bus;

   wherein the memory controller is capable of initiating burst mode operation based, at least in part, on receipt of a request from the CPU;

   wherein the request is to include a memory address, a word count, and a read or a write control transfer designation; and

   wherein the memory controller is to process the request and take control of the system transfer bus.

3.221231 Illustrative Claim Example

For this situation, consider, again, a competitor who is selling memory with a memory controller[180] that would infringe claim 1 if combined with the other claim elements in the manner recited. As before, a memory manufacturer who competes with a patentee memory manufacturer supplies the memory and memory controller to a company that integrates this into a computing system with a CPU, system bus, and so on. Again, direct infringement is established by activities of the company that performs the integration. However, again,

180. The analysis might be limited to the memory controller but it would be unusual to sell a memory controller without the memory if it is intended to operate embedded on the same integrated circuit.

the patentee may not want to sue that party, who may even be a current customer. Rather, the patentee would like to sue its competitor.

As before, if the company performing the integration is a foreign entity performing the integration outside the United States, technically, there is no infringement under section 271(a) by virtue of the assembly abroad, thus, meaning no indirect infringement under section 271(b).[181] However, fortunately, there are other subsections of 271 to address this.[182]

Assuming this is not a foreign entity situation, for inducing infringement, as for contributory infringement, the patentee must establish that the competitor knew of the patent and knew that using the component in the recited combination would result in infringement of the apparatus claim in this example. It may be that the competitor did not know of the patent. For example, the patentee may have only *after* sale found out about a system to implement burst mode using memory and a memory controller manufactured by someone else and then provided notice. However, in this situation, in comparison with the previous method example, if direct infringement continues after notice is provided, which is reasonably likely, then it may be possible to establish intent. That is, the competitor will likely provide the memory and controller for an infringing system again *after* being put on notice. Continued direct infringement of the previous method claim, in comparison, does not necessarily provide a basis for asserting inducement (unless by an infringing sale) if the knowledge was not present at the time of the inducement.

---

181. *See* Deepsouth Packing Co. v. Laitram Corp., 406 U.S. 518, 528 (1972).
182. 35 U.S.C. § 271(f) (2022) states:

> (1) Whoever without authority supplies or causes to be supplied in or from the United States all or a substantial portion of the components of a patented invention, where such components are uncombined in whole or in part, in such manner as to actively induce the combination of such components outside of the United States in a manner that would infringe the patent if such combination occurred within the United States, shall be liable as an infringer.
>
> (2) Whoever without authority supplies or causes to be supplied in or from the United States any component of a patented invention that is especially made or especially adapted for use in the invention and not a staple article or commodity of commerce suitable for substantial noninfringing use, where such component is uncombined in whole or in part, knowing that such component is so made or adapted and intending that such component will be combined outside of the United States in a manner that would infringe the patent if such combination occurred within the United States, shall be liable as an infringer.

Section (1) is similar to inducement and section (2) is similar to contributory infringement. *See also* Waymark Corp. v. Porta Sys. Corp., 245 F.3d 1364 (Fed. Cir. 2001) regarding liability under section 271(f)(2) for exportation of a component, in which the court noted that "infringement without a completed infringing embodiment is not the norm in patent law, but it is reasonable in the context of 271(f)(2)."

As was noted for section 271(c), assuming knowledge could be established, there may be decent arguments of substantial noninfringing uses for the memory and memory controller depending on the facts.[183] Thus, there may be no claim of contributory infringement.

Nonetheless, this may be an inducing infringement situation, under section 271(b). It is likely that with the memory and memory controller instructions on use are provided. If so, it is well established, assuming the requisite knowledge, this is sufficient to establish inducing infringement.[184]

Now, compare the preceding situation, with asserting a claim directed only to the memory and memory controller. Following is the claim from Chapter 1 directed to memory and a memory controller.[185]

I claim:

1. An apparatus comprising:

   random access memory (RAM) and a memory controller;

   wherein the memory controller is capable of initiating burst mode operation based, at least in part, on receipt of a request from a central processing unit (CPU);

   wherein the request is to include a memory address, a word count, and a read or a write control transfer designation; and

   wherein the memory controller is to process the request and take control of a system transfer bus.

As suggested with the prior example, this claim avoids the potential issues associated with proving intent or active inducement. One should also appreciate that the component sold (even assuming, for example, it's a staple

183. *See* discussion in section 3.22 and its subsections addressing this issue.

184. *See, e.g.*, Arthrocare Corp. v. Smith & Nephew, Inc. 406 F.3d 1465 (2005) (affirming a "jury's induced infringement verdict where defendant distributed 'sales literature' and 'manuals' that instructed how to use product in infringing manner").

185. If the memory controller is sold stand-alone, then we would not have direct infringement, but, again, an indirect infringement claim. However, since memory is almost always, if not always, sold with an embedded controller, this should not be an issue. Nonetheless, someone very conservative might prefer a claim only to the memory controller.

article of commerce capable of substantial noninfringing use) is nonetheless an *unpatented* product with respect to initially presented claim 1 of Example 3.3. Before the 1952 patent act, attempting to assert a patent against such a product, in some courts, amounted to patent misuse. However, section 271(d) (which remains in the current statute) clarified that bringing such a claim is not patent misuse.[186]

3.23 Claim Drafting Principles Based on DOE Framework

Previously, direct, literal patent infringement was discussed along with claim drafting principles that emanate from legal doctrines associated with direct, literal infringement and claim construction. Now, we discuss direct, nonliteral patent infringement, also known as the doctrine of equivalents (DOE), and principles for claim drafting that emanate from legal doctrines around the DOE.

We begin with an overview of the DOE. As with indirect patent infringement, the DOE introduces more legal hurdles to finding patent infringement than direct, literal patent infringement. Thus, the latter is preferred. Nonetheless, the world of patent infringement is not always ideal. For example, a case filed as a claim for direct, literal infringement may become a DOE case after some discovery. Generally, claims under the DOE are today viewed as weaker than claims for literal infringement. Notably, however, recently some cases under the DOE have resulted in liability.[187]

When drafting patent claims, although literal infringement is most important, there are ways to potentially increase the chances of liability under the DOE, if that should be needed, as shall be discussed.

At a high level, there are three doctrinal legal considerations that affect whether there might be liability under the DOE. The first is the function-way-result (FWR) test or the insubstantial differences test, the second is prosecution history estoppel (PHE), and the third is how the prior art may limit the scope of the DOE. For example, the federal circuit in *Pennwalt v. Durand*[188] stated (emphasis supplied):

---

186. *See* Dawson Chem. Co. v. Rohm & Haas Co., 448 U.S. 176 (1980).

187. *See* Eli Lilly & Co. v. Hospira, Inc., 933 F.3d 1320 (Fed. Cir. 2019) (narrowing amendment did not create prosecution history estoppel; no disclosure-dedication; district court did not err in finding insubstantial differences); Ajinomoto Co., Inc. v. Int'l Trade Comm'n, 932 F.3d 1342 (Fed. Cir. 2019) (affirming equivalents determination).

188. 833 F.2d 931 (Fed. Cir. 1987).

> Under the doctrine of equivalents, **infringement may be found (but not necessarily) if an accused device performs substantially the same overall function or work, in substantially the same way, to obtain substantially the same overall result as the claimed invention.** *Perkin-Elmer Corp. v. Computervision Corp.*, 732 F.2d 888, 901-02, 221 USPQ 669, 679 (Fed. Cir.), *cert. denied*, 469 U.S. 857, 105 S.Ct. 187, 83 L.Ed.2d 120 (1984); *Graver Tank*, 339 U.S. at 608, 70 S.Ct. at 856. That formulation, however, does not mean one can ignore claim limitations. As this court recently stated in *Perkin-Elmer Corp. v. Westinghouse Elec. Corp.*, 822 F.2d 1528, 3 USPQ2d 1321 (Fed. Cir. 1987):
>
> The doctrine of equivalents is limited in that the doctrine will not extend **(1) to cover an accused device in the prior art, and (2) to allow the patentee to recapture through equivalence certain coverage given up during prosecution.** *Loctite Corp. v. Ultraseal Ltd.*, 781 F.2d 861, 870, 228 USPQ 90, 96 (Fed. Cir. 1985).

Hence, this quotation outlines the three legal considerations discussed earlier. Each is described next with respect to one or more legal decisions.

3.231 Decision Examples

3.2311 Hilton-Davis Decision—Equivalence and More

Hilton-Davis[189] is a Supreme Court case that reaffirmed the DOE as a fixture of U.S. Patent Law and also reaffirmed some principles that had emerged from the federal circuit; however, it also addressed prosecution history estoppel (PHE) and introduced new principles around this latter doctrine.

Hilton-Davis and Warner Jenkins both manufactured dyes from which impurities were to be removed. Hilton-Davis' '746 patent, which issued in 1985, disclosed an improved purification process involving the "ultrafiltration" of dye through a porous membrane at pH levels between 6.0 and 9.0. The inventors limited their claim's pH element during patent prosecution after the patent examiner objected because of a perceived overlap with an earlier "Booth" patent, which disclosed an ultrafiltration process operating at a pH above 9.0. In 1986, petitioner developed its own ultrafiltration process, which operated at a pH level of 5.0.

Hilton-Davis sued for infringement of the '746 patent, relying solely on the "doctrine of equivalents," under which a product or process that does not literally infringe upon the express terms of a patent claim may nonetheless be found to infringe if there is "equivalence" between elements of the accused

189. 520 U.S. 17 (1997).

product or process and the claimed elements of the patented invention.[190] Over Warner Jenkins' objections, the equivalence issue was included among those issues sent to the jury, which found that Warner Jenkins infringed upon the '746 patent. The district court, among its rulings, entered a permanent injunction against Warner Jenkins. The en banc federal circuit affirmed, holding that the doctrine of equivalents continues to exist, that the question of equivalence is for the jury to decide, and that the jury had substantial evidence from which to conclude that petitioner's process was not substantially different from the process disclosed in the '746 patent.

The Supreme Court granted certiorari and reversed and remanded. It agreed with the federal circuit that the DOE was alive and well, rejecting various arguments that the 1952 act had eliminated it or that it should be more limited. It also addressed application of the equivalence test, including the linguistic formulation, and prosecution history estoppel (PHE).

There was disagreement on the federal circuit about whether the legal test for equivalence should be applied to a patent claim as a whole or limitation by limitation. The Supreme Court in this regard, stated[191] (bolded emphasis supplied):

> We do, however, share the concern of the dissenters below that the doctrine of equivalents, as it has come to be applied since *Graver Tank*, has taken on a life of its own, unbounded by the patent claims. There can be no denying that the doctrine of equivalents, when applied broadly, conflicts with the definitional and public-notice functions of the statutory claiming requirement. Judge Nies identified one means of avoiding this conflict:
>
> [A] distinction can be drawn that is not too esoteric between substitution of an equivalent for a component *in* an invention and enlarging the metes and bounds of the invention *beyond* what is claimed.
>
> Where a claim to an invention is expressed as a combination of elements, as here, 'equivalents' in the sobriquet 'Doctrine of Equivalents' refers to the equivalency of an *element* or *part* of the invention with one that is substituted in the accused product or process.
>
> This view that the accused device or process must be more than 'equivalent' *overall* reconciles the Supreme Court's position on infringement by equivalents with its concurrent statements that 'the courts have no right to enlarge a patent beyond the scope of its claims as allowed by the Patent Office.' [Citations omitted.] The 'scope' is not enlarged if courts do not go beyond the substitution of equivalent elements." 62 F. 3d, at 15731574 (dissenting opinion) (emphasis in original).

190. *See* Graver Tank & Mfg. Co. v. Linde Air Products Co., 339 U.S. 605, 609 (1950).
191. 520 U.S. 17, 28–30 (1997).

> We concur with this apt reconciliation of our two lines of precedent. **Each element contained in a patent claim is deemed material to defining the scope of the patented invention, and thus the doctrine of equivalents must be applied to individual elements of the claim, not to the invention as a whole.** It is important to ensure that the application of the doctrine, even as to an individual element, is not allowed such broad play as to effectively eliminate that element in its entirety. So long as the doctrine of equivalents does not encroach beyond the limits just described, or beyond related limits to be discussed *infra* this page and 31-34, 39, n. 8, and 39-40, we are confident that the doctrine will not vitiate the central functions of the patent claims themselves.

There was also discussion of the proper test for equivalency. The Supreme Court stated:[192]

> All that remains is to address the debate regarding the linguistic framework under which "equivalence" is determined. Both the parties and the Federal Circuit spend considerable time arguing whether the so-called "triple identity" test-focusing on the *function* served by a particular claim element, the *way* that element serves that function, and the *result* thus obtained by that element-is a suitable method for determining equivalence, or whether an "insubstantial differences" approach is better. There seems to be substantial agreement that, while the triple identity test may be suitable for analyzing mechanical devices, it often provides a poor framework for analyzing other products or processes. On the other hand, the insubstantial differences test offers little additional guidance as to what might render any given difference "insubstantial."
>
> In our view, the particular linguistic framework used is less important than whether the test is probative of the essential inquiry: Does the accused product or process contain elements identical or equivalent to each claimed element of the patented invention? Different linguistic frameworks may be more suitable to different cases, depending on their particular facts. A focus on individual elements and a special vigilance against allowing the concept of equivalence to eliminate completely any such elements should reduce considerably the imprecision of whatever language is used. An analysis of the role played by each element in the context of the specific patent claim will thus inform the inquiry as to whether a substitute element matches the function, way, and result of the claimed element, or whether the substitute element plays a role substantially different from the claimed element. With these limiting principles as a backdrop, we see no purpose in going further and micromanaging the Federal Circuit's particular word choice for analyzing

192. 520 U.S. 17, 39–40 (1997).

> equivalence. We expect that the Federal Circuit will refine the formulation of the test for equivalence in the orderly course of case-by-case determinations, and we leave such refinement to that court's sound judgment in this area of its special expertise. (emphasis in original)

While the Court expressed no particular preference as to the legal test and both the FWR (called the triple identity test by the Court) and the insubstantial differences test have both been used by the federal circuit, it appears that the FWR test is generally used more frequently.[193]

In general, regarding the FWR test, typically if there is a feature in the accused device argued to be an equivalent of a limitation, it may typically meet the substantially same "function" component of the FWR test. However, more frequently, that feature fails the substantially same "way" component of the FWR test.

This approach by the FWR test is sometimes criticized because saying the feature does not meet "substantially the same way" may simply be little more than saying it does not literally meet the limitation at issue, which will by design usually fail if the criticism is accurate. It is true that the DOE is generally considered weaker than literal infringement; however, whether the equivalent meets "substantially the same way" amounts to a judgment that comprehends the claim language, the specification description and the prosecution history.[194]

Likewise, whether the argued equivalent meets "substantially the same way," it still must also meet "substantially the same result." For example, the argued equivalent might provide an *inferior* or even a *superior* result compared with the literal claim limitation at issue.

One claim drafting guideline to deduce from the FWR test has been discussed previously in a different context. Previously, we discussed the legal issues associated with functional claiming.[195] Those considerations may be applied here.

As the discussion of the FWR test and the insubstantial differences test suggests, generally limitations that are functional are more likely to be satisfied by the accused device or service with respect to an accused device or service in which a feature is argued to be met by equivalence, assuming the

---

193. This is not based on a formal survey but is rather based on having read a number of DOE cases. *See also* Mas-Hamilton v. LaGard, 156 F.3d 1206 (Fed. Cir. 1998) ("One way to determine if substantial differences exist is to apply the function-way-result analysis of Graver Tank. . . .").

194. *See* Pennwalt v. Durand 833 F.2d 931 (Fed. Cir. 1987) (en banc).

195. *See* section 2.1111.

functional language does not result in application of section 112(f). A similar observation may be made regarding the insubstantial differences test. To the extent that the limitation is more functional than structural, for example, it seems more likely that the insubstantial differences test may be met as to an accused device or service. Based on the face of the claim, functional limitations appear to be broader than structural limitations; however, it is not always easy to predict whether such limitations will be interpreted as the words appear in the claim due to section 112(f).

Resolving this issue requires the exercise of legal judgment. Some claim terms appear to be *sufficiently* structural so as to not invoke section 112(f). Further, in some other federal circuit cases, functional language was permissibly used and did *not* invoke 112(f).[196] That is, the cases suggest that functional language may in some situations properly and appropriately be employed in claims without using the means-plus-function format of section 112(f) and without necessarily be interpreted under that subsection. Presumably, despite the functional language, the claim still recited *sufficient* structure to avoid invoking section 112(f).

With this in mind, it is suggested a mix of structural and functional language be used so that the claim language at issue is not entirely devoid of structure. Consider Example 2.3 from Chapter 2 with claim language such as:

> wherein the memory controller is capable of initiating burst mode operation based, at least in part, on receipt of an externally derived request from an external central processing unit (CPU);
>
> wherein the request is to include a memory address, a word count, and a read or a write control transfer designation; and

---

196. *See, e.g.*, K-2 Corp. v. Salomon S.A., 191 F.3d 1356, 1363 (Fed. Cir. 1999) (functional language "for substantially preventing movement" did not invoke 112(6)); BASF Corp. v. Johnson Matthey Inc., 875 F.3d 1360 (Fed. Cir. 2017) (functional phrase "effective to catalyze" did not involve 112(6)); *see also* Enzo Biochem, Inc. v. Applera Corp., 599 F.3d 1325, 1332–33 (Fed. Cir. 2010), *reh'g and reh'g en banc denied*, 605 F.3d 1347 (Fed. Cir. 2010), ("when a claim limitation is defined in 'purely functional terms,' a determination of whether the limitation is sufficiently definite is 'highly dependent on context (e.g., the disclosure in the specification and the knowledge of a person of ordinary skill in the relevant art area).'"; Miken Composites, L.L.C. v. Wilson Sporting Goods Co., 515 F.3d 1331 (Fed. Cir. 2008) (Court stated that while the term "insert" has "functional attributes," it was still a structural component); Plastic Container Corp. v. Cont'l Plastics of Oklahoma, Inc., 607 F.2d 885, 203 USPQ 27, 650, 651 (10th Cir. 1979), *cert. denied*, 444 U.S. 1018 (1980), *on remand*, 515 F. Supp. 834, 214 USPQ 530 (W.D. Okla. 1980), *aff'd in part, reversed in part*, 708 F.2d 1554, 219 USPQ 26 (10th Cir. 1983) ("the idea that functional language ipso facto cannot precisely define novelty in structure was laid to rest in In re Swinehart. . . ."); *In re* Swinehart, 439 F.2d 210, 212, 169 USPQ 226, 228 (CCPA 1971) ("[T]here is nothing intrinsically wrong with [employing functional limitations] in drafting patent claims.").

> wherein the memory controller is to process the request and take control of an external system transfer bus.

The claim, here, recites "the memory controller is capable of initiating burst mode operation" and "the memory controller is to process the request and take control of an external system transfer bus." The term "memory controller" is likely structural, but the other recited limitations are more functional; however, a memory controller may be argued to support such functions.

Example 2.6 from Chapter 2 uses a similar approach reciting "network device," a potentially structural device, but adding functional limitations such as "to emulate," "to encapsulate," and "to communicate." Again, these could be argued to be operations a network device may support. With even more attention, these positions might be made even clearer through claim language and specification language. The point, here, is to pay attention to the use of structural versus function language in the claim and attempt to use *some* functionality to increase the chances of meeting the FWR or insubstantial differences test of equivalency due to the presence of functional language while not being so functional so that 112(f) is invoked. Of course, easier said than done.

Hilton-Davis also addressed the issue of PHE. On this issue the Court stated[197] (emphasis supplied):

> We are left with the problem, however, of what to do in a case like the one at bar, where the record seems not to reveal the reason for including the lower pH limit of 6.0. In our view, holding that certain reasons for a claim amendment may avoid the application of prosecution history estoppel is not tantamount to holding that the *absence* of a reason for an amendment may similarly avoid such an estoppel. Mindful that claims do indeed serve both a definitional and a notice function, we think the better rule is to place the burden on the patent holder to establish the reason for an amendment required during patent prosecution. The court then would decide whether that reason is sufficient to overcome prosecution history estoppel as a bar to application of the doctrine of equivalents to the element added by that amendment. **Where no explanation is established, however, the court should presume that the patent applicant had a substantial reason related to patentability for including the limiting element added by amendment. In those circumstances, prosecution history estoppel would bar the application of the doctrine of equivalents as to that element. The presumption we have described, one subject to rebuttal if an appropriate reason for a required amendment is established, gives proper deference to the role of claims in defining an invention and providing public notice, and to**

197. 520 U.S. 17, 33–34 (1997).

the primacy of the PTO in ensuring that the claims allowed cover only subject matter that is properly patentable in a proffered patent application. Applied in this fashion, prosecution history estoppel places reasonable limits on the doctrine of equivalents, and further insulates the doctrine from any feared conflict with the Patent Act.

Because respondent has not proffered in this Court a reason for the addition of a lower pH limit, it is impossible to tell whether the reason for that addition could properly avoid an estoppel. Whether a reason in fact exists, but simply was not adequately developed, we cannot say. On remand, the Federal Circuit can consider whether reasons for that portion of the amendment were offered or not and whether further opportunity to establish such reasons would be proper.

3.2312 Festo *Decision—Prosecution History Estoppel*

In *Festo Corp. v. Shoketsu Kinzoku Kogyo Kabushiki*[198] the Supreme Court again took up the relationship between the DOE and PHE. *Hilton-Davis* and *Festo* together reset the law regarding PHE in the United States.

Festo Corporation owned two patents for an improved magnetic rodless cylinder, a piston-driven device that relied on magnets to move objects in a conveying system. The patent applications were amended during the prosecution proceedings. The application for the first patent, the Stoll Patent, was amended after the patent examiner rejected the initial application because the exact method of operation was unclear and some claims were made in an impermissible way. The inventor, Dr. Stoll, submitted a new application designed to meet the examiner's objections and also added certain references to cited prior art. The second patent, the Carroll Patent, was also amended during a reexamination proceeding. The prior art references were added to this amended application as well. Both amended patents added a new limitation-that the inventions contain a pair of sealing rings, each having a lip on one side, which would prevent impurities from getting on the piston assembly. The amended Stoll Patent added the further limitation that the outer shell of the device, the sleeve, be made of a magnetizable material.

After Festo began selling its rodless cylinder, respondents (referred to as SMC) entered the market with a device similar, but not identical, to the ones disclosed by Festo's patents. SMC's cylinder, rather than using two one-way sealing rings, employed a single sealing ring with a two-way lip. Furthermore, SMC's sleeve was made of a nonmagnetizable alloy. SMC's device did not fall

198. 535 U.S. 722 (2002).

within the literal claims of either patent, but Festo contended that it was so similar that it infringed under the doctrine of equivalents.

SMC, however, contended that Festo was estopped from making this argument because of the prosecution history of its patents. The sealing rings and the magnetized alloy in the Festo product were both disclosed for the first time in the amended applications. In SMC's view, these amendments narrowed the earlier applications, surrendering alternatives that are the very points of difference in the competing devices-the sealing rings and the type of alloy used to make the sleeve. As Festo narrowed its claims in these ways in order to obtain the patents, said SMC, Festo was now estopped from saying that these features are immaterial and that SMC's device is an equivalent.

Regarding PHE, the Court stated[199] (emphasis supplied):

> Prosecution history estoppel ensures that the doctrine of equivalents remains tied to its underlying purpose. Where the original application once embraced the purported equivalent but the patentee narrowed his claims to obtain the patent or to protect its validity, the patentee cannot assert that he lacked the words to describe the subject matter in question. The doctrine of equivalents is premised on language's inability to capture the essence of innovation, but a prior application describing the precise element at issue undercuts that premise. **In that instance the prosecution history has established that the inventor turned his attention to the subject matter in question, knew the words for both the broader and narrower claim, and affirmatively chose the latter.**

According to the Court, in such a situation, the question is not whether there is estoppel, but rather *the scope of the estoppel*. In this regard, the Court stated[200] (emphasis supplied):

> Just as Warner-Jenkinson held that the patentee bears the burden of proving that an amendment was not made for a reason that would give rise to estoppel, we hold here that the patentee should bear the burden of showing that the amendment does not surrender the particular equivalent in question. This is the approach advocated by the United States, see Brief for United States as *Amicus Curiae* 22-28, and we regard it to be sound. The patentee, as the author of the claim language, may be expected to draft claims encompassing readily known equivalents. A patentee's decision to narrow his claims through amendment may be presumed to be a general disclaimer of the territory between the original claim and the amended claim. *Exhibit Supply*, 315 U. S., at 136-137 ("By the amendment [the patentee] recognized and emphasized

199. 535 U.S. 722, 733–34 (2002).
200. *Id.* at 740–41.

> the difference between the two phrases and proclaimed his abandonment of all that is embraced in that difference"). **There are some cases, however, where the amendment cannot reasonably be viewed as surrendering a particular equivalent. The equivalent may have been unforeseeable at the time of the application; the rationale underlying the amendment may bear no more than a tangential relation to the equivalent in question; or there may be some other reason suggesting that the patentee could not reasonably be expected to have described the insubstantial substitute in question. In those cases the patentee can overcome the presumption that prosecution history estoppel bars a finding of equivalence.**

It therefore should be reasonably clear from the prior discussion that (1) a claim should not be amended in a manner which is narrowing *unless* absolutely required, especially if addressing formalities unrelated to prior art; and (2) the record should clarify the rationale for an amendment, especially if a claim is being narrowed, so that it might be possible to later argue the estoppel is not a complete bar to all equivalents because "[t]he equivalent may have been unforeseeable at the time of the application; the rationale underlying the amendment may bear no more than a tangential relation to the equivalent in question; or there may be some other reason suggesting that the patentee could not reasonably be expected to have described the insubstantial substitute in question."[201]

3.2313 Dolly v. Spalding *Decision—Interpreting Claim Language to Exclude Equivalents*

An important aspect related to claim drafting and the DOE is illustrated by *Dolly v. Spalding*.[202] *Dolly* predates the Supreme Court decisions just discussed but remains a feature of DOE jurisprudence that the federal circuit has repeated in various cases over the years. It illustrates that it is important to draft a good claim of literal scope not only because the DOE is generally a weaker claim than literal infringement, but also because drafting a narrow claim may also have the undesired effect of restricting the range of equivalents available, if any. After *Dolly*, the federal circuit in a later case clarified that application of the DOE is the exception, rather than the rule.[203] These cases have consistent themes—it is that the precise claim limitations matter. The DOE is not a license to erase such limitations. Thus, the claim drafting

---

201. For a recent example of disclaimer, *see* Genuine Enabling Tech. LLC v. Nintendo Co., Ltd., 2022 WL 982246, — F.4th — (Fed. Cir. Apr. 1, 2022).

202. 16 F.3d 394 (Fed. Cir. 1994).

203. *See, e.g.*, Schoell v. Regal Marine Indus., Inc., 247 F.3d 1202, 1210 (Fed. Cir. 2001).

principle, previously articulated in a different context,[204] is to *draft the broadest claim of literal scope that the prior art will permit (depending somewhat on context).*

The *Dolly* case concerned a patent that disclosed a portable, adjustable child's chair that also served as a booster seat or a highchair. The '638 patent carried the title "Portable Adjustable Child's Chair." The claimed chair had a series of channels into which the seat panels would slide, thereby adjusting the seat height to accommodate a growing child. The chair also had a detachable tray, means for retaining the child in the seat, and means for securing the chair to a standard kitchen chair for use as a highchair.

Claim 19, the only claim at issue, was dependent upon claims 16 and 17. Claims 16, 17, and 19 stated:

> 16. A portable adjustable child's chair, comprising:
>
> (a) a contoured seat panel;
>
> (b) a contoured back panel;
>
> (c) two side panels having on their inner surfaces facing each other a plurality of generally horizontal grooves or channels to slidably receive said seat panel whereby said seat panel may be raised or lowered; and
>
> (d) a stable rigid frame which is formed in part from said side panels and which along with said seat panel and said back panel provides a body supporting feature, said stable rigid frame being self-supporting and free-standing, whereby said child's chair is readily portable and easily stored.
>
> 17. The portable adjustable child's chair of claim 16 further comprising:
>
> a serving tray; and
>
> means for removably attaching said tray to said child's chair.
>
> ....
>
> 19. The portable adjustable child's chair of claim 17 further comprising means for retaining the occupant in said child's chair and means for securely attaching said child's chair to an existing chair or other support.

Evenflo produced the "Snack & Play" chair, a portable adjustable child's chair that also converted into a booster seat or highchair. The Snack & Play chair consisted of four interlocking panels, a tray, and two sets of straps. The Snack & Play chair completely disassembled for easy portability and storage. The purchaser would assemble the components to form a chair. In disassembled form, the Snack & Play chair consisted of four panels—a back panel, a

204. *See* section 1.31, discussing this principle.

seat panel, and two side panels. During assembly, the back panel tabs would slide into receiving grooves on the side panels, the seat would slide into one of three slots on the side panels and would engage a receiving slot on the back panel to make a stable chair. The seat height was adjustable because the assembler can choose from among three slots on the side panels when attaching the seat panel. The Snack & Play had no additional frame or components supporting the side, back, and seat panels.

The district court had granted a preliminary injunction to Dolly against Evenflo based on the doctrine of equivalents. The federal circuit reversed. At a high level, the principle at work is that if a patent claim is overly narrowly and/or if the invention barely gets over 103 in terms of innovation, the patent claim will be given a restricted range of equivalents, if any.[205] Specifically, the federal circuit stated[206] (emphasis supplied):

> The doctrine of equivalents cannot extend or enlarge the scope of the claims. *Wilson Sporting Goods Co. v. David Geoffrey & Assocs.*, 904 F.2d 677, 684, 14 USPQ2d 1942, 1948 (Fed. Cir.), *cert. denied*, 498 U.S. 992, 111 S. Ct. 537, 112 L. Ed. 2d 547 (1990). "The claims—i.e. the scope of patent protection as defined by the claims—remain the same and application of the doctrine expands the right to exclude to 'equivalents' of what is claimed." *Id.* The doctrine of equivalents is not a license to ignore claim limitations. *See Pennwalt Corp.*, 833 F.2d at 935.
>
> Claim 16's language requiring a stable rigid frame independent of seat and back panels is not a requirement solely for literal infringement. This limitation applies under the doctrine of equivalents as well. "Under the doctrine of equivalents, the accused device and the claimed invention cannot work in 'substantially the same way' if a limitation (including its equivalent) is missing." *Valmont Indus. v. Reinke Mfg.*, 983 F.2d 1039, 1043 n. 2, 25 USPQ2d 1451, 1455 n. 2 (Fed. Cir. 1993). The Snack & Play chair lacks a stable rigid frame separate from the panels. The Snack & Play also lacks a structure to which additional components are added to form the body supporting feature. Rather, the Snack & Play chair achieves its function without a stable rigid frame independent of the various panels. In the absence of the stable rigid frame limitation or its equivalent, the Snack & Play chair does not infringe.
>
> . . .

205. *See* Sage Products, Inc. v. Devon Indus., 126 F.3d 1420 (Fed. Cir. 1997) ("[A]s between the patentee who had a clear opportunity to negotiate broader claims but did not do so, and the public at large, it is the patentee who must bear the cost of its failure to seek protection for this foreseeable alteration of its claimed structure.").

206. *Dolly*, 16 F.3d 394 (Fed. Cir. 1994).

> **In short, the concept of equivalency cannot embrace a structure that is specifically excluded from the scope of the claims.** A stable rigid frame assembled from the seat and back panels is not the equivalent of a separate stable rigid frame which the claim language specifically limits to structures exclusive of seat and back panels. The district court erred by failing to give effect to this claim limitation in applying the doctrine of equivalents to the Snack & Play chair.

Dolly and similar cases, such as *Sage Products*,[207] therefore, illustrate that where the innovation barely manages to get over section 103 and/or the claim language is apparently narrower than needed based on simple inspection of the patent claim, then the range of equivalents, if any, will be restricted.

3.2314 Wilson Sporting Goods *Decision—Prior Art Limit on Equivalency*

Wilson Sporting Goods[208] is an important case to understand in connection with the DOE. The facts and law are complex, but we should be able to simplify the facts for these purposes.

The invention at issue concerned the arrangement of dimples on a golf ball. Apparently, the arrangement affects the distance a golf ball will go after being hit with a golf club. Golfers prefer golf balls that sail further. Wilson had sued Dunlop on its patent and obtained a ruling that the claims were valid and infringed under the DOE.

Dunlop challenged the ruling arguing that an interpretation that concludes its golf balls infringe under the DOE would violate the principle that the prior art limits the scope of equivalents under the DOE. In a well-reasoned and insightful opinion, Judge Rich set forth some key principles for making such a determination and ultimately agrees with Dunlop.

Judge Rich begins with the question: why should the prior art be a limitation on the range of permissible equivalents? According to Judge Rich (emphasis supplied):

> **The answer is that a patentee should not be able to obtain, under the doctrine of equivalents, coverage which he could not lawfully have obtained from the PTO by literal claims.** . . . Thus, since prior art always

207. *See* Sage Products, Inc. v. Devon Indus., 126 F.3d 1420 (Fed. Cir. 1997) ("[A]s between the patentee who had a clear opportunity to negotiate broader claims but did not do so, and the public at large, it is the patentee who must bear the cost of its failure to seek protection for this foreseeable alteration of its claimed structure.").

208. 904 F.2d 677 (Fed. Cir. 1990). The case was written by the esteemed Judge Rich, who was a giant in the field of Patent Law in the United States.

> limits what an inventor could have claimed, it limits the range of permissible equivalents of a claim.
>
> Whether prior art restricts the range of equivalents of what is literally claimed can be a difficult question to answer. To simplify analysis and bring the issue onto familiar turf, it may be helpful to conceptualize the limitation on the scope of equivalents by visualizing a hypothetical patent claim, sufficient in scope to literally cover the accused product. The pertinent question then becomes whether that hypothetical claim could have been allowed by the PTO over the prior art. If not, then it would be improper to permit the patentee to obtain that coverage in an infringement suit under the doctrine of equivalents. If the hypothetical claim could have been allowed, then prior art is not a bar to infringement under the doctrine of equivalents.

Hence, Judge Rich introduces hypothetical claim analysis, an invaluable tool to perform an evaluation of whether the prior art limits the scope of equivalents. The judge then states:

> The specific question before us, then, is whether Wilson has proved that a hypothetical claim, similar to claim 1 but broad enough to literally cover Dunlop's balls, could have been patentable.

He answers that with respect to the one independent claim of the patent at issue such a hypothetical claim would be unpatentable.

The judge then provides a dramatic insight regarding the dependent claims. The issue here is patent infringement. Normally, if the independent claim is not infringed that is the end of the matter. *However, Judge Rich realizes that principle only works for literal infringement, not infringement under the DOE.* The judge states (emphasis supplied):

> Before separately analyzing the asserted dependent claims, we should first explain why we are bothering to do so. This court has stated: "It is axiomatic that dependent claims cannot be found infringed unless the claims from which they depend have been found to have been infringed." *Wahpeton Canvas Co., Inc. v. Frontier, Inc.*, 870 F.2d 1546, 1553 & n. 9, 10 USPQ2d 1201, 1208 & n. 9 (Fed. Cir. 1989). While this proposition is no doubt generally correct, it does not apply in the circumstances of this case. . . . **The dependent claims, of course, are narrower than claim 1; therefore, it does not automatically follow that the ranges of equivalents of these narrower claims would encompass the prior art, because of their added limitations. . . .**

To comprehend the judge's point, consider this example. Suppose someone has a patent claim on a cycle with three wheels in accordance with the following claims:

EXAMPLE 3.5

I claim:

1. An apparatus comprising:

   a cycle including a cycle frame and three wheels attached to the cycle frame in a manner to rotate, during use of the cycle, so that the cycle is able to move forward.

2. The apparatus of claim 1, further comprising: handlebars attached to the cycle frame and a hand brake attached to one of the handlebars for at least one of the wheels.

Suppose a competitor comes out with a bicycle. We assume the claims were allowed on the first office action and that there is at least a colorable argument, such that factual issues are present to be resolved, that two wheels are the equivalent of three wheels in this context. Also assume two wheeled cycles are in the prior art.

The issue should now be reasonably clear. As to claim 1, a hypothetical claim with two wheels would very likely be unpatentable in this scenario due to the assumed prior art. However, the addition of handlebars and a hand brake in claim 2 suggests that claim 2 could potentially be infringed under the DOE without the prior art showing a two wheeled cycle necessarily limiting the scope of the DOE. For the accused product to infringe claim 2 under the DOE, it, however, should have handlebars and a hand brake.

This point leads to a claim drafting principle discussed previously[209] in an entirely different context. However, the same principle assists with potential infringement under the DOE, as discussed in a later section of this chapter.[210] The principle is to cover commercially desirable embodiments in dependent claims. Here, this makes sense since, in this manner, if those features in dependent claims are copied, it increases the chances of patent infringement under the DOE of the dependent claim with the commercial features likely to be copied, although the prior art may limit infringement under the DOE of a claim from which the claim depends.

---

209. *See* the subsections of section 2.15, discussing dependent claims.

210. *See* section 3.233, discussing using dependent claims for commercial features likely to be copied.

3.232 Focus on Literal Infringement Rather than the DOE When Drafting

Several principles for patent claim drafting emerge from the prior discussion of the DOE. First and foremost, when drafting patent claims, the focus should be on literal infringement and getting the broadest claim in terms of literal scope (depending somewhat on context), rather than focusing on the DOE. The DOE is the exception rather than the rule. It is a much harder case to make out and generally a weaker assertion than literal infringement in light of the multiple legal hurdles that exist. Understanding the DOE and being mindful about it may potentially avoid drafting overly narrow claims;[211] however, it would be the tail wagging the dog, so to speak, to sacrifice literal scope in favor of the DOE.

The principle to draft the broadest claim the prior art will allow (depending on context, of course) was previously articulated in another context.[212] Here, consideration of the DOE reaffirms that principle.

3.233 Use Dependent Claims for Commercial Aspects Most Likely to Be Copied

Another principle that emanates from our consideration of the DOE, also previously discussed in another context,[213] concerns drafting dependent claims. In general, it is prudent to include in the dependent claims commercial aspects related to the invention that are more likely to be copied.

Previously, this made sense as a fallback position in case the independent claim, for example, was of questionable validity, while potentially bolstering a claim for willful patent infringement on the right circumstances.[214]

Here, however, the previous analysis involving the DOE and hypothetical claims also suggests such an approach. For example, it may be that the prior art limits equivalents as to base claim features, which is the broadest claim with respect to literal scope. However, by including in the dependent claims features likely to be copied, it increases the chances of patent infringement under the DOE of the dependent claim with the commercial features likely to be copied, although the prior art may limit infringement under the DOE of a claim from which the claim depends. That is, a feature in the dependent claim that is copied may remove the prior art from consideration that restricted the

211. *See* section 3.234, discussing how narrow claims may limit the doctrine of equivalents.
212. *See* section 1.31, discussing the advantages and disadvantages of broad claims.
213. *See* section 2.15 and subsections thereof, discussing dependent claim considerations.
214. *Id.*

range of equivalents for the feature in the base claim believed to be infringed by an equivalent, much like illustrated with Example 3.5.[215]

3.234 Do Not Draft Claims in a Manner That Is Clearly Narrower than Needed and Easily Designed around Almost by Inspection of the Patent Claim

Dolly and similar cases, such as *Sage Products*,[216] illustrate that where the innovation barely manages to get over section 103 and/or the claim language is apparently narrower than needed by simple inspection, then the range of equivalents, if any, will be restricted. In *Dolly*, the innovation was slight *and* the claim language used was easily designed around. In *Sage*, again, the innovation was slight *and* the claim language used was easily designed around. It is well-established that the more innovative the invention, the greater the range of equivalents under the DOE.[217] Likewise, it is the limitations of a patent claim that define the invention.[218] Each limitation of a patent claim is considered material.[219] Again, form becomes substance for patent claim language.[220] Lazy or sloppy claim drafting will not only affect literal claim scope, it may also work against finding infringement by equivalents.

For example, here is the independent claim from *Sage Products:*

---

1. A disposal container comprising:
   a. a hollow upstanding container body,
   b. *an elongated slot at the top of the container body* for permitting access to the interior of the container body,
   c. barrier means disposed adjacent said slot for restricting access to the interior of said container body, at least a portion of said barrier means comprising

---

215. *See* section 3.2314, discussing prior art as a limit on the DOE.

216. *See* Sage Products, Inc. v. Devon Indus., 126 F.3d 1420 (Fed. Cir. 1997) ("[A]s between the patentee who had a clear opportunity to negotiate broader claims but did not do so, and the public at large, it is the patentee who must bear the cost of its failure to seek protection for this foreseeable alteration of its claimed structure.").

217. *See, e.g.*, Insta-Foam Prod., Inc. v. Universal Foam Sys., Inc., 906 F.2d 698, 704, 15 U.S.P.Q.2d (BNA) 1295, 1299 (Fed. Cir. 1990).

218. *See, e.g.*, Phillips v. AWH, 415 F.3d 1303 (Fed. Cir. 2005) (en banc).

219. *See* Hilton-Davis, 520 U.S. 17 (1997).

220. *See* section 2.1123, which discusses this principle.

i. a first constriction extending over said slot, and

ii. a complementary second constriction extending beneath said slot, and

d. a closure disposed adjacent said slot.

The italicized portions represent those limitations that were argued to be infringed by equivalents.

Regarding the DOE, the federal circuit affirmed the district court ruling on summary judgment that there was no infringement by equivalents. The federal circuit stated[221] (emphasis supplied):

> Once again, this case raises the question of why the law restricts application of the doctrine of equivalents without further fact finding in some cases, *see, e.g., id.; Dolly*, 16 F.3d at 400, 29 USPQ2d at 1771, while in other cases the law imposes no such restriction, *see, e.g., Hilton Davis Chem. Co. v. Warner-Jenkinson Co.*, 114 F.3d 1161, 1163-64, 43 USPQ2d 1152, 1154-55 (Fed. Cir. 1997) (in banc) (after remand from the Supreme Court; order permitting factual analysis of equivalence to stand). The claim at issue defines a relatively simple structural device. **A skilled patent drafter would foresee the limiting potential of the "over said slot" limitation. No subtlety of language or complexity of the technology, nor any subsequent change in the state of the art, such as later-developed technology, obfuscated the significance of this limitation at the time of its incorporation into the claim.** *See, e.g., Pennwalt*, 833 F.2d at 938, 4 USPQ2d at 1742 ("[T]he facts here do not involve later-developed computer technology which should be deemed within the scope of the claims to avoid the pirating of an invention."). If Sage desired broad patent protection for any container that performed a function similar to its claimed container, it could have sought claims with fewer structural encumbrances. Had Sage done so, then the Patent and Trademark Office (PTO) could have fulfilled its statutory role in helping to ensure that exclusive rights issue only to those who have, in fact, contributed something new, useful, and unobvious. **Instead, Sage left the PTO with manifestly limited claims that it now seeks to expand through the doctrine of equivalents. However, as between the patentee who had a clear opportunity to negotiate broader claims but did not do so, and the public at large, it is the patentee who must bear the cost of its failure to seek protection for this foreseeable alteration of its claimed structure.** *Cf. Maxwell v. J. Baker, Inc.*, 86 F.3d 1098,

221. *See* Sage Products, Inc. v. Devon Indus., 126 F.3d 1420 (Fed. Cir. 1997).

1108, 39 USPQ2d 1001, 1007 (Fed. Cir. 1996), *cert. denied,* ___ U.S. ___, 117 S.Ct. 1244 (1997) (discussing danger of allowing patentee to file and prosecute narrow claims and then, during the course of litigation, expand its exclusive rights under the doctrine of equivalents, thereby avoiding examination of the broad subject matter).

This court does not imply that Sage's representation before the Patent and Trademark Office was inadequate. To the contrary, it appears that the claim precisely defines the structure elaborated in the written description and drawings. The public record reflects a manifest intention to claim this structure and no more. Whether actual or constructive, that intention now binds Sage.

This court recognizes that such reasoning places a premium on forethought in patent drafting. Indeed this premium may lead to higher costs of patent prosecution. However, the alternative rule—allowing broad play for the doctrine of equivalents to encompass foreseeable variations, not just of a claim element, but of a patent claim—also leads to higher costs. Society at large would bear these latter costs in the form of virtual foreclosure of competitive activity within the penumbra of each issued patent claim. Because the doctrine of equivalents blurs the line of demarcation between infringing and non-infringing activity, it creates a zone of uncertainty, into which competitors tread only at their peril. *Cf. Markman v. Westview Instruments, Inc.,* ___ U.S. ___, 116 S.Ct. 1384, 1396 (1996) (discussing the importance of certainty in defining the scope of exclusive rights). **Given a choice of imposing the higher costs of careful prosecution on patentees, or imposing the costs of foreclosed business activity on the public at large, this court believes the costs are properly imposed on the group best positioned to determine whether or not a particular invention warrants investment at a higher level, that is, the patentees.**

In sum, the '728 patent claims a precise arrangement of structural elements that cooperate in a particular way to achieve a certain result. Devon achieves a similar result—restricted entry to a medical disposal container—but it does so by a different arrangement of elements. Because this issued patent contains clear structural limitations, the public has a right to rely on those limits in conducting its business activities. This court will not effectively remove such a limitation under a doctrine designed to prevent "fraud on a patent." Accordingly, this court affirms the judgment of the district court that Devon does not infringe the '728 patent, either literally or under the doctrine of equivalents.

3.235 Rewriting Claims Versus Amending Claims

A question may arise in the context of PHE whether it would be better to entirely rewrite a claim or to make a "surgically focused" amendment to the claim language. Before *Festo* and *Hilton-Davis*, anecdotally, there was a view among some practitioners that rewriting a claim, although much more work, might potentially create less estoppel by narrowing some parts of a newly crafted claim while at the same time broadened the claim in other ways. Whether previously true, how might such an approach play out today?

Generally, the recommendation here is to *not* worry so much about PHE and, *instead*, focus on literal scope. If a better claim in terms of scope may result from rewriting the claim, then do so. How it likely will be analyzed is substantially in accordance with *Festo*. That is, the portions narrowed may be analyzed for scope of estoppel in light of the remarks, whether the equivalent in question was foreseeable, and whether the rationale for amendment is tangentially related to the equivalent in question. Perhaps, however, if the court is unable to figure these things out, complete estoppel might be presumed. It may depend on a variety of issues tied to the language, the art and the interaction between the PTO and the patentee's legal representative.

Regardless, instead, focus on literal scope. If a focused amendment is more likely to result in allowance and a claim of broad scope, then make a focused amendment. In either case, explain the rationale for the amendment or the claim rewrite so as not to create a presumption of complete estoppel.

Certainly, rewriting the claim is more difficult. In either case, the examiner will do a new search. It may be that rewriting the claim raises enough new issues that ultimately a continuation to continue prosecution will be needed. Thus, the guidance is to do what is best to get the best patent claim of literal scope without introducing unnecessary delay due to prosecution.

Thus, the guidance is to do what is best to get the best patent claim of literal scope without introducing unnecessary delay due to prosecution.

4

PCDP Basics: Drilling Down on Claim Diversity

High-Level Principles of This Chapter:[1]

- Employ a "hedge" strategy to claiming through patent claim diversity (consider using the following claim types to enhance claim diversity: component level claims, system level claims; means plus function claims; method of using claims; method of making claims; composition of matter claims; Beauregard claims; and/or Markush Group claims);
- Draft the patent claims to expressly recite the broadest and the narrowest embodiments of the invention, including multiple claims for multiple embodiments between the broadest and the narrowest embodiments.

In the foregoing three chapters, the basics of patent claims and patent law were introduced. We also introduced a few basic claim drafting principles and provided an introduction to various types of patent claims. Having established that foundation, these next three chapters are more directly focused on the tactics and strategy of patent claim drafting practice itself. The sections are mostly organized to represent specific claim drafting principles. The sections highlight the principles and the subsections go on to provide explanation, examples, and so on, regarding the particular principles identified.

This chapter, Chapter 4, deals primarily with the fundamentals of patent claim diversity and drills down, through examples, into drafting strategies that employ the different claim types that were previously introduced. Chapter 5 deals with the basic principles of good claim drafting. Chapter 6 then deals with more advanced principles of good claim drafting.

1. *See* List of Claim Drafting Principles, Appendix A.

4.1 Employ a "Hedge" Strategy to Claiming—Use Patent Claim Diversity

As explained, at the time a patent application is filed, the patentee has one view of the prior art. However, that is a view that evolves throughout the life of a patent. During prosecution, prior art is uncovered that was not known at the time of filing. Likewise, the patent issuing is not the end of the matter. The claims of a patent are presumed valid. If the patent is challenged or asserted, then more art comes to the fore. Even after a litigation, more prior art may be uncovered in later litigations. A patent is not held valid by a court. Rather, a patent is presumed valid. A court at best may declare a patent *not invalid*. Consequently, it is still possible for validity of the patent claims to be tested.

In such a situation, a prudent drafter would be wise to employ a wide spectrum of patent claims from quite broad to quite narrow with claims also falling in the range of intermediate scope. Likewise, various claim types should be employed, and in the dependent claims, features should be mixed and matched based on judgment about which features are likely to provide strong patentability arguments and which features are likely to be copied by others who may sell similar products or provide similar services.

4.11 The Patent Claims Should Expressly Recite the Broadest and Narrowest Embodiments of the Invention, Including Multiple Claims for Multiple Embodiments between the Broadest and the Narrowest

For good practice, the patent claims should include claims of varying scope. It is specifically recommended that multiple embodiments be *disclosed and claimed*, including the broadest and the narrowest embodiments of the invention, and embodiments between the broadest and the narrowest. There are several reasons for this recommendation.

For one thing, as previously suggested, it is a good principle of claim drafting to make the drafter's intent as clear as possible from the face of the claims themselves. Drafting the claims to expressly cover multiple embodiments assists this effort. It makes clearer to others looking at the claims what is intended to be a broad claim, an intermediate claim, and a narrow claim, and how the words of the claims and the order of the claims are structured to communicate such claim breadth and claim narrowness. Of course, it is likewise important that the specification also recite these embodiments, and they be clearly understood to present examples of broad, intermediate, and narrow scope, although preferably without using such labels per se.[2]

Another advantage of this approach is that it reduces the risk of limitations being read into the claims from the specification. It is difficult to predict when a court will read a limitation from the specification into the claims and when it will not.[3]

This was done, for example, in *Toro v. White Consolidated*.[4] The federal circuit limited the term "including" to mean "permanently affixed to and included as part of. . . ." In *Toro*, the patent at issue disclosed and claimed a convertible vacuum-blower for use in vacuuming or blowing leaves and small debris, depending on the selected mode. The design employed a removable cover which was *physically attached* to a restriction ring. The restriction ring was used to increase the velocity of air in the blower mode by reducing the diameter of the air intake opening. The accused product, on the other hand, had a restriction ring *physically separate from* the cover. Therefore, because the federal circuit reached a different construction of the word "including," the federal circuit reversed the district court's summary judgment of patent infringement.

Likewise, *Watts v. XL Systems*[5] and *Wang Laboratories v. America Online*[6] were two more cases where limitations were read from the specification into the claims. Of course, these are not the only examples. For example, in *SciMed Life Systems v. Advanced Cardiovascular Systems*,[7] a claim for a catheter, having guide wire and inflation lumens that were "separate" from one another,

---

2. It is important to remember that while we recommend drafting claims as broad as the prior art will allow (depending, of course, on context), there remains uncertainty as to whether you have the closest and most relevant prior art. Thus, those intermediate and narrow claims may become quite important.

See, e.g., the recent case, Neenah, Inc. v. Schwendimann, IPR2021-00016, Paper 26 (PTAB Apr. 12, 2022), in which the Patent Trial and Appeal Board (PTAB) determined that all challenged claims were unpatentable as anticipated. The patent owner argued that the claims required each material to be present "in a sufficient amount to actually provide the desired characteristic." According to the Board, construing the claim by function would improperly import limitations into the claims.

PTAB found that, based on the language of the claims, "there is no express requirement of a specific amount of a film forming binder, a wax emulsion, or retention aid, in any of the challenged claims. Nor is there an express requirement in any of the challenged claims that the film forming binder, wax emulsion, or retention aid perform a particular function."

3. *See* section 2.1414, discussing importing claim limitations from the specification.

4. 199 F.3d 1295, 1301 (Fed. Cir. 1999).

5. 232 F.3d 877 (Fed. Cir. 2000).

6. 197 F.3d 1377 (Fed. Cir. 1999).

7. 242 F.3d 1337 (Fed. Cir. 2001).

was interpreted to read only on coaxial lumens and not side-by-side lumens. Likewise, in *Bell Atlantic v. Covad Communications*,[8] the federal circuit interpreted a claim to an ADSL data transmission system with adjustable variable rate functionality that employed the term "mode." The federal circuit interpreted the language to cover only three specific "modes" of operation recited in the specification. Furthermore, in *Renishaw v. Marposs*,[9] the federal circuit interpreted the term "when," used in a claim to a touch probe for automated manufacturing, to mean the probe was triggered as soon as possible after contact with the work piece rather than simply "at or after the time that" contact with the work piece occurred.

The point, of course, is not to list every case where a limitation was ever read from the specification into the claims, but, rather, to demonstrate that the risk this may happen is substantial. However, drafting the claims so that multiple embodiments are covered, including the broadest and the narrowest, should reduce this risk.

Because these embodiments are specifically covered in the claims, it makes it less likely that a court will read a limitation into a claim where the limitation is not specifically intended.[10] In many of the cases just cited, one of the difficulties was that the specification recited only one or only a few embodiments. This situation made it easier for the court to read limitations from the specification into the claim or claims at issue. In contrast, the more embodiments in the specification *with corresponding claims*, the more likely it is that a court will not read a limitation into a claim where that limitation is not intended.

> The more embodiments in the specification with corresponding claims, the more likely it is that a court will not read a limitation into a claim where that limitation is not intended.

Another advantage of this approach is that it reduces the risk that claims will be held invalid for lack of written description. Several well-known federal circuit cases, including *Gentry Gallery v. Berkline*,[11] *Tronzo v. Biomet*,[12] and *Toro*

8. 262 F.3d 1258 (Fed. Cir. 2001).
9. 158 F.3d 1243 (Fed. Cir. 1998).
10. *See, e.g.*, Interdigital Commons v. ITC, 690 F.3d 1315, 1324 (Fed. Cir. 2012) (The doctrine of claim differentiation disfavors reading a limitation from a dependent claim into an independent claim.).
11. 134 F.3d 1473 (Fed. Cir. 1998).
12. 156 F.3d 1154 (Fed. Cir. 1998).

v. Ariens,[13] have found patent claims to be invalid under 35 USC section 112 for failing to satisfy the written description requirement. In these cases, the court determined that the specification failed to provide support for recited limitations in the claims. This is a risk associated with disclosing a single or only a few embodiments. By, instead, describing and claiming multiple embodiments from broadest to narrowest, the risk of lack of written description is reduced because explicit textual support is provided at the time of filing, at a minimum, by the claims themselves.

By describing and claiming multiple embodiments from broadest to narrowest, the risk of lack of written description is reduced because explicit textual support is provided at the time of filing, at a minimum, by the claims themselves.

One risk avoided, then, is that a court will conclude in later litigation that added claims are broader than the specification intended to support those claims. For example, in *Gentry*, the patent related to a section sofa having two parallel reclining seats. In the embodiment disclosed in the specification, two push button recliner controls were mounted on a console positioned between the two recliners. The broadest claim at filing specified the location of the controls as upon the center console; however, claims were later added that did not specify the location of the recliner controls specifically. The federal circuit, therefore, held the later-added claims to be invalid because the patent did not support location of the recliner controls other than on the console.

The recommended approach also avoids the risk that a court will conclude that a narrow claim is not supported by the specification. For example, in *Purdue Pharma v. Faulding*,[14] the claims related to a method for treating pain by administering an analgesic. A claim added after filing related to concentration in a patient's blood (defined by a ratio) 24 hours after administration. The claim specified the ratio as greater than 2. According to the court, the examples in the specification did not emphasize this limitation as "an important defining quality of the formulation." Thus, the court held the claim invalid for failing to satisfy the written description requirement under 35 USC section 112.

13. 232 F.3d 915 (Fed. Cir. 2000) (nonprecedential).
14. 230 F.3d 1320 (Fed. Cir. 2000).

An independent advantage, of course (i.e., of having a set of claims of varying scope that includes narrow claims, intermediate claims, and broad claims), is that this increases the chances of capturing infringers while decreasing the chances of reading on the prior art. The more different ways an invention is claimed, the more opportunities exist to capture infringers that might otherwise escape liability. Likewise, even if a thorough prior art search may have taken place, there is still some uncertainty regarding whether the best and closest prior art has been found. Also, it may be that a search has not been conducted. In both instances, claiming the invention a variety of ways from broad to narrow helps mitigate that risk by providing more opportunities to avoid potentially difficult prior art that may later crop up.

> An independent advantage of having a set of claims of varying scope that includes narrow claims, intermediate claims, and broad claims is that this increases the chances of capturing infringers while decreasing the chances of reading on the prior art.

4.12 Examples of Varying Claim Types

Of course, one way to vary claim scope is to create a diverse claim set by varying scope through the language of the claim. However, in that case, often you may employ the same claim type as you linguistically vary the scope. On the other hand, by example,[15] we saw previously that you may vary the claim type, which often impacts the set of rights obtained if issued. Typically, when you vary the claim type, some linguistic accommodation of language also is made as well.

In general, then, you should create diverse claims both through linguistic changes in scope and by employing many different claim types. In this section, we discuss the most common claim types used and, where appropriate, discuss the advantages and disadvantages of each. No one claim will necessarily address all potential ways that an invention may be protected, particularly where a variety of commercial embodiments may be of interest to the market. Thus, as with varying claim scope, varying claim type is a sort of hedge considering the future uncertainty surrounding how the technology at issue might ultimately be adopted for use in the market.

15. *See* the sections and subsections of Chapter 2.

In this section, we discuss a host of claim types that may be employed to capture an invention. Specifically, we discuss component claims, system claims, means and step plus function claims, product-by-process claims, method of using claims, method of making claims, Beauregard claims, and Markush claims.[16] We have touched on many of these earlier by example, and, here, we discuss them primarily as a refresh or review of these claim types, since knowing the different types is fundamental to claim drafting, with additional illustrative examples and some added claim drafting subtleties.

4.121 Component Level Claims

In prior chapters, we have discussed the difference between component level claims and system level claims, including examples of each.[17] These concepts arise frequently enough and are important enough that we are providing additional illustrative examples of these concepts.

Previously,[18] we discussed some semiconductor technology, as follows:

A metal oxide semiconductor (MOS) transistor body made from silicon may be biased in a manner to reduce noise for analog signals being transmitted via an electrical or electronic switch that includes the transistor. MOS transistors may be P-channel (also called P-type) MOS (PMOS) transistors or N-channel (also called N-type) MOS (NMOS) transistors. For example, an electronic switch may comprise a radio frequency (RF) switch, which is used, for example, in cell phones. A similar body biasing mechanism may be used in the MOS transistor of a modulator, as may be employed in radio communications, for example.

The switch or modulator may be implemented in an integrated circuit (IC) and the IC may be part of a module. In addition to Silicon, a transistor made from Gallium Arsenide (GaAs) may be body biased to reduce noise as well for similar applications. Typically, an electronic switch has multiple signal paths, such as a path to pass an analog signal, which may be implemented as a pass gate, and a path to not pass the analog signal, which may be implemented as a shunt gate. It is a transistor in the shunt gate that is electrically body biased when OFF while the pass gate is ON to pass an analog signal. This electrical body biasing of the transistor in the shunt gate reduces noise that might otherwise corrupt the analog signal passing through the pass gate of the switch.

---

16. Jepson claims were introduced in section 2.1151 of Chapter 2 and are further discussed in section 7.5 of Chapter 7 in connection with EPO claim format issues.

17. *See* section 1.211 and its subsections, providing various illustrative examples.

18. *See* section 3.2141, discussing this example.

Following is an example component level claim, capturing a transistor capable of being appropriately electrically body biased to reduce noise that might otherwise corrupt an analog signal that might pass through a separate transistor that is close in proximity to the transistor having its body being negatively biased. Without the strong negative bias claimed, mutual electrical effects between the transistors that are close together may result in corruption of an analog signal passing through a transistor that is ON. That is, without the negative bias, negative charge may accumulate in the body of the transistor that is OFF proximate to its gate and the analog signal, that is varying, may induce movement of that negative charge within the transistor body. That charge movement, occurring in the transistor that is OFF, may then, through mutual electrical effects, corrupt the analog signal passing through the transistor that is ON.

4.1211 Illustrative Claim Example

EXAMPLE 4.1

I claim:

1. A device comprising: at least one N-type metal oxide semiconductor field effect transistor (NMOSFET), the at least one NMOSFET including a source, a gate, a drain and a body;

   wherein the at least one NMOSFET is further included in an electrical configuration at least to control the at least one NMOSFET transistor to either an OFF state or an ON state;

   wherein the electrical configuration is at least further to electrically bias the body of the at least one NMOSFET at least in a portion of the OFF state of the at least one NMOSFET to a DC voltage level substantially more negative than at least one of the following: ground, the DC voltage level of the source, and the DC voltage level of the drain.

Appreciate that in some respects this claim is rather *specific*, but in other ways it is quite *open ended*. As mentioned previously, good claims achieve a "balance between precision, breadth and vagueness."[19] The claim specifically

19. *See* section 2.141 and its subsections, discussing this principle.

covers "at least one N-type metal oxide semiconductor field effect transistor." Any device that has an NMOSFET body biased as claimed would infringe. There would not be a reason to bias an NMOSFET body as claimed, other than to avoid the signal corruption explained earlier.

However, while the claim is *clear* as to the type of transistor and to the type and amount of bias on the body, it is quite *vague* about how that bias is implemented. It states: "the at least one NMOSFET is further included in an electrical configuration" and "the electrical configuration is at least further to electrically bias the body of the at least one NMOSFET."

Furthermore, observe the use of the language "at least in a portion of the OFF state of the at least one NMOSFET." This language is to address an issue like the issue of "when" in the *Renishaw* case, previously discussed.[20] That is, it may be a challenge to legally establish that a bias is applied precisely at the time and only at the time the transistor is in the OFF state. This language makes it clear that such precise timing is not required.

As a claim to a component, this claim is extremely powerful. The transistor may be included in an electrical switch. The electrical switch may be one of many switches on an integrated circuit (IC). Although not required for infringement, all the transistors for all the switches on the IC may operate in this manner. Likewise, the IC could be included in a module and the module may be part of a consumer device, such as a cell phone, as simply one example of a consumer device that uses such switches. Note that due to the "comprising," all these things—switch, IC, module, and cellphone, would, at least theoretically, be included within the scope of the claim without being expressly "called out" as such in claim 1.

Claim 1, therefore, carries a threat of an injunction against anyone who manufactures or deals in these parts. Also, since many of these parts are manufactured abroad and imported into the United States, there may also be a threat of an exclusion order from the International Trade Commission (ITC), potentially keeping infringing parts from entering the United States.[21] Exclusion orders from the ITC are much easier to get than injunctions from a federal court. One problem, however, for such an exclusion order, may be how to distinguish infringing product from noninfringing product by inspection, since an exclusion order is enforced by U.S. Customs, who must inspect imported goods to find infringing product. Regardless, this is not a bad component claim. One would expect it to worry anyone using this technology without a patent license.

20. *See* section 2.1414, discussing the Renishaw case.
21. *See* section 3.11, discussing patent enforcement in the ITC.

One issue, however, may relate to monetary damages. One issue is royalty base. Unfortunately, the law of damages for patent infringement may be more of an art than a science. However, typically, damages may be based on a reasonable royalty rather than lost profits.[22]

Relying on the reasonable royalty remedy in the statute requires considering a hypothetical transaction.[23] In that transaction, usually there is a royalty rate and a royalty base. The royalty base represents the value of what the claim covers. So, for a chip that sells potentially for a few dollars, what is the value of a transistor on a chip that may contain tens of thousands of transistors. Considering even that the transistors in the switches of the IC may all be biased in this manner, perhaps, a few cents? Now we consider the royalty rate. Again, this is mostly speculation, but a 10 percent royalty rate might be considered on the high side. Thus, while the claim may pose quite a threat in terms of the ability to potentially stop the manufacturer or distributer, it may be less of a monetary threat, although with high product volume it might be a reasonable monetary threat.

Of course, it is easy to add dependent claims that include higher levels of integration and that would certainly be something to be done. However, quite frequently, in an assertion posture, focus is placed on the base claim, unless it is believed invalid due to art, for example. It seems like it might be a challenge to convince someone to ignore the base claim and only consider the dependent claims to determine a royalty base. In a litigation, again, this may arise as a "hypothetical" negotiation, in which many, many factors are considered.[24]

4.122 System Level Claims

There are a variety of reasons one might employ system level claims. A system integrator is, in a sense, the flip side of a component manufacturer. The two frequently have a symbiotic relationship. A component manufacturer is a supplier to a system integrator. Similarly, a system integrator is a customer of a component manufacturer. It follows many of the claim drafting considerations

---

22. Lost profits may arise, but usually does so in very specific situations. *See* 35 U.S.C. § 384 (2022). It states, in part: "Upon finding for the claimant the court shall award the claimant damages adequate to compensate for the infringement, but in no event less than a reasonable royalty for the use made of the invention by the infringer, together with interest and costs as fixed by the court."

23. *See* Finjan, Inc. v. Blue-Coat Sys., Inc., 879 F.3d 1299 (Fed. Cir. 2018); Mfg. Co. v. Briggs & Stratton Power Products Grp., 879 F.3d 1332 (Fed. Cir. 2018).

24. *See* section 6.41 and its subsections, discussing drafting patent claims with monetary damages in mind.

for system level claims overlap with claim drafting considerations for component level claims.

One may genuinely ask whether an approach of using a system level independent claim has advantages over an approach in which there is a component level independent claim, with aspects of the overall system being added via dependent claims. There are various considerations, but there is no clear answer to such a question.

One consideration may be that a system level claim may make it clearer that specific end products infringe, which may be beneficial in some circumstances. If dealing with U.S. Customs, as one example, and trying to enforce an exclusion order issued by the ITC against importation of consumer end products into the United States, a system level claim, such as to a consumer electronic device, may be much more likely to be enforced. One would not expect Customs to tear apart end products to look for infringing components. Yet, in theory at least, using dependent claims to cover the system should have this same legal advantage. That is, the dependent claims may be asserted and may also result in an exclusion order, although an independent system claim might be considered to more clearly be a system.

One might also imagine that a system that is a combination of more elements may at least arguably be more likely to be patentable. In other words, the component interactions may provide potential patentability arguments.[25] Yet, in theory at least, again, using dependent claims to cover the system should have this same legal advantage. That is, those same arguments could be made with respect to the dependent claims that might have been made regarding an independent claim that incorporates the limitations of such dependent claims.

Still, a tangible benefit may relate to how patent prosecution typically proceeds for a pending patent application. Examiners usually focus on the independent claims. An independent claim of multiple components might potentially be slightly more likely to be allowed than a dependent claim that amounts to the same elements and limitations. That is, for a simple component claim, the examiner may reject the independent claim and then, in passing, also reject the dependent claims, without much consideration,[26] even though there may be additional technical arguments in favor of patentability for the dependent claims. The patent prosecutor may, in our hypothetical, then, in a response to a rejection, make an argument regarding the dependent claims separately from the independent claim, if this happens (i.e., the

25. Although that potential benefit may not necessarily be immediately apparent in this example.

26. Granted that this may not be legally appropriate, it does happen at times.

examiner rejects the dependent claims without much consideration). At that point, however, the examiner may be reluctant to modify his decision, having previously rejected all the claims.

Both approaches have some merit, that is, an independent claim for the system and a separate component level independent claim using dependent claims to then cover the system. In some cases, therefore, a drafter may employ both approaches.[27]

Typically, a component claim is more valuable against a component manufacturer for asserting direct patent infringement and a system level claim is more valuable against a system integrator for asserting direct patent infringement. For example, a system integrator may have a contractual indemnity against patent infringement for components that it purchases. However, typically, such indemnities are limited to the part sold. One could certainly make a direct infringement claim against the system integrator with a component claim if the component is a part of the system. The component claim would be directly infringed. However, because of contractual indemnities from component manufacturers, a component claim against a system integrator may be less valuable than a system level claim.[28] The system claim may threaten the core business with no indemnity; whereas the component claim is not directed to a core business of the integrator and the integrator may have a contractual indemnity against patent infringement.

Despite these latter potential considerations, if your client is a system integrator, it may generally profess to have no interest in covering a component manufacturer and not want to incur the extra claim fees associated with employing both approaches (e.g., system claim approach and component claim approach), although employing both approaches would provide an ability to go after a component manufacturer/supplier as well as a systems integrator. Specifically, a new application is permitted three independent claims and 20 total claims before incurring extra claim fees.[29]

---

27. But not in a manner so that claim scope is identical in all respects between an independent claim of one claim set and a dependent claim of another set, which might otherwise produce a rejection.

28. *But see* section 6.4 and its subsections, discussing using higher levels of integration in claim drafting.

29. *See* Manual of Patent Examining Procedure (MPEP) § 607 (2020). This lack of interest by a system integrator may *change* if the system integrator's memory supplier expands its business to system integration and becomes a direct competitor. *See* section 1.1.

Another consideration as to the two approaches might relate to monetary damages.[30] This may matter in several ways, potentially; however, damages law is quite unclear in this regard. By claiming a system, one might, in an appropriate situation, try to argue for purposes of assessing damages that an entire market value effect occurs with sales of an entire system, potentially justifying damages be calculated using the entire system as a royalty base.[31]

In essence, the notion is that the whole is greater than the sum of the parts. This might be a reason to favor a system level claim as an independent claim, for example, in appropriate situations.[32] However, the entire market value principle is a challenge to establish legally. Damages based on a reasonable royalty tend to more frequently use the "smallest saleable unit," rather than the entire market value, as a royalty base. The smallest saleable unit, here, might be argued to be an integrated circuit, for example, which would at least be better than a transistor as a royalty base.

Consistent with the entire market value suggestion, however, one might attempt to draft a claim to potentially increase the royalty base by including language directed to a communications device, such as a wireless phone, for example, that claims a module specifically, assuming that a module is likely to be integrated. A system claim at a higher integration level, such as a consumer product, may be beneficial to assert against end products that use the system.

The strategy here is to increase the royalty base through claim drafting. Several factors affect how a court may determine royalty base for damages; however, one factor is definitely how the invention is claimed. Here, there are a variety of levels of integration one might seek to employ—switch, integrated circuit, module, communications device. The preferred level, of course, depends on likely targets.

It might be appropriate to have several system claims at different levels of integration. The two that appear promising here are the module and the communications device. Modules are common enough these days that a chip manufacturer may still be likely to integrate the chip into a module. Whereas a chip may be worth a few dollars, such as $3, a module may be worth tens

---

30. *See* section 4.1211, providing an illustrative example of dependent claims for a component level claim.

31. *See* Finjan, Inc. v. Blue-Coat Sys., Inc., 879 F.3d 1299 (Fed. Cir. 2018); Mfg. Co. v. Briggs & Stratton Power Products Grp., 879 F.3d 1332 (Fed. Cir. 2018). *See* section 6.4 and its subsections, discussing how potential for monetary damages may affect claim drafting.

32. For example, with the sample claims that follow, one might argue that the claimed mechanism to reduce noise in an analog signal drives the sale of a wireless phone. This position is not without merit.

of dollars, such as \$30 to \$50. However, a communications device would be worth hundreds of dollars at least. Thus, in this example, higher levels of integration might increase a potential royalty base by a factor of ten per level, roughly.

4.1221 Illustrative Claim Examples

EXAMPLE 4.2

I claim:

1. An RF module comprising: at least one integrated circuit chip;

   the at least one integrated circuit chip included in the RF module and further including at least one field effect transistor, the at least one field effect transistor including a gate, a drain, a source, and a body;

   wherein, during at least a portion of an off state, the body of the at least one field effect transistor is to be electrically biased to have a voltage level substantially more negative than the lowest voltage level of the following: ground, the DC voltage level of the source of the at least one field effect transistor, and the DC voltage level of the drain of the at least one field effect transistor.

The preceding claim integrates the transistor at the module level, although the integrated circuit is also recited. The term "module" is used in the preamble and in the claim body to address the argument that the preamble is not limiting. Note that the claim recites an "RF module," which is probably the most likely implementation. Nonetheless, "RF" is a limitation that may be omitted here and added through a dependent claim. The broadened base claim is shown in Example 4.3.

EXAMPLE 4.3

I claim:

1. A module comprising: at least one integrated circuit chip;

   the at least one integrated circuit chip included in the module and further including at least one field effect transistor, the at least one field effect transistor including a gate, a drain, a source, and a body;

wherein, during at least a portion of an off state, the body of the at least one field effect transistor is to be electrically biased to have a voltage level substantially more negative than the lowest voltage level of the following: ground, the DC voltage level of the source of the at least one field effect transistor, and the DC voltage level of the drain of the at least one field effect transistor.

So as not to create the impression of form versus substance, it might be prudent to include some dependencies that focus on the module itself as distinguished from the IC. For example, a module likely includes multiple ICs , which may be clarified through a dependency without giving up scope. Likewise, a module likely includes special packaging which might be claimed as a dependency.

A similar approach might be employed to claim a communications device. Likewise, features of the communications device might be claimed, such as for a wireless smart phone, a tablet, or a laptop. Likewise, dependencies may include that the IC or module is included in the communications channel of a communications device and may be coupled to an antenna of the device, and so on.

Additional dependencies may drill down on features of the technology since not all the prior art is necessarily known (i.e., as a hedge against presently unknown prior art). For example, the passing transistor and shunting transistor structure may be claimed for an electrical switch. Also, implementation technologies likely to be used, such as silicon on insulator transistor structure and/or thin-film silicon structures may be claimed, as examples to narrow the claim. Features of the biasing structure might also be claimed. Note that similar features could be dependences for the preceding example claim 4.1, illustrating a component level claim.[33]

Among other lessons, these examples illustrate the importance of understanding the technology being claimed, including aspects, such as its technical value, its commercial value, how it might be distributed or sold, how use might be detected, how it might be used, how it might potentially change, and how it might be designed around.[34]

In our examples, we typically have described a technical problem (e.g., here, corruption of an analog signal) that was present before the invention

33. *See* section 4.131 and its subsections illustrating intermediate and narrow scope claims.

34. *See, e.g.*, the sections and subsections of Chapters 5 and 6 discussing many of these principles/issues.

and the claim is intended to cover a possible technical solution to the technical problem. This approach is more typical of patent prosecution in Europe, but it is a helpful way to think about technology and patent claims.[35] This approach becomes especially important in connection with software-related inventions, discussed later.[36]

Often, claim drafting amounts to making explicit what in layman's terms might be understood without being expressly stated. For example, as one illustration, the language "during at least a portion of an off state" makes explicit what might be understood by a layperson. However, if not clarified expressly with claim language, you are stuck with the exact language used, as happened in *Renishaw* with the use of "when," since the burden is typically on the drafter as the "least cost avoider" to make sure the language is clear regarding its scope.[37]

> Often, claim drafting amounts to making explicit what in layman's terms might be understood without being expressly stated. . . . the burden is typically on the drafter as the "least cost avoider" to make sure the language is clear regarding its scope.

4.123 Means Plus Function/Step Plus Function Claims

As is well-known, 35 USC section 112(f) (previously, 35 USC section 112, paragraph 6) specifically authorizes by statute a special claim type, but also specifies how that claim type must be construed. The statute states:

> **An element in a claim** for a combination **may be expressed as a means** or a step **for performing a specified function without the recital of structure**, material, or acts in support thereof, and such claim shall be construed to cover the corresponding structure, materials, or acts described in the specification and equivalents thereof.[38] (emphasis supplied)

35. *See* Chris Konkol, *The "Problem Solved" in In re Wright and In re Dillon*, IDEA: J.L. & Tech. 131 (1990).
36. *See* section 5.44 and its subsections.
37. *See* Sage Products v. Devon, 126 F.3d 1420 (Fed. Cir. 1997).
38. 35 U.S.C. § 112(f) (2022).

The statute has been interpreted, in essence, to mean that a claim element (note that a "means plus function" claim must be a claim for a combination) may be expressed in the form "means for [function]," such as "means for transmitting," and this functional form is permissible, providing the element is construed appropriately. More specifically, the element is construed to cover the embodiment or embodiments, that is, the "corresponding structure, material, or acts," in the specification, and "equivalents thereof." Thus, if the specification describes a wire coupled to a signal generator, for example, then the "means for transmitting" is likely to be construed to be the wire (and equivalents thereof).

In one sense, the concept of the statute is that you may claim an element in terms of what it does (function), rather than what it is (embodiments). For years, patent attorneys were of the view that such claims would obtain a broad construction since they were broad on their face and, perhaps, due to the presence of the language "and equivalents thereof" in the statute. However, in the late 80s and early 90s, in a sequence of cases, the federal circuit made clear that 112, 6 (now, 112(f)) was a claim *narrowing* statute rather than a claim broadening statute.[39]

The rationale was largely based on the history of the statute, which was passed to overrule a Supreme Court case, *Haliburton Oil Well Cementing Co. v. Walker*,[40] that had held functional claims at the point of novelty to be invalid as being overly broad. Thus, in the federal circuit's view, while Congress intended to overrule that case, it also intended such claims to be narrow. Thus, the additional range provided by "equivalents thereof" was interpreted to be quite narrow.[41] Furthermore, the federal circuit made clear that the term "equivalents" in 112(f) and the doctrine of equivalents (DOE) are separate and distinct concepts.[42] To put a finer point on it, the equivalents in 112(f) is technically considered to be *a part of the literal scope* of the means plus function claim, whereas the DOE is a type of nonliteral paint infringement.[43]

The state of the law regarding the construction of means plus function claims[44] may be stated as follows. To infringe a claim including such an element, the accused product must perform the function recited in the element

39. *See* Johnson v. IVAC, 885 F.2d 1574, 1580 (Fed. Cir. 1989).

40. 329 U.S. 1 (1946).

41. *See, e.g.*, Valmont v. Reinke, 983 F.2d 1039, 1043 (Fed. Cir. 1993).

42. *See* Valmont, 983 F.2d at 1043 n.14.

43. *See* Chapter 3 discussion of DOE.

44. For our purposes, a means plus function claim is a claim with at least one means plus function clause.

identically. Furthermore, the accused product must be the same as the embodiment or embodiments shown in the specification to be corresponding to that function, or the accused product must be an equivalent to the embodiment or embodiments shown in the specification. Here, "an equivalent" is construed narrowly to mean an insubstantial change which adds nothing of significance to the structure, material, or acts disclosed in the patent specification.[45]

The state of the law regarding the construction of means plus function claims may be stated as follows. To infringe a claim including such an element, the accused product must perform the function recited in the element *identically*. Furthermore, the accused product must be the same as the embodiment or embodiments shown in the specification to be corresponding to that function, or the accused product must be an equivalent to the embodiment or embodiments shown in the specification. Here, "an equivalent" is construed narrowly to mean an insubstantial change which adds nothing of significance to the structure, material, or acts disclosed in the patent specification.

The line of precedent on step plus function claims[46] is much shorter than means plus function claims, despite the same statutory origin. Thus, section 112(f) has also been interpreted to mean that:

> An element in a claim for a combination may be expressed as a . . . step for performing a specified function without the recital of . . . acts in support thereof, . . .

According to the federal circuit, "step" in a method claim is the corresponding word for "means" in an apparatus claim.[47] Likewise, whereas a means plus function element avoids the need to recite "structure" in the claim, likewise, a step plus function claim avoids the need to recite "acts." While federal circuit has yet to interpret a method claim to be a step plus function claim, the interpretation would be like that indicated earlier for means plus function claims.

45. *See* Valmont, 983 F.2d at 1043 n.14.

46. A step plus function claim has a similar definition for our purposes as a means plus function claim. That is, a claim with at least one step plus function clause.

47. *See* O.I. Corp. v. Tekmar, 115 F.3d 1576, 1583 (Fed. Cir. 1997).

While the federal circuit has yet to interpret a method claim to be a step plus function claim, the interpretation would be similar to that indicated earlier for means plus function claims.

In an apparatus claim, a means plus function element may recite function in place of structure via reciting "means for [function]." In a method claim, due to the statute, a step plus function element may recite function in place of "acts" via the claim language "step for [function]." In the absence of the word step, it is expected, like in the absence of "means," by analogy, an adversary trying to make this argument must rebut a presumption against application of 112(f) by arguing that the claim recites a "function" rather than "acts." That is, by analogy, the language would be argued to be devoid of "action," and assuming successful rebuttal of the presumption, would, therefore, be interpreted as functional.

What might be an example? Consider a method claim element such as: generating a Fast Fourier Transform (FFT) signal from an audio signal. Is this a function or an act? That is a reasonably tricky question and may depend quite heavily on the specification description. Typically, generating an FFT involves many separate signal processing operations that individually could be "acts." Is this example language above (i.e., "generating . . .") referring to all such acts together or is this more like a function by simply reciting a statement of a result? How would one of ordinary skill interpret this language? The point is that, in general, due at least partially to the inherent nature of language, it may be more challenging to argue that a function is recited versus an act, in comparison with arguing that a function is recited versus structure. Of course, good specification drafting may also make such an argument that such a claim be interpreted under section 112(f) even more challenging.

Again, there is not much case law on step plus function elements of combination claims, as suggested,[48] although they may be thought of as the method analog of a means plus function element of an apparatus claim. In general, claim elements interpreted under section 112(f) tend to be construed more narrowly than claim elements not interpreted under section 112(f).

---

48. *See* Seal-Flex Inc. v. Athletic Track & Court Constr., 172 F.3d 836 (Fed. Cir. 1999). A concurrence by Judge Rader suggests that "comprising the steps of" would not be a problem, but best to avoid such questions by good drafting practice.

However, by their very nature, regarding specifically the action elements of a method claim, such as "transmitting," "encapsulating," and so on, these are less likely to be construed under section 112(f). This is based on analysis of the language of 112(f) and the reasoning of *Seal-flex*.[49] Thus, invoking section 112(f) to interpret an act or action as a "step plus function" element is believed to not be particularly likely. Nonetheless, we recommend avoiding use of the word "step" in claims unless the intention is to deliberately invoke 112(f).

4.1231 Mas-Hamilton *Decision*

The *Mas-Hamilton* case is instructive regarding interpretation of means plus function claims. There were several independent claims. One had a means plus function clause, but the others did not. Nonetheless, all were interpreted under section 112, paragraph 6 (now 112(f)). This ultimately determined the outcome of the case because all the claims were limited to the embodiment described in the specification.

Per Judge Michel, the court stated (emphasis supplied):

> Claim 1 requires, *inter alia:*
>
> lever operating means for positively driving said lever toward said cam in response to continued dial rotation after said combination has been entered, ...
>
> Looking to the specification to determine the structure that the inventor intended to perform the specified function, *i.e.*, positively driving the lever toward the cam, we note that the "lever operating means" includes, at least, a solenoid, spherical detent 96, solenoid housing 62, boss 92, and pin 54. *See* Fig. 1, *ante*. A solenoid is an electrically energized coil of insulated wire which produces a magnetic field within the coil to provide power. *See McGraw-Hill Dictionary of Scientific and Technical Terms* 1863 (Sybil P. Parker ed.' 5th ed.1994). In operation, the solenoid is actuated to move a plunger 98 to its rightmost position. . . . **The solenoid, therefore, is a required structure for the "lever operating means" because it provides the power that operates the lever.**
>
> . . .
>
> The accused X-07 lock does not use a solenoid to provide power to move the lever. It uses, instead, a stepper motor. **A stepper motor is an electric motor that rotates in short and essentially uniform angular movements rather than continuously. *See McGraw-Hill, ante,* at 1918. As the district court aptly pointed out in its section 112, ¶ 6 analysis, the solenoid is continuously operated and hence requires considerable power.** *Mas-Hamilton,* 21 F.Supp.2d at 733. **"In contrast, the stepper motor used in**

49. *Id.*

> **the X-07 lock is actuated by a short electrical pulse, remains in its second state without application of power, [and] is returned manually to its original state."** ***Id.*** In addition, the stepper motor translates its power into rotational motion, whereas the claimed solenoid uses linear motion. Hence, we hold that the district court did not clearly err in determining that the stepper motor of the accused X-07 lock is not a structural equivalent under section 112 to the claimed solenoid. The **"lever operating means" limitation, therefore, is not literally met by the accused device which substitutes a stepper motor; and hence, the accused X-07 lock does not literally infringe claim 1.**

The court also concluded no infringement under the doctrine of equivalents with respect to the claim.

Claim 3 was also an independent claim. The court stated:

> Claim 3 requires, *inter alia:*
>
> > a substantially non-resilient lever moving element for moving the lever from its disengaged position for engaging the protrusion of the lever with the cam surface on the cam wheel so that the rotation of the cam wheel thereafter in the given direction changes the locking mechanism from the locked condition to the unlocked condition; . . . .

The district court determined this to also be a means plus function claim and the federal circuit agreed. The appellate court stated (emphasis supplied):

> The district court determined that a "lever moving element" had not been shown to have a generally understood structural meaning in the art. *See Mas-Hamilton*, 21 F.Supp.2d at 730-31. We agree. *See Greenberg*, at 1583, 39 USPQ2d at 1786, (**holding that "what is important is not simply that [the element at issue] is defined in terms of what it does, but that the term, as the name for a structure, has a reasonably well understood meaning in the art."**). La Gard has not directed this court to any evidence demonstrating that the district court erred in determining that the term "lever moving element" lacks a reasonably well understood meaning in the relevant lock art.

Thus, the same analysis regarding the solenoid and stepper motor applied here. The court employed a similar analysis to claims 34 and 43. It stated (emphasis supplied):

> Claims 34 and 43 both require, *inter alia:*
>
> a movable link member for holding the lever out of engagement with the cam surface before entry of a combination and for releasing the lever after entry of the combination;
>
> '656 Pat., col. 17, ll. 45-48, col. 18, ll. 51-54. The district court construed this limitation under section 112, ¶ 6 as in means-plus-function format.

> *Mas-Hamilton*, 21 F.Supp.2d at 725. The district court determined that there was no evidence that a "movable link member" has a well-understood structural meaning in the art. *See id.* (citing *Greenberg*, 91 F.3d at 1583, 39 USPQ2d at 1786).
>
> La Gard argues on appeal that the district court erred in interpreting this claim limitation under section 112, ¶ 6. According to La Gard, the district court erred by considering the claim term "movable" to invoke section 112, ¶ 6. We agree with La Gard that the claim term "movable" *alone* does not cause the claim to be read in means-plus-function format. However, we note that the subsequent functional language requires two functions: (1) "for holding the lever out of engagement with the cam surface before entry of a combination," and (2) "for releasing the lever after entry of the combination." Such language is precisely what was intended by the statutory phrase in section 112, ¶ 6 requiring that means-plus-function limitations provide "a specified function." 35 U.S.C. § 112, ¶ 6. **Further, we do not see that the remaining terms in the claim limitation other than those defining the two functions, *i.e.*, "a movable link member," provide any structure as necessary to remove this limitation from the ambit of section 112, ¶ 6. We hold, therefore, that the district court's statement that the term "movable" caused section 112, ¶ 6 to apply, is at most harmless error because the limitation at issue was properly construed in means-plus-function format.**

Thus, despite that one independent claim employed "means" and the others did not, the claims, in particular and including, those that did not recite "means," were still interpreted under 112, paragraph 6 (now 112(f)). It could be argued the use of means in one claim and not the others suggested an intent to avoid 112, 6 as to the other claims; however, the position of the court seems to be despite any possible intention as to scope, the command of the statute will not be ignored. Rather, to avoid interpretation under 112, 6 requires use of claim terms that connote sufficient structure.

4.1232 Braun Medical *Decision*

The relevant statute, section 112(f), states:

> An element in a claim for a combination may be expressed as a means or a step for performing a specified function without the recital of structure, material, or acts in support thereof, and such claim shall be construed to cover the **corresponding** structure, materials, or acts described in the specification and equivalents thereof.[50] (emphasis supplied)

50. 35 U.S.C. § 112(f) (2022).

The *Braun* decision addresses the "corresponding" language used in the statute. Interestingly, the case was tried to a jury before the Supreme Court handed down its *Markman* ruling. However, the appeal to the federal circuit was after that ruling. The federal circuit determined it was harmless error for the jury to construe the claim since the federal circuit agreed with the jury decision.

The limitation at issue stated: "means with the other body element for holding said disc firmly against said first means in such a manner that said disc is restrained from sideways movement." Thus, it was construed under 112, 6.

The jury determined that "[c]laim one claims only the traverse bar and equivalents thereof." Because the accused product lacked a traverse bar or an equivalent thereof, the jury returned a verdict of no infringement either literally or under the doctrine of equivalents. The jury relied on the description in the specification, which explicitly stated that the traverse cross bar 15 is a structure that is designed to hold the flexible disc firmly against the triangular member 40 so as to restrain sideways movement.

However, Braun argued that "the specification shows a valve seat, and this valve seat functions to hold the flexible disc firmly against the triangular member." The court stated (emphasis supplied):

> Section 112, paragraph 6 states that a means-plus-function claim "shall be construed to cover the corresponding structure . . . described in the specification." **We hold that, pursuant to this provision, structure disclosed in the specification is "corresponding" structure only if the specification or prosecution history clearly links or associates that structure to the function recited in the claim.** This duty to link or associate structure to function is the quid pro quo for the convenience of employing § 112, ¶ 6. *See O.I. Corp. v. Tekmar Co.*, 115 F.3d 1576, 1583, 42 USPQ2d 1777, 1782 (Fed.Cir. 1997). Our holding in this regard is also supported by our precedent stating that claims drafted in means-plus-function format are subject to the definiteness requirement of the patent law.
>
> . . .
>
> Although Fig. 3 of the patent shows a valve seat, neither the specification nor the prosecution history contains any indication that the valve seat structure corresponds to the recited function, i.e., that it holds the flexible disc against the triangular member so as to restrain sideways movement. This lack of association between the valve seat and the recited function is especially striking given the explicitly clear association provided between the traverse cross bar and the recited function. Because Braun's specification does not adequately disclose the valve seat as structure that holds the disc firmly in place, Braun has failed to particularly point out and distinctly claim that particular means. *Cf. Athletic Alternatives, Inc. v. Prince Mfg., Inc.*, 73 F.3d 1573,

> 1581, 37 USPQ2d 1365, 1372 (Fed.Cir.1996) (rejecting the patentee's broad interpretation of the claim because the patentee particularly pointed out and distinctly claimed only the narrower interpretation); *Fonar Corp. v. General Elec. Co.*, 107 F.3d 1543, 1551-52, 41 USPQ2d 1801, 1807 (Fed.Cir.1997) (explaining that although the specification states that other wave forms may be used, it fails to specifically identify those wave forms and thus the § 112, ¶ 6 claim is limited to the generic gradient wave form actually disclosed). In sum, Braun's specification does not describe the valve seat as a structure that holds the disc firmly in place in such manner that it is restrained from sideways movement. Therefore, we agree with the jury's determination that the means recited in the fifth limitation refers only to the traverse cross bar.

Thus, the court affirmed the jury decision of no infringement relying on the fact that there was no indication that the valve seat could be used to perform the recited function.

4.1233 Williamson v. Citrix *Decision*

Williamson is an important case because it signals a greater willingness on the part of the federal circuit to conclude that a claim may be construed under section 112(f) despite *not* reciting the word "means." The case was decided en banc because it overruled prior precedent. Previously, the federal circuit had indicated that use of the word "means" received a *strong* presumption that the claim should be construed under section 112(f) and, likewise, lack of the word "means" received a *strong* presumption that the claim should *not* be construed under section 112(f). In *Williamson*, the federal circuit determined that this presumption should not be considered a "strong" presumption.

In its claim construction order, the district court had concluded that the limitation of claim 8, "distributed learning control module," was a means-plus-function term under 35 U.S.C. section 112, para. 6. The district court then evaluated the specification and concluded that it failed to disclose the necessary algorithms *for performing all the claimed functions.*[51] The district court thus held claim 8 and its dependent claims 9–16 invalid as indefinite under section 112, paragraph 2. *To be clear, lack of corresponding structure for a claim construed under section 112, paragraph 6 led to invalidity of the claim* <u>*under section 112, paragraph 2*</u>.

Williamson conceded that under the district court's claim construction, none of appellees' accused products infringed independent claims 1 and 17 or their respective dependent claims 2–7 and 18–24, and that claims 8–16 were invalid. The parties stipulated to final judgment. Williamson then appealed.

---

51. A risk to keep in mind when drafting claims.

The '840 patent described methods and systems for "distributed learning" that utilized industry standard computer hardware and software linked by a network to provide a classroom or auditorium-like metaphor—that is, a "virtual classroom" environment. The objective was to connect one or more presenters with geographically remote audience members. The disclosed inventions purported to provide "the benefits of classroom interaction without the detrimental effects of complicated hardware or software, or the costs and inconvenience of convening in a separate place." There were three main components of the "distributed learning" system set forth in the '840 patent: (1) a presenter computer, (2) audience member computers, and (3) a distributed learning server. The distributed learning server implemented a "virtual classroom" over a computer network, such as the internet, to facilitate communication and interaction among the presenter and audience members.

The key disputed term was the "distributed learning control module." The court began its analysis by stating (emphasis added):

> In making the assessment of whether the limitation in question is a means-plus-function term subject to the strictures of § 112, para. 6, our cases have emphasized that the essential inquiry is not merely the presence or absence of the word "means" but whether the words of the claim are understood by persons of ordinary skill in the art to have a sufficiently definite meaning as the name for structure. *Greenberg*, 91 F.3d at 1583 ("What is important is . . . that the term, as the name for structure, has a reasonably well understood meaning in the art."). When the claim uses the word "means," our cases have been consistent in looking to the meaning of the language of the limitation in assessing whether the presumption is overcome. We have also traditionally held that when a claim term lacks the word "means," the presumption can be overcome and § 112, para. 6 will apply if the challenger demonstrates that the claim term fails to "recite[ ] sufficiently definite structure" or else recites "function without reciting sufficient structure for performing that function." *Watts v. XL Sys., Inc.*, 232 F.3d 877, 880 (Fed.Cir.2000).
>
> . . .
>
> **Our consideration of this case has led us to conclude that such a heightened burden is unjustified and that we should abandon characterizing as "strong" the presumption that a limitation lacking the word "means" is not subject to § 112, para. 6.** That characterization is unwarranted, is uncertain in meaning and application, and has the inappropriate practical effect of placing a thumb on what should otherwise be a balanced analytical scale. It has shifted the balance struck by Congress in passing § 112, para. 6 and has resulted in a proliferation of functional claiming untethered to § 112, para. 6 and free of the strictures set forth in the statute. . . .

Regarding the particular claim limitation at issue, the court stated (emphasis added):

> We begin with the observation that the claim limitation in question is not merely the introductory phrase "distributed learning control module," but the entire passage "distributed learning control module for receiving communications transmitted between the presenter and the audience member computer systems and for relaying the communications to an intended receiving computer system and for coordinating the operation of the streaming data module." **This passage, as lengthy as it is, is nonetheless in a format consistent with traditional means-plus-function claim limitations. It replaces the term "means" with the term "module" and recites three functions performed by the "distributed learning control module."**
>
> **"Module" is a well-known nonce word that can operate as a substitute for "means" in the context of § 112, para. 6.** As the district court found, "'module' is simply a generic description for software or hardware that performs a specified function." J.A. 31. Generic terms such as "mechanism," "element," "device," and other nonce words that reflect nothing more than verbal constructs may be used in a claim in a manner that is tantamount to using the word "means" because they "typically do not connote sufficiently definite structure" and therefore may invoke § 112, para. 6. *Mass. Inst. of Tech. & Elecs. for Imaging, Inc. v. Abacus Software*, 462 F.3d 1344, 1354 (Fed. Cir.2006); *see generally* M.P.E.P. § 2181.

Regarding corresponding structure in the specification, the court stated:

> Having found that the "distributed learning control module" is subject to application of § 112, para. 6, we next determine whether the specification discloses sufficient structure that corresponds to the claimed function. We conclude that it does not.
>
> . . .
>
> Structure disclosed in the specification qualifies as "corresponding structure" if the intrinsic evidence clearly links or associates that structure to the function recited in the claim. *Id.* (citing *B. Braun Med., Inc. v. Abbott Labs.*, 124 F.3d 1419, 1424 (Fed.Cir.1997)). Even if the specification discloses corresponding structure, the disclosure must be of "adequate" corresponding structure to achieve the claimed function. *Id.* at 1311–12 (citing *In re Donaldson Co.*, 16 F.3d 1189, 1195 (Fed.Cir.1994) (en banc)). Under 35 U.S.C. § 112, paras. 2 and 6, therefore, if a person of ordinary skill in the art would be unable to recognize the structure in the specification and associate it with the corresponding function in the claim, a means-plus-function clause is indefinite. *Id.* at 1312 (citing *AllVoice Computing PLC v. Nuance Commc'ns, Inc.*, 504 F.3d 1236, 1241 (Fed.Cir.2007)).

Thus, the appellate court agreed with the district court especially in light of the modified presumption.

4.1234 Advantages and Disadvantages of Means Plus Function/Step Plus Function Claims

Employing claims that *are intended* to invoke section 112(f), that is, means and step plus function claims, has become an issue surrounded with some controversy. Some lawyers feel strongly that such claims should be avoided due to their narrow interpretation, whereas other lawyers feel that the law may change again and such claims could become useful someday. Furthermore, there are situations where under current law these claims may have value. We do not necessarily recommend that means or step plus function claims be used or that they be avoided. *Rather, our recommendation is that if you draft claims in a way that is clearly intended to invoke section 112(f) (e.g., by using the word "means"), then you should also specifically include an alternate set of claims that is specifically drafted so as not to invoke section 112(f).* Likewise, because claims may inadvertently invoke section 112(f) without the use of the terms "means" or "step," it is also recommended that you take care to avoid section 112(f) even when not employing these terms.

We do not necessarily recommend that means or step plus function claims be used or that they be avoided. Rather, our recommendation is that if you draft claims in a way that is clearly intended to invoke section 112(f) (e.g., by using the word "means"), then you should also specifically include an alternate set of claims that is specifically drafted so as not to invoke section 112(f) Likewise, because claims may inadvertently invoke section 112(f) without the use of the terms "means" or "step," it is also recommended that you take care to avoid section 112(f) even when not employing these terms.

One potential advantage of employing section 112(f) is that it provides the capability to literally cover a wide variety of associated devices where no specific word exists that might ordinarily be employed in a claim to cover them. Thus, if a means plus function claim is employed and the *identical* function is met by a set of described devices, so long as it is clear in the specification that the embodiments described *correspond* to the identified function, then such devices should quite arguably be covered literally by the claim.

Employing a means plus function claim may also provide a useful technique, for example, to address the issue in *Johnson & Johnston*, where subject matter disclosed in the specification was inadvertently dedicated to the public because the subject matter was not specifically covered by any of the claims of the patent. That is, because claims under section 112(f) are interpreted to cover embodiments in the specification, then there is a reasonable likelihood that a means plus function claim may cover an embodiment that you did not specifically otherwise cover with a patent claim.

A major disadvantage of means and step plus function claims is that they are generally construed to be narrow. In fact, as the federal circuit has stated, section 112(f) was intended as a claim narrowing rather than a claim broadening provision. Rather than working like the doctrine of equivalents, the provision functions more like the reverse doctrine of equivalents.[52]

On the other hand, in a crowded field, a means plus function claim may provide some advantages. It is narrow, which may assist in distinguishing from the prior art. However, its scope may nonetheless still be quite arguable since it is a matter of interpretation what features from the specification embodiment(s) are part of the claim. This uncertainty as to scope, again, in a crowded field may have value. Furthermore, whether something qualifies as an "equivalent" is a question of fact.[53] Thus, one may argue this issue should be decided by a jury; which in some situations may provide a procedural advantage.

One aspect of the narrow nature of such claims is that the recited function of the claim must be met *identically* by the accused product. This leaves little room for so-called play at the joints in terms of the claim drafting. Thus, it may, perhaps, be better to recite broad literal functions when employing such claims, but it is also important to make sure such functions are supported, as discussed immediately following. In contrast, for example, to meet the doctrine of equivalents,[54] the function (under the function, way, result test) only needs to be "substantially similar," something that is looser than "identical." Thus, the federal circuit has even suggested that a modified function-way-result test may be employed when construing claims under section 112(f) where the function is met identically.[55]

52. *See* Valmont, 983 F.3d at 1042.

53. *See, e.g.*, Overhead Door Corp. v. Chamberlain Grp., Inc., 194 F.3d 1261, 1273, 52 USPQ2d 1321, 1329 (Fed. Cir. 1999) (a genuine fact issue arose whether for purposes of 112, 6, the accused software was equivalent to the patent's software).

54. *See* discussion in Chapter 3.

55. *See* Kemco v. Control Papers, 208 F.3d 1352 (Fed. Cir. 2000).

Another narrow aspect of claims under section 112(f) is that the specification must include "corresponding structure, material or acts in support thereof," and it must be clear from the specification that such structure, material, or acts *correspond* to the recited function. For example, in *B. Braun Medical v. Abbott Lab.*,[56] the federal circuit determined that a means plus function claim directed to a valve was not infringed where a structure included in the specification that would have arguably supported the infringement was not associated with the recited function in the specification (or prosecution history). Furthermore, in *Cardiac Pacemakers v. St. Jude Medical*,[57] the federal circuit invalidated a claim including a means plus function clause because the specification failed to disclose any structure for performing the recited function.

Means plus function elements are also construed to *only* cover the embodiment or embodiments described in the specification "and equivalents thereof." However, because "equivalents thereof" is construed narrowly, this is another aspect of their construction that makes these claims narrow. An equivalent for purposes of literal infringement under 112(f) is an insubstantial change which adds nothing of significance.[58] Likewise, another narrowing aspect of "equivalents thereof" is the time at which whether something is an "equivalent" is evaluated. The federal circuit has stated that this is at the time the patent issues.[59] This is directly in contrast to the doctrine of equivalents, where whether something is an "equivalent" is evaluated at the time of the infringement, usually a later time.[60] Because known interchangeability is a factor in determining whether something is an equivalent,[61] evaluation of this at the time the patent issues should tend to narrow the claim.

Consistent with the preceding, the doctrine of equivalents has a limited role in connection with claims construed under section 112(f). Generally, with only limited exception, for example, if a means plus function element is not infringed by the accused device, then there also will *not* be infringement under the doctrine of equivalents. As indicated earlier, primary differences that may in only limited circumstances make the DOE applicable, include the time of evaluating an equivalent, and that the function element for the DOE need not be met in the accused product identically. However, one important difference between such claims and the DOE that tends to make claims evaluated under

56. 124 F.3d 1419 (Fed. Cir. 1997).
57. 296 F.3d 1106 (Fed. Cir. 2002).
58. *See* Valmont, 983 F.3d at 1043 n.14.
59. *See* Al-Site Corp. v. VSI Int'l, 174 F.3d 1308, 1320–21 (Fed. Cir 1999).
60. *See* Warner-Jenkinson v. Hilton Davis Chem., 520 U.S. 17, 29 (1997).
61. *See id.*

section 112(f) *less* narrow is that whether the accused product is the same or "an equivalent" is evaluated "overall";[62] in contrast, the DOE is evaluated element-by-element.[63] An element-by-element analysis usually produces a narrower result than an "overall" analysis, as performed under section 112(f).

4.1235 Illustrative Claim Example—Functional Claiming With and Without Use of "Means" or "Step"

A risk exists under federal circuit law that a claim employing functional language that does not use the word "means" or "step" may, nonetheless, be construed under section 112(f). The federal circuit, however, has recognized that some words, while functional in nature, have acquired accepted meanings that make them less functional.[64] For example, in *Personalized Media Communications v. ITC*,[65] the federal circuit determined that the language "digital detector" employed in a claim should not be construed under section 112(f) reversing the ITC's conclusion to the contrary. Likewise, in *Apex v. Raritan Computer*,[66] the federal circuit determined that "circuit" should not be construed under section 112(f).

> As previously indicated, to avoid invoking 112, 6, it is recommended that words that are more concrete in meaning be employed where possible. Many examples of such words exist and, in fact, are in common use in patent claiming. For example, in addition to "detector" and "circuit," others include "memory," "processor," "pump," "adder," "generator," "transmitter," "receiver," etc.

Some of the complex legal issues related to functional language in patent claims emanate from how the federal circuit has interpreted section 112(f). The provision, to be invoked for an element of a patent claim, appears to require the formulation "means for [function]." However, there is federal circuit case law in which section 112(f) is invoked to interpret an element of a claim although the word "means" does not appear in the claim.[67]

62. *See* Odetics v. Storage Tech., 185 F.3d 1259 (Fed. Cir. 1999).
63. *See* Pennwalt v. Durand-Wayland, 833 F.3d 931 (Fed. Cir. 1987) (en banc).
64. *See, e.g.*, Mas-Hamilton v. LaGard, 156 F.3d 1206 (Fed. Cir. 1998).
65. 161 F.3d 696 (Fed. Cir. 1998).
66. 325 F.3d 1364 (Fed. Cir. 2003).
67. *See, e.g.*, Williams v. Citrix, 792 F.3d 1339 (Fed. Cir.) (en banc); Cole v. Kimberly–Clark Corp., 102 F.3d 524, 531 (Fed. Cir. 1996); *see also* Greenberg v. Ethicon Endo–Surgery, Inc., 91 F.3d 1580, 1584 (Fed. Cir. 1996).

This may occur, for example, where the claim term or terms at issue do *not* recite sufficient structure.[68] There is a presumption that the absence of use of "means" in language of a patent claim should *not* be construed under section 112(f), but that presumption may be rebutted. The primary case is *Williamson v. Citrix Online*, decided en banc, which referred to use of "nonce words" for elements of a claim, such as the word "module," which in the context of the claim was not a recognized term of art. "Nonce words" refers to made up words that seek to make a functional limitation appear structural. The federal circuit stated (note that 112(f) has replace 112, para. 6):

> Our consideration of this case has led us to conclude that such a heightened burden is unjustified and that we should abandon characterizing as "strong" the presumption that a limitation lacking the word "means" is not subject to § 112, para. 6. That characterization is unwarranted, is uncertain in meaning and application, and has the inappropriate practical effect of placing a thumb on what should otherwise be a balanced analytical scale. It has shifted the balance struck by Congress in passing § 112, para. 6 and has resulted in a proliferation of functional claiming untethered to § 112, para. 6 and free of the strictures set forth in the statute. Henceforth, we will apply the presumption as we have done prior to *Lighting World*, without requiring any heightened evidentiary showing and expressly overrule the characterization of that presumption as "strong." We also overrule the strict requirement of "a showing that the limitation essentially is devoid of anything that can be construed as structure."
>
> The standard is whether the words of the claim are understood by persons of ordinary skill in the art to have a sufficiently definite meaning as the name for structure. *Greenberg*, 91 F.3d at 1583. When a claim term lacks the word "means," the presumption can be overcome and § 112, para. 6 will apply if the challenger demonstrates that the claim term fails to "recite sufficiently definite structure" or else recites "function without reciting sufficient structure for performing that function." *Watts*, 232 F.3d at 880. The converse presumption remains unaffected: "use of the word 'means' creates a presumption that § 112, ¶ 6 applies." *Personalized Media*, 161 F.3d at 703.

Some terms, as a result, appear to be sufficiently structural to not invoke section 112(f).[69] A few example claim terms in which there have been court

68. *See, e.g.*, Williams v. Citrix, 792 F.3d 1339 (Fed. Cir.) (en banc); Cole v. Kimberly-Clark Corp., 102 F.3d 524, 531 (Fed. Cir. 1996); *see also* Greenberg v. Ethicon Endo-Surgery, Inc., 91 F.3d 1580, 1584 (Fed. Cir. 1996).

69. *See* Dyfan, LLC v. Target Corp., 28 F.4th 1360 (Fed. Cir. 2022); Zeroclick v. Apple, 891 F.3d 1003, 1008 (Fed. Cir. 2018) ("the mere fact that the disputed limitations incorporate functional language does not automatically convert the words into means for performing such functions"). *See Greenberg*, 91 F.3d at 1583 ("Many devices take their names from the functions they perform. The examples are innumerable, such as 'filter,' 'brake,' 'clamp,' 'screwdriver,' or

rulings indicating some claim terms are structural rather than functional include: processor; circuit or circuitry; and digital detector. There are many other case examples that could also be cited. More specifically, as an example of the reasoning used, the federal circuit case, *Personalized Media Communications v. Thomson*,[70] states (emphasis supplied):

> 'Detector' is not a generic structural term such as 'means,' 'element,' or 'device; nor is it a coined term lacking a clear meaning, such as 'widget' or 'ram-a-fram.' **Instead, as noted by the ALJ by reference to dictionary definitions, 'detector' had a well-known meaning to those of skill in the electrical arts connotative of structure,** . . . .

Further, in some other federal circuit cases, functional language was permissibly used and did *not* invoke section 112(f).[71] That is, these cases suggest that functional language may in some situations be properly and appropriately employed in claims *without* using the means-plus-function format of section 112(f) and *without* necessarily being interpreted under that subsection. Presumably, despite the functional language, the claim still recited sufficient structure to avoid invoking section 112(f). We recommend using both approaches to provide diversity and to signal a different intended scope for the separate claims.[72]

'lock.'"); VDPP v. Vizio, case no. 21-2040 (Mar. 25, 2022 Fed. Cir.) ("processor" and "storage" do not invoke 112(f)) (nonprecedential).

70. 532 F.3d 1318, 1329 (Fed. Cir 1998). It is noted that Personalized Media Comm'ns v. Thomson was decided before en banc decision Williams v. Citrix.

71. *See, e.g.*, K-2 Corp. v. Salomon S.A., 191 F.3d 1356, 1363 (Fed. Cir. 1999) (functional language "for substantially preventing movement" did not invoke 112(6)); BASF Corp. v. Johnson Matthey Inc., 875 F.3d 1360 (Fed. Cir. 2017) (functional phrase, "effective to catalyze," did not involve 112(6)); *see also* Enzo Biochem, Inc. v. Applera Corp., 599 F.3d 1325, 1332–33 (Fed. Cir. 2010), *reh'g and reh'g en banc denied*, 605 F.3d 1347 (Fed. Cir. 2010) ("when a claim limitation is defined in 'purely functional terms,' a determination of whether the limitation is sufficiently definite is 'highly dependent on context (e.g., the disclosure in the specification and the knowledge of a person of ordinary skill in the relevant art area)'"); Miken Composites, L.L.C. v. Wilson Sporting Goods Co., 515 F.3d 1331 (Fed. Cir. 2008) (Court stated that while the term "insert" has "functional attributes," it was still a structural component.); Plastic Container Corp. v. Cont'l Plastics of Okla., Inc., 607 F.2d 885, 203 USPQ 27, 650, 651 (10th Cir. 1979), *cert. denied*, 444 U.S. 1018 (1980), *on remand*, 515 F. Supp. 834, 214 USPQ 530 (W.D. Okla. 1980), *aff'd in part, reversed in part*, 708 F.2d 1554, 219 USPQ 26 (10th Cir. 1983) ("the idea that functional language ipso facto cannot precisely define novelty in structure was laid to rest in In re Swinehart. . . ."); *In re* Swinehart, 439 F.2d 210, 212, 169 USPQ 226, 228 (CCPA 1971) ("[T]here is nothing intrinsically wrong with [employing functional limitations] in drafting patent claims.").

72. *But see* Mas-Hamilton v. LaGard, 156 F.3d 1206 (Fed. Cir. 1998) (claim without "means" interpreted under 112, 6 despite a separate independent claim that employed "means").

Some features, unfortunately, may not have a feasible way to be claimed structurally. In that situation, it is suggested a mix of structural and functional language be used so that at least the claim language at issue is not entirely devoid of structure. Consider Example 2.3 from Chapter 2 (which is similar to Example 3.3 from Chapter 3) with claim language such as:

> wherein the memory controller is capable of initiating burst mode operation based, at least in part, on receipt of an externally derived request from an external central processing unit (CPU);
>
> wherein the request is to include a memory address, a word count, and a read or a write control transfer designation; and
>
> wherein the memory controller is to process the request and take control of an external system transfer bus.

The claim, here, recites "the memory controller is capable of initiating burst mode operation" and "the memory controller is to process the request and take control of an external system transfer bus." The term "memory controller" is likely structural, but the other recited limitations are more functional; however, a memory controller may be argued to support such functions.

Example 2.6 from Chapter 2 (which is similar to Example 3.2 from Chapter 3) uses a similar approach reciting "network device," a potentially structural device, but adding functional limitations such as "to emulate," "to encapsulate," and "to communicate." Again, these could be argued to be operations a network device may support. With even more attention, these positions might be made even clearer through claim language and specification language. The point, here, is to pay attention to the use of structural versus functional language in the claim and attempt to hedge your bets so that your claim is not construed to be limited to, essentially, your specification embodiment due to invocation of section 112(f).

The point, here, is to pay attention to the use of structural versus functional language in the claim and attempt to hedge your bets so that your claim is not construed to be limited to, essentially, your specification embodiment due to invocation of section 112(f).

Previously, in Example 4.1, a component claim was illustrated. Following is an Example claim 4.4, using means plus function language.

EXAMPLE 4.4

I claim:

1. A device comprising: at least one N-type metal oxide semiconductor field effect transistor (NMOSFET), the at least one NMOSFET including a source, a gate, a drain and a body;

   wherein the at least one NMOSFET is further included in a configuration means at least to control the at least one NMOSFET transistor to either an OFF state or an ON state;

   wherein the configuration means comprises an electrical bias means to at least electrically bias the body of the at least one NMOSFET at least in a portion of the OFF state of the at least one NMOSFET to a DC voltage level substantially more negative than at least one of the following: ground, the DC voltage level of the source, and the DC voltage level of the drain.

This claim should provide some diversity because Example 4.1 should not be construed under section 112(f), while this claim should be construed under section 112(f). The analysis of claim scope, therefore, should be significantly different.

It is also a good idea to be mindful of the consequences should, despite your best drafting efforts, your claim be construed under section 112(f) during examination or in litigation. In the event section 112(f) is invoked, the specification *must* provide sufficient *corresponding* structure for the recited function. That is, for the function or functions recited in the claim, the specification *must* describe *corresponding* structure able to perform the recited function or functions or the claim will be invalid if issued. Here, *corresponding* suggests that the specification is written to clearly associate the function and the structure in the description in a manner such that one of ordinary skill would comprehend the association.

If an element is construed under section 112(f) and the statutory requirements regarding corresponding structure are satisfied, then the claim covers, by express statutory direction:

> . . . the *corresponding* structure, material, or acts described in the specification *and equivalents* . . . (emphasis supplied).

Thus, the claim, by statute, construed *literally* under section 112(f) may be infringed by embodiments in your specification that *correspond* to the functional language or by a *112(f) equivalent* of what is shown in the specification; however, the scope of such *112(f) equivalents* is generally exceedingly narrow.[73]

In the area of software, in particular, the algorithm is considered the structure at issue under section 112(f).[74] For this reason, not infrequently, claims interpreted under section 112(f) that relate to software are held invalid as not appropriately describing structure or enough structure. That is, generally it is not sufficient to merely provide a functional description.[75] Enough detail must be described to, in effect, show possession, which means sufficient detail of *how to perform the function* so that one of ordinary skill would know the scope being claimed with respect to implementing the function or operation claimed.[76]

Likewise, if a function is claimed that is not described to this level, the claim is held invalid. Therefore, in drafting claims, care is warranted to not inadvertently claim a function that is believed to be well understood, such as "transmit a signal" or "receive a signal," but for which the specification does not actually provide an implementation description.

Therefore, in drafting, care is warranted to not inadvertently claim a function that is believed to be well understood, such as "transmit a signal" or "receive a signal," but for which the specification does not actually provide an implementation description.

4.124 Structure Versus Function Revisited

Use of functional language may be challenging due primarily to 35 USC section 112(f).[77] Some functional terms, however, appear to be sufficiently

73. *See, e.g.*, Valmont v. Reinke, 983 F.2d 1039 (Fed. Cir. 1993).

74. *See, e.g.*, Eon Corp. IP Holdings, LLC v. AT&T Mobility, LLC, 785 F.3d 616, 621 (Fed. Cir. 2015).

75. *See* Blackboard, Inc. v. Desire2Learn, Inc., 574 F.3d 1371, 1383–85, 91 USPQ2d 1481, 1491–93 (Fed. Cir. 2009); Noah Systems v. Intuit, 675 F.3d 1302 (Fed. Cir. 2012).

76. *See* Blackboard, Inc. v. Desire2Learn, Inc., 574 F.3d 1371, 1383–85, 91 USPQ2d 1481, 1491–93 (Fed. Cir. 2009); Noah Systems v. Intuit, 675 F.3d 1302 (Fed. Cir. 2012).

77. Note that § 112(f) also refers to "materials" suggesting applicability to composition of matter claims as well.

structural to not invoke section 112(f). Further, in some federal circuit cases, functional language was permissibly used and did *not* invoke section 112(f).[78]

A line of federal circuit authority is directed to claiming a device with a so-called *capability* of infringing. One way to view such cases is as another spin on functional language. It is not uncommon to see language in claims such as "adapted to," "configured to," in connection with functional language. Other formulations include "capable of," "the capability to," as well as ". . . for . . ." (which is similar to "means for" and may be more likely to invoke section 112(f)), and ". . . to. . . ."

There could be issues with some of these formulations, particularly "adapted to" and "configured to." For one thing, examiners do not like them, so they are reasonably likely to be rejected. Second, there is some federal circuit law that has construed some of these linguistic formulations narrowly (although, interestingly, without invoking section 112(f)).[79] Third, one could make the noninfringement argument that the accused product is not "configured" or "adapted." This might be an especially strong argument in connection with software, which is often configured. Usually the word "adapted," "configured," and so on is not needed. Thus, including it suggests some intent that it have meaning, which in reality may not be the case.

One case addressing these functional phrases is *Aspex Eyewear v. Marchon Eyewear*.[80] In that case, the district court had construed "adapted to" narrowly

---

78. *See, e.g.*, K-2 Corp. v. Salomon S.A., 191 F.3d 1356, 1363 (Fed. Cir. 1999) (functional language "for substantially preventing movement" did not invoke 112(6)); BASF Corp. v. Johnson Matthey Inc., 875 F.3d 1360 (Fed. Cir. 2017) (functional phrase, "effective to catalyze," did not involve 112(6)); *see also* Enzo Biochem, Inc. v. Applera Corp., 599 F.3d 1325, 1332–33 (Fed. Cir. 2010), *reh'g and reh'g en banc denied*, 605 F.3d 1347 (Fed. Cir. 2010), ("when a claim limitation is defined in 'purely functional terms,' a determination of whether the limitation is sufficiently definite is 'highly dependent on context (e.g., the disclosure in the specification and the knowledge of a person of ordinary skill in the relevant art area).'"); Miken Composites, L.L.C. v. Wilson Sporting Goods Co., 515 F.3d 1331 (Fed. Cir. 2008) (Court stated that while the term "insert" has "functional attributes," it was still a structural component.); Plastic Container Corp. v. Cont'l Plastics of Okla., Inc., 607 F.2d 885, 203 USPQ 27, 650, 651 (10th Cir. 1979), *cert. denied*, 444 U.S. 1018 (1980), *on remand*, 515 F. Supp. 834, 214 USPQ 530 (W.D. Okla. 1980), *aff'd in part, reversed in part*, 708 F.2d 1554, 219 USPQ 26 (10th Cir. 1983) ("the idea that functional language ipso facto cannot precisely define novelty in structure was laid to rest in In re Swinehart. . . ."); *In re* Swinehart, 439 F.2d 210, 212, 169 USPQ 226, 228 (CCPA 1971) ("[T]here is nothing intrinsically wrong with [employing functional limitations] in drafting patent claims.").

79. *See* Aspex Eyewear, Inc. v. Marchon Eyewear, Inc., 672 F.3d 1335 (Fed. Cir. 2012); *In re* Giannelli, 739 F.3d 1375 (Fed. Cir. 2014).

80. 672 F.3d 1335 (Fed. Cir. 2012).

and the construction was challenged on appeal. The federal circuit agreed with the narrow construction, stating (emphasis supplied):

> Aspex's first objection to the court's ruling on that limitation is that it construes the phrase "adapted to" too narrowly; that phrase, according to Aspex, should be interpreted to mean "suitable for" rather than "made to." As the parties have noted, the phrase "adapted to" is sometimes used in claim drafting to carry the broader meaning proposed by Aspex, and sometimes to carry a narrower meaning closer to that proposed by the defendants. **In this case, we conclude that the narrower meaning is correct.**
>
> In common parlance, the phrase "adapted to" is frequently used to mean "made to," "designed to," or "configured to," but it can also be used in a broader sense to mean "capable of" or "suitable for." *See* Webster's Third New International Dictionary 24 (1968) ("suited by nature, character, or design to a particular use, purpose, or situation"); 1 Oxford English Dictionary 139 (2d ed. 1989) ("fitted; fit, suitable . . . modified to fit new situations"). The way the phrase is used in amended claim 23 of the '545 patent supports the district court's conclusion that a narrower definition, such as "configured to," applies here. *See Sta-Rite Indus., LLC v. ITT Corp.*, 682 F. Supp. 2d 738, 753 (E.D. Tex. 2010) (construing "adapted to," in context, to mean "designed or configured to," not "having the capacity to"); *Boston Scientific Corp. v. Cordis Corp.*, 2006 U.S. Dist. LEXIS 94329, 2006 WL 3782840 (N.D. Cal. Dec. 20, 2006) (construing "adapted to," in light of patent as a whole, to mean "configured to," not "capable of").

Two years later, the federal circuit used similar analysis to reverse and remand the Board's affirmance of an examiner's obviousness rejection. In the case *In re Giannelli*,[81] the court stated (emphasis supplied):

> The claims of the '261 application specifically require a "first handle portion adapted to be moved from a first position to a second position by a pulling force . . . in a rowing motion." Response to Office Action, No. 10/378,261, at 2 (Apr. 12, 2006). We have noted that, "the phrase 'adapted to' is frequently used to mean 'made to,' 'designed to,' or 'configured to,' . . ." *Aspex Eyewear, Inc. v. Marchon Eyewear, Inc.*, 672 F.3d 1335, 1349 (Fed.Cir.2012). **Although the phrase can also mean "'capable of' or 'suitable for,'" *id.*, here the written description makes clear that "adapted to," as used in the '261 application, has a narrower meaning, viz., that the claimed machine is designed or constructed to be used as a rowing machine whereby a pulling force is exerted on the handles.**

81. 739 F.3d 1375 (Fed. Cir. 2014).

> The written description of the '261 application describes how the position of the handles relative to the primary and secondary lever arms and the resistance mechanism renders them "adapted" to be moved by the user's pulling force. For example, the application states that the exercise machine "enables a user to maintain biomechanical alignment of the user's wrist and forearm during performance of the exercise, while maintaining a consistent resistance applied to the muscles, in the stability of an exercise machine." '261 application, at 3. The location of those handles relative to the other components is one of their structural attributes that enables performance of the rowing motion against the selected resistance. '261 application, at 4 ("The declining, substantially linear path [of the pulled handles] enables the user to maintain proper biomechanical alignment of the force angle being applied to the grip. This allows for a fairly consistent torque application at the shoulder throughout the range of motion of the exercise."). Consequently, the relevant question before the Board was whether the apparatus described in the '447 patent was " 'made to,' 'designed to,' or 'configured to,' " allow the user to perform a rowing exercise by pulling on the handles as claimed in the '261 application.
>
> . . .
>
> Because the Board's analysis began with the premise that "adapted to" meant "capable of," its affirmance of the examiner's rejection also contained no explanation why or how a person having ordinary skill in the art would modify the prior art chest press machine to arrive at the apparatus of the '261 application. And because the initial burden was not met, Giannelli was not obligated to submit additional evidence to rebut the examiner's findings of pulling capability. *See In re Rijckaert*, 9 F.3d 1531, 1532 (Fed.Cir.1993) ("Only if that burden [of establishing a prima facie case] is met, does the burden of coming forward with evidence or argument shift to the applicant."). The Board thus erred in affirming the conclusion of the examiner that the '447 patent apparatus rendered obvious the claimed invention of the '261 application.

Good practice, therefore, suggests avoiding formulations like "adapted to" or "configured to" and the like. Instead, just say "to. . . ."

Good practice suggests avoiding formulations like "adapted to" or "configured to" and the like. Instead, just say "to. . . ."

Language such as "capable of" or "the capability to" seems to more often receive a broader scope from courts, as stated in the previous two cases. This approach to claiming may be quite powerful in some situations. For example, software or semiconductor chips may have many different features. A customer may not necessarily use or even be aware of all such features. Yet, it may be powerful to draft a claim such that so long as the software or chip, for example, has the capability to perform the feature, direct patent infringement is present.

Two cases that relate to this issue are *Intel v. U.S.ITC*[82] and *Fantasy Sports.*[83] A crucial issue seems to be the presence of a limitation that may be met by an accused product even if not activated or used by a customer, as an example.

In general, the topic of claiming a device capable to infringe may be tricky in some situations. In the *Intel* case, an early and influential case on this topic, the feature was so-called page mode addressing. Generally, to use page mode addressing required setting a bit in a chip. However, the language of the claim was such that as long as the capability to use page mode addressing was present in a device, such as enabled by setting a bit, then infringement was present *even if the bit was not actually set.*

The claim at issue recited:

---

1. In an integrated circuit, read-only memory having n address lines used for accessing p words in one addressing mode, an improvement for providing an alternate addressing mode, comprising:

   programmable selection means for selecting said alternate addressing mode; storage means for storing at least one signal; an address buffer coupled to one of said n address lines, said buffer also being coupled to said storage means and said programmable selection means, the output of said buffer being controlled by said signal stored in said storage means when said alternate addressing mode is selected, whereby when said alternate addressing mode is selected said p words in said memory may be selected with less than n address signals.

Cleverly, the claim recited: "programmable selection means . . . when said alternate addressing mode is selected said p words in said memory may be selected with less than n address signals." The issue, therefore, was whether

82. 946 F.2d 821, 832 (Fed. Cir. 1991).
83. 287 F.3d 1108 (Fed. Cir. 2002).

the alleged infringing product necessarily infringed if it had this alternative addressing mode capability, but the mode was not being used.

In affirming the ITC ruling finding infringement, the federal circuit stated (emphasis supplied):

> Both the multiplexer and the address buffer use an addressing signal to select a particular memory cell from an incoming address pin or latch. Thus, the accused circuits infringe claim 1 under the doctrine of equivalents because they perform substantially the same function in substantially the same way to obtain the same result as the invention claimed in the '084 patent.
>
> . . .
>
> GI/M also contends that the Commission's finding of infringement under the doctrine of equivalents is incorrect because, although GI/M's "old" design 51 Series EPROMs are capable of performing page mode addressing, the EPROMs were never sold to operate in page mode. No customer was ever told how to convert the chip to page mode operation—or even that such conversion was possible. GI/M argues that an alleged infringer must intend its parts to be used in an infringing fashion and cites *Fromberg, Inc. v. Thornhill*, 315 F.2d 407, 415, 137 USPQ 84, 89 (5th Cir. 1963), in support of its argument. As noted by Intel, there is no intent element to direct infringement. See 35 U.S.C. § 271(b) and (c). Fromberg deals with induced and contributory infringement and is therefore inapposite. **Because the language of claim 1 refers to "programmable selection means" and states "whereby when said alternate addressing mode is selected" (emphases added), the accused device, to be infringing, need only be capable of operating in the page mode. Contrary to GI/M's argument, actual page mode operation in the accused device is not required.**

More recent cases employ a similar analysis. For example, in *Fantasy_Sports v. SportsLine*,[84] the federal circuit reversed and remanded a district court ruling of summary judgment of no infringement due to the presence of genuine and material issues of fact requiring resolution.

The issue was whether the accused software met a limitation or, instead, was modifiable to meet the limitation. The former would be infringing, whereas the latter would not. The court referenced the *Intel* case in its discussion. The federal circuit stated (some emphasis in original and some added):

> *Intel* involved a claim to a memory chip in an integrated circuit having, *inter alia*, "*programmable* selection means for selecting [an] alternate addressing mode." *Id.* at 831, 20 USPQ2d at 1170 (emphasis added). The defendant in *Intel* argued that even though its products could be modified to infringe that claim, the fact that those products were capable of infringing alone could not

84. 287 F.3d 1108 (Fed. Cir. 2002).

support a finding of infringement. *Id.* at 832, 20 USPQ2d at 1171. Although we concluded that the defendant's products did infringe, we explained our basis for doing so as follows: "Because *the language of claim 1* refers to '*programmable* selection means' . . . the accused device, to be infringing, need only be capable of operating in the page mode." *Id.* (emphases added). *Intel* therefore does not stand for the proposition, as argued by Fantasy, that infringement may be based upon a finding that an accused product is merely capable of being modified in a manner that infringes the claims of a patent. *See High Tech Med. Instrumentation, Inc. v. New Image Indus., Inc.*, 49 F.3d 1551, 1555-56, 33 USPQ2d 2005, 2008-09 (Fed. Cir. 1995) (distinguishing *Intel* and holding that the fact that the accused device could be altered in way that satisfies the claim term "rotatably coupled" did not *per se* justify a finding of infringement); *see also Telemac Cellular Corp. v. Topp Telecom, Inc.*, 247 F.3d 1316, 1330, 58 USPQ2d 1545, 1554 (Fed. Cir. 2001) ("[T]hat a device is capable of being modified to operate in an infringing manner is not sufficient, by itself, to support a finding of infringement."). **Rather, as in every infringement analysis, the language of the claims, as well as the nature of the accused product, dictates whether an infringement has occurred.**

In the present case, claim 1 is directed to "[a] computer for playing football," and thus the claims of the '603 patent read on a computer executing fantasy football game software. Claim 1 also sets forth a number of functionally defined means that that software must contain, including a "means for scoring . . . bonus points" for unusual scoring plays. Software is a set of instructions, known as code, that directs a computer to perform specified functions or operations. Thus, the software underlying a computer program that presents a user with the ability to select among a number of different options must be written in such a way as to enable the computer to carry out the functions defined by those options when they are selected by the user. Therefore, although a user must activate the functions programmed into a piece of software by selecting those options, the user is only activating means that are *already present in the underlying software*. Otherwise, the user would be required to alter the code to enable the computer to carry out those functions. Accordingly, in order to infringe the '603 patent, the code underlying an accused fantasy football game must be written in such a way as to enable a user of that software to utilize the function of awarding bonus points for unusual plays such as out-of-position scoring, without having to modify that code. In other words, an infringing software must include the "means for scoring . . . bonus points" regardless whether that means is activated or utilized in any way.

A recent federal circuit case may muddy slightly how to interpret such limitations; however, the basic conclusion regarding claims that include limitations with the capability to infringe remains intact, or so it appears. In *INVT*

SPE LLC v. International Trade Commission,[85] the federal circuit affirmed the International Trade Commission's (ITC) determination that the respondents did not violate 19 U.S.C. § 1337. INVT had alleged that the importation and sale of LTE-compliant personal electronic devices infringed U.S. Patent Nos. 6,760,590 ("the '590 patent") and 7,848,439 ("the '439 patent"). The ITC determined that the asserted claims were not essential to the LTE standard and that the accused products did not infringe the asserted claims.

However, before reaching this conclusion, it was necessary to construe the claims at issue, in particular, the claims of the '439 patent, which related to wireless communication systems, specifically an improvement to adaptive modulation and coding (AMC), which is a technique used to transmit signals in an orthogonal frequency division multiplexing (OFDM) system. Claim 1 of the '439 patent recited:

> 1. A communication apparatus comprising:
>
> > [a] a channel estimating section that carries out a channel estimation per subband;
> >
> > [b] a parameter deciding section that decides modulation parameters and coding parameters per subband group comprised of a plurality of the subbands, based on a result of the channel estimation per subband;
> >
> > [c] a parameter information transmission section that transmits, to a communicating party, parameter information indicating the modulation parameters and the coding parameters decided at the parameter deciding section;
> >
> > [d] a receiving section that receives a signal containing data modulated and encoded on a per subband group basis at the communicating party using the modulation parameters and the coding parameters of the parameter information transmitted at the parameter information transmission section;
> >
> > [e] a data obtaining section that demodulates and decodes the received signal received at the receiving section on a per subband group basis using the modulation parameters and the coding parameters decided at the parameter deciding section, and obtains the data contained in the received signal; and
> >
> > [f] a pattern storage section that stores in advance patterns for selecting subbands constituting the subband groups wherein the parameter

85. *See* INVT SPE LLC v. ITC, Appeal No. 2020-1903 (Fed. Cir. Aug. 31, 2022).

> deciding section decides the modulation parameters and the coding parameters per subband group comprised of the subbands selected based on the patterns stored in the pattern storage section.

INT asserted that compliance with the LTE communications standard required infringing this claim. The key limitations in dispute were elements [d] and [e], which stated:

> [d] a receiving section that receives a signal containing data modulated and encoded on a per subband group basis at the communicating party using the modulation parameters and the coding parameters of the parameter information transmitted at the parameter information transmission section;
>
> [e] a data obtaining section that demodulates and decodes the received signal received at the receiving section on a per subband group basis using the modulation parameters and the coding parameters decided at the parameter deciding section, and obtains the data contained in the received signal.

At the ITC, a dispute regarding interpretation of these elements related to whether this language required "actual operation" or merely "the capability for performing." The ITC determined that the language required actual operation; however, the ITC also determined that the language was not shown to be LTE compliant and also determined separately that the accused devices had not been shown to meet the claim language at issue regardless of whether it was LTE compliant.

On appeal, INT challenged the interpretation of the claims as requiring actual operation. In this regard, the federal circuit agreed with INT that the language required the capability for performing rather than actual operation, but, nonetheless, concluded that the language still had not been shown to be LTE compliant and also that the accused devices had not been shown to meet the limitations at issue.

Here, the federal circuit stated (emphasis supplied):

> Our cases have held that sometimes a device only needs to be "capable of operating" according to a claimed limitation, for a finding of infringement. *See Finjan*, 626 F.3d at 1204. Other times, a device does not infringe unless it actually operates as claimed. *See ParkerVision, Inc. v. Qualcomm Inc.*, 903 F.3d 1354, 1361 (Fed. Cir. 2018) (*discussing Ball Aerosol & Specialty Container, Inc. v. Ltd. Brands, Inc.*, 555 F.3d 984 (Fed. Cir. 2009)). **Whether infringement requires actual performance of the recited functions by the accused device depends on the claim language.** *See Finjan*, 626 F.3d 1204 (*citing Fantasy Sports Props. v. Sportsline.com, Inc.*, 287 F.3d 1108, 1118 (Fed. Cir. 2002)); *see also ParkerVision, Inc.*, 903 F.3d at 1361 (articulating a distinction between configuration-type and capability type claims).

Possibly the most straightforward example of this is the common distinction between method claims and apparatus claims. *See, e.g.*, *Finjan*, 626 F.3d at 1203–05. In *Finjan*, this court held that Finjan's "non-method claims describe capabilities without requiring that any software components be 'active' or 'enabled.'" *Id.* at 1204–05. The court, therefore, upheld a finding of infringement for products in which the accused proactive-scanning software module was locked when sold by the defendants. *Id.* at 1205; *see also id.* at 1203–04 (*distinguishing Southwest Software, Inc. v. Harlequin Inc.*, 226 F.3d 1280, 1291 (Fed. Cir. 2000), in which the accused software product required a manual step to activate the patented feature, but the claim at issue was a method claim). In contrast, Finjan's method claims were not infringed by the accused products because those claims required actual performance of each claimed step; there was no evidence that proactive scanning was performed in the United States. *Id.* at 1206 ("To infringe a method claim, a person must have practiced all steps of the claimed method." (*quoting Lucent Techs. v. Gateway, Inc.*, 580 F.3d 1301, 1317 (Fed. Cir. 2009))). *Cf. ParkerVision, Inc.*, 903 F.3d at 1363 (similarly differentiating apparatus claims and method claims in the patent invalidity context). However, differences exist between apparatus claims as well, depending on the claim language. **We have construed some apparatus claims to require an infringing device to actually perform and operate according to the functional terms recited in the claim.** The intervenors cite two such cases, *Cross Medical* and *Ball Aerosol*. *See Intervenors' Br.* 64, 67–68. We have construed other apparatus claims to require only capability, such as in *Finjan* and *Silicon Graphics*.

. . .

. . .

In *Cross Medical*, we rejected the argument that the limitation "anchor seat means which has a lower bone interface operatively joined to said bone segment" could be met merely by an interface that was capable of contacting bone. *Cross Med. Prods., Inc. v. Medtronic Sofamor Danek, Inc.*, 424 F.3d 1293, 1305–06 (Fed. Cir. 2005). **Instead, the claim language "operatively joined" required that the interface and the bone segment be connected and in contact such that the device effectively performed posterior stabilization.** *Id.* at 1306. Direct infringement did not occur until the device was connected to the bone, which a surgeon performed, not the allegedly infringing device maker. *Id.* at 1310–14.

. . .

. . . Intervenors emphasize that the *Cross Medical* claims included the present-tense verb "has," similar to the present-tense verbs "demodulates" and "decodes" in the '439 claims. But this court's construction in *Cross Medical* was based on "operatively joined," not "has." Intervenors do not provide any analysis of *Ball Aerosol*. While the *Ball Aerosol* claim is atypical for its recitation, within a mechanical device claim, of how a component is to be used or operated—somewhat akin to computer device claims, which commonly include functional language—it ultimately has little relevance for construing INVT's claims.

Because of the nature of the technology, computer and software claims typically use functional language to define the invention. Functional language is used to define and delimit otherwise generic or interchangeable general purpose computer hardware, which can be programmed to perform an unlimited array of functions. In other words, the recited operative steps a computer- or software-based device undertakes is what defines what a computer-implemented invention is. We have frequently construed such functional language as not requiring actual performance of those operative steps for infringement purposes. Moreover, we have not required claims to adhere to a specific grammatical form to find that the claim is drawn to capability, contrary to the Commission's and the intervenors' contentions.

. . .

The FID relied primarily on *Finjan* and the absence of "for performing"-type claim language, providing little else for why the '439 claims require actual operation. The intervenors argue that simple-present-tense words are enough to require actual operation, *see Intervenors' Br.* 65, 67, but *Silicon Graphics* shows that is not true. **In fact, based on just claim language, we see very little significance in the difference between a limitation that might recite "a data obtaining section for demodulating and decoding" (*Finjan*-style) and one that recites "a data obtaining section that demodulates and decodes" (the actual '439 claim language), for determining on which side of the capability/actual-operation line the claims fall.**

Like with the claims in *Finjan* and *Silicon Graphics*, we find that the asserted '439 claims are directed to capability—as in a device that includes "software components with specific purposes," programmed to have the ability to perform the operative steps: namely, a "receiving section" that can receive a signal containing data modulated and encoded using the parameters decided at user device, and a "data obtaining section" that can demodulate and decode the signal using the parameters decided at the user device. *Finjan*, 626 F.3d at 1204–05. **In other words, the claims recite a device with the capability of performing the recited functions when in operation without any modification or further programming.**

Thus, the court interpreted the language of the claim, such as, "a data obtaining section that demodulates and decodes" to recite a device with the capability of performing the recited functions apparently in part because the language at issue involves a device that includes "software components with specific purposes," programmed to have the ability to perform the operative steps. Despite this, however, the court affirmed as to non-infringement.

For our purposes, in light of this precedent, the analysis seems clear. If the claim requires that a device have the capacity to perform a function, one who makes, uses, or sells, and so on, a device with that capacity without the patent owner's authority is a direct infringer even if the capacity is not actually used.[86]

To illustrate such a claim for such a situation, consider, for example, this technical problem. On modern computers, the address space of programs are typically provided a special region of memory described as the stack. The stack is primarily intended for fast allocation and deallocation of regions of memory, called frames, for use by a particular function operation (a function operation refers to code to perform an operation; the term is intended to distinguish it from a mathematical function). Data objects allocated in a frame of a particular function operation are considered to be "private" to that frame by default; however, there are ways for unscrupulous individuals to violate this protocol and improperly access the frame of a particular function operation. This may occur via malware with the intention to interfere with normal computer operation. Furthermore, there are no standard methods to prevent this from occurring at program runtime in state-of-the-art computers today.

One way to prevent such malware interference is to limit access to the stack memory locations of the particular function operation by another function operation *unless* the other function operation has had a *pointer granting access passed to it* by the particular function operation during the execution of the processor instructions.

This may, for example, be a feature included in a microprocessor in which the feature may be turned on and off. Next is a possible claim.

86. It is noted that there appears to be some tension between this case and the case, IPXL Holdings v. Amazon, 430 F.3d 1377, 1384 (Fed. Cir. 2005). *See also* section 5.6 and its subsections, discussing the issue of mixing statutory classes. However, it may be that the IPXL v. Amazon line of authority had not been argued and, furthermore, the court seems here to have interpreted the claim language in a manner that may not make the claim language indefinite because it involves a device that includes "software components with specific purposes," programmed to have the ability to perform the operative steps. We, nonetheless, continue to recommend drafting apparatus claims in a manner to avoid the risk of mixing statutory classes. Even in this case, the court acknowleged *"[p]ossibly the most straightforward example of this [difference] is the common distinction between method claims and apparatus claims."*

EXAMPLE 4.5

I claim:

1. An apparatus comprising: an integrated circuit; wherein the integrated circuit comprises a processor;

   wherein the processor comprises memory management capability with memory to be connected to the processor and to be accessed during execution of one or more programs, wherein the execution of the one or more programs comprises execution of processor instructions by the processor;

   wherein the memory management capability includes the capability to maintain flow control between the execution of function operations to be implemented via the processor instructions;

   wherein the capability to maintain flow control between the execution of function operations to be implemented via the processor instructions comprises the processor, during execution of the processor instructions, to limit access of another function operation to read from or write to stack memory address locations to be reserved for a particular function operation unless the another function operation has had a pointer to grant access passed to it by the particular function operation during the execution of the processor instructions.

Thus, the claim recites

> the memory management capability includes the capability to maintain flow control between the execution of function operations . . . ;
> wherein the capability to maintain flow control between the execution of function operations . . . comprises the processor, during execution of the processor instructions, to limit access of another function operation to read from or write to stack memory address locations to be reserved for a particular function operation unless the another function operation has had a pointer to grant access passed to it by the particular function operation during the execution of the processor instructions.

A processor with this capability whether activated or used would therefore infringe this claim.

4.125 Product-by-Process Claims

For many years it remained unclear how product-by-process claims should be interpreted.[87] This was due to two federal circuit panels that reached different outcomes. *Scripps Clinic & Research Foundation v. Genentech, Inc.*, a 1991 federal circuit decision, stated that a product-by-process claim was *not* limited to products prepared by the process recited in the claims.[88] However, in *Atlantic Thermoplastics Co., Inc. v. Faytex Corp.*, a 1992 federal circuit decision, a different three-judge panel ruled that "[P]rocess terms in product-by-process claims serve as limitations in determining infringement."[89]

These potentially inconsistent rulings, however, did not necessarily foreclose use of such claims since one case discussed applying a process limitation for purposes of infringement, whereas the other case was less clear. Rather, the uncertainty provided a potential opportunity to argue for a desired interpretation, depending on issues related to invalidity or infringement. For a knowledgeable practitioner, product-by-process claims might be included, but with recognition of the interpretation risk. However, after nearly two decades, the federal circuit ultimately resolved the panel inconsistency, and the interpretation of such claims is now clear.[90] As a result of this interpretation, such claims are not generally advisable unless it is the *only* way to claim the subject matter at issue. Part of the reason for this is that the process limitations *are not* considered for purposes of validity, but the process limitations *are* considered for purposes of infringement.

Product-by-process claims represent one of the few situations where claims are interpreted differently for validity than they are for infringement. As the court said in *Abbott Labs*:

> The impact of these different analyses is significant. For product-by-process claims, that which anticipates if earlier does not necessarily infringe if later.

---

87. *See* Atlantic Thermoplastics Co., Inc. v. Faytex Corp., 970 F.2d 834, 23 USPQ2d 1481 (Fed. Cir. 1992), *suggestion for reh'g en banc declined*, 974 F.2d 1279, 23 USPQ2d 1801, 974 F.2d 1299, 24 USPQ2d 1138 (Fed. Cir. 1992).

88. *See* Scripps Clinic & Rsch. Found. v. Genentech, Inc., 927 F.2d 1565, 18 USPQ2d 1001 (Fed. Cir. 1991).

89. *See* Atlantic Thermoplastics Co., Inc. v. Faytex Corp., 970 F.2d 834, 23 USPQ2d 1481 (Fed. Cir. 1992).

90. *See* Abbott Laboratories v. Sandoz, Inc., 566 F.3d 1282 (Fed. Cir. 2009) (en banc).

That is because a product in the prior art made by a different process can anticipate a product-by-process claim, but an accused product made by a different process cannot infringe a product-by-process claim.[91]

The format of a product-by-process claim might look like:

1. An apparatus comprising: product X;

    wherein product X is to be produced by:

    action 1;

    action 2; and

    action 3.

One issue to be aware of in this context is inadvertent use of "product-by-process" limitations.[92] Words that may be the past tense of a verb that suggests a process, as illustrated in Example 2.17 of Chapter 2, for example, may have some risk. There, "coating," "blended," or "disposed over" are illustrative examples. A common word used that may be another example is "formed." The nature of materials technology may often lend itself to this sort of description. This sort of language is highlighted here because, if interpreted to be a product by process limitation, the language would be subject to the rules governing product-by-process claims, which increases risk of invalidity.[93]

4.1251 Advantages and Disadvantages

Although previously it was thought there was some advantage to the use of product-by-process claims due to the uncertainty in the law regarding their scope for validity and infringement, in 2009 the federal circuit resolved the issue in an en banc decision.[94] As a result, the process limitations of a product-by-process claim *are not* considered for purposes of validity, but the process limitations of the claim *are* considered for purposes of infringement. As the court said in *Abbott Labs*:

> The impact of these different analyses is significant. For product-by-process claims, that which anticipates if earlier does not necessarily infringe if later.

91. *See* Abbott Laboratories v. Sandoz, Inc., 566 F.3d 1282 (Fed. Cir. 2009).

92. *See* section 1.2212 discussing product-by-process claims as an example of a legal change that may impact patent strategy and tactics.

93. *See* section 1.2212, also discussing product-by-process claims; *see also* Kamstrup A/S v. Axioma Metering UAB, 43 F.4th 1374 (Fed. Cir. 2022) (affirming that the PTAB properly construed a product-by-process claim element as not entitled to patentable weight).

94. *See* Abbott Laboratories v. Sandoz, Inc., 566 F.3d 1282 (Fed. Cir. 2009).

> That is because a product in the prior art made by a different process can anticipate a product-by-process claim, but an accused product made by a different process cannot infringe a product-by-process claim.[95]

This, of course, means that to be patentable, the claim must distinguish from the prior art *without* considering the process limitations. However, if that is the case, why include the process limitations, in the independent claim at least? One might include process limitations in a dependent claim. However, in that case, the dependent claim would not help distinguish from the prior art. Thus, these claims offer some disadvantages with few advantages.

One situation where a product-by-process might arguably be of use is where there is no other way to describe the product being made by the particular process; however, even in this case, if true, it would seem that the claim would not be patentable because the process limitations are ignored. If one could write a patentable claim despite ignoring the process limitations, then the situation would appear to be the one just described. That is, one could write a patentable independent claim without process limitations, which would capture more infringers.

There might be a possible advantage to a product-by-process claim, assuming a patentable claim may be crafted. Previously, the power of a product by process claim was typically seen with a manufacturing process. A method claim to the process is only infringed by the manufacturer. Once something is made by the process and sold, it is beyond the scope of the process claim. However, with a product-by-process claim, in theory at least, a distributer or purchaser of the manufactured product would be suable based on a product within the scope of the claim.

However, again, the situation sort of begs the question. If one could write a product-by-process claim that is patentable when ignoring the process limitations, what value do the process limitations add? It seems the value is in the product related limitations regardless of process.

The next section, however, discusses a very specific situation where one may get the power of a product-by-process claim, as just described, without the disadvantages of federal circuit jurisprudence in which the validity and infringement considerations are not in balance.

---

95. *See id.*

4.1252 *Illustrative Claim Example—Capturing Product-by-Process Infringement With and Without Product-By-Process Claims (e.g., 35 USC § 271(g))*

For starters, there may be a bit of subtlety in appreciating how a product-by-process claim might differ from an apparatus claim directed to the product or differ from a claim to the particular process. Consider first the following relatively simple process claim directed to manufacturing a thin-film silicon-on-insulator (SOI) integrated circuit. At one time, the following claim would have been new and non-obvious.

EXAMPLE 4.6

I claim:

1. A method of fabrication comprising:

   fabricating an integrated circuit (IC);

   wherein the fabricating includes forming at least a plurality of N-type metal oxide semiconductor field effect transistors (NMOSFETs) by forming a source, a drain, a gate and a body for respective NMOSFETs of the plurality in a thin-film silicon layer of a silicon-on-insulator (SOI) substrate;

   wherein the forming the source, the drain, the gate and the body for the respective NMOSFETs of the plurality comprises:

      forming the gate from a conductive layer and an oxide layer over the thin film silicon layer of the SOI substrate; and

      forming two N+ regions in the thin film silicon layer of the SOI substrate via ion implantation or diffusion to form the source, the drain, and the body;

   wherein the fabricating further includes fabricating one or more layers of metallization over the thin film silicon layer; and

   coupling the one or more layers of metallization to the plurality of NMOSFETs into an electrical configuration.

Next, consider a claim for fabricating an RF switch in a thin-film silicon-on-insulator (SOI) integrated circuit. Perhaps one might try to argue this is a product-by-process claim, but by its terms it is a method claim.

EXAMPLE 4.7

I claim:

1. A method of fabricating an RF switch comprising:

fabricating an integrated circuit (IC) that includes the RF switch;

wherein the fabricating includes forming at least a plurality of N-type metal oxide semiconductor field effect transistors (NMOSFETs) by forming a source, a drain, a gate and a body for respective NMOSFETs of the plurality in a thin-film silicon layer of a silicon-on-insulator (SOI) substrate;

wherein the forming the source, the drain, the gate and the body for the respective NMOSFETs of the plurality comprises:

forming the gate from a conductive layer and an oxide layer over the thin film silicon layer of the SOI substrate; and

forming two N+ regions in the thin film silicon layer of the SOI substrate via ion implantation or diffusion to form the source, the drain, and the body;

wherein the fabricating further includes fabricating one or more layers of metallization over the thin film silicon layer;

wherein the one or more layers of metallization to couple the plurality of NMOSFETs into a stack to pass an RF signal through the stack of NMOSFETs in an ON state of the stack of NMOSFETs;

wherein the one or more layers of metallization to couple the plurality of NMOSFETs of the stack to not pass an RF signal through the stack of NMOSFETs in an OFF state of the stack of NMOSFETs; and

wherein the one or more layers of metallization to couple an electrical bias to the body of the respective NMOSFETs at least in a portion of the OFF state of the stack to have a DC voltage level substantially more negative than a lowest voltage level of the following: ground, a DC voltage level of the source of the respective NMOSFETs, and a DC voltage level of the drain of the respective NMOSFETs.

One might perhaps argue that the last three wherein clauses are not in method format. Thus, to keep the claim "clean," so to speak, the method claim might, instead, be crafted as follows:

EXAMPLE 4.8

I claim:

1. A method of fabricating an RF switch comprising:

   fabricating an integrated circuit (IC) that includes the RF switch;

   wherein the fabricating includes forming at least a plurality of N-type metal oxide semiconductor field effect transistors (NMOSFETs) by forming a source, a drain, a gate and a body for respective NMOSFETs of the plurality in a thin film silicon layer of a silicon on insulator (SOI) substrate;

   wherein the fabricating further includes fabricating one or more layers of metallization over the thin film silicon layer;

      coupling the plurality of NMOSFETs into a stack via the one or more layers of metallization to pass an RF signal through the stack of NMOSFETs in an ON state of the stack of NMOSFETs;

      coupling the plurality of NMOSFETs of the stack via the one or more layers of metallization to not pass an RF signal through the stack of NMOSFETs in an OFF state of the stack of NMOSFETs; and

      coupling an electrical bias to the body of the respective NMOSFETs via the one or more layers of metallization at least in a portion of the OFF state of the stack to have a DC voltage level substantially more negative than a lowest voltage level of the following: ground, a DC voltage level of the source of the respective NMOSFETs, and a DC voltage level of the drain of the respective NMOSFETs.

Now, it appears a challenge to argue this is not a method claim. Next, consider the following, which might be considered a product-by-process claim.

EXAMPLE 4.9

I claim:

1. A device comprising: a plurality of N-type metal oxide semiconductor field effect transistors (NMOSFETs), respective NMOSFETs of the plurality including a source, a gate, a drain and a body;

   wherein the plurality of NMOSFETs are to be fabricated on an integrated circuit;

   the respective NMOSFETs are to be fabricated from the source, the drain, the gate and the body that are to be formed in a thin-film silicon layer of a silicon-on-insulator substrate;

   wherein the source, the drain, the gate and the body for the respective NMOSFETs of the plurality are to be formed in a manner that comprises the following:

      the gate is to be formed from a conductive layer and an oxide layer over the silicon layer of the SOI substrate; and

      two N+ regions are to be formed in the silicon layer of the SOI substrate via ion implantation or diffusion to form the source, the drain, and the body;

   wherein one or more layers of metallization are to be fabricated over the silicon layer;

   wherein the one or more layers of metallization are to couple the plurality of NMOSFETs into a stack to pass an RF signal through the stack of NMOSFETs in an ON state of the stack of NMOSFETs;

   wherein the one or more layers of metallization are to couple the plurality of NMOSFETs of the stack to not pass an RF signal through the stack of NMOSFETs in an OFF state of the stack of NMOSFETs; and

   wherein the one or more layers of metallization are to couple an electrical bias to the body of the respective NMOSFETs at least in a portion of the OFF state of the stack to have a DC voltage level substantially more negative than a lowest voltage level of the following: ground, a DC voltage level of the source of the respective NMOSFETs, and a DC voltage level of the drain of the respective NMOSFETs.

However, appreciate that there is not a tremendous amount of process in this claim. For the claim to be patentable, the key features are in the structure. Perhaps one could argue that "fabricated" and "formed" are structural limitations, although this seems like a long shot in this context. Nonetheless, appreciate that many of these linguistic issues are subtle and subject to interpretation and argument and the specification description may shift the balance as well regarding interpretation issues.

Here is another example of a product-by-process claim for a different technology:

EXAMPLE 4.10

I claim:

1. An apparatus comprising: a mesh;

   the mesh including plastic;

   the plastic heated to a temperature sufficient to make the plastic malleable;

   the malleable plastic then rolled, extruded, and cut to form a mesh-shaped plastic;

   the mesh-shaped plastic then being cooled to a temperature sufficient to harden the plastic of the mesh-shaped plastic after having been rolled, extruded, and cut.

One important legal opportunity to be aware of in connection with method of manufacture claims is section 271(g). This section provides the ability to potentially get a type of product-by-process claim without the invalidity disadvantages discussed earlier. The section states:

> (g) Whoever without authority imports into the United States or offers to sell, sells, or uses within the United States a product which is made by a process patented in the United States shall be liable as an infringer, if the importation, offer to sell, sale, or use of the product occurs during the term of such process patent. In an action for infringement of a process patent, no remedy may be granted for infringement on account of the noncommercial use or retail sale of a product unless there is no adequate remedy under this title for infringement on account of the importation or other use, offer to sell, or sale of that product. A product which is made by a patented process will, for purposes of this title, not be considered to be so made after—

(1) it is materially changed by subsequent processes; or

(2) it becomes a trivial and nonessential component of another product.

Note the specific language "a product which is *made* by a process patented in the United States" (emphasis supplied). This provision has been interpreted to be limited to manufacturing.[96] This provision as well as section 271(f) are directed to "extraterritorial activities" that may ultimately result in liability for patent infringement in the United States.

For example, it is becoming more common for companies, so-called fabless design houses, to outsource chip manufacturing to others. Coming up with the design does not generally by itself directly infringe a patent claim.[97] Yet, a company making the chip for someone else could infringe a manufacturing claim absent extraterritorial considerations.[98]

Let's consider a situation in which a foundry *outside* the United States performs the claim of Example 2.14 or the claim of Example 4.6 for a U.S. company who then imports the manufactured IC into the United States. That U.S. company, while having not performed the process itself, is nonetheless liable for infringement in federal court assuming (g)(1) and (g)(2) do not apply. Furthermore, those in the chain of distribution may similarly be sued in federal court as an infringer, subject to the defenses in the statute, such as a noncommercial use, a retail sale, or the conditions of subsections (g)(1) or (g)(2).

This section, in effect, gives one the equivalent of a product-by-process patent claim for this situation, but without the invalidity concerns previously raised for a product-by-process claim.[99] Furthermore, the federal circuit has ruled that the two defenses in (g)(1) and (g)(2) are not legally applicable in proceedings before the International Trade Commission (ITC), a quasi-judicial governmental body that hears and decides complaints regarding importations that may be in violation of certain U.S. trade regulation laws, including intellectual property laws.[100] Thus, one may potentially stop importation of the

96. *See* Bayer v. Houses Pharmaceuticals, 340 F.3d 1367 (Fed. Cir. 2003).

97. Although it might be a basis for a claim for indirect infringement; *see* section 3.22, discussing indirect infringement.

98. *See* section 4.127, discussing method of making claims. Direct infringement is generally easier to prove than indirect infringement, as discussed in Chapter 3.

99. *See* section 1.2212, discussing product-by-process claims; *see* Jennewein Biotechnologie GMBH v. ITC 2021 U.S. App. LEXIS 28200 (Sept. 17, 2021 Fed. Cir.); Kinik v. ITC, 362 F.3d 1359 (Fed. Cir. 2004).

100. *See* Jennewein Biotechnologie GMBH v. ITC 2021 U.S. App. LEXIS 28200 (Sept. 17, 2021 Fed. Cir.); Kinik v. ITC, 362 F.3d 1359 (Fed. Cir. 2004).

chips at the border of the United States without a concern regarding potential defenses under (g)(1) and (g)(2).[101]

4.126 Method of Using Claims

As suggested, these sections are a refresh or review of basic claim types, since a lot of ground has been covered since the earlier discussion. To keep things interesting, we provide different examples for discussion. One point to be made early is that one might attempt to draft method claims, particularly method of using claims, at different levels of integration just as was illustrated for apparatus claims. Some examples are provided next.

To refresh some basic concepts, recall that method patent claims also employ a preamble, a transition word, and a claim body. Each also ends with a period.

Likewise, as for apparatus claims, method claims obey the single infringer rule. One party should control the set of acts, actions, or operations recited in the claim. If some actions are done by one party, and some actions are done by another party acting independently, then it may be that no one will infringe the patent claim.[102]

Recall, at one of the most basic levels, the set of rights granted by these different categories of patent claims is different. An apparatus claim provides the full set of statutory rights, that is, make, use, sell, and so on.[103] On the other hand, due to an inherent nature, a method claim essentially covers "use," as in a method of using, or "make," as in a method of making or manufacturing. At least partially for this reason, apparatus claims are usually perceived to be more valuable than method claims. However, do not read this to suggest that method claims are not valuable. In various situations, having a method claim may be important to have as an arrow in your quiver. It is recommended to nearly always include method claims with apparatus claims for claim diversity. Many patents are written that do not follow this simple principle.

Usually, an invention will more easily be claimed as one or the other, that is, as a method or as an apparatus. For example, software operation is usually more easily described as a method. Although not a requirement, it seems

---

101. Another feature of section 271(g) is that a single entity need not perform all the claim elements. That is, as to the method claim, there is liability without meeting the single infringer rule. *See* Syngenta v. Willowood, 944 F.3d 1344 (Fed. Cir. 2019).

102. *See, e.g.*, Akamai v. Limelight, 572 U.S. 915, 921–22 (2014); Muniauction, Inc. v. Thompson Corp., 532 F.3d 1318 (Fed. Cir. 2008); BMC v. Paymentech, 489 F.3d 1373, 1379–81 (Fed. Cir. 2007).

103. *See* 35 U.S.C. § 271(a) (2022).

logical when beginning to draft claims for an invention to begin with the claim type that is more easily drafted due to the inherent nature of the invention.

> When beginning to draft claims for an invention, begin with the claim type that is more easily drafted due to the inherent nature of the invention.

Regardless, do not pass on the opportunity to claim an invention in method terms (e.g., method of using and/or method of making in addition to apparatus terms). A litany of good reasons to do this exist. A method may stand up to prior art even in situations where an apparatus claim may not. Depending on the limitations of the patent claim, a method claim may be infringed where an apparatus claim is not, it may be infringed in a different manner, or it may result in greater damages. Further, a pure method claim generally is much less likely to be construed under section 112(f). The failure to claim a method described in the specification also has the potential to dedicate to the public subject matter that might have otherwise been covered by a method claim.[104] Other good reasons also exist to include method claims, but these reasons should be more than sufficient.

> It is recommended to nearly always include method claims with apparatus claims for claim diversity.

One aspect to appreciate is the difference in drafting a method claim versus drafting an apparatus claim that flows directly from the preceding discussion about the set of rights associated with each. A method claim recites actions or acts. A method claim is infringed by performing an action, an act or an operation, such as when "using" something or "making" something. Hence, the claim elements of a method claim are actions like "receiving," "transmitting," and so on, that is, words ending in "ing."

104. *See* Johnson & Johnston Assocs. v. R.E. Serv. Co., 285 F.3d 1046m 1054 (Fed. Cir. 2002) (en banc) ("As stated in Maxwell, when a patent drafter discloses but declines to claim subject matter, as in this case, this action dedicates that unclaimed subject matter to the public.").

One way to think of a method claim, for drafting purposes, is like a cooking recipe. It specifies the steps to follow. Usually, therefore, method claims are easier to draft than their apparatus counterparts. As has been stated, an apparatus may be *capable of* performing an action, an act or an operation, but it is considered prudent to not claim an apparatus in a manner that suggests that it is actually performing such actions or operations.[105] Thus, an apparatus claim either recites structural elements, such as a processor or memory, or it recites that such elements are able to perform an action to make it clear that the action itself is not being claimed. Claiming the action itself is the domain of method claims.[106]

> One way to think of a method claim is like a cooking recipe. It specifies the steps to follow.

4.1261 Illustrative Claim Example

The opportunity to claim a method even in situations where that is *not necessarily* the feature that is inventive should also not be overlooked. For example, consider an analog or digital circuit invention capable of being embedded in a silicon chip in which the arrangement of the circuit is truly the inventive feature. Still, a method of using patent claim, for example, may be drafted that provides claim diversity.

Consider Examples 4.1, 4.2, and 4.3 from earlier in the chapter. The innovation relates to the circuit structure; however, method of using claims of value are able to be formulated.

Here is an example of a method claim for operating a module.

---

105. *See, e.g.*, IPXL Holdings v. Amazon, 430 F.3d 1377, 1384 (Fed. Cir. 2005). *See* section 5.6 and its subsections, discussing not mixing statutory classes in a patent claim.

106. *Cf.* INVT SPE LLC v. ITC, Appeal No. 20-1903 (Fed. Cir. August 31, 2022) (distinguishing between actual operation and capability of operating or performing for apparatus claims, particularly for software on a device, which tends to be functional, without discussing indefiniteness issue of mixing method and apparatus limitations), discussed in subsections 4.124 and 4.1272.

EXAMPLE 4.11

I claim:

1. A method of operating a module, the module including at least one integrated circuit chip comprising a plurality of series N-type metal oxide semiconductor (NMOS) field effect transistors configured in a series connected stack configuration that comprises at least one series NMOS field effect transistor including a body, the at least one series NMOS field effect transistor either to pass an RF signal in a series enable state or to not pass the RF signal in a series disable state, the method further comprising:

   electrically biasing the body of the at least one series NMOS field effect transistor of the module in the series disable state to have a voltage level substantially more negative than the lowest voltage level of the following: ground, a DC voltage level of a source of the at least one series NMOS field effect transistor of the module, and a DC voltage level of a drain of the at least one series NMOS field effect transistor of the module.

Observe this is a one action method claim. This should not be an issue unless it is interpreted under section 112(f), which requires that such claims are for combinations. Also, observe that the hardware limitations are in the preamble so that the claim body is essentially a "pure" method. Also notice that to address a potential argument that the preamble language directed to "module" is not necessarily limiting, "module" is also used in the claim body.

The point here is that while different substantive rights may flow from different claim types, creating different claim types is largely an exercise in drafting.

> The point here is that while different substantive rights may flow from different claim types, creating different claim types is largely an exercise in drafting.

One notable potential weakness in this claim is the language "a plurality of series N-type metal oxide semiconductor (NMOS) field effect transistors *configured in* a series connected stack configuration." It is not uncommon to see language in claims such as "adapted to," "configured to," particularly in connection with functional language, as occurs here.

There could be several problems with such language. For one thing, examiners do not like it, so it is reasonably likely to be rejected. Second, there is some federal circuit law that has construed such language narrowly.[107] Third, one could make the noninfringement argument that the accused product is not "configured" or "adapted." This might be an especially strong argument in connection with software, which is often configured. Usually the word "adapted," "configured" and so on is not needed. Here, for example, the claim might read:

---

1. A method of operating a module, the module including at least one integrated circuit chip comprising a plurality of N-type metal oxide semiconductor (NMOS) field effect transistors in a series connected stack configuration that comprises at least one NMOS field effect transistor including a body, the at least one NMOS field effect transistor either to pass an RF signal in a series enable state or to not pass the RF signal in a series disable state, the method further comprising:

   electrically biasing the body of the at least one NMOS field effect transistor of the module in the series disable state to have a voltage level substantially more negative than the lowest voltage level of the following: ground, a DC voltage level of a source of the at least one series NMOS field effect transistor of the module, and a DC voltage level of a drain of the at least one NMOS field effect transistor of the module.

> Good practice suggests avoiding formulations like "adapted to" or "configured to" and the like. Instead, just say "to. . . ."

107. *See* Aspex Eyewear, Inc. v. Marchon Eyewear, Inc., 672 F.3d 1335 (Fed. Cir. 2012); *In re* Giannelli, 739 F.3d 1375 (Fed. Cir. 2014).

With that said, the original language here is probably quite innocuous. The original claim language simply says the transistors are configured in a configuration, somewhat awkward, admittedly, but not indefinite. Furthermore, since this is hardware, it is virtually assured that the claim language is met. Nonetheless, good practice suggests avoiding formulations like "adapted to" or "configured to" and the like. Instead, just say "to. . . ."

Here, the claim example omits thin-film and silicon-on-insulator limitations. These are left for dependent claims because the electrical biasing limitation is believed to patentably distinguish the claim.

Here is a similar claim approach directed to a method of operating a communication device, rather than a module.

EXAMPLE 4.12

I claim:

1. A method of operating a communication device, the communication device including at least one integrated circuit chip comprising a plurality of series N-type metal oxide semiconductor (NMOS) field effect transistors in a series connected stack configuration that comprises at least one series NMOS field effect transistor including a body, the at least one series NMOS field effect transistor either to pass an RF signal in a series enable state or to not pass the RF signal in a series disable state, the method further comprising:

   electrically biasing the body of the at least one series NMOS field effect transistor of the communication device in the series disable state to have a voltage level substantially more negative than the lowest voltage level of the following: ground, the DC voltage level of the source of the at least one series NMOS field effect transistor of the communication device, and the DC voltage level of the drain of the at least one series NMOS field effect transistor of the communication device.

The points made earlier regarding Example 4.11 apply here to Example 4.12 as well, although arguably the royalty base is greater. A smart phone, for example, might sell for around $1,000 or more these days. Furthermore, the technology of the claim is critical to wireless cellphone operation. Without it, the signal would be corrupted; hence, providing a basis to argue that the entire market principle for damages should apply.[108]

Now, of course, it is highly likely that the choice of royalty base will necessarily affect the royalty rate. That is, one might expect that the royalty rate may be reduced by orders of magnitude. With that said, however, a royalty base of $1,000 is much more appealing from a negotiation point of view than one of a few cents, as in the earlier transistor claim example. All of these points are matters of negotiation, while the law of damages, which is fluid, so to speak, operates as the backdrop. Thus, it may be that a larger royalty base provides room to be more flexible on royalty rate in a negotiation and still come out ahead relative to a royalty base based on a transistor innovation, as here, for example.

As another approach to a method claim for this technology, consider the following:

EXAMPLE 4.13

I claim:

1. A method of operating an RF module comprising at least one integrated circuit chip, the method comprising:

   inputting an input RF signal and one or more control signals to the RF module;

   outputting an output RF signal from the RF module;

   controlling, based at least in part on the one or more control signals, a silicon on insulator (SOI) N-type metal oxide semiconductor (NMOS) field effect transistor (FET) series connected stack configuration to either an OFF state or an ON state, the SOI NMOS FET stack configuration, comprising a plurality of NMOS FET transistors, being implemented on the at least one integrated circuit chip; and

   electrically biasing, based at least in part on the one or more control signals, a body of at least one NMOS FET transistor of the plurality of NMOS FET transistors of the SOI NMOS FET stack configuration with a bias voltage substantially more negative than ground during at least a portion of the OFF state of the at least one NMOS FET transistor.

108. *See* section 6.4 discussing damages considerations in claim drafting.

There are several notable differences from Example 4.11. However, like 4.11, module and integrated circuit are used in the claim body. A dramatic difference is that while Example 4.11 had essentially one recited action, this claim has four. These are: inputting, outputting, controlling, and electrically biasing. Thus, an aspect of the claim is inputting signals and outputting signals. This is usually performed by most chips, but not always necessarily called out in the claim.

Another dramatic difference is how hardware aspects of the claim are handled. In this instance, they are not recited in a preamble, but are rather recited as needed within the claim body, like the approach discussed in connection with inferential claiming.[109] Some differences that could have been handled more like previous claims is the recitation of "ground" rather than three possible voltage levels. As a practical matter, in most cases, ground will be the lowest voltage level. This, therefore, simplifies the claim. Likewise, although SOI is recited, as for Example 4.11, a thin-film silicon layer is left to be recited in dependencies.

EXAMPLE 4.14

I claim:

1. A method of operating a communication device including an RF module that further includes at least one integrated circuit chip, the method comprising:

   controlling a silicon on insulator (SOI) N-type metal oxide semiconductor (NMOS) field effect transistor (FET) series connected stack configuration to either an OFF state or an ON state, the SOI NMOS FET stack configuration, comprising a plurality of NMOS FET transistors, being implemented on the at least one integrated circuit chip of the RF module of the communication device; and

   electrically biasing a body of at least one NMOS FET transistor of the plurality of NMOS FET transistors of the SOI NMOS FET stack configuration with a bias voltage substantially more negative than ground during at least a portion of the OFF state of the at least one NMOS FET transistor of the RF module of the communication device.

109. *See* section 2.1413, discussing inferential claiming.

Again, a communication device instead of a module is recited so that the points made earlier regarding Example 4.12 may apply here to Example 4.14 as well.

One practice that used to be common was to recite in the claim "A method comprising the steps of": This practice is less common today and, here, we also suggest avoiding it. At least one reason is to prevent someone from arguing that your method claim has a "step plus function" element recited that should properly be interpreted under section 112(f).

Most method claims recite some tangible components as limitations, such as discussed in connection with the distinction between function and structure. However, care is warranted here. If a method claim recites a lot of tangible components, such as hardware, for example, and is sloppy, someone may argue it is not clear whether the claim is a method or an apparatus claim. There is not much, if any law, on this specific situation, but the legal argument follows from cases that have held claims invalid that were ostensibly apparatus claims but used too much language that typically appears in method claims.[110] Judgment and/or claim diversity should be a guide here. Two different approaches to this were just discussed and illustrated.

It also is a good idea to stick to the form of a method claim, including with "wherein" clauses in the claim and with dependencies.[111]

Another useful point about method claims is that the acts, actions, or operations (e.g., elements) may be done in any order unless the language expressly states an order or through its language implies an order.[112]

4.1262 New Use of an Old Device

One situation to be aware of is that a new use of an old or known device may be patentable;[113] however, it is also important to understand the parameters that affect patentability in this situation. The doctrine of inherent anticipation may limit patentability if the new use is based on an inherent characteristic of the old or known device.[114] However, if the feature is not inevitably present

110. *See, e.g.*, IPXL Holdings v. Amazon, 430 F.3d 1377, 1384 (Fed. Cir. 2005). *See* section 5.6 and its subsections, discussing this claim drafting issue.

111. *See* discussion of method claims in Chapter 2.

112. *Id.*

113. *See, e.g.*, Sean Seymore, *Patenting New Uses of Old Inventions*, 73(2) Vanderbilt L. Rev. 479–543 (2020); Perricone v. Medicis Pharm. Corp., 432 F.3d 1368, 1378 (Fed. Cir. 2005) ("New uses of old products or processes are indeed patentable subject matter."). One case example is *Glaxosmithkline v. Teva* 7 F.4th 1320 (Fed. Cir. 2021) in which a drug for hypertension, carvedilol, was found to also decrease mortality for congestive heart failure.

114. *See, e.g.*, Seymore, *supra* note 113; Atlas Powder Co. v. Ireco Inc., 190 F.3d 1342, 1347 (Fed. Cir. 1999).

as "the natural result flowing from the operation [of the prior art] as taught," then it is not inherent.[115]

This inherency issue may be a technical challenge in the chemical or pharmaceutical arts, the so-called unpredictable arts.[116] The article "Patenting New Uses of Old Inventions," provides a good hypothetical example of an anti-depressant drug in which the patent has expired and is re-patented as a treatment for irritable bowel syndrome, migraines, fibromyalgia, and functional dyspepsia. However, if the drug is able to operate as a treatment because it inhibits the uptake of serotonin in the brain, then this may not really be a new use since this may be how it *inherently* operated as an anti-depressant.

Although still a real issue, it may be less of a technical issue generally for mechanical arts, electrical arts and for software, the so-called predictable arts. Typically, the science behind operation of such technical innovations are better understood than in the unpredictable arts.

A new use is a method of using claim. The general principles of drafting method claims will therefore apply; however, also beware that the claim you draft is *sufficiently specific* lest the examiner give you a rejection by, in effect, taking the position that what you are claiming is inherent to an old structure. For example, in *King Pharmaceuticals, Inc. v. Eon Labs, Inc.*,[117] the federal circuit stated: "[u]nder the principles of inherency, if a structure in the prior art necessarily functions in accordance with the limitations of a process or method claim of an application, the claim is anticipated."

In prosecution, as an illustration, the examiner will attempt to provide a basis in fact and/or technical reasoning to reasonably support the determination that the allegedly inherent characteristic necessarily flows from the teachings of the applied prior art.[118] If a prior art device, in its normal and usual operation, would necessarily perform the method claimed, then the method claimed is anticipated by the prior art device.[119] Furthermore, when the prior art device or product is the same as the device described in the specification, the MPEP allows the examiner to presume that it will inherently perform

115. *See, e.g.*, Seymore, *supra* note 113; *In re* Oelrich, 666 F.2d 578, 581 (C.C.P.A. 1981) (quoting Hansgirg v. Kemmer, 102 F.2d 212, 214 (1939)); *see also* Transclean Corp. v. Bridgewood Servs., 290 F.3d 1364, 1373 (Fed. Cir. 2002) ("[A]nticipation by inherent disclosure is appropriate only when the reference discloses prior art that must necessarily include the unstated limitation.").

116. *See* Chapter 2 regarding discussion of predictable versus unpredictable arts.

117. 616 F.3d 1267, 1275–76 (Fed. Cir. 2010).

118. *See* Ex parte Levy, 17 U.S.P.Q.2d (BNA) 1461, 1464 (B.P.A.I. 1990).

119. *See In re* Best, 562 F.2d 1252, 1255 (C.C.P.A. 1977).

the claimed method.[120] In this situation, a prima facie case of anticipation has been made by the examiner and the burden then shifts to the applicant. This is similar to the situation previously described regarding functionality where the PTO may shift the burden to the applicant.[121] If the PTO were to do this it may require seeking to prove the characteristic is not in the prior art (e.g., proving a negative proposition, which is usually a challenge), amending the claim, or arguing that for some reason the PTO has inappropriately shifted the burden (e.g., because what is described in the specification is not the same as the prior art device).

Also recognize the disadvantages of the situation. The method claim should be specific enough to convince the examiner to allow it and yet the device is also known. In other words, it may be a challenge to obtain an allowable claim sufficiently specific and representing enough of a technical advance over the known device that also has market value because it is able to capture potential infringers.

4.1263 Use Infringement of a System Claim

Another issue to consider when drafting relates to the difference between use infringement of an apparatus or system-type claim, such as a server as one example, versus infringement of a method of using claim directed to the server. Perhaps surprisingly, the federal circuit employs different legal analyses to the two situations.

One of the first cases to squarely raise this issue was *NTP, Inc. v. Research in Motion, Ltd.*[122] The federal circuit distinguished claims to an apparatus or system from claims to a process, in particular, in terms of whether a system or process has been used so as to fall within section 271(a). It held that, for a claimed system, components of a claimed system are "used collectively." On the other hand, a claimed process is used on a step-by-step basis. In the case, it was argued that use by RIM's customers of the overall system resulted in indirect infringement by RIM for which RIM should be liable. Thus, the fundamental issue was whether RIM's customers directly infringed the claims at issue by use of RIM's email system under section 271(a). Interestingly, the case also partly turned-on extraterritoriality because RIM had its server/relay station in Canada, not in the United States.[123]

120. *See* MPEP § 2112 (2021).
121. *See* section 2.1111, discussing burden shifting in connection with functionality.
122. 418 F.3d 1282, 1319 (Fed. Cir. 2005), *cert. denied*, 546 U.S. 1157 (2006).
123. *Cf.* 35 U.S.C. § 271(f), (g) (2022) addressing extraterritorial patent infringement.

The court stated:

> The use of a claimed system under section 271(a) is the place at which the system as a whole is put into service, *i.e.*, the place where control of the system is exercised and beneficial use of the system obtained. . . .
>
> . . .
>
> Under section 271(a), the concept of 'use' of a patented method or process is fundamentally different from the use of a patented system or device. *In re Kollar*, 286 F.3d 1326, 1332 (Fed. Cir. 2002) (recognizing 'the distinction between a claim to a product, device, or apparatus, all of which are tangible items, and a claim to a process, which consists of a series of acts or steps. . . . [A process] consists of doing something, and therefore has to be carried out or performed.'); *see Joy Techs., Inc. v. Flakt, Inc.*, 6 F.3d 770, 773 (Fed. Cir. 1993) ('The law is unequivocal that the sale of equipment to perform a process is not a sale of the process within the meaning of section 271(a).'). Although the Supreme Court focused on the whole operable assembly of a system claim for infringement in *Deepsouth*, there is no corresponding whole operable assembly of a process claim. A method or process consists of one or more operative steps, and, accordingly, 'it is well established that a patent for a method or process is not infringed unless all steps or stages of the claimed process are utilized.' *Roberts Dairy Co. v. United States*, 530 F.2d 1342, 1354, 208 Ct. Cl. 830 (Ct. Cl. 1976).
>
> Because a process is nothing more than the sequence of actions of which it is comprised, the use of a process necessarily involves doing or performing each of the steps recited. This is unlike use of a system as a whole, in which the components are used collectively, not individually. We therefore hold that a process cannot be used 'within' the United States as required by section 271(a) unless each of the steps is performed within this country.

This approach distinguishing use infringement of an apparatus claim from infringement of a method of using claim was carried forward and refined in later cases, such as *Centillion Data Systems, LLC v. QWest Communications International, Inc.*[124] and *Intellectual Ventures I LLC v. Motorola Mobility LLC.*[125] These cases require that, for patent infringement, the user put the system into service by control over the system as a whole and by obtaining benefit from it, in particular, as to *each element of the claim*. Thus, on this basis, in *Centillion*, the federal circuit found infringement and, in *Motorola Mobility*, it did not.

In *Centillion*, the court stated:[126]

> In order to "put the system into service," the end user must be using all portions of the claimed invention. For example, in NTP, the end user was "using"

124. 631 F.3d 1279 (Fed. Cir. 2011).
125. 870 F.3d 1320 (Fed. Cir. 2017).
126. Centillion Data Sys., LLC v. QWest Comm'ns Int'l, Inc, 631 F.3d 1279 (Fed. Cir. 2011).

> every element of the system by transmitting a message. It did not matter that the user did not have physical control over the relays, the user made them work for their patented purpose, and thus "used" every element of the system by putting every element collectively into service.

Thus, physical possession was and is not a requirement for use infringement.

By contrast, in *Motorola Mobility*, the accused infringer's customers did not obtain a benefit from the generation of delivery reports, which was an element of the claim at issue. There was no evidence the customers ever generated a delivery report. Instead, the evidence was that reports were generated by centers operated by the customers' wireless service carriers.[127]

Here, a lesson may be to take care when drafting complex apparatus/system claims that may involve use infringement by customers for services offered by a party that may actually own and maintain the overall system, such as where services are provided to mobile devices, for example. *That is, do not include limitations that would not actually be initiated by the users and from which they will not actually benefit.*

Likewise, in this section, we are focused on drafting method of using claims. Thus, a question might be: are we able to draft *method of using* claims that would capture a system owner/operator directly for use of an innovation by a customer?

Consider this situation. So-called visual voicemail was invented well before the introduction of the iPhone. This refers to the feature in which voicemails are transcribed so that the party to whom the voicemail is directed may read the content rather than listen to it. Visual voicemail, when invented, was one feature of an overall voicemail management system, with an inbox, somewhat similar, but distinctly separate from an email inbox. At the time of the invention, cellphone voicemail capability was limited to serially going through and listening to voicemail messages forwarded to a wireless handset from a voicemail server.

In general, the visual voicemail innovation was initially directed at wireless handsets. The handsets might transcribe and display in a voicemail inbox received voicemails that a mobile device had at least partially transcribed. Alternately or additionally, the innovation was directed to a wireless handset that might receive transcribed voicemails from a voicemail server and display partial transcriptions in a voicemail inbox.

---

127. *See* Intellectual Ventures I LLC v. Motorola Mobility LLC, 870 F.3d 1320 (Fed. Cir. 2017).

For example, in this latter approach, a wireless carrier might charge for a transcription service included with its voicemail service. The wireless carrier, for example, may employ a voicemail server with the capability to transcribe audio voicemails and then forward the audio voicemail and the transcription to a wireless cellphone to the wireless handset. If the wireless subscriber has signed up for the transcription service, the wireless carrier would also provide software executable on the wireless handset to handle the processing and display of the voicemails and associated at least partial transcriptions in a voicemail inbox.

The question, then, might be, how to draft an apparatus and method claim intended to capture wireless providers that provide such a voicemail transcription service based on use of the service by one or more subscribers? Following is an example of a possible method of using claim.

EXAMPLE 4.15

I claim:

1. A method of processing voicemail messages at a voicemail server, the method comprising:

   capturing a plurality of received voicemail messages in an audio format to provide a plurality of audio-formatted voicemail messages;

   converting the plurality of audio-formatted voicemail messages to a plurality of corresponding text representations of the voicemail messages; and

   initiating communication of the text representations of the voicemail messages and the audio-formatted voicemail messages to a mobile device, wherein a respective text representation comprises a representation of an at least partial text transcription of a corresponding converted audio-formatted voicemail message, the at least partial text transcriptions of the voicemail messages to be displayed via a visual voicemail inbox of a voicemail system integrated as part of the mobile device.

One reason for writing the claim to refer to a plurality of voicemail messages, which might otherwise be an "out" if someone argues they do not process a plurality of such messages, is to argue the innovation is associated with the feature of displaying *multiple* messages in a single voicemail inbox; however, one might, instead, start with a claim to individual messages and move this feature to a dependent claim. Since this claim is drafted as a method,[128] deliberately, there is not a lot of extra description regarding the server hardware, such as a processor, memory, instructions, and so on. Such hardware recitation would seem unnecessary and also should not really help much with respect to patent eligibility and section 101,[129] which is often the reason why some practitioners include hardware recitations. Also, that material should already be provided in the specification and could be added to the claim later, during prosecution if needed.

It appears that a voicemail server is able to perform the acts recited in the claim. Thus, by writing a method of using claim that reads on a voicemail server able to perform transcription that would be owned and operated by a wireless service provider, more complex questions about customer initiation of service, customer control, and/or customer benefit seem to be avoided here.

Appreciate the tricky part to drafting this claim and the hook it provides vis-a-vis wireless carriers. Ultimately, the innovation here is really associated with display of one or more at least partial transcriptions in a voicemail inbox (i.e., separate from an email inbox) on a wireless handset. It is true that wireless carriers, like AT&T do sell handsets; however, the handsets are manufactured by others, such as Apple. Furthermore, it is likely that a wireless carrier selling a handset manufactured by someone else gets a contractual indemnity against patent infringement.

So how do we capture the wireless providers in a core business, such as wireless services, since they do not actually perform the displaying and so on? The wireless provider not only transcribes the audio voicemails, but it must also send "at least partial transcriptions" in a *format* capable of being displayed by a handset. There is really no way around doing that in the model of forwarding a transcription described.

The claim, therefore, has specific language directed to a "text representation" of the voicemail message as "a representation of an at least partial text transcription" in which the "at least partial text transcriptions of the voicemail messages [are] to be displayed via a visual voicemail inbox of a voicemail system integrated as part of the mobile device. Thus, regardless of the *format* (i.e., "representation" in the claim) actually sent, a *communication* that is *convertible* to an at least partial text transcription by a wireless handset would appear to otherwise meet the language of the claim.

128. *See* discussion of drafting method claims in Chapter 2.

129. *See* discussion of patent eligibility in section 5.44 and its subsections.

From the method claim, it should be easy to see how to handle an apparatus claim. It is quite similar to the approach for a Beauregard claim.[130] However, here, since this is an apparatus claim, there is not much harm in including more apparatus limitations, such as processors, memory, and so on. All servers will meet such limitations.

EXAMPLE 4.16

I claim:

1. An apparatus comprising: a server;

   wherein the server comprises one or more processors, wherein the one or more processors are coupled to one or more physical memories via one or more buses;

   wherein at least one of the one or more physical memories comprise stored instructions executable by the one or more processors; and

   wherein at least one of the one or more physical memories is capable of storing in one or more memory locations as physical memory states any results from execution by the one or more processors of the stored executable instructions;

   wherein the stored executable instructions comprise instructions, as a result of execution, at least to:

   capture a plurality of messages in an audio format to provide a plurality of audio-formatted voicemail messages; convert the plurality of audio-formatted voicemail messages to a plurality of corresponding text representations of the voicemail messages; and initiate communication of the text representations of the voicemail messages and the audio formatted voicemail messages to a mobile device, wherein a respective text representation comprises a representation of an at least partial text transcription of a corresponding converted audio-formatted voicemail message, the at least partial text transcriptions of the voicemail messages to be displayed via a visual voicemail inbox of a voicemail system integrated as part of the mobile device.

130. *See* section 4.128.

It also appears here that as to this claim, the wireless provider will meet the control and benefit test described earlier. Observe also that this claim uses a format similar to the format for a Beauregard claim described previously and later in this chapter.[131]

4.127 Method of Making Claims

Method of making claims have been covered in some detail in Chapters 1 and 2.

Method of making claims follow the same rules as method of using claims, although directed to different substantive rights (i.e., the right to make). Thus, they employ a preamble, transition word and body, and end with a period. They follow the single infringer rule, of course. They cover actual operations, acts, or actions, rather than the capability to perform an operation, act or action. The elements consequently also use words ending in "ing." Similarly, there is no inherent order associated with the elements unless expressly stated or implied.

4.1271 Illustrative Claim Example

Following are two method of manufacturing claims related to the technology example used as an illustration for this chapter. The two examples are similar but have some differences regarding specific limitations. These two examples are intended to illustrate possible differences in recitation of hardware-type limitations in method claims.

EXAMPLE 4.17

I claim:

1. A method of fabrication comprising:

   fabricating an integrated circuit (IC);

   wherein the fabricating includes forming at least a plurality of N-type metal oxide semiconductor field effect transistors (NMOSFETs) by forming a source, a drain, a gate and a body for respective NMOSFETs of the plurality in a thin film silicon layer of a silicon on insulator (SOI) substrate;

131. *See* section 2.1411, discussing Beauregard claims. Section 4.128 of this chapter also discusses Beauregard claims.

wherein the forming the source, the drain, the gate and the body for the respective NMOSFETs of the plurality comprises:

forming the gate from a conductive layer and an oxide layer over the thin film silicon layer of the SOI substrate; and

forming two N+ regions in the thin film silicon layer of the SOI substrate via ion implantation or diffusion to form the source, the drain, and the body;

and wherein the fabricating further includes:

fabricating one or more layers of metallization over the thin film silicon layer; and coupling the one or more layers of metallization to the plurality of NMOSFETs into an electrical configuration.

The preceding claim is directed to manufacturing a thin-film silicon-on-insulator (SOI) integrated circuit. Thus, for this situation, the innovation resides in the operation "forming a source, a drain, a gate and a body for respective NMOSFETs of the plurality in a thin-film silicon layer of a silicon-on-insulator (SOI) substrate," which at one time would have been new and nonobvious. Note the method format of using "fabricating," "forming," and even "coupling." The hardware recitations are made quite minimal in this example.

The next example has more hardware-type recitations since it is specifically directed to fabricating a radio frequency (RF) switch.

EXAMPLE 4.18

I claim:

1. A method of fabricating an RF switch comprising:

fabricating an integrated circuit (IC) that includes the RF switch;

wherein the fabricating includes forming at least a plurality of N-type metal oxide semiconductor field effect transistors (NMOSFETs) by forming a source, a drain, a gate and a body for respective NMOSFETs of the plurality in a thin film silicon layer of a silicon on insulator (SOI) substrate; and wherein the fabricating further includes fabricating one or more layers of metallization over the thin film silicon layer;

coupling the plurality of NMOSFETs into a stack via the one or more layers of metallization to pass an RF signal through the stack of NMOSFETs in an ON state of the stack of NMOSFETs;

coupling the plurality of NMOSFETs of the stack via the one or more layers of metallization to not pass an RF signal through the stack of NMOSFETs in an OFF state of the stack of NMOSFETs; and

coupling an electrical bias to the body of the respective NMOSFETs via the one or more layers of metallization at least in a portion of the OFF state of the stack to have a DC voltage level substantially more negative than a lowest voltage level of the following: ground, a DC voltage level of the source of the respective NMOSFETs, and a DC voltage level of the drain of the respective NMOSFETs.

In this claim, although directed to a thin-film silicon-on-insulator integrated circuit, a further innovation relates to the recited operation:

> coupling an electrical bias to the body of the respective NMOSFETs . . . at least in a portion of the OFF state of the stack to have a DC voltage level substantially more negative than a lowest voltage level of the following: ground, a DC voltage level of the source of the respective NMOSFETs, and a DC voltage level of the drain of the respective NMOSFETs.

Thus, for these examples, the innovation is not necessarily related to the fabrication details. Also, observe that unlike a product-by-process claim, an RF switch sold by a distributor although made by the claimed process would *not* make the distributor liable for direct infringement. However, as noted, product-by-process claims have potential legal issues. On the other hand, if someone imports an RF switch made abroad by a patented process that would infringe these method claims if performed in the United States, per the language of 271(g), he may be liable as an infringer, although he may not have performed the process (emphasis supplied):

> (g) Whoever without authority imports into the United States or offers to sell, sells, or uses within the United States a product which is made by a process patented in the United States **shall be liable as an infringer**, if the importation, offer to sell, sale, or use of the product occurs during the term of such process patent.

Also, an entity may indirectly infringe, for example, if they encouraged the direct infringement in the U.S., such as by specifying the design and fabrication process, even in another country. Note that unlike 271(a) and 271(c), the language of 271(b) does *not* limit itself to the U.S. It states:

> (b) Whoever actively induces infringement of a patent shall be liable as an infringer.

4.1272 Making a Device Capable of Infringing

Example 4.18 in a back-handed way raises the issue of making a device *capable* of infringing. This is another way to consider the issue raised in section 4.124 "STRUCTURE VERSUS FUNCTION REVISITED."

Specifically, the limitations "to pass an RF signal through the stack of NMOSFETs in an ON state," "to not pass an RF signal through the stack of NMOSFETs in an OFF state," and "an electrical bias to [be coupled to] the body of the respective NMOSFETs . . . at least in a portion of the OFF state" raise the issue of whether an IC manufactured with this capability might necessarily infringe even if the capability were not being used by a customer, for example. One might, for example, also imagine a patent claim like Example 4.1:

I claim:

1. A device comprising: at least one N-type metal oxide semiconductor field effect transistor (NMOSFET), the at least one NMOSFET including a source, a gate, a drain and a body;

   wherein the at least one NMOSFET is further included in an electrical configuration at least to control the at least one NMOSFET transistor to either an OFF state or an ON state;

   wherein the electrical configuration is at least further to electrically bias the body of the at least one NMOSFET at least in a portion of the OFF state of the at least one NMOSFET to a DC voltage level substantially more negative than at least one of the following: ground, the DC voltage level of the source, and the DC voltage level of the drain.

For this claim, limitations "to control the at least one NMOSFET transistor to either an OFF state or an ON state" and "to electrically bias the body of the at least one NMOSFET at least in a portion of the OFF state of the at least one NMOSFET" raise an issue regarding *making* an IC that might include this capability, but in which the capability might be latent and not used.[132]

In general, the topic of claiming a device capable to infringe may be tricky in some situations. One of the early and highly influential cases addressing this legal issue is *Intel v. U.S. ITC*.[133] The claim at issue recited:

---

1. In an integrated circuit, read-only memory having n address lines used for accessing p words in one addressing mode, an improvement for providing an alternate addressing mode, comprising:

   programmable selection means for selecting said alternate addressing mode; storage means for storing at least one signal; an address buffer coupled to one of said n address lines, said buffer also being coupled to said storage means and said programmable selection means, the output of said buffer being controlled by said signal stored in said storage means when said alternate addressing mode is selected,

   whereby when said alternate addressing mode is selected said p words in said memory may be selected with less than n address signals.

Cleverly, the claim recites: "programmable selection means . . . when said alternate addressing mode is selected said p words in said memory may be selected with less than n address signals." The issue, therefore, was whether the alleged infringing product necessarily infringed if it had this alternative addressing mode capability, but the mode was not being used.

In affirming the ITC ruling finding infringement, the federal circuit stated (emphasis supplied):

> Both the multiplexer and the address buffer use an addressing signal to select a particular memory cell from an incoming address pin or latch. Thus, the accused circuits infringe claim 1 under the doctrine of equivalents because

---

132. Granted that this is probably not a case where such a capability would be included and then not employed.

133. 946 F.2d 821 (Fed. Cir. 1991).

they perform substantially the same function in substantially the same way to obtain the same result as the invention claimed in the '084 patent.

. . .

GI/M also contends that the Commission's finding of infringement under the doctrine of equivalents is incorrect because, although GI/M's "old" design 51 Series EPROMs are capable of performing page mode addressing, the EPROMs were never sold to operate in page mode. No customer was ever told how to convert the chip to page mode operation--or even that such conversion was possible. GI/M argues that an alleged infringer must intend its parts to be used in an infringing fashion and cites *Fromberg, Inc. v. Thornhill*, 315 F.2d 407, 415, 137 USPQ 84, 89 (5th Cir. 1963), in support of its argument. As noted by Intel, there is no intent element to direct infringement. *See* 35 U.S.C. § 271(b) and (c). Fromberg deals with induced and contributory infringement and is therefore inapposite. **Because the language of claim 1 refers to "programmable selection means" and states "whereby when said alternate addressing mode is selected" (emphases added), the accused device, to be infringing, need only be capable of operating in the page mode. Contrary to GI/M's argument, actual page mode operation in the accused device is not required.**

More recent cases employ a similar analysis. For example, in *Fantasy Sports v. SportsLine*,[134] the federal circuit reversed and remanded a district court ruling of summary judgment of no infringement due to the presence of genuine and material issues of fact requiring resolution.

The issue was whether the accused software met a limitation or, instead, was modifiable to meet the limitation. The former would be infringing, whereas the latter would not. The court referenced the *Intel* case in its discussion. The federal circuit stated (some emphasis in original and some added):

Intel involved a claim to a memory chip in an integrated circuit having, *inter alia*, "*programmable* selection means for selecting [an] alternate addressing mode." *Id.* at 831, 20 USPQ2d at 1170 (emphasis added). The defendant in *Intel* argued that even though its products could be modified to infringe that claim, the fact that those products were capable of infringing alone could not support a finding of infringement. *Id.* at 832, 20 USPQ2d at 1171. Although we concluded that the defendant's products did infringe, we explained our basis for doing so as follows: "Because *the language of claim 1* refers to '*programmable* selection means' . . . the accused device, to be infringing, need only be capable of operating in the page mode." *Id.* (emphases added). *Intel* therefore does not stand for the proposition, as argued by Fantasy, that infringement may be based upon a finding that an accused product is merely capable

134. 287 F.3d 1108 (Fed. Cir. 2002).

of being modified in a manner that infringes the claims of a patent. *See High Tech Med. Instrumentation, Inc. v. New Image Indus., Inc.*, 49 F.3d 1551, 1555-56, 33 USPQ2d 2005, 2008-09 (Fed. Cir. 1995) (distinguishing *Intel* and holding that the fact that the accused device could be altered in way that satisfies the claim term "rotatably coupled" did not *per se* justify a finding of infringement); *see also Telemac Cellular Corp. v. Topp Telecom, Inc.*, 247 F.3d 1316, 1330, 58 USPQ2d 1545, 1554 (Fed. Cir. 2001) ("[T]hat a device is capable of being modified to operate in an infringing manner is not sufficient, by itself, to support a finding of infringement."). **Rather, as in every infringement analysis, the language of the claims, as well as the nature of the accused product, dictates whether an infringement has occurred.**

In the present case, claim 1 is directed to "[a] computer for playing football," and thus the claims of the '603 patent read on a computer executing fantasy football game software. Claim 1 also sets forth a number of functionally defined means that that software must contain, including a "means for scoring . . . bonus points" for unusual scoring plays. Software is a set of instructions, known as code, that directs a computer to perform specified functions or operations. Thus, the software underlying a computer program that presents a user with the ability to select among a number of different options must be written in such a way as to enable the computer to carry out the functions defined by those options when they are selected by the user. Therefore, although a user must activate the functions programmed into a piece of software by selecting those options, the user is only activating means that are *already present in the underlying software*. Otherwise, the user would be required to alter the code to enable the computer to carry out those functions. Accordingly, in order to infringe the '603 patent, the code underlying an accused fantasy football game must be written in such a way as to enable a user of that software to utilize the function of awarding bonus points for unusual plays such as out-of-position scoring, without having to modify that code. In other words, an infringing software must include the "means for scoring . . . bonus points" regardless whether that means is activated or utilized in any way.

A recent federal circuit case may muddy slightly how to interpret such limitations; however, the basic conclusion regarding claims that include limitations with the capability to infringe remains intact, or so it appears. In *INVT SPE LLC v. International Trade Commission*,[135] the federal circuit affirmed the International Trade Commission's (ITC) determination that the respondents did not violate 19 U.S.C. § 1337. INVT had alleged that the importation and sale of LTE-compliant personal electronic devices infringed U.S. Patent Nos. 6,760,590 ("the '590 patent") and 7,848,439 ("the '439 patent"). The ITC

135. *See* INVT SPE LLC v. ITC, Appeal No. 2020-1903 (Fed. Cir. Aug. 31, 2022).

determined that the asserted claims were not essential to the LTE standard and that the accused products did not infringe the asserted claims.

However, before reaching this conclusion, it was necessary to construe the claims at issue, in particular, the claims of the '439 patent, which related to wireless communication systems, specifically an improvement to adaptive modulation and coding (AMC), which is a technique used to transmit signals in an orthogonal frequency division multiplexing (OFDM) system. Claim 1 of the '439 patent recited:

1. A communication apparatus comprising:

   [a] a channel estimating section that carries out a channel estimation per subband;

   [b] a parameter deciding section that decides modulation parameters and coding parameters per subband group comprised of a plurality of the subbands, based on a result of the channel estimation per subband;

   [c] a parameter information transmission section that transmits, to a communicating party, parameter information indicating the modulation parameters and the coding parameters decided at the parameter deciding section;

   [d] a receiving section that receives a signal containing data modulated and encoded on a per subband group basis at the communicating party using the modulation parameters and the coding parameters of the parameter information transmitted at the parameter information transmission section;

   [e] a data obtaining section that demodulates and decodes the received signal received at the receiving section on a per subband group basis using the modulation parameters and the coding parameters decided at the parameter deciding section, and obtains the data contained in the received signal; and

   [f] a pattern storage section that stores in advance patterns for selecting subbands constituting the subband groups wherein the parameter deciding section decides the modulation parameters and the coding parameters per subband group comprised of the subbands selected based on the patterns stored in the pattern storage section.

INT asserted that compliance with the LTE communications standard required infringing this claim. The key limitations in dispute were elements [d] and [e], which state:

> [d] a receiving section that receives a signal containing data modulated and encoded on a per subband group basis at the communicating party using the modulation parameters and the coding parameters of the parameter information transmitted at the parameter information transmission section;
>
> [e] a data obtaining section that demodulates and decodes the received signal received at the receiving section on a per subband group basis using the modulation parameters and the coding parameters decided at the parameter deciding section, and obtains the data contained in the received signal.

At the ITC, a dispute regarding interpretation of these elements related to whether this language required "actual operation" or merely "the capability for performing." The ITC determined that the language required actual operation; however, the ITC also determined that the language was not shown to be LTE compliant and also determined separately that the accused devices had not been shown to meet the claim language at issue regardless of whether it was LTE compliant.

On appeal, INT challenged the interpretation of the claims as requiring actual operation. In this regard, the federal circuit agreed with INT that the language required the capability for performing rather than actual operation, but, nonetheless, concluded that the language still had not been shown to be LTE compliant and also that the accused devices had not been shown to meet the limitations at issue.

Here, the federal circuit stated (emphasis supplied):

> Our cases have held that sometimes a device only needs to be "capable of operating" according to a claimed limitation, for a finding of infringement. *See Finjan*, 626 F.3d at 1204. Other times, a device does not infringe unless it actually operates as claimed. *See* ParkerVision, Inc. v. Qualcomm Inc., 903 F.3d 1354, 1361 (Fed. Cir. 2018) (discussing Ball Aerosol & Specialty Container, Inc. v. Ltd. Brands, Inc., 555 F.3d 984 (Fed. Cir. 2009)). **Whether infringement requires actual performance of the recited functions by the accused device depends on the claim language.** *See Finjan*, 626 F.3d 1204 (*citing* Fantasy Sports Props. v. Sportsline.com, Inc., 287 F.3d 1108, 1118 (Fed. Cir. 2002)); *see also ParkerVision, Inc.*, 903 F.3d at 1361 (articulating a distinction between configuration-type and capability type claims).
>
> **Possibly the most straightforward example of this is the common distinction between method claims and apparatus claims.** *See, e.g., Finjan*, 626 F.3d at 1203–05. In *Finjan*, this court held that Finjan's "non-method claims describe capabilities without requiring that any software components be 'active' or 'enabled.'" *Id.* at 1204–05. The court, therefore, upheld a finding

of infringement for products in which the accused proactive-scanning software module was locked when sold by the defendants. *Id.* at 1205; *see also id.* at 1203–04 (distinguishing Southwest Software, Inc. v. Harlequin Inc., 226 F.3d 1280, 1291 (Fed. Cir. 2000), in which the accused software product required a manual step to activate the patented feature, but the claim at issue was a method claim). In contrast, *Finjan's* method claims were not infringed by the accused products because those claims required actual performance of each claimed step; there was no evidence that proactive scanning was performed in the United States. *Id.* at 1206 ("To infringe a method claim, a person must have practiced all steps of the claimed method." (quoting Lucent Techs. v. Gateway, Inc., 580 F.3d 1301, 1317 (Fed. Cir. 2009))). *Cf.* ParkerVision, Inc., 903 F.3d at 1363 (similarly differentiating apparatus claims and method claims in the patent invalidity context). However, differences exist between apparatus claims as well, depending on the claim language. **We have construed some apparatus claims to require an infringing device to actually perform and operate according to the functional terms recited in the claim.** The intervenors cite two such cases, *Cross Medical* and *Ball Aerosol. See Intervenors' Br.* 64, 67–68. We have construed other apparatus claims to require only capability, such as in *Finjan* and *Silicon Graphics.*

. . .

. . .

In *Cross Medical*, we rejected the argument that the limitation "anchor seat means which has a lower bone interface operatively joined to said bone segment" could be met merely by an interface that was capable of contacting bone. Cross Med. Prods., Inc. v. Medtronic Sofamor Danek, Inc., 424 F.3d 1293, 1305–06 (Fed. Cir. 2005). **Instead, the claim language "operatively joined" required that the interface and the bone segment be connected and in contact such that the device effectively performed posterior stabilization.** *Id.* at 1306. Direct infringement did not occur until the device was connected to the bone, which a surgeon performed, not the allegedly infringing device maker. *Id.* at 1310–14.

. . .

. . . Intervenors emphasize that the *Cross Medical* claims included the present-tense verb "has," similar to the present-tense verbs "demodulates" and "decodes" in the '439 claims. But this court's construction in *Cross Medical* was based on "operatively joined," not "has." Intervenors do not provide any analysis of *Ball Aerosol.* While the *Ball Aerosol* claim is atypical for its recitation, within a mechanical device claim, of how a component is to be used or operated—somewhat akin to computer device claims, which commonly include functional language—it ultimately has little relevance for construing INVT's claims.

> **Because of the nature of the technology, computer and software claims typically use functional language to define the invention. Functional language is used to define and delimit otherwise generic or interchangeable general purpose computer hardware, which can be programmed to perform an unlimited array of functions. In other words, the recited operative steps a computer- or software-based device undertakes is what defines what a computer-implemented invention is. We have frequently construed such functional language as not requiring actual performance of those operative steps for infringement purposes. Moreover, we have not required claims to adhere to a specific grammatical form to find that the claim is drawn to capability,** contrary to the Commission's and the intervenors' contentions.
>
> . . .
>
> The FID relied primarily on *Finjan* and the absence of "for performing"-type claim language, providing little else for why the '439 claims require actual operation. The intervenors argue that simple-present-tense words are enough to require actual operation, see *Intervenors' Br.* 65, 67, but *Silicon Graphics* shows that is not true. **In fact, based on just claim language, we see very little significance in the difference between a limitation that might recite "a data obtaining section for demodulating and decoding" (*Finjan*-style) and one that recites "a data obtaining section that demodulates and decodes" (the actual '439 claim language), for determining on which side of the capability/actual-operation line the claims fall.**
>
> Like with the claims in *Finjan* and *Silicon Graphics*, we find that the asserted '439 claims are directed to capability—as in a device that includes "software components with specific purposes," programmed to have the ability to perform the operative steps: namely, a "receiving section" that can receive a signal containing data modulated and encoded using the parameters decided at user device, and a "data obtaining section" that can demodulate and decode the signal using the parameters decided at the user device. *Finjan*, 626 F.3d at 1204–05. **In other words, the claims recite a device with the capability of performing the recited functions when in operation without any modification or further programming.**

Thus, the court interpreted the language of the claim, such as, "a data obtaining section that demodulates and decodes" to recite a device with the capability of performing the recited functions apparently in part because the language at issue involves a device that includes "software components with specific purposes," programmed to have the ability to perform the operative steps. Despite this, however, the court affirmed as to non-infringement.

For our purposes, in light of this precedent, the analysis seems clear. If the claim requires that a device have the capacity to perform a function, one who makes a device with that capacity without the patent owner's authority is a direct infringer even if the maker's customers do not use the capacity.[136]

4.128 Beauregard Claims[137]

35 USC section 101 is the statutory source for court pronouncements regarding what is statutory subject matter, that is, subject matter that is capable of being claimed by a patent claim. A line of Supreme Court cases[138] has indicated that mathematical algorithms are not patentable subject matter. However, this line of authority, for a while, left unclear whether software, for example, computer programs, were patentable subject matter.

Today, although the Supreme Court has not specifically opined on the latter issue, it is generally accepted, based both on court decisions and PTO policy, that computer programs are an acceptable subject for patent claiming. To many, the case *In re Beauregard*,[139] which has led to a particular claiming style referred to as "Beauregard" claims,[140] was an important turning point.

In some ways, it is ironic, because there is no federal circuit decision in the *Beauregard* case itself; however, many people believe they know how the case would have come out if the federal circuit had decided it—in favor of the patentee. The case itself was between IBM and the PTO over a claiming style that claimed software embodied on a storage medium of some sort, such as a floppy, disk, or CD. Here is one example of such a claim:

> An article comprising: a storage medium having stored thereon, instructions, that when executed, result in performance of the following method:

---

136. It is noted that there appears to be some tension between this case and the case, IPXL Holdings v. Amazon, 430 F.3d 1377, 1384 (Fed. Cir. 2005). *See also* section 5.6 and its subsections, discussing the issue of mixing statutory classes. However, it may be that the IPXL v. Amazon line of authority had not been argued and, furthermore, the court seems here to have interpreted the claim language in a manner that may not make the claim language indefinite because it involves a device that includes "software components with specific purposes," programmed to have the ability to perform the operative steps. We, nonetheless, continue to recommend drafting apparatus claims in a manner to avoid the risk of mixing statutory classes. Even in this case, the court acknowledged *"[p]ossibly the most straightforward example of this [difference] is the common distinction between method claims and apparatus claims."*.

137. *See also* section 2.1141, introducing Beauregard claims.

138. *See* Diamond v. Diehr, 450 U.S. 175 (1981).

139. 53 F.3d 1583 (Fed. Cir. 1995).

140. *See also* section 2.1141.

Action A;

Action B;

Action C.

The PTO, at the time, would likely have taken the position that a claim like this one constitutes unpatentable subject matter, like the position it initially took in the *Beauregard* case itself.

However, while the case was on appeal before the federal circuit and waiting to be heard, the Patent Commissioner asked that the case be dismissed, settling the dispute. Soon after that occurred, in 1996, the PTO then published guidelines regarding this claim type.[141] Since then, probably tens of thousands, if not hundreds of thousands, of patents have issued from the PTO containing such so-called Beauregard claims.[142]

4.1281 Advantages and Disadvantages

One advantage of employing Beauregard claims, of course, is that it provides the capability to pursue an infringer where the infringement occurs because infringing software is merely stored, such as on a server, a hard drive, a CD, or even a floppy. Therefore, it is recommended that Beauregard claims nearly always be employed in patent applications where a potential embodiment of the invention includes software. It is also noted that several different forms of Beauregard claims are possible. The form of such a claim from the prior section is improved in the next section.

> One advantage of employing Beauregard claims is that it provides the capability to pursue an infringer where the infringement occurs because infringing software is merely stored, such as on a server, a hard drive, a CD, or even a floppy. Therefore, it is recommended that Beauregard claims nearly always be employed in patent applications where a potential embodiment of the invention includes software.

It is also noted that another similar claim type had at one time cropped up as well, although it was quite experimental at the time it was introduced. Some

141. *See* MPEP § 2106 (2022).
142. This is an educated guess, not based on any careful study.

refer to these as "propagating signal" claims. The idea here was to claim the signals themselves as subject matter, that is, "signals per se."

Although, as with Beauregard claims, such claims have many potential forms, one example of such a claim might be:

> A signal comprising: propagating energy that, when received, results in performance of the following method:
>
> Action A;
>
> Action B;
>
> Action C.

However, as to the latter claim type, it was ultimately ruled to be non-statutory.[143] Use of this claim type, therefore, of course, is not recommended.

4.1282 Examples of Various Approaches to Beauregard Claiming

The general idea is to claim software stored on a "storage medium," such as on a flash drive, a hard disk drive, and so on. However, the claim recites features of the software in a manner so that it is clear the software is *not* operating, analogous to the manner of claiming previously mentioned for apparatus claims. These claims have become quite commonly used most likely because anyone in the chain of distribution of the software can be sued. Software is always stored on some type of storage medium.

Although most of these claims refer to a "machine readable storage medium" or "computer readable storage medium," a question may be whether this is narrower than needed. Why not just recite "storage medium"?

Similarly, a lot of examples do not clearly distinguish the claim preamble from the claim body. Some claims, for example, recite "A computer readable storage medium having stored thereon executable computer instructions comprising . . . ."

In this latter claim, is the transition word "having" or is it "comprising"? If it is "having," then the claim is subject to the argument that it is not an "open format claim." Furthermore, is this format non-statutory because "computer readable storage medium" is the preamble and, consequently, not necessarily limiting? Recall that the federal circuit never resolved the issue regarding whether the claim in the *Beauregard* case was necessarily statutory.

143. *See In re* Nuijten, 500 F.3d 1346 (Fed. Cir. 2007).

Consider this hypothetical claim example:

> A storage medium having stored thereon computer readable software instructions that, when executed by a computer, cause to be performed a method of transmitting signals over a network comprising:
>
> Action A;
>
> Action B;
>
> Action C.

From the face of this claim, it is not entirely clear whether the entire preamble is "a storage medium" or whether it is everything that precedes the word "comprising." One problem with this ambiguity is that it permits an opponent to take the position that best suits his or her case and it permits a court to go along with that position. As previously indicated, preambles are not always limiting, whereas the words in the body of the claim are.[144] Thus, in this example, it is not entirely clear whether the words between "having" and "comprising" necessarily limit the scope of the claim or not.

A clearer approach would be to recite:

> An article comprising:
>
> a storage medium including stored thereon...

Here, it is clear that "comprising" is the transition word and that "storage medium" is within the claim body.

Another issue that may arise with this claim type is whether it might be interpreted to cover "signals per se,"[145] an issue discussed as non-statutory in the previous section. This concern is based in part on the notion that the PTO is permitted to apply the broadest reasonable interpretation (BRI) to a claim. In theory, perhaps a wire transmitting an electrical signal along it, as a type of transitory storage medium for the signal, would qualify as a "storage medium." Whether this is a real concern or not, some examiners will not issue a Beauregard claim unless it recites "non-transitory," so that it clearly does not cover signals per se. For this reason, it is a good idea to describe a "non-transitory storage medium" in your specification so that there is clear written description support, if needed, for the following:

---

144. *See* sections 2.12, 2.14 and their subsections, discussing the patent claim preamble and patent claim body for a patent claim.

145. *See In re* Nuijten, 500 F.3d 1346 (Fed. Cir. 2007).

An article comprising:

a non-transitory storage medium including stored thereon executable instructions to . . .

Appreciate that "non-transitory" does not exclude memory states stored on a temporary basis (versus a transitory basis), as is done with random access memory, for example. However, clarifying this in the specification would be prudent.

Another issue to appreciate is that the language of the claim reciting features of the software may be functional, raising the issues described regarding structural and functional language.[146]

Fortunately, there is another formulation for a Beauregard claim that may address this concern. It uses a concept explained previously with respect to method claims. Method claims are more difficult to attack as being functional because they recite "acts" or "actions."[147] Hence, a Beauregard claim might, instead, have the following form:

An article comprising: a non-transitory storage medium;

wherein the storage medium includes stored thereon executable instructions; and

wherein the instructions are executable to perform a method comprising the following:

Action A;

Action B; and

Action C.

This may to a large extent address the functionality issue, although one may wonder if the claim could then be attacked as having unclear scope for mixing method claim terminology with apparatus claim terminology, potentially making it indefinite, an issue previously raised.[148] However, a federal circuit case addressed a similar issue in at least two cases where an apparatus was described in a patent claim using terms ending in "ing," similar to the approach shown, in which the "actions" of this claim would recite operations using words that end in "ing." The court determined that such a claim was not indefinite because for the claim at issue it was clear that a method was *not*

146. *See* discussion of structural versus functional claiming in Chapter 2.

147. *See* section 2.1121, discussing functionality in the context of method of using claims.

148. *See, e.g.*, IPXL Holdings v. Amazon, 430 F.3d 1377, 1384 (Fed. Cir. 2005). *See also* section 5.6 and its subsections, discussing the issue of mixing statutory classes.

being claimed. This case provides a strong reasoned basis for concluding that such a claim as the preceding would not be indefinite for mixing statutory classes if carefully drafted.[149]

To demonstrate this, recall Example 2.12 providing this method claim as an illustration:

I claim:

A method comprising:

emulating one or more network devices of at least a second broadcast domain;

encapsulating one or more signal packets from at least a first broadcast domain to be directed to a network device of the at least a second broadcast domain; and

communicating the encapsulated one or more signal packets to at least one tunnel server.

Using the alternate Beauregard claim format immediately preceding, a Beauregard claim might be:

I claim:

1. An article comprising: a non-transitory storage medium;

wherein the storage medium includes stored thereon executable instructions; and wherein the instructions are executable to perform a method comprising the following:

emulating one or more network devices of at least a second broadcast domain;

149. *See* Microprocessor Enhancement Corp. v. Texas Instruments Inc. 520 F.3d 1367 (Fed. Cir. 2008); HTC Corp. v. IPCom GmbH & Co., 667 F.3d 1270, 101 U.S.P.Q.2d 1518 (Fed. Cir. 2012).

encapsulating one or more signal packets from at least a first broadcast domain to be directed to a network device of the at least a second broadcast domain; and

communicating the encapsulated one or more signal packets to at least one tunnel server.

4.129 Markush Group Claims

Another claim type frequently in use, in particular, in the chemical area, is referred to as a Markush group or Markush expression, after the case on which it is based, *Ex Parte Markush*.[150] Markush groups are seen most frequently in the unpredictable arts but may also be employed in the predictable arts.

Markush groupings are, in general, fine to employ; however, it is important to employ a good form for such a claim. The concept of the claim is to name a genus of certain specified claim elements, such as, for example, materials, when there is no commonly accepted generic expression to cover the subject matter to be claimed.[151] A common claim form is, for example:

A process for etching silicon, comprising:

treating the surface of the silicon with an acid selected from the group consisting of sulfuric acid, nitric acid, and phosphoric acid.

However, this may not the preferred form. One reason is that the use of "consisting of" introduces some risk that the claim may be construed narrowly to cover using only acid and nothing else. Instead, a better form introduces a "comprising" before the Markush group so that it is clear the claim element is not necessarily limited to the Markush group, such as the following:[152]

150. 1925 C.D. 126; 340 O.G. 839.
151. *See* MPEP section 2173.05(h) (2022).
152. *See* Amgen v. Amneal Pharm. LLC, 945 F.3d 1368 (2020).

A process for etching silicon, comprising:

> treating the surface of the silicon with a substance **comprising** an acid selected from the group consisting of sulfuric acid, nitric acid, and phosphoric acid.

This claim may yet be further refined. What if someone used a combination of acids? Would there be infringement? Probably, because the combination would literally include one of the recited acids and we have introduced a "comprising." Still, it would be better if it were clearer that combinations of acids from the group infringe. Here is one way to do this:

A process for etching silicon, comprising:

> treating the surface of the silicon with a substance comprising at least one acid selected from the group consisting of sulfuric acid, nitric acid, and phosphoric acid.

Now, it is clearer that a combination of acids from the group infringe. Perhaps, yet another way, that is arguably even clearer, might be:

A process for etching silicon, comprising:

> treating the surface of the silicon with a substance comprising at least one acid selected from the group consisting of sulfuric acid, nitric acid, phosphoric acid and any combinations thereof.

Likewise, it may be appropriate to, instead, employ the form "consisting essentially of" in some situations, but beware of the potential risks of indefiniteness.[153]

153. *See* discussion of "consisting essentially of" in Chapter 2.

> Markush groupings are fine to employ; however, it is important to employ the best form of such a claim. . . . a better form introduces a comprising before the Markush group so that it is clear the claim element is not necessarily limited to the Markush group, ...

Appreciate that a Markush group has certain legal requirements that, if not met, may invalidate the claim. Also, appreciate that where a Markush group lists several elements of the group, if any one member of the group is found in the prior art, along with the other limitations of the claim, then the claim would be anticipated. MPEP section 2117 discusses features of a Markush group:

> A "Markush" claim recites a list of alternatively useable members. *In re Harnisch*, 631 F.2d 716, 719-20 (CCPA 1980); *Ex parte Markush*, 1925 Dec. Comm'r Pat. 126, 127 (1924). The listing of specified alternatives within a Markush claim is referred to as a Markush group or Markush grouping. *Abbott Labs v. Baxter Pharmaceutical Products, Inc.*, 334 F.3d 1274, 1280-81, 67 USPQ2d 1191, 1196-97 (Fed. Cir. 2003) (citing to several sources that describe Markush groups). Claim language defined by a Markush grouping requires selection from a closed group "consisting of" the alternative members. *Id.* at 1280, 67 USPQ2d at 1196. *See* MPEP § 2111.03, subsection II, for a discussion of the term "consisting of" in the context of Markush groupings.
>
> . . .
>
> Inventions in metallurgy, refractories, ceramics, chemistry, pharmacology and biology are most frequently claimed under the Markush formula, but purely mechanical features or process steps may also be claimed by using the Markush style of claiming. *See, e.g., Fresenius USA, Inc. v. Baxter Int'l, Inc.*, 582 F.3d 1288, 1297-98 (Fed. Cir. 2009)(claim to a hemodialysis apparatus required "at least one unit selected from the group consisting of (i) a dialysate-preparation unit, (ii) a dialysate-circulation unit, (iii) an ultrafiltrate-removal unit, and (iv) a dialysate-monitoring unit" and a user/machine interface operably connected thereto); *In re Harnisch*, 631 F.2d 716, 206 USPQ 300 (CCPA 1980)(defining alternative moieties of a chemical compound with Markush groupings).
>
> A Markush grouping is proper if the members of a group share a single structural similarity and a common use.
>
> *See* MPEP § 2111.03 and MPEP § 2173.05(h) for discussions of when a Markush grouping may be indefinite under 35 U.S.C. 112(b) (e.g., if the list of alternatives is not a closed grouping, or if a Markush group is so expansive

that persons skilled in the art cannot determine the metes and bounds of the claimed invention).

. . .

A Markush claim may be rejected under judicially approved "improper Markush grouping" principles when the claim contains an improper grouping of alternatively useable members. A Markush claim contains an "improper Markush grouping" if either: (1) the members of the Markush group do not share a "single structural similarity" or (2) the members do not share a common use. See, e.g., *the Supplementary Examination Guidelines for Determining Compliance with 35 U.S.C. 112 and for Treatment of Related Issues in Patent Applications* ("*Supplementary Guidelines*"), 76 Fed. Reg. 7162, 7166 (February 9, 2011).

As noted in the MPEP, Markush groups work for both the predictable and unpredictable arts. For example, a large group of dependent claims might be combined into a single Markush group claim. With that said, it is suggested that Markush groups be limited to the areas in which they are more commonly used, such as metallurgy, refractories, ceramics, chemistry, pharmacology, and biology. Rather, use of a Markush group may make a straightforward claim more confusing, particularly with respect to the proper use of "and" versus "or." One example of such confusion is the case *Superguide v. Direct TV*,[154] discussed later.

4.1291 Advantages and Disadvantages

An advantage of a Markush group is that it is a way to claim subject matter broadly. That is, a Markush group permits a claim to read on many embodiments, particularly with respect many substances. However, we shall also see that this may be accomplished without a Markush group.[155]

Of course, extremely broad claims also have risks, particularly in the unpredictable arts.[156] For example, claims may be held invalid for lack of enablement or lack of written description.[157]

There are other risks as well. For one thing, the language may fail to meet the legal requirements of a Markush group.[158] In addition, the wording might be improper. That is, the language may use "or" rather than "and."

---

154. 358 F.3rd 870 (Fed. Cir. 2004).

155. *See* the discussion in next section; *see* Amgen v. Sanofi, 987 F.3d 1080 (Fed. Cir. 2021), *cert. granted*, __ U.S. __ (2022), in which billions of potential substances fell within the scope of the claims at issue. The claims used the technique described in the next section.

156. *See* discussion of the unpredictable arts in Chapter 2.

157. *Id.*

158. *See* section 4.1292, discussing Markush groups with examples.

One issue to appreciate with Markush groups is that they came into existence at a time when the PTO took the position that the use of "or" was considered indefinite since it permitted the claim to cover alternatives. Today, courts and even the PTO both recognize that "or" does not necessarily make a claim indefinite.[159]

The Markush group claim format was an approach to get the equivalent of "or" without using the word expressly.[160] That is, the formulation "at least one . . . selected from the group consisting of A, B, *and* C" is equivalent to "at least one of the following: A, B, *or* C." This may create some confusion regarding proper use of "and" versus "or." A good example is the case *Superguide v. Direct TV*.[161] The claim construction issue concerned the language "at least one of A, B, and C." The federal circuit stated (emphasis supplied):

> The next phrase for construction is "at least one of" which appears in Claim 1: **at least one of a desired program start time, a desired program end time, a desired program service *and* a desired program type.** SuperGuide and Gemstar argue that only one of the four criteria is necessary; Defendants assert that one of each is necessary. . . . SuperGuide's position that "at least one of" refers only to one category of the criteria instead of to one of each category "would contradict the clear purpose of the invention as described in the written description, depicted in [Figure 4a], and recited in claim 1. Such an assertion would also impermissibly read the preferred embodiment out of claim 1." *Crystal Semiconductor*, 246 F.3d at 1349; *accord, Sandisk Corp. v. Lexar Media, Inc.*, 91 F. Supp. 2d 1327, 1330-32 (N.D.Cal. 2000) (Claim language "partitioning the memory cells within the individual sectors into at least a user data portion and an overhead portion" meant the memory cells within the individual sectors were partitioned "into at least a user data portion and an overhead portion."). Here, the claim language is "at least one of" followed by the term "a desired," a term which is repeated for each category. **More-over, the final category is introduced by "*and*** a desired" **which is conjunctive not disjunctive. Thus, the phrase "at least one of" means at least one of each desired criterion; that is, at least one of a desired program start time, a desired program end time, a desired program service and a desired program type.**

Consequently, of course, there was no infringement. Although it is only a theory, the formulation construed in *Superguide* shows up frequently enough

159. Although, once in a while, an examiner will issue an indefiniteness rejection for the use of "or."

160. Of course, since such a claim was definite, one would think that would have been a clear basis to conclude use of "or" is not necessarily indefinite.

161. 358 F.3d 870 (Fed. Cir. 2004).

in claims that it suggests some practitioners are confused about the usage of "and" in a Markush group and the use of "or" in a claim that does not employ a Markush group.

Superguide is not the only federal circuit case to implicate use of "and" versus use of "or."[162] This issue, that is, use of "and" versus "or" in a claim, is sufficiently unclear but is important enough with respect to infringement[163] that it is recommended to, in general, use "and/or" in claims except where it makes no sense and to address this in the specification.[164] For example, language such as the following may be employed:

> Unless otherwise indicated, in the context of the present patent application, the term "or" if used to associate a list, such as A, B, or C, is intended to mean A, B, and C, here used in the inclusive sense, as well as A, B, or C, here used in the exclusive sense. With this understanding, "and" is used in the inclusive sense and intended to mean A, B, and C; whereas "and/or" can be used in an abundance of caution to make clear that all of the foregoing meanings are intended, although such usage is not required.[165]

4.1292 Examples—Claiming Subject Matter With and Without Markush Groups

Following are two examples of claims employing a Markush group in the formulation we described earlier so that, for example, "substance" is not limited to the particular Markush group.

EXAMPLE 4.19

I claim:

1. A process for etching silicon, comprising:

    treating the surface of the silicon with a substance comprising at least one acid selected from the group consisting of sulfuric acid, nitric acid, phosphoric acid, and any combinations thereof.

162. *See* Kustom Signals, Inc. v. Applied Concepts, 264 F.3d 1326 (Fed. Cir. 2001); Brown v. 3M, 265 F.3d 1349 (Fed. Cir. 2001); *cf.* Kaufman v. Microsoft, case 21-1634 (Fed. Cir. May 20, 2022) (affirming interpretation of "and" in claim as meaning "or" based on usage in specification).

163. Consider the Superguide case in which the use of "and" resulted in no infringement.

164. *See* Appendix B, providing sample application boilerplate for a patent specification.

165. *See* Ex Parte Gross (PTAB 2014) (approving use of "and/or" in patent claims); *cf.* Kaufman v. Microsoft, case 21-1634 (Fed. Cir. May 20, 2022) (affirming interpretation of "and" in claim as meaning "or" based on usage in specification).

EXAMPLE 4.20

I claim:

1. A semiconductor device comprising:

   a substrate, the substrate comprising at least one material selected from the group consisting of silicon, sapphire, gallium arsenide, magnesium oxide, zinc oxide, silicon carbide, and any combinations thereof;

   a crystalline buffer layer on the substrate consisting essentially of gallium nitride; and

   a growth layer on the buffer layer, the growth layer comprising gallium nitride and a first dopant material.

As noted, however, an equivalent claim for Example 4.19 might be:

I claim:

1. A process for etching silicon, comprising:

   treating the surface of the silicon with a substance comprising at least one of the following: sulfuric acid, nitric acid, or phosphoric acid.

A similar formulation might be:

I claim:

1. A process for etching silicon, comprising:

   treating the surface of the silicon with a substance comprising at least one of the following: sulfuric acid, nitric acid, phosphoric acid, or any combination thereof.

Another similar formulation might be (in conjunction with the boilerplate specification language proposed earlier):

I claim:

1. A process for etching silicon, comprising:

   treating the surface of the silicon with a substance comprising at least one of the following: sulfuric acid, nitric acid, and/or phosphoric acid.

Note that the MPEP suggests these formulations will be viewed as Markush groups. In general, any formulation involving alternatives appears to be considered a Markush group based on the MPEP. Of course, the examiner must recognize and appreciate the issue. It does not appear that case law has adopted this view.[166] It is in part for these reasons that it is recommended that Markush groups be used with claims in the unpredictable arts but that the preceding alternative formulations be used in the predictable arts. That is, this recommendation is an attempt to balance prosecution risk with enforcement risk.

> It is recommended that Markush groups be used with claims in the unpredictable arts but that the preceding alternative formulations be used in the predictable arts. That is, this recommendation is an attempt to balance prosecution risk with enforcement risk.

4.130 Composition of Matter Claims

Compositions of matter more frequently arise in the unpredictable arts, such as chemistry or biotechnology, although not necessarily. A composition of matter is not limited to chemistry or biotechnology. Also, some chemistry has become reasonably predictable from being well studied, such as silicon-related

166. It is noted, however, that the EPC appears to have a view similar to the MPEP. *See* Chapter 7, discussing claim drafting issues for the EPC.

processing for manufacture of silicon chips. In general, any type of composition of matter, so long as it would have been novel, non-obvious, and useful within the relevant time frame would be appropriate to claim. These claims can be quite important.

We have discussed that apparatus claims cover make, use, sell, and so on, whereas method claims cover make or use. One might think of this as a type of claim domination. That is, anything that infringes the dominated claim infringes the dominant claim, but there are other things that also infringe the dominant claim. Apparatus claims, for example, may dominate related method claims, such as method of using claims because apparatus claims cover make, use, sell, and so on. In a similar manner, composition of matter claims may dominate related apparatus claims and method claims.

The Supreme Court[167] has stated "composition of matter" means "all compositions of two or more substances and all composite articles, whether they be the results of chemical union, or of mechanical mixture, or whether they be gases, fluids, powders or solids." Composite articles may also be claimed as articles of manufacture—such as roofing, a bathtub or countertop, a door jamb, and so on.

Typically, the claim recites the constituent components and how they are to be combined, such as amounts and conditions (e.g., temperature, pressure, flow rates, catalysts, etc.). The purpose or use of the composition may or may not be stated. Likewise, a composition of matter claim may cover short-lived or intermediate compositions of an overall chemical process.

Composition of matter claims may at times use a transition word other than "comprising." The word comprising is understood to be open form. For some composition of matter claims, this may produce a rejection or result in invalidity either for undue breath in the unpredictable arts or for failing to enable or provide written description support for the full scope of the claim.[168] For example, it may require quite specific conditions to produce a particular composition of matter. Using "comprising," however, would imply the composition of matter could be produced with other conditions or substances, for example. Thus, the claim would on its face appear to cover many more inoperative embodiments

---

167. *See* Diamond v. Deihr, 450 U.S. 175 (1981).

168. *See* Juno Therapeutics, Inc. v. Kite Pharma, Inc. 10 F.4th 1330 (Fed. Cir. 2021) (written description);Trustees of Boston v. Everlight, 896 F.3d 1357 (Fed. Cir. 2018) (enablement); Durel Corp. v. Osram Sylvania, 256 F.3d 1298, 1306–07 (Fed. Cir. 2001) (a significant number of inoperative embodiments within the scope of the claims might be sufficient to prove invalidity); *see also* Atlas Powder v. DuPont, 750 F.2d 1569, 1576–77 (Fed. Cir. 1984). *See* EMI Grp. North America, Inc. v. Cypress Semiconductor Corp., 268 F.3d 1342 (Fed. Cir. 2001) (claims reciting scientific process found to be impossible are invalid). *See also* Sean Seymore, *Heightened Enablement in the Unpredictable Arts*, 56 UCLA L. Rev. 127 (2008).

than operative embodiments[169] or the claim could be said to fail to be enabled or fail to be described sufficiently as to its full scope,[170] rendering it invalid.

To address this, such claims often use "consisting of" or "consisting essentially of" as the transition,[171] referred to as closed form and partially closed form, respectively. These transitions have a specifically understood meaning that relates to canons of construction regarding patent claims, as has been explained and as shall also be explained later; however, there are federal circuit cases as well that have deviated from these understood meanings when interpreting a claim. One may view these canons and meanings as a type of "first order" analysis or, perhaps, as a weak presumption. In the appropriate circumstances, depending on claim wording, the specification, the file history, the technology, and so on, a federal court may be willing to deviate from the applicable understood meaning(s) or canon(s).

With this in mind, "consisting of" is used to claim only the elements and limitations as recited in the claim body (e.g., closed form).[172] "Consisting essentially of" is used to claim the elements and limitations only as recited in the claim body *including* any additional unclaimed constituents that are of a nature or an amount to not alter the character of what is otherwise intended to be claimed as something that would have been novel subject matter (e.g., partially closed form).[173] More discussion on the important topic of transition words is included in Chapter 2.[174]

However, one important aspect to know about transition words or phrases, especially in connection with compositions of matter, is that different transition words or phrases may be used within the claim to limit or enlarge

169. *See* Durel Corp. v. Osram Sylvania, 256 F.3d 1298, 1306–07 (Fed. Cir. 2001) (a significant number of inoperative embodiments within the scope of the claims might be sufficient to prove invalidity); *see* Atlas Powder v. DuPont, 750 F.2d 1569, 1576–77 (Fed. Cir. 1984). *See also* EMI Group v. Cypress Semiconductor, 268 F.3d 1342 (Fed. Cir. 2001) (claims reciting scientific process found to be impossible are invalid).

170. *See* Juno Therapeutics, Inc. v. Kite Pharma, Inc. 10 F.4th 1330 (Fed. Cir. 2021) (written description); Trustees of Boston v. Everlight, 896 F3.d 1357 (Fed. Cir. 2018) (enablement); Durel Corp. v. Osram Sylvania, 256 F.3d 1298, 1306–07 (Fed. Cir. 2001) (a significant number of inoperative embodiments within the scope of the claims might be sufficient to prove invalidity); *see* EMI Group v. Cypress Semiconductor, 268 F. 3d 1342 (Fed. Cir. 2001) (claims reciting scientific process found to be impossible are invalid); Atlas Powder v. DuPont, 750 F.2d 1569, 1576–77 (Fed. Cir. 1984). *See also* Seymore, *supra* note 168.

171. *See* section 2.13 and its subsections, describing transition words or phrases.

172. *See* AFG Indus. v. Cardinal, 239 F.3d 1236 (Fed. Cir. 2001); *cf.* Norian Corp. v. Stryker Corp., 363 F.3d 1321 (Fed. Cir.2004) (claim includes ordinary impurities of recited elements).

173. *See* PPG Indus. v. Guardian Indus., 156 F.3d 1351 (Fed. Cir. 1998); *see also* section 2.13 and its subsections, describing transition words or phrases.

174. *See* section 2.13 and its subsections, describing transition words or phrases.

scope as well. This technique was discussed previously in the prior section on Markush groups. Now, we illustrate it with another example of a composition of matter claim.

EXAMPLE 4.21

I claim:

1. A substance comprising: a flash fusible toner comprising a binder resin which includes a bisphenol A polyester containing an aliphatic dicarboxylic acid selected from the group consisting of succinic acid, glutaric acid and adipic acid.

Another thing to appreciate about this claim is that it is very similar to the claim in the federal circuit case, *In re Baird*.[175] That case held the fact that a compound recited in a claim may be encompassed by a disclosed generic formula would not have by itself necessarily rendered that compound obvious, citing *In re Jones*.[176]

This, then, is an example where the details of Markush group claiming and use of different transition words may result in a valuable claim. In *In re Baird*, the claim was held to not have been obvious despite the disclosure of the recited compound in the prior art.

At times, for example, the same chemical compound may exist in different forms, such as, for example, depending on how the compound may be crystallized. Crystallization in different forms may lead to very different properties in different forms for the same compound. This property of a compound is referred to as polymorphism. Thus, if a compound has many, many so-called polymorphs, disclosure of the compound, a genus, would not necessarily have rendered obvious specific polymorphs of the compound.

The same might be the case in the predictable arts as it is for the unpredictable arts, if perhaps less likely. For example, one could imagine the disclosure of a generic form of an invention that would not have rendered obvious a species version because the species version may be constructed to address problems not addressed or even recognized in connection with the generic form.

175. 16 F.3d 380 (Fed. Cir. 1994).
176. 958 F.2d 347, 350, 21 USPQ2d 1941, 1943 (Fed. Cir. 1992).

Consider, as one example, the Fast Fourier Transform (FFT) algorithm. The basic ideas were popularized in 1965, but some algorithms had been derived as early as 1805. In 1994, Gilbert Strang described the FFT as "the most important numerical algorithm of our lifetime," and it was included in Top 10 Algorithms of 20th Century by the IEEE magazine, Computing in Science & Engineering. Yet, there are *many* patents on specific implementations of the FFT, for example, to take advantage of improvements developed over the years in memory technology, processor technology, and so on.

4.131 In General, Draft Claims of Varying Scope

For good practice, the patent claims should include claims of varying scope. It is specifically recommended that multiple embodiments be disclosed and claimed, including the broadest and the narrowest embodiments of the invention, and embodiments between the broadest and the narrowest. There are several reasons for this recommendation.

For one thing, as previously indicated several times, it is a good principle of claim drafting to make the drafter's intent as clear as possible from the face of the claims themselves. Drafting the claims to expressly cover multiple embodiments assists this effort. It makes clearer to others looking at the claims what is intended to be a broad claim, an intermediate claim, and a narrow claim, and how the words of the claims and the order of the claims are structured to communicate breadth and narrowness. Of course, it is likewise important that the specification also recite these embodiments, and via explanation thereof present them as broad, intermediate, and narrow (but without using that express language).

Another advantage of this approach is that it reduces the risk of limitations being read into the claims from the specification. It is difficult to predict when a court will read a limitation from the specification into the claims and when it will not. However, drafting the claims so that multiple embodiments are covered, including the broadest and the narrowest, reduces the risk a court will read a limitation from the specification into the claims. Because these embodiments are specifically covered in the claims, it makes it a less likely occurrence when not intended.

In many reported cases, one of the difficulties was that the specification recited only one or only a few embodiments. This situation made it easier for the court to read limitations from the specification into the claim or claims at issue. In contrast, the more embodiments with corresponding claims, the more likely it is that a court will not read a limitation into a claim where that limitation is not intended.

> The more embodiments in the specification with corresponding claims, the more likely it is that a court will not read a limitation into a claim where that limitation is not intended.

Another advantage of this approach is that it reduces the risk that claims will be held invalid for lack of written description. This is a risk associated with disclosing a single or only a few embodiments. By, instead, describing and claiming multiple embodiments from broadest to narrowest, the risk of lack of written description is significantly reduced because explicit textual support is provided at the time of filing, at a minimum, by the claims themselves.

> By describing and claiming multiple embodiments from broadest to narrowest, the risk of lack of written description is significantly reduced because explicit textual support is provided at the time of filing, at a minimum, by the claims themselves.

One risk avoided, then, is that a court will conclude in later litigation that added claims are broader than the specification intended to support those claims.

An independent advantage, of course, of having a set of claims of varying scope that includes narrow claims, intermediate claims, and broad claims is that this increases the chances of capturing infringers while decreasing the chances of reading on the prior art. The more different ways an invention is claimed, the more opportunities exist to capture infringers that might otherwise escape liability. Likewise, although a thorough prior art search may have taken place, there is usually still some uncertainty regarding whether the best and closest prior art has been found. Also, it may be that a search has not been conducted. In both instances, claiming the invention a variety of ways from broad to narrow helps mitigate that risk by providing more opportunities to avoid potentially difficult prior art that may later crop up.

An independent advantage of having a set of claims of varying scope that includes narrow claims, intermediate claims, and broad claims is that this increases the chances of capturing infringers while decreasing the chances of reading on the prior art.

4.1311 Examples of Broad Scope Claims

As an illustration of drafting claims from broad to narrow scope, the previous technology examples related to transistor body biasing and visual voicemail are employed. Note that these are two quite different technologies.

Observe that we provide a single set of claims for each as an example; however, a patent application would include other claim sets with different independent claims and likely different claim types. For example, we illustrate transistor body biasing with apparatus claims, but we would also expect, perhaps, a set with a different apparatus claims and a set with an independent method of using claim in a complete application. One might also employ means plus function claims and/or method of making claims, provided the client is willing to absorb extra claim fees. We begin with a broad independent claim in these examples.

EXAMPLE 4.22

I claim:

1. An RF module comprising: at least one integrated circuit chip;

   the at least one integrated circuit chip included in the RF module and further including at least one field effect transistor, the at least one field effect transistor including a gate, a drain, a source, and a body;

   wherein, during at least a portion of an off state, the body of the at least one field effect transistor is to be electrically biased to have a voltage level substantially more negative than the lowest voltage level of the following: ground, the DC voltage level of the source of the at least one field effect transistor, and the DC voltage level of the drain of the at least one field effect transistor.

Example Features Recited:

1. Claim recites an RF module.
2. Claim recites the RF module includes an integrated circuit chip.
3. Claim recites that the integrated circuit chip includes at least one field effect transistor including a gate, a drain, a source, and a body.
4. Claim recites the at least one field effect transistor is in the off state.
5. Claim recites the body of the at least one field effect transistor is electrically biased to a voltage level.
6. Claim recites the voltage level of the electrical bias is substantially more negative than the lowest voltage level of ground, the DC voltage level of the source, and the DC voltage level of the drain.

Observe that while claim 1 is reasonably broad, it clearly has specific limitations that permit the ability to distinguish even this broad claim from the prior art. The reasons for these features should be clear from the prior technology discussion.[177] Most are for patentability arguments, but the recitation of a module and an integrated circuit is to aid enforcement.

EXAMPLE 4.23

I claim:

1. A method of processing voicemail messages at a voicemail server, the method comprising:

   capturing a plurality of received voicemail messages in an audio format to provide a plurality of audio-formatted voicemail messages;

   converting the plurality of audio-formatted voicemail messages to a plurality of corresponding text representations of the voicemail messages; and

   initiating communication of the text representations of the voicemail messages and the audio-formatted voicemail messages to a mobile device, wherein a respective text representation comprises a representation of an at least partial text transcription of a corresponding converted audio-formatted voicemail message, the at least partial text transcriptions of the voicemail messages to be displayed via a visual voicemail inbox of a voicemail system integrated as part of the mobile device.

177. *See* section 3.2141, discussing this technology example.

Example Features Recited:

1. Claim recites processing of voicemail messages (plural) at a voicemail server.
2. Claim recites capturing audio-formatted voicemail messages and converting to text representations.
3. Claim clarifies and recites that a text representation comprises a representation of an at least partial text transcription of a corresponding audio-formatted voicemail message.
4. Claim recites that communication of the text representations of the voicemail messages and the audio-formatted voicemail messages is to a mobile device and is initiated.
5. Claim recites that the at least partial text transcriptions of the voicemail messages are to be displayed via a visual voicemail inbox of a voicemail system integrated as part of the mobile device.

Observe, as before, that while claim 1 is reasonably broad, it clearly has specific limitations that permit the ability to distinguish even this broad claim from the prior art. The reasons for these features should be clear from prior discussion.[178]

4.1312 Examples of Intermediate and Narrow Scope Claims

Continuing with the two previous technical examples, here, for the transistor body biasing technology example, are claims 2-10, which might be half of the claims of a complete patent application. Usually, patent applications are filed with 20 claims and three independent claims. The other ten claims might be another independent claim with nine dependent claims, or two more independent claims each with four dependent claims.

EXAMPLE 4.24

2. The RF module of claim 1, wherein the at least one field effect transistor comprises a N-type metal oxide semiconductor (NMOS) field effect transistor.

3. The RF module of claim 1, wherein the at least one field effect transistor is implemented in a silicon-on-insulator technology.

4. The RF module of claim 1, wherein the voltage level substantially more negative than the lowest voltage level is more than one volt more negative than the lowest voltage level.

178. *See* section 4.1263, discussing this technology example.

5. The RF module of claim 1, wherein the body of the at least one field effect transistor is electrically coupled to an accumulated charge sink.

6. The RF module of claim 1, wherein the at least one field effect transistor during the at least a portion of the off state is to be electrically biased so as to improve the linearity of the at least one field effect transistor relative to the at least one field effect transistor not electrically biased to have a voltage level substantially more negative than the lowest voltage level of the following: ground, the DC voltage level of the source of the at least one field effect transistor, and the DC voltage level of the drain of the at least one field effect transistor.

7. The RF module of claim 1, wherein the at least one field effect transistor during the at least a portion of the off state is to be electrically biased so as to reduce non-linear harmonic and/or intermodulation distortion of RF signals to be propagated by the module, reduction via the at least one field effect transistor being relative to the at least one field effect transistor not electrically biased to have a voltage level substantially more negative than the lowest voltage level of the following: ground, the DC voltage level of the source of the at least one field effect transistor, and the DC voltage level of the drain of the at least one field effect transistor.

8. The RF module of claim 7, wherein the power of a third harmonic of the RF signals to be propagated via the RF module is to be lower than -30 dBm at an operating power of +35 dBm power.

9. The RF module of claim 1, wherein the at least one field effect transistor is included in a stack of field effect transistors included in an RF switch, the RF switch being included in the at least one integrated circuit chip.

10. The RF module of claim 1, wherein the body of the at least one field effect transistor is electrically coupled to at least two accumulated charge sinks.

Example Features Recited:

1. Claims recite NMOS FETs.
2. Claims recite silicon-on-insulator (SOI) technology.
3. Claims recite "substantially more negative" is more than one volt "more negative."
4. Claims recite an accumulated charge sink.
5. Claims recite linearity improvement relative to a transistor without a body biased electrically negative so as to be in the off state.

6. Claims recite reduction of nonlinear harmonic and/or intermodulation distortion relative to a transistor without a body biased electrically negative so as to be in the off state.
7. Claims recite the power of a third harmonic of the RF signals to be propagated via the RF module is to be lower than –30 dBm at an operating power of +35 dBm power.
8. Claims recite that the at least one transistor is included in a transistor stack.

All these claims via dependency are necessarily narrower than claim 1. Some are not significantly narrower than claim 1, whereas some claims do seem narrow, such as claim 7, for example.

EXAMPLE 4.25

2. The method of claim 1, and further comprising:

   receiving and processing the plurality of text representations for display of the at least partial text transcriptions via the visual voicemail inbox of the voicemail system integrated as part of the mobile device.

3. The method of claim 1, wherein the initiating communication of the text representations of the voicemail messages and the audio-formatted voicemail messages to the mobile device further includes initiating communication of one or more voicemail identifiers for respective voicemail messages of the plurality of voicemail messages, the one or more voicemail identifiers also displayable with the at least partial text transcriptions via the visual voicemail inbox as one or more visual voicemail indicators.
4. The method of claim 3, wherein, for a particular voicemail message, the one or more visual voicemail indicators include at least one of the following: a time of a telephone call associated with the particular voicemail message; a date of the telephone call associated with the particular voicemail message; and/or a telephone number for the telephone call associated with the particular voicemail message.
5. The method of claim 3, wherein the initiating communication further includes initiating communication of a plurality of telephone numbers associated with the plurality of voicemail messages, the telephone numbers displayable via the visual voicemail inbox as one of the one or more visual voicemail indicators in a manner so that the telephone numbers are selectable to call at least one of the telephone numbers.

6. The method of claim 1, wherein the initiating communication comprises initiating communication of one or more voicemail identifiers for respective voicemail messages to the mobile device displayable via the visual voicemail inbox as one or more visual voicemail indicators for respective voicemail messages along with the at least partial text transcription of the respective voicemail messages via the visual voicemail inbox of the voicemail system integrated as part of the mobile device.

7. The method of claim 1, wherein the initiating communication further includes initiating communication of the text representations of the voicemail messages and the audio-formatted voicemail messages, wherein the text transcriptions respectively comprise an at least partial text transcription displayable in a manner so that a displayed telephone number in at least one of the at least partial text transcriptions is selectable to call the telephone number that is displayed.

Example Features Recited:

1. Claims recite receiving and processing the plurality of text representations for display.
2. Claims recite initiating communication of one or more voicemail identifiers for respective voicemail messages.
3. Claims recite particulars regarding voicemail indicators, for example, a time of a telephone call associated with the particular voicemail message; a date of the telephone call associated with the particular voicemail message; and/or a telephone number for the telephone call associated with the particular voicemail message.
4. Claims recite that displayable telephone numbers are selectable to call at least one of the telephone numbers.
5. Claims recite a displayed telephone number in at least one of the at least partial text transcriptions is selectable to call the telephone number that is displayed.

All these claims via dependency are necessarily narrower than claim 1. In general, all seem of intermediate scope or narrower. Note how all are written in method claim format.

4.1313 Use Picture Claims

A picture claim refers to a claim that includes all or nearly all the limitations of the narrowest embodiment of an invention. Such a claim, in essence, is sufficiently detailed as to form or create a "picture." Although we have recommended that you use claim differentiation as one technique for claiming the narrow embodiments, we also recommend the use of picture claims separately as well. Picture claims, of course, provide some of the advantages previously discussed. For example, they reduce the risk of lack of written description; however, there are additional advantages as well.

Although we have recommended that you use claim differentiation as one technique for claiming the narrow embodiments, we also recommend the use of picture claims separately as well.

Employing picture claims may avoid the need to add rewritten claims in response to a PTO rejection. This, of course, has the potential to reduce prosecution history estoppel, although it will depend on the circumstances.[179] In addition, it is likely to save prosecution time by avoiding the need for an amendment, as just indicated, and, therefore, avoid the need to wait for the examiner's response to that amendment. Therefore, it may save money for your client, as well as a portion of the patent term.[180]

Another benefit of a picture claim is that it may lead to having at least one claim allowed in the first office action.[181] If not, this also gives you a good sense of where the examiner stands regarding your added limitations, suggesting you have work ahead to further distinguish from the art or to convince the examiner he has overlooked something.

Typically, a picture claim is an independent claim. This means it should get serious consideration from the examiner, which is desirable. One technique that is not as good might be to have, through a series of related dependencies, a claim that is a picture claim in theory because it includes all the important limitations. There are several reasons this is not as good. First, not being an independent claim, it may not get as much examiner attention. Furthermore, from the face of the claim, all its limitations are not immediately apparent.

179. *See* Honeywell Int'l v. Hamilton Sundstrand Corp., 370 F.3d 1131 (Fed. Cir. 2004) (en banc).

180. Delays in prosecution may affect the term of the patent. *See* 35 U.S.C. § 154 (2022).

181. On the other hand, some have expressed the concern that due to presence of the picture claim, perhaps that is all the examiner is willing to allow. If so, this would certainly be a disadvantage of a picture claim.

Rather, one needs to trace through a series of dependencies to appreciate its limitations. For this reason, it may not appear as narrow to the examiner.

Finally, employing picture claims may reduce the risk of dedicating disclosed subject matter to the public by forcing the patent drafter to be careful and claim everything that is disclosed. In *Johnson & Johnston v. R.E. Service*[182] the federal circuit held, en banc, that subject matter disclosed in a specification that is not claimed is dedicated to the public. Of course, a picture claim would not necessarily have solved the problem in that case. The claims at issue related to fabrication of a printed circuit board. The claims recited aluminum and the patentee was attempting to use the doctrine of equivalents to also encompass steel, although steel had been disclosed as a possible material in the specification. Therefore, in some sense, the claim at issue in *Johnson & Johnston* was too narrow. However, writing picture claims is a good claim drafting practice to ensure that nothing mentioned in the specification that should be claimed is overlooked. As mentioned in connection with the discussion of means plus function claims,[183] including such claims is another way to avoid the problem in *Johnson & Johnston*.

There was a time when picture claims were commonly employed. Today, with the costs of filing having gone up considerably and with an increased focus on cost cutting, such claims are no longer typical. However, their benefits have been overlooked. A picture claim might be a third independent claim in a set of 20 claims or it might be a fourth independent claim in a set of 20 claims, at an additional cost of around $200 for a large entity. Given its potential benefits, it seems worth it.

182. 285 F.3d 1046 (Fed. Cir. 2002) (en banc).

183. *See* discussion of means plus function claims in Chapter 2 and in this chapter.

5
More PCDP Basics

High-Level Principles of This Chapter:[1]

- Use claim preambles that are short and avoid introducing limitations;
- Make where the preamble and transition phrase ends and the claim body begins clear with punctuation;
- Use "comprising" as the transition word in the predictable arts;
- Use varying transitional phrases ("consisting of" and/or "consisting essentially of") to vary claim scope in the unpredictable arts;
- Draft the patent claims before the specification;
- Use dependent claims for claim differentiation and to cover commercial embodiments (e.g., those most likely to be copied);
- Use claim terms that have express definitions in the specification;
- Have the closest *known* prior art in mind when drafting the claims;
- Do not draft claims that read on *known* prior art;
- Have a good faith argument to patentably distinguish the broadest claims;
- Avoid drafting claims in a manner that leaves the statutory class of the claim unclear (avoid apparatus-type limitations in method claims and method-type limitations in apparatus claims);
- When creating claim dependencies, skip some intermediate dependent claims for claim diversity.

1. *See* List of Claim Drafting Principles, Appendix A.

Chapter 4 drilled down in some detail into various types of claims to assist in achieving patent claim diversity when drafting claims. Chapter 5 deals with the basic principles of good claim drafting. Chapter 6 then deals with more advanced principles of good claim drafting.

5.1 Claim Preambles Should Be Short and Avoid Introducing Limitations

The notion of a patent claim preamble is very similar in concept to the notion of a preamble to a contract in contract law. In contract law, the preamble of a contract typically states the purpose or reason for the contract but does not form part of the formal agreement itself. Thus, typically, but not always, the preamble is not used to interpret the agreement, since that is not its purpose. Sometimes, if the language of the agreement itself is ambiguous, then a court may use the preamble to assist in resolving the ambiguity.[2]

Analogous principles apply to claim preambles. The preamble of a patent claim is a statement of intended use or purpose for the subject matter being claimed. Therefore, typically, it is not part of the subject matter itself and is not usually a limitation on the subject matter being claimed. However, because this is only usually true and not always true, preambles can prove troubling when drafting patent claims. When drafting claims, certainty is preferred, if possible.

Despite the principle that claim preambles are usually a statement of purpose and should not limit the scope of the patent claims, as in contract law, this principle is not always followed by courts. For example, in *Catalina Marketing v. Coolsavings.com*,[3] the federal circuit noted that no litmus test defines when a preamble limits claim scope.

Claim preambles, therefore, present a variety of risks. One risk is that the preamble will inadvertently introduce an unintended limitation into the claims. This is what most commonly occurs. However, another risk is that

2. Here is a simple example of a preamble of a contract:

In order to permit each party to this agreement to conduct research and development in the field of semiconductor technology and manufacturing without the concerns of inadvertent patent infringement, the parties have determined that a patent cross-license in the field of semiconductor technology and manufacturing would be in their mutual best interests. The parties, therefore, agree as follows:

3. 289 F.3d 801, 808 (Fed. Cir. 2002).

you may, in fact, intend the preamble as a limitation of the claim to distinguish from the prior art; but a court may, instead, conclude that the preamble is not a limitation and, therefore, hold the claim invalid. Likewise, if a court construes the preamble to be a limitation, then there is always the risk that the court will conclude that the limitation is not adequately supported by the specification. Good patent claim drafting practice dictates that claim preambles should be short and to the point to reduce these risks.

One possible approach to drafting preambles is limiting the preamble to recite only the statutory class of the invention, such as "A method comprising,"[4] and so on. However, such a restrictive approach is not necessary and may not be preferred from a drafting perspective. However, again, it is recommended that care be used to draft the preamble and ensure that it is short and to the point.

Method claims deserve special mention in the context of preambles. It is common practice when drafting method claims to use the preamble to provide antecedent basis for words that are then used in the body of the claim. Here is a simple example:

> A method of cooking pasta comprising:
> placing the pasta in boiling water; and
> waiting until the pasta becomes at least slightly tender.

As is clear in this example, the preamble provides antecedent basis for the word "pasta." In this case, there is little doubt, therefore, that the preamble will be construed to be limiting. This is because the words of the preamble are also referenced in the body of the claim. Of course, in this simple example, the claim could have been drafted so that the preamble did not provide antecedent basis; however, for more complex method claims, drafting the claim so that the preamble does not serve this function can be much trickier, depending upon the situation.

> It is recommended that care be used to draft the preamble and ensure that it is short and to the point.

4. Note that "comprising" is actually not part of the preamble, but is the transition word, as explained in more detail *supra*.

5.11 For Method Claims, Avoid "A Method Comprising the Steps Of"

For years, it also used to be common practice to add to the end of a preamble of a method claim, the language "the steps of," as in "A method comprising the steps of:"

It is recommended that this formulation *not* be employed. Using the word "step" anywhere in the claim, including in the preamble,[5] creates the risk that the patent claim will be interpreted to be a step plus function claim under 35 USC section 112(f) (previously, 35 USC § 112, paragraph 6).[6] Because such claims are typically given a narrow construction by courts, good practice suggests that this be avoided.

5.12 Avoid Preambles That Refer to Non-Statutory Subject Matter

Another issue that has sometimes arisen with preambles is the issue of non-statutory subject matter. 35 USC section 101 defines subject matter that may properly be claimed in a U.S. patent. However, a line of U.S. Supreme Court cases, culminating with *Diamond v. Diehr*,[7] have interpreted that section to mean that an "algorithm, or mathematical formula, is like a law of nature, which cannot be the subject of a patent."[8]

Despite this relatively clear prohibition, surprisingly, over the years, there have still been examples of patent claims with preambles, such as "an algorithm comprising" or "a mathematical algorithm comprising." It is recommended that preambles claiming non-statutory subject matter, or even preambles that might arguably claim non-statutory subject matter, be avoided, including such preambles as "a formula comprising." Even preambles such as "software comprising" or "a computer program comprising" are not recommended. Another example of a non-statutory preamble is "the signal comprising."[9]

---

5. Technically, one might argue that "the steps of" is part of the body rather than the preamble, although it is usually followed with a colon. Since we recommend against use, we need not formally analyze whether "the steps of" is in the preamble or the body. If interpreted as part of the body, that just makes the step plus function issue that much riskier.
6. *See* discussion of step plus function claims in Chapter 4 and in Chapter 2.
7. 450 U.S. 175 (1981).
8. *Id.* at 186
9. *See* discussion in this chapter of "signal propagating" claim in section 4.128 and its subsections.

Instead, use a preamble that comports with the language of 35 USC section 101 regarding eligible subject matter.[10]

> It is recommended that preambles claiming non-statutory subject matter, or even preambles that might arguably claim non-statutory subject matter, be avoided, including such preambles as "a formula comprising" or even "software comprising" or "a computer program comprising."

5.13 Where the Preamble Ends Should Be Clear

As indicated previously, a principle to which one should adhere when drafting claims is to endeavor to make the drafter's intent clear from the face of the claim. Otherwise, a risk is incurred that a court will interpret the claim in a way other than was intended. One example where this might occur is where it is not clear from the face of the claim where the preamble ends. Here is a simple, yet common, example:[11]

> A storage medium having stored thereon machine-readable instructions that, when executed by a computer, cause to be performed a method of transmitting signals over a network comprising:
> Action A;
> Action B;
> Action C.

From the face of this claim, it is not entirely clear whether the preamble is "a storage medium" or whether it is everything that precedes the word "comprising." One problem with this ambiguity is that it permits an opponent to take the position that best suits his or her case and it permits a court to go along with that position. As previously indicated, preambles are not always limiting, whereas the words in the body of the claim are. Thus, in this example, it is not entirely clear whether the words between "having" and "comprising" necessarily limit the scope of the claim or not.

Of course, some patent practitioners may believe that there is minimal risk that a court will construe the preamble to be anything other than "storage medium." This assessment might even be accurate in some cases. Still,

10. *See* discussion in section 2.1 and its subsections.
11. *See* discussion of Beauregard claims in Chapter 4 and Chapter 2.

in other claim situations, the risk or ambiguity may be greater. The point is why incur any risk at all, when the claim may be drafted so that there is no ambiguity and no risk? It is relatively easy to draft the claim so that where the preamble ends is clear. However, if the claim is not drafted so that this is clear, then there is greater uncertainty regarding which portions of the claim are limiting and which portions are not. Good practice suggests that even potentially small unnecessary risks, such as ambiguity regarding where the preamble ends, should. be avoided, if possible.

Good practice suggests that even potentially small unnecessary risks, such as ambiguity regarding where the preamble ends, should be avoided, if possible.

5.14 List of Examples of Preambles

Chapter 2 provides a list of potential claim preambles and cites additional resources as well.[12] That section is cross-referenced here rather than repeat the subject matter.

5.2 In the Predictable Arts, Use "Comprising" as the Transition Word

A long line of patent cases has construed claims so that when the word "comprising" is employed as the transition word, the claim is open. For example, a statement of this basic proposition is contained in the federal circuit case *Invitrogen v. Biocrest*.[13] This means the claim is construed to cover more than simply all the elements and limitations provided in the body of the claim. The claim is interpreted so that, if all the listed elements and limitations are present, then the claim is met, even if other aspects of the so-called accused product or accused process are not explicitly listed in the claim. That is, those other aspects do not prevent the accused product or process from falling within the scope of the claim.

12. See section 2.122, providing a variety of examples of preamble.
13. 327 F.3d 1364 (Fed. Cir. 2003).

In virtually all cases in the predictable arts, "comprising" should be used as the transition word. This is because it would be unusual in the predictable arts to find all the elements and limitations of a claim present in the accused product or process, but still find that the inventive concept was not being employed, regardless of what else might also be present in the accused product or process.

It is also a good idea to follow the word "comprising" by a colon. This will make it clear that comprising is intended to be the transition word and that everything that follows the colon is intended to be the body of the claim. Again, as previously discussed, it is best to have it be clear which portion of the claim is the preamble, which is portion is the transition word, and which is the body. This will make it more clear which words of the claim are intended as limitations and which words are not.

> In virtually all cases in the predictable arts, "comprising" should be used as the transition word. It is also a good idea to follow the word "comprising" by a colon. This will make it clear that comprising is intended to be the transition word and that everything that follows the colon is intended to be the body of the claim.

Using any words other than "comprising" as the transition word in the predictable arts[14] is not recommended because there is some risk that the claim will otherwise not be interpreted to be "open." For example, in *Crystal v. Tritech*,[15] the federal circuit stated that if the transition word employed is "having," the claim may be interpreted to be open or closed, depending on the context. Here, context refers to the claim language itself, the other claims, the specification, and the file history. Likewise, use of the word "comprising" elsewhere in the claim other than as the transition word is subject to interpretation, meaning that if it is used other than as a transition word, then it may not automatically be interpreted to be open (although one would expect it to be in most cases).[16] In others words, making clear in the specification that it is intended to be open may be a good idea.

---

14. See discussion of predictable and unpredictable arts in Chapter 2.

15. 246 F.3d 1336, 1338 (Fed. Cir. 2001).

16. *See* Moleculon Rsch. v. CBS, 793 F.2d 1261, 1271 n.8 (Fed. Cir.), *cert. denied*, 479 U.S. 1030 (1987).

It is also a good idea to ensure that the rest of the claim is not drafted to imply that the claim is closed, despite the presence of the transition word "comprising." If this were the case, it could trump the use of "comprising" to indicate the intent that the claim be construed to be open. For example, if the claim were to recite: "An apparatus comprising: only one widget," the claim may not be interpreted to be open since it seems clear from the body that the claim is not intended to cover more than one widget. Furthermore, the federal circuit has stated several times that use of the word "comprising" is not an excuse to ignore claim limitations.[17] Therefore, if the body of the claim were to imply that the scope of the claim is closed or in some way limited, it is not likely that the use of "comprising" would overcome that implication. This is perhaps analogous to the notion that the doctrine of equivalents cannot be used to erase or ignore claim limitations.[18] In both contexts, the limitations present in the body of the claim are given serious weight.

Of course, the other claims, the specification and the prosecution history may all be employed to further support or aid the interpretation that a particular claim should be construed as open from the use of "comprising" as the transition word, and it is recommended that this be done. For example, the dependent claims may be employed to add elements to the base claim. By using dependent claims to add elements, the drafter could be interpreted to be demonstrating that the base claim itself is not intended to be closed or partially closed, but, instead, open. Additionally, the specification itself may use the word "comprising" in a variety of open-ended contexts to describe one or more embodiments, thereby shoring up the intended open-ended meaning, for example.

It is true that the interpretation of "comprising" as open-ended when used as a transition word has significant precedent behind it; however, again, good practice indicates that the application should be drafted to avoid what might appear at the time of drafting to be even a potentially small risk or aberration. For example, if a claim recited: "An apparatus comprising: an adder," would it be unreasonable for a defendant to argue that the claim *cannot* be construed to cover a subtractor? This is despite the notion that subtraction is merely adding a negative number. Perhaps in some contexts the answer is "yes," but not necessarily in all contexts. Thus, additional support in the specification for an open-ended interpretation of the claims in most situations is probably warranted.

---

17. *See, e.g.*, Spectrum v. Sterilite, 164 F.3d 1372, 1386 (Fed. Cir. 1998).

18. *See, e.g.*, Pennwalt Corp. v. Durand-Wayland, 833 F.2d 931 (Fed. Cir. 1987) (en banc); Dolly v. Spalding & Evenflo, 16 F.3d 394, 398 (Fed. Cir. 1994).

Another issue that has not been heavily litigated, but that may sometimes arise is whether "comprising" is to be interpreted as meaning *physically* or *structurally* open-ended or is it broad enough to encompass the notion of the claim being also *functionally* open-ended. For example, if a claim recites: "A system comprising: A, B, and C." Does this mean that A, B, and C must be part of the same physical system, although these are distinct components, or, alternatively, does it mean that any time you have A, B, and C functionally associated, the claim is satisfied?

It is likely that there is no single answer to this question, and it will, instead, be resolved based on the particular context, that is, the other claims, the specification, and the file history. For example, in the case *Toro v. White Consolidated*,[19] the federal circuit interpreted the word "including" used in the body of a claim to mean "permanently affixed to and included as part of. . . ." However, it would probably be a mistake to extrapolate this case to mean that "including" used in the body of the claim *always* means "permanently affixed to."

In *Toro*, the patent at issue disclosed and claimed a convertible vacuum-blower for use in vacuuming or blowing leaves and small debris, depending on the selected mode. The design employed a removable cover which was *physically attached* to a restriction ring. The restriction ring was used to increase the velocity of air in the blower mode by reducing the diameter of the air intake opening. The accused product, on the other hand, had a restriction ring *physically separate from* the cover. Therefore, because of its construction of the word "including" indicated earlier, the federal circuit reversed the district court's summary judgment of patent infringement.

Other cases have also interpreted either "including" or "comprising" in the body of the claim to essentially mean "physically apart of."[20] Nonetheless, these results are also based on the particular context.[21] Therefore, as has previously been indicated, for good claim drafting practice, it is best to make your intention as clear as possible on the face of the claims, and draft the remainder of the application and the file history to be consistent with that intention.

---

19. 199 F.3d 1295, 1301 (Fed. Cir. 1999).

20. *See* Senior Tech. v. R. F. Tech., 2001 U.S. App Lexis 4179 (Fed. Cir. 2001) (nonprecedential); Multitech v. Microsoft, 2002 U.S. Dist. Lexis 15960 (D. Minn. 2002) (nonprecedential).

21. *Toro*, 199 F.3d at 1301.

5.21 Use Varying Transitional Phrases to Vary Claim Scope in the Unpredicable Arts

Just as "comprising" used as the transitional word has acquired an open meaning, "consisting of" and "consisting essentially of" have acquired a closed meaning and a partially closed meaning, respectively.[22] Because these terms used as transition words or phrases generally restrict the scope of a claim, they are not recommended for use in the predictable arts; however, they are sometimes used in the unpredictable arts where, despite their apparent narrow orientation, they provide protection. For example, their use may be appropriate where only a certain specified combination of elements may produce the desired result, such as with a particular composition of matter.[23] However, in the predictable arts, such claims may be quite easy to design around. Consider, for example, the claim: "An apparatus consisting of: A, B, and C." This claim could easily be avoided in the predictable arts by simply adding another element to the combination.

> Because "consisting of" and "consisting essentially of" used as transition words generally restrict the scope of a claim, they are not recommended for use in the predictable arts; however, they are sometimes used in the unpredictable arts where, despite their apparent narrow orientation, they provide protection.

5.211 "Consisting Of" and "Consisting Essentially Of"

"Consisting of" and "consisting essentially of" as transitional phrases have been covered.[24] Therefore, this is merely a refresh/review.

Let us consider some major technological and scientific areas: mechanical devices, electrical or electronic devices, software, materials science, chemistry, and biotechnology. In this order, these technologies represent a spectrum in which, moving from left to right, the technologies become less predictable. By

22. *See, e.g.*, PPG Indus. v. Guardian Indus., 156 F.3d 1351 (Fed. Cir. 1998); *In re* Certain Slide Fastener Stringers, 216 USPQ 907 (US ITC 1981); *ex parte* Grasselli, 231 USPQ 395 (Bd. App. 1983).

23. See discussion of transitional phrases in Chapter 2. Also see discussion of compositions of matter in Chapter 4 and in Chapter 2.

24. See section 2.13 and its subsections, discussing these transitional phrases.

predictable, we mean that given an invention or innovation, it becomes more difficult to extrapolate from that invention or innovation to additional possible related technology that would be enabled from knowing the invention and the state of the art.

Chemistry and biotechnology tend to be highly experimental sciences in which the properties of various combinations of known technical components are more unexpected than for mechanical devices, electronic devices, and software.[25] Hence, in patent law, the latter technologies are characterized more generally as being in the predictable arts and the former technologies are characterized as being in the unpredictable arts.[26]

Imagine, for example, a chemical invention (e.g., composition of matter) such that the properties of the constituents are nothing like the properties of the result, as is usually the case in the chemical arts. Furthermore, for patentability under section 103, often the compounds or composition of matter that results should have improved and unexpected properties relative to similar, previously known formulations.

Typically, formations of such compounds require precise conditions. Important considerations with a composition of matter claim may include "the type[s] of reactions, the state of the art, the representative nature of the examples, and the breadth of the claims."[27] If one were to use of the word "comprising" in a patent claim for a compound formulation, the patent claim could sweep in a host of other possible constituents, conditions, chemical catalysts, and so on, that may not produce the desired result being described and

---

25. *See* Sean Seymore, *Heightened Enablement in the Unpredictable Arts*, 56 UCLA L. Rev. 127 (2008). *See In re* Rainer, 377 F.2d 1006, 1012 (C.C.P.A. 1967) (Important considerations include "the type[s] of reactions, the state of the art, the representative nature of the examples, and the breadth of the claims."). *See also* PPG Indus., Inc. v. Guardian Indus. Corp., 75 F.3d 1558, 1564 (Fed. Cir. 1996) (explaining that "enablement is lacking . . . , because the undescribed embodiments cannot be made, based on the disclosure . . . without undue experimentation"); *In re* Prutton, 200 F.2d 706 (C.C.P.A. 1952) (holding that claims to a class of chemical compounds which were sufficiently broad to involve some speculation lack enablement notwithstanding the presence of the operative specific examples within the class); *In re* Fisher, 427 F.2d 833 (C.C.P.A. 1970).

26. *Compare In re* Vaeck, 947 F.2d 488, 496 (Fed. Cir. 1991) (noting that the requisite level of disclosure for an invention involving predictable mechanical or electrical elements is less than that required for the unpredictable arts) *with* PPG Indus., Inc. v. Guardian Indus. Corp., 75 F.3d 1558, 1564 (Fed. Cir. 1996) (explaining that "enablement is lacking . . . , because the undescribed embodiments cannot be made, based on the disclosure . . . without undue experimentation"); *see In re* Prutton, 200 F.2d 706 (C.C.P.A. 1952) (holding that claims to a class of chemical compounds which were sufficiently broad to involve some speculation lack enablement notwithstanding the presence of the operative specific examples within the class).

27. *See In re* Rainer, 377 F.2d 1006, 1012 (C.C.P.A. 1967).

sought to be claimed and patented. In such a case, then, the claim may be invalid because its full scope would not and possibly could not be enabled or may not be sufficiently described, as is legally required.[28] That is, the specification may describe precise conditions to produce a chemical compound, as a working example, perhaps; however, the claim language with "comprising" as the transition word may sweep in other subject matter that has not been enabled or even described because the described conditions will not produce compounds literally covered by the claim or, perhaps even, compounds literally covered by the claim may not even be possible to produce.[29]

Thus, in the so-called unpredictable arts, a transitional phrase is called for to limit scope and thereby avoid invalidity for lack of enablement or lack of written description of subject matter that an open form transition word would likely bring within the scope of the claim. Claim drafters may, instead, with other types of transitional phrases vary claim scope linguistically to capture more than the working examples described in the specification *without* use of an open form transition word. As one example, precisely varying specified parameters defined by the specification and claim permits one to achieve a desired claim scope.[30]

Again, this difference in transitional phrases is a result of the inherent nature of the technology involved. In the predictable arts, a broad claim that uses the open form "comprising" may still be enabled and potentially be sufficiently described to its full scope from only one embodiment due the nature of the technology and the state of the art.[31]

---

28. *See* Juno Therapeutics, Inc. v. Kite Pharma, Inc. 10 F.4th 1330 (Fed. Cir. 2021) (written description); Trustees of Boston v. Everlight, 896 F3.d 1357 (Fed. Cir. 2018) (enablement); Durel Corp. v. Osram Sylvania, 256 F.3d 1298, 1306–07 (Fed. Cir. 2001) (a significant number of inoperative embodiments within the scope of the claims might be sufficient to prove invalidity); *see also* Atlas Powder v. DuPont, 750 F.2d 1569, 1576–77 (Fed. Cir. 1984).

29. For example, this would require undue experimentation. *See* Trustees of Boston v. Everlight, 896 F3.d 1357 (Fed. Cir. 2018) (enablement); Durel Corp. v. Osram Sylvania, 256 F.3d 1298, 1306–07 (Fed. Cir. 2001) (a significant number of inoperative embodiments within the scope of the claims might be sufficient to prove invalidity); *see also* Atlas Powder v. DuPont, 750 F.2d 1569, 1576–77 (Fed. Cir. 1984).

30. *See* Example 2.15 in Chapter 2.

31. *See, e.g.*, Leibel-Flarsheim v. Medrad, 358 F.3d 898, 905 (Fed. Cir. 2004); Spectra-Physics, Inc. v. Coherent, Inc., 827 F.2d 1524, 1533 (Fed. Cir. 1987) ("[i]f an invention pertains to an art where the results are predictable, e.g., mechanical as opposed to chemical arts, a broad claim can be enabled by disclosure of a single embodiment, and is not invalid for lack of enablement simply because it reads on another embodiment of the invention which is inadequately disclosed"). However, there are cases where the federal circuit concluded a claim was not enabled by a single embodiment. Thus, it is best to provide multiple embodiments. *See* section 4.11 and its subsections.

To address this issue for the unpredictable arts, patent claims in the unpredictable arts often use "consisting of" or "consisting essentially of" as the transition, referred to as closed form and partially closed form, respectively. These transitions have a specific meaning based on canons of construction regarding patent claims, as explained later; however, there are federal circuit cases as well that have deviated from these canons when interpreting a claim. One may view these canons as a type of "first order" analysis or, perhaps, as a weak presumption. In the appropriate circumstances, depending on claim wording, the specification, the file history, the technology, and so on, a federal court may be willing to deviate from the canon.

With this in mind, "consisting of" is used to claim the elements and limitations as recited in the claim body (e.g., closed form).[32] "Consisting essentially of" is used to claim the elements and limitations as recited in the claim body including any additional unclaimed constituents that are of a nature or an amount to not alter the character of what is otherwise intended to be claimed as something that would have been novel subject matter (e.g., partially closed form).[33]

A similar result, therefore, would follow if "consisting essentially of" were used in such a manner. This transitional phrase is referred to as partially closed, because it includes within its scope the addition of unspecified elements or ingredients that do not significantly modify or affect the basic (and novel) characteristics of the recited elements or limitations. Again, such a form may be typically useful in the unpredictable arts, such as in chemistry, where it may be difficult or unusual to have materials in a pure form, or it is desirable to prevent someone from avoiding the claim simply by adding impurities.[34]

---

32. *See* AFG Industries v. Cardinal, 239 F.3d 1236 (Fed. Cir. 2001); *Cf.* Norian Corp. v. Stryker Corp., 363 F.3d 1321 (Fed. Cir. 2004) (claim includes ordinary impurities of recited elements). *See* section 2.113.

33. *See* PPG Indus. v. Guardian Indus., 156 F.3d 1351 (Fed. Cir. 1998). *See* section 2.113. Note that use of "consisting essentially of" was recently held to raise an indefiniteness issue. In HZNP Medicines LLC v. Actavis Laboratories UT, Inc., 940 F.3d 680 (Fed. Cir. 2019), the phrase "consisting essentially of" was found indefinite. This was because a basic and novel property was indefinite. However, with this transition phrase, unclaimed constituents are to be of a nature or an amount to not alter the character of what is otherwise intended to be claimed as something that would have been novel subject matter. Hence, claim scope was unclear.

34. However, be aware of the potential risk of indefiniteness with this transitional phrase. PPG Indus. v. Guardian Indus., 156 F.3d 1351 (Fed. Cir. 1998). *See* section 2.113. Note that use of "consisting essentially of" was recently held to raise an indefiniteness issue. In HZNP Medicines LLC v. Actavis Laboratories UT, Inc., 940 F.3d 680 (Fed. Cir. 2019), the phrase "consisting essentially of" was found indefinite. This was because a basic and novel property was indefinite. However, with this transition phrase, unclaimed constituents are to be of a nature or

5.3 Use Multiple Verbal Formulations or Approaches That Are Logically Consistent to Capture and Characterize the Inventive Concept

One of the issues that makes claim drafting a difficult enterprise is that the attorney drafting the claims is essentially required to describe with words something that, in theory, was not previously known or did not previously exist. Given that the invention is new, it is frequently difficult to know which aspects will become valuable in time versus which aspects, while still new, will not. The now-famous case, *Autogiro Co. of America v. United States*,[35] recognized this conundrum quite eloquently:

> An invention exists most importantly as a tangible structure or a series of drawings. A verbal portrayal is usually an afterthought written to satisfy the requirements of patent law. This conversion of machine to words allows for unintended idea gaps which cannot be satisfactorily filled. Often the invention is novel and words do not exist to describe it. The dictionary does not always keep abreast of the inventor. It cannot. Things are not made for the sake of words, but words for things.

Thus, by its very nature, the process of reducing an invention to words runs a risk of being flawed, incomplete, or at least, when the time comes to attempt to assert the claims, not particularly valuable or useful.

One way to attempt to mitigate this situation is to avoid being locked into a single particular mode of thought or single way of characterizing the invention. This usually will not happen automatically or without forethought, however. It is, therefore, recommended that you *affirmatively* take steps to avoid being locked into one particular way of thinking about or characterizing the invention.

This is another reason why it is good practice to disclose multiple embodiments and multiple ways of implementing specific features of the embodiments. Doing so will allow you to also claim the invention in multiple ways, reducing the risk that, when it comes time to prosecute the claims or assert the patent, you are stuck in a particular phraseology that ultimately proves to not advance your cause, but is too late to change.

Thus, it is specifically recommended that you not rely on only one particular set of phrases throughout the claims (and specification) to characterize

---

an amount to not alter the character of what is otherwise intended to be claimed as something that would have been novel subject matter. Hence, claim scope was unclear.

35. 384 F.2d 391, 397 (Ct. Cl. 1976).

what is inventive or unique about the subject matter being claimed. This may be accomplished several different ways.

One way is to include claims that are broad, intermediate, and narrow, and to use claim differentiation to potentially broaden the interpretation of the base claims. Another recommended technique is to include entirely different sets of claims that take entirely different approaches to the subject matter. It is important to recognize that the phrase or phrases you might otherwise exclusively rely upon may be construed against you, either from an infringement perspective, or from a validity perspective. Thus, it is recommended that you develop several "fallback" verbal formulations to "cover" these possibilities.

> Another recommended technique is to include entirely different sets of claims that take entirely different approaches to the subject matter. It is important to recognize that the phrase or phrases you might otherwise exclusively rely upon may be construed against you, either from an infringement perspective, or from a validity perspective. Thus, it is recommended that you develop several "fallback" verbal formulations to cover these possibilities.

In addition to the benefits discussed earlier, this approach also has the added benefit that it is likely to increase the breadth of the claims. Varying use of terminology with reference to different embodiments is likely to broaden the scope of the invention. In particular, the federal circuit has made it clear that use of claim terms in varying senses in the specification generally implies breadth.[36] Likewise, the federal circuit has implied narrow intent from use throughout the specification of the same term to mean the same thing.[37] Thus, using varying terminology, rather than simply employing varying senses, should also imply breadth.

It is noted, however, that using varying terminology is not the same as using synonyms for what may be essentially the same feature in a single family of dependencies. This last practice is to be avoided. It is likely that you will create ambiguity and/or other interpretation problems if you use different words to essentially refer to the same thing *unless* you clarify expressly that this is what you are doing. For example, you might state: "Without loss of generality

36. *See, e.g.*, Johnson Worldwide v. Zebco, 175 F.3d 985, 991 (Fed. Cir. 1999).
37. *See* Bell Atlantic v. Covad, 262 F.3d 1262, 1270 (Fed. Cir. 2001).

and not intending to limit the scope of claimed subject matter, the following terms are used interchangeably throughout this patent application."[38] Likewise, again, it is good practice to use *varying* terminology when you intend *different* scope.

When developing alternative formulations of the claims, it would also be wise to avoid being limited by the current state of the technology. Patents, of course, potentially have a 20-year plus term. Many changes in technology and variations in implementation may occur during such an extended period, especially with the current pace of technological change. Consider, for example, a vacuum tube versus a transistor. Claims to a vacuum tube circuit, if properly drafted, would apply to the same circuit implemented with a transistor. As is well-known, both may, for example, be employed to implement an amplifier or an electronic switch. Thus, claims referring to amplification or an amplifier or to an electronic switch would arguably not be limited to a vacuum tube, assuming a patent written before the invention of the transistor remained in force after the transistor was invented.

Given the potential that state of the art technology has to limit the scope of claims, it is, thus, worthwhile spending time considering potential current and future implementations of various aspects of the invention. It is also worthwhile to consider the maturity of the technology when drafting the claims. For example, is the technology in the research stage, the early development stage, the prototype stage, or the production stage etc.? This consideration has the potential to impact not only the claim breadth, but also alternative applications of the technology and its patentability. For example, for technology in the research stage, the claims should be extremely broad; whereas for technology in the production stage, narrower claims may be acceptable and still provide valuable protection.

To illustrate the concept of multiple verbal formulations, consider the claim from Example 1.9:

38. Even then, great care is warranted when trying to use words interchangeably. *See* Aqua-Aerobic Sys., Inc. v. Aerators Inc., 211 F.3d 1241 (Fed. Cir. 2000) (different phrases interpreted differently, even if the drafter intended them to have the same meaning); Epcon Gas Sys., Inc. v. Bauer Compressors, Inc., 279 F.3d 1022 (Fed. Cir. 2002) (construing "substantially below" and "substantially constant" differently because of what the court found to be "subtle differences" in the way the terms were used in the claim).

I claim:

1. A method of forming a virtual private network comprising:

   communicating one or more signal packets between respective physically separate broadcast domains via a gateway device included in the respective physically separate broadcast domains, wherein the communicating the one or more signal packets comprises:

      encapsulating the one or more signal packets in the respective physically separate broadcast domains to be communicated; and

      communicating the encapsulated signal packets between the respective gateway devices and at least one tunnel server so that the one or more signal packets are communicated between the respective physically separate broadcast domains.

Following is a different method claim based on the same technology.[39] Observe that while the same technology is at issue, really this new claim employs a different approach to capturing the concept of the technology than the previous claim. The previous claim is more about encapsulation and transmission via a tunnel server. This claims the technology at a higher level and is more about bypassing network address translation, although the tunnel server is also mentioned.

EXAMPLE 5.1

I claim:

1. A method comprising:

   overlaying at least one private network on networking infrastructure and/or computing infrastructure via network connectivity, wherein the at least one private network comprises two or more separate logical broadcast domains and a controller, the controller being outside the two or more separate logical broadcast domains;

39. *See* technology description in section 1.2113.

communicating selected signal packets from one network device in one of the two or more separate logical broadcast domains transmitted to one network device in another of the two or more separate logical broadcast domains via at least one tunnel server outside the two or more separate logical broadcast domains, the at least one tunnel server provisioned by the controller;

wherein the communicating selected signal packets further comprises communicating the selected signal packets from the one network device in the one of the two or more separate logical broadcast domains transmitted to the one network device in the another of the two or more separate logical broadcast domains as if the logical broadcast domains are not separate, which comprises communicating the selected signal packets in a manner to by-pass network address translation.

Thus, here, at least two distinct approaches to capturing essentially the same technology is demonstrated.

5.31 Identify Features of the Invention Independent of the Particular Embodiments

When drafting claims from the information in an invention disclosure, it can be important to identify features of the invention that are innovative independent of many of the specific implementation details for a particular embodiment. This may sound easier said than done, but it is a facility that one acquires from drafting claims for different inventions from scratch. A crucial aspect involves interviewing the inventor and having him explain the state of the art, the innovative aspects of the invention, and why he sees those aspects as innovative.

Often, inventors will believe to be innovative it is sufficient that the invention has never been done before. Inventors think that if it would have been obvious, the invention would have been implemented by someone. Unfortunately, this reasoning will not convince the PTO. That it has not been previously implemented and/or was not previously known really goes to novelty rather than non-obviousness. However, it may be a starting point. What are the technical reasons the invention was not previously implemented? This may help explain the innovation in a manner that might be divorced from a particular embodiment.

One of the more important skills to develop is the ability to interview the inventor and with a series of questions get him to articulate the innovation, although before coming to see you, he may have had no idea of what that might be. One helpful technique is to take a somewhat practical approach to the invention using the problem-solution approach mentioned in Chapter 1.

One might begin by asking about a problem the invention is intended to address. Is it an existing and known problem or is it a new, unrecognized problem? It might be both depending how one looks at it, but that is useful information as well.

A known problem might be a device that uses too much power or uses too much memory. These are typically known technical problems, depending on context. The invention might relate to reducing electrical interference. You get the idea. If it is a known problem, the next question is why not use off the shelf approaches to this problem? There may be deficiencies in the existing, off the shelf approaches. Now the innovation is taking shape. The invention solves an existing, known problem, but it does so in a manner that has an advantage over state of the art approaches. Now we are getting somewhere.

If it does not solve a known, existing problem, then it may, instead, solve an otherwise unrecognized problem. That is, a problem that is not yet known in the prior art because it has not yet been recognized. On this point, there is well-established law that the mere recognition of a previously unaddressed problem may be sufficient to impart patentability to an invention, even if once the problem is recognized, the solution employed might have been obvious.[40] Of course, it might also be that the problem is unrecognized *and* the solution would not have been obvious. However, the point is that this line of questioning should uncover the innovation if the other line of questioning does not.

It is not the case, of course, that how the invention is implemented is unimportant. Rather, the claims should cover the implementation. However, it should more typically be handled with dependent claims so that the independent claim is *not* limited to the particular embodiment.

5.311 Illustrative Claim Example—Chair

To, perhaps, gain a better appreciation of trying to identify an innovation not necessarily limited to a particular embodiment, let's return to a previous example from Chapter 2.[41] Consider Example 2.2, now Example 5.2. Also, recall our drafting principle, a good claim is an appropriate balance between breadth, vagueness, and precision.

40. *See, e.g.*, Eibel Process Co. v. Minn. & Ontario Paper Co., 261 U.S. 45 (1923).
41. *See* section 2.141, discussing this example.

EXAMPLE 5.2

I claim:

1. An apparatus comprising:

 a substantially horizontally oriented, rectangularly shaped seat including four corners;

 wherein attached to a respective corner of the seat is a substantially vertically oriented leg such that the legs point in the same direction away from the seat, are oriented to be substantially mutually parallel, and are of substantially the same length.

This sample claim has precision and some breadth. More to the point, however, what is the innovation sought to be captured? It is not clear from the claim language. By focusing on the innovation, the aspects involving breadth and vagueness, which are better able to be balanced, along with balancing precision, may also perhaps be better developed.

It is important, however, in performing such an evaluation, to consider the closest *known* prior art. This is a hypothetical situation. In this hypothetical world, chairs have not been invented yet. So, what did people use to sit in groups or to sit on after becoming tired from a lot of walking, etc.? Perhaps, they used very large rock formations, the ground, or trees that had fallen due to windstorms and the like. Of course, these "prior art" approaches are not convenient. To sit in groups, for example, you would need a bunch of fallen trees or boulders close together.

So, with this background, what might one conclude is innovative about a chair? It appears to be that it is portable. That is, it provides a place to sit that is easily and conveniently portable. What would that look like in a patent claim body? Perhaps, something like this.

EXAMPLE 5.3

I claim:

An apparatus comprising: a portable seat.

Of course, this is a stylized example and, hence, here results in a possibly overly broad claim, but it *does* begin the process of formulating the claim, primarily, the claim body. A portable seat seems like it might have been novel and unobvious in light of prior art such as the ground or fallen trees. Also, it is useful.

Appreciate, however, if allowable, what this potentially captures compared with the previous claim. Many potential follow-on improvements—wheel chairs, swivel chairs, ergonomic chairs, even exercise balls, and so on. Many things that the previous claim would not have captured. Patents have a 20-year term. With the pace of technical change, it might be surprising how quickly products built on a fundamental concept, such as this example, might develop.

Someone, a lawyer most likely, may argue that a small boulder could be a portable seat. That may be a good point, again, Example 5.3 was a starting point. Perhaps, to distinguish from the known prior art, the claim should be:

EXAMPLE 5.4

I claim:

1. An apparatus comprising: a portable seat;

   wherein the portable seat includes a back oriented to be roughly perpendicular to the portable seat.

So, the claim body now includes elements (seat and back) and limitations ("portable," "oriented to be roughly perpendicular") which provide relationships between the elements.[42]

5.312 Employ a Hierarchy of Claim Terms

This was discussed in Chapter 3,[43] and, again, is provided here as a refresh/review.

For purposes of drafting the claims and the specification, it is desirable to create and employ a hierarchy of terms that relate to the subject matter of the

42. Alternatively, perhaps, Example 5.3 is claim 1 and Example 5.4 is a claim 2 that is dependent providing additional features.

43. *See* section 3.2141, discussing a hierarchy of claim terms.

invention. The point of doing so is to make clear the scope intended for certain terms and then support that with specification description. This is at least one reason that it usually makes sense to draft a set of claims before drafting the specification. That set of claims may be updated, modified, and grow as you draft the specification, but it crystallizes your thinking initially and creates a list of terms.

As should now be clear, how terms are used in the specification and claims is legally significant. Thus, creating an initial set of claims that may be viewed as hierarchical would be prudent. The hierarchy relates to narrower or more specific embodiments, that is, differing scope. In this manner, terms are able to be used consistently so as not to create ambiguity while still being clear regarding intended scope.

5.313 Illustrative Example

Figure 3.1 and the associated claim example related to the transistor body biasing technology example previously introduced. Therefore, this example will use the visual voicemail technology example from Examples 4.23 and 4.25 of Chapter 4. A possible hierarchy might be what is shown in Figure 5.1.

5.32 Use Dependent Claims for Claim Differentiation and to Cover Commercial Embodiments

Claim differentiation is a doctrine where different patent claims are presumed to be of different scope. Unfortunately, it is not always clear when the federal circuit will choose to apply it. In *Comark*, for example, previously discussed, the court stated:

> [A]s the district court correctly pointed out, Harris's proposed construction of claim 1 would violate the doctrine of claim differentiation by rendering claim 2 superfluous. While we recognize that the doctrine of claim differentiation is not a hard and fast rule of construction, it does create a presumption that each claim in a patent has a different scope. "There is presumed to be a difference in meaning and scope when different words or phrases are used in separate claims. To the extent that the absence of such difference in meaning and scope would make a claim superfluous, the doctrine of claim differentiation states the presumption that the difference between claims is significant." [citations omitted][44]

44. 156 F.3d at 1187.

Figure 5.1 Yet Another Example of Hierarchy of Claim Terms

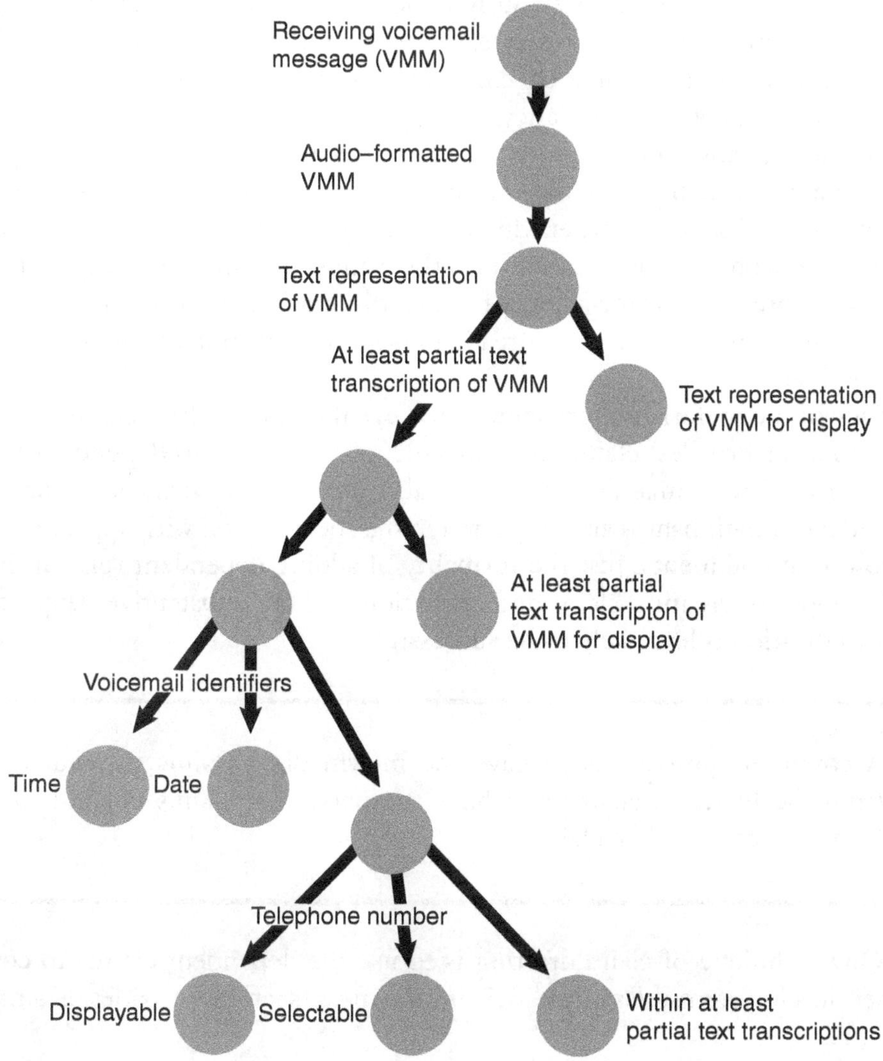

In contrast, in *Toro v. White Consolidated*,[45] also previously discussed, the federal circuit rejected the argument that claim differentiation should apply, stating that it was only a presumption and could not overcome the specification and prosecution history. There are, of course, many other examples where the court has endorsed it and many other examples where the court has refused to follow it.

45. 199 F.3d at 1302.

Despite this inconsistent treatment, it is still worthwhile to consider when drafting the claims. As was previously indicated, in some cases, at least, it will be followed and, therefore, it may assist in obtaining the claim construction sought. For example, it may be employed to make the intent of the claim drafter clearer, as with dependency.

By structuring the dependency relationships carefully, ambiguity is reduced about which claims the drafter considers to be the broadest and the narrowest. As discussed earlier, this tends to reduce the risk that limitations will be read from the specification into the claims. As a simple example, it will be much more difficult for a court to read a limitation from the specification into a claim if that limitation is already present in a claim depending from the claim at issue.[46]

One of the preferred approaches is to have the intermediate claims dependent from the broadest claims and have the narrowest claims dependent from the intermediate claims. Of course, it is also important to make sure that the dependency relationships are supported in the specification with appropriately narrower embodiments. Just the formality of adding dependent relationships in the hopes of creating claim differentiation without substantive support in the specification is less likely to be successful.

> A common approach is to have the intermediate claims dependent from the broadest claims and have the narrowest claims dependent from the intermediate claims.

One technique of claim drafting is to use the dependent claims to cover higher level systems. Example 5.5 in the next section provides a simple example.

5.321 Illustrative Claim Example

Chapter 2 discusses flip chip technology that at the appropriate time would have been a new and non-obvious technology.[47] Following is an example using dependencies around a base claim.

46. *See, e.g.*, Interdigital Commons v. ITC, 690 F.3d 1315, 1324 (Fed. Cir. 2012) (The doctrine of claim differentiation disfavors reading a limitation from a dependent claim into an independent claim.).

47. *See* section 2.1123, discussing this technology example.

EXAMPLE 5.5

I claim:

1. An apparatus comprising: a flip chip.
2. The apparatus of claim 1, wherein the flip chip is incorporated in an integrated circuit chip (IC).
3. The apparatus of claim 2, wherein the IC is part of an electronic circuit.
4. The apparatus of claim 3, wherein the electronic circuit is attached to a circuit board.
5. The apparatus of claim 4, wherein the circuit board is incorporated in a mobile device.
6. The apparatus of claim 5, wherein the mobile device is wirelessly communicatively couplable to other mobile devices via a satellite system.

In this example, each claim adds a new, higher level of system integration beyond the previous claim. Of course, this is an extreme case for the purpose of illustration. Depending on the situation, it may not be possible to continually increase levels of integration with each dependency. Furthermore, as explained later,[48] this technique of each claim being dependent from the immediately preceding claim should not be used exclusively or it may introduce other risks.[49]

Nonetheless, using dependencies to cover higher levels of system integration provides several advantages, including directing the claims at a variety of infringers. In the prior example, potential infringers that are potentially covered include: the chip manufacturer, the circuit board assembler, the mobile device manufacturer, and the wireless service provider. In theory, of course, the base claim to the flip chip could be asserted against these parties. However, directing the claims in this manner may address issues not handled by the flip chip claim and, therefore, be more useful for enforcement.

48. *See* section 5.7.

49. Later, we refer to this technique of each claim being dependent from the immediately preceding claim, as "the house that jack built" because the approach is to keep building on something previously built, as in building a house from the foundation up. *See id.*

> Using dependencies to cover higher levels of system integration provides several advantages, including directing the claims at a variety of infringers.

For example, it is common for a components manufacturer to offer patent indemnity. However, by drafting the claims in this manner, the indemnity may not be particularly useful for some of the dependent claims, since the indemnity will only cover the component sold and nothing more, typically.

Likewise, as shall be discussed later in connection with advanced claiming considerations, it may be possible to draft claims, in conjunction with this technique, to avoid certain defenses that might otherwise be available, such as exhaustion or an implied patent license.[50] For example, suppose the IC manufacturer is a licensed supplier. It still might be possible in the right circumstances and with some clever claim drafting to assert claims against others in the manufacturing chain, such as the circuit board assembler or the cell phone manufacturer.

Finally, this approach potentially increases the royalty base in a patent licensing context. For example, if the flip chip claim were the only assertable claim and it was asserted against a mobile device manufacturer, the manufacturer might argue that, because the flip chip itself is only worth a fraction of a cent out of a $1,000 mobile device, the royalty it should pay should not be very large. However, including a claim directed to the mobile device may potentially undermine that position, granted that it is a dependent rather than an independent claim.[51]

5.4 Draft the Claims Before the Specification

It is considered good practice, in general, to draft the claims before the specification. It permits you to make sure, when drafting the specification, that you have described the invention completely, both narrowly and broadly. In general, it is probably more difficult to broaden the specification once you have written it, than it is to narrow it, which may explain at least partly the focus on getting a good initial independent claim that is as broad as is reasonably

50. See discussion of implied licensing and exhaustion in Chapter 6.
51. See discussion of damages considerations later in this chapter.

possible.[52] Thus, by formulating the claims before the specification, you "should" be able to ensure that you have support for your broadest claims.

The word "should" has quotes around it because the drafting process is more dynamic than simply first draft the claims, and then draft the specification. More typically, a working set of claims is drafted, then the specification is started. As the specification is flushed out, a better understanding of the technology usually results, leading to changes to improve the claims along the way. Furthermore, once the specification is mostly written, there may be an attempt to draft additional claims to have a complete claim set of around 20 total claims and three independent claims.

However, by seeking to draft in the initially recommended order, you can endeavor to make sure that the exact same terminology that is employed in the claims is also employed in the specification. This is a good drafting practice because even slight changes in terminology may create interpretive problems or potentially even written description problems. If you were to write the specification first, you may be more likely to change and perhaps inconsistently employ the relevant terminology as you draft the claims, and it then would be more problematic to attempt to ensure that the specification and claims are consistent.

Another advantage of writing the claims before the specification is that it permits you to make sure that all key terms in the claims are clearly and carefully defined to provide the appropriate coverage. As has been previously discussed,[53] claim terms are given their ordinary and customary meaning, unless it's clear in the specification that they are intended to have a different meaning. One unfortunate result of this law is that unless you define your key terms in the specification, you may never be sure of the claim coverage until litigation ensues. You may want to rely on the ordinary and customary meaning, but it may not be entirely clear what that is. Therefore, it is recommended that once you have drafted the claims, you review them and pick out the key terms and make sure those terms are clearly and crisply defined to resolve potential ambiguities that might otherwise crop up later, such as in litigation.

As illustrations, consider these definitional questions: is a set-top box a "computer"? Is a cell phone a "computer"? Is a microcontroller a "processor"? By defining the key terms of your claims in the specification, you are able to anticipate and answer questions, such as these, that otherwise might be unclear.

---

52. However, as discussed in detail in Chapter 1, that is not necessarily always the chosen approach.

53. See discussion of claim interpretation in Chapter 3.

> It is recommended that once you have drafted the claims, you review them and pick out the key terms and make sure those terms are clearly and crisply defined to resolve potential ambiguities that might otherwise have cropped up later, such as in litigation.

Furthermore, there are potential legal issues that are easier to address in this early drafting stage rather than later.

5.41 Potential Written Description Issues

Of course, many written description-type issues are possible. However, the focus here is primarily issues that relate to the process of drafting the claims of the patent application. Regarding claim drafting, one of the more common issues is to *modify* the claims in a way not ultimately reflected in the specification. This may occur because as one refines a set of claims, perhaps after the specification is mostly complete, it may be an oversight to not reflect some claim refinements in the specification itself.

Fortunately, if this happens and the examiner, for example, raises a written description issue, most of the time it is correctible. Nonetheless, it would be much better if this did not happen because there might be other legal issues from this oversight beyond written description support.

In general, the claim, if in the originally filed patent application, is usually considered to support itself, since the originally filed claims are part of the written description.[54] In this case, the specification could be amended to include the claim language without raising a new matter issue. However, a risk, apart from the written description issue, is that the claim language may be unclear without more supporting description. Thus, for example, it may raise an indefiniteness issue.[55] Furthermore, there have been cases in which *an original claim* has been invalidated under the written description requirement. An example of this is the federal circuit case, discussed later in more detail, *Lizardtech, Inc. v. Earth Res. Mapping, Inc.*[56]

54. *See, e.g.*, Mentor Graphics Corp. v. Eve-Usa, Inc., 870 F.3d 1298 (Fed. Cir. 2017). *Cf.* Kennecott Corp. v. Kyocera Int'l, Inc., 835 F. 2d 1419 (Fed. Cir. 1987) (claim supported because although words are missing from the specification, the specification provided inherent support).

55. *See* discussion of indefiniteness later in this chapter.

56. 424 F.3d 1336 (Fed. Cir. 2005).

Much more deadly is to amend a claim in prosecution in a manner without written description support. Unfortunately, the contours of written description support are not precise. Typically, if this occurs, it may be that the attorney did not realize the claim was not supported, perhaps relying on his imperfect memory of the specification.[57]

Several well-known federal circuit cases, including *Gentry Gallery v. Berkline*,[58] *Tronzo v. Biomet*,[59] and *Toro v. Ariens*,[60] have found patent claims to be invalid under 35 USC section 112 for failing to satisfy the written description requirement. In these cases, the court determined that the specification failed to provide support for recited limitations in the claims. In these cases, the claims were amended in prosecution in ways that were not supported by the written description. This is a risk often associated with disclosing a single or only a few embodiments. By, instead, describing and claiming multiple embodiments from broadest to narrowest, as has been mentioned, the risk of lack of written description is reduced because explicit textual support is provided at the time of filing, at a minimum, by the claims themselves.

The apparent problem is that if not supported, the claim is invalid. However, a *more pernicious* problem also exists due to the AIA. A real risk exists that, if this is a continuation claiming priority from a pre-AIA patent application, that now post-AIA, rather than pre-AIA, law applies to the continuation. This issue was discussed in Chapter 1.[61] It relates to AIA transition provisions for situations where a post-AIA filed patent application claims priority to a pre-AIA original patent application filing.

The upshot of the AIA transition provisions may be summarized as follows: if a patent claim is added *at any time* that does not have written description support in the original pre-AIA patent application filing, all the claims of a patent application filed on or after March 16, 2013, are subject to *post*-AIA section 102 and *post*-AIA section 103. Furthermore, once such a patent claim is added, this consequence cannot be undone. Once these statutory sections apply to all the claims of a patent application, for example, as a result of adding new subject matter without written description support in the original pre-March 16, 2013, filing, such as by adding a patent claim, even if later the new subject matter is removed, such as cancelling the claim (because, for example, it constitutes new subject matter), those statutory sections will continue to

57. Suggesting that a reread of the specification is always a good idea if amending claims.
58. 134 F.3d 1473 (Fed. Cir. 1998).
59. 156 F.3d 1154 (Fed. Cir. 1998).
60. 232 F.3d 915 (Fed. Cir. 2000) (nonprecedential).
61. *See* section 1.3321, discussing claiming priority and the AIA.

apply to all of the claims of the patent application filed on or after March 16, 2013. Furthermore, recent PTAB cases support this interpretation.[62]

Now let us think for a moment about the potential consequences of the post-AIA provisions applying to a continuation application for the preceding scenario. For one thing, more prior art may now be citable against the patent claims. For example, if the date of invention under subsection 102(g)(2) (pre-AIA) is much earlier than cited prior art, one will be legally foreclosed from arguing that the invention predates the prior art because it was conceived and reduced to practice before the date of the prior art. However, potentially even more troubling, suppose the inventor had engaged in pre-filing commercialization activities with respect to his invention, but it took place within a year of the actual filing date, such as "on sale" or "public use" activities. Recall that the interpretation of post-AIA section 102 around these events is not settled, but *Helsinn* potentially implies that these events may bar an invention. Under these circumstances and this interpretation of post-AIA section 102, then, further prosecution, in theory, via the continuation patent application, potentially may be barred.

This is "in theory" because this all may happen inadvertently. For example, claims may be added that a judge in *later litigation* concludes do not have written description support in the original filing. At that time, then, the consequences of this on the validity of a patent that issued from the continuation patent application would need to be evaluated. This provides an additional reason to make sure that drafted patent claims have written description support in a patent application or claim amendment to be filed.

> This [the AIA transition provisions] provides an additional reason to make sure that drafted patent claims have written description support in a patent application or claim amendment to be filed.

62. *See* Microsurgical Tech., Inc. v. Regents of the Univ. of Colo., PGR2021-00026, Paper 12 (PTAB, 2021); Rockwool Int'l A/S v. Knauf Insulation, Inc., PGR2022-00022, Paper 10 (PTAB, July 6, 2022).

Of course, if you add new subject matter to a claim you might also get a rejection under section 132[63] for having new matter; however, primarily the issue is really one of lack of written description support.

Another possible issue may arise related to the specification description under 112(f)—although the issue is characterized as indefiniteness, it is really a matter of not providing enough description.[64] For example, it may be that a functional claim without the word "means" (or, perhaps, with the word "means") may be held to include a limitation that is to be construed under section 112(f). It, therefore, is a good idea to be mindful of the consequences should, despite your best drafting efforts, your claim be construed under section 112(f) during examination or in litigation.

In the event section 112(f) is invoked, the specification *must* provide sufficient *corresponding* structure for the recited function. That is, for the function or functions recited in the claim, the specification *must* describe *corresponding* structure able to perform the recited function or functions or the claim will be held invalid if tested. Here, *corresponding* suggests that the specification is written to clearly associate the function of the claim and the structure in the description in a manner such that one of ordinary skill would comprehend the association.

If an element is construed under section 112(f) and the statutory requirements regarding corresponding structure are satisfied, then the claim covers, by express statutory direction:

> . . . the **corresponding** structure, material, or acts described in the specification **and equivalents** . . . (emphasis supplied).

Thus, the claim, by statute, construed *literally* under section 112(f) may be infringed by embodiments in your specification that *correspond* to the functional language or by a *112(f) equivalent* of what is shown in the specification; however, the scope of such *112(f) equivalents* is generally exceedingly narrow.[65]

In the area of software, in particular, the software algorithm is considered the structure at issue under section 112(f).[66] For this reason, not infrequently, claims interpreted under section 112(f) that relate to software are held invalid

---

63. 35 U.S.C. § 132 (2022) states, in pertinent part: "No amendment shall introduce new matter into the disclosure of the invention."

64. See discussion later in this chapter regarding indefiniteness.

65. *See, e.g.*, Valmont v. Reinke, 983 F.2d 1039 (Fed. Cir. 1993).

66. *See, e.g.*, Eon Corp. IP Holdings, LLC v. AT&T Mobility, LLC, 785 F.3d 616, 621 (Fed. Cir. 2015).

as not appropriately describing structure or enough structure. They are invalidated as being indefinite, under section 112, second paragraph. However, in reality, insufficient description has been provided. That is, generally it is *not* sufficient to merely provide a functional description.[67] Enough detail must be described to, in effect, show possession, which means sufficient detail of *how to perform the function* so that one of ordinary skill *would know the scope being claimed* with respect to implementing the function or operation claimed.[68]

If a function is claimed under section 112(f) that is not described to this level, the claim will be held invalid if tested. Therefore, in drafting claims, care is warranted to not inadvertently claim a function that is believed to be well understood, such as "transmit a signal" or "receive a signal," but for which the specification does not provide an implementation description because it is not appreciated that the claims will be interpreted under section 112(f).

Therefore, in drafting, care is warranted to not inadvertently claim a function that is believed to be well understood, such as "transmit a signal" or "receive a signal," but for which the specification does not provide an implementation description because it is not appreciated that the claims will be interpreted under section 112(f).

5.411 Use Express Definitions of Claim Terms

Many good reasons exist to define claims terms expressly in the specification.[69] Previously, we discussed this recommendation from the perspective of claim interpretation, which is quite important. In addition, however, doing so provides clear written description support as well.

Federal circuit jurisprudence has held that claim terms may be defined in the specification expressly or by implication. We recommend that all *important* claim terms be expressly defined in the specification.[70] Of course, once this has been done, the claims must be properly drafted to implement the definition provided, an important and still challenging claim drafting exercise.

---

67. *See* Blackboard, Inc. v. Desire2Learn, Inc., 574 F.3d 1371, 1383–85, 91 USPQ2d 1481, 1491–93 (Fed. Cir. 2009); Noah Systems v. Intuit, 675 F.3d 1302 (Fed. Cir. 2012).

68. *See* Blackboard, Inc. v. Desire2Learn, Inc., 574 F.3d 1371, 1383–85, 91 USPQ2d 1481, 1491–93 (Fed. Cir. 2009); Noah Systems v. Intuit, 675 F.3d 1302 (Fed. Cir. 2012).

69. *See* discussion in Chapter 3 of expressly defining claim terms.

70. *See* example in section 3.123.

One problem with defining claim terms by implication, rather than with express language, is that whether this has occurred (e.g., the claim terms are defined) may be arguable, and the ultimate decision is usually left to someone else other than the patentee, such as a judge in a suit, a competitor in a negotiation, and so on. Furthermore, what is required to define a claim term by implication is not entirely clear.

Cases in which claim terms were found to be defined in the specification by implication[71] include *Covad Communications*[72] and *Scimed.*[73] On the other hand, *Sony v. Thorner*[74] suggests that the federal circuit may, instead, be reluctant to conclude a claim term has been defined by implication. As suggested previously,[75] the line may be a fine one between reading limitations from the specification into the claims, highlighted in *Phillips* as something to avoid, and providing a special meaning to a claim term. It also appears that different panels of judges may reach different conclusions, further confounding the issue.

Thus, it is recommended that important claim terms be expressly defined; however, in a manner consistent with ordinary and customary meaning. In this way, two risks are addressed. One risk relates to whether the patentee has imparted a special meaning to the claim term. The other risk relates to whether the ordinary meaning includes the intended meaning. Again, by following this approach, either position may be argued. It may turn out, depending on the circumstances, one position is preferred. However, by an approach that supports either position, the opportunity is preserved to take a preferred position later.

It is recommended that important claim terms be expressly defined; however, in a manner consistent with ordinary and customary meaning. In this way, two risks are addressed. One risk relates to whether the patentee has imparted a special meaning to the claim term. The other risk relates to whether the ordinary meaning includes the intended meaning.

71. *See* sections 3.123 and 3.212, and their subsections, discussing defining claim terms expressly and by implication.

72. 262 F.3d 1258 (Fed. Cir. 2001).

73. 242 F.3d 1337 (Fed. Cir. 2001). *See also* Microsoft Corp. v. Multi-Tech Systems, Inc., 357 F.3d 1340, 1347 (Fed. Cir. 2004), *cert. denied*, 543 U.S. 821 (2004) (citing and applying SciMed.); Alloc, Inc. v. U.S. Int'l Trade Comm'n, 342 F.3d 1361, 1370, 68 USPQ2d 1161 (Fed. Cir. 2003), *cert. denied*, 541 U.S. 1063 (2004) (citing and applying SciMed.).

74. 669 F.3d 1362 (Fed. Cir. 2012); *see* discussion in section 2.1414.

75. *See* discussion in section 2.1414.

5.412 *Lizardtech* Decision

The *Lizardtech*[76] decision is a groundbreaking one for the written description requirement, although it was not entirely unexpected that such a decision might eventually be handed down, given federal circuit emphasis in earlier cases that the written description may limit claim scope and similar statements. Essentially, the case held that a claim that was originally filed with the patent application failed to have written description support because the scope of the claim exceeded what was described in the specification (and file history). The claim at issue was a valiant attempt by the claim drafter to capture more scope, but it ultimately did not succeed.

In hindsight, at best, what the drafter might have done was to have the inventors come up with additional embodiments and then draft different claims to these embodiments that might have potentially "snagged" the infringer in this case. Though feasible, such is usually considered above and beyond the duty of the drafter, unless the client has indicated that the application should receive "special" treatment and additional budget is provided to support such activities.

The technology in the case is a bit complex, involving the discrete wavelet transform or DWT. The bottom line is that the DWT is useful in compression of images because if done properly, it results in lossless compression. However, for images that are sufficiently large, for processing purposes, it is easier to break an image into tiles and process the tiles in parallel, for example. However, this approach produces undesirable edge effects or artifacts from combining the separate tiles to reconstruct the original image. The technology at issue in the case solves this issue. It provided a technique that produced a seamless full image without artifacts from processing the tiles appropriately and combining the results.

There were three independent claims. Two were directed to the technique described in the specification. As to those claims, the district court issued a noninfringement ruling predicated on its interpretation of the "maintaining updated sums" limitation in the two claims, which addresses how a "seamless DWT of the image" is formed. The district court construed that limitation to mean "summing the DWT coefficients of one tile together with overlapping DWT coefficients from one or more adjacent tiles." It was clear that the accused product did not sum DWT coefficients of one tile with "overlapping DWT coefficients from one or more adjacent tiles" to form a seamless DWT of an image.

76. 424 F.3d 1336 (Fed. Cir. 2005).

The third claim, claim 21, did not have the specific limitations that resulted in noninfringement. The appellate court, on its review, stated:

> The fact that claim 21 is directed to creating a seamless DWT does not mean that the claim is valid, however. The problem is that the specification provides only one method for creating a seamless DWT, which is to "maintain updated sums" of DWT coefficients. That is the procedure recited by claim 1. Yet claim 21 is broader than claim 1 because it lacks the "maintain updated sums" limitation. Thus, a person of ordinary skill in the art would understand that claim 21 is directed to a seamless DWT. But because there are no limitations in claim 21 as to how the seamless DWT is accomplished, claim 21 refers to taking a seamless DWT generically. It is also clear that claim 21 cannot be directed to creating a seamless DWT only in the way that claim 1 recites, i.e., by maintaining updated sums of DWT coefficients. To do so would impermissibly read a limitation into claim 21 and would make it essentially redundant of claim 1.
>
> The trouble with allowing claim 21 to cover all ways of performing DWT-based compression processes that lead to a seamless DWT is that there is no support for such a broad claim in the specification. The specification provides only a single way of creating a seamless DWT, which is by maintaining updated sums of DWT coefficients. There is no evidence that the specification contemplates a more generic way of creating a seamless array of DWT coefficients.
>
> . . .
>
> The "written description" clause of section 112 has been construed to mandate that the specification satisfy two closely related requirements. First, it must describe the manner and process of making and using the invention so as to enable a person of skill in the art to make and use the full scope of the invention without undue experimentation. *See Tyler v. City of Boston*, 7 Wall. 327, 74 U.S. 327, 330, 19 L.Ed. 93 (1868); *AK Steel Corp. v. Sollac Ugine*, 344 F.3d 1234, 1244 (Fed. Cir. 2003). Second, it must describe the invention sufficiently to convey to a person of skill in the art that the patentee had possession of the claimed invention at the time of the application, i.e., that the patentee invented what is claimed. *See O'Reilly v. Morse*, 56 U.S. (15 How.) 62, 112-13, 14 L.Ed. 601 (1853) (denying a claim for use of "electro-magnetism, however developed for marking or printing intelligible characters . . . at any distances" because others "may discover a mode of writing or printing at a distance . . . without using any part of the process or combination set forth in the plaintiff's specification"); *Moba, B.V. v. Diamond Automation, Inc.*, 325 F.3d 1306, 1320-21 (Fed. Cir. 2003).
>
> Those two requirements usually rise and fall together. That is, a recitation of how to make and use the invention across the full breadth of the claim is ordinarily sufficient to demonstrate that the inventor possesses the full scope

> of the invention, and vice versa. This case is no exception. Whether the flaw in the specification is regarded as a failure to demonstrate that the patentee possessed the full scope of the invention recited in claim 21 or a failure to enable the full breadth of that claim, the specification provides inadequate support for the claim under section 112, paragraph one.
>
> . . . Placed in that context, it is unnecessary to spell out every detail of the invention in the specification; only enough must be included to convince a person of skill in the art that the inventor possessed the invention and to enable such a person to make and use the invention without undue experimentation. In this case, however, LizardTech has failed to meet either requirement. After reading the patent, a person of skill in the art would not understand how to make a seamless DWT generically and would not understand LizardTech to have invented a method for making a seamless DWT, except by "maintaining updating sums of DWT coefficients."

Thus, the court held claim 21 invalid as not being supported by the written description. As suggested earlier, the lesson might be to encourage the inventors to come up with additional embodiments to be claimed differently.

The lesson might be to encourage the inventors to come up with additional embodiments to be claimed differently.

5.413 Negative Limitations

One situation that has potential to create a written description issue is a negative limitation. There was a time that negative limitations were not permitted, at least by the PTO, because rather than saying what is covered, they recite what is not covered.[77] Although they are not verboten any longer, they may present tricky issues compared with other types of limitations. Negative limitations may be overly broad, so clarification in the specification is a good idea. That is, perhaps a narrower embodiment that could be covered with a positive recitation could be described and included as a dependent claim. Negative limitations might also create written description issues, primarily if not expressly described.

However, the law seems to be, as with other limitations, express language may not *necessarily* be required to satisfy written description. It is sufficient

77. See MPEP § 2173.05(i) (2022).

that one of ordinary skill upon reading the specification would conclude that the claim language reflects what has been invented.[78] However, best to avoid such a situation by being express regarding the negative limitation since then whether the negative limitation is supported should not be arguable with the decision left to another. It is also worth noting that whether prior art shows a negative limitation appears to be just as, if not more, lenient.[79]

5.42 Avoid Potential Enablement Issues

Like written description, other issues, like enablement, though mostly about the specification, still have the potential to render claims invalid or to result in rejection during examination. It is well beyond the scope of this work to address these issues in any comprehensive manner since the focus here is about drafting patent claims. Rather, the point is to alert a claim drafter to a few of the pitfalls.

In the predictable arts, if there is full written description support for all the claims and if the claims cover the full range of embodiments, it is pretty likely that enablement has been met. One way, perhaps to tell, is to make sure you, the drafter, could implement the invention from the specification description. Typically, but not necessarily, patent attorneys are probably below ordinary skill or just barely make it, particularly with respect to the most relevant technology for the invention. Patent attorneys simply cannot be experts in everything. Also, because this is the predictable arts, some "play" should be present at the margins. That is, there are many things that may not need to be described since some technical matters are within the knowledge of one of ordinary skill.

What may be most important is enabling the feature that makes the invention innovative. Most description for an invention in the predictable arts is known and the description is provided for written description support and for

---

78. *See* Almirall, LLC v. Amneal Pharms. LLC, 28 F.4th 265 (Fed. Cir. 2022); Novartis Pharm. Corp. v. Accord Healthcare, Inc., 38 F.4th 1013 (Fed. Cir. 2022); Inphi Corp. v. Netlist, Inc., 805 F.3d 1350, 1356 (Fed. Cir. 2015) (there is no "new and heightened standard for negative claim limitations"); Santarus v. Par Pharm., 694 F.3d 1344, 1350–51 (Fed. Cir. 2012); Nike, Inc. v. Adidas AG, 812 F.3d 1326, 1348 (Fed. Cir. 2016); All Dental Prodx, LLC v. Advantage Dental Prod., Inc., 309 F.3d 774, 779 (Fed. Cir. 2002) ("[T]he failure of the specification to specifically mention a limitation that later appears in the claims is not a fatal one when one skilled in the art would recognize upon reading the specification that the new language reflects what the specification shows has been invented.").

79. *See* Daniel Hanson, *Proving a Negative Claim Limitation: A Tale of Three Nonprecedential Cases*, IPWatchdog (Sept. 12, 2019, 1:15 PM), https://www.ipwatchdog.com/2019/09/12/proving-a-negative-claim-limitation-a-tale-of-three-nonprecedential-cases/id=113260/.

claim interpretation, rather than enablement. However, the feature that makes the invention innovative is critical to describe. Thus, in the predictable arts, enablement is usually not an issue unless the invention is not enabled regarding the best mode and/or regarding what is believed to be the true innovation.

Such confidence may not be appropriate as to the unpredictable arts. In that case, the inventors may provide the best insights into whether enablement has been met. Furthermore, the level of detail needed to be enabling is expected to vary with technical area for the unpredictable arts. It is common to provide actual working examples or even prophetic examples, suitably identified as such. Satisfying enablement and written description may be challenging issues in some areas of the unpredictable arts. Thus, care is warranted.

5.43 Avoid Potential Indefiniteness Issues

In more recent years, indefiniteness has become a much more important issue than many years ago, although in general, the federal circuit tends to find claims definite. A watershed event was the *Nautilus* case in which the Supreme Court altered the legal standard for indefiniteness.[80] The standard had been whether the claim language was "insolubly ambiguous" considering the claims, the specification, and the file history. The Supreme Court modified the standard, recognizing the inherent limits of language, to whether the language, again, considering the claims, the specification and the file history, "fails to inform, with reasonable certainty, those skilled in the art about the scope of the invention."[81]

We have mentioned several ways indefiniteness might become as issue. A common situation might be to amend a claim in prosecution and use words not in the specification, claims, or file history. Although it is not a guarantee that such language will be found indefinite, such a situation is not a desirable one.

---

80. *See* Nautilus, Inc. v. Biosig Instruments, Inc., 134 S. Ct. 2120 (2014).

81. As stated, the federal circuit tends to hold claims definite. *See, e.g.*, Niazi Licensing Corp. v. St. Jude Med. S.C., Inc., 30 F.4th 1339 (Fed. Cir. 2022) (reversing district court finding claims indefinite); U. of Massachusetts v. L'Oreal S.A., 36 F.4th 1374 (Fed. Cir. 2022) (vacating district court finding claims indefinite); ImmunoGen, Inc. v. Hirshfeld, 2021-1939, 2022 WL 885774, at *2 (Fed. Cir. Mar. 25, 2022) (vacating district court holding "AIBW" indefinite); ClearOne, Inc. v. Shure Acq. Holdings, Inc., 35 F.4th 1345 (Fed. Cir. 2022) (affirming PTAB determination that newly added claim language was not indefinite); Dyfan, LLC v. Target Corp., 28 F.4th 1360, 1364 (Fed. Cir. 2022) (claimed "code" was not in means plus function format and not indefinite for lack of structural equivalents in the specification).

Other typical situations include use of language to suggest a subjective standard rather than an objective one or simply nonsensical language.[82] In this regard, words of degree may create indefiniteness issues without clarification as to how the language is to be applied.[83] Another problematic situation may be in which several equally valid measures to evaluate a claimed property exist and the specification does not identify the one that should be used.[84] It is worthy of mention that the PTO employs a different standard for indefiniteness than in *Nautilus* based on the rationale that there is no presumption of validity in prosecution.[85]

Previously, indefiniteness issues with respect to means plus function claims were discussed and this may be an issue particularly with respect to software, as previously discussed.[86]

Likewise, we have previously pointed out that claims which leave unclear the statutory category of the claimed subject matter may be indefinite.[87] We discuss this latter issue in more detail later in this chapter.[88]

Finally, simply sloppy drafting may lead to indefiniteness. Examples are included later in this chapter.[89]

5.44 Avoid Potential Patent Eligibility Issues

Since the *Mayo*[90] and *Alice*[91] decisions from the Supreme Court, patent eligibility has increasingly become an issue that has proven to affect more types of claims than expected. It is to the point where claims cannot be drafted and, likewise, a specification cannot be drafted, without serious consideration of whether this issue has been adequately handled.

---

82. *See* Interval Licensing v. AOL, 896 F.3d 1335 (Fed. Cir. 2018); Halliburton Energy Services Inc. v. M-I L, 514 F.3d 1244, 1251 (Fed. Cir. 2008).

83. *See* discussion in Chapter 2 regarding words of degree.

84. *See* Dow Chem. Co. v. Nova Chemicals Corp. (Canada), 803 F.3d 620, 633–35 (Fed. Cir. 2015).

85. *See* MPEP § 2173 (2022).

86. *See* section 4.123 and its subsections.

87. *See* discussion in connection with method and apparatus claims in Chapter 2 and discussion later in this chapter.

88. *See* section 5.6 and its subsections.

89. *See* section 5.8 and its subsections.

90. *See* Mayo Collaborative Servs. v. Prometheus Labs., Inc., 566 U.S. 66, 71, 101 USPQ2d 1961, 1965 (2012).

91. *See* Alice Corp. Pty. Ltd. v. CLS Bank Int'l, 573 U.S. 208, 216, 110 USPQ2d 1976, 1980 (2014).

> It is to the point where claims cannot be drafted and, likewise, a specification cannot be drafted, without serious consideration of whether this issue has been adequately handled.

There are several pieces to this puzzle to consider. Initially, one should at least understand the *Mayo-Alice* framework as articulated by the Supreme Court. It is articulated reasonably clearly in MPEP section 2106 (I) (2022).

<u>2106 Patent Subject Matter Eligibility</u>

I. TWO CRITERIA FOR SUBJECT MATTER ELIGIBILITY

First, the claimed invention must be to one of the four statutory categories. 35 U.S.C. 101 defines the four categories of invention that Congress deemed to be the appropriate subject matter of a patent: processes, machines, manufactures and compositions of matter. The latter three categories define "things" or "products" while the first category defines "actions" (i.e., inventions that consist of a series of steps or acts to be performed). *See* 35 U.S.C. 100(b) ("The term 'process' means process, art, or method, and includes a new use of a known process, machine, manufacture, composition of matter, or material."). *See* MPEP § 2106.03 for detailed information on the four categories.

Second, the claimed invention also must qualify as patent-eligible subject matter, i.e., the claim must not be directed to a judicial exception unless the claim as a whole includes additional limitations amounting to significantly more than the exception. The judicial exceptions (also called "judicially recognized exceptions" or simply "exceptions") are subject matter that the courts have found to be outside of, or exceptions to, the four statutory categories of invention, and are limited to abstract ideas, laws of nature and natural phenomena (including products of nature). *Alice Corp. Pty. Ltd. v. CLS Bank Int'l*, 573 U.S. 208, 216, 110 USPQ2d 1976, 1980 (2014) (*citing Ass'n for Molecular Pathology v. Myriad Genetics, Inc.*, 569 U.S. 576, 589, 106 USPQ2d 1972, 1979 (2013). *See* MPEP § 2106.04 for detailed information on the judicial exceptions.

Because abstract ideas, laws of nature, and natural phenomenon "are the basic tools of scientific and technological work," the Supreme Court has expressed concern that monopolizing these tools by granting patent rights may impede innovation rather than promote it. *See Alice Corp.*, 573 U.S. at 216, 110 USPQ2d at 1980; *Mayo Collaborative Servs. v. Prometheus Labs., Inc.*, 566 U.S. 66, 71, 101 USPQ2d 1961, 1965 (2012). However, the Court has also emphasized that an invention is not considered to be ineligible for patenting simply because it involves a judicial exception. *Alice Corp.*, 573 U.S. at

217, 110 USPQ2d at 1980-81 (*citing Diamond v. Diehr*, 450 U.S. 175, 187, 209 USPQ 1, 8 (1981)). *See also Thales Visionix Inc. v. United States*, 850 F.3d. 1343, 1349, 121 USPQ2d 1898, 1902 (Fed. Cir. 2017) ("That a mathematical equation is required to complete the claimed method and system does not doom the claims to abstraction."). Accordingly, the Court has said that integration of an abstract idea, law of nature or natural phenomenon into a practical application may be eligible for patent protection. *See, e.g., Alice*, 573 U.S. at 217, 110 USPQ2d at 1981 (explaining that "in applying the §101 exception, we must distinguish between patents that claim the 'buildin[g] block[s]' of human ingenuity and those that integrate the building blocks into something more" (*quoting Mayo*, 566 U.S. at 89, 110 USPQ2d at 1971) and stating that *Mayo* "set forth a framework for distinguishing patents that claim laws of nature, natural phenomena, and abstract ideas from those that claim patent-eligible applications of those concepts"); *Mayo*, 566 U.S. at 80, 84, 101 USPQ2d at 1969, 1971 (noting that the Court in *Diamond v. Diehr* found "the overall process patent eligible because of the way the additional steps of the process integrated the equation into the process as a whole," but the Court in *Gottschalk v. Benson* "held that simply implementing a mathematical principle on a physical machine, namely a computer, was not a patentable application of that principle"); *Bilski v. Kappos*, 561 U.S. 593, 611, 95 USPQ2d 1001, 1010 (2010) ("*Diehr* explained that while an abstract idea, law of nature, or mathematical formula could not be patented, 'an application of a law of nature or mathematical formula to a known structure or process may well be deserving of patent protection.'" (*quoting Diamond v. Diehr*, 450 U.S. 175, 187, 209 USPQ 1, 8 (1981)) (emphasis in original)); *Diehr*, 450 U.S. at 187, 192 n.14, 209 USPQ at 10 n.14 (explaining that the process in *Parker v. Flook* was ineligible not because it contained a mathematical formula, but because it did not provide an application of the formula). *See Diamond v. Diehr*, 450 U.S. 175, 209 USPQ 1 (1981); *Gottschalk v. Benson*, 409 U.S. 63, 175 USPQ 673 (1972); *Parker v. Flook*, 437 U.S. 584, 198 USPQ 193 (1978).

The Supreme Court in *Mayo* laid out a framework for determining whether an applicant is seeking to patent a judicial exception itself, or a patent-eligible application of the judicial exception. *See Alice Corp.*, 573 U.S. at 217-18, 110 USPQ2d at 1981 (*citing Mayo*, 566 U.S. 66, 101 USPQ2d 1961). This framework, which is referred to as the *Mayo* test or the *Alice/Mayo* test, is discussed in further detail in subsection III, below. The first part of the *Mayo* test is to determine whether the claims are directed to an abstract idea, a law of nature or a natural phenomenon (i.e., a judicial exception). *Id.* If the claims are directed to a judicial exception, the second part of the *Mayo* test is to determine whether the claim recites additional elements that amount to significantly more than the judicial exception. *Id. citing Mayo*, 566 U.S. at 72-73, 101 USPQ2d at 1966). The Supreme Court has described the second part of the test as the "search for an 'inventive concept.'" *Alice Corp.*, 573 U.S.

at 217-18, 110 USPQ2d at 1981 (*citing Mayo*, 566 U.S. at 72-73, 101 USPQ2d at 1966).

The *Alice/Mayo* two-part test is the only test that should be used to evaluate the eligibility of claims under examination. While the machine-or-transformation test is an important clue to eligibility, it should not be used as a separate test for eligibility. Instead it should be considered as part of the "integration" determination or "significantly more" determination articulated in the *Alice/Mayo* test. *Bilski v. Kappos*, 561 U.S. 593, 605, 95 USPQ2d 1001, 1007 (2010). See MPEP § 2106.04(d) for more information about evaluating whether a claim reciting a judicial exception is integrated into a practical application and MPEP § 2106.05(b) and MPEP § 2106.05(c) for more information about how the machine-or-transformation test fits into the *Alice/Mayo* two-part framework. Likewise, eligibility should not be evaluated based on whether the claim recites a "useful, concrete, and tangible result," *State Street Bank*, 149 F.3d 1368, 1374, 47 USPQ2d 1596, 1602 (Fed. Cir. 1998) (*quoting In re Alappat*, 33 F.3d 1526, 1544, 31 USPQ2d 1545, 1557 (Fed. Cir. 1994)), as this test has been superseded. *In re Bilski*, 545 F.3d 943, 959-60, 88 USPQ2d 1385, 1394-95 (Fed. Cir. 2008) (*en banc*), *aff'd by Bilski v. Kappos*, 561 U.S. 593, 95 USPQ2d 1001 (2010). *See also TLI Communications LLC v. AV Automotive LLC*, 823 F.3d 607, 613, 118 USPQ2d 1744, 1748 (Fed. Cir. 2016) ("It is well-settled that mere recitation of concrete, tangible components is insufficient to confer patent eligibility to an otherwise abstract idea"). The programmed computer or "special purpose computer" test of *In re Alappat*, 33 F.3d 1526, 31 USPQ2d 1545 (Fed. Cir. 1994) (*i.e.*, the rationale that an otherwise ineligible algorithm or software could be made patent-eligible by merely adding a generic computer to the claim for the "special purpose" of executing the algorithm or software) was also superseded by the Supreme Court's *Bilski* and *Alice Corp.* decisions. *Eon Corp. IP Holdings LLC v. AT&T Mobility LLC*, 785 F.3d 616, 623, 114 USPQ2d 1711, 1715 (Fed. Cir. 2015) ("[W]e note that *Alappat* has been superseded by *Bilski*, 561 U.S. at 605–06, and *Alice Corp. v. CLS Bank Int'l*, 573 U.S. 208, 110 USPQ2d 1976 (2014)"); *Intellectual Ventures I LLC v. Capital One Bank (USA), N.A.*, 792 F.3d 1363, 1366, 115 USPQ2d 1636, 1639 (Fed. Cir. 2015) ("An abstract idea does not become nonabstract by limiting the invention to a particular field of use or technological environment, such as the Internet [or] a computer"). Lastly, eligibility should not be evaluated based on whether the claimed invention has utility, because "[u]tility is not the test for patent-eligible subject matter." *Genetic Techs. Ltd. v. Merial LLC*, 818 F.3d 1369, 1380, 118 USPQ2d 1541, 1548 (Fed. Cir. 2016).

Thus, as stated, the first part of the *Mayo-Alice* test is to determine whether the claims are directed to an abstract idea, a law of nature or a natural phenomenon (i.e., a judicial exception). If the claims are directed to a judicial exception, the second part of the test is to determine whether the claim recites additional elements that amount to significantly more than the judicial exception.[92] This involves looking at the elements and limitations of the claim individually and as an ordered combination to determine, either individually or as an ordered combination, whether the claim amounts to more than simply known, routine, or conventional technology.

5.441 Illustrative Claim Example—Software: VisiCalc

More typically, in connection with the predictable arts, the issue under the first part of the test relates to whether the claim is directed to an abstract idea. The term "abstract" was not defined by the Court in *Alice*. Furthermore, the meaning imparted to the term from *Alice* and from subsequent federal circuit cases is likely different from what might be expected.

Rather, the language of *Alice* and certainly the direction of the jurisprudence since then has been *to assess whether an innovation is truly being claimed.*[93] One way to view this is that the Court is asking whether the innovation is abstract or is it concrete (meaning, largely, that it is identifiable, specific, technical, and innovative, as discussed in more detail later), meaning, again, is this *truly* an innovation or just smoke and mirrors to make it look like there is an innovation? The subsequent case law seems to bear out this view.

Let's consider, as an example, the early days of computers and the creation of VisiCalc. If today's law were to have been applied then, in particular, *Mayo-Alice*, would a patent claim covering VisiCalc be patent eligible? The answer truly depends on the claim itself. *So, unlike other countries, in the United States, how the claim is drafted may critically affect eligibility.*

> ... unlike other countries, in the United States, how the claim is drafted may critically affect eligibility.

92. If the claims are not directed to a judicial exception, then the claims are patent eligible, as explained in the MPEP.

93. *See* Howard Skaist, *Alice Corp. and Patent Claiming: A Simple Example*, PatentlyO (Aug. 28, 2014), https://patentlyo.com/patent/2014/08/claiming-simple-example.html.

Prior to *Alice* and *Mayo*, a claim drafter might have written the following claim:

EXAMPLE 5.6

I claim:

1. A method comprising: implementing a spreadsheet on a computer.

Appreciate, here, as we have suggested previously, most skilled practitioners tend to make sure that *a spectrum* of claims is included, at least for considerations related to section 103. Drafting a *spectrum* of claims around patent eligibility may *now* be a best practice to consider *for addressing 101 issues.*

Appreciate, here, as we have suggested, most skilled practitioners tend to make sure that *a spectrum* of claims is included, at least for considerations related to section 103 Drafting a *spectrum* of claims around patent eligibility may *now* be a best practice to consider *for addressing 101 issues.*

The preceding claim, thus, is in line with claims previously adjudicated before the Court. That is, the claim on its face does not appear to communicate details about the innovation itself. Rather, this claim would likely be held patent ineligible under the *Mayo-Alice* approach.

Spreadsheets are of long-standing use. The aspect of the claim calling out implementation on a computer likewise, on its face at least, does not constitute a sufficiently meaningful addition. It might be argued that computer implementation is faster than performing spreadsheet calculations on paper, but merely being faster is not sufficient, generally, to pass muster under *Mayo-Alice*.

How might such a claim, then, otherwise have been deemed patentable under sections 102 and 103, *before* the *Alice* and *Mayo* decisions?

It is important to realize that when technology is implemented, rarely does it just result in being faster *and nothing more*. Usually, the implementation provides other advantages. *Here, referring to this simple example as an illustration, VisiCalc made a type of functionality possible via computer that had not existed before.*

Thus, there are quite reasonable arguments for patentability of claim 1 under sections 102 and 103 (and *before Mayo-Alice*).

Under section 102, is the claim novel? It would seem so. While spreadsheets were known and computers were known, VisiCalc is likely the first spreadsheet to be implemented on a computer.

Section 103 is more challenging than 102 in this example, as is usually the case; nonetheless, there are good arguments, such as the point articulated earlier. Per section 103 and case law, the claim must be viewed *as a whole*, and this includes advantages that would necessarily flow from the claim language as a whole. *Thus, implementing a spreadsheet on a computer permits new functionality, such as implementing user-selected operations within cells.* The power of this feature may not be understated. It is why spreadsheets have become largely essential tools throughout the world. They have literally changed how the world operates.

This example also demonstrates the *challenge* faced by the PTO and courts as well to evaluate broad claims under 102 and 103 *before* the *Mayo-Alice* framework. With a doctrine like the one articulated for 103, patent attorneys became quite adept at drafting broad patent claims because under 103 *the innovation does not need to be recited in the claim language.* ***The key to understanding the power of section 103 is that claim language dissection is not permitted. This is well-established patent law.*** This is also part of the essence of viewing the claim "as a whole."

Enter section 101. Whereas viewing the claim "as a whole" under 103 is statutory, viewing the claim as a whole under section 101 is judge made and, consequently, capable of being changed.[94] Before *Alice* and *Mayo*, under section 101, claim dissection was already beginning to happen. For example, one doctrine, such as "extra solution activity" stated that such activity did not "make statutory" an otherwise non-statutory claim and another doctrine stated that limiting a claim to a particular technology did not transform a non-statutory claim into a statutory one. These doctrines could be viewed as examples of claim dissection at the margin. However, appreciate also that while a large overlap between being statutory and being patent eligible exists, the two have become separate considerations. *Thus, one way to view the two-part test is as a type of claim dissection under 101 despite the teachings of* Diamond v. Diehr. *Rather, the two-part test effectively breaks the Diehr analysis into two-parts to, in effect, permit claim dissection.*

The first part of the *Mayo-Alice* framework is the "dissection" part asking what the claim is "directed to." The second part is the "as a whole" part, which

94. *See* Diamond v. Diehr, 450 U.S. 175 (1981).

might find a claim patent eligible despite being too abstract if dissected. *Here, "abstract" meaning the proposed technical innovation based on the claim language is not sufficiently concrete, largely meaning not sufficiently identifiable, specific, technical, and innovative.*

Note also that "innovative" here is not the same as being unobvious. Rather, if there are no factual issues that arise in the analysis (e.g., via judicial or examiner notice, known art, or some other way), the innovative evaluation might be seen as "like" a judgment on the pleadings. That is, if we take what the patentee says as true, is this claim *sufficiently* technical, identifiable, specific and innovative for section 101 patent eligibility? That is, sufficiently concrete. If not, then it is deemed "abstract." This is one way to view the analysis at a high level.

Returning to our example, if such an aspect of VisiCalc, described earlier as the innovation, were particularly claimed, perhaps, such a claim would be deemed eligible under the analysis in *Alice*. For example, consider the following claims, recognizing that this example is not intended to illustrate the best claims possible, but is just a simple example to illustrate considerations raised by the *Mayo-Alice* framework.

EXAMPLE 5.7

I claim:

1. A method comprising:

   generating and displaying a matrix of cells comprising an electronic spreadsheet on a computer, the electronic spreadsheet implementing one or more user-specified operations in which one or more operands for the one or more user-specified operations are entered in one or more particular cells of the matrix and results of performing the one or more user-specified operations on the one or more operands are retained in the particular cells and/or one or more other particular cells of the matrix with or without display thereof.

2. The method of claim 1, and further comprising: displaying on the computer, in the particular cells and/or the other particular cells, after the one or more operands are entered, the results of performing the one or more user-specified operations on the one or more operands.

3. The method of claim 1, wherein, the implementing comprises: implementing one or more other user-specified operations for the particular

cells and/or the other particular cells on the results of performing the one or more user-specified operations on the one or more operands, which are retained in the particular cells and/or the other particular cells of the matrix with or without display thereof.

Observe these are method claims. Software tends to be more easily claimed as a method. Likewise, a benefit is that functionality typically is less of an issue for method claims. Claim 1 is intended to cover using cells to implement user-specified operations with or without display of the results. This is so that one dependent claim may cover displaying the results (claim 2), while another claim may cover using the results as operand inputs for one or more "other" user specified functions (claim 3).

The first part of *Mayo-Alice* is to determine whether the claims are directed to an abstract idea, a law of nature or a natural phenomenon (i.e., a judicial exception). If the claims are directed to a judicial exception, the second part of the test is to determine whether the claim recites additional elements that amount to significantly more than the judicial exception.

Analyzing these claims under the first part of Mayo-Alice, as we suggested, *if we take what the patentee says as true, is this claim* ***sufficiently*** *technical, identifiable, specific and innovative (i.e., concrete; not abstract)?*

Arguably so. Probably the most challenging issue with these claims is whether they are sufficiently *technical*. That is, do they address a *technical* problem? Correctly characterizing this as a solution to a technical problem may be critical here.[95]

Keep in mind that this claim is for a time when the IBM PC, for example, was quite new; whereas today this may seem straight-forward, it was not at the time VisiCalc was invented. The specification should describe in specific details the technical hurdles related to implementation of the claims. This is likely both a hardware and software problem and solution, which should be described. Such explanation would also provide written description support for narrower dependent claims.

One should be clear that this approach was not used previously in the prior art. That is, this is not a case of taking something previously done and simply implementing it by computer. *Rather, new computer functionality is enabled here.*

95. Note the similarity with EPC law. See Chapter 7, discussing EPC law.

This distinguishes the case from *Alice*. Providing new computer functionality has also been shown to be an aspect of patent eligibility.[96] *Here, the new functionality is permitting or enabling user-specified operations within cells of a spreadsheet.* This functionality enables a user to program solutions to extremely complex problems much more quickly and much more easily. Whereas previously it might have taken someone with a degree in programming days to program and troubleshoot something reasonably complex; with this technology, someone with only a high school diploma may effectively generate a programmed solution to such a problem within hours.

Furthermore, this is not a case of pre-empting all possible solutions, which has also been shown to be an aspect of patent eligibility (that is, pre-emption of all possible solutions suggests patent ineligibility).[97] For example, programmable calculators exist, as does computer programming itself. Rather, this is a very particular implementation in which user-selected operations are implemented within cells.

One issue to also appreciate here is that although the desire is to have the PTO issue the claim, the courts and the PTO are not fully aligned on patent eligibility. Thus, it may be important when drafting claims to be patent eligible to provide a basis for eligibility that will be sufficient if the claim were to be tested in litigation. As we discuss later in more detail, it is not too difficult to draft a claim that satisfies the PTO requirement of an application, per PTO guidelines. However, meeting that requirement may not satisfy a court.[98] Hence, we are focusing here on the two-part test and case law in connection with drafting a patent eligible claim.

---

96. For example, the PTO-issued November 2, 2016, patent eligibility guidance (see https://www.uspto.gov/patents/laws/examination-policy/subject-matter-eligibility-examination-guidance-date), states (emphasis supplied):

> An "improvement in computer-related technology" is *not limited to* improvements in the operation of a computer or a computer network per se, but may also be claimed *as a set of "rules" (basically mathematical relationships) that improve computer-related technology by allowing computer performance of a function not previously performable by a computer.*

See also McRO v. Bandai, 837 F.3d 1299 (Fed. Cir. 2016).

97. *See, e.g.*, McRO v. Bandai, 837 F.3d 1299 (Fed. Cir. 2016).

98. *See, e.g.*, *In re* Killian, 45 F.4th 1373 (Fed. Cir. 2022), stating the following:

> Although there is no single, inflexible rule for the abstract idea inquiry, our court has provided guidance as to what constitutes an abstract idea. We have explained that, first, "[t]he 'abstract idea' step of the inquiry calls upon us to look at the 'focus of the claimed advance over the prior art' to determine if the claim's 'character as a whole' is directed to excluded subject matter." *Affinity Labs.* Once we identify the "focus of the asserted claims," we may consider whether the claims "fall into a familiar class of claims directed to' a patent-ineligible concept." *Elec. Power Grp.*

Thus, to summarize the prior discussion of the first part of the test, an important point under the *Mayo-Alice* Framework is to appreciate that "not abstract'" does not mean "physical" (although the claim subject matter must be physical as well to be statutory). Rather, it means an "identifiable," "specific," "concrete," "technical," and "innovative" improvement recited on the face of the claim at issue.

An aspect of this, if responding to a 101 rejection, for example, includes pointing out that the claim is not directed to any of the problematic areas, like a mathematical algorithm, mental steps, organizing human activities, and/or a fundamental or long-standing practice. Thus, one should draft the claim to avoid these problematic areas. If, under scrutiny, however, such arguments are weak or suspect in light of the drafted claim, then the claim language may need to be re-formulated to more clearly recite an approach that, as an example, addresses a previously unaddressed ***technical*** problem or that addresses a ***technical*** problem in a way that is better than otherwise known approaches.

We have provided still further guidance for those familiar classes of claims. For example, in the context of claims to results, we have explained that claims that "simply demand the production of a desired result . . . without any limitation on how to produce that result" are directed to an abstract idea. *Interval Licensing*. In the context of mental processes . . . we have explained that if a claim's steps "can be performed in the human mind, or by a human using a pen and paper," and the elements in the claim do not contain a sufficient inventive concept under *Alice/Mayo* step two, the claim is for a patent-ineligible abstract idea. *Ericsson Inc. v. TCL Commc'n Tech. Holdings Ltd.*, 955 F.3d 1317, 1327 (Fed. Cir. 2020) And we have explained that "[i]nformation as such is an intangible"; accordingly, "gathering and analyzing information of a specified content, then displaying the results" without "any particular assertedly inventive technology for performing those functions" is an abstract idea. *Elec. Power Grp.* We have provided further guidance for "cases involving software innovations," where the abstract idea "inquiry often turns on whether the claims focus on 'the specific asserted improvement in computer capabilities . . . or, instead, on a process that qualifies as an 'abstract idea' for which computers are invoked merely as a tool.'" *Finjan*.

Our case law also provides guidance as to "inventive concept," particularly in the context of claims for computer implementations of abstract ideas. We have explained that claims for methods that "improve an existing technological process" include an inventive concept at step two. *BASCOM*. And claims that "recite a specific, discrete implementation of the abstract idea" rather than "preempt[ing] all ways of" achieving an abstract idea using a computer may include an inventive concept. *Id.* But claims to "an abstract idea implemented on generic computer components, without providing a specific technical solution beyond simply using generic computer concepts in a conventional way" do not pass muster at step two. *Id.* "Neither attempting to limit the use of [the idea] to a particular technological environment nor a wholly generic computer implementation is sufficient." *buySAFE*.

Thus, one should draft a claim in which it may be shown that what is being claimed is, again, an "identifiable," "specific," "technical," and "innovative" improvement.

If, again, responding to a rejection under 101, often the examiner will overgeneralize the claim language and/or assert that the claim merely covers data processing, which is not generally patent eligible. It may be helpful to remind the examiner to not overly generalize the claim language, point to the specific claim language at issue, and also point out that the claim language and the specification explicitly refer to "signals and/or states,"[99] which qualifies as physical manifestations, unlike "data," which does not. Cases that support this include *Digitech*[100] and even older precedent like *Arrhythmia*.[101]

It may also be appropriate to point to and discuss the case, *Electric Power Group*.[102] The claims related to systems and methods for performing real-time performance monitoring of an electric power grid by collecting data from multiple data sources, analyzing the data, and displaying the results. Regarding the first step of *Mayo-Alice*, the court stated:

> The claims in this case fall into a familiar class of claims "directed to" a patent-ineligible concept. The focus of the asserted claims, as illustrated by claim 12 quoted above, is on collecting information, analyzing it, and displaying certain results of the collection and analysis. We need not define the outer limits of "abstract idea," or at this stage exclude the possibility that any particular inventive means are to be found somewhere in the claims, to conclude that these claims focus on an abstract idea—and hence require stage-two analysis under § 101.
>
> Information as such is an intangible. *See Microsoft Corp. v. AT & T Corp.*, 550 U.S. 437, 451 n.12, 127 S. Ct. 1746, 167 L. Ed. 2d 737 (2007); *Bayer AG v. Housey Pharms., Inc.*, 340 F.3d 1367, 1372 (Fed. Cir. 2003). Accordingly, we have treated collecting information, including when limited to particular content (which does not change its character as information), as within the realm of abstract ideas. *See, e.g., Internet Patents*, 790 F.3d at 1349; *OIP Techs., Inc. v. Amazon. com, Inc.*, 788 F.3d 1359, 1363 (Fed. Cir. 2015); *Content Extraction & Transmission LLC v. Wells Fargo Bank, Nat'l Ass'n*, 776 F.3d 1343, 1347

99. *See* Appendix B with sample application boilerplate for a patent specification.

100. *See* Digitech v. Electronics for Imaging, 758 F. 3d 1344 (Fed. Cir. 2014).

101. *See* Arrhythmia Rsch. Tech. Inc. v. Corazonix Corp., 958 F.2d 1053 (Fed. Cir. 1992). The case Enfish, LLC v. Microsoft Corp., 822 F.3d 1327 (Fed. Cir. 2016) is also helpful to cite here due to its language:

Much of the advancement made in computer technology consists of improvements to software that, by their very nature, may not be defined by particular physical features but rather *by logic structures and processes*. We do not see in Bilski and Alice, or our cases, an exclusion to patenting this large field of technological progress (emphasis supplied).

102. *See* Elec. Power Group, LLC v. Alstom S.A., 830 F.3d 1350 (Fed. Cir. 2016).

(Fed. Cir. 2014); *Digitech Image Techs., LLC v. Elecs. for Imaging, Inc.*, 758 F.3d 1344, 1351 (Fed. Cir. 2014); *CyberSource Corp. v. Retail Decisions, Inc.*, 654 F.3d 1366, 1370 (Fed. Cir. 2011). In a similar vein, we have treated analyzing information by steps people go through in their minds, or by mathematical algorithms, without more, as essentially mental processes within the abstract-idea category. *See, e.g., TLI Commc'ns*, 823 F.3d at 613; *Digitech*, 758 F.3d at 1351; *SmartGene, Inc. v. Advanced Biological Labs.*, SA, 555 F. App'x 950, 955 (Fed. Cir. 2014); *Bancorp Servs., L.L.C. v. Sun Life Assurance Co. of Canada (U.S.)*, 687 F.3d 1266, 1278 (Fed. Cir. 2012); *CyberSource Corp. v. Retail Decisions, Inc.*, 654 F.3d 1366, 1372 (Fed. Cir. 2011); *SiRF Tech., Inc. v. Int'l Trade Comm'n*, 601 F.3d 1319, 1333 (Fed. Cir. 2010); *see also Mayo*, 132 S. Ct. at 1301; *Parker v. Flook*, 437 U.S. 584, 589-90, 98 S. Ct. 2522, 57 L. Ed. 2d 451 (1978); *Gottschalk v. Benson*, 409 U.S. 63, 67, 93 S. Ct. 253, 34 L. Ed. 2d 273 (1972). And we have recognized that merely presenting the results of abstract processes of collecting and analyzing information, without more (such as identifying a particular tool for presentation), is abstract as an ancillary part of such collection and analysis. *See, e.g., Content Extraction*, 776 F.3d at 1347; *Ultramercial, Inc. v. Hulu, LLC*, 772 F.3d 709, 715 (Fed. Cir. 2014).

Here, the claims are clearly focused on the combination of those abstract-idea processes. The advance they purport to make is a process of gathering and analyzing information of a specified content, then displaying the results, and not any particular assertedly inventive technology for performing those functions. They are therefore directed to an abstract idea.

Regarding the second step, the court stated:

When we turn to stage two of the *Alice* analysis and scrutinize the claim elements more microscopically, we find nothing sufficient to remove the claims from the class of subject matter ineligible for patenting. Most obviously, limiting the claims to the particular technological environment of power-grid monitoring is, without more, insufficient to transform them into patent-eligible applications of the abstract idea at their core. *See Alice*, 134 S. Ct. at 2358; *Mayo*, 132 S. Ct. at 1294; *Bilski v. Kappos*, 561 U.S. 593, 610-11, 130 S. Ct. 3218, 177 L. Ed. 2d 792 (2010); *Diamond v. Diehr*, 450 U.S. 175, 191, 101 S. Ct. 1048, 67 L. Ed. 2d 155 (1981); *buySAFE, Inc. v. Google, Inc.*, 765 F.3d 1350, 1355 (Fed. Cir. 2014). More particularly, a large portion of the lengthy claims is devoted to enumerating types of information and information sources available within the power-grid environment. But merely selecting information, by content or source, for collection, analysis, and display does nothing significant to differentiate a process from ordinary mental processes, whose implicit exclusion from § 101 undergirds the information-based category of abstract ideas.

However, the *main* problem appeared to be the general and all encompassing nature of the claims. In this regard, the court stated: Nothing in the

> claims, understood in light of the specification, requires anything other than off-the-shelf, conventional computer, network, and display technology for gathering, sending, and presenting the desired information. That is so even as to the claim requirement of "displaying concurrent visualization" of two or more types of information, '710 patent, col. 31, line 37, even if understood to require time-synchronized display: nothing in the patent contains any suggestion that the displays needed for that purpose are anything but readily available. We have repeatedly held that such invocations of computers and networks that are not even arguably inventive are "insufficient to pass the test of an inventive concept in the application" of an abstract idea. *buySAFE*, 765 F.3d at 1353, 1355; *see, e.g.*, *Mortg. Grader, Inc. v. First Choice Loan Servs. Inc.*, 811 F.3d 1314, 1324-25 (Fed. Cir. 2016); *Intellectual Ventures I LLC v. Capital One Bank (USA)*, 792 F.3d 1363, 1370 (Fed. Cir. 2015); *Internet Patents*, 790 F.3d at 1348-49; *Content Extraction*, 776 F.3d at 1347-48.

The court went on to distinguish two cases, in particular, *Bascom*, which is discussed more later. It stated:

> Nor do the claims here require an arguably inventive distribution of functionality within a network, thus distinguishing the claims at issue from those in *Bascom*, 827 F.3d 1341, 2016 U.S. App. LEXIS 11687, 2016 WL 3514158, *at *6* (at pleading stage finding sufficient inventive concept in "the installation of a filtering tool at a specific location, remote from the endusers, with customizable filtering features specific to each end user"). The claims in this case specify what information in the power-grid field it is desirable to gather, analyze, and display, including in "real time"; but they do not include any requirement for performing the claimed functions of gathering, analyzing, and displaying in real time by use of anything but entirely conventional, generic technology. The claims therefore do not state an arguably inventive concept in the realm of application of the information-based abstract ideas.

Thus, unlike *Electric Power Group* and more like *Bascom*, the claims here, one would argue, are specific and innovative as to the operations at issue.

In this manner, through argument, one may refocus the examiner's attention on more appropriate considerations for patent eligibility, such as the technical problems that are being addressed through express claim language and associated discussion contained in the specification describing the technical problem.

Usually when addressing an overgeneralization of claim language by an examiner, again, it may be helpful to highlight and repeat the exact language of the claim and point out the improvement over the state of the art to make the overgeneralization quite clear and specific for the examiner.

Likewise, as alluded to previously, one should draft the claim so that one may emphasize that the claim does not tie up fundamental scientific building blocks, again, through the specificity of claim language and how that language relates to a particular technical issue.

Thus, one may assert that, as a whole, the claim is patent eligible and not directed to an abstract idea. Because the improvement is identifiable, specific, technical, and innovative (such as not a long standing practice), the discussion of the problem and the improvement distinguishes the claim from the one in *Alice*. Likewise, emphasizing that the subject matter claimed is not a long-standing practice further distinguishes *Alice*, not unlike how the *DDR*[103] court compared a website to a kiosk to conclude the subject matter to be patent eligible because of significant technical differences. That is, per *DDR*, mere analogies are inadequate in a discussion involving *specific* and *technical* improvements. The technical advances, such as new computer functionality, or the internet, as another example, creates new problems that require new solutions.[104]

However, for the sake of argument, this could also be a case, for example, in which whether the first part of the test is met is on the borderline. Case law suggests that the second part of the test is to address such situations.[105] Thus, under the second part of the test, the benefits that flow from the claim may also be important. That is, for the analysis to be conducted, the claim elements are viewed individually or in combination to determine whether they amount to more than the judicial exception. Here, meaning the claim elements viewed individually or in combination, are more than simply well-known, routine, or conventional technology.

Thus, in our example, for claim drafting and for analysis, one should also consider the second step—which *Bascom* clarifies is used for close call cases. That is, for example, even if the examiner might be "on the fence" on the first step (simply for the sake of legal argument), the claim *still* may pass muster through application of the second step. *Bascom* clarifies (and it is reiterated in the PTO guidelines) that even if individual elements of a claim are known,

---

103. *See* DDR Holdings v. Hotels.com, 773 F.3d 1245, 1258 (Fed. Cir. 2014).

104. On this point, DDR Holdings v. Hotels.com, 773 F.3d 1245, 1258 (Fed. Cir. 2014), states (emphasis supplied):

> The dissent suggests that the "store within a store" concept, such as a warehouse store that contains a kiosk for selling a third-party partner's cruise vacation packages, is the pre-Internet analog of the '399 patent's asserted claims. Dissenting Op. 1264. While that concept may have been well-known by the relevant timeframe, that practice did not have to account for the ephemeral nature of an Internet 'location' or the near-instantaneous transport between these locations made possible by standard Internet communication protocols, ***which introduces a problem that does not arise in the 'brick and mortar' context.***

105. *See* Bascom v. AT&T, 827 F.3d 1341 (Fed. Cir. 2016).

conventional, and so on, nonetheless, a *non-generic/non-conventional arrangement* of known elements is still able to be patent eligible. Thus, *DDR* and/or *Bascom* provide a good basis for distinguishing the improvement as non-conventional.[106] *Amdocs v. Opennet*[107] is also on point in this regard.

It is worth pointing out that prior technical arguments made under the first part of the test may also come into play under the second part of the test, but with a different emphasis (e.g., viewed through a different lens, so to speak).[108] In this example, then, for a case such as this, and, in general, one may draft the claim to provide technical arguments able at least in part to show that the technology at issue involves a computer-related technical problem, illustrating that the problem addressed does *not* relate to a problem addressed by a long-standing practice and, rather, here, for example, provides new functionality. Also suggesting that it is sufficiently identifiable, specific, technical, and innovative (i.e., concrete) that it is not abstract.

Even assuming, without agreeing, this example is a close call case; nonetheless, the language used to draft this claim is intended to transform an otherwise arguably abstract idea to patent eligible subject matter, such as through a non-generic or non-conventional arrangement. That is, the claim should be drafted with this in mind. For example, in claim 1, the language:

> the electronic spreadsheet implementing one or more user-specified operations in which one or more operands for the one or more user-specified operations are entered in one or more particular cells . . . and results of

---

106. In *Bascom*, 827 F.3d 1341 (Fed. Cir. 2016), the federal circuit disagreed with the district court's holding that the ordered combination of limitations was noninventive and held that the claimed technical improvement transformed the abstract idea into patent-eligible subject matter under the second step. The federal circuit recognized that courts commonly consider whether various claim elements simply recite "well-understood, routine, conventional activities." But the federal circuit further stated that "[t]he inventive concept inquiry requires *more than* recognizing that each claim element, by itself, was known in the art . . . *an inventive concept can be found in the non-conventional and non-generic arrangement* of known, conventional pieces" (emphasis supplied).

Amdocs v. Opennet, 841 F.3d 1288 (Fed. Cir. 2016), is yet another decided federal circuit case suggesting that, even assuming the claim were directed to an abstract idea, other aspects of the claim transform it to be patent-eligible subject matter. For example, in that case, the court stated (emphasis supplied):

> "Claim 1 involves some arguably conventional components (e.g., gatherers), but the claim also involves limitations that when considered individually and as an ordered combination recite an inventive concept through the system's distributed architecture. . . . *This arrangement is not so broadly described to cause preemption concerns.* Instead, it is narrowly circumscribed to the particular system outlined. As in *BASCOM*, this is a technical improvement over prior art technologies and served to improve the performance of the system itself."

107. 841 F.3d 1288 (Fed. Cir. 2016).

108. *See* Elec. Power Grp., LLC v. Alstom S.A., 830 F.3d 1350 (Fed. Cir. 2016).

> performing the one or more user-specified operations on the one or more operands are retained in the particular cells and/or one or more other particular cells . . .

could and should be argued to be a non-generic and non-conventional arrangement that provides new functionality to the platform.

This part of the analysis, however, also involves some of the factual aspects of the inquiry, such as in the *Berkheimer* case[109] and the requirements set out by the PTO in the so-called *Berkheimer* memorandum, related to what is known, routine or conventional.[110] Along these lines, an effective point to be made is that *Berkheimer* specifically says a feature shown in the prior art does not *necessarily* establish that the feature is conventional. Thus, for our example, one might point out that, *a fortiori*, the elements or limitations at issue cannot be conventional because (assuming this is accurate) the examiner has not even found prior art showing the elements or limitations at issue (e.g., in response to a rejection under section 102 or 103 made along with the rejection under 101).

Likewise, when drafting the claim, it follows one would use claim language to provide linguistic support for legal arguments to distinguish the claim from known prior art. This may seem like simply drafting to avoid 102 and 103; however, it is much more than that. It is drafting the claim to support arguments so that *on the face of the claim*, based on the language of the claim itself, it is clear that the subject matter is identifiable, it is specific, it is technical, and it is innovative so that when the elements and limitations are viewed individually and in combination, it is more than simply known, routine, or conventional technology.

Having provided an illustration of claim drafting and associated analysis to address section 101 patent eligibility in light of federal circuit case law, we now address drafting the claim to satisfy the PTO, based on its guidelines. To be more specific, how would the previous example claim *before Alice* (Example

---

109. Berkheimer v. HP Inc., 881 F.3d 1360, 1367 (Fed. Cir. 2018).

110. The *Berkheimer* memorandum provides that "an additional element (or combination of elements) is *not* well-understood, routine or conventional *unless* the examiner finds, and expressly supports a rejection in writing with, one or more of the following:

- A citation to an express statement in the specification or to a statement made by an applicant during prosecution that demonstrates the well-understood, routine, conventional nature of the additional element(s).
- A citation to one or more of the court decisions discussed in MPEP § 2106.05(d)(II) as noting the well-understood, routine, conventional nature of the additional element(s).
- A citation to a publication that demonstrates the well-understood, routine, conventional nature of the additional element(s).
- A statement that the examiner is taking official notice of the well-understood, routine, conventional nature of the additional element(s)." (emphasis supplied)

5.6) fare under the current *subject matter eligibility guidance (i.e., published in January 2019)*?[111] Furthermore, how might that claim be re-drafted to hopefully improve the chances that the claim will pass muster under that same new guidance?

One problem, however, as illustrated starkly by the previous hypothetical examples, is that claims drafted in light of the *Alice* decision are generally *narrower* than they would have been otherwise. Perhaps, for example, one could write better (e.g., broader) claims to pass muster under the *Mayo-Alice* framework in light of the PTO guidelines as a sort of hedge regarding breadth while at the same time increasing claim diversity.

To refresh, the "before" claim from earlier (Example 5.6) recited:

1. A method comprising: implementing a spreadsheet on a computer.

The primary change under the January 2019 subject matter guidance was to so-called step 2A (using the terminology of the PTO; effectively the first part of the *Mayo-Alice* framework), that is whether the claim is directed toward a judicial exception, such as an abstract idea.

The *January 2019 subject matter guidance* adds a first prong and a second prong to Step 2A of the PTO guidelines. Following the first prong of the PTO guidance, an examiner is to determine whether the claim recites a judicial exception, in this case an abstract idea, by referring to subject matter groupings. The subject matter groupings are specified as: mathematical concepts, certain methods of organizing human behavior, and mental processes. These are essentially the areas discussed previously as problematic areas to avoid when drafting the claim.

The guidance is quite specific in saying that the claim must "recite" subject matter that falls within the enumerated groupings to raise an issue regarding patent eligibility. One could argue that the claim does not "recite" subject matter that falls into the enumerated groupings. Nonetheless, this claim is not going to get through the PTO unchallenged under section 101. One could easily imagine an examiner asserting that the claim recites a mental process despite the language directed to a computer. An examiner might say, for example, that implementing a spreadsheet can be a mental process and that the language "implementing . . . on a computer" is nothing more than clever patent drafting without a substantive limit on scope.

---

111. The PTO's current eligibility guidance is found in the MPEP and particularly sections 2103 through 2106.07(c). *See* https://www.uspto.gov/patents/laws/examination-policy/subject-matter-eligibility.

How, then, might the claim be re-drafted to overcome such a rejection, but still retain some measure of breadth? Here is one attempt, capturing the inventive concept of Example 5.7, while achieving some greater breadth.

EXAMPLE 5.8

I claim:

1. A method comprising: implementing a spreadsheet via a computer, including determining contents of one or more cells thereof, based at least in part on one or more user-specified operations to be applied to signals and/or states to be provided as operands for the one or more user-specified operations.

This re-drafted claim at least arguably does not recite a mental process. Rather, the claim language is pretty specific to make it clear that physical processes are taking place. For example, it describes applying operations to signals and/or states. Thus, at least two out of three groupings have been drafted around, since it does not recite a mathematical process, as such.

Still, an examiner might say that a spreadsheet is a long-standing, fundamental economic practice or one that is a method of organizing human activities, demonstrating one danger with this latter particular grouping. It is, by its very nature, a bit vague. At least partly due to its vagueness, it would not be *entirely* unreasonable for an examiner to suggest that a spreadsheet might fall into this grouping.

Fortunately, all is not lost. Even if one fails to pass muster under the first prong, an opportunity to satisfy section 101 under the second prong remains under the PTO guidelines. Here, the guidance says that if the recited exception is integrated into a practical application, then the claim is still patent-eligible.

This is an area where one *cannot* be sure that meeting this will satisfy a federal court; however, if a claim is issued, it is presumed valid and previously we drafted *narrower* claims intended to be included and provide some comfort regarding satisfying section 101 for federal court litigation.

Specifically, the guidance says that to meet the second prong the claim is to integrate the judicial exception into a *practical application that imposes a meaningful limit* on the judicial exception, such that the claim is more than a drafting effort to monopolize the judicial exception. One could argue that Example 5.7 already does this. As suggested previously, this is not a case of pre-empting all possible solutions, which has also been shown to be an aspect of patent eligibility (that is, pre-emption of all possible solutions suggests patent ineligibility).[112] For example, programable calculators exist, as does computer programming itself. Rather, this is a very particular implementation in which user-selected operations are implemented within cells.

However, to bolster such a position, we could also via claim language make it clear that some sort of result is generated, so that, *as a whole*, the claim comprises an improvement over a spreadsheet generated by hand, for example, as follows:

EXAMPLE 5.9

I claim:

1. A method comprising: implementing a spreadsheet via a computer, including: determining contents of one or more cells thereof, based at least in part on one or more user-specified operations to be applied to signals and/or states to be provided as operands for the one or more user-specified operations; and generating output signals and/or states based at least in part on the determining, wherein the generating includes generating a report or a display that comprises at least a table portion or a sub-portion of the spreadsheet.

Now, it seems that it would be challenging to assert that a practical application with meaningful limits has *not* been claimed. Furthermore, if needed, more dependent claims could be used to flush out more application specific features. Thus, it would seem, we have successfully written or could successfully write a claim that is patent-eligible under the PTO guidance.

5.442 Medical Diagnostic Methods

After *Mayo*, claims directed to medical diagnosis became another area that had problems related to patent eligibility. Often, a diagnosis claim relates to measuring something, for example, regarding the human body, and making a diagnosis based on the measurement. Because the first part of the test asks whether the claim is directed to a judicial exception, these types of claims are

112. *See* McRO v. Bandai, 837 F.3d 1299 (Fed. Cir. 2016).

determined to be patent ineligible because ultimately this diagnosis at least in part based on a measurement of the human body is viewed as tantamount to claiming a law of nature.

The result has been the invalidation of patents claiming medical diagnostic methods that make use of commonly known laboratory and analytical techniques to diagnose naturally occurring physical phenomena, even where the diagnosis itself might be novel. That is, the measurement involves measuring something that occurs in nature and drawing a conclusion (e.g., making a diagnosis) based on a correlation of some sort between the measurement and a medical condition. Medical diagnostic patents might do better regarding eligibility by claiming innovative methods and/or practical applications, rather than the observation of biological or other physical effects using known techniques, not unlike the approach described earlier.

Specifically, courts have found that diagnostic method claims directed primarily to a correlation that exists in nature related to a natural phenomenon are not patent-eligible. A good example is the *Ariosa v. Sequenom* decision.[113] The federal circuit held that claims directed to a method of detecting fetal DNA in a mother's serum or plasma sample were patent-ineligible, as being directed to a natural phenomenon. The court acknowledged that the discovery of cell-free fetal DNA (cffDNA) present in a mother's circulating blood was a major scientific breakthrough; nonetheless, the claims were ultimately found to be primarily directed to a natural phenomenon—the presence of fetal DNA in a mother's serum or plasma. The claims recited conventional techniques for detecting the DNA. This, therefore, failed to transform the claims into patent eligible subject matter.

A *claiming approach to address this issue is to draft a claim that uses the measurement in a manner that is more than simply making a diagnosis*. For example, perhaps the measurement leads to a new and innovative *treatment* or perhaps the measurement leads to a new and innovative *preparation of a sample* of some sort. That is, the claim is drafted in a manner so that the claim does not amount to simply a law of nature or little more than a law of nature when viewing the elements and limitations either individually or as an ordered combination.

Analogously, as discussed previously with software, as just discussed, this means drafting the claim in a manner to show that the claim recites a technique that is identifiable, specific, technical, and innovative (e.g., concrete), meaning, here, that the claim is more than simply a diagnosis based upon a measurement.

113. 788 F.3d 1371 (Fed. Cir. 2015).

For example, some court decisions illustrate that method of treatment claims may be patent-eligible. For example, in *Vanda Pharmaceuticals v. West-Ward Pharmaceuticals*,[114] the claim at issue was directed to the *identification* of a genetic variant regarding individuals as poor metabolizers of a compound used to treat schizophrenia, and *administering* specific and different amounts of the compound to individuals, depending on whether they harbor the genetic variant. Thus, the administering the compound amounted to more than simply diagnosis and claiming a law of nature.

Similarly, in *Endo Pharmaceuticals v. Teva Pharmaceuticals*,[115] the claims were directed to treating pain in a renally impaired patient with a compound, in which the creatinine clearance rate of the patient was *measured*, and *a lower dosage of the compound was administered* to the patient, depending on the patient's clearance rate. The federal circuit found the claims at issue to be patent-eligible, as being directed to "a specific method of treatment for specific patients using a specific compound at specific doses to achieve a specific outcome."

Hence, a drafting technique here is to incorporate additional features related to treatment so that the claims represent practical applications of underlying natural phenomena. Again, this is similar to the approach, just discussed in the prior section, to draft the claim so that the claim covers a practical application in a manner that is identifiable, specific, technical, and innovative (e.g., concrete), as previously discussed.

More recently, the federal circuit, in *Illumina v. Arisa*,[116] deemed claims to be patent-eligible and distinguished them from the claims in *Ariosa v. Sequenom*. The court stated: "This is not a diagnostic case. And it is not a method of treatment case. It is a method of preparation case." Similar to our criteria regarding, identifiable, specific, technical, and innovative, the claims involved *specific processing* of size discrimination, *selecting* DNA fragments above a specified size threshold; and *physical* processing that *changed the composition* of the mixture, resulting in a DNA fraction different from that occurring naturally.

Thus, again, following the analogy with the software area, conventional techniques may be used in an unconventional approach. If the method a patent applicant seeks to protect uses conventional operations, for example, perhaps the claims may be tailored in a way to exploit a new observation or to generate a new result.

Some additional suggestions include, similar to preceding suggestions regarding the software illustrative example: focus the claims on actions (instead

114. 887 F.3d 1117 (Fed. Cir. 2018).
115. 919 F.3d 1347 (Fed. Cir. 2019).
116. 952 F.3d 1367 (Fed. Cir. 2020).

of correlations, for example); describe the method with specificity; focus the claims on the particular technology or systems at issue; and, in general, do not concede or state that an aspect of the claim is conventional or routine.

5.5 Have the Closest *Known* Prior Art in Mind when Drafting the Claims

As indicated previously, although you may have conducted a search, you may not know until sometime later (if ever) whether the art you have is, in fact, the closest; however, you should nonetheless treat the *known* art as if it is and draft the claims accordingly.

There is an interesting tension here between drafting broad claims while also not committing inequitable conduct. Inequitable conduct considerations have become complex. There are the ethical conduct rules that guide one's behavior in representing a client before the PTO[117] and there is also the

117. See 37 C.F.R. §§ 1.56, 1.57 (2022). Sections a and b of § 1.56 state:

(a) A patent by its very nature is affected with a public interest. The public interest is best served, and the most effective patent examination occurs when, at the time an application is being examined, the Office is aware of and evaluates the teachings of all information material to patentability. Each individual associated with the filing and prosecution of a patent application has a duty of candor and good faith in dealing with the Office, which includes a duty to disclose to the Office all information known to that individual to be material to patentability as defined in this section. The duty to disclose information exists with respect to each pending claim until the claim is cancelled or withdrawn from consideration, or the application becomes abandoned. Information material to the patentability of a claim that is cancelled or withdrawn from consideration need not be submitted if the information is not material to the patentability of any claim remaining under consideration in the application. There is no duty to submit information which is not material to the patentability of any existing claim. The duty to disclose all information known to be material to patentability is deemed to be satisfied if all information known to be material to patentability of any claim issued in a patent was cited by the Office or submitted to the Office in the manner prescribed by §§ 1.97(b)-(d) and 1.98. However, no patent will be granted on an application in connection with which fraud on the Office was practiced or attempted or the duty of disclosure was violated through bad faith or intentional misconduct. The Office encourages applicants to carefully examine:

(1) Prior art cited in search reports of a foreign patent office in a counterpart application, and

(2) The closest information over which individuals associated with the filing or prosecution of a patent application believe any pending claim patentably defines, to make sure that any material information contained therein is disclosed to the Office.

(b) Under this section, information is material to patentability when it is not cumulative to information already of record or being made of record in the application, and

defense of inequitable conduct because a patent may have been procured by fraud on the PTO.[118] The two are not identically the same, although there is a lot of overlap. For inequitable conduct to be committed, deliberate conduct is required. In general, under both, there is a duty to disclose information material to patentability.[119] It is even more complex in that there may also be antitrust implications,[120] which is yet something else, but which has overlap with inequitable conduct.

It is helpful to appreciate your ethical duty before the PTO is referred to as "the duty of candor."[121] That is, you are supposed to be "candid" with the examiner. Of course, a major tension exists between that duty and your duty of zealous advocacy. However, the rationale for a duty of "candor," which may not be present in other forums, is because patent prosecution is ex parte. That is, there is no zealous advocate on the other side pointing out all the arguments you omitted that suggest the claims should *not* be allowed. This is not to suggest you need to do the examiner's job for him, but you should appreciate how an objective third-party, such as a tribunal or court, may view your conduct before the PTO. It is important to not misstate, overstate, or mislead the examiner. Misstatements, overstatements, or misleading statements, once realized, should be corrected *on the record.*

It is important to not misstate, overstate, or mislead the examiner. Misstatements, overstatements, or misleading statements, once realized, should be corrected *on the record.*

---

(1) It establishes, by itself or in combination with other information, a prima facie case of unpatentability of a claim; or

(2) It refutes, or is inconsistent with, a position the applicant takes in:

(i) Opposing an argument of unpatentability relied on by the Office, or

(ii) Asserting an argument of patentability.

A prima facie case of unpatentability is established when the information compels a conclusion that a claim is unpatentable under the preponderance of evidence, burden-of-proof standard, giving each term in the claim its broadest reasonable construction consistent with the specification, and before any consideration is given to evidence which may be submitted in an attempt to establish a contrary conclusion of patentability.

118. *See, e.g.*, Therasense, Inc. v. Becton, Dickinson & Co., 649 F.3d 1276, 1290 (Fed. Cir. 2011) (en banc).

119. *See* 37 C.F.R. §§ 1.56, 1.57 (2022).

120. *See, e.g.*, Walker Process Equip., Inc. v. Food Mach. & Chem. Corp., 382 U.S. 172 (1965).

121. *See* 37 C.F.R. §§ 1.56, 1.57 (2022).

Therefore, while you might choose to take an aggressive posture and draft the broadest claims to the edge of the art in a 102/103 sense,[122] care is also warranted. It is true at least in theory that even a word difference in a claim may be sufficient to patentably distinguish an invention from the closest prior art. On the other hand, if the patent you get for a client ends up being litigated, you can be sure that the adversary will do *everything possible* to create an issue of fact that inequitable conduct was committed *somehow*.

Furthermore, it is not unusual for more *presently* valuable patentable technology to be only slightly ahead of the prior art. Thus, it is prudent to err here on the side of caution. Not only regarding the claims you present, but also regarding the prior art you disclose.

That is, review the claims with the inventors and quiz him, her, or them, regarding the closest *known* art. Also, make sure that it is understood that an examiner may combine art so that art may be *material* though standing alone it does not necessarily render the claims unpatentable.[123]

5.51 Understanding Potential Inequitable Conduct Issues: *Therasense*

To prevail on a claim of inequitable conduct in a patent case, as set forth in *Therasense*,[124] the accused infringer must prove by clear and convincing evidence that the patentee: (a) *knew* of the reference or prior commercial sale, etc., (b) *knew* that it was *material*, and (c) made a *deliberate* decision to withhold it. However, knowledge may be, and usually is, inferred from circumstantial evidence.[125] That is, typically, there is no direct evidence of a deliberate intent to deceive.

Therasense v. Becton, Dickinson[126] was decided en banc.[127] In general, two significant issues before and after *Therasense* that govern whether inequitable conduct has been committed relate to "materiality" and "intent." For example, if an applicant fails to disclose to the examiner, during prosecution of a patent application, prior art of which the applicant is aware, then inequitable conduct

122. *But see* section 1.31, discussing advantages and disadvantages of broad claims.

123. *See* 37 C.F.R. §§ 1.56, 1.57 (2022).

124. *See* Therasense, Inc. v. Becton, Dickinson & Co., 649 F.3d 1276, 1290 (Fed. Cir. 2011) (en banc).

125. *Id.*

126. 649 F.3d 1276 (Fed. Cir. 2011).

127. This means the 11 judges of the federal circuit heard the case, rather than the usual three-judge panel. Thus, the case has special precedential significance. Since it was heard by the 11-member court, the case can only be overturned by a decision of the U.S. Supreme Court (or, perhaps, a later en banc panel).

may be found if the prior art is determined to be *material to patentability* and if the failure to disclose the material prior art is *done with a specific intent to deceive the PTO.*

However, in *Therasense*, the majority raised the intent standard. It rejected a "sliding scale" approach previously employed in which balancing intent and materiality took place. It also adopting a "but-for" standard for materiality for many situations. Thus, the court stated in *Therasense*:

> This court holds that, as a general matter, the materiality required to establish inequitable conduct is but-for materiality. When an applicant fails to disclose prior art to the PTO, that prior art is but-for material if the PTO would not have allowed a claim had it been aware of the undisclosed prior art. Hence, in assessing the materiality of a withheld reference, **the court must determine whether the PTO would have allowed the claim if it had been aware of the undisclosed reference.** In making this patentability determination, the court should apply the preponderance of the evidence standard and give claims their broadest reasonable construction. *See* Manual of Patent Examining Procedure ('MPEP') §§706, 2111 (8th ed. Rev. 8, July 2010). (emphasis supplied)

The majority also provided an "exception" for *affirmative* egregious conduct, stating (emphasis supplied):

> Although but-for materiality generally must be proved to satisfy the materiality prong of inequitable conduct, **this court recognizes an exception in cases of affirmative egregious misconduct.** This exception to the general rule requiring but-for proof incorporates elements of the early unclean hands cases before the Supreme Court, which dealt with 'deliberately planned and carefully executed scheme[s]' to defraud the PTO and the courts. *Hazel-Atlas*, 322 U.S. at 245. When the patentee has engaged in affirmative acts of egregious misconduct, such as the filing of an unmistakably false affidavit, the misconduct is material. *See Rohm & Haas Co. v. Crystal Chem. Co.*, 722 F.2d 1556, 1571 (Fed. Cir. 1983) ('there is no room to argue that submission of false affidavits is not material'); *see also Refac Int'l, Ltd. v. Lotus Dev. Corp.*, 81 F.3d 1576, 1583 (Fed. Cir. 1996) (finding the intentional omission of declarant's employment with inventor's company rendered the affidavit false and that '[a]ffidavits are inherently material').

Thus, *Therasense* did away with balancing of intent and materiality. *The inequitable conduct elements of materiality and intent must each be evaluated independently. After* a patent challenger has established the underlying factual elements of materiality and intent, the district court must engage in an overall balancing of the evidence to determine whether the scales tilt to a conclusion that inequitable conduct occurred. If they do, the court will hold the patent unenforceable for inequitable conduct. *Thus, even if both materiality and intent are established by clear and convincing evidence, a court need not necessarily reach the conclusion that inequitable conduct occurred.*

The balancing comes *after both* elements of materiality and intent have been established by clear and convincing evidence. Once these proofs have been made, a district court must balance the facts as proven and the equities of the case to determine whether the severe penalty of unenforceability should be imposed.

Therasense also changed the intent requirement. A breach of a patent applicant's duty of disclosure to the USPTO, without more, does not establish the defense of inequitable conduct. *The party asserting the defense must establish that material information was withheld (or falsely submitted) with a specific intent to deceive the USPTO.* Each element must be established by clear and convincing evidence. In addition, when an inequitable conduct charge is based on an applicant's failure to disclose prior art to the USPTO, *clear and convincing evidence must show that the applicant made a* ***deliberate*** *decision* ***to withhold a known material reference.***

Thus, the "specific intent" called for by the federal circuit in *Therasense* mandates both *knowledge and deliberate action by the patent applicant.* When alleged inequitable conduct involves the withholding of prior art from the USPTO, an accused infringer *must prove by clear and convincing evidence* that *the applicant knew of the reference, knew that it was material, and made a deliberate decision to withhold it.*

Intent is generally inferred from the evidence because direct evidence is rarely available; nonetheless, even where intent is inferred, the inference must be based not only on sufficient evidence and be reasonable in light of that evidence, but *it must also be the single most reasonable inference able to be drawn from the evidence to meet the clear and convincing standard.* Thus, it is also worth noting that intent may *not* be inferred where there are multiple reasonable inferences that could be made. On this point, the federal circuit stated:

> We have . . . held that because direct evidence of deceptive intent is rarely available, such intent can be inferred from indirect and circumstantial evidence. . . . . But such evidence must still be clear and convincing, and inferences drawn from lesser evidence cannot satisfy the deceptive intent requirement. . . . **Further, the inference must not only be based on sufficient evidence and be reasonable in light of that evidence, but it must also be the single most reasonable inference able to be drawn from the evidence to meet the clear and convincing standard. *Scanner Techs. Corp. v. ICOS Vision Sys. Corp.*, 528 F.3d 1365, 1376 (Fed. Cir. 2008)**

('Whenever evidence proffered to show either materiality or intent is susceptible of multiple reasonable inferences, a district court clearly errs in overlooking one inference in favor of another equally reasonable inference.'). (emphasis supplied)

5.52 Do Not Draft Claims That Read on *Known* Prior Art

Knowingly submitting claims that read on the prior art violates one's ethical duties before the PTO, even if that prior art has been disclosed appropriately.[128] This should also be considered an example of an affirmative act of egregious misconduct because you are representing that you believe the claim is patentable when you know that the claim reads on prior art.[129]

Of course, it must be done knowingly. However, state of mind is inferred from the circumstances.[130] Is a jury likely to believe it was done inadvertently? In other words, taking an aggressive posture as an advocate may be warranted, but be careful not to take an *overly* aggressive posture.[131]

> In other words, taking an aggressive posture as an advocate may be warranted, but be careful not to take an *overly* aggressive posture. . . . One way to do this is to review the broadest claims and make sure that you have *reasonable* arguments that distinguish the claim from the closest *known* art under sections 102 *and* 103.

One way to do this is to review the broadest claims and make sure that you have *reasonable* arguments that distinguish the claim from the closest *known* art under sections 102 *and* 103. If it turns out the claims read on prior art *not* known by you or the inventors, no violation has occurred. In fact, if a claim issues that later is found to read on prior art that was *not* known to you, the inventors and the examiner, the claim may be invalid, but again, no

128. *See* 37 C.F.R. §§ 1.56, 1.57 (2022).

129. *See* Therasense, Inc. v. Becton, Dickinson & Co., 649 F.3d 1276, 1290 (Fed. Cir. 2011) (en banc).

130. *Id.*

131. In general, the underlying principle is to not let your client's problem become your problem.

inequitable conduct is present. Furthermore, until proven to be invalid, once issued, the claim is presumed valid.

Thus, the sin is not obtaining a patent with invalid claims, but rather having done so by not disclosing known, material art and/or by knowingly (or perhaps more accurately, by deliberately) submitting a claim that reads on known prior art. Appreciate, again, that for a violation the prior art must be *known*. An analogy may be helpful here. Suppose you are putting your house on the market for sale. Suppose it has the original roof. You may wonder if the roof should be replaced. However, at this point, other than the fact that it is the original roof, that is, other than pure speculation, you have no reason to believe it needs to be replaced. So, you have nothing to disclose about it to a perspective buyer other than it is the original roof, which should be apparent from your realtor's documents and disclosures.

However, suppose on your own initiative, you have a roofer come look at the roof before you put your house on the market and he tells you the roof is damaged and in need of significant repair or in need of replacement. Now, if you do not tell this to a perspective buyer, you have committed common law fraud. Inequitable conduct is a type of common law fraud committed before the PTO.

Thus, if you submit a broad claim and, for example, have not performed a search, though you may wonder why the claimed subject matter has not been done before, if that is merely speculation, and you otherwise have no reason to believe it has been done previously, then you have breached no duty. That is, you have not committed inequitable conduct. On the other hand, if you or the inventors know of material art that you or they deliberately withhold because of concern that the examiner may not allow the broad claims or if your claim *deliberately* reads on prior art you are submitting (and perhaps you believe the examiner will not look closely enough at the submitted art to appreciate it), then you have committed inequitable conduct.

Generally, most lawyers are not about to commit inequitable conduct. Why should they? It's the client's invention and they get paid whether the patent issues or not. So, how is it that inequitable conduct is asserted in so many litigations? It is advocacy by the attorneys representing the defendant/alleged infringer. Therefore, it is important in your conduct before the PTO to consider borderline situations that someone may later assert was deliberately withholding material prior art or deliberately submitting a claim that reads on a known reference. In general, err on the side of caution by submitting more rather than less prior art. Of course, there have also been a few cases of inequitable conduct with allegations around *deliberately burying a material reference* in a lot of submitted prior art, but such cases are quite rare and in balancing the risk, are not worth the worry.

> In general, err on the side of caution by submitting more rather than less prior art.

5.53 Have a Good Faith Argument to Patentably Distinguish the Broadest Claims

As previously indicated, having a good faith argument for patentably distinguishing the claimed invention under sections 102 and 103 from prior art known at the time of filing is a good practice. One advantage of doing this is that it forces the drafter to rigorously determine whether the claims being submitted are either too narrow or too broad.

> As previously indicated, having a good faith argument for patentably distinguishing the claimed invention under sections 102 and 103 from prior art known at the time of filing is a good practice. One advantage of doing this is that it forces the drafter to rigorously determine whether the claims being submitted are either too narrow or too broad.

A review with the inventors would be a good idea. This may accomplish several things. It will assist you in determining that you have successfully formulated appropriately distinguishing technical arguments. It should also potentially ferret out prior art that may not have come up previously that you would be better off disclosing to the PTO. Seeing the words of the claim and how it could be interpreted tends to trigger the inventors' minds in new ways. That is, the language of the claims tends to assist the inventors in seeing their invention in a way perhaps not fully appreciated previously, potentially leading to additional prior art to be disclosed. *On this point, consider that a patent is stronger if closer prior art is considered during examination.* Thus, while we are not necessarily recommending that a search needs to be performed,[132] it is

132. *See* section 1.32, discussing advantages and disadvantages of performing a search.

important to disclose all the *known* art that is material at the time of patent application filing.

Another advantage of a review with the inventors, consistent with the preceding point regarding a rigorous review of the claims, is that it may uncover deficiencies in claim scope. For example, it would be a good idea to ask the inventors about potential design around opportunities[133] to see if the claim may be modified to cover those situations.

5.6 Avoid Drafting Claims in a Manner That Leaves the Statutory Class Unclear

This principle has been previously discussed and not adhering to it may lead to an indefinite claim. In these sections, we consider this and additional reasons to follow this principle.

5.61 Avoid Apparatus-Type Limitations in Method Claims and Avoid Method-Type Limitations in Apparatus Claims

Method claims may, if well-drafted, provide one possible advantage over apparatus claims in that the subject matter of the claim may be covered quite broadly using method language, whereas apparatus claims tend to include more specific limitations that are often narrower. This may be because, in many instances, method elements tend to be more functional in nature.[134] Consider, for example, a corkscrew. To claim the apparatus, one may need to be rather specific in describing particular elements, such as the screw itself. However, a method claim directed to its operation may be broader since it may simply recite "attaching securely" to the wine cork or some similar broad characterization, and then "applying a force" to remove the cork.

For this reason alone, it is recommended that apparatus limitations in method claims be avoided as much as possible. Including such limitations ultimately undermines the potential breadth of using method claims. *Hence, the principle previously articulated, to attempt to include <u>only</u> those apparatus limitations needed to perform the claimed method.*

---

133. *See* section 6.5 and its subsections, discussing addressing potential design around opportunities.

134. *See* discussion in sections 2.112 and 4.126 and related subsections.

Of course, it is not always easy to remove the apparatus limitations and still have a claim that is distinguishable from the art; nonetheless, it is certainly worth the effort to try. It may be surprising how much we tend to let apparatus limitations slip into such claims when they are either unnecessary or may, with only modest effort, be drafted around. It generally requires focusing on what the apparatus does functionally and how it operates, rather than its structure. As an intermediate step, for example, it might be helpful to first try to draft a means plus function claim to the apparatus.

> It is recommended that apparatus limitations in method claims be avoided as much as possible. Including such limitations ultimately undermines the potential breadth of using method claims.

As a reminder, since we are discussing method claims, in addition to the overuse of apparatus-type limitations, there are other pitfalls associated with the use of method claims. For example, it is important to avoid embedding an implied order in the elements of the claim unless that order is intended and is necessary. Black letter law dictates that the elements of a method claim do not need to be performed in a particular order to infringe the claim, unless the order is expressly or impliedly included in the claim.

Consider, for example, baking a cake:

A method of baking a cake comprising:
placing dry ingredients together in a container;
mixing wet ingredients together with the dry ingredients in the container to produce batter;
pouring the batter from the container into a baking pan;
heating the baking pan holding the batter until the batter solidifies and rises.

As is apparent in this simple example, the claim appears to require that the dry ingredients be mixed before the wet ingredients. This may be the most logical order, the natural order, or the preferred order; however, it is probably not necessary that it be done in this order to bake the cake. Therefore, it is important to make sure and draft such a claim so that this order is not necessary, at least in the broadest claim. For example, the placing and mixing operations may be combined in one action or the first action may be omitted entirely, as follows.

A method of baking a cake comprising:
mixing wet ingredients together with dry ingredients in a container to produce batter;
pouring the batter from the container into a baking pan;
heating the baking pan holding the batter until the batter solidifies and rises.

It is important to avoid embedding an implied order in the elements of the claim unless that order is actually intended and is necessary.

Also, as a reminder regarding method claims, it is also wise when employing method claims to not overlook other related method claiming opportunities. For example, it is important to be aware that a method claim can cover a new use for an old device or apparatus.[135] For example, a new use for a composition of matter, or a new application of a known circuit may be claimed.

Likewise, when preparing a method claim, it is always worth considering whether a subset of what it being claimed might be independently patentable. For example, if a method of manufacturing a plastic coating is being claimed, it may include a novel method of annealing that is independent of the overall manufacturing process. Therefore, both could be independently claimed as patentable inventions.

Also, it is helpful to be cognizant that 35 USC section 271(g) provides potential foreign coverage for methods that are performed abroad if the product produced is imported into the United States. This section provides the ability to sue a foreign competitor in the United States that may be manufacturing the patented invention abroad[136] using a patented process. Therefore, you may be well advised to include such method claims in an application where foreign competitors are known to exist.

135. *See* section 4.1262, discussing claiming a new use of an old device.
136. *See* sections 4.1252 and 4.127 and their subsections, discussing 271(g).

It is important to be aware that a method claim can cover a new use for an old device or apparatus. Likewise, when preparing a method claim, it is always worth considering whether a subset of what it being claimed might be independently patentable. Also, it is helpful to be cognizant that 35 USC section 271(g) provides potential foreign coverage for manufacturing methods that are performed abroad if the product produced is imported into the United States.

Just as apparatus-type limitations should be avoided with method claims, also method-type limitations should be avoided with apparatus claims. One advantage that apparatus claims have over method claims is that the subject matter of the claim does not need to be in operation to infringe. To be more specific, apparatus claims potentially cover making, using, selling, offering to sell, or importing the claimed invention. However, in addition to creating a risk of indefiniteness, including method-type limitations may undermine the ability to capture this broad set of rights by narrowing scope unnecessarily.[137] The case *IPXL v. Amazon* is a good example regarding how mixing statutory classes may create indefiniteness.

In addition to creating a risk of indefiniteness, including method-type limitations may undermine the ability to capture a broad set of rights by narrowing scope unnecessarily.

5.611 *IPXL v. Amazon* Decision

IPXL v. Amazon involved a suit against Amazon for infringing the claims of a patent owned by IPXL Holdings. The district court found the claims at issue not infringed and invalid. Some claims were held to be invalid as anticipated but claim 25 was held invalid as being indefinite.

137. *Cf.* INVT SPE LLC v. HTC, Appeal No. 20-1903 (Fed. Cir. Aug. 31, 2022) (distinguishing between actual operation and capability of operating or performing for apparatus claims, particularly for software on a device, which tends to be functional, without discussing indefiniteness issue of mixing method and apparatus limitations), discussed in sections 4.124 and 4.1272.

IPXL appealed the decision and the federal circuit affirmed as to invalidity and, therefore, did not reach the issue of noninfringement. Regarding claim 25, in particular, the court stated (emphasis supplied):

> The district court found that claim 25 is indefinite under 35 U.S.C. § 112, as it attempts to claim both a system and a method for using that system. Section 112, paragraph 2, requires that the claims of a patent "particularly point out and distinctly claim the subject matter which the applicant regards as his invention." 35 U.S.C. § 112 (2000). A claim is considered indefinite if it does not reasonably apprise those skilled in the art of its scope. *Amgen, Inc. v. Chugai Pharm. Co.*, 927 F.2d 1200, 1217 (Fed. Cir. 1991).
>
> Whether a single claim covering both an apparatus and a method of use of that apparatus is invalid is an issue of first impression in this court. The Board of Patent Appeals and Interferences ("Board") of the PTO, however, has made it clear that reciting both an apparatus and a method of using that apparatus renders a claim indefinite under section 112, paragraph 2. *Ex parte Lyell*, 17 USPQ2d 1548 (1990). As the Board noted in *Lyell*, "the statutory class of invention is important in determining patentability and infringement." *Id.* at 1550 (*citing In re Kuehl*, 475 F.2d 658, 665 (1973); *Rubber Co. v. Goodyear*, 9 Wall. 788, 76 U.S. 788, 796, 19 L.Ed. 566 (1869)). The Board correctly surmised that, as a result of the combination of two separate statutory classes of invention, a manufacturer or seller of the claimed apparatus would not know from the claim whether it might also be liable for contributory infringement because a buyer or user of the apparatus later performs the claimed method of using the apparatus. *Id.* Thus, such a claim "is not sufficiently precise to provide competitors with an accurate determination of the 'metes and bounds' of protection involved" and is "ambiguous and properly rejected" under section 112, paragraph 2. *Id.* at 1550-51. This rule is well recognized and has been incorporated into the PTO's Manual of Patent Examination Procedure. § 2173.05(p)(II) (1999) ("A single claim which claims both an apparatus and the method steps of using the apparatus is indefinite under 35 U.S.C. 112, second paragraph."); *see also* Robert C. Faber, Landis on Mechanics of Patent Claim Drafting § 60A (2001) ("Never mix claim types to different classes of invention in a single claim.").
>
> **Claim 25 recites both the system of claim 2 and a method for using that system.** The claim reads:
>
>> The system of claim 2 [including an input means] wherein the predicted transaction information comprises both a transaction type and transaction parameters associated with that transaction type, and the user uses the input means to either change the predicted transaction information or accept the displayed transaction type and transaction parameters.
>
> '055 patent, col. 22, ll. 8-13 (emphasis added).

> **Thus, it is unclear whether infringement of claim 25 occurs when one creates a system that allows the user to change the predicted transaction information or accept the displayed transaction, or whether infringement occurs when the user actually uses the input means to change transaction information or uses the input means to accept a displayed transaction. Because claim 25 recites both a system and the method for using that system, it does not apprise a person of ordinary skill in the art of its scope, and it is invalid under section 112, paragraph 2.**

IPXL was followed in later federal circuit and district court cases.[138]

5.612 Illustrative Claim Examples

In this example, we demonstrate reducing hardware limitations for a method claim. Following are two method claims previously provided. Furthermore, the method claims even take different approaches to handling the apparatus limitations.[139] However, the scope is somewhat similar to the apparatus claim discussed in the sections of this chapter addressing component and system claims.[140] This might be considered a weakness here because these claims are not taking full advantage of the opportunity to use a method claim to capture greater scope than an apparatus claim.

EXAMPLE 5.10

I claim:

1. A method of operating an RF module comprising at least one integrated circuit chip, the method comprising:

   inputting an RF signal and one or more control signals to the RF module;

   outputting an RF signal from the RF module;

   controlling, based at least in part on the one or more control signals, a silicon on insulator (SOI) N-type metal oxide semiconductor (NMOS) field effect transistor (FET) series connected stack configuration to either an OFF state or an ON state, the SOI NMOS

138. *See* Microprocessor Enhancement Corp. v. Texas Instruments Inc., 520 F.3d 1367 (Fed. Cir. 2008); Lecat's Ventriloscope v. MT Tool & Mfg., 351 F. Supp. 3d 1100 (N.D. Ill. 2018).

139. *See* section 4.126 and its subsections, discussing method of using claims.

140. *See* sections 4.121, 4.122 and related subsections, discussing component and system level claims.

FET stack configuration, comprising a plurality of NMOS FET transistors, being implemented on the at least one integrated circuit chip; and

electrically biasing, based at least in part on the one or more control signals, a body of at least one NMOS FET transistor of the plurality of NMOS FET transistors of the SOI NMOS FET stack configuration with a bias voltage substantially more negative than ground during at least a portion of the OFF state of the at least one NMOS FET transistor.

I claim:

1. A method of operating a module, the module including at least one integrated circuit chip comprising a plurality of N-type metal oxide semiconductor (NMOS) field effect transistors in a series connected stack configuration that comprises at least one NMOS field effect transistor including a body, the at least one NMOS field effect transistor either to pass an RF signal in an enable state or to not pass the RF signal in a disable state, the method further comprising:

electrically biasing the body of the at least one NMOS field effect transistor of the module in the disable state to have a voltage level substantially more negative than the lowest voltage level of the following: ground, a DC voltage level of a source of the at least one NMOS field effect transistor of the module, and a DC voltage level of a drain of the at least one NMOS field effect transistor of the module.

Here, however, is another claim, demonstrating a method claim with fewer hardware limitations and, thus, greater scope.

EXAMPLE 5.11

I claim:

1. A method of reducing nonlinearity for an analog signal comprising:

passing the analog signal through at least one N-type metal oxide semiconductor field effect transistor (NMOSFET) in the ON state; and negatively biasing a body of at least another NMOSFET in an OFF state to reduce the nonlinearity of the analog signal, the at least another NMOSFET proximate to the at least one NMOSFET.

This claim has stripped the claimed subject matter to bare essentials. The only hardware limitations relate to the two NMOSFETs. Likewise, the actions are "passing" and "negatively biasing." Also, appreciate that here the technology is quite intimately tied to hardware. That is, it is difficult to claim the technology without at least reciting the two NMOSFETs. Still, this claim significantly reduces the hardware limitations, resulting in a much broader claim. We also could write the claim so that the hardware is in the preamble, but this would not seem to "buy" much since, again, the transistors need to be mentioned in the actions performed.

Following is a simple example of reducing method language for an apparatus claim. It is easy to see in this example how method language may inadvertently find its way into an apparatus claim, which, again, may be quite risky, as demonstrated by the *IPXL* case. The italicized language has a risk of making the claim indefinite or limiting claim scope since it may be interpreted to suggest that the circuit is operating rather than being capable of operating.

EXAMPLE 5.12

I claim:

1. An apparatus comprising:

   a bandgap circuit;

   the bandgap circuit *producing a fixed voltage*, the fixed voltage *corresponding* to the bandgap.

A better approach would be:

EXAMPLE 5.13

I claim:

1. An apparatus comprising:

a bandgap circuit;

the bandgap circuit *being capable of producing a fixed voltage*, the fixed voltage *to correspond* to the bandgap.

Or, perhaps, even more simply:

---

1. An apparatus comprising:

   a bandgap circuit;

   the bandgap circuit *to produce a fixed voltage*, the fixed voltage *to correspond* to the bandgap.

Here, the claim is drafted to make it clear that the circuit is not operating, but, rather, that the circuit has the capability of operating in a particular manner.[141]

5.7 Skip Some Intermediate Dependent Claims for Greater Diversity

This addresses the situation where every patent claim in a claim set is dependent from the immediately prior claim. More specifically, claim 2 depends from claim 1, claim 3 depends from claim 2, claim 4 depends from claim 3, and so on. Example 5.5 of Chapter 5 illustrates it perfectly, which is one reason why it is also recommended that the system integration approach to dependent claims not be relied upon exclusively. One way to remember this principle is to avoid the problem of "the house that jack built." In other words, avoid claiming in perfect sequence, similar to an approach for building a house, for example, after the foundation, add floors; after the floors, add walls; after the walls, add a ceiling, after the ceiling, add a roof, and so on.

It is recommended that you avoid this approach primarily as a diversified strategy to claim drafting. Suppose, for example, that one of the intermediate

141. *See* INVT SPE LLC v. HTC, Appeal No. 20-1903 (Fed. Cir. Aug. 31, 2022) (distinguishing between actual operation and capability of operating or performing for apparatus claims), discussed in sections 4.124 and 4.1272.

claims in the chain has a problem that either makes it easy to avoid infringement or that makes the claim invalid for reasons not related to art (so that additional narrowing of the claim may not make it valid). In these circumstances, all the remaining claims may suffer from the same difficulty and, therefore, lose their value to the patentee. If claims are written so that not every claim is dependent from all the prior claims, the risk is reduced that a problem with a prior claim will "infect" the remaining claims.

> If claims are written so that not every claim is dependent from all the prior claims, the risk is reduced that a problem with a prior claim will "infect" the remaining claims.

5.8 Avoid Sloppy Drafting Practices

There are innumerable sloppy techniques for drafting claims. The problem, of course, is that sloppiness increases the potential for problems when interpreting claims, potentially resulting in noninfringement or, perhaps, invalidity, such as for indefiniteness.

In 2014, the U.S. Supreme Court issued a decision changing the standard used to determine whether claims are indefinite. This standard should be kept in mind when preparing patent claims. In *Nautilus, Inc. v. Biosig Instruments, Inc.*,[142] the new standard for indefiniteness became "failing to inform those of ordinary skill regarding the scope of the claim with reasonable certainty." The Court stated:

> In place of the "insolubly ambiguous" standard, we hold that a patent is invalid for indefiniteness if its claims, read in light of the specification delineating the patent, and the prosecution history, fail to inform, with reasonable certainty, those skilled in the art about the scope of the invention.

The Court's holding affects whether the claims particularly point out and distinctly claim the invention, as required by statute.

A few of the more common sloppiness problems are discussed next.

142. 134 S. Ct. 2120 (2014).

5.81 Double Inclusion

One common problem is referred to as "double inclusion." This refers to including the same element in a claim twice under two different names. For example,

---

1. An apparatus comprising:

   a bottle having a neck with a cylindrical-shaped opening; and a cork stopper sized to fit securely within the cylindrical-shaped opening.

2. The apparatus of claim 1, and further comprising:

   means for corking the cylindrical-shaped opening.

As should be apparent, this is likely to create difficulties of various sorts, most likely invalidity for indefiniteness. For example, is the "cork stopper" of claim 1 the "means for corking" of claim 2?

> One common problem is referred to as "double inclusion." This refers to including the same element in a claim twice under two different names.

5.82 Singular and Plural Elements

Another example of sloppy claim drafting relates to whether claim elements are plural or singular. It is wise to take care and ensure that singular and plural elements are *only* used where appropriate in claim language. Sometimes a specification may include boilerplate language directed to this issue.[143]

Realize that a plural claim element may provide a wonderful noninfringement argument where the particular element is singular in the accused product.[144] This may seem like a simple point; however, consider the case,

143. *See* Appendix B, providing an example of sample patent application boilerplate.

144. *See* Apple Inc. v. MPH Techs. Oy, 28 F.4th 254 (Fed. Cir. 2022) (a plural term is presumed to refer to two or more absent a clear disclosure to the contrary).

Superior Fireplace v. Majestic Products.[145] This case may be an example of a patent attorney's worst nightmare.

Another example of sloppy claim drafting relates to singular and plural elements. It is wise to take care and ensure that singular and plural elements are *only* used where appropriate in claim language. A plural claim element may provide a wonderful noninfringement argument where the particular element is singular in the accused product.

The invention related to a fireplace, and the submitted claims included a reference to a firebox with a "rear wall." During prosecution, the attorney and the examiner had several interviews which resulted in amendment of the claims. Although it appears from the record that the portion of the claim relating to the "rear wall" had not specifically been amended by Superior, nonetheless, due to an examiner's amendment, an "s" was inserted, resulting in issued claims that referred to "rear walls" rather than "rear wall." After suing Majestic on the patent, Superior submitted a certificate of correction to make the term singular, as had been originally intended, and the PTO issued the certificate. However, the federal circuit declared the certificate of correction invalid, as having broadened the claim, something that may only occur through a broadening reissue within two years of patent issuance. In this case, the correction was more than two years after patent issuance.[146] Thus, Superior was stuck with the plural "rear walls," which, of course, in this case, the accused product did not meet.

5.83 Redundant Terms

Redundancy in claims often happens; however, this is also some small risk at least that redundancy may lead to interpretation issues. "Double inclusion" discussed earlier is one type of redundancy; however, it is not the only example. For example, it is not uncommon to see the following formulation in a patent claim: "a receiver for receiving signals." On its face, perhaps this formulation might be harmless; however, It would be better if, instead, this element had been recited as: "a signal receiver."

145. 270 F.3d 1358 (Fed. Cir. 2001).

146. The certificate of correction was filed and issued after the two-year deadline for a broadening reissue.

In addition, a current concern when drafting claims is to avoid unintentionally invoking 35 USC section 112(f). Current federal circuit law indicates it is possible for a claim to be interpreted under this provision even without express use of the word "means" in the claim. If this occurs, the claim typically receives a narrower interpretation.

The former claim language, reciting "a receiver for receiving signals," thus, would probably be an example in which an opponent, hoping for a narrow construction, would attempt to argue that section 112(f) should apply, based at least on its similarity to "means for receiving signals" arguing that if this had been intended to be structure, the language "signal receiver" would have been used; whereas, the formulation "receiver for receiving" implies function. Of course, a court may not necessarily apply section 112(f) to interpret such language, if it were argued; nonetheless, good practice suggests that it would be better to avoid the risk. Thus, this is another reason to avoid the formulation "receiver for receiving signals." On the other hand, if the intent is to invoke section 112(f), then perhaps it would be better to recite: "means for receiving signals," rather than "a receiver for receiving signals," making the intention clearer.

5.84 Lack of Antedecent Basis

Another common problem is lack of antecedent basis. This is not always a problem, depending on the context. There are federal circuit cases that state that lack of antecedent basis does not *necessarily* make a claim indefinite.[147] For example, elements that are considered inherent are often recited without creating antecedent basis, but this should not create an indefiniteness issue. Nonetheless, out of an abundance of caution, it seems wise to provide antecedent basis rather than make a claim susceptible to an indefiniteness argument.

For example, consider:

---

1. An apparatus comprising:

   a bandgap circuit;

   the bandgap circuit to produce a fixed voltage, the fixed voltage to correspond to the size of the bandgap.

---

147. *See, e.g.*, Bose Corp. v. JBL, Inc., 274 F.3d 1354, 1359 (Fed. Cir. 2001); Slimfold Mfg. Co. v. Kinkead Indus., Inc., 810 F.2d 1113, 1117 (Fed. Cir. 1987).

See section 2.1411.

Here, no formal antecedent basis for "size" was provided. Nonetheless, there is probably no harm or ambiguity because it is inherent that a bandgap has a particular size. However, in other circumstances, failing to provide antecedent basis can create problems. For example,

---

1. An apparatus comprising:

   a cylindrical-shaped container including an opening at an end of the cylindrical-shaped container.

2. The apparatus of claim 1, wherein the opening at the other end includes a cover.

Again, the potential issues should be apparent. Claim 2 may not necessarily be indefinite despite the lack of antecedent basis for "the opening at the other end," but why take the risk?

> Another common problem is lack of antecedent basis.

5.85 Inconsistent Use of "Said" or "The"

Another problem similar in kind to the preceding examples is the inconsistent use of "the" and "said" in connection with a claim element. It is probably best to choose one (that is, either use "the" or use "said") and stick with it throughout the claims. Otherwise, an opponent may argue that these refer to two different elements rather than the same element, potentially creating indefiniteness. *We generally recommend using "the" throughout.*

Some practitioners profess to prefer using "the" so that a patent claim is easier to be understood by a lay person, such as members of a jury, for example. However, some prefer "said" due to its historical roots.

Here, however, "the" is recommended over "said" for a different reason. For a set of claims with dependencies, especially during a prosecution that may have many months (or even years) between office action responses, it becomes surprisingly easy to inadvertently intermix the use of "said" with "the" potentially raising difficult and undesired questions of interpretation.

> Another problem similar in kind to the preceding examples is the inconsistent use of "the" and "said" in connection with a claim element. It is probably best to choose one and stick with it throughout the claims. . . . We generally recommend using "the" throughout.

5.86 Inconsistent Use of Term Modifiers

Another common situation of sloppy drafting is improperly adding a modifier. For example,

---

1. An apparatus comprising:

   a container and a platform;

   wherein the container is attached to the platform.

2. The apparatus of claim 1, wherein the circular platform is capable of rotating.

From these claims, we can infer that the platform in claim 1 is circular; however, again, this sloppy drafting may leave this open to interpretation if an opponent wished to challenge that construction. Perhaps claim 1 is intended to be broader than having a circular platform. Hence, this is a good case for finding indefiniteness. Sometimes this is referred to as inferential claiming, although not all inferential claiming should necessarily be avoided.[148]

> Another common situation of sloppy drafting is improperly adding a modifier.

148. *See* section 2.1413, discussing inferential claiming.

5.87 Sloppy Use of Conjunctions and Disjunctions

We previously discussed issues related to use of "and" versus "or."[149] It is quite important to review claims and make sure the proper language is employed. Often, this issue is addressed at least partially with patent application boilerplate.[150] However, even with application boilerplate, there are situations that may trip up a patent claim drafter.

As one example, the following claim would be interpreted in a manner so that it would be probably not be infringed:

> An apparatus comprising: a substance including a halogen comprising at least one of the following: Chlorine, Fluorine, and Iodine.

The reason is because the use of "and" indicates the substance must include all three halogens.[151] Again, for such situations, it is not uncommon to see boilerplate in the specification to assist in addressing the issue. Here, it is recommended to, in general, use "and/or" in claims except where it makes no sense and to address this in the specification.[152] For example, language such as the following may be employed in the specification:

Unless otherwise indicated, in the context of the present patent application, the term "or" if used to associate a list, such as A, B, or C, is intended to mean A, B, and C, here used in the inclusive sense, as well as A, B, or C, here used in the exclusive sense. With this understanding, "and" is used in the inclusive sense and intended to mean A, B, and C; whereas "and/or" can be used in an abundance of caution to make clear that all of the foregoing meanings are intended, although such usage is not required.[153]

Thus, the claim could be written:

> An apparatus comprising: a substance including a halogen comprising at least one of the following: Chlorine, Fluorine and/or Iodine.

5.9 Employ Simple and Well-Established Drafting Principles

Some simple, easy to follow principles of claim drafting you may already know. In general, these are simply rules for good writing, such as to be terse, precise, revise often, and follow the rules of grammar.

149. *See* section 4.129 and its subsections.
150. *See* Appendix B, providing sample patent application boilerplate.
151. *See* Superguide v. Direct TV, 358 F.3d 870 (Fed. Cir. 2004).
152. *See* Appendix B, providing sample patent application boilerplate.
153. *See* Ex Parte Gross (PTAB 2014) (approving use of "and/or" in patent claims).

5.91 Be Terse

Fewer words provide fewer limitations, meaning claims are usually broader. Furthermore, wordiness in claims gives more language for an opponent to attack as indefinite, not supported or not infringed. It may also make the claim more cumbersome and harder to follow. Therefore, as in writing ordinary prose, wordiness is discouraged.

5.92 Be Precise

The importance of being precise when drafting patent claims cannot be understated. Remember the guidance: a good claim is an appropriate balance between precision, breadth, and ambiguity. Precise language is critical to good claim drafting.

Imprecise language usually follows from imprecise thinking about the invention. Therefore, precise language forces the claim drafter to be more precise in his or her thinking. Of course, at times, there may be a tension between being precise and being terse. This is where experience in claim drafting and the principles we have discussed (or will discuss) are intended to assist.

However, being precise does not imply or mean being narrow. It is important to realize this distinction. People often confuse vagueness with breadth; however, claim language may be broad and still be precise. Here is a simple example: all wirelessly transmitted signals. The language is precise as to what is included, while also being quite broad.

A good example of imprecise claim drafting are the claims in *Hewlett Packard v. Pitney Bowes.*[154] The invention related to laser printing technology in which beams of light were applied to photoreceptors to form areas of discharge. The areas of discharge then attracted toner. However, the claims *inconsistently* referred to a "spot." In some cases, "spot" in the claims referred to a spot formed by the beam of light and, in other cases, "spot" in the claims referred to the area of discharge formed. The claims at issue in the case were:

---

1. A method of producing on a photoreceptor an image of generated shapes made up of spots, comprising:

   directing a plurality of beams of light towards a photoreceptor, each beam of light generating a spot on the photoreceptor and controlling a parameter of the light beams to produce spots of different sizes

154. 182 F.3d 1298 (Fed. Cir. 1999).

whereby the appearance of smoothed edges are given to the generated shapes.

2. The method of claim 1 wherein the parameter controlled is light beam intensity.
3. Apparatus for producing on a photoreceptor an image of generated shapes made up of spots, comprising:

   means for directing a plurality of beams of light toward a photoreceptor to generating [sic] a plurality of spots on the photoreceptor and means for generating spots of different sizes whereby the appearance of smoothed edges are given to the generated shapes.

The meaning of "spot" became a hotly contested issue in litigation. Depending on whether "spot" was interpreted in the claims to refer to a spot formed by the beam of light or to refer to an area of discharge formed affected whether there was infringement.

Tremendous amounts of time and money were spent debating this interpretive issue. Ultimately, the case settled without trial. It is fair to say that a more precisely worded claim would probably have affected how this case ultimately was resolved.

Likewise, federal circuit law is relatively clear that vague words used in the claims require resort to the specification for interpretation. This is more likely to narrow the claim rather than broaden it, *unless* the vague word or words have been carefully defined in the specification to have a broad meaning based on forethought. For example, many cases are to the same effect as *Johnson Worldwide*,[155] which states:

> Our case law demonstrates two situations where a sufficient reason exists to require the entry of a definition of a claim term other than its ordinary and accustomed meaning. The first arises if the patentee has chosen to be his or her own lexicographer by clearly setting forth an explicit definition for a claim term. [citations omitted] The second is where the term or terms chosen by the patentee so deprive the claim of clarity that there is no means by which the scope of the claim may be ascertained from the language used.

---

155. 175 F.3d at 990.

In other words, it is better if claims are drafted so that resort to the specification to provide a meaning other than the ordinary and customary meaning occurs when it is intended, that is to provide a clearly set forth meaning.

5.93 Write and Revise

New or relatively inexperienced attorneys often have the most problems beginning a set of claims. Partly for this reason, it is recommended, rather than spending a *significant* amount of time *thinking* about *precisely* how to word a claim to an invention, to, instead, put something on paper sooner and spend the additional time revising it.

This, in essence, gives you a "working document." People often find it easier to revise something, though not completely thought out, than to create something. This approach will make it easier to separate the process of creation from the process of critiquing. Trying to create *and* critique in your head in one step is more likely to inhibit your writing, rather than make the process proceed more quickly.

> It is recommended, rather than spending a *significant* amount of time *thinking* about *precisely* how to claim the invention, to, instead, put something on paper sooner and spend the additional time revising it.

5.94 Follow Rules of Grammar

The final simple rule is an important one. Endeavor to follow the rules of good grammar. This may seem like a challenge given how claims are constructed. Typically, claims violate a basic rule of grammar because a claim looks a lot like a run-on sentence. However, aside from that, because a claim is, in effect, a sentence starting with "I claim," "We claim," or something similar and ending in a period, generally rules of grammar should be followed to avoid creating interpretive ambiguities. For example, a clause of a claim should have a subject, a verb, and potentially an object.

Good grammar is what judges, especially those less familiar with reading claims, would expect. To the extent that rules of grammar (and punctuation) are not followed, it may either lead to an unexpected interpretation or to indefiniteness in an extreme case.

To the extent that rules of grammar (and punctuation) are not followed, it may either lead to an unexpected interpretation or to indefiniteness in an extreme case.

6

Advanced PCDP

High-Level Principles of This Chapter:[1]

- Draft claims in anticipation of the first office action and in light of expected obviousness arguments;
- Review the claims in light of the Broadest Reasonable Interpretation (BRI);
- Use the dependent claims to establish fallback positions in addition to claim differentiation;
- Draft claims to cover a variety of potential infringers;
- Draft claims in a manner to avoid covering multiple independent parties acting together (i.e., make sure the claims have a single direct infringer);
- Use the dependent claims to cover higher levels of product integration;
- Draft the claims to make "design around" more difficult;
- Draft the claims to increase the relative ease of detecting (and proving) infringement;
- Draft some claims that are structural and draft some claims that are functional;
- Claim the environment of the invention in the dependent claims (i.e., keep the invention terminology broad while narrowing the environment of the invention);
- Employ more than one statutory class to claim the invention—but do so in different claims sets;
- Employ the same statutory class to cover rights of different scope;
- Draft claims to reduce the risk of exhaustion or implied patent licensing, if possible.

1. See List of Claim Drafting Principles, Appendix A.

This chapter is focused on treating some more advanced considerations, although some of these concepts have been introduced in various places throughout the preceding chapters.

As a reminder, it is often a good idea to draft a broad initial claim; however, as previously explored, drafting a broad initial claim may not necessarily always be the goal.[2] As previously suggested, in general, a good patent claim is one that is a balance between breadth, precision, and ambiguity.

In general, to write a broad initial patent claim involves identifying subject matter that constitutes the minimum set of features, described in their broadest terms, that will provide the desired result from use of the technology. It is one thing to encourage identifying the minimum number, yet broadest set of features, and it is another thing to do it. It is difficult to tell someone how to do this successfully.

In general terms, one should attempt to transcend the actual embodiment and identify the so-called gist of the invention.[3] Doing this also permits one to draft claims of varying scope. One should ask: what is it that makes what the inventor has come up with inventive? However, an example is necessary to best illustrate this process.

> In general terms, one should attempt to transcend the actual embodiment and identify the so-called gist of the invention. Ask: what is it that makes what the inventor has come up with inventive?

Imagine, for example, a world in which chairs have not yet been invented and a tree stump represents the state of the art in terms of sitting technology.[4] In other words, the known state of the art is that people walk until they find a tree stump to sit upon. Your client, however, found this to be an inconvenient set of circumstances, and invented a chair, that is, a device having a seat, four legs, and a back. You recognize that you are on the cusp of breakthrough technology and want to protect the invention as much as legally possible. Do you think that the best claim would be one that recites the seat, back, and legs?

---

2. *See* section 1.31, discussing the advantages and disadvantages of drafting the broadest claim possible.

3. Although this notion may now be disfavored since the claim is to be viewed as a whole. *See* 35 U.S.C. § 103 (2022).

4. *See* section 5.311, discussing this example.

Clearly, the back may be omitted in the broadest claim. Likewise, the number of legs is not critical. So, does the broadest claim recite a seat and a set of legs? A problem with this approach is that it continues to focus on the specific embodiment, missing what is *truly* innovative about this new technology. If the broadest claim were one that recited a seat coupled to a set of legs, many potential "downstream" technologies would be left uncovered, including wheel chairs, swivel chairs, ergonomic chairs and a host of other sitting devices. All these technologies, however, build upon what your client has invented. Therefore, you need to draft a claim sufficiently broad so that he or she is entitled to at least a piece of the action, so to speak.

In more general terms, then, what is it that the inventor has invented? Often, focusing on the problem solved assists in writing a broader claim. Thus, it is important to thoroughly understanding the invention. For example, figuring out what was the problem, the source of the problem and/or other stimuli leading to the invention would be useful questions to ask the inventor(s) to aid in this inquiry. Nonetheless, you should always take care when using this information to draft the claims. For example, what is viewed as inventive or innovative will usually change with time. Thus, timing, as in the time of filing, may be an important consideration. Furthermore, often it is the recognition of the problem, rather than its solution, which is inventive.[5] In general, endeavor to use motivation for the invention to assist you in drafting broader claims, rather than to narrow the claims.

Applying this to our example, what is the problem that the inventor recognized? It may be fair to say that he or she recognized that places to sit were not portable. If this problem has not been previously recognized in the prior art, what would be wrong with attempting to draft a claim that broad, this is, directed to "a portable seat"? Specific embodiments may then be covered in the dependent claims, using a cascaded approach from broad to medium to narrow, where the narrow claims cover the patentee's embodiment (i.e., the seat, back and four legs) and, perhaps, approaches your client may believe a competitor might consider using. Again, the point is to move beyond the specific embodiment provided by the inventor to the inventive concept underlying the invention itself.

5. *See, e.g.*, Eibel Process Co. v. Minn. & Ontario Paper Co., 261 U.S. 45 (1923); *In re* Peehs, 612 F.2d 1287, 1290 (CCPA 1980).

6.1 Draft Claims in Anticipation of the First Office Action and in Light of Expected Obviousness Arguments

The benefits of drafting claims in anticipation of a first office action are many. This is one reason it is desirable to be aware of prior art at least as good as will be cited by the examiner, if possible. By anticipating the first office action and drafting the claims appropriately, the need to amend may potentially be avoided. That is, you may already have formulated an argument for patentability and drafted a claim reflecting that argument before the application is even filed.

This potentially reduces estoppel, results in quicker prosecution, saves the client money, and increases the patent term. In addition, if done properly, it also potentially reduces the risk that limitations will be imported from the specification or that written description problems will occur.

It should not be difficult from being aware of the closest *known* prior art to anticipate a typical 103 rejection. The rejection anticipated is under 103 because the claims should be written to clearly distinguish over any potential 102 art, although it is expected that potential 102 art may figure prominently in a 103 rejection.

To make out a *prima facia* case under section 103, the examiner must establish (1) that the proposed combination of prior art references includes all the limitations of the rejected claim in the manner recited in the rejected claim; and (2) that there is motivation in the prior art to make the proposed combination.[6]

Typically, showing that element (1) is not met is the strongest argument against a 103 rejection. Often, the examiner will cite art that might be analogous in some way to the language of the claim or it may in some hypertechnical way appear to meet the elements, but not in the manner expressly recited in the claim.

If you review your claims, you probably will be able to figure out those aspects the examiner would easily locate from searching and those aspects that you think should be more challenging to locate from searching or that he simply will not find. Thus, of course, focus on the latter over the former in terms of anticipating how you might respond.

It might, however, be that all the elements would not be difficult to locate and that you believe the strongest argument is that there should not be a

6. *See* MPEP § 2141 (2022).

motivation in the prior art to make the proposed combination, that is, the prior art does not recognize the desirability and advantages of making the proposed combination. This unfortunately does tend to be a more challenging argument to make successfully. That is, examiners tend to not take such arguments as seriously, despite that such arguments are legitimate ones for patentability. As well, having the particular art that the examiner may be relying upon to make a rejection will help (which is highly unlikely, if not possible, when merely anticipating the rejection), since it may be that the aspects of the documents he seeks to combine are not readily combinable or it may be that how the elements are depicted in the cited documents does not resemble the manner in which the examiner has sought to combine the elements for his rejection, suggesting that the prior art does not truly provide the appropriate motivation for the combination.

In anticipation of such a rejection, it may also be helpful to consider why you think the prior art may not provide a motivation for the proposed combination. It may be helpful to consider why others have not hit upon the invention. Typically, there is an underlying fact or several underlying facts that are not well-known in the art and that often provide some basis for the invention. It is helpful to try to uncover from interviewing the inventor(s) this basis or these bases to later argue that the proposed combination lacks motivation. It would also be a good idea that these notions, once explained by the inventor(s), also be articulated reasonably clearly with respect to "a particular embodiment" in the specification. This should be possible since when anticipating this first office action, you are drafting the patent claims and, therefore, have not yet filed the patent application.

One thing, however, to also keep in mind is that the prior art may not necessarily motivate one to combine the elements *for the exact reason that these elements are combined in the invention at issue.* Yet, despite this, the invention may be unpatentable as having been obvious. Rather, any *legitimate* reason to combine these elements, that is, any legitimate reason for one of ordinary skill in the art to make the proposed combination, is sufficient for a 103 rejection.[7] *Nonetheless, there must be a legitimate reason for one of ordinary skill to be motivated to combine the cited references in the manner asserted by the examiner.* Often, therefore, the examiner will come up with a strawman, not well-thought-out, or possibly not a true technical reason to make the proposed combination. Also, sometimes the examiner fails to provide any motivation at all. Either way, the examiner's motivation, if provided in the office action, and not a truly

7. *See, e.g., In re* Wright 848 F.2d 1216, 6 USPQ2d 1959 (Fed. Cir. 1988).

legitimate and technical basis for making the combination of references in the manner recited in the claim, should be attacked as not sufficient. However, in anticipation, the specification should describe the actual motivation, again, with respect to a "particular embodiment." Depending on the details of the invention and the references cited, this description may demonstrate to the examiner that his proposed motivation is lacking in substance compared with a real or true technical motivation.

Likewise, to the extent the dependent claims may be crafted to bring out such a motivation, one may try to do that.

As an example, consider the following claim:

EXAMPLE 6.1

I claim:

1. A method comprising: implementing a spreadsheet on a computer.[8]

Previously, we suggested that such a claim might be attacked as patent-ineligible under section 101. However, the examiner may see this as such an easy rejection under 103, he may not raise 101. Or, perhaps, this claim is presented in a patent application participating in the pilot program in which 101 rejections are not handled until all other rejections are resolved.[9] Either way, it is possible that such a claim may receive a rejection under 103.[10]

A typical rejection would cite a document with a computer and a document with a spreadsheet and assert that the motivation to combine them is speed, accuracy, convenience, etc. Thus, here is one example of anticipating the first office action.

One way to respond might be to point out that none of the documents show "implementing" on a computer. However, the examiner may have a document showing something being implemented. However, one may argue, quite legitimately, *even with these references before him or her, this would not have made obvious to one of ordinary skill in the art how to implement a spreadsheet on a computer*. One may also argue the benefits that flow from the claim as a whole.

8. *See* section 5.44, discussing potential eligibility issues.

9. *See* https://www.uspto.gov/patents/initiatives/patent-application-initiatives/deferred-subject-matter-eligibility-response regarding deferred subject matter eligibility response.

10. Patent eligibility might not be raised also because we assumed that VisiCalc has not been invented or that this patent application is for VisiCalc.

However, it would be far more persuasive to add limitations directed to the functionality that one may believe will not be found in the prior art, that is, performing operations within cells.[11] Thus, including claims with such limitations in the dependent claims may be another way to anticipate the first office action. So that, if the examiner provides such a rejection, without amendment, those dependent claims may be argued. Consequently, such limitations, such as in Example 5.7 of section 5.441, may be of value both to respond to a rejection under section 101 and to respond to a rejection under section 103. This is not an uncommon occurrence for subject matter subject to a patent eligibility challenge, such as software.

6.11 Make Sure Key Claim Terms Are Clearly Defined

This point has been discussed previously.[12] In general, claim terms are presumed to be used in a manner consistent with ordinary and customary meaning.[13] On the other hand, a patentee is entitled to be his own lexicographer by making clear the meaning he or she ascribes to the claim terminology at issue.[14]

We recommend that key claim terms be defined, but preferably in a manner consistent with ordinary and customary meaning. Thus, under either principle mentioned earlier, the term should receive the expected construction. In general, the goal is to have the intended meaning be clear from the claim language (and specification, if needed) with a high degree of certainty that a court or third-party will agree with that intended meaning as much as is feasible.

In general, the goal is to have the intended meaning be clear from the claim language (and specification, if needed) with a high degree of certainty that a court or third-party will agree with that intended meaning as much as is feasible.

Another benefit of an express definition is that it provides written description support for a claim amendment, if needed to be made at a later time. This

11. *See* section 5.44 for examples of how to frame such limitations.
12. See discussion in Chapter 3 regarding express versus implied meaning of claim terms.
13. *See, e.g.*, Phillips v. AWH Corp., 376 F.3d 1382 (Fed. Cir. 2004) (en banc).
14. *Id.*

point is an important one. Although one may be willing to argue to the ends of the earth with an examiner about whether the art being cited should fall within the scope of the terms used in the claim, and the examiner may even be taking a seriously unreasonable position, by having needed language to distinguish from such art present in the specification, the path of least resistance may be to amend the language so that the examiner is no longer able to take such a position.[15]

6.111 Consider Claims in Light of the Broadest Reasonable Interpretation (BRI)

When reviewing draft claims, it is often easy to lose sight of the principle that during ex parte examination of an originally filed patent application, the claim terms are given their broadest reasonable interpretation. This is yet another reason to expressly define important claim terms. That is, it may make it that much clearer how the examiner's position on interpretation of a claim term is an unreasonable one.[16]

Without a definition, examiners have a *surprising amount of discretion* to state what they consider a claim term to mean. They should apply the ordinary and customary meaning; however, the proof to establish that may not be readily available during a simple prosecution and may be subject to interpretation as well. Defining the term expressly in the specification is a much easier route from a proof perspective.

Furthermore, if the examiner still does not relent, then language from the specification definition may be added to the claim without being concerned about written description support, as suggested in the preceding discussion.

6.12 Use Dependent Claims to Establish Fallback Position (and for Claim Differentiation)

We have discussed a variety of reasons to include dependent claims—all of them quite useful from a claim drafting perspective. For example, they reduce the risk of a limitation being read into the base claim from which the dependent claim depends. They also provide written description support. They provide an additional basis to patentably distinguish from the art. They narrow scope which may remove problematic art but may still be broad enough to capture an

15. Likewise, broader claims, if believed appropriate, might be pursued via a continuation once the pending claims are allowed.

16. *See In re* Smith, 815 F.3d 816 (Fed. Cir. 2016) (providing an example in which an examiner's position even under BRI was held to be unreasonable).

infringer. Thus, *they establish a fallback position that may still be legally viable.* They also help clarify the scope of the base claim, which is another way of saying they help establish claim differentiation. They may also be used to capture the more important commercial embodiments while still implying greater claim scope.[17] They may also remove indefiniteness issues present for the base claim.[18]

6.13 Draft Claims to Avoid Potential Written Description/New Matter/Indefiniteness/ Patent Eligibility Issues

This was covered in detail in Chapter 5.[19] This is provided here primarily as a reminder/refresh regarding these considerations. Thus, it is important to avoid written description issues, especially with original claims, as shown by the *Lizardtech* decision.[20] Likewise, it is prudent to review claims to uncover potential indefiniteness issues that may be handled through redrafting or additional specification clarification.[21] Similarly, it is also wise to identify potential patent eligibility issues and redraft claims appropriately as a technique to handle the issue before it is raised.[22]

6.2 Draft Claims to Cover a Variety of Potential Infringers

It is also worthwhile to think about the claims from the perspective of capturing potential infringers. One way to do this is to consider the commercial value considerations with reference to why someone else may want to use the technology at issue. Does it reduce costs? Improve performance? Does it relate to compatibility? For example, is it related to a published standard, or does it address compatibility of widely used software or hardware? Does it have potential mass market appeal? Viewing the technology from the perspective of its commercial value should make it easier to draft claims that will capture perspective infringers since this allows you to focus on the features that others will want to use and/or copy.

---

17. *See* section 3.233, discussing the legal analysis for this approach.

18. *See* section 3.1232, discussing clarifying relative claim terms to remove indefiniteness, and example 3.1, providing an illustrative example.

19. *See* section 5.4 and its subsections.

20. *Id.*

21. *Id.*

22. *Id.*

> Viewing the technology from the perspective of its commercial value should make it easier to draft claims that will capture perspective infringers since this allows you to focus on the features that others will want to use and/or copy.

It is also helpful to view the claims from the perspective of how they may be used by the patentee to gain commercial advantage. For example, who are potential injunction targets? Typically, this will be the patentee's competitors. Are there companies who are potential cross-licensing targets for the patentee? Usually, this will include companies that could have patents to cover the patentee's products and who might use those patents to generate revenue. Are there potential pure licensing revenue targets for the technology? Frequently, this might include potential suppliers or customers. It is suggested that you not omit such companies from claim coverage simply due to existing business relationships with the patentee. Such relationships may change over time. Also, what about currently existing licenses and cross-licenses that may matter with respect to this technology? Sometimes such agreements may even impact the desire to file the patent application at all. Are such licenses so-called capture period licenses, meaning that patents filed or issued during a specific period remain licensed even after the term of the agreement ends, or is it a "guillotine" license, meaning that patents become unlicensed once the agreement expires? As should be clear, the answers to these questions do not only affect how the claims should be crafted but may ultimately affect whether the patent is worth pursuing since accurate answers ultimately may impact the value of the patent to the patentee.

A related consideration, although one that more frequently is an issue in foreign filing than claim drafting, is the location of these potential target companies. Where are manufacturing sites for target companies? Where are major markets for these companies? Where are corporate headquarters for these companies? It is sometimes difficult to reflect these considerations in the claims but be aware of 271(f) and 271(g) which affect the ability to assert patent claims against companies in the United States that "infringe" abroad. For example, section 271(g) permits suit against someone who performs a process abroad that is patented in the United States, and then imports the product of that process.[23] Likewise, 271(f) is meant to address various situa-

23. *See* section 4.1252, discussing § 271(g).

tions where acts of indirect infringement occur abroad (as if the patent were enforceable abroad), but some portion of the acts occur in the United States.[24] Without these statutes, such indirect activities may otherwise not be actionable. However, due to these statutes, indirect infringement activities pursued abroad that have a connection to the United States, as defined by these statutes, may result in actions filed against those companies in the United States for indirect patent infringement.

With the growth of the internet, a more common claim drafting problem is multiparty claims, discussed in detail in the next section.[25] Patent claims that require several parties to be working in unison for direct infringement to occur are not really infringed by anyone. This is to be distinguished from the typical or usual patent infringement situation, where there is one direct infringer and others who may aid and abet the direct infringer, making those other parties indirect infringers. For example, a claim directed to multiple servers and multiple clients where each client and each server is owned by a different party will not generally result in patent infringement.[26] The claims must, in effect, be drafted from the perspective of a particular infringer. In this example, it would be wise to draft separate claims directed to individual server owners and separate claims directed to individual client owners.

---

24. 35 U.S.C. § 271(f) (2022) states:

(1) Whoever without authority supplies or causes to be supplied in or from the United States all or a substantial portion of the components of a patented invention, where such components are uncombined in whole or in part, in such manner as to actively induce the combination of such components outside of the United States in a manner that would infringe the patent if such combination occurred within the United States, shall be liable as an infringer.

(2) Whoever without authority supplies or causes to be supplied in or from the United States any component of a patented invention that is especially made or especially adapted for use in the invention and not a staple article or commodity of commerce suitable for substantial noninfringing use, where such component is uncombined in whole or in part, knowing that such component is so made or adapted and intending that such component will be combined outside of the United States in a manner that would infringe the patent if such combination occurred within the United States, shall be liable as an infringer.

Section (1) is similar to inducement and section (2) is similar to contributory infringement. *See also* Waymark Corp. v. Porta Systems Corp., 245 F.3d 1364 (Fed. Cir. 2001) regarding liability under section 271(f)(2) for exportation of a component, in which the court noted that "infringement without a completed infringing embodiment is not the norm in patent law, but it is reasonable in the context of 271(f)(2)."

25. *See* section 6.3 and its subsections, discussing the single infringer principle.

26. *Id.*

> Patent claims that require several parties to be working in unison for direct infringement to occur are not really infringed by anyone. This is to be distinguished from the usual or typical patent infringement situation, where this is one direct infringer, but others who aid and abet the direct infringer, making those other parties indirect infringers.

Example 5.5 of section 5.31 gives an example of covering a variety of potential infringers with an independent claim and then several dependent claims, repeated here for convenience as Example 6.2. It is a good idea to consider different potential markets and the different potential infringers that claims may be drafted to cover, including manufacturers, resellers, system integrators, end users, and so on.

EXAMPLE 6.2

I claim:

1. An apparatus comprising: a flip chip.
2. The apparatus of claim 1, wherein the flip chip is incorporated in an integrated circuit chip (IC).
3. The apparatus of claim 2, wherein the IC is part of an electronic circuit.
4. The apparatus of claim 3, wherein the electronic circuit is attached to a circuit board.
5. The apparatus of claim 4, wherein the circuit board is incorporated in a mobile device.
6. The apparatus of claim 5, wherein the mobile device is wirelessly communicatively couplable to other mobile devices via a satellite system.

6.3 Draft Claims to Avoid Covering Multiple Independent Parties Operating Together

Surprisingly, the single infringer doctrine, also referred to as divided infringement, does not have a long historical pedigree in case law. However, before federal circuit cases addressing it were handed down, patent claim drafters at least instinctively knew that a single entity must, in effect, perform all the elements and limitations of a claim for direct infringement liability. This follows logically from the all elements rule and from 35 USC section 271(a).

We have emphasized the point that claims should cover a single infringer previously because it is a common claim drafting error, and it may be fatal to any claim for patent infringement. Now, we discuss some of the cases behind the doctrine.

6.31 Single Infringer Doctrine

The widely known federal circuit case to directly state the principle appears to be *BMC Resources v. Paymentech*,[27] a case from 2007. In that case, some steps of a method claim were performed by one party and the remaining steps were performed by another party. In that case, the federal circuit stated (emphasis supplied):

> Infringement requires, as it always has, a showing that a defendant has practiced each and every element of the claimed invention. *Warner-Jenkinson*, 520 U.S. at 40, 117 S.Ct. 1040 (element-by-element analysis for doctrine of equivalents). This holding derives from the statute itself, which states "whoever without authority makes, uses, offers to sell, or sells any patented invention within the United States, or imports into the United States any patented invention during the term of the patent therefor, infringes the patent." 35 U.S.C. § 271(a) (2000). Thus, liability for infringement requires a party to make, use, sell, or offer to sell the patented invention, meaning the entire patented invention.
>
> Where a defendant participates in infringement but does not directly infringe the patent, the law provides remedies under principles of indirect infringement. However, this court has held that inducement of infringement requires a predicate finding of direct infringement. *Dynacore*, 363 F.3d at 1272.
>
> Two such cases that have found that a party cannot be liable for direct infringement because the party did not perform all the steps are *Fromson v. Advance Offset Plate, Inc.*, 720 F.2d 1565, 1568 (Fed. Cir.1983) (finding no direct infringement by manufacturer who performed the first step of a process claim even where its customer performed the other step of the claim) and *Cross Medical Products*, 424 F.3d at 1311 (rejecting patentees' efforts to combine the acts of surgeons with those of a medical device manufacturer to find direct infringement of an apparatus claim).

27. 498 F.3d 1373 (Fed. Cir. 2007).

Courts faced with a divided infringement theory have also generally refused to find liability where one party did not control or direct each step of the patented process. *See BMC Resources, Inc. v. Paymentech, L.P.*, 2006 WL 306289 (N.D.Tex. Feb. 9, 2006) ("No court has ever found direct infringement based on the type of arms-length business transaction presented here."); *Faroudja Labs. v. Dwin Elecs., Inc.*, 1999 WL 111788, 1999 U.S. Dist. LEXIS 22987 (N.D. Cal. Feb. 24, 1999); *Mobil Oil Corp. v. Filtrol Corp.*, 501 F.2d 282, 291-92 (9th Cir.1974) (expressing doubt over the possibility of divided infringement liability).

A party cannot avoid infringement, however, simply by contracting out steps of a patented process to another entity. In those cases, the party in control would be liable for direct infringement. It would be unfair indeed for the mastermind in such situations to escape liability. District courts in those cases have held a party liable for infringement. *See Shields v. Halliburton Co.*, 493 F.Supp. 1376, 1389 (W.D.La.1980).

This court acknowledges that the standard requiring control or direction for a finding of joint infringement may in some circumstances allow parties to enter into arms-length agreements to avoid infringement. Nonetheless, this concern does not outweigh concerns over expanding the rules governing direct infringement. For example, expanding the rules governing direct infringement to reach independent conduct of multiple actors would subvert the statutory scheme for indirect infringement. **Direct infringement is a strict-liability offense, but it is limited to those who practice each and every element of the claimed invention**. By contrast, indirect liability requires evidence of "specific intent" to induce infringement. Another form of indirect infringement, contributory infringement under § 271(c), also requires a mens rea (knowledge) and is limited to sales of components or materials without substantial noninfringing uses. Under BMC's proposed approach, a patentee would rarely, if ever, need to bring a claim for indirect infringement.

The concerns over a party avoiding infringement by arms-length cooperation can usually be offset by proper claim drafting. A patentee can usually structure a claim to capture infringement by a single party. *See Mark A. Lemley et al., Divided Infringement Claims*, 33 AIPLA Q.J. 255, 272-75 (2005). In this case, for example, BMC could have drafted its claims to focus on one entity. The steps of the claim might have featured references to a single party's supplying or receiving each element of the claimed process. However, BMC chose instead to have four different parties perform different acts within one claim. BMC correctly notes the difficulty of proving infringement of this claim format. Nonetheless, this court will not unilaterally restructure the claim or the standards for joint infringement to remedy these ill-conceived claims. *See Sage Prods. Inc. v. Devon Indus. Inc.*, 126 F.3d 1420, 1425 (Fed. Cir.1997) ("[A]s between the patentee who had a clear opportunity to negotiate broader claims but did not do so, and the public at large, it is the patentee who must bear the cost of its failure to seek protection for this foreseeable alteration of its claimed structure.")

Thus, the court did acknowledge the corner case where the actions of one party are directed by another. This might be analogized to either agency law or perhaps joint venture law, in which two parties, for example, without a formal arrangement, may be considered a single entity in the eyes of the law.

However, if the parties are operating independent of one another, then there would be no liability. For this reason, as the court suggests, claims should be written from the perspective of a single party that will perform every element and limitation. Not long after *BMC Resources*, the court decided *Muniauction.*[28] In *Muniauction*, again, it was clear that not all steps of a method claim were performed by one party. However, the district court decision did not have the benefit of the ruling in *BMC Resources.* On appeal, several of the claims found infringed were held invalid as obvious. For the remaining claims held to be infringed, the question involved whether there was "direction and control" by one party of another, an issue alluded to by the court in *BMC* case. Here, the court stated:

> Accordingly, where the actions of multiple parties combine to perform every step of a claimed method, the claim is directly infringed only if one party exercises "control or direction" over the entire process such that every step is attributable to the controlling party, i.e., the "mastermind." *Id.* at 1380-81. At the other end of this multi-party spectrum, mere "arms-length cooperation" will not give rise to direct infringement by any party. *Id.* at 1371.
>
> . . .
>
> Under *BMC Resources*, the control or direction standard is satisfied in situations where the law would traditionally hold the accused direct infringer vicariously liable for the acts committed by another party that are required to complete performance of a claimed method. 498 F.3d at 1379; *accord Int'l Rectifier v. Samsung Elecs. Co.*, 361 F.3d 1355, 1361 (Fed. Cir. 2004) (reversing district court's ruling that Samsung violated a permanent injunction prohibiting infringement in the United States on the grounds that Samsung did not control or participate in the extraterritorial activities of a third party such that the acts of the third party were not attributable to Samsung). In this case, Thomson neither performed every step of the claimed methods nor had another party perform steps on its behalf, and Muniauction has identified no legal theory under which Thomson might be vicariously liable for the actions

28. *See* Muniauction, Inc. v. Thomson Corp., 532 F.3d 1318 (Fed. Cir. 2008).

of the bidders. Therefore, Thomson does not infringe the asserted claims as a matter of law.

Observe that a similar "direction and control" test arises under use infringement of a system claim.[29]

6.32 Illustrative Claim Example

The divided infringement issue may arise in a host of possible situations; however, it has become particularly prevalent because a variety of technologies require client and server interactions in which the client and the server are operated by otherwise independent parties. For example, long before Apple Music and similar services, there was Napster. Napster is credited with being the first peer-to-peer network for sharing music. Putting copyright issues aside, before Napster, others had the idea for peer-to-peer sharing of digital music and attempted to obtain patent protection. Thus, consider this example claim.

EXAMPLE 6.3

I claim:

1. A method of sharing digital music comprising:

   initiating and establishing a network connection between a first computer and a second computer; and

   sharing one or more digital music files on the first computer with the second computer via the network connection so that the second computer is able to independently play the shared one or more digital music files.

Of course, this claim might raise a number of issues today, including, perhaps, patent eligibility. Even at the time of Napster, there might have been a question of having been obvious. However, we put those issues aside for purposes of illustration.

It would also not be fair to say that *no one* necessarily infringes this claim. Rather, an entity or person that owns or directs and controls both the first and

29. *See* section 4.1263, discussing use infringement of a system claim.

the second computer might infringe. Of course, detecting such infringement is problematic. It might be possible to argue with evidence that Apple infringes if Apple is transporting digital music between its servers, for example.

Could one argue that Apple infringes when a user downloads music from its servers? Apple provides software to assist in downloading the music. However, could it be argued that Apple initiates and establishes the network connection? It seems it is the user that initiates the network connection, granted that the details of the technology may matter here. Is the user under Apple's direction and control? Unlikely. However, Apple probably performs the second operation of sharing the one or more digital music files.

Thus, it should be clear from this example, that it might have been possible to draft a claim that would more clearly be infringed had it properly been written from the perspective of the first computer.

6.4 Use Dependent Claims to Cover Higher Levels of Product Integration

Previously, we have given several examples of using higher levels of product integration in claims. This is also another approach to covering a variety of infringers, hence, Example 6.2 is a good example, repeated here for convenience.

I claim:

1. An apparatus comprising: a flip chip.
2. The apparatus of claim 1, wherein the flip chip is incorporated in an integrated circuit chip (IC).
3. The apparatus of claim 2, wherein the IC is part of an electronic circuit.
4. The apparatus of claim 3, wherein the electronic circuit is attached to a circuit board.
5. The apparatus of claim 4, wherein the circuit board is incorporated in a mobile device.
6. The apparatus of claim 5, wherein the mobile device is wirelessly communicatively couplable to other mobile devices via a satellite system.

This principle was also discussed in connection with examples of component level claims versus system level claims.[30] Following are several examples in which higher levels of product integration are included in dependent or in independent claims.

Example 6.4 demonstrates in claim 1 a memory controller component base claim. Although a CPU is recited as a limitation, it is not a claim element that must be present for infringement.[31] Claim 2 is a dependent claim that expressly recites the CPU as a claim element. Example 6.5 is similar in concept except that claim 1 includes the CPU as a claim element and claim 2 recites a higher level of integration, such as in a tablet, laptop computer, and so on.

EXAMPLE 6.4

I claim:

1. An apparatus comprising:

   random access memory (RAM) and a memory controller;

   wherein the memory controller is capable of initiating burst mode operation based, at least in part, on receipt of a request from a central processing unit (CPU);

   wherein the request is to include a memory address, a word count, and a read or a write control transfer designation; and

   wherein the memory controller is to process the request and take control of a system transfer bus.

2. The apparatus of claim 1, comprising: the CPU and the system transfer bus, wherein the CPU is external to the RAM and the system transfer bus is external to the RAM.

30. See, for example, discussions in Chapter 1 and Chapter 4.
31. See section 2.141 and its subsections, discussing the body of a patent claim.

EXAMPLE 6.5

I claim:

1. An apparatus comprising:

   random access memory (RAM), a memory controller, a central processing unit (CPU), and a system bus;

   wherein the memory controller is capable of initiating burst mode operation based, at least in part, on receipt of a request from the CPU;

   wherein the request is to include a memory address, a word count, and a read or a write control transfer designation; and

   wherein the memory controller is to process the request and take control of the system transfer bus.

2. The apparatus of claim 1, wherein the RAM, memory controller, CPU and system transfer bus are incorporated together in at least one of the following: a desktop computer, a laptop computer, a tablet, a smart phone and/or a server.

Examples 6.6 and 6.8 illustrate two approaches to a method of operating a module or RF module and examples 6.7 and 6.9 show a comparable method claim except directed to operating a device integrating the technology at a higher level, here, a communication device. Of course, for claims 6.6 and 6.8, a device integrating the technology at a higher level might have been recited in a dependent claim, rather than as an independent claim, as in 6.7 and 6.9.

EXAMPLE 6.6

I claim:

1. A method of operating a module, the module including at least one integrated circuit chip comprising a plurality of N-type metal oxide semiconductor (NMOS) field effect transistors in a series connected stack configuration that comprises at least one NMOS field effect transistor including a body, the at least one NMOS field effect transistor either to

pass an RF signal in a series enable state or to not pass the RF signal in a series disable state, the method further comprising:

electrically biasing the body of the at least one NMOS field effect transistor of the module in the series disable state to have a voltage level substantially more negative than the lowest voltage level of the following: ground, a DC voltage level of a source of the at least one series NMOS field effect transistor of the module, and a DC voltage level of a drain of the at least one NMOS field effect transistor of the module.

EXAMPLE 6.7

I claim:

1. A method of operating a communication device, the communication device including at least one integrated circuit chip comprising a plurality of series N-type metal oxide semiconductor (NMOS) field effect transistors in a series connected stack configuration that comprises at least one series NMOS field effect transistor including a body, the at least one series NMOS field effect transistor either to pass an RF signal in a series enable state or to not pass the RF signal in a series disable state, the method further comprising:

   electrically biasing the body of the at least one series NMOS field effect transistor of the communication device in the series disable state to have a voltage level substantially more negative than the lowest voltage level of the following: ground, the DC voltage level of the source of the at least one series NMOS field effect transistor of the communication device, and the DC voltage level of the drain of the at least one series NMOS field effect transistor of the communication device.

EXAMPLE 6.8

I claim:

1. A method of operating an RF module comprising at least one integrated circuit chip, the method comprising:

   inputting an input RF signal and one or more control signals to the RF module;

outputting an output RF signal from the RF module;

controlling, based at least in part on the one or more control signals, a silicon on insulator (SOI) N-type metal oxide semiconductor (NMOS) field effect transistor (FET) series connected stack configuration to either an OFF state or an ON state, the SOI NMOS FET stack configuration, comprising a plurality of NMOS FET transistors, being implemented on the at least one integrated circuit chip; and

electrically biasing, based at least in part on the one or more control signals, a body of at least one NMOS FET transistor of the plurality of NMOS FET transistors of the SOI NMOS FET stack configuration with a bias voltage substantially more negative than ground during at least a portion of the OFF state of the at least one NMOS FET transistor.

EXAMPLE 6.9

I claim:

1. A method of operating a communication device including an RF module that further includes at least one integrated circuit chip, the method comprising:

controlling a silicon on insulator (SOI) N-type metal oxide semiconductor (NMOS) field effect transistor (FET) series connected stack configuration to either an OFF state or an ON state, the SOI NMOS FET stack configuration, comprising a plurality of NMOS FET transistors, being implemented on the at least one integrated circuit chip of the RF module of the communication device; and

electrically biasing a body of at least one NMOS FET transistor of the plurality of NMOS FET transistors of the SOI NMOS FET stack configuration with a bias voltage substantially more negative than ground during at least a portion of the OFF state of the at least one NMOS FET transistor.

These examples show that innumerable ways to claim higher levels of integration are possible.

6.41 Damages Issues

Generally, the value of a patent relates to how it might be used. There are three things at a high level that one may do with a patent.[32] One may rely on its exclusive power to increase barriers to entry for a market in which one sells a product or service, one may license it for value, or one may trade it for access to someone else's patented technology. The last two things could also be viewed as one, so that ultimately, one may rely on its exclusionary power or one may effectively trade it for value.

This is similar in principle to how the remedies in federal court mostly work as well. One may seek and obtain an injunction or one may seek and obtain monetary damages, or both.

The question for the claim drafter is how a formulation of the claims may affect these options or remedies. The options available in federal court serve as a backdrop to patent assertion, but typically the patent value is realized in private negotiations assuming rational parties and an enforceable patent.

The injunction side of remedies or exclusionary power is understood and reasonably predictable. This remedy has, in effect, guided much of our discussion. The process of reading a claim on an accused process or product captures this option. That is, an injunction will foreclose making, using, and selling anything within the scope of the claims (and potentially, something falling within the doctrine of equivalents, if raised and won).

The damages, trade for value, or royalty revenue side of remedies is less certain and less predictable unfortunately. It is driven in many cases by aspects beyond the control of the claim drafter, such as previous licenses or licenses by others for similar technology, markets, costs, profits, the relation of the parties, and a host of other factors. Here, there are not many hard and fast rules because these factors vary significantly with the situation. This also tends to make the legal principles less clear as well.

Nonetheless, the law does impose some structure here. Under 35 USC section 284, one may recover lost profits and "in no event less than a reasonable royalty."[33] The fundamental notion is to adequately compensate the patent holder as if the infringement had not taken place.[34] In general, if the

---

32. *See* discussion in Chapter 1 of patent strategy.

33. 35 U.S.C. § 284 (2022) states in part: "Upon finding for the claimant the court shall award the claimant damages adequate to compensate for the infringement, but in no event less than a reasonable royalty for the use made of the invention by the infringer, together with interest and costs as fixed by the court."

34. *See, e.g.*, Aro v. Convertible Top Replacement, 377 U.S. 476, 507 (1964) stating a plaintiff can recover as damages "the difference between his pecuniary condition after the infringement,

infringement had not taken place, then the patent holder would have had more profits. Hence, the patent holder is entitled to lost profits. Typically, lost profits is also the greater recovery than a reasonable royalty, but, in general, is a greater challenge to prove in many situations. That is, it must be proven that "but for" the infringement, the patent holder would have made more sales and/or would not have had to lower its prices.[35] In a two-supplier market, this may be relatively easy to show, but that type of simple market is relatively unusual. Thus, in many situations, sufficient evidence to make out a strong or credible lost profits case is not available because of the complexity of the market and the availability of reasonable alternative noninfringing substitutes.[36] Where there are reasonable alternative substitutes, it is difficult to prove "but for" causation, as required to recover lost profits.

Fortunately, the statute provides a damages floor, which is the reasonable royalty measure of recovery. Here, the notion is, again, that the patent holder should be adequately compensated as if the infringement did not take place. Hence, the patent holder should be compensated as if the defendant had taken a license.

This brings us to the made-up world of the hypothetical negotiation. Here, the landmark case is the *Georgia-Pacific*[37] decision which lists 15 factors that continue to this day to drive the reasonable royalty damages recovery. These factors are:

1. The royalties received by the patent owner for the licensing of the patent-in-suit, proving or tending to prove an established royalty;
2. The rates paid by the licensee for the use of other patents comparable to the patent-in-suit;
3. The nature and scope of the license, as exclusive or non-exclusive, or as restricted or non-restricted in terms of territory or with respect to whom the manufactured product may be sold;
4. The licensor's established policy and marketing program to maintain its patent monopoly by not licensing others to use the invention or by granting licenses under special conditions designed to preserve that monopoly;

---

and what his condition might have been if the infringement had not occurred."

35. *See* Richard Cauley, Winning The Patent Damages Case (2009).

36. *Id.*

37. Georgia-Pacific Corp. v. U.S. Plywood Corp., 318 F. Supp. 1116 (S.D.N.Y. 1970), *mod. and aff'd*, 446 F.2d 295 (2d Cir. 1971), *cert. denied*, 404 U.S. 870 (1971).

5. The commercial relationship between the licensor and the licensee, such as whether they are competitors in the same territory in the same line of business, or whether they are inventor and promoter;
6. **The effect of selling the patented specialty in promoting sales of other products of the licensee; the existing value of the invention to the licensor as a generator of sales of its non-patented items; and the extent of such derivative or convoyed sales;**
7. The duration of the patent and the term of the license;
8. The established profitability of the product made under the patent; its commercial success; and its current popularity;
9. **The utility and advantages of the patent property over the old modes or devices, if any, that had been used for working out similar results;**
10. **The nature of the patented invention; the character of the commercial embodiment of it as owned and produced by the licensor; and the benefits to those who have used the invention;**
11. **The extent to which the infringer has made use of the invention, and any evidence probative of the value of that use;**
12. The portion of the profit or of the selling price that may be customary in the particular business or in comparable businesses to allow for the use of the invention or analogous inventions;
13. **The portion of the realizable profit that should be credited to the invention as distinguished from non-patented elements, the manufacturing process, business risks, or significant features or improvements added by the infringer;**
14. The opinion testimony of qualified experts; and
15. The amount that a licensor (such as the patent owner) and a licensee (such as the infringer) would have agreed upon (at the time the infringement began) if both had been reasonably and voluntarily trying to reach an agreement; that is, the amount that a prudent licensee—who desired, as a business proposition, to obtain a license to manufacture and sell a particular article embodying the patented invention—would have been willing to pay as a royalty and yet be able to make a reasonable profit, and which amount would have been acceptable by a prudent patent owner who was willing to grant a license.

It is the last factor, number 15, that summarizes the concept of the hypothetical negotiation itself:

The amount that a licensor (such as the patent owner) and a licensee (such as the infringer) would have agreed upon (at the time the infringement began) if both had been reasonably and voluntarily trying to reach an agreement; that is, the amount that a prudent licensee—who desired, as a business proposition, to obtain a license to manufacture and sell a particular article embodying the patented invention—would have been willing to pay as a royalty and yet be able to make a reasonable profit, and which amount would have been acceptable by a prudent patent owner who was willing to grant a license.

As suggested, these factors eschew hard and fast rules and relate in many cases to aspects beyond the control of the claim drafter, such as previous licenses under the patent, licenses by others for similar technology, markets, costs, profits, the relation of the parties, when the infringement took place, the time remaining on the patent, and a host of other factors.

Nonetheless, there are some factors that do appear to have the potential to be influenced by how the claims are drafted. These factors have been highlighted in bold, in particular, factors 6, 9, 10, 11, and 13. However, even here, how these factors translate into claim language is difficult to intuit.

Also, one should not lose sight of the practical reality that the possibility of an injunction may also affect the damages analysis.[38] That is, between a willing licensor and a willing licensee, the royalty will be higher to the extent that the possibility of an enforceable injunction limits the options available to the prospective licensee. Similarly, it is also clear that claim language and claim construction may potentially affect damages recovery.[39] Thus, we attempt to uncover the few principles that might be emergent from the case law.

6.411 Entire Market Value Principle

It seems clear that the "entire market value" principle cuts across all approaches to damages recovery. The entire market principle might be viewed as a sort of exception in damages law. That is, despite the patented feature being only a portion of the product sold with many unpatented features, it permits recovery for lost profits, for example, if it can be shown that the patented feature drives consumer demand for the end product or that the patented features and unpatented features of an end product worked together as a single functional unit.

Courts are not always clear regarding the damages theory being applied, that is lost profits, a reasonable royalty, or both. In *Del Mar Avionics, Inc. v.*

---

38. *See* Cauley, *supra* note 35; Mark Lemley & Carl Shapiro, *Patent Holdup and Royalty Stacking*, 95 Texas L. Rev. 1991 (2007).

39. *See* Metabolite Labs., Inc. v. Lab. Corp. of Am. Holdings, 370 F.3d 1354, 1364 (Fed. Cir. 2004) ("the invitation to apply a different claim construction for computation of damages than for infringement liability" was rejected by the court).

Quinton Instrument Co. (1987),[40] however, the federal circuit noted that "in appropriate circumstances the patentee may prove the extent of its lost profits by the 'entire market value rule,' . . . based on a showing that the patentee could reasonably anticipate the sale of the unpatented components together with the patented components. . . ." Notably, a similar "entire market" principle applies with respect to recovery based on a reasonable royalty damages measure.[41]

Clearly, the plaintiff prefers application of this principle while the defendant would prefer that it not be applied. Again, the goal is to compensate the patent holder for the infringement. Thus, to the extent one or more patented features influences the price or sale of other unpatented components or features, it seems an argument exists to apply the entire market principle.[42] Ultimately, it likely will come down to how persuasive the evidence is for its application or non-application.

On the other hand, cases also recognize that to the extent this principle may overcompensate the plaintiff, that may potentially be handled via an appropriate royalty rate.[43] Thus, a line of federal circuit cases suggest that the problem of apportionment, that is, valuing a patented feature or component of a complex multicomponent, may be handled in this manner.[44]

The view we have come to, therefore, is that an argument for application of an entire market principle, either on its own or as a step in an apportionment analysis, will be stronger to the extent that the claim covers the entire accused end product rather than merely a particular feature or improvement.

---

40. 836 F.2d 1320 (Fed. Cir. 1987).

41. *See, e.g.*, Lucent Techs., Inc. v. Gateway, Inc., 580 F.3d 1301, 1324 (Fed. Cir. 2009). *See, e.g.*, Lucent Techs. Inc. v. Microsoft Corp., 544 F. Supp. 2d 1080, 1105–06 (S.D. Cal. 2008), discussing federal circuit cases.

42. *See, e.g.*, Deere Co. v. Int'l Harvester Co., 710 F.2d 1551 (Fed. Cir. 1983) ("the district court did nothing more or less than take into account the impact of anticipated collateral sales of an admittedly noninfringing product line on the respective bargaining positions of the parties engaged in theorized licensing negotiations. We consider this an eminently reasonable approach to the willing seller-willing buyer analysis. . . .").

43. *See* Lucent Techs., Inc. v. Gateway, Inc., 580 F.3d 1301 (Fed. Cir. 2009), stating: "Although our law states certain mandatory conditions for applying the entire market value rule, courts must nevertheless be cognizant of a fundamental relationship between the entire market value rule and the calculation of a running royalty damages award. Simply put, the base used in a running royalty calculation can always be the value of the entire commercial embodiment, as long as the magnitude of the rate is within an acceptable range (as determined by the evidence). Indeed, '[a]ll running royalties have at least two variables: the royalty base and the royalty rate.'"

44. *See, e.g.*, Lucent Techs., Inc. v. Gateway, Inc., 580 F.3d 1301, 1324 (Fed. Cir. 2009). *See, e.g.*, Lucent Techs. Inc. v. Microsoft Corp., 544 F. Supp. 2d 1080, 1105–06 (S.D. Cal. 2008), discussing federal circuit cases.

Even to the extent that the royalty rate would be adjusted for a larger base, we still believe from a damages recovery or a negotiation standpoint, one would be better off with the larger base because typically the whole has more value than the sum of the parts.

On the other hand, as has been discussed, if the infringer only makes the component, as opposed to the end product, this approach may represent the difference between a case for direct infringement versus indirect infringement.[45] For this and other reasons, we have emphasized *both* component and system level claims with the recognition that different situations may prefer one or the other.[46]

For illustrative claim examples, one may simply look to the several component and system level claim examples discussed in prior chapters.[47]

6.412 Smallest Saleable Unit Principle

The smallest saleable unit developed in the case law for situations where it was expected, even with adjusting for apportionment via the royalty rate, still using the entire market value would tend to overcompensate the plaintiff.[48]

A similar strategy may be employed as just described with this principle as well. That is, assuming the smallest saleable unit is larger than the particular feature to be patented, draft the claim so that it at least covers the smallest saleable unit. This strategy was alluded to previously in examples in which it was suggested that a patent claim be written to cover an integrated circuit or a module, as an example.[49] That is, these examples involve situations in which the integrated circuit or module would likely be used in a computer or a cell phone. However, it might be a stretch to expect a royalty base of a computer or cell phone using the entire market principle. Thus, instead, an integrated circuit or module is used, as the largest likely royalty base for an infringing commercial embodiment. That is, the patented feature would likely be a small part thereof.

Thus, in general, the difference in treatment of apportionment lies in the federal circuit's view of the scope of the claims compared to the accused products.[50] Where a claim covers an entire product, apportionment is required in

---

45. *See* section 3.22 and its subsections.

46. *See* discussion regarding system versus component claims in Chapters 1, 2, and 4.

47. *Id.*

48. *See, e.g.*, Ericsson, Inc. v. D-Link Sys., Inc., 773 F.3d 1201, 113 U.S.P.Q.2d (BNA) 1001 (Fed. Cir. 2014).

49. See, for example, discussions in Chapters 1 and 4.

50. *Compare* Exmark Mfg. Co. v. Briggs & Stratton Power Prods. Grp., 879 F.3d 1332 (Fed. Cir. 2018) *with* Finjan, Inc. v. Blue Coat Sys., Inc., 879 F.3d 1299 (Fed. Cir. 2018).

the royalty rate to account for the value the novel features add to the conventional features covered by the claim. That is, one will argue for the entire market value principle based on the claim itself, consumer demand, and/or whether the patented and conventional features form a functional unit. *In this case, conventional features that are included in the claim are included in the royalty base where the claim covers a complete product and the royalty rate may, consequently, be apportioned to account for what the patented feature may add.* Where a claim covers only a portion of a multicomponent product, apportionment is required in the royalty base to account for the patented and unpatented features in the smallest saleable unit as well as in the royalty rate. In other words, *if a claim covers only part of a product, both the royalty base and the royalty rate may be apportioned.* Furthermore, the royalty rate calculation must tie the facts of the case to the royalty rate determination. Hence, as suggested in the previous section, if one is able to draft a claim in a manner to make the entire market value royalty base more likely at the margin, that appears to be a laudable goal.

6.5 Draft Claims to Make "Design Around" More Difficult

It is best if the claims may be drafted so that the only design around alternative is the prior art. It is impossible to cover the prior art with a claim, of course; however, presumably, the prior art approaches are inferior and less desirable than employing the technology associated with the invention. Preventing design around is such an important consideration that it may be a factor in the application of the doctrine of equivalents (DOE).

It is best if the claims may be drafted so that the only design around alternative is the prior art. It is impossible to cover the prior art with a claim, of course; however, presumably, the prior art approaches are inferior and less desirable than employing the technology associated with the invention.

For example, in *Sage Products v. Devon*,[51] the federal circuit held that no equivalents to the literal claims existed because the claims were drafted in a manner that made it "foreseeable" at the time of drafting that they could be

51. 126 F.3d 1420 (Fed. Cir. 1997).

easily designed around. This is sometimes referred to as the "foreseeability" limit to the DOE. Of course, this case may be unusual due to the simplicity of the invention and how easily the claims were to design around. The invention related to a receptacle for used medical debris, such as hypodermic needles. The concept, therefore, was that once the debris was placed in the receptacle it should not be easily removable. The claims, however, specifically recited elements, such as a precise location for the opening of the receptacle relative to the "top," etc.

Nonetheless, the Supreme Court case, *Festo v. Shoketsu Kinzoku Kogyo Kabushiki Co.*[52] also lends credence to the notion that design around potential of the claims has become significant in relation to the DOE. In that case, the Supreme Court created a presumption with respect to prosecution history estoppel in connection with an amendment of the claims. The Court stated:

> A patentee's decision to narrow his claims through amendment may be **presumed** to be a general disclaimer of the territory between the original claim and the amended claim.[53] (emphasis added)

However, according to the Court, the patentee is entitled to rebut this presumption:

> The patentee must show that at the time of the amendment one skilled in the art could not reasonably be expected to have drafted a claim that would have literally encompassed the alleged equivalent.[54]

Thus, it is fair to say that after *Festo* design around considerations took on additional importance in connection with claim drafting.

> It is fair to say that after *Festo* design around considerations took on new importance in connection with claim drafting.

It is important to consult with the inventors and technical personnel to make sure that all possible alternatives are thoroughly considered, evaluated, and, if appropriate, disclosed and claimed. Note that in addition to addressing the design around issues, as just discussed, including such claims as alternatives should also reduce the risk of a limitation being imported from the

52. 535 U.S. 722 (2002).
53. *Id.* at 740.
54. *Id.* at 741.

specification into the claims and reduce the risk that a court will conclude that the claims are not adequately supported in the specification.

A valuable technique is to review the claims with the inventors word by word. This will uncover both design around opportunities and potentially the closest prior art known to the inventor, which, in most if not all cases, must then be disclosed to the PTO. Another helpful exercise is to ask the inventors how they might attempt to design around their own invention once you have shown them the claims.

> As was suggested previously, a valuable technique is to review the claims with the inventors word by word. This will uncover both design around opportunities and potentially the closest prior art known to the inventor, which, in most if not all cases, must then be disclosed to the PTO. Another helpful exercise is to ask the inventors how they might attempt to design around their own invention, once you have shown them the claims.

6.51 Illustrative Claim Examples

Following are examples of claims easily designed around. Potential ways to design around Example 6.10 include the shape of the seat, its orientation, the number and orientation of the legs, etc. Inherently, a claiming approach that relies on claiming embodiments rather than the inventive concept invites design around opportunities.

EXAMPLE 6.10

I claim:

1. An apparatus comprising:

   a substantially horizontally oriented, rectangularly shaped seat including four corners;

   wherein attached to a respective corner of the seat is a substantially vertically oriented leg such that the legs point in the same direction away from the seat, are oriented to be substantially mutually parallel, and are of substantially the same length.

Instead, this might be claimed as a portable seat, which captures more effectively the inventive concept or innovation.[55]

Following is a more subtle potential design around example.

EXAMPLE 6.11

I claim:

1. A method of forming a virtual private network comprising:

   communicating one or more signal packets between respective physically separate broadcast domains via a gateway device included in the respective physically separate broadcast domains, wherein the communicating the one or more signal packets comprises:

      encapsulating the one or more signal packets in the respective physically separate broadcast domains to be communicated; and

      communicating the encapsulated signal packets between the respective gateway devices and at least one tunnel server so that the one or more signal packets are communicated between the respective physically separate broadcast domains.

If this were the initial claim, one might argue implicitly that a broadcast domain includes more than one network device. This is further suggested by the reference to a gateway device, suggesting a gateway for other network devices on the domain. However, it is possible for a domain to consist of one device.

There are several ways to attempt to handle this potential design around opportunity. For one thing, "gateway device" may be changed to "network device," since a gateway device is really a network device, particularly in an embodiment employing a single device domain, as illustrated here.

I claim:

1. A method of forming a virtual private network comprising:

   communicating one or more signal packets between respective physically separate broadcast domains via a network device included

55. See section 5.311, discussing this example in more detail.

in the respective physically separate broadcast domains, wherein the communicating the one or more signal packets comprises:

encapsulating the one or more signal packets in the respective physically separate broadcast domains to be communicated; and

communicating the encapsulated signal packets between respective network devices and at least one tunnel server so that the one or more signal packets are communicated between the respective physically separate broadcast domains.

Furthermore, adding a dependent claim reciting a single network device domain would leave little doubt regarding an embodiment with a single network device and that the base claim is intended to cover domains of one network device or more than one network device.

2. The method of claim 1, wherein at least one of the respective physically separate broadcast domains comprises a stand-alone network device.

However, one weakness with this claim is that it is not provided in method claim format, as shown here.

2. The method of claim 1, wherein the communicating one or more signal packets between the respective physically separate broadcast domains comprises communicating the one or more signal packets between the respective broadcast domains in which at least one physically separate broadcast domain comprises a stand-alone network device.

6.6 Draft Claims to Increase Relative Ease of Detecting (and Proving) Infringement

This is another area where it is recommended that you consult closely with the inventors and technical personnel who are familiar with the technology to ensure that this issue is addressed as completely as possible. There are a variety of ways that patent infringement is typically detectable. Therefore, ask technical personnel about whether those ways might apply and then draft the claims to enhance the possibility of detection.

> There are a variety of ways that patent infringement is typically detectable. Therefore, ask technical personnel about whether those ways might apply and then draft the claims to enhance the possibility of detection.

For example, often certain features are likely to be mentioned in advertising literature, on a website, in a data sheet, etc. One instance of this is a feature related to a published standard. If so, this is a feature where detecting its presence is relatively easy and claiming that feature will likely improve the value of the claims to the patentee. Of course, claiming features that are apparent rather than latent, or features that are relatively easy to test, such as those related to the input or output terminals of a chip, for example, is recommended. Also, claiming the ultimate end product in addition to the process of producing it, assuming that is possible, will make detecting infringement easier. This assumes the end product is easier to obtain and test than the process for making it. For example, if the invention is a process of applying a moisture resistant coating to integrated circuits, claim the moisture resistant chip as well. Frequently, detecting infringement of the manufacturing process is difficult because it requires access the potential infringer's factory; however, the chip may usually be purchased and closely examined.

It is also helpful to think in terms of features that will quickly eliminate products that do not infringe from consideration, even if it may not definitely produce an infringing product without significantly more investigation. Such features have the beneficial effect of limiting the scope of products to investigate to a reasonable number. For example, if the invention will reduce power consumption over the prior art, this may be a feature worth claiming even assuming there may be other reasons unrelated to the invention that may also reduce power consumption. At least those products that do not reduce power consumption measurably are easy to eliminate early. This is often an overlooked technique to improve ease of detecting infringement. Features that improve the ability to detect infringement add value, even where presence of the feature is not dispositive of infringement.

In addition to detecting infringement, the ability to easily prove infringement if a lawsuit were to result can be quite important (or where there is a significant threat of a lawsuit, such as a private negotiation). As claim drafters, we try to precisely identify what makes the invention innovative, which has been espoused throughout this book, because it is an issue important in prosecution and may be important to establish validity in other circumstances. However, this precise aspect may at times be quite a challenge to prove. It might be helpful in such circumstances to look for a sort of "proxy" measurement or feature that also relates to the innovation but is much easier to demonstrate with evidence. Again, consulting the inventors, as the technical experts, may be useful here.

6.61 Illustrative Claim Examples

Following is a claim to the switch technology we have used to illustrate some claim drafting principles.[56]

EXAMPLE 6.12

I claim:

1. A device comprising: at least one integrated circuit; the at least one integrated circuit comprising:

   a shunt transistor having a first node coupled to a port and a second node coupled to ground, the shunt transistor comprising an accumulated charge control N-type MOSFET (NMOSFET) and wherein:

      the accumulated charge control NMOSFET comprises a gate, a drain, a source, a gate oxide layer, and a body, and an accumulated charge sink region connected to the body;

      the shunt transistor to couple the first port with the second port in a shunt transistor first state;

      the shunt transistor to isolate the first port from the second port in a shunt transistor second state, and wherein the shunt transistor is to have a bias voltage applied to the accumulated charge sink region to remove or otherwise control, via the

56. See section 4.131 and its subsections, discussing this example.

accumulated charge sink region, charge that, without the bias voltage applied, would accumulate in the body in the shunt transistor second state; and

the bias voltage to be substantially negative with respect to ground.

Here, the invention is claimed in terms of the innovation. That is, to remove or otherwise control (e.g., limit) negative charge that might otherwise accumulate in the body of a transistor. It is this negative charge accumulation in a transistor (termed here "a shunt transistor") proximate to a transistor passing an analog signal that would otherwise corrupt the analog signal being passed.

While a technically accurate patent claim, an issue might be proving that negative charge would accumulate in the transistor body but for the claimed technology. The problem is that it would require building computer models of transistor operation to prove this. This could be done but it would be expensive and, of course, one can expect a battle of experts regarding the transistor models before a judge and jury who are unlikely to understand the transistor models of the technology enough to assess who should be believed.

However, if the shunt transistor body is properly biased in the off state, then signal corruption or nonlinear harmonics are reduced. Therefore, instead, simply claim the bias voltage as applied in the off state of the shunt transistor for the broadest claim. This is easier to prove. It also is broader than example 6.12. The charge accumulation aspects may also be claimed in dependencies as fallback positions if needed to distinguish from prior art.

In addition, other more detectable and provable features may be included in dependent claims, as illustrated here.

EXAMPLE 6.13

I claim:

1. A device comprising: at least one integrated circuit chip; the at least one integrated circuit chip including at least one N-type metal oxide semiconductor field effect transistor (NMOSFET);

   wherein at least one NMOSFET transistor of the plurality includes a source, a gate, a drain and a body;

wherein the at least one NMOSFET transistor is further included in an electrical configuration within the at least one integrated circuit chip, the electrical configuration to at least control the at least one NMOSFET transistor to either an ON state or an OFF state based at least on one or more control signals; and wherein the electrical configuration is at least further to electrically bias the body of the at least one NMOSFET transistor to a DC voltage level substantially more negative than ground at least in a portion of the OFF state of the at least one NMOSFET transistor.

2. The device of claim 1, wherein the at least one field effect transistor is implemented in a silicon-on-insulator technology.
3. The device of claim 1, wherein the voltage level substantially more negative than ground is more than one volt more negative than ground.
4. The device of claim 1, wherein the at least one field effect transistor during the at least a portion of the off state is to be electrically biased so as to improve the linearity of the at least one field effect transistor relative to the at least one field effect transistor not electrically biased to have a voltage level substantially more negative than ground.
5. The device of claim 1, wherein the at least one field effect transistor during the at least a portion of the off state is to be electrically biased so as to reduce nonlinear harmonic and/or intermodulation distortion of signals to be propagated by the integrated circuit, reduction via the at least one field effect transistor being relative to the at least one field effect transistor not electrically biased to have a voltage level substantially more negative than ground.

Claim 2 refers to silicon-on-insulator technology, which is relatively easy to detect and prove. Claim 3 refers to a specific voltage amount below ground. Claims 4 and 5 refer to measures easy to detect and prove—improved signal linearity and reduced nonlinear harmonic and/or intermodulation distortion, respectively. These features, such as the latter two, are not only easy to detect and prove but also provide further distinctions from the prior art beyond the base claim.

6.7 Draft Some Claims That Are Structural and Draft Some Claims That Are Functional

The notion of functionality refers to claiming an invention is terms of "what it does" rather than "what it is." For example, claiming a nut and bolt or a staple versus claiming the function of attaching. Technically, there is nothing wrong with drafting claims that are functional, despite the fact that some examiners will reject such claims as indefinite under 35 USC § 112, second paragraph. The MPEP itself recognizes that functional claims are permitted.[57] Likewise, there are lines of precedent acknowledging that functional claims are appropriate, including federal circuit cases.[58] Thus, the issue for the claim drafter is not whether functional claims are permitted, but whether such claims will provide an advantage over claims that include structure.

> The issue for the claim drafter is not whether functional claims are permitted, but whether or not such claims will provide an advantage over claims that include structure.

Today, perhaps the greatest risk of functional claiming is that that claim will be construed to be a "means plus function" claim under 35 USC § 112(f) despite the absence of the word "means" in the claims. This has been discussed extensively previously.[59] However, as a slight refresh, this occurred in *Mas-Hamilton v. LaGard.*[60] The invention related to a locking mechanism that was actuated by the electromagnetic pull of a solenoid. The patentee claimed this feature as a "substantially non-resilient lever moving element." It is worth noting that the patent also included a separate set of claims that specifically claimed this feature in means plus function format. Despite that and the presumption that where the word "means" is absent, 112, 6 (currently, 112(f)) is not invoked, the federal circuit interpreted the former claim (i.e., reciting a "sub-

57. *See* MPEP 2173.05(g) (2022).

58. *See, e.g., In re* Schreiber, 128 F.3d 1473 (Fed. Cir. 1997); *In re* Swinehart, 439 F.2d 210 (C.C.P.A. 1971).

59. *See* section 4.123 and its subsections.

60. 156 F.3d 1206 (Fed. Cir. 1998).

stantially non-resilient lever moving element") to be a means plus function claim that must be construed under 112, paragraph six. The accused product used a stepper motor instead of a solenoid to actuate the locking mechanism. Under the analysis applied to means plus function claims, therefore, the accused product was held to not infringe.

The federal circuit indicated the policy behind its decision is that it should not be possible to draft a claim element in a way that encompasses *any* structure which accomplishes the stated function. Thus, as suggested previously,[61] one way to avoid the result in *Mas-Hamilton* is to employ a recited element that has a well-understood meaning in the art. Examples include words such as memory, processor, etc. While these terms are technically functional, over time they have acquired an accepted meaning in the art so that the federal circuit may not consider them to be purely functional when used in a patent claim. It is noted that several recent cases suggest the federal circuit remains quite receptive to this argument.[62]

However, again, to refer to the issue at hand, the question for the patent drafter is whether to employ functional claims. We recommend that functional claims be employed, but not be exclusively relied upon. In our view, the issue comes down to this: functional claims have the capability to be broader than structural claims, if not construed to invoke 112(f). However, if construed under 112(f) then functional claims will likely be narrower in scope than structural claims. As with most of the issues related to claiming, it is extremely difficult to predict which functional claims a court will decide should be construed under 112(f) and which claims it will decide should not. Thus, we recommend employing functional claims because there is a reasonable chance that they will not be construed under 112(f), particularly if they are drafted as recommended, that is, by using functional terms that arguably have reasonably well understood meanings.[63]

This principle has been illustrated in several of the prior examples.[64]

---

61. *See* section 4.123 and its subsections.

62. *See, e.g.*, Dyfan, LLC v. Target Corp., 28 F.4th 1360 (Fed. Cir. 2022); VDPP v. Vizio, case no. 21-2040, (Mar. 25, 2022 Fed. Cir.) ("processor" and "storage" do not invoke 112(f)) (nonprecedential).

63. Furthermore, an opponent will have the same difficulty predicting how such a functional claim is necessarily going to be construed. Therefore, in a private negotiation, such a claim will have some negotiating leverage.

64. *See* section 4.123 and its subsections.

We recommend that functional claims be employed, but not be exclusively relied upon. In our view, the issue comes down to this: functional claims have the capability to be broader than structural claims, if not construed to invoke 112(f).

6.8 Claim The Environment of the Invention in Dependent Claims

While drafting broad patent claims is a laudable and valiant endeavor, it is important to remember that not all inventions are technological breakthroughs. Therefore, it is important to discuss the situation where the invention is just a relatively minor improvement on existing technology. Depending on the circumstances, for example, such claims may still provide commercial value, in some cases, significant commercial value. Performing a search should help uncover situations where the art may be close.[65] However, regardless, it is always a good idea to make sure that you have claims directed to the "environment" of the invention.

It is always a good idea to make sure that you have claims directed to the "environment" of the invention.

This is meant to refer to details regarding the application of the invention that may largely be technologically independent from how the invention works.[66] Consider, for example, a simple implementation of a look-up table in a digital memory and nothing else. It is likely that a broad claim directed to such an invention is unlikely to make it through the PTO successfully. Such techniques have been known and applied for years. However, at the same

65. Although we are not necessarily recommending that a search be performed. *See* section 1.32, discussing the advantages and disadvantages of searching.

66. Although, to be clear, it may be the environment of the invention that ultimately gives the invention a significant part of its value, as explained in more detail in this section.

time, it is reasonably likely if not highly likely that a table look-up invention, in a properly focused technical environment, and properly claimed, will make it through the PTO and also stand-up in litigation. Suppose, for example, that in wireless networking technology, a table look-up implementation for directing packets from their source to their selected destination was an important aspect in a network interface card for providing the desired connection speed and, that, before that, complex and time-consuming algorithms and memory accesses had to be employed. A similar point could be made in the microprocessor or graphics processor environment. As has been discussed elsewhere, it is often the recognition of the problem that makes the invention patentable.[67]

Therefore, claiming the environment of the invention provides a number of advantages. It should be done in the narrower dependent claims and, therefore, it takes advantage of claim differentiation. Further, it also addresses the issues of written description and claim construction that have been previously discussed by providing additional embodiments to describe and claim. It also preserves validity, as just suggested. While the invention recited independent of the environment may or may not be patentable, claimed within the technical environment, there is a much better chance that the invention will withstand attacks on validity based upon prior art.

> While the invention recited independent of the environment may or may not be patentable, claimed within the technical environment there is a much better chance that the invention will withstand attacks on validity based upon prior art.

6.81 Keep the Invention Terminology Broad while Narrowing the Environment of the Invention

Previously, we suggested that one seek to identify the smallest set of features needed for the invention/innovation as a starting point. We believe that remains correct in the appropriate circumstances (e.g., seeking patent claims that are broad). The following principles are follow-on principles for dependent claims.

---

67. *See, e.g.*, Eibel Process Co. v. Minn. & Ontario Paper Co., 261 U.S. 45 (1923); *see also* section 1.33 and its subsections.

We have discussed the problem-solution approach to claim drafting.[68] In some sense, the problem often helps define the invention by setting out the environment in which the invention arises.

Once the invention is realized for a particular environment, analogous environments in which the invention may be employed often become apparent. Hence, the broadest claim relates to the minimum set of features, described in the broadest terminology *and cast in the broadest environment.*[69] With this construct, the ways to narrow the subject matter relate to: adding more features and narrowing (i.e., clarifying) the terminology. As discussed with respect to dependent claims, this involves the two respective formulations discussed:[70]

(1) "comprising:" or "further comprising:" (adding more features); and

(2) "wherein" (narrowing/clarifying terminology).

The construct of narrowing the environment, however, as implied, may provide yet another way to look at narrowing the claims that may use either of these two formulations and, in some cases, may use both.

This notion is to narrow the environment while seeking to keep the terminology broad, as applicable (that is, in some cases, narrowing the environment may also call for narrowing terminology that describes the invention). Narrowing the environment also allows one to claim the commercial embodiment, or at least the commercial environment, but does so in dependent claims, as has previously been recommended.

6.82 Illustrative Claim Examples

Example 6.14 is primarily to cover a door jamb which is a component of a door frame; however, the technology could be used with any frame. Hence, claim 1 is written more broadly than a door frame. The dependent claims including a window frame; however, claims 2–6 (particularly, 3–6) are used to narrow the environment, potentially providing additional ways to distinguish from prior art that may be cited or applied.

---

68. *See* Chris Konkol, *The "Problem Solved" in In re Wright and In re Dillon*, IDEA J. of Law & Tech. 131 (1990).

69. Again, assuming claim breath is a goal. *See* section 1.31, discussing advantages and disadvantages of seeking broad claims.

70. *See* section 2.152, discussing claim drafting approaches to narrowing a claim.

EXAMPLE 6.14

I claim:

1. A frame comprising: a composite, the composite comprising:

   at least one first member comprising a composite material;

   at least one second member coupled to the first member, the second member comprising one or more materials; and

   an at least partially blended composite coating disposed over the first and the second members, the coating capable of providing structural support to the frame.

2. The frame of claim 1, wherein the frame comprises a window frame.
3. The frame of claim 1, wherein the frame comprises a door frame and the composite comprises a door jamb.
4. The frame of claim 3, wherein the door frame includes a bottom piece of the door frame and the bottom piece of the door frame comprises the door jamb.
5. The frame of claim 4, wherein the door frame includes a top piece and two side pieces.
6. The frame of claim 5, wherein one or more pieces of the door frame respectively comprise any one or any combination of the following: a metallic material, a mineral material, a ceramic material, a plastic material or a hard fibrous material.
7. The frame of claim 1, wherein the coating is further capable of facilitating dimensional stability of the door frame.
8. The frame of claim 1, wherein the coating comprises any combination of the following: resin, substantially spherical structures, glass objects, polyvinyl acetate, a surfactant, glass micro spheres or a wetting agent.
9. The frame of claim 1, wherein the one or more materials of the second member comprise any one or any combination of the following: a metallic material, a mineral material, a ceramic material, a plastic material or a hard fibrous material.

Example 6.15 is the electronic switch we have previously considered that reduces analog signal corruption. It was primarily intended for wireless handsets but has a host of other applications, as recited in claim 2, such as a frequency mixer, a set top box, a smart TV, a TiVo device, a smart console for an automobile, or an analog signal measurement device. The other dependent claims begin to narrow the environment, such as claims 6–8. For example, claim 6 recites an RF switch and includes a stack of transistors which permits higher voltage operation. Claim 7 recites the transistor as a transistor for a shunt path to ground, as used in a switch, and claim 8 recites a pass transistor path, as would be present in the electronic switch.

EXAMPLE 6.15

I claim:

1. A module comprising: at least one integrated circuit chip;

   the at least one integrated circuit chip included in the module and further including at least one field effect transistor, the at least one field effect transistor including a gate, a drain, a source, and a body;

   wherein, during at least a portion of an off state, the body of the at least one field effect transistor is to be electrically biased to have a voltage level substantially more negative than the lowest voltage level of the following: ground, the DC voltage level of the source of the at least one field effect transistor, and the DC voltage level of the drain of the at least one field effect transistor.

2. The module of claim 1, wherein the module is incorporated in at least one of the following: a frequency mixer, a wireless handset, a set top box, a smart TV, a TiVo device, a smart console for an automobile, or an analog signal measurement device.

3. The module of claim 1, wherein the at least one field effect transistor comprises a N-type metal oxide semiconductor (NMOS) field effect transistor.

4. The module of claim 1, wherein the at least one field effect transistor is implemented in a silicon-on-insulator technology.

5. The module of claim 1, wherein the voltage level substantially more negative than the lowest voltage level is more than one volt more negative than the lowest voltage level.

6. The module of claim 1, wherein the at least one field effect transistor is included in a stack of field effect transistors included in a radio frequency (RF) switch, the RF switch being included in the at least one integrated circuit chip.

7. The module of claim 1, wherein the at least one field effect transistor comprising a shunt transistor having a first node coupled to a first port and a second node coupled to ground, the shunt transistor to couple the first port with the ground in an on state, the shunt transistor to isolate the first port from the ground in an off state.

8. The module of claim 7, comprising:

   a second port; and another field effect transistor comprising a pass transistor having a first node coupled to the first port and a second node coupled to a second port, the pass transistor comprising a second gate, a second drain, a second source, and a second body,

   the pass transistor to couple the first port with the second port in an on state;

   the pass transistor to isolate the first port from the second port in an off state and wherein, during at least a portion of the off state of the pass transistor, the body of the pass transistor is to be electrically biased to have a voltage level substantially more negative than the lowest voltage level of the following: ground, the DC voltage level of the source of the pass transistor, and the DC voltage level of the drain of the pass transistor.

9. The module of claim 8, wherein the ports comprise RF ports.

6.9 Employ More Than One Statutory Class to Claim the Invention—But Do So in Different Claim Sets; Employ the Same Statutory Class to Cover Rights of Different Scope

As many practicing attorneys may already realize, it is typical for an invention to lend itself to a particular statutory class. As an example, software typically lends itself more to method claims, whereas a chip or circuit tends to lend itself more to apparatus claims. Despite this, it is recommended that you make the effort to claim the invention using a different statutory class in addition to the statutory class that seems most natural. The justifications are those that we have discussed earlier, for example, diversity in claiming approach, covering different rights, avoiding dedicating subject matter to the public, and reducing the need to modify the claims later (and thus reducing risks such as estoppel, written description or claim construction issues).

As a technical matter, it is legally proper to mix statutory classes in the same set of claims. For example, one may depend an apparatus claim from a method claim where the apparatus claim implements the method, if properly drafted. However, it is suggested that this practice be avoided primarily because it is believed the risk of drafting an indefinite claim is higher in this situation. That is, without careful drafting, there is greater risk that it may not be clear that claim 2 (the dependent claim) is an apparatus claim in the previous hypothetical. For example, in *IPXL v. Amazon*[71] a claim was held invalid because apparatus and method type language included in the same claim made it unclear whether the claim was a method claim or an apparatus claim.

Along similar lines, for the preceding reason, when adapting the claims to a different statutory class, you should also be mindful to employ proper language for the type of statutory class. Apparatus claims should recite structure or the capability to perform acts, whereas method claims should recite performing the acts themselves using words that end in "ing."

If moving between apparatus and method claims, one should also be mindful to *more than* simply repeat the limitations in a slightly modified form if possible. This relates in many respects to a prior discussion regarding the trade-offs between apparatus and method claims.[72] For example, because method claims have the potential to be broader by avoiding apparatus-type limitations, when adapting an apparatus invention to method form, you should try to ensure that the limitations are appropriately modified to take advantage of that additional scope.

> It is recommended that you make the effort to claim the invention using a different statutory class. The justifications are those that we have discussed earlier, for example, diversity in claiming approach, covering different rights, and reducing the need to modify the claims later (and thus reducing risks such as estoppel, written description or claim construction issues). However, when adapting the claims to a different statutory class, you should also be mindful to *more than* simply repeat the limitations in a slightly modified form if possible.

71. 430 F.3d 1377, 1384 (Fed. Cir. 2005); *see also* section 5.6 and its subsections discussing mixing statutory classes in one claim.

72. *See* Chapter 4 discussion regarding method claims.

Consider, for example, an invention directed to an optical waveguide or optical switch and waveguide of some sort. Typically, this type of an invention would lend itself well to an apparatus claim. The limitations may refer to materials employed to fabricate the waveguide, such as a transmission layer and a cladding layer, or to particular circuitry for optical switch operation. When claiming this technology in method form, however, such limitations are typically not desirable. Instead, it would, perhaps, be wise to refer to actions, such as transmitting or receiving radiation from one point to another, and/or actions of the switch and/or waveguide in operation.

If, instead, the apparatus limitations were included in the method claim, such as with a "providing" element, for example, the value of employing method form, in addition to apparatus form, may be largely vitiated, even assuming the claim raises no indefiniteness issues. In such a form, this may cover little to nothing more via the method claim than has already been covered with the apparatus claim itself.

Likewise, when starting with a method claim and attempting to draft an apparatus claim directed to the technology, such as in the case of software, for example, simply writing a means plus function claim from the method elements, or a purely functional claim, where the apparatus elements track the method elements, will not necessarily produce the best protection for the invention. Although there is federal circuit law that states that in such an instance the claims must be construed separately and independently,[73] the claims are still likely to be construed similarly since virtually the same words are being employed.[74] Thus, this still may not produce as good protection as if an attempt were made to draft an apparatus claim having structural elements mixed with functional elements in language that is not identical or almost identical to the language of the method claim.

Sometimes the opportunity to cover a significantly *different* scope of rights using the *same* statutory class is also overlooked in connection with a particular patent application. Consider, for example, technology directed to fabrication of a processor of some sort, such as a microprocessor. Typically, this would be covered using a method claim. Likewise, as the prior section discussed, it may be wise to include an apparatus claim to cover the result of the fabrication process (note: here, we are not intending to refer to product-by-process claims[75]). However, there may also be sub-methods of the method

---

73. *See, e.g.*, Generation II Orthotics v. Medical Tech., 263 F.3d 1356, 1368 (Fed. Cir. 2001).

74. Of course, that *might* be the drafters desire in some situations, in which case, it would then be acceptable.

75. *See* section 4.125 and its subsections, discussing product-by-process claims.

claim that are protectible as well. Likewise, a method claim may be directed to using a particular apparatus, separate from method claims directed to manufacture of the apparatus. Thus, in the latter situation, a significantly different scope would be covered using the same statutory class.

The same might be said regarding the apparatus claims. Through the use of combination claims and sub-combinations claims, rights having different scope may be covered, such as component and system,[76] via the same statutory class.

> A method claim may be directed to using a particular apparatus, separate from method claims directed to manufacture of the apparatus. Thus, a significantly different scope may be covered using the same statutory class. The same might be said regarding the apparatus claims. Through the use of combination claims and sub-combinations claims, rights having different scope may be covered via the same statutory class.

A chip may also be claimed that is intended to be included in a system so that infringement occurs even where the chip is sold without the system. For example, a component claim may look like:

EXAMPLE 6.16

I claim:

1. An apparatus comprising: a memory integrated circuit chip, including a memory controller to implement burst mode memory operation, for a computer system including the capability to activate the burst mode memory operation.

Infringement is present if the chip sold has the recited capability, whether the feature claimed is in use. A similar result occurred in *Intel v. ITC*.[77] The

76. *See* sections 4.121 and 4.122 and their subsections, discussing component and system claims.

77. 946 F.2d 821, 832 (Fed. Cir. 1991).

claim at issue was directed to page mode operation; however, the claim was drafted so that infringement occurred if the chip had the capability, regardless of whether that capability was being employed during operation of the chip. It required the setting of a particular bit to put the chip in that mode and that feature was specifically claimed. Therefore, the federal circuit concluded that infringement could still occur whether the bit was actually set, such as by a particular operating system.[78]

There are many examples where this technique might be useful. As illustrations, a transmitter and receiver, a television and TV remote, and a processor and memory may be claimed like this. Thus, components may be claimed so that they infringe whether sold separately or sold in a complete system.

6.10 Draft Claims to Reduce the Risk of Exhaustion or Implied Patent Licensing

When attempting to protect technology with various types of patent claims, such as a component and a system, different methods, or a method and apparatus, the doctrine of patent exhaustion and the doctrine of implied patent licenses may come into play. Doctrinally, the notion of exhaustion is that if you sell (or license a manufacturer who then sells) a product that is "covered" by a claim in a patent (i.e., reads on the product), then the claim (or claims) that cover (i.e., read on) the product are "exhausted," meaning that you may not ever assert the claim(s) against that specific product item sold.[79]

Technically, exhaustion applies to an entire patent. That is, one may either sell product under the patent or license another to sell under the patent.[80] Once a sale of a product occurs in which a claim of the patent reads on the product, the patent with those claims is exhausted.[81] However, after the Supreme Court decision in *Quanta*, what constitutes patent exhaustion became understood to be more than having a claim read on the product sold. For example, the sale of a component of a claim typically was viewed previously as not necessarily creating exhaustion as to the patent claim, but as a

78. *See* section 4.124.

79. *See, e.g.*, Quanta Comput., Inc. v. LG Elecs., Inc., 553 U.S. 617, 128 S. Ct. 2109 (2008).

80. Although through express language a license may be limited to specific patent claims so that there may be a question as to whether or not all the claims are exhausted if a product is sold in which one of the licensed claims reads on the product. *Cf.* Quanta Comput., Inc. v. LG Elecs., Inc., 553 U.S. 617, 128 S. Ct. 2109 (2008).

81. *See id.*, it's as if the entire patent is expressly licensed.

possible implied license situation.[82] However, this latter situation was clarified by the Supreme Court to potentially constitute patent exhaustion as well, depending on the facts.

An implied patent license need not apply to an entire patent since its doctrinal underpinnings rely on contract law. Thus, the doctrine of implied patent licenses, in general, is not the same legal doctrine as patent exhaustion. This former doctrine may arise, for example, if a component of a patent claim was sold or if a method claim covered use of a product sold. That is, depending on the circumstances, a license to certain patent claims might be implied by the sale. One requirement, however, was (and is) that the product sold not be capable of substantial noninfringing uses with respect to a claim or claims at issue.[83]

Years ago, by using different statutory classes and/or by using the same statutory class to cover different sets of rights, such as a combination and subcombination, as discussed in the preceding section, it was believed that these doctrines might be avoided or at least the risk of these doctrines being applicable in a given situation could be reduced through claim drafting in combination with contractual provisions. Thus, in addition to clever drafting of patent claims, attempts were made to limit both of these doctrines with contractual provisions. So-called post-sale contractual restrictions, for example, were used in an attempt to limit the scope of exhaustion. In yet another scenario, if you were to sell a component covered by a patent claim in which either a system claim or a method claim recited the component itself; typically, it would be argued that the system or method claims were not necessarily exhausted in some situations.[84] However, several Supreme Court cases have all but made it clear that many of these attempts will not work legally. Furthermore, today, the distinction between patent exhaustion and an implied patent license is blurrier than it was previously.

6.101 *Quanta* Decision

Quanta[85] is an important exhaustion case because it expanded the notion of patent exhaustion beyond the contours set by the federal circuit, which represented the prevailing understanding at the time. It was understood that exhaustion applied if a product was sold that was covered by a claim of a patent

82. *See* Met-Coil Systems Corp. v. Korners Unlimited, 803 F.2d 684 (Fed. Cir. 1986).
83. *Id.*
84. Often, these situations were accompanied by contractual provisions that expressly stated no intent to grant an implied patent license.
85. 553 U.S. 617, 128 S. Ct. 2109 (2008).

(i.e., the claim read on the product). That is, if the claim read on the product sold, the claim was exhausted and, hence, the patent was exhausted. The idea was that the patentee could either sell under the patent or license the patent. That is how the patentee extracts value from the patent.

The facts of *Quanta* were that Quanta purchased Intel parts and combined them with non-intel parts to make computer systems. These computer systems as sold were accused to infringe patents owned by LG Electronics (LGE). Quanta offered as its defense, exhaustion, because LGE had licensed Intel under the patents. However, Quanta did not license Intel to make the computer systems (e.g., to make the combination that resulted in the accused infringement). Furthermore, Intel, per its agreement with LGE, was required to and did notice its customers that it did not possess such a license in order to make clear to its customers that it was not passing on a license to make the system combination.

However, the Supreme Court ruled that the Intel-LGE agreements did not attempt to speak to exhaustion. Furthermore, the Court ruled that the Intel parts "substantially embodied" the invention of the LGE patents because the Intel parts merely needed to be connected to generic memory to produce what was alleged to infringe the patent claims. In other words, exhaustion applied, via the concept of the product sold "substantially embodying" the invention, to the claims, although the claims did not "read on" what was sold.

6.102 *Lexmark* Decision

Lexmark[86] is another important patent exhaustion decision. The federal circuit previously had made clear that it was permissible to contract around exhaustion.[87] That is, according to the federal circuit, if a state law contract made clear that patent exhaustion did not apply, and the contract was otherwise legal, then the contract rendered patent exhaustion inapplicable in patent law, which is federal, not state, law. The Supreme Court corrected that view in *Lexmark*.

The federal circuit had assumed patent exhaustion rested on the authority granted by the patentee under the patent; however, according to the Supreme Court, it rests on the principle of not permitting restraints on alienation. Thus, post-sale contractual restrictions on patented products are unenforceable in patent law, although they may be enforceable under state contract law. That is, once the patented product is sold, the patent claim (and, thus, the

86. *See* Impression Products, Inc. v. Lexmark Int'l Inc., 581 U.S. ___, 137 S. Ct. 1523 (2017).
87. *See* Mallinckrodt, Inc. v. Medipart, Inc., 976 F.2d 700 (Fed. Cir. 1992).

patent) is exhausted regardless of agreed upon post-sale contractual restrictions that may be enforceable in state court.

In *Lexmark*, Lexmark had patents on its ink cartridges. It had a return program where purchasers could pay less for those cartridges if they agreed after use to return them to Lexmark and not sell them to entities who would buy them, refill them with ink, and sell them to others. Impression Products was an entity that obtained empty ink cartridges and refilled them for sale. Some of those ink cartridges were return program cartridges and some were ink cartridges that had been sold abroad by Lexmark.

Lexmark sued Impression Products arguing patent infringement. Impression Products defended based on patent exhaustion. Lexmark argued that patent exhaustion did not apply to the return program cartridges based on an enforceable contact and did not apply to the cartridges sold abroad since they were sold outside the United States (i.e., arguing U.S. law on exhaustion should not apply). The federal circuit held for Lexmark via summary judgment both as to the cartridges from the return program and the cartridges purchased abroad.

The Supreme Court reversed as to both rulings. It determined patent exhaustion applied to both types of cartridges.

6.103 *Met-Coil* Decision

Met-Coil Systems Corp. was the assignee of U.S. Patent No. 4,466,641, which claimed an apparatus and method for connecting sections of metal ducts of the kind used in heating and air conditioning systems. Under the claimed invention, the ends of the metal duct sections were bent to form integral flanges. Then specially shaped corner pieces were snapped in place, and the sections are then bolted together. Met-Coil made and sold roll-forming machines that its customers used to bend integral flanges so as to practice the claimed invention. Met-Coil also sold the specially shaped corner pieces for use with the integral flanges. Korners Unlimited, Inc. made corner pieces for use with Met-Coil's integral flanges and sold them to purchasers of Met-Coil's machines. Met-Coil sued Korners for inducing infringement.

Kroners had moved for summary judgment. The basis of Korners' motion for summary judgment was that Met-Coil, by selling the roll-forming machine, granted an implied license under the patent to its customers. Because of that license, Korners contended that Met-Coil's customers cannot infringe the claims of the patent and, thus, Korners can neither induce infringement nor contribute to patent infringement. The district court had ruled that an implied license had been granted with the sale of the machines.

The federal circuit affirmed the district court. The appellate court stated (emphasis supplied):

> On appeal, Met-Coil urges that the district court erred. . . . To support that proposition, Met-Coil cites *Bandag, Inc. v. Al Bolser's Tire Stores, Inc.*, 750 F.2d 903, 223 USPQ 982 (Fed. Cir. 1984). In that case, the owner of a patent claiming a method for retreading tires sued a retreader who had purchased retreading equipment from a former licensee of the patent owner. This court set out two requirements for the grant of an implied license by virtue of a sale of nonpatented equipment used to practice a patented invention. **First, the equipment involved must have no noninfringing uses.** *Id.* at 924, 223 USPQ at 998. In *Bandag*, the retreading equipment had noninfringing uses, so no license could be implied. To the contrary, Met-Coil's machines have no non-infringing use. **Second, the circumstances of the sale must "plainly indicate that the grant of a license should be inferred."** *Id.* at 925, 223 USPQ at 998, quoting *Hunt v. Armour Co.*, 185 F.2d 722, 729, 88 USPQ 53, 58 (7th Cir. 1950). The circumstances of the sale in *Bandag*, purchase of the equipment from the former licensee of the patent owner, did not plainly indicate that the grant of a license should be inferred.

Here, the appellate court agreed that there was no noninfringing use other than in practicing the patent and that the circumstances of the sale plainly indicated that the grant of an implied license should be inferred.

6.104 Drafting Techniques to Reduce Risk of Patent Exhuastion and/or an Implied Patent License

In comparison with exhaustion, there are approaches to reducing risks of creating an implied patent license that are reasonably clear. However, to be effective, typically, the patent claims need to also be drafted to reduce risk of exhaustion. Either would make the patent claims effectively unenforceable in a situation in which, it is assumed, the patentee would like the patent claims to be enforceable, such as with respect to a competitor.

A primary consideration for drafting patent claims to reduce the risk of granting an implied patent license through the sale of a patented product is to ensure that suitable or "reasonable"[88] noninfringing uses of the product sold are present. That is, the *product* as sold should be capable of substantial noninfringing uses with respect to the patent *claim or claims* at issue. Notably, if accomplished, this should eliminate potential for also bringing a charge of contributory infringement based on the patent claims, which may not be

88. *See, e.g.*, Glass Equip. Dev. v. Besten, 174 F.3d 1337, 1343 (Fed. Cir. 1999).

desirable.[89] Furthermore, this might be a real challenge because as a claim drafter, one may not know what future products the patentee might sell or license others to sell. However, with that said, there is no real harm in asking the patentee and taking that information into consideration in drafting the claims.

To illustrate this drafting approach, consider, for example, the situation for a graphics processor manufacturer. Let's simplify this complex analysis by assuming exhaustion of a component may be handled by claiming more than a component. That is, for traditional exhaustion, a claim is exhausted if the claim reads on the product sold by the patentee or his licensee. Before *Quanta*, this was believed to be the case; however, today, exhaustion is much more complex in accordance with *Quanta*. However, with this more simplified approach as a start, a system claim may look like:

EXAMPLE 6.17

I claim:

1. A system comprising: a graphics processor coupled to memory.

In this example, the manufacturer probably has not managed to avoid an implied patent license, even under the assumption that exhaustion is not applicable because the claim does not read on the graphics processor as sold. The reason an implied license is not avoided is that the processor cannot be used without coupling it to memory. Thus, the product sold, that is, the graphics processor, does not have substantial noninfringing uses. Suppose, however, the claim recited:

EXAMPLE 6.18

I claim:

1. A system comprising: a graphics processor coupled to random access memory (RAM), wherein the RAM has an access time of 50 nanoseconds or less.

89. Although a claim for inducing infringement may still be available. *See* section 3.22 and its subsections.

Assuming that the processor could be coupled to other more generic types of memory and/or RAM with slower access times, then arguably no implied license is granted;[90] however, because most of the valuable uses of the processor will be with RAM having relatively high speed (e.g., above 50 ns access time), little may have been given up in this example, that is, restricting the scope of the claim in this manner covers the valuable uses with fast memory while making it arguable that sale of the graphics processor does not impliedly license the claim.

> A primary consideration for drafting patent claims to reduce the risk of granting an implied patent license through the sale of a patented product is to ensure that suitable or "reasonable" noninfringing uses of the product sold are present.

This approach may be counterintuitive to most patent attorneys. It suggests that claims should be drafted to deliberately leave some uses not covered by the patent claims, rather than to cover as much with the claims as possible. However, also recognize that this is being suggested in a unique situation.

The suggestion is that when patenting a product that will be sold (or expressly licensed as a product that will be manufactured and sold), include claims that cover *more than* the product itself, which may assist in reducing the risk of exhaustion, as discussed later. Further, include claims such that noninfringing uses of the product sold exist to reduce the risk of an implied patent license. Of course, the uncovered uses should preferably be inferior or less valuable uses than those covered by the patent claims.

To explain the analysis further, the idea here is to avoid the implication *in law* of a grant of an implied patent license. If one sells a product (or licenses a product for manufacture and sale) and all its reasonable uses will result in patent infringement, then a court will likely conclude that a patent license is implied in law, if not also, in fact.[91]

This entire approach, however, is merely to give the patent more vitality than to simply protect the product, a situation that may also be viewed with

90. It is also a good idea to include labels on the product or language in applicable order forms or agreements that clarify that no implied patent license is intended to be granted; however, that issue is not one related to claim drafting. *See* Met-Coil Systems Corp. v. Korners Unlimited, 803 F.2d 684 (Fed. Cir. 1986).

91. *See* Met-Coil Systems Corp. v. Korners Unlimited, 803 F.2d 684 (Fed. Cir. 1986).

suspicion by a court. If the goal were merely to protect the product itself, then the patent becomes diminished in value once a large market for the product develops based on the patentee's own sales. That is, if the patentee has flooded the market with its product, then a patent on the product should be less valuable; the patentee has already obtained most of its value for the product. Thus, such attempts as described here to reduce the risk of an implied patent license or exhaustion may be viewed by a court as an attempt to, in effect, "double dip." Courts view such attempts with extreme suspicion.

Hence, for this situation, one should not cover the product as sold with a claim of the patent or risk exhausting the entire patent.[92] If it is unclear whether protecting the product would be more valuable, one approach might be to have separate patents, one directed to the product as sold and one with claims directed to more than the product as sold, such as just described and as further explained later. If later it becomes clear that the patent with claims that cover more than the product is more valuable, then the patent with claims that cover the product as sold can be disclaimed, if needed (or vice versa).

> The suggestion is that, in a unique situation of patenting a product that will be sold (or expressly licensed as a product that will be manufactured and sold), first, include claims that cover *more than* the product itself, which may assist in reducing the risk of exhaustion, as discussed later. Second, include claims such that noninfringing uses of the product sold exist to reduce the risk of an implied patent license. Of course, the uncovered uses should preferably be inferior or less valuable uses than those covered by the claims.

As an example, consider the claim drafting principle "batteries not included." This refers to the notion that it is usually best to not claim the power source in connection with a particular technology. One reason, of course, is that it provides an easy design around for those interested in using the technology without infringing the patent claims. In fact, most technology is sold without the power source anyway. However, a claim that includes the power source may likewise grant an implied license with the sale of the product. If you include the power source in the claim, then, perhaps, at least

92. Later in this section approaches to draft claims to address exhaustion are discussed.

arguably, the product sold has no noninfringing uses, assuming that there is no feasible way to use the product without a power source.[93]

> Keep in mind the claim drafting principle "batteries not included." This refers to the notion that it is usually best to not claim the power source in connection with a particular technology.

Now, however, we must address the thorny issue of exhaustion. As mentioned previously, *Quanta*, to some extent, made less-clear differences between situations that might result in patent exhaustion and situations that might result in an implied patent license. Prior to *Quanta*, what we refer to here as "traditional exhaustion" required that a patent claim "read" on a product as sold, whether sold by a licensee or by the patentee. However, *Quanta* clarified the concept of a product that "substantially embodies" a patent (in the language of the Supreme Court), so that this latter principle, as previously understood, can no longer be maintained. Therefore, we introduce here the terminology of "*Quanta*-type exhaustion" to refer to a situation, such as in *Quanta*, where a claim does not read on product sold, but nonetheless the product sold may be held to "substantially embody" a patent, such that the entire patent is exhausted. We refer to the situation where a claim of a patent reads on a product as sold, such that the entire patent is exhausted, as "traditional exhaustion."

It may not always be possible to avoid patent exhaustion. However, limiting the potential scope of exhaustion via claim drafting, if possible, remains beneficial, such as by not exhausting claims of related patents with respect to one's competitors. Although it may vary significantly depending on products, markets and technologies, it is believed that the situation in *Quanta* may not be a typical technology situation. If this belief is correct, *Quanta* probably creates less risk regarding patent exhaustion than may be perceived.

For example, one might have the perception that, as a result of *Quanta*, any product sale has the potential to exhaust significant portions of one's patent portfolio. It is believed, however, that these perceptions may be an overstatement of the impact of the decision and that the decision may, instead, represent a so-called corner case. That is, *Quanta* addresses what may be a narrowly circumscribed factual situation.

---

93. *Cf.* Anton/Bauer v. Pag, 329 F.3d 1343 (Fed. Cir. 2003).

In *Quanta*, LGE was asserting its patents against Quanta. Quanta was a system integrator that provided complete systems that included Intel processors and chipsets connected to system memory. Thus, the Intel processors and chipsets when connected to memory were able to implement the patented features. LGE had granted a license to Intel. However, the license agreement contained language that clarified that LGE did not grant Intel an implied license. Since Intel did not have an implied license neither did Quanta.

However, the district court ruled that patent exhaustion applied, although the patent claims did *not* read on the Intel product as sold. Thus, this was *not* a case of traditional exhaustion. The federal circuit reversed based on its understanding of the principles around patent exhaustion. However, the Supreme Court reversed the federal circuit, concluding that the license to Intel exhausted the asserted patent claims, although the claims at issue did *not* read on the Intel product as sold.

Specifically, the Supreme Court, in explaining the situation at hand in *Quanta*, stated:

> Like the Univis lens blanks, the Intel Products constitute a material part of the patented invention and **all but completely practice the patent**. Here, as in *Univis*, the incomplete article substantially embodies the patent because **the only step necessary** to practice the patent is the application of common processes or the addition of standard parts. (emphasis supplied)

The Court further stated:

> Naturally, the Intel Products cannot carry out these functions unless they are attached to memory and buses, **but those additions are standard components in the system**, providing the material that enables the microprocessors and chipsets to function. The Intel Products were specifically designed to function only when memory or buses are attached; **Quanta was not required to make any creative or inventive decision when it added those parts.**

Therefore, Quanta had to do no more than connect processors, chipsets, and memory. Rather, according to the Court, Quanta did not modify the Intel products at all:

> **Quanta does not modify the Intel components** and follows Intel's specifications to incorporate the parts into its own systems. (emphasis supplied)

More typically, however, a company may bundle its own technology along with components that it may purchase to produce a complete or final product for market, *which may, at times, involve significant technical modifications made to the purchased components, such as, for compatibility*, in comparison with the situation of *Quanta* or even *Univis Lens*, a predecessor Supreme Court case relied upon in *Quanta*.

The Court's language in *Quanta* implies at least three possible legal differences that may be used in claim drafting to provide a distinction from the facts of *Quanta*. One potential distinction suggests that *Quanta*-type exhaustion may be limited to situations in which a product is being "finished." For example, in explaining the reasoning of *Univis Lens*, the *Quanta* Court, quoting in part the *Univis Lens* Court, stated: (emphasis added)

> The Court assumed that the Univis patents containing claims for finished lenses were practiced in part by the wholesalers and finishing retailers who ground the blanks into lenses, and held that the sale of the lens blanks exhausted the patents on the finished lenses. *Univis*, 316 U. S., at 248–249. The Court explained that the lens blanks "embodi[ed] essential features of the patented device and [were] without utility until . . . ground and polished as the finished lens of the patent." *Id.*, at 249. The Court noted that:
>
> "where one has sold an uncompleted article which, because it embodies essential features of his patented invention, is within the protection of his patent, and has destined the article to be finished by the purchaser in conformity to the patent, he has sold his invention so far as it is or may be embodied in that particular article." *Id.*, at 250–251.
>
> In sum, the Court concluded that **the traditional bar on patent restrictions following the sale of an item applies when the item sufficiently embodies the patent—even if it does not completely practice the patent—such that its only and intended use is to be finished under the terms of the patent.**

Likewise, later in the *Quanta* opinion, the Court stated:

> First, *Univis* held that "the authorized sale of an article which is capable of use only in practicing the patent is a relinquishment of the patent monopoly with respect to the article sold." *Id.* at 249. The lens blanks in *Univis* met this standard because they were "without utility until [they were] ground and polished as the finished lens of the patent." *Ibid.* Accordingly, "the only object of the sale [was] to enable the [finishing retailer] to grind and polish it for use as a lens by the prospective wearer." *Id.*

The language of the Court cited here suggests a possibility that exhaustion may be limited to situations in which the "only and intended use" of the product sold is to be finished; that is, in this situation, the product "substantially embodies" the patent.

Likewise, the Court stated (emphasis added):

> But we think that the nature of **the final step,** rather than whether it consists of adding or deleting material, is the relevant characteristic. In each case, **the final step to practice the patent is common and noninventive**: grinding a lens to the customer's prescription, or connecting a microprocessor or chipset to buses or memory.

The Court later stated (emphasis supplied):

> But this is simply a rephrasing of its argument that combining the Intel Products with other components adds more than **standard finishing to complete a patented article. As explained above, making a product that substantially embodies a patent is, for exhaustion purposes, no different from making the patented article itself.** In other words, **no further "making"** results from the addition of standard parts—here, the buses and memory—to a product that already substantially embodies the patent.

Again, these passages might imply that some type of ministerial "product finishing" may be a feature of exhaustion in situations like this. If so, reducing risk of exhaustion may involve drafting a claim that covers more than the product, but in which the covered combination is created by adding significant technology rather than making standardized electrical connections (as in *Quanta*) or performing standard grinding and polishing (as in *Univis Lens*), for example.

Furthermore, other language may suggest that perhaps what is sold must embody the essential features of the invention. The following are sample passages from the *Quanta* opinion (emphasis supplied):

> We agree with Quanta that *Univis* governs this case. As the Court there explained, exhaustion was triggered by the sale of the lens blanks because **their only reasonable and intended use** was to practice the patent and **because they "embodie[d] essential features of [the] patented invention."** 316 U. S., at 249–251. Each of those attributes is shared by the microprocessors and chipsets Intel sold to Quanta under the License Agreement.
>
> . . .
>
> Second, the lens blanks in *Univis* **"embodie[d] essential features of [the] patented invention."** *Id.*, at 250–251. The essential, or inventive, feature of the Univis lens patents was the fusing together of different lens segments to create bi- and tri-focal lenses.
>
> . . .
>
> The Intel Products **embody the essential features** of the LGE Patents **because they carry out all the inventive processes** when combined, according to their design, with standard components.

> . . .
>
> The relevant consideration is whether the Intel Products that partially practice a patent—**by, for example, embodying its essential features—** exhaust *that* patent.
>
> . . .
>
> Intel's microprocessors and chipsets **substantially embodied** the LGE Patents **because they had no reasonable noninfringing use and included all the inventive aspects** of the patented methods.

However, some of the language cited here may be read to instead suggest that exhaustion applies where there are no reasonable noninfringing uses, not unlike the approach applied in *Met-Coil,* which relates to implied patent licensing. Additional language in the opinion may also be cited to support that view (emphasis supplied):

> Here, LGE has suggested **no reasonable use** for the Intel Products other than incorporating them into computer systems that practice the LGE Patents. Nor can we can discern one: A microprocessor or chipset cannot function until it is connected to buses and memory. And here, as in *Univis*, the only apparent object of Intel's sales to Quanta was to permit Quanta to incorporate the Intel Products into computers that would practice the patents.
>
> . . .
>
> Intel's microprocessors and chipsets substantially embodied the LGE Patents **because they had no reasonable noninfringing use and included all the inventive aspects of the patented methods.**

Still other language, however, in addition to some of the language cited earlier, suggests that if something creative or inventive was added then exhaustion might not apply. The Court stated (emphasis supplied):

> Here, as in *Univis*, the incomplete article substantially embodies the patent **because the only step necessary to practice the patent is the application of common processes or the addition of standard parts.**
>
> . . .
>
> Quanta **was not required to make any creative or inventive decision** when it added those parts. . . .

In light of the passages from the *Quanta* opinion cited earlier, one might craft claims along the following lines in an attempt to avoid exhaustion from the sale of a product related to the claims of the patent. First, the claims should cover more than the product as sold so that *the claims do not literally cover what is sold.* Second, the claims should meet one or more (perhaps even all, if possible) of the following:

(1) what is covered by the claims is something that is a complete product and what is sold is either a different complete product or an incomplete product that requires much more than some type of common, well-known or merely ministerial type of finishing or completion to provide the complete product that is claimed,
(2) what is covered by the claims is something that embodies all the essential features of the patented invention and what is sold does not embody all of those essential features,
(3) what is sold is intended to be substantially modified by the purchaser and in a manner that may possibly be covered by the claims (and perhaps such modifications are creative or inventive modifications[94]) and/or
(4) what is sold has reasonable alternative uses beyond practicing what is covered by the claims.

Again, the concept is to have what is sold by the patentee or licensee be different from the claims in a technically substantive manner, rather than a technically ministerial manner. These specific points, of course, focus on the situation in *Quanta*. There may be other ways to accomplish this for other situations. Drafting such claims might be a real challenge because, as a claim drafter, one may not know what future products the patentee might sell or license others to sell. However, with that said, there is no real harm in asking the patentee and taking that information into consideration in drafting the claims. Consider, for example, a scenario in which a company might patent its software executing on a standard computing platform; however, other companies may purchase/license that software and modify it by adding their own technology to produce a special purpose computing platform. Likewise, hardware system integrators may similarly take flash memory and load bios or other low-level programs, add other software and integrate the chip into a motherboard of a computing platform which may then be sold. These may be scenarios where the claims cover something other than a product as sold, what is sold does not "substantially embody" the invention of the claims, and the claims may otherwise have value if not exhausted. Claims might likewise be drafted so that a reasonable noninfringing alternative use of the product is present. This latter point is similar to the approach that has been suggested to reduce the risk that claims may be impliedly licensed by the sale of a component, for example.

94. Software might be a good example.

7

EPC Practice and Claim Drafting Issues

There are many issues of European patent practice that might be discussed in light of the European Patent Convention (EPC). However, that is beyond the scope of this work. This section is intended simply as a quick introduction to a few important differences from U.S. practice that relate to claim preparation.

It is also helpful to understand how these issues may typically arise procedurally based on an initially domestically filed patent application, which is often the case. That is, frequently the United States is a preferred initial jurisdiction in which to file a patent application.

Under the Paris Convention, which is an international treaty related to international filing of patent applications, if a patent application is initially filed in a Paris Convention member jurisdiction, then a counterpart patent application, if filed within 12 months of the initial filing in another Paris Convention member jurisdiction, will be accorded priority as if it had been filed the same day as the initial filing. Virtually all countries in the world of commercial interest are members of the Paris Convention.[1] Thus, if a patent application is filed in the United States and a counterpart patent application is filed in the European Patent Office (EPO) within 12 months, the EPO application is accorded priority based on the U.S. application. The EPO is the office designated for filing for members of the European Patent Convention (EPC).

Thus, the EPO does not constitute a patent office for a particular country. Instead, many countries (over 40) in Europe (and even some technically not in Europe) are members of the European Patent Convention. By agreement, the member countries agree to follow the rules of the EPC, which are carried out by the EPO. Thus, if the EPO grants a patent application, then it can be issued in selected member countries (also referred to here as "local countries") through a process referred to as validation that involves paying fees and observing other local country formalities but does not require further

1. However, Taiwan is not a member of the Paris Convention. Also, be aware another treaty that arises in connection with foreign patent practice, the Patent Cooperation Treaty (PCT), may not necessarily include all countries of commercial interest.

substantive examination. After issuance by the local country, issues regarded that country's issued patent law, such as infringement or validity, are handled by the courts of that local country.

Rather than filing in the EPO, for many European Convention countries, it is possible, instead, to "directly file" in selected member countries of the EPO,[2] but, if filing in multiple countries, that would require multiple prosecutions under each local country's rules and in each local country's language. Thus, filing in the EPO saves costs with one prosecution in one of three select languages (German, French, or English) under a single set of rules.[3] Thus, this is legally appealing as well as a way to reduce costs.[4]

7.1 Prior Art

Article 54 of the EPC defines the state of the art and, consequently, prior art. It states in pertinent part:

> (1) An invention shall be considered to be new if it does not form part of the state of the art.
>
> (2) The state of the art shall be held to comprise everything made available to the public by means of a written or oral description, by use, or in any other way, before the date of filing of the European patent application.
>
> (3) Additionally, the content of European patent applications as filed, the dates of filing of which are prior to the date referred to in paragraph 2 and which were published on or after that date, shall be considered as comprised in the state of the art.

This is different than section 102, discussed extensively in Chapter 1. Europe is said to observe an "absolute novelty" standard with respect to prior art since anything made available to the public in any way before the application filing date is considered prior art. On the other hand, "offers for sale" do not put an invention in the public domain for an EPC country, in contrast with the United States. Also, commercial use in secret, which may constitute a "public use" in the United States, should not put an invention in the public domain in an EPC country since it is not "made available to the public." It is worthy

2. France is one example of a country in which one may not directly file.

3. Be aware, however, that translation errors, unfortunately, may potentially have a detrimental impact on legal rights.

4. Another option with respect to patent filing in Europe not yet available as of the date of preparation of this book, but which will soon be available, is the Unified Patent and its associated Unified Patent Court. It is expected to be available April, 2023.

of note that Article 54(3) is analogous to pre-AIA section 102(e) or post-AIA section 102(a)(2).

7.2 Excluded Subject Matter: Computer Programs; Methods of Diagnosis, Treatment, and Surgery

Under Article 52(2)(c) of the EPC, various types of subject matter, including software, are not patentable, meaning that European patents cannot be granted for such subject matter. Article 52 states:

> (1) European patents shall be granted for any inventions, in all fields of technology, provided that they are new, involve an inventive step and are susceptible of industrial application.
>
> (2) The following in particular shall not be regarded as inventions within the meaning of paragraph 1:
>
> (a) discoveries, scientific theories and mathematical methods;
>
> (b) aesthetic creations;
>
> (c) schemes, rules and methods for performing mental acts, playing games or doing business, and programs for computers;
>
> (d) presentations of information.
>
> (3) Paragraph 2 shall exclude the patentability of the subject-matter or activities referred to therein only to the extent to which a European patent application or European patent relates to such subject-matter or activities as such.

However, it has been established that computer programs having "technical character" do not fall within the exclusion.[5] The Guidelines state:[6]

> Computer programs are excluded from patentability under Art. 52(2)(c) and (3) if claimed as such. However, following the generally applicable criteria for Art. 52(2) and (3) (GII, 2), the exclusion does not apply to computer programs having a technical character.
>
> Art. 52(2)(c)
>
> In order to have a technical character, and thus not be excluded from patentability, a computer program must produce a "further technical effect" when run on a computer. A "further technical effect" is a technical effect going beyond the "normal" physical interactions between the program (software) and the computer (hardware) on which it is run. The normal physical

5. *See* Guidelines for Examination, Part G, Chapter II, Section 3.6 (2022).
6. *Id.*

effects of the execution of a program, e.g. the circulation of electrical currents in the computer, are not in themselves sufficient to confer technical character to a computer program (T 1173/97 and G 3/08).

Examples of further technical effects which confer technical character to a computer program are the control of a technical process or of the internal functioning of the computer itself or its interfaces (see GII, 3.6.1).

The presence of a further technical effect is assessed without reference to the prior art. It follows that the mere fact that a computer program serving a non-technical purpose requires less computing time than a prior-art program serving the same non-technical purpose does not on its own establish the presence of a further technical effect (T 1370/11). Likewise, comparing a computer program with how a human being would perform the same task is not a suitable basis for assessing if the computer program has a technical character (T 1358/09).

If a further technical effect of the computer program has already been established, the computational efficiency of an algorithm affecting the established technical effect contributes to the technical character of the invention and thus to inventive step (e.g. where the design of the algorithm is motivated by technical considerations of the internal functioning of the computer; see also GII, 3.3).

A computer program cannot derive a technical character from the mere fact that it has been designed such that it can be automatically performed by a computer. "Further technical considerations", typically related to the technical considerations of the internal functioning of the computer, going beyond merely finding a computer algorithm to perform a task are needed. They have to be reflected in claimed features that cause a further technical effect (G 3/08).

If a claim is directed to a computer program which does not have a technical character, it is objected to under Art. 52(2)(c) and (3). If it passes the test for having technical character, the examiner then proceeds to the questions of novelty and inventive step (see GVI and GVII, in particular GVII, 5.4).

Computer-implemented inventions

"Computer-implemented invention" is an expression intended to cover claims which involve computers, computer networks or other programmable apparatus wherein at least one feature is realised by means of a computer program. Claims directed to computer-implemented inventions may take the forms described in FIV, 3.9 and subsections.

A computer program and a corresponding computer-implemented method are distinct from each other. The former refers to a sequence of computer-executable instructions specifying a method while the latter refers to a method being actually performed on a computer.

Claims directed to a computer-implemented method, a computer-readable storage medium or a device cannot be objected to under Art. 52(2) and (3) as any method involving the use of technical means (e.g. a computer) and any technical means itself (e.g. a computer or a computer-readable storage medium) have technical character and thus represent inventions within the meaning of Art. 52(1) (T 258/03, T 424/03, G 3/08).

Regarding technical character, the Guidelines further state:[7]

If a method has a technical character over and above the mere fact that it is computer-implemented, a corresponding computer program specifying that method produces a further technical effect when run on a computer. For example, a computer program which specifies a method of controlling an anti-lock braking system in a car, determining emissions by an X-ray device, compressing video, restoring a distorted digital image, or encrypting electronic communications brings about a further technical effect when it is run on a computer (see GII, 3.3).

Furthermore, if a computer program is designed based on specific technical considerations of the internal functioning of the computer on which it is to be executed, such as by being adapted to the specific architecture of the computer, it may be considered to produce a further technical effect. For example, computer programs implementing security measures for protecting boot integrity or countermeasures against power analysis attacks have a technical character since they rely on a technical understanding of the internal functioning of the computer.

Similarly, computer programs controlling the internal functioning or operation of a computer, such as processor load balancing or memory allocation, normally produce a further technical effect (see, however, GVII, 5.4.2.3 for an example of a case where the controlling is based on a non-technical scheme).

Programs for processing code at low level, such as builders or compilers, may well have a technical character. For example, when building runtime objects from development objects, regenerating only those runtime objects resulting from modified development objects contributes to producing the further technical effect of limiting the resources needed for a particular build.

The rationale seems to be that a solution to a technical problem should not be excluded from being patented simply because software may be involved in implementing the solution.

To understand technical effect, perhaps a good example is the invention in *Diamond v. Diehr*.[8] A computer was used to do computations, but the invention was much more than the computations performed by the computer.

7. *Id.*
8. 450 U.S. 175 (1981).

The patent application was for a "[process] for molding raw, uncured synthetic rubber into cured precision products." The process of curing synthetic rubber depends on a number of factors including time, temperature and thickness of a mold. Using the Arrhenius equation $k = Ae^{\frac{-E_a}{RT}}$ it is possible to calculate when to open a press and remove cured, molded rubber. The problem was that, at the time of the invention, there was no disclosed way to obtain an accurate measure of the temperature without opening the press. In the traditional method, the temperature of the mold press, which was apparently set at a fixed temperature and was controlled by thermostat, fluctuated due to the opening and closing of the press. The invention solved this problem by using embedded thermocouples to constantly check the temperature, and then feeding the measured values into a computer. The computer then used the Arrhenius equation to calculate when sufficient energy had been absorbed so that the molding machine should open the press. Thus, while software was involved, the invention was of a technical character.

Some have observed that with the *Mayo-Alice* framework,[9] the United States appears to be becoming more like European law. The federal circuit has, for example, emphasized that to be patent eligible an invention must address a *technical* problem.[10] Nonetheless, even with the *Mayo-Alice* framework, software is more likely to be patentable in the United States than in Europe.

Similarly, Article 53 provides additional exceptions to patentability. It states:

> European patents shall not be granted in respect of:
>
> > (a) inventions the commercial exploitation of which would be contrary to "ordre public" or morality; such exploitation shall not be deemed to be so contrary merely because it is prohibited by law or regulation in some or all of the Contracting States;
> >
> > (b) plant or animal varieties or essentially biological processes for the production of plants or animals; this provision shall not apply to microbiological processes or the products thereof;
> >
> > (c) methods for treatment of the human or animal body by surgery or therapy and diagnostic methods practised on the human or animal body; this provision shall not apply to products, in particular substances or compositions, for use in any of these methods.

9. *See* section 5.44 and its subsections, discussing patent eligibility of software.
10. *Id.*

Consequently, methods of diagnosis, treatment, or surgery are not patentable.[11] However, these exceptions are narrowly applied. For example, products for use in medical methods are patentable.[12]

The Guidelines for Examination in this regard state:[13]

> European patents are not to be granted in respect of "methods for treatment of the human or animal body by surgery or therapy and diagnostic methods practised on the human or animal body; this provision shall not apply to products, in particular substances or compositions, for use in any of these methods." Hence, patents may be obtained for surgical, therapeutic or diagnostic instruments or apparatuses for use in such methods. The manufacture of prostheses or artificial limbs could be patentable. For instance, a method of manufacturing insoles in order to correct the posture or a method of manufacturing an artificial limb is patentable. In both cases, taking the imprint of the footplate or a moulding of the stump on which an artificial limb is fitted is clearly not of a surgical nature. Furthermore, the insoles as well as the artificial limb are manufactured outside the body. However, a method of manufacturing an endoprosthesis outside the body, but requiring a surgical step to be carried out for taking measurements, would be excluded from patentability under Art. 53(c) (see T 1005/98).
>
> Art. 53(c)
>
> The exception under Art. 53(c) does not extend to new products, particularly substances or compositions, for use in these methods of treatment or diagnosis.
>
> Where a substance or composition is already known, (notional) novelty can be derived from a new medical use in accordance with Art. 54(4) and (5).
>
> Pursuant to Art. 54(4), a known substance or composition may still be patented for use in a method referred to in Art. 53(c) if the known substance or composition has not previously been disclosed for use for any such method ("first medical use"). A claim to a known substance or composition for the first use in surgical, therapeutic and/or diagnostic methods must be in a form such as: "Substance or composition X" followed by the indication of the use, for instance ". . . for use as a medicament" or ". . . for use in therapy/in vivo diagnostics/surgery" (see GVI, 7.1).
>
> Art. 54(4)
>
> Furthermore, if the known substance or composition was previously disclosed for use in surgery, therapy or diagnostic methods practised on the human or animal body, a patent may still be obtained according to Art. 54(5)

11. This also is analogous to U.S. law; *see* section 5.44 and its subsections, discussing methods of diagnosis.

12. Compare this with 35 U.S.C. § 287(c) (2022).

13. Guidelines for Examination, Part G, Chapter II, Section 4.2 (2022).

for any second or further use of the substance in these methods provided that said use is novel and inventive ("further medical use"). A claim to a further medical use of a known substance must be in the form: "Substance or composition X" followed by the indication of the specific therapeutical/in vivo diagnostic/surgical use, for instance, ". . . for use in treating disease Y" (see GVI, 7.1).

The Guidelines for Examination also state:[14]

Exceptions under Art. 53(c) are confined to methods for treatment of the human or animal body by surgery or therapy and diagnostic methods practised on the human or animal body. It follows that other methods of treatment of living human beings or animals (e.g. treatment of a sheep in order to promote growth, to improve the quality of mutton or to increase the yield of wool) or other methods of measuring or recording characteristics of the human or animal body are patentable, provided that such methods are of a technical and not essentially biological character (see GII, 5.4.2). For example, an application containing claims directed to the purely cosmetic treatment of a human by administration of a chemical product is considered as being patentable (see T 144/83). A cosmetic treatment involving surgery or therapy would, however, not be patentable (see below).

Art. 53(c)

To be excluded from patentability, a treatment or diagnostic method must actually be carried out on the living human or animal body. A treatment of or diagnostic method practised on a dead human or animal body would therefore not be excluded from patentability by virtue of Art. 53(c). Treatment of body tissues or fluids after they have been removed from the human or animal body, or diagnostic methods applied thereon, are not excluded from patentability as long as these tissues or fluids are not returned to the same body. Thus the treatment of blood for storage in a blood bank or diagnostic testing of blood samples is not excluded, whereas a treatment of blood by dialysis with the blood being returned to the same body would be excluded.

Regarding methods which are carried out on or in relation to the living human or animal body, it must be borne in mind that the intention of Art. 53(c) is only to free from restraint non-commercial and non-industrial medical and veterinary activities. Interpretation of the provision must avoid the exceptions from going beyond their proper limits (see G 5/83, G 1/04, and G 1/07).

Whether or not a method is excluded from patentability under Art. 53(c) cannot depend on the person carrying it out (see G 1/04 and G 1/07, Reasons 3.4.1).

14. *Id.*

However, in contrast to the subject-matter referred to in Art. 52(2) and (3) which is only excluded from patentability if claimed as such, a method claim is not allowable under Art. 53(c) if it includes at least one feature defining a physical activity or action that constitutes a method step for treatment of the human or animal body by surgery or therapy. In that case, whether or not the claim includes or consists of features directed to a technical operation performed on a technical object is legally irrelevant to the application of Art. 53(c) (see G 1/07, Reasons 3.2.5).

Claims to medical devices, computer programs and storage media which comprise subject-matter corresponding to that of a method for treatment of the human or animal body by surgery or therapy or to that of a diagnostic method practised on the human or animal body are not to be objected to under Art. 53(c), because only method claims may fall under the exception of Art. 53(c).

7.3 Novelty and Inventive Step

The EPC has a novelty requirement and, comparable to non-obviousness, it has a requirement of inventive step. Article 54 clarifies novelty, recited previously, and Article 56 clarifies inventive step. It states:

> An invention shall be considered as involving an inventive step if, having regard to the state of the art, it is not obvious to a person skilled in the art. If the state of the art also includes documents within the meaning of Article 54, paragraph 3, these documents shall not be considered in deciding whether there has been an inventive step.

To evaluate patentability in the EPC, first, one should ask whether the subject matter at issue is technical. This requirement was discussed earlier in connection with software. If the subject matter does not qualify as technical, then in general, in the EPC, it is not patentable. One, of course, should also make sure it does not fall within any of the exceptions, such as in Article 52 or 54, previously discussed.

If the subject matter is arguably technical, then the question of novelty is evaluated. Note that the EPC does not have a disclosure of prior art requirement, in comparison with 37 CFR section 1.56 in the United States. However, to evaluate novelty, one needs access to the closest *known* prior art. As in the United States, under a rigorous comparison, if there is no difference between the subject matter at issue and the closest prior art, then the subject matter is not novel. Recall, here, our red doorknob versus blue doorknob example.[15]

---

15. *See* section 1.31, discussing this example.

A few other points regarding novelty in the EPC. Prior EPO applications may render subject matter not novel. However, notably, prior EPO applications of the applicant are not considered under inventive step. Furthermore, a new use of a known substance or compound would be considered novel, much like in the United States. The EPC, again, is a first to file system, there is no grace period, and publications anywhere in the world are considered when evaluating novelty.

As suggested earlier, when evaluating inventive step, the problem should be a technical problem. For example, it should relate to a technical field. If the problem is not technical, then as previously suggested, the subject matter is excluded from patentability. Likewise, nontechnical aspects of the subject matter (e.g., claim limitations) may be ignored for evaluating inventive step.

A useful question, suggested during the discussion of section 103, is whether the technical problem is addressed in the prior art. To restate the question: what is the problem addressed by the subject matter that is not addressed in the prior art? This approach may be even more helpful in Europe than in the United States. Along these lines, for prosecution in the EPC, it may be more effective to point out advantages the subject matter has over the prior art than to simply identify missing features. Thus, EPO examiners tend to be more responsive to arguments that prior art is in an unrelated field than U.S. examiners.

7.4 Clarity, Sufficiency, and Claim Support

The European Patent Convention (EPC) does not have a written description requirement as such, but it does have a sufficiency of disclosure requirement contained in Article 83 of the EPC. It states:[16]

> The European patent application shall disclose the invention in a manner sufficiently clear and complete for it to be carried out by a person skilled in the art.

For example, the European Guidelines for Examination in pertinent part state:[17]

> A detailed description of at least one way of carrying out the invention must be given. Since the application is addressed to the person skilled in the art, it is neither necessary nor desirable that details of well-known ancillary features

16. Article 83 EPC (2022).
17. Part F, Chapter III, Section 1 (sufficiency of disclosure) (2022).

are given, but the description must disclose any feature essential for carrying out the invention in sufficient detail to render it apparent to the skilled person how to put the invention into practice. A single example may suffice, but where the claims cover a broad field, the application is not usually regarded as satisfying the requirements of Art. 83 unless the description gives a number of examples or describes alternative embodiments or variations extending over the area protected by the claims. However, regard must be had to the facts and evidence of the particular case. There are some instances where even a very broad field is sufficiently exemplified by a limited number of examples or even one example (see also FIV, 6.3). In these latter cases the application must contain, in addition to the examples, sufficient information to allow the person skilled in the art, using common general knowledge, to perform the invention over the whole area claimed without undue burden and without needing inventive skill (see T 727/95). In this context, the "whole area claimed" is to be understood as substantially any embodiment falling within the ambit of a claim, even though a limited amount of trial and error may be permissible, e.g. in an unexplored field or when there are many technical difficulties (see T 226/85 and T 409/91).

A basis for the requirement of support for patent claims is contained in Article 84.[18] It states:

> The claims shall define the matter for which protection is sought. They shall be clear and concise and be supported by the description.

As to the difference between support and sufficiency of disclosure, the European Guidelines for Examination in pertinent part state:[19]

> Although an objection of lack of support is an objection under Art. 84, it can often, as in the above examples, also be considered as an objection of insufficient disclosure of the invention under Art. 83 (see FIII, 1 to 3), the objection being that the disclosure is insufficient to enable the skilled person to carry out the "invention" over the whole of the broad field claimed (although sufficient in respect of a narrow "invention"). Both requirements are designed to reflect the principle that the terms of a claim must be commensurate with, or be justified by, the invention's technical contribution to the art. Therefore, the extent to which an invention is sufficiently disclosed is also highly relevant to the issue of support. The reasons for failure to meet the requirements of Art. 83 may in effect be the same as those that lead to the infringement of Art. 84 as well, namely that the invention, over the whole range claimed,

18. Article 84 EPC (2022).
19. Part F, Chapter IV, Section 6.4 (2022).

> extends to technical subject-matter not made available to the person skilled in the art by the application as filed (see T 409/91, Reasons 2 and 3.3 to 3.5).

In many ways, this sounds similar to U.S. law. However, one should be aware that *European requirements for claim support are much more exacting than the requirements of U.S. law* although the requirements sound quite similar.

In many ways, this sounds similar to U.S. law. However, one should be aware that *European requirements for claim support are much more exacting than the requirements of U.S. law* although the requirements sound quite similar.

For example, the European Guidelines for Examination in pertinent part state:[20]

> A claim in generic form, i.e. relating to a whole class, e.g. of materials or machines, may be acceptable even if of broad scope, if there is fair support in the description and there is no reason to suppose that the invention cannot be worked through the whole of the field claimed. Where the information given appears insufficient to enable a person skilled in the art to extend the teaching of the description to parts of the field claimed but not explicitly described by using routine methods of experimentation or analysis, the division raises a reasoned objection, and invites the applicant to establish, by suitable response, that the invention can in fact be readily applied on the basis of the information given over the whole field claimed or, failing this, to restrict the claim accordingly.

The question of support is illustrated by the following examples, which appear in the Guidelines:

> (i) a claim relates to a process for treating all kinds of "plant seedlings" by subjecting them to a controlled cold shock so as to produce specified results, whereas the description discloses the process applied to one kind of plant only. Since it is well-known that plants vary widely in their properties, there are well-founded reasons for believing that the process is not applicable to all plant seedlings. Unless the applicants can provide convincing evidence that the process is nevertheless generally applicable, they must restrict their claim to the particular kind of plant referred to in the description. A mere assertion that the process is applicable to all plant seedlings is not sufficient;

20. Part F, Chapter IV, Section 6.3 (2022).

(ii) a claim relates to a specified method of treating "synthetic resin mouldings" to obtain certain changes in physical characteristics. All the examples described relate to thermoplastic resins and the method is such as to appear inappropriate to thermosetting resins. Unless the applicants can provide evidence that the method is nevertheless applicable to thermosetting resins, they must restrict their claim to thermoplastic resins;

(iii) a claim relates to improved fuel oil compositions which have a given desired property. The description provides support for one way of obtaining fuel oils having this property, which is by the presence of defined amounts of a certain additive. No other ways of obtaining fuel oils having the desired property are disclosed. The claim makes no mention of the additive. The claim is not supported over the whole of its breadth and objection arises.

In the United States, the standard is whether one of ordinary skill would know what was meant. In application, this appears to be a much looser standard than in the EPO. The European Guidelines say that "fair support in the description" is required. Although the Guidelines do not actually say express support is required, it does *not* appear that the notion of what one of ordinary skill might already know is heavily incorporated into the analysis in comparison to U.S. law. Thus, a good rule of thumb might be to make sure all claim elements and limitations are clearly and expressly supported in the description. For example, combinations of features may not support a claim to an individual feature without express language directed to the individual features themselves. Thus, again, care is warranted.

Thus, a good rule of thumb might be to make sure all claim elements limitations are clearly and expressly supported in the description.

Also be wary that Article 123 forbids subject matter beyond the content of the application, which may lead to a trap that may invalidate a patent for lack of description support. For example, suppose an amendment includes added subject matter that extends beyond the content of the application, in violation of Article 123(2). Normally, the amendment would be canceled if the application were still pending. However, assuming the patent is issued, and this is raised, such as in an opposition, cancelling the amendment would extend the protection of the patent after grant beyond the protection conferred by the patent, which is also not permissible under Article 123(3). Thus, the patent would need to be revoked.

Article 84 also indicates that the claims must have clarity, meaning that the claims must be clear and concise. For this reason, in the claims and in the specification, vague language referring to "spirit of invention" or the like should be omitted. Also, equivalents should not be discussed as such, because this might be interpreted to refer to subject matter "instead" of what is in the description. Finally, the term "example" might be preferred over the term "embodiment."

It is also noted that incorporation by reference is not permitted in the EPC and there is no best mode requirement.

7.5 Improvement Claim Format

Previously, in connection with Jepson claims, the European style/format for a claim was introduced.[21] As noted, the European format is quite similar to the Jepson-type claim in the U.S. Consequently, the risks associated with Jepson claims also apply to claims written in the European style. Care in drafting is warranted here.

Rules 43(1)(a) and (b) of the regulations implementing the EPC state:

> (1) The claims shall define the matter for which protection is sought in terms of the technical features of the invention. Wherever appropriate, claims shall contain:
>
> > (a) a statement indicating the designation of the subject-matter of the invention and those technical features which are necessary for the definition of the claimed subject-matter but which, in combination, form part of the prior art;
> >
> > (b) a characterising portion, beginning with the expression "characterised in that" or "characterised by" and specifying the technical features for which, in combination with the features stated under sub-paragraph (a), protection is sought.

The Guidelines state:[22]

> Rule 43(1)(a) and (b) define the two-part form which a claim must have "wherever appropriate."
>
> The first part or "preamble" needs to contain a statement indicating "the designation of the subject-matter of the invention", i.e. the general technical class of apparatus, process, etc. to which the invention relates, followed by a statement of "those technical features which are necessary for the definition

21. *See* section 2.1151, discussing Jepson claims.
22. Guidelines for Examination, Part F, Chapter IV, Section 2.2 (2022).

of the claimed subject-matter but which, in combination, are part of the prior art." This requirement to state prior-art features in the first part of the claim is applicable only to independent claims and not to dependent claims (see FIV, 3.4). It is clear from the wording of Rule 43 that it is necessary only to refer to those prior-art features which are relevant to the invention. For example, if the invention relates to a photographic camera but the inventive step relates entirely to the shutter, it would be sufficient for the first part of the claim to read: "A photographic camera including a focal plane shutter" and there is no need to refer also to the other known features of a camera such as the lens and view-finder.

The second part or "characterising portion" needs to state the features which the invention adds to the prior art, i.e. the technical features for which, in combination with the features stated in the first part, protection is sought.

If a single document in the state of the art according to Art. 54(2), e.g. cited in the search report, reveals that one or more features in the second part of the claim were already known in combination with all the features in the first part of the claim and in that combination have the same effect as they have in the full combination according to the invention, the division will require that such feature or features be transferred to the first part.

Where, however, a claim relates to a novel combination, and where the division of the features of the claim between the preamble and the characterising part could be made in more than one way without inaccuracy, applicants must not be pressed, unless there are very substantial reasons, to adopt a different division of the features from that which they have chosen, if their version is not incorrect. If the applicant insists on including more features in the preamble than can be derived from the closest available prior art, this is accepted.

If no other prior art is available, this first part of the claim could be used to raise an objection on the ground of lack of inventive step (see GVII, 5.1, last paragraph).

The two-part claim is preferred by EPO examiners but is not always required. An issue may be whether to start with it or not in part because how the claims may be modified may affect interpretation of the U.S. counterpart case and in part because the two-part claim form also necessarily needs express support in the EPO. Still, it appears that this claim type may be handled with careful drafting as suggested with Jepson claims.[23]

As with Jepson claims, it is important to confirm (1) what you believe is prior art is, in fact, prior art, and (2) the characterization you provide in the preamble is an accurate description of the prior art. Several claim drafting examples are provided in the section discussing Jepson claims.

23. *See* section 2.1151, discussing Jepson claims.

7.6 Means Plus Function Claims

Quite typically, as discussed previously,[24] a patent application is first filed in the U.S. and then filed in other jurisdictions, such as the European Patent Office (EPO). In this situation, one should be mindful of claiming approaches specific to the United States, such as means plus function claims. These claims are permissible, but whereas in the United States such claims are construed narrowly, in the EPO, these claims will be construed quite broadly. It might be that if construed based on the face of the claim, such claims are clearly unpatentable based on prior art. Thus, rather than waste money, it might be prudent to modify or remove these claims before filing abroad.

The Guidelines[25] state:

> A claim may broadly define a feature in terms of its function, i.e. as a functional feature, even where only one example of the feature has been given in the description, if the skilled person would appreciate that other means could be used for the same function (see also FIV, 2.1 and 4.10). For example, "terminal position detecting means" in a claim might be supported by a single example comprising a limit switch, it being evident to the skilled person that e.g. a photoelectric cell or a strain gauge could be used instead. In general, however, if the entire contents of the application are such as to convey the impression that a function is to be carried out in a particular way, with no intimation that alternative means are envisaged, and a claim is formulated in such a way as to embrace other means, or all means, of performing the function, then objection arises. Furthermore, it may not be sufficient if the description merely states in vague terms that other means may be adopted, if it is not reasonably clear what they might be or how they might be used.

7.7 Unity

Article 82 specifies unity of invention, which is analogous to restriction practice[26] in the United States. It states:

> The European patent application shall relate to one invention only or to a group of inventions so linked as to form a single general inventive concept.

Thus, the claims of a patent application must relate to one inventive concept or technical problem. It may be permissible if several claimed solutions relate

24. *See* section 7.0, discussed the Paris Treaty Convention.
25. *See* Guidelines, Part F, Chapter IV, Section 6.3 (2022).
26. *See* subsection 2.11231, discussing restriction practice in the United States.

to identification of the problem. Otherwise, if there are several solutions, these other separate solutions are separate inventions requiring separate applications. However, if a method and apparatus are related, that may be permitted.

Procedurally, handling multiple claimed "solutions" is also similar to the United States. That is, only one "solution" is searched. The unsearched claimed "solutions" are canceled but may be claimed in a divisional patent application to retain priority.

7.8 Claim Formalities and Fees

Article 43(7) states:

> Where the European patent application contains drawings including reference signs, the technical features specified in the claims shall preferably be followed by such reference signs relating to these features, placed in parentheses, if the intelligibility of the claim can thereby be increased. These reference signs shall not be construed as limiting the claim.

The United States has no such requirement. The risk is that such reference numerals may be used to interpret the claims in the United States. Unfortunately, there is not a good way around this issue other than to be quite circumspect when adding references numerals from the specification into the claims. Despite that the last sentence says the reference numerals shall not limit the claims, such a statement is not binding on a federal court interpreting the corresponding claims of an issued U.S. patent.

In the EPO, an application is permitted 15 total claims without incurring extra fees. Typically, only one independent claim is searched. The others are generally unsearched and handled with divisionals, as described earlier with respect to unity of invention.[27]

It is common practice to try to limit fees using multiply dependent claims. Unlike the United States, charges are based on the number of actual claims, rather than the number of "dependencies" created. It is also possible to depend a multiply dependent claim from a multiply dependent claim. Care may be called for, however, to not inadvertently claim unsupported subject matter via a multiply dependent claim. Furthermore, a multiply dependent claim may add an unsearched dependency as well. Markush group or other ways of claiming alternative approaches may also be used to reduce the number of claims.

27. *See* section 7.7, discussing unity of invention.

Appendix A
List of Claim Drafting Principles

Introductory Principles

- Identify the business strategy and the patent strategy objective for pursuing patent protection;
- Anticipate the possibility of changes in the law, the technology and/or the business dynamics as you formulate and draft patent claims;
- Understand what constitutes prior art;
- Avoid making prior art admissions;
- Understand the basic types of patent claims and what they are used to cover;
- Understand the constituent parts of a patent claim (preamble, transition phrase, and claim body) and how to draft a patent claim so that the separate parts are clearly identifiable;
- Understand the basic mechanics of how to formulate and draft a patent claim.

Claim Drafting Basic Principles

- Understand the differences between direct patent infringement and indirect patent infringement as well as the differences between literal patent infringement and nonliteral patent infringement;
- At the start of drafting, consider the types of direct infringement and the business and economic considerations surrounding the invention;
- Draft short claims;
- Make claim coverage clear from the face of the claim (i.e., based on the language used for the claim);
- Use words in the claims consistent with their understood meaning;
- Use words in the claims with broadly understood meanings where appropriate;

- Employ a hierarchy of claim terms for the independent and dependent claims;
- Avoid overly specific modifiers in the independent claims;
- Draft claims that will be directly infringed (rather than indirectly infringed);
- Draft claims that will be literally infringed (rather than nonliterally infringed);
- Avoid drafting claims clearly narrower than needed and easily designed around;
- Employ a "hedge" strategy to claiming through patent claim diversity (consider using the following claim types to enhance claim diversity: component level claims, system level claims; means plus function claims; method of using claims; method of making claims; composition of matter claims; Beauregard claims; and/or Markush Group claims);
- Draft the patent claims to expressly recite the broadest and the narrowest embodiments of the invention, including multiple claims for multiple embodiments between the broadest and the narrowest embodiments;
- Use claim preambles that are short and avoid introducing limitations;
- Make where the preamble and transition phrase ends and the claim body begins clear with punctuation;
- Use "comprising" as the transition word in the predictable arts;
- Use varying transitional phrases ("consisting of" and/or "consisting essentially of") to vary claim scope in the unpredictable arts;
- Draft the patent claims before the specification;
- Use dependent claims for claim differentiation and to cover commercial embodiments (e.g., those most likely to be copied);
- Use claim terms that have express definitions in the specification;
- Have the closest *known* prior art in mind when drafting the claims;
- Do not draft claims that read on *known* prior art;
- Have a good faith argument to patentably distinguish the broadest claims;
- Avoid drafting claims in a manner that leaves the statutory class of the claim unclear (avoid apparatus-type limitations in method claims and method-type limitations in apparatus claims);
- When creating claim dependencies, skip some intermediate dependent claims for claim diversity.

Claim Drafting Advanced Principles

- Draft claims in anticipation of the first office action and in light of expected obviousness arguments;
- Review the claims in light of the Broadest Reasonable Interpretation (BRI);
- Use the dependent claims to establish fallback positions in addition to claim differentiation;
- Draft claims to cover a variety of potential infringers;
- Draft claims in a manner to avoid covering multiple independent parties acting together (i.e., make sure the claims have a single direct infringer);
- Use the dependent claims to cover higher levels of product integration;
- Draft the claims to make "design around" more difficult;
- Draft the claims to increase the relative ease of detecting (and proving) infringement;
- Draft some claims that are structural and draft some claims that are functional;
- Claim the environment of the invention in the dependent claims (i.e., keep the invention terminology broad while narrowing the environment of the invention);
- Employ more than one statutory class to claim the invention—but do so in different claims sets;
- Employ the same statutory class to cover rights of different scope;
- Draft claims to reduce the risk of exhaustion or implied patent licensing if possible.

Appendix B

Sample Patent Application Boilerplate

Title

BACKGROUND

1. Field

[0001] This disclosure relates to -----.

2. Information

[0002] In certain types of situations,------.

BRIEF DESCRIPTION OF DRAWINGS

[0003] Claimed subject matter is particularly pointed out and distinctly claimed in the concluding portion of the specification. However, both as to organization and/or method of operation, together with objects, features, and/or advantages thereof, it may best be understood by reference to the following detailed description if read with the accompanying drawings in which:

FIG. 1 is an illustration of an embodiment of a __________;

FIG. 2 is an illustration of an embodiment of a ___________;

FIG. 3 is a schematic diagram of an embodiment of a __________;

FIG. 4 is an illustration of an embodiment of a _________; and

FIG. 5 is . . . _____.

[0004] Reference is made in the following detailed description to accompanying drawings, which form a part hereof, wherein like numerals may designate like parts throughout that are corresponding and/or analogous. It will be appreciated that the figures have not necessarily been drawn to scale, such as for simplicity and/or clarity of illustration. For example, dimensions of some aspects may be exaggerated relative to others. Furthermore, structural and/or other changes may be made without departing from claimed subject matter. It should also be noted that directions and/or references, for example, such as up, down, top, bottom, and so on, may be used to facilitate discussion of drawings and are not intended to restrict application of claimed subject matter. Therefore, the following detailed description is not to be taken to limit claimed subject matter and/or equivalents. Further, it is to be understood that other embodiments may be utilized. Also, embodiments have been provided of claimed subject matter and it is noted that, as such, those illustrative embodiments are inventive and/or unconventional; however, claimed subject matter is not limited to embodiments provided primarily for illustrative purposes. Thus, while advantages have been described in connection with illustrative embodiments, claimed subject matter is inventive and/or unconventional for additional reasons not expressly mentioned in connection with those embodiments. In addition, references throughout this specification to "claimed subject matter" refer to subject matter intended to be covered by one or more claims, and are not necessarily intended to refer to a complete claim set, to a particular combination of claim sets (e.g., method claims, apparatus claims, etc.), or to a particular claim.

Detailed Description

[0005] References throughout this specification to one implementation, an implementation, one embodiment, an embodiment, and/or the like means that a particular feature, structure, characteristic, and/or the like described in relation to a particular implementation and/or embodiment is included in at least one implementation and/or embodiment of claimed subject matter. Thus, appearances of such phrases, for example, in various places throughout this specification are not necessarily intended to refer to the same implementation and/or embodiment or to any one particular implementation and/or embodiment. Furthermore, it is to be understood that particular features, structures, characteristics, and/or the like described are capable of being combined in various ways in one or more implementations and/or embodiments and, therefore, are within intended claim scope. In general, of course, as has always been the case for the specification of a patent application, these and other issues have a potential to vary in a particular context of usage. In other words, throughout the patent application, particular context of description and/or usage provides helpful guidance regarding reasonable inferences to be drawn; however, likewise, "in this context" in general without further qualification refers to the context of the present patent application.

[0006] BEGIN APPLICATION TECHNICAL DESCRIPTION HERE

[0007] END APPLICATION TECHNICAL DESCRIPTION HERE

[0008] In the context of the present patent application, the term "connection," the term "component" and/or similar terms are intended to be physical, but are not necessarily always tangible. Whether or not these terms refer to tangible subject matter, thus, may vary in a particular context of usage. As an example, a tangible connection and/or tangible connection path may be made, such as by a tangible, electrical connection, such as an electrically conductive path comprising metal or other conductor, that is able to conduct electrical current between two tangible components. Likewise, a tangible connection path may be at least partially affected and/or controlled, such that, as is typical, a tangible connection path may be open or closed, at times resulting from influence of one or more externally derived signals, such as external currents and/or voltages, such as for an electrical switch. Non-limiting illustrations of an electrical switch include a transistor, a diode, etc. However, a "connection" and/or "component," in a particular context of usage, likewise, although physical, can also be non-tangible, such as a connection between a client and a server over a network, particularly a wireless network, which generally refers to the ability for the client and server to transmit, receive, and/or exchange communications, as discussed in more detail later.

[0009] In a particular context of usage, such as a particular context in which tangible components are being discussed, therefore, the terms "coupled" and "connected" are used in a manner so that the terms are not synonymous. Similar terms may also be used in a manner in which a similar intention is exhibited. Thus, "connected" is used to indicate that two or more tangible components and/or the like, for example, are tangibly in direct physical contact. Thus, using the previous example, two tangible components that are electrically connected are physically connected via a tangible electrical connection, as previously discussed. However, "coupled," is used to mean that potentially two or more tangible components are tangibly in direct physical contact. Nonetheless, "coupled" is also used to mean that two or more tangible components and/or the like are not necessarily tangibly in direct physical contact, but are able to co-operate, liaise, and/or interact, such as, for example, by being "optically coupled." Likewise, the term "coupled" is also understood to mean indirectly connected. It is further noted, in the context of the present patent application, since memory, such as a memory component and/or memory states, is intended to be non-transitory, the term physical, at least if used in relation to memory necessarily implies that such memory components and/or memory states, continuing with the example, are tangible.

[0010] Additionally, in the present patent application, in a particular context of usage, such as a situation in which tangible components (and/or similarly, tangible materials) are being discussed, a distinction exists between being "on" and being "over." As an example, deposition of a substance "on" a substrate refers to a deposition involving direct physical and tangible contact without an intermediary, such as an intermediary substance, between the substance deposited and the substrate in this latter example; nonetheless, deposition "over" a substrate, while understood to potentially include deposition "on" a substrate (since being "on" may also accurately be described as being "over"), is understood to include a situation in which one or more intermediaries, such as one or more intermediary substances, are present between the substance deposited and the substrate so that the substance deposited is not necessarily in direct physical and tangible contact with the substrate.

[0011] A similar distinction is made in an appropriate particular context of usage, such as in which tangible materials and/or tangible components are discussed, between being "beneath" and being "under." While "beneath," in such a particular context of usage, is intended to necessarily imply physical and tangible contact (similar to "on," as just described), "under" potentially includes a situation in which there is direct physical and tangible contact, but does not necessarily imply direct physical and tangible contact, such as if one or more intermediaries, such as one or more intermediary substances, are present. Thus, "on" is understood to mean "immediately over" and "beneath" is understood to mean "immediately under."

[0012] It is likewise appreciated that terms such as "over" and "under" are understood in a similar manner as the terms "up," "down," "top," "bottom," and so on, previously mentioned. These terms may be used to facilitate discussion, but are not intended to necessarily restrict scope of claimed subject matter. For example, the term "over," as an example, is not meant to suggest that claim scope is limited to only situations in which an embodiment is right side up, such as in comparison with the embodiment being upside down, for example. An example includes a flip chip, as one illustration, in which, for example, orientation at various times (e.g., during fabrication) may not necessarily correspond to orientation of a final product. Thus, if an object, as an example, is within applicable claim scope in a particular orientation, such as upside down, as one example, likewise, it is intended that the latter also be interpreted to be included within applicable claim scope in another orientation, such as right side up, again, as an example, and vice versa, even if applicable literal claim language has the potential to be interpreted otherwise. Of course, again, as always has been the case in the specification of a patent application, particular context of description and/or usage provides helpful guidance regarding reasonable inferences to be drawn.

[0013] Unless otherwise indicated, in the context of the present patent application, the term "or" if used to associate a list, such as A, B, or C, is intended to mean A, B, and C, here used in the inclusive sense, as well as A, B, or C, here used in the exclusive sense. With this understanding, "and" is used in the inclusive sense and intended to mean A, B, and C; whereas "and/or" can be used in an abundance of caution to make clear that all of the foregoing meanings are intended, although such usage is not required. In addition, the term "one or more" and/or similar terms is used to describe any feature, structure, characteristic, and/or the like in the singular and/or the plural, "and/or" is also used to describe a plurality and/or some other combination of features, structures, characteristics, and/or the like. Likewise, the term "based on" and/or similar terms are understood as not necessarily intending to convey an exhaustive list of factors, but to allow for existence of additional factors not necessarily expressly described.

[0014] Furthermore, it is intended, for a situation that relates to implementation of claimed subject matter and is subject to testing, measurement, and/or specification regarding degree, that the particular situation be understood in the following manner. As an example, in a given situation, assume a value of a physical property is to be measured. If alternatively reasonable approaches to testing, measurement, and/or specification regarding degree, at least with respect to the property, continuing with the example, is reasonably likely to occur to one of ordinary skill, at least for implementation purposes, claimed subject matter is intended to cover those alternatively reasonable approaches unless otherwise expressly indicated. As an example, if a plot of measurements over a region is produced and implementation of claimed subject matter refers to employing a measurement of slope over the region, but a variety of reasonable and alternative techniques to estimate the slope over that region exist, claimed subject matter is intended to cover those reasonable alternative techniques unless otherwise expressly indicated.

[0015] To the extent claimed subject matter is related to one or more particular measurements, such as with regard to physical manifestations capable of being measured physically, such as, without limit, temperature, pressure, voltage, current, electromagnetic radiation, etc., it is believed that claimed subject matter does not fall within the abstract idea judicial exception to statutory subject matter and/or patent eligibility. Rather, it is asserted, that physical measurements are not mental steps and, likewise, are not abstract ideas.

[0016] It is noted, nonetheless, that a typical measurement model employed is that one or more measurements may respectively comprise a sum of at least two components. Thus, for a given measurement, for example, one component may comprise a deterministic component, which in an ideal sense, may comprise a physical value (e.g., sought via one or more measurements), often in the form of one or more signals, signal samples and/or states, and one component may comprise a random component, which may have a variety of sources that may be challenging to quantify. At times, for example, lack of measurement precision may affect a given measurement. Thus, for claimed subject matter, a statistical or stochastic model may be used in addition to a deterministic model as an approach to identification and/or prediction regarding one or more measurement values that may relate to claimed subject matter.

[0017] For example, a relatively large number of measurements may be collected to better estimate a deterministic component. Likewise, if measurements vary, which may typically occur, it may be that some portion of a variance may be explained as a deterministic component, while some portion of a variance may be explained as a random component. Typically, it is desirable to have stochastic variance associated with measurements be relatively small, if feasible. That is, typically, it may be preferable to be able to account for a reasonable portion of measurement variation in a deterministic manner, rather than a stochastic matter as an aid to identification and/or predictability.

[0018] Along these lines, a variety of techniques have come into use so that one or more measurements may be processed to better estimate an underlying deterministic component, as well as to estimate potentially random components. These techniques, of course, may vary with details surrounding a given situation. Typically, however, more complex problems may involve use of more complex techniques. In this regard, as alluded to above, one or more measurements of physical manifestations may be modelled deterministically and/or stochastically. Employing a model permits collected measurements to potentially be identified and/or processed, and/or potentially permits estimation and/or prediction of an underlying deterministic component, for example, with respect to later measurements to be taken. A given estimate may not be a perfect estimate; however, in general, it is expected that on average one or more estimates may better reflect an underlying deterministic component, for example, if random components that may be included in one or more obtained measurements, are considered. Practically speaking, of course, it is desirable to be able to generate, such as through estimation approaches, a physically meaningful model of processes affecting measurements to be taken.

[0019] In some situations, however, as indicated, potential influences may be complex. Therefore, seeking to understand appropriate factors to consider may be particularly challenging. In such situations, it is, therefore, not unusual to employ heuristics with respect to generating one or more estimates. Heuristics refers to use of experience related approaches that may reflect realized processes and/or realized results, such as with respect to use of historical measurements, for example. Heuristics, for example, may be employed in situations where more analytical approaches may be overly complex and/or nearly intractable. Thus, regarding claimed subject matter, an innovative feature may include, in an example embodiment, heuristics that may be employed, for example, to estimate and/or predict one or more measurements.

[0020] A "signal measurement" and/or a "signal measurement vector" may be referred to respectively as a "random measurement" and/or a "random vector," such that the term "random" may be understood in context with respect to the fields of probability, random variables and/or stochastic processes. A random vector may be generated by having measurement signal components comprising one or more random variables. Random variables may comprise signal value measurements, which may, for example, be specified in a space of outcomes. Thus, in some contexts, a probability (e.g., likelihood) may be assigned to outcomes, as often may be used in connection with approaches employing probability and/or statistics. In other contexts, a random variable may be substantially in accordance with a measurement comprising a deterministic measurement value or, perhaps, an average measurement component plus random variation about a measurement average. The terms "measurement vector," "random vector," and/or "vector" are used throughout this document interchangeably. In an embodiment, a random vector, or portion thereof, comprising one or more measurement vectors may uniquely be associated with a distribution of scalar numerical values, such as random scalar numerical values (e.g., signal values and/or signal sample values), for example. Thus, it is understood, of course, that a distribution of scalar numerical values, for example, without loss of generality, substantially in accordance with the foregoing description and/or later description, is related to physical measurements, and is likewise understood to exist as physical signals and/or physical signal samples.

[0021] The terms "correspond", "reference," "associate," and/or similar terms relate to signals, signal samples and/or states, e.g., components of a signal measurement vector, which may be stored in memory and/or employed with operations to generate results, depending, at least in part, on the above-mentioned, signal samples and/or signal sample states. For example, a signal sample measurement vector may be stored in a memory location and further referenced wherein such a reference may be embodied and/or described as a stored relationship. A stored relationship may be employed by associating (e.g., relating) one or more memory addresses to one or more other memory addresses, for example, and may facilitate an operation, involving, at least in part, a combination of signal samples and/or states stored in memory, such as for processing by a processor and/or similar device, for example. Thus, in a particular context, "associating," "referencing," and/or "corresponding" may, for example, refer to an executable process of accessing memory contents of two or more memory locations, e.g., to facilitate execution of one or more operations among signal samples and/or states, wherein one or more results of the one or more operations may likewise be employed for additional processing, such as in other operations, or may be stored in the same or other memory locations, as may, for example, be directed by executable instructions. Furthermore, terms "fetching" and "reading" or "storing" and "writing" are to be understood as interchangeable terms for the respective operations, e.g., a result may be fetched (or read) from a memory location; likewise, a result may be stored in (or written to) a memory location.

[0022] It is further noted that the terms "type" and/or "like," if used, such as with a feature, structure, characteristic, and/or the like, using "optical" or "electrical" as simple examples, means at least partially of and/or relating to the feature, structure, characteristic, and/or the like in such a way that presence of minor variations, even variations that might otherwise not be considered fully consistent with the feature, structure, characteristic, and/or the like, do not in general prevent the feature, structure, characteristic, and/or the like from being of a "type" and/or being "like," (such as being an "optical-type" or being "optical-like," for example) if the minor variations are sufficiently minor so that the feature, structure, characteristic, and/or the like would still be considered to be substantially present with such variations also present. Thus, continuing with this example, the terms optical-type and/or optical-like properties are necessarily intended to include optical properties. Likewise, the terms electrical-type and/or electrical-like properties, as another example, are necessarily intended to include electrical properties. It should be noted that the specification of the present patent application merely provides one or more illustrative examples and claimed subject matter is intended to not be limited to one or more illustrative examples; however, again, as has always been the case with respect to the specification of a patent application, particular context of description and/or usage provides helpful guidance regarding reasonable inferences to be drawn.

[0023] With advances in technology, it has become more typical to employ distributed computing and/or communication approaches in which portions of a process, such as signal processing of signal samples, for example, may be allocated among various devices, including one or more client devices and/or one or more server devices, via a computing and/or communications network, for example. A network may comprise two or more devices, such as network devices and/or computing devices, and/or may couple devices, such as network devices and/or computing devices, so that signal communications, such as in the form of signal packets and/or signal frames (e.g., comprising one or more signal samples), for example, may be exchanged, such as between a server device and/or a client device, as well as other types of devices, including between wired and/or wireless devices coupled via a wired and/or wireless network, for example.

[0024] An example of a distributed computing system comprises the so-called Hadoop distributed computing system, which employs a map-reduce type of architecture. In the context of the present patent application, the terms map-reduce architecture and/or similar terms are intended to refer to a distributed computing system implementation and/or embodiment for processing and/or for generating larger sets of signal samples employing map and/or reduce operations for a parallel, distributed process performed over a network of devices. A map operation and/or similar terms refer to processing of signals (e.g., signal samples) to generate one or more key-value pairs and to distribute the one or more pairs to one or more devices of the system (e.g., network). A reduce operation and/or similar terms refer to processing of signals (e.g., signal samples) via a summary operation (e.g., such as counting the number of students in a queue, yielding name frequencies, etc.). A system may employ such an architecture, such as by marshaling distributed server devices, executing various tasks in parallel, and/or managing communications, such as signal transfers, between various parts of the system (e.g., network), in an embodiment. As mentioned, one non-limiting, but well-known, example comprises the Hadoop distributed computing system. It refers to an open source implementation and/or embodiment of a map-reduce type architecture (available from the Apache Software Foundation, 1901 Munsey Drive, Forrest Hill, MD, 21050-2747), but may include other aspects, such as the Hadoop distributed file system (HDFS) (available from the Apache Software Foundation, 1901 Munsey Drive, Forrest Hill, MD, 21050-2747). In general, therefore, "Hadoop" and/or similar terms (e.g., "Hadoop-type," etc.) refer to an implementation and/or embodiment of a scheduler for executing larger processing jobs using a map-reduce architecture over a distributed system. Furthermore, in the context of the present patent application, use of the term "Hadoop" is intended to include versions, presently known and/or to be later developed.

[0025] In the context of the present patent application, the term network device refers to any device capable of communicating via and/or as part of a network and may comprise a computing device. While network devices may be capable of communicating signals (e.g., signal packets and/or frames), such as via a wired and/or wireless network, they may also be capable of performing operations associated with a computing device, such as arithmetic and/or logic operations, processing and/or storing operations (e.g., storing signal samples), such as in memory as tangible, physical memory states, and/or may, for example, operate as a server device and/or a client device in various embodiments. Network devices capable of operating as a server device, a client device and/or otherwise, may include, as examples, dedicated rack-mounted servers, desktop computers, laptop computers, set top boxes, tablets, netbooks, smart phones, wearable devices, integrated devices combining two or more features of the foregoing devices, and/or the like, or any combination thereof. As mentioned, signal packets and/or frames, for example, may be exchanged, such as between a server device and/or a client device, as well as other types of devices, including between wired and/or wireless devices coupled via a wired and/or wireless network, for example, or any combination thereof. It is noted that the terms, server, server device, server computing device, server computing platform and/or similar terms are used interchangeably. Similarly, the terms client, client device, client computing device, client computing platform and/or similar terms are also used interchangeably. While in some instances, for ease of description, these terms may be used in the singular, such as by referring to a "client device" or a "server device," the description is intended to encompass one or more client devices and/or one or more server devices, as appropriate. Along similar lines, references to a "database" are understood to mean, one or more databases and/or portions thereof, as appropriate.

[0026] It should be understood that for ease of description, a network device (also referred to as a networking device) may be embodied and/or described in terms of a computing device and vice versa. However, it should further be understood that this description should in no way be construed so that claimed subject matter is limited to one embodiment, such as only a computing device and/or only a network device, but, instead, may be embodied as a variety of devices or combinations thereof, including, for example, one or more illustrative examples.

[0027] A network may also include now known, and/or to be later developed arrangements, derivatives, and/or improvements, including, for example, past, present and/or future mass storage, such as network attached storage (NAS), a storage area network (SAN), and/or other forms of device readable media, for example. A network may include a portion of the Internet, one or more local area networks (LANs), one or more wide area networks (WANs), wire-line type connections, wireless type connections, other connections, or any combination thereof. Thus, a network may be worldwide in scope and/or extent. Likewise, sub-networks, such as may employ differing architectures and/or may be substantially compliant and/or substantially compatible with differing protocols, such as network computing and/or communications protocols (e.g., network protocols), may interoperate within a larger network.

[0028] In the context of the present patent application, the term sub-network and/or similar terms, if used, for example, with respect to a network, refers to the network and/or a part thereof. Sub-networks may also comprise links, such as physical links, connecting and/or coupling nodes, so as to be capable to communicate signal packets and/or frames between devices of particular nodes, including via wired links, wireless links, or combinations thereof. Various types of devices, such as network devices and/or computing devices, may be made available so that device interoperability is enabled and/or, in at least some instances, may be transparent. In the context of the present patent application, the term "transparent," if used with respect to devices of a network, refers to devices communicating via the network in which the devices are able to communicate via one or more intermediate devices, such as one or more intermediate nodes, but without the communicating devices necessarily specifying the one or more intermediate nodes and/or the one or more intermediate devices of the one or more intermediate nodes and/or, thus, may include within the network the devices communicating via the one or more intermediate nodes and/or the one or more intermediate devices of the one or more intermediate nodes, but may engage in signal communications as if such intermediate nodes and/or intermediate devices are not necessarily involved. For example, a router may provide a link and/or connection between otherwise separate and/or independent LANs.

[0029] In the context of the present patent application, a "private network" refers to a particular, limited set of devices, such as network devices and/or computing devices, able to communicate with other devices, such as network devices and/or computing devices, in the particular, limited set, such as via signal packet and/or signal frame communications, for example, without a need for re-routing and/or redirecting signal communications. A private network may comprise a standalone network; however, a private network may also comprise a subset of a larger network, such as, for example, without limitation, all or a portion of the Internet. Thus, for example, a private network "in the cloud" may refer to a private network that comprises a subset of the Internet. Although signal packet and/or frame communications (e.g. signal communications) may employ intermediate devices of intermediate nodes to exchange signal packets and/or signal frames, those intermediate devices may not necessarily be included in the private network by not being a source or designated destination for one or more signal packets and/or signal frames, for example. It is understood in the context of the present patent application that a private network may direct outgoing signal communications to devices not in the private network, but devices outside the private network may not necessarily be able to direct inbound signal communications to devices included in the private network.

[0030] The Internet refers to a decentralized global network of interoperable networks that comply with the Internet Protocol (IP). It is noted that there are several versions of the Internet Protocol. The term Internet Protocol, IP, and/or similar terms are intended to refer to any version, now known and/or to be later developed. The Internet includes local area networks (LANs), wide area networks (WANs), wireless networks, and/or long haul public networks that, for example, may allow signal packets and/or frames to be communicated between LANs. The term World Wide Web (WWW or Web) and/or similar terms may also be used, although it refers to a part of the Internet that complies with the Hypertext Transfer Protocol (HTTP). For example, network devices may engage in an HTTP session through an exchange of appropriately substantially compatible and/or substantially compliant signal packets and/or frames. It is noted that there are several versions of the Hypertext Transfer Protocol. The term Hypertext Transfer Protocol, HTTP, and/or similar terms are intended to refer to any version, now known and/or to be later developed. It is likewise noted that in various places in this document substitution of the term Internet with the term World Wide Web ("Web") may be made without a significant departure in meaning and may, therefore, also be understood in that manner if the statement would remain correct with such a substitution.

[0031] Although claimed subject matter is not in particular limited in scope to the Internet and/or to the Web; nonetheless, the Internet and/or the Web may without limitation provide a useful example of an embodiment at least for purposes of illustration. As indicated, the Internet and/or the Web may comprise a worldwide system of interoperable networks, including interoperable devices within those networks. The Internet and/or Web has evolved to a public, self-sustaining facility accessible to potentially billions of people or more worldwide. Also, in an embodiment, and as mentioned above, the terms "WWW" and/or "Web" refer to a part of the Internet that complies with the Hypertext Transfer Protocol. The Internet and/or the Web, therefore, in the context of the present patent application, may comprise a service that organizes stored digital content, such as, for example, text, images, video, etc., through the use of hypermedia, for example. It is noted that a network, such as the Internet and/or Web, may be employed to store electronic files and/or electronic documents.

[0032] The terms electronic file and/or the term electronic document are used throughout this document to refer to a set of stored memory states and/or a set of physical signals associated in a manner so as to thereby at least logically form a file (e.g., electronic) and/or an electronic document. That is, it is not meant to implicitly reference a particular syntax, format and/or approach used, for example, with respect to a set of associated memory states and/or a set of associated physical signals. If a particular type of file storage format and/or syntax, for example, is intended, it is referenced expressly. It is further noted an association of memory states, for example, may be in a logical sense and not necessarily in a tangible, physical sense. Thus, although signal and/or state components of a file and/or an electronic document, for example, are to be associated logically, storage thereof, for example, may reside in one or more different places in a tangible, physical memory, in an embodiment.

[0033] A Hyper Text Markup Language ("HTML"), for example, may be utilized to specify digital content and/or to specify a format thereof, such as in the form of an electronic file and/or an electronic document, such as a Web page, Web site, etc., for example. An Extensible Markup Language ("XML") may also be utilized to specify digital content and/or to specify a format thereof, such as in the form of an electronic file and/or an electronic document, such as a Web page, Web site, etc., in an embodiment. Of course, HTML and/or XML are merely examples of "markup" languages, provided as non-limiting illustrations. Furthermore, HTML and/or XML are intended to refer to any version, now known and/or to be later developed, of these languages. Likewise, claimed subject matter are not intended to be limited to examples provided as illustrations, of course.

[0034] In the context of the present patent application, the term "Web site" and/or similar terms refer to Web pages that are associated electronically to form a particular collection thereof. Also, in the context of the present patent application, "Web page" and/or similar terms refer to an electronic file and/or an electronic document accessible via a network, including by specifying a uniform resource locator (URL) for accessibility via the Web, in an example embodiment. As alluded to above, in one or more embodiments, a Web page may comprise digital content coded (e.g., via computer instructions) using one or more languages, such as, for example, markup languages, including HTML and/or XML, although claimed subject matter is not limited in scope in this respect. Also, in one or more embodiments, application developers may write code (e.g., computer instructions) in the form of JavaScript (or other programming languages), for example, executable by a computing device to provide digital content to populate an electronic document and/or an electronic file in an appropriate format, such as for use in a particular application, for example. Use of the term "JavaScript" and/or similar terms intended to refer to one or more particular programming languages are intended to refer to any version of the one or more programming languages identified, now known and/or to be later developed. Thus, JavaScript is merely an example programming language. As was mentioned, claimed subject matter is not intended to be limited to examples and/or illustrations.

[0035] In the context of the present patent application, the terms "entry," "electronic entry," "document," "electronic document," "content," "digital content," "item," and/or similar terms are meant to refer to signals and/or states in a physical format, such as a digital signal and/or digital state format, e.g., that may be perceived by a user if displayed, played, tactilely generated, etc. and/or otherwise executed by a device, such as a digital device, including, for example, a computing device, but otherwise might not necessarily be readily perceivable by humans (e.g., if in a digital format). Likewise, in the context of the present patent application, digital content provided to a user in a form so that the user is able to readily perceive the underlying content itself (e.g., content presented in a form consumable by a human, such as hearing audio, feeling tactile sensations and/or seeing images, as examples) is referred to, with respect to the user, as "consuming" digital content, "consumption" of digital content, "consumable" digital content and/or similar terms. For one or more embodiments, an electronic document and/or an electronic file may comprise a Web page of code (e.g., computer instructions) in a markup language executed or to be executed by a computing and/or networking device, for example. In another embodiment, an electronic document and/or electronic file may comprise a portion and/or a region of a Web page. However, claimed subject matter is not intended to be limited in these respects.

[0036] Also, for one or more embodiments, an electronic document and/or electronic file may comprise a number of components. As previously indicated, in the context of the present patent application, a component is physical, but is not necessarily tangible. As an example, components with reference to an electronic document and/or electronic file, in one or more embodiments, may comprise text, for example, in the form of physical signals and/or physical states (e.g., capable of being physically displayed). Typically, memory states, for example, comprise tangible components, whereas physical signals are not necessarily tangible, although signals may become (e.g., be made) tangible, such as if appearing on a tangible display, for example, as is not uncommon. Also, for one or more embodiments, components with reference to an electronic document and/or electronic file may comprise a graphical object, such as, for example, an image, such as a digital image, and/or sub-objects, including attributes thereof, which, again, comprise physical signals and/or physical states (e.g., capable of being tangibly displayed). In an embodiment, digital content may comprise, for example, text, images, audio, video, and/or other types of electronic documents and/or electronic files, including portions thereof, for example.

[0037] Also, in the context of the present patent application, the terms attributes (e.g., one or more attributes) and/or parameters (e.g., one or more parameters) refer to material descriptive of a collection of signal samples, such as one or more electronic documents and/or electronic files, and exist in the form of physical signals and/or physical states, such as memory states. For example, one or more parameters and/or attributes, such as referring to an electronic document and/or an electronic file comprising an image, may include, as examples, time of day at which an image was captured, latitude and longitude of an image capture device, such as a camera, for example, etc. In another example, one or more parameters and/or attributes relevant to digital content, such as digital content comprising a technical article, as an example, may include one or more authors, for example. Claimed subject matter is intended to embrace meaningful, descriptive parameters and/or attributes in any format, so long as the one or more parameters and/or attributes comprise physical signals and/or states, which may include, as examples, collection name (e.g., electronic file and/or electronic document identifier name), technique of creation, purpose of creation, time and date of creation, logical path if stored, coding formats (e.g., type of computer instructions, such as a markup language) and/or standards and/or specifications used so as to be protocol compliant (e.g., meaning substantially compliant and/or substantially compatible) for one or more uses, and so forth.

[0038] Signal packet communications and/or signal frame communications, also referred to as signal packet transmissions and/or signal frame transmissions (or merely "signal packets" or "signal frames"), may be communicated between nodes of a network, where a node may comprise one or more network devices and/or one or more computing devices, for example. As an illustrative example, but without limitation, a node may comprise one or more sites employing a local network address, such as in a local network address space. Likewise, a device, such as a network device and/or a computing device, may be associated with that node. It is also noted that in the context of this patent application, the term "transmission" is intended as another term for a type of signal communication that may occur in any one of a variety of situations. Thus, it is not intended to imply a particular directionality of communication and/or a particular initiating end of a communication path for the "transmission" communication. For example, the mere use of the term *in and of itself* is not intended, in the context of the present patent application, to have particular implications with respect to the one or more signals being communicated, such as, for example, whether the signals are being communicated "to" a particular device, whether the signals are being communicated "from" a particular device, and/or regarding which end of a communication path may be initiating communication, such as, for example, in a "push type" of signal transfer or in a "pull type" of signal transfer. In the context of the present patent application, push and/or pull type signal transfers are distinguished by which end of a communications path initiates signal transfer.

[0039] Thus, a signal packet and/or frame may, as an example, be communicated via a communication channel and/or a communication path, such as comprising a portion of the Internet and/or the Web, from a site via an access node coupled to the Internet or vice versa. Likewise, a signal packet and/or frame may be forwarded via network nodes to a target site coupled to a local network, for example. A signal packet and/or frame communicated via the Internet and/or the Web, for example, may be routed via a path, such as either being "pushed" or "pulled," comprising one or more gateways, servers, etc. that may, for example, route a signal packet and/or frame, such as, for example, substantially in accordance with a target and/or destination address and availability of a network path of network nodes to the target and/or destination address. Although the Internet and/or the Web comprise a network of interoperable networks, not all of those interoperable networks are necessarily available and/or accessible to the public.

[0040] In the context of the particular patent application, a network protocol, such as for communicating between devices of a network, may be characterized, at least in part, substantially in accordance with a layered description, such as the so-called Open Systems Interconnection (OSI) seven layer type of approach and/or description. A network computing and/or communications protocol (also referred to as a network protocol) refers to a set of signaling conventions, such as for communication transmissions, for example, as may take place between and/or among devices in a network. In the context of the present patent application, the term "between" and/or similar terms are understood to include "among" if appropriate for the particular usage and vice versa. Likewise, in the context of the present patent application, the terms "compatible with," "comply with" and/or similar terms are understood to respectively include substantial compatibility and/or substantial compliance.

[0041] A network protocol, such as protocols characterized substantially in accordance with the aforementioned OSI description, has several layers. These layers are referred to as a network stack. Various types of communications (e.g., transmissions), such as network communications, may occur across various layers. A lowest level layer in a network stack, such as the so-called physical layer, may characterize how symbols (e.g., bits and/or bytes) are communicated as one or more signals (and/or signal samples) via a physical medium (e.g., twisted pair copper wire, coaxial cable, fiber optic cable, wireless air interface, combinations thereof, etc.). Progressing to higher-level layers in a network protocol stack, additional operations and/or features may be available via engaging in communications that are substantially compatible and/or substantially compliant with a particular network protocol at these higher-level layers. For example, higher-level layers of a network protocol may, for example, affect device permissions, user permissions, etc.

[0042] A network and/or sub-network, in an embodiment, may communicate via signal packets and/or signal frames, such as via participating digital devices and may be substantially compliant and/or substantially compatible with, but is not limited to, now known and/or to be developed, versions of any of the following network protocol stacks: ARCNET, AppleTalk, ATM, Bluetooth, DECnet, Ethernet, FDDI, Frame Relay, HIPPI, IEEE 1394, IEEE 802.11, IEEE-488, Internet Protocol Suite, IPX, Myrinet, OSI Protocol Suite, QsNet, RS-232, SPX, System Network Architecture, Token Ring, USB, and/or X.25. A network and/or sub-network may employ, for example, a version, now known and/or later to be developed, of the following: TCP/IP, UDP, DECnet, NetBEUI, IPX, AppleTalk and/or the like. Versions of the Internet Protocol (IP) may include IPv4, IPv6, and/or other later to be developed versions.

[0043] Regarding aspects related to a network, including a communications and/or computing network, a wireless network may couple devices, including client devices, with the network. A wireless network may employ stand-alone, ad-hoc networks, mesh networks, Wireless LAN (WLAN) networks, cellular networks, and/or the like. A wireless network may further include a system of terminals, gateways, routers, and/or the like coupled by wireless radio links, and/or the like, which may move freely, randomly and/or organize themselves arbitrarily, such that network topology may change, at times even rapidly. A wireless network may further employ a plurality of network access technologies, including a version of Long Term Evolution (LTE), WLAN, Wireless Router (WR) mesh, 2nd, 3rd, 4th, and/or 5th generation (2G, 3G, 4G, and/or 5G) cellular technology and/or the like, whether currently known and/or to be later developed. Network access technologies may enable wide area coverage for devices, such as computing devices and/or network devices, with varying degrees of mobility, for example.

[0044] A network may enable radio frequency and/or other wireless type communications via a wireless network access technology and/or air interface, such as Global System for Mobile communication (GSM), Universal Mobile Telecommunications System (UMTS), General Packet Radio Services (GPRS), Enhanced Data GSM Environment (EDGE), 3GPP Long Term Evolution (LTE), LTE Advanced, Wideband Code Division Multiple Access (WCDMA), Bluetooth, ultra-wideband (UWB), 802.11b/g/n, and/or the like. A wireless network may include virtually any type of now known and/or to be developed wireless communication mechanism and/or wireless communications protocol by which signals may be communicated between devices, between networks, within a network, and/or the like, including the foregoing, of course.

[0045] In one example embodiment, as shown in FIG. 2, a system embodiment may comprise a local network (e.g., device 204 and medium 240) and/or another type of network, such as a computing and/or communications network. For purposes of illustration, therefore, FIG. 2 shows an embodiment 200 of a system that may be employed to implement either type or both types of networks. Network 208 may comprise one or more network connections, links, processes, services, applications, and/or resources to facilitate and/or support communications, such as an exchange of communication signals, for example, between a computing device, such as 202, and another computing device, such as 206, which may, for example, comprise one or more client computing devices and/or one or more server computing device. By way of example, but not limitation, network 208 may comprise wireless and/or wired communication links, telephone and/or telecommunications systems, Wi-Fi networks, Wi-MAX networks, the Internet, a local area network (LAN), a wide area network (WAN), or any combinations thereof.

[0046] Example devices in FIG. 2 may comprise features, for example, of a client computing device and/or a server computing device, in an embodiment. It is further noted that the term computing device, in general, whether employed as a client and/or as a server, or otherwise, refers at least to a processor and a memory connected by a communication bus. A "processor," for example, is understood to connote a specific structure such as a central processing unit (CPU) of a computing device which may include a control unit and an execution unit. In an aspect, a processor may comprise a device that interprets and executes instructions to process input signals to provide output signals. As such, in the context of the present patent application at least, computing device and/or processor are understood to refer to sufficient structure within the meaning of 35 USC § 112(f) so that it is specifically intended that 35 USC § 112(f) not be implicated by use of the term "computing device," "processor" and/or similar terms; however, if it is determined, for some reason not immediately apparent, that the foregoing understanding cannot stand and that 35 USC § 112(f), therefore, necessarily is implicated by the use of the term "computing device," "processor" and/or similar terms, then, it is intended, pursuant to that statutory section, that corresponding structure, material and/or acts for performing one or more functions be understood and be interpreted to be described at least in figure(s) **[FIGURE NUMBERS TO BE PROVIDED]** and in the text associated with the foregoing figure(s) of the present patent application.

[0047] Referring now to FIG. 2 in an embodiment, first and third devices 202 and 206 may be capable of rendering a graphical user interface (GUI) for a network device and/or a computing device, for example, so that a user-operator may engage in system use. Device 204 may potentially serve a similar function in this illustration. Likewise, in FIG. 2, computing device 202 ("first device" in figure) may interface with computing device 204 ("second device" in figure), which may, for example, also comprise features of a client computing device and/or a server computing device, in an embodiment. Processor (e.g., processing device) 220 and memory 222, which may comprise primary memory 224 and secondary memory 226, may communicate by way of a communication bus 215, for example. The term "computing device," in the context of the present patent application, refers to a system and/or a device, such as a computing apparatus, that includes a capability to process (e.g., perform computations) and/or store digital content, such as electronic files, electronic documents, measurements, text, images, video, audio, etc. in the form of signals and/or states. Thus, a computing device, in the context of the present patent application, may comprise hardware, software, firmware, or any combination thereof (other than software per se). Computing device 204, as depicted in FIG. 2 is merely one example, and claimed subject matter is not limited in scope to this particular example.

[0048] For one or more embodiments, a device, such as a computing device and/or networking device, may comprise, for example, any of a wide range of digital electronic devices, including, but not limited to, desktop and/or notebook computers, high-definition televisions, digital versatile disc (DVD) and/or other optical disc players and/or recorders, game consoles, satellite television receivers, cellular telephones, tablet devices, wearable devices, personal digital assistants, mobile audio and/or video playback and/or recording devices, Internet of Things (IOT) type devices, or any combination of the foregoing. Further, unless specifically stated otherwise, a process as described, such as with reference to flow diagrams and/or otherwise, may also be executed and/or affected, in whole or in part, by a computing device and/or a network device. A device, such as a computing device and/or network device, may vary in terms of capabilities and/or features. Claimed subject matter is intended to cover a wide range of potential variations. For example, a device may include a numeric keypad and/or other display of limited functionality, such as a monochrome liquid crystal display (LCD) for displaying text, for example. In contrast, however, as another example, a web-enabled device may include a physical and/or a virtual keyboard, mass storage, one or more accelerometers, one or more gyroscopes, global positioning system (GPS) and/or other location-identifying type capability, and/or a display with a higher degree of functionality, such as a touch-sensitive color 2D or 3D display, for example.

[0049] As suggested previously, communications between a computing device and/or a network device and a wireless network may be in accordance with known and/or to be developed network protocols including, for example, global system for mobile communications (GSM), enhanced data rate for GSM evolution (EDGE), 802.11b/g/n/h, etc., and/or worldwide interoperability for microwave access (WiMAX). A computing device and/or a networking device may also have a subscriber identity module (SIM) card, which, for example, may comprise a detachable or embedded smart card that is able to store subscription content of a user, and/or is also able to store a contact list. It is noted, however, that a SIM card may also be electronic, meaning that is may simply be stored in a particular location in memory of the computing and/or networking device. A user may own the computing device and/or network device or may otherwise be a user, such as a primary user, for example. A device may be assigned an address by a wireless network operator, a wired network operator, and/or an Internet Service Provider (ISP). For example, an address may comprise a domestic or international telephone number, an Internet Protocol (IP) address, and/or one or more other identifiers. In other embodiments, a computing and/or communications network may be embodied as a wired network, wireless network, or any combinations thereof.

[0050] A computing and/or network device may include and/or may execute a variety of now known and/or to be developed operating systems, derivatives and/or versions thereof, including computer operating systems, such as Windows, iOS, Linux, a mobile operating system, such as iOS, Android, Windows Mobile, and/or the like. A computing device and/or network device may include and/or may execute a variety of possible applications, such as a client software application enabling communication with other devices. For example, one or more messages (e.g., content) may be communicated, such as via one or more protocols, now known and/or later to be developed, suitable for communication of email, short message service (SMS), and/or multimedia message service (MMS), including via a network, such as a social network, formed at least in part by a portion of a computing and/or communications network, including, but not limited to, Facebook, LinkedIn, Twitter, and/or Flickr, to provide only a few examples. A computing and/or network device may also include executable computer instructions to process and/or communicate digital content, such as, for example, textual content, digital multimedia content, and/or the like. A computing and/or network device may also include executable computer instructions to perform a variety of possible tasks, such as browsing, searching, playing various forms of digital content, including locally stored and/or streamed video, and/or games such as, but not limited to, fantasy sports leagues. The foregoing is provided merely to illustrate that claimed subject matter is intended to include a wide range of possible features and/or capabilities.

[0051] In FIG. 2, computing device 202 may provide one or more sources of executable computer instructions in the form physical states and/or signals (e.g., stored in memory states), for example. Computing device 202 may communicate with computing device 204 by way of a network connection, such as via network 208, for example. As previously mentioned, a connection, while physical, may not necessarily be tangible. Although computing device 204 of FIG. 2 shows various tangible, physical components, claimed subject matter is not limited to a computing device having only these tangible components as other implementations and/or embodiments may include alternative arrangements that may comprise additional tangible components or fewer tangible components, for example, that function differently while achieving similar results. Rather, examples are provided merely as illustrations. It is not intended that claimed subject matter be limited in scope to illustrative examples.

[0052] Memory 222 may comprise any non-transitory storage mechanism. Memory 222 may comprise, for example, primary memory 224 and secondary memory 226, additional memory circuits, mechanisms, or combinations thereof may be used. Memory 222 may comprise, for example, random access memory, read only memory, etc., such as in the form of one or more storage devices and/or systems, such as, for example, a disk drive including an optical disc drive, a tape drive, a solid-state memory drive, etc., just to name a few examples.

[0053] Memory 222 may be utilized to store a program of executable computer instructions. For example, processor 220 may fetch executable instructions from memory and proceed to execute the fetched instructions. Memory 222 may also comprise a memory controller for accessing device readable-medium 240 that may carry and/or make accessible digital content, which may include code, and/or instructions, for example, executable by processor 220 and/or some other device, such as a controller, as one example, capable of executing computer instructions, for example. Under direction of processor 220, a non-transitory memory, such as memory cells storing physical states (e.g., memory states), comprising, for example, a program of executable computer instructions, may be executed by processor 220 and able to generate signals to be communicated via a network, for example, as previously described. Generated signals may also be stored in memory, also previously suggested.

[0054] Memory 222 may store electronic files and/or electronic documents, such as relating to one or more users, and may also comprise a computer-readable medium that may carry and/or make accessible content, including code and/or instructions, for example, executable by processor 220 and/or some other device, such as a controller, as one example, capable of executing computer instructions, for example. As previously mentioned, the term electronic file and/or the term electronic document are used throughout this document to refer to a set of stored memory states and/or a set of physical signals associated in a manner so as to thereby form an electronic file and/or an electronic document. That is, it is not meant to implicitly reference a particular syntax, format and/or approach used, for example, with respect to a set of associated memory states and/or a set of associated physical signals. It is further noted an association of memory states, for example, may be in a logical sense and not necessarily in a tangible, physical sense. Thus, although signal and/or state components of an electronic file and/or electronic document, are to be associated logically, storage thereof, for example, may reside in one or more different places in a tangible, physical memory, in an embodiment.

[0055] Algorithmic descriptions and/or symbolic representations are examples of techniques used by those of ordinary skill in the signal processing and/or related arts to convey the substance of their work to others skilled in the art. An algorithm is, in the context of the present patent application, and generally, is considered to be a self-consistent sequence of operations and/or similar signal processing leading to a desired result. In the context of the present patent application, operations and/or processing involve physical manipulation of physical quantities. Typically, although not necessarily, such quantities may take the form of electrical and/or magnetic signals and/or states capable of being stored, transferred, combined, compared, processed and/or otherwise manipulated, for example, as electronic signals and/or states making up components of various forms of digital content, such as signal measurements, text, images, video, audio, etc.

[0056] It has proven convenient at times, principally for reasons of common usage, to refer to such physical signals and/or physical states as bits, values, elements, attributes, parameters, symbols, characters, terms, numbers, numerals, measurements, content and/or the like. It should be understood, however, that all of these and/or similar terms are to be associated with appropriate physical quantities and are merely convenient labels. Unless specifically stated otherwise, as apparent from the preceding discussion, it is appreciated that throughout this specification discussions utilizing terms such as "processing," "computing," "calculating," "determining," "establishing," "obtaining," "identifying," "selecting," "generating," and/or the like may refer to actions and/or processes of a specific apparatus, such as a special purpose computer and/or a similar special purpose computing and/or network device. In the context of this specification, therefore, a special purpose computer and/or a similar special purpose computing and/or network device is capable of processing, manipulating and/or transforming signals and/or states, typically in the form of physical electronic and/or magnetic quantities, within memories, registers, and/or other storage devices, processing devices, and/or display devices of the special purpose computer and/or similar special purpose computing and/or network device. In the context of this particular patent application, as mentioned, the term "specific apparatus" therefore includes a general purpose computing and/or network device, such as a general purpose computer, once it is programmed to perform particular functions, such as pursuant to program software instructions.

[0057] In some circumstances, operation of a memory device, such as a change in state from a binary one to a binary zero or vice versa, for example, may comprise a transformation, such as a physical transformation. With particular types of memory devices, such a physical transformation may comprise a physical transformation of an article to a different state or thing. For example, but without limitation, for some types of memory devices, a change in state may involve an accumulation and/or storage of charge or a release of stored charge. Likewise, in other memory devices, a change of state may comprise a physical change, such as a transformation in magnetic orientation. Likewise, a physical change may comprise a transformation in molecular structure, such as from crystalline form to amorphous form or vice versa. In still other memory devices, a change in physical state may involve quantum mechanical phenomena, such as, superposition, entanglement, and/or the like, which may involve quantum bits (qubits), for example. The foregoing is not intended to be an exhaustive list of all examples in which a change in state from a binary one to a binary zero or vice versa in a memory device may comprise a transformation, such as a physical, but non-transitory, transformation. Rather, the foregoing is intended as illustrative examples.

[0058] Referring again to FIG. 2, processor 220 may comprise one or more circuits, such as digital circuits, to perform at least a portion of a computing procedure and/or process. By way of example, but not limitation, processor 220 may comprise one or more processors, such as controllers, microprocessors, microcontrollers, application specific integrated circuits, digital signal processors, programmable logic devices, field programmable gate arrays, the like, or any combination thereof. In various implementations and/or embodiments, processor 220 may perform signal processing, typically substantially in accordance with fetched executable computer instructions, such as to manipulate signals and/or states, to construct signals and/or states, etc., with signals and/or states generated in such a manner to be communicated and/or stored in memory, for example.

[0059] FIG. 2 also illustrates device 204 as including a component 232 operable with input/output devices, for example, so that signals and/or states may be appropriately communicated between devices, such as device 204 and an input device and/or device 204 and an output device. A user may make use of an input device, such as a computer mouse, stylus, track ball, keyboard, and/or any other similar device capable of receiving user actions and/or motions as input signals. Likewise, for a device having speech to text capability, a user may speak to a device to generate input signals. A user may make use of an output device, such as a display, a printer, etc., and/or any other device capable of providing signals and/or generating stimuli for a user, such as visual stimuli, audio stimuli and/or other similar stimuli.

[0060] In the preceding description, various aspects of claimed subject matter have been described. For purposes of explanation, specifics, such as amounts, systems and/or configurations, as examples, were set forth. In other instances, well-known features were omitted and/or simplified so as not to obscure claimed subject matter. While certain features have been illustrated and/or described herein, many modifications, substitutions, changes and/or equivalents will now occur to those skilled in the art. It is, therefore, to be understood that the appended claims are intended to cover all modifications and/or changes as fall within claimed subject matter.

CLAIMS:

1. A method comprising: . . .

    . . .

. . .

11. An apparatus comprising: . . .

    . . .

ABSTRACT

Briefly, embodiments, such as methods and/or systems of ____________, for example, are described.

Figure 2

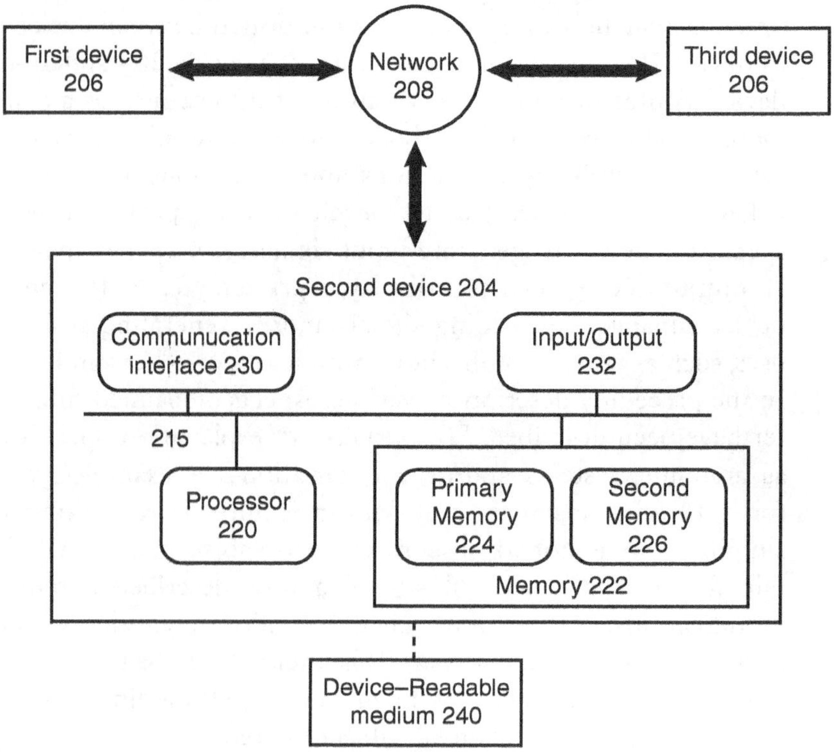

Index

affidavit evidence, 91
affirmative egregious misconduct, 485, 488. *See also* inequitable conduct
America Invents Act (AIA)
  defined terms, 101
  enactment, 2n5
  prior art, 2, 7, 64, 75, 99–109, 452
  transition provisions, 106, 108–109
  written description issues, 108–109, 451–452
"and/or," 506
antecedent basis, lack of, 503–504
anticipation requirement. *See* novelty/anticipation requirement
apparatus claims
  Beauregard claims and, 51–52, 385
  breadth of, 491
  claim diversity with, 44–45, 555–558
  for component manufacturer, 20–24, 25–28
  contributory infringement, 280–284
  dependent claims, 124, 127
  examples and illustrations, 119–132, 498–499
  inducing infringement, 289–292
  inferential claiming, 125, 192–197
  manufacture claims and, 161
  means plus function elements, 331
  mechanics of, 119–132
  method claims and, 25–28, 44–46, 132, 147–153, 356, 369–371, 377, 393–394, 491–499, 555–557
  method-type limitations in, 494–496, 498–499, 555–556
  for network provider, 44–46, 48–49, 52
  patent infringement, 280–284, 289–292, 379–385, 557–558
  patent strategy, 20–24, 25–28, 32, 44–46, 48–49, 52
  statutory class, 115, 116–118, 491–499, 554–558
  structural vs. functional limitations, 123, 127–132, 356, 393–394
  for system integrator, 32
  use infringement, 379–385
apparatus means plus function claims. *See* means plus function claims
article of manufacture claims. *See* manufacture claims

Beauregard claims
  advantages and disadvantages of, 397–398
  apparatus claims and, 51–52, 385
  approaches to, 398–402
  claim diversity with, 51–52, 396–402
  defined, 51
  examples and illustrations, 161–166
  mechanics of, 161–166
  patent strategy, 51–52
  structural vs. functional limitations, 163–166, 400–402
Braun decision, 334–336, 341

breadth of claims, 62–112
overview, 62–65
broad claim advantages and disadvantages, 7, 9, 12–13, 65, 66–73, 269n131, 512–513
broad claim examples, 415–417
claim body and, 186–188
claim diversity and, 314–318, 413–422, 437, 499–500
commercial motivations, 10–13, 65nn151–152
dependent claims, 205–214, 446, 550–554
DOE considerations, 308–310
environment of the inventions and, 550–554
examiners' standing on, 69–70
functional and structural language, 548
independent claims, 205–214, 269–272, 448–449
intermediate claim examples, 417–420
intermediate dependent claims, skipping, 499–500
means plus function claims narrowing, 340–341
narrow claim advantages and disadvantages, 25, 35, 64–65, 71, 97–98, 269n131, 308–310
narrow claim examples, 417–420
negotiation effects, 69–70, 270–271
patent eligibility and, 478–479
picture claims, 420–422
precision and, 66, 68, 507
prior art and, 9, 35, 43, 62–66, 73–112, 270–272, 301, 414, 490–491
short claims and, 269–272
statutory class and, 491
statutory issues, 62–64
technological changes, 6, 66
vagueness and, 66–68, 186, 507
verbal formulations increasing, 437
broadest reasonable interpretation (BRI), 81–82, 163, 246–247, 270, 518
business strategy
anticipating changes, 53, 60–62
commercial motivation for patent claims, 9–13, 65nn151–152, 251–252, 448, 519–520
patent strategy driven by, 13–62

candor, duty of, 483n117, 484
capacity for infringing, making device with, 388–396
CIP (continuation-in-part) patent application, 106, 108
claim body, 185–204
apparatus claims, 122, 192–197
Beauregard claims, 162–163
breadth, vagueness, and precision balance in, 186–188
elements, limitations, and associated relationships, 185, 189–191, 194–195
examples and illustrations, 4, 187–197
improvement claims, 167–169
inferential claiming, 192–197
interpretation of, 197–204
mechanics, 3–5, 113–114, 185–204
method claims, 195–196, 426n5
prior art distinguished in, 187–188
redefining terms, 200–204
specifications, 197–204 (*see also* specifications; written descriptions)
step plus function elements, 426n5
structural vs. functional vs. process limitations, 191–192
theory of, 185–204
claim construction, 215–311. *See also* mechanics
overview, 215–216
categories of claim terminology, 244–249

clarity of claims in, 252–258
for direct, literal patent infringement, 249–272
DOE framework-based, 250, 292–311
drafting principles, 249–311 (*see also* claim drafting)
express vs. implied meaning in, 242–243
hierarchy of claim terms in, 262–267, 443–445
for indirect infringement, 250–251, 272–292
interchangeable terms in, 266, 438
intrinsic vs. extrinsic evidence distinction for, 224–249
ITC investigation and, 219–224
legal framework for, 216–249
Markman decision/hearings and, 216–219, 221–222, 224, 252
ordinary and customary meaning in, 224–225, 232, 234–241, 242, 244, 258–260
overly-specific modifiers avoided in, 268–269
patentee as lexicographer, 241–249, 517
Phillips decision and, 225–226, 227, 229–234, 236–240, 241–242, 252
rewriting vs. amending claims, 310–311
short and concise claims in, 269–272
Vitronics decision and, 224–225, 226–228, 229, 233–234, 236, 252–253, 259–260
words consistent with understood meaning in, 258–260
words with broadly understood meanings in, 260–262
claim differentiation, doctrine of, 206–208, 444–448, 519
claim diversity
overview, 313, 318–319
apparatus claims, 44–45, 555–558
Beauregard claims, 51–52, 396–402
breadth of claims and, 314–318, 413–422, 437, 499–500
component claims, 319–322, 557–558
composition of matter claims, 409–413
dependent claims for, 206–208, 444–448, 519
as hedge strategy, 314–422 (*see also* hedge strategy)
intermediate dependent claims skipped for, 499–500
Markush group claims, 402–409
means plus function/step plus function claims, 328–347
method claims, 26, 37–38, 132, 369–396, 439–440, 555–557
patent eligibility and, 383, 466, 478
product-by-process claims, 360–369
statutory class use, 554–558
structural and functional language for, 123, 130, 347–360, 547–549
system claims, 322–328
varying scope with, 413–422
varying terminology, 436–440
verbal formulations, 436–448
claim drafting. *See also* Patent Claim Drafting Practice; *specific claim types*
anticipating first office action, 514–517
breadth of claims (*see* breadth of claims)
business and economic considerations in, 251–252 (*see also* commercial issues)
of claim body (*see* claim body)
claim diversity and (*see* claim diversity)
clarity of claims in, 252–258, 413
complexity and challenge, 2–13
damages, 532–538 (*see also* damages)

claim drafting *(continued)*
dependent claims (*see* dependent claims)
design around avoidance, 308, 327, 432, 491, 538–542
for direct, literal infringement avoidance, 249–272
DOE framework-based, 250, 292–311
enablement issues, 459–460 (*see also* enablement)
EPC practices, 573–589 (*see also* European Patent Convention)
functional language (*see* functional language)
grammar rules, 509–510
hierarchy of claim terms in, 262–267, 443–445
implied patent licensing risk reduction, 558–571 (*see also* patent licensing)
indefiniteness issues, 460–461, 519 (*see also* indefiniteness)
independent claims (*see* independent claims)
for indirect infringement avoidance, 250–251, 272–292
inequitable conduct and, 483–490
mechanics of (*see* mechanics)
modifiers in, 268–269, 505
multiparty claim avoidance, 521, 522–527
patent eligibility issues, 461–483, 519 (*see also* patent eligibility)
patent exhaustion risk reduction, 558–571 (*see also* patent exhaustion)
for patent infringement avoidance, 249–292, 519–522, 524–527
for patent infringement detection, 542–546
patent strategy and (*see* patent strategy)
of preamble (*see* preamble)
precision, 507–509 (*see also* precision)
principles, advanced, 511–571
principles, basic, 423–510
principles, for claim construction, 249–311
principles, list of, 591–593
principles, simple and well-established, 506–510
prior art issues, 483–491 (*see also* prior art)
rewriting vs. amending claims, 310–311
short and concise claims in, 269–272
sloppy techniques, avoiding, 500–506
of specifications (*see* specifications)
statutory class issues, 491–499, 554–558 (*see also* statutory classes; *specific classes*)
structural language (*see* structural language)
terseness, 507
of transition word (*see* transition word)
verbal formulations, 436–448
words consistent with understood meaning in, 258–260
words with broadly understood meanings in, 260–262
writing then revising, 509
written description issues, 450–459, 519 (*see also* written descriptions)
claim estoppel, 71–72
claims, patent. *See* patent claims
commercial issues
commercialization of inventions, 83–85, 92–93, 103–104, 109, 452, 565
commercially copyable aspects of dependent claims, 305–306, 307–308, 448, 551

as motivation for claims, 9–13, 65nn151–152, 251–252, 448, 519–520
royalties (*see* royalties)
staple vs. non-staple articles of commerce, 276–277
common ownership, 100, 103
component claims
claim diversity with, 319–322, 557–558
commercial motivation for, 11–13
damages, 322
examples and illustrations, 320
patent infringement, 273
patent strategy, 34–36
system claims vs., 322–325, 557–558
component manufacturer, patent strategy, 18–30, 31, 34
composition of matter claims
claim diversity with, 409–413
examples and illustrations, 153–161
Markush groups, 159, 183, 412
mechanics of, 153–161
product-by-process claims and, 160
statutory class, 115, 116–118
structural vs. functional limitations, 160–161
transition word, 157–159, 179–183, 410–412, 433–434
computer programs, 575–578, 581. *See also* software claims
computer readable medium claims. *See* Beauregard claims
computer-implemented inventions, 576–578
conjunctions, sloppy use of, 506
contempt power, 222
continuation patent application, 69, 106–109
continuation-in-part (CIP) patent application, 106, 108
contracts
indemnity clauses, 12, 34, 324, 383
patent claims vs., 171
patent exhaustion and implied license restrictions, 559, 560–561, 567
preambles, 424
contributory infringement, 275–284
of apparatus claim component, 280–284
direct infringement required for, 275
intent and knowledge required for, 275, 276, 278–279, 282–283
of method claim component, 277–280
non-staple articles of commerce and, 276–277
single infringer principle, 524
statutory foundations, 273, 274–275, 282n162
copyrights, 14
costs. *See* financial considerations
covenant not to sue, 71
CRM (computer readable medium) claims. *See* Beauregard claims

damages
claim drafting, 532–538
component claims, 322
entire market value principle, 34–35, 325, 535–537
factors driving, 533–535
method claims, 374–375
patent litigation, 219, 221–222
patent strategy, 34
royalty-based, 34, 322, 325–326, 374–375, 532–538
smallest saleable unit principle, 34, 325, 537–538
statutory foundations, 532–533
system claims, 325–326
definiteness requirement, 63, 208. *See also* indefiniteness
definitions, 200–204, 449–450, 454–455, 508–509, 517–518

dependent claims
adding new element via, 210–214
anticipating first office action with, 516–517
apparatus claims, 124, 127
breadth of, 205–214, 446, 550–554 (*see also* breadth of claim)
claim differentiation doctrine and, 206–208, 444–448, 519
commercially copyable aspects of, 305–306, 307–308, 448, 551
DOE and, 305–306, 307–308
environment of the inventions in, 549–554
examples and illustrations, 4, 446–448
fallback position established with, 43, 46, 68, 307, 518–519
filing fees, 204–205n171, 212, 324, 589
independent claim relationship, 204–214 (*see also* independent claims)
intermediate, skipping, 499–500
mechanics of, 204–214
method claims, 140–145, 214, 529–531
order of, 212–214, 446
patent infringement detection with, 545–546
patent strategy, 22, 32–35, 43–44, 46–48
as prior art hedge, 206, 208
product integration coverage, 322, 527–531
system claims, 323–324, 327
theory of, 204–210
transition word, 208, 210
design around opportunities, 308, 327, 432, 491, 538–542
dictionaries, use of, 236–241
diligence evidence, 91
direct infringement
claim drafting, 249–272
defined, 250, 272
indirect infringement requiring, 274, 275, 284, 523
literal, 249–272, 307
multiparty claims, 521
nonliteral, 250, 251 (*see also* doctrine of equivalents)
patent strategy and, 35–36, 38
single infringer principle, 523–525
statutory foundations, 250
discovery, 220
disjunctions, sloppy use of, 506
divided infringement. *See* single infringer principle
divisional patent application, 106, 107, 151, 153, 589
doctrine of equivalents (DOE)
breadth of claims and, 308–310
claim drafting based on, 250, 292–311
claim language interpretation equivalents, 301–304
dependent claims and, 305–306, 307–308
design around factors, 308, 538–539
Dolly v. Spalding decision, 301–304
equivalents in section 112(f), 329, 341
Festo decision, 299–301
foreseeability limit to, 538–539
function-way-result test, 292, 295–298, 340
Hilton-Davis decision, 293–299
individual elements vs. invention as whole, 294–295
insubstantial differences test, 292, 295–298
legal clarification of, 57, 58–59
literal infringement focus vs., 307
means plus function claims, 329, 340–342

novelty/anticipation and, 17
patent infringement, 17, 57, 58–59, 250, 292–311, 329, 340–342, 538–539
prior art limiting scope of, 292–293, 304–306
prosecution history estoppel, 292, 293–294, 298–301
rewriting vs. amending claims, 310–311
Wilson Sporting Goods decision, 304–306
doctrine of inherent anticipation, 377–379
DOE. *See* doctrine of equivalents
Dolly v. Spalding decision, 301–304
double inclusion, 501
double patenting, 62, 151–153

eligibility. *See* patent eligibility
enablement, 179nn122–123, 181, 255, 433nn25–26, 459–460
entire market value principle, 34–35, 325, 535–537
environment of the invention, 549–554
EPC. *See* European Patent Convention
EPO (European Patent Office), 573–574
equivalents, doctrine of. *See* doctrine of equivalents
estoppel, 71–72, 82, 292, 293–294, 298–301, 421
European Patent Convention (EPC), 573–589
claim formalities and fees, 589
clarity, sufficiency, and claim support requirements, 582–586
computer programs and computer-implemented inventions, 575–578, 581
excluded subject matter, 575–581
filing in EPO, 573–574
improvement claims, 167, 169, 586–587
Markush group claims, 409n166
means plus function claims, 588
medical diagnosis, treatment, and surgery method claims, 578–581
novelty and inventive step requirements, 574, 581–582
prior art, 104, 111, 574–575, 581–582
public accessibility and use, 104, 574
unity of invention, 150n61, 588–589
European Patent Office (EPO), 573–574
ex parte litigation. *See* patent prosecution
exclusion, right of, 15, 114, 177, 220, 222
express meaning of claim terms, 242–243. *See also* definitions
extrinsic evidence
defined, 224
intrinsic, distinguished, 224–249
ordinary and customary meaning in, 224–225, 232, 234–241, 242, 244
patentee as lexicographer, 241–249
Phillips decision on, 225–226, 227, 229–234, 236–240, 241–242
reliability of, 232–233

fallback position, establishing, 43, 46, 52, 68, 97, 307, 437, 518–519
Festo decision, 299–301
filing date
effective, 101–102, 235
first-to-file patent system, 75, 82n181, 83, 89, 92, 102
patent term from, 151–153
financial considerations
commercial issues (*see* commercial issues)
cost of patent claims, 74–75, 150–151 (*see also filing fees this heading*)

financial considerations *(continued)*
cost of patent prosecution, 69
cost of picture claims, 422
cost of prior art searches, 8, 73–75
damages (*see* damages)
filing fees, 52, 74–75, 107, 148, 151, 204–205n171, 212, 324, 589
royalties (*see* royalties)
first office action, anticipating, 514–517
first-to-file patent system, 75, 82n181, 83, 89, 92, 102
first-to-invent patent system, 75, 82–83, 89, 92
foreign entities. *See also* European Patent Convention
extraterritorial infringement, 30, 39, 136, 146–147, 368–369, 379
indirect infringement, 281–282, 290, 520–521
ITC enforcement (*see* International Trade Commission)
method claims, 493–494
fraud, 310, 483n117, 484, 486, 489. *See also* inequitable conduct
functional claims. *See* means plus function claims; step plus function claims
functional language
apparatus claims, 123, 127–132, 356, 393–394
Beauregard claims, 163–166, 400–402
claim body, 191–192
for claim diversity, 123, 130, 347–360, 547–549
composition of matter claims, 160–161
DOE, 296–298
means plus function claims, 130, 139, 342–347, 547–548
method claims, 138–141, 356, 373, 388–396, 400–401
software claims, 347–348, 351–353, 356–358, 395, 453–454
specifications, 453–454
function-way-result (FWR) test, 292, 295–298, 340

good faith, 9, 76, 271n135, 483n117, 490–491
grammar rules, 509–510

hedge strategy, 314–422
overview, 314
Beauregard claims as, 396–402
breadth of claims and, 314–318, 413–422
claim diversity as, 314–422 (*see also* claim diversity)
component claims as, 319–322
composition of matter claims as, 409–413
dependent claims, 206, 208
Markush group claims as, 402–409
means plus function/step plus function claims as, 328–347
method of making claims as, 367–371, 385–396
method of using claims as, 369–385
product-by-process claims as, 360–369
structural and functional language for, 347–360
system claims as, 322–328
hierarchy of claim terms, 262–267, 443–445
Hilton-Davis decision, 293–299

implication claiming, 192n148. *See also* inferential claiming
implied meaning of claim terms, 242–243
implied patent licensing, 36, 558–571

improvement claims
  environment of the invention, 549–550
  EPC standards, 167, 169, 586–587
  examples and illustration, 166–169
  Jepson claims, 110–112, 166–169, 175, 586, 587
  mechanics of, 166–169
  patent eligibility, 470n96, 475
  preamble, 167–169, 175, 586
imputed infringement, 273n139
indefiniteness. *See also* definiteness requirement; vagueness
  avoiding issues with, 460–461, 519
  breadth of claims and, 66n153, 68
  dependent claims, 208, 519
  grammar misuse creating, 509
  inferential claiming, 192–197
  legal standard for, 246, 460–461, 500
  Markush group claims, 403, 404, 406
  sloppy techniques and, 500–501, 503–504, 505
  statutory class clarity lack as, 491, 494–496, 498
  terms of degree and, 244n81, 246, 461
  transition word, 435n34
  written description issues, 450, 453–454
independent claims
  adding new element to, 210–214
  breadth of, 205–214, 269–272, 448–449 (*see also* breadth of claim)
  defined, 22
  dependent claim relationship, 204–214 (*see also* dependent claims)
  example, 4
  filing fees, 52, 204–205n171, 212, 324
  method of making, 493
  overly-specific modifiers avoided in, 268–269
  patent strategy, 22, 32–35, 52
  picture claims as, 421
  product integration coverage, 529–531
  short and concise, 269–272
  system claims, 32–35, 323–325
indirect infringement
  claim drafting, 250–251, 272–292
  contributory, 273, 274–284, 524
  defined, 250–251, 272
  direct infringement required for, 274, 275, 284, 523
  foreign entities, 281–282, 290, 520–521
  inducing, 273, 275, 276–277, 282, 284–292, 523, 524
  intent and knowledge required for, 273–292
  literal, 273
  nonliteral, 273
  patent strategy and, 35–36
  single infringer principle, 523–524
  statutory foundations, 250–251, 273, 274–275, 282, 521n24
  unpatented products, 284, 292
inducing infringement, 284–292
  of apparatus claims, 289–292
  direct infringement required for, 284, 523
  intent and knowledge required for, 284–285, 287, 290–291
  of method claims, 286–289
  single infringer principle, 523, 524
  staple articles of commerce and, 276–277
  statutory foundations, 273, 275, 282
inequitable conduct, 483–490
inferential claiming, 125, 141, 174, 192–197, 211, 376, 505
infringement. *See* patent infringement
inherent anticipation, doctrine of, 377–379

injunctions, 219–220, 321, 532, 535
insubstantial differences test, 292, 295–298
inter partes reviews (IPRs), 3n7, 8, 22, 71, 86
interchangeable terms, 266, 438
interferences, 92
International Trade Commission (ITC)
  claim construction and, 219–224
  on component claims, 321
  enforcement authority, 33n71, 147
  on method of making claims, 147, 391–393
  on product-by-process claims, 368
  on structural vs. functional limitations, 354–355
  on system claims, 323
intrinsic evidence
  categories of claim terminology, 244–249
  defined, 224
  express vs. implied meaning of, 242–243
  extrinsic, distinguished, 224–249
  ordinary and customary meaning in, 224–225, 232, 234–241, 242, 244
  patentee as lexicographer, 241–249
  pecking order of, 225–234
  Phillips decision on, 225–226, 227, 229–234, 236–240, 241–242
  Vitronics decision on, 224–225, 226–228, 229, 233–234, 236
invention(s)
  abandoned, suppressed, or concealed, 91–92
  affidavit evidence, 91
  "as a whole," 96–97, 118–119, 185–186, 294–295, 467–468, 480
  claimed, defined, 101
  commercialization or public use, 83–85, 92–93, 103–104, 109, 452, 565
  common ownership of, 100, 103
  computer-implemented, 576–578 (*see also* software claims)
  conception of, 89–91
  corroboration of, 90–91
  defined, 15
  design around opportunities, 308, 327, 432, 491, 538–542
  diligence evidence, 91
  environment of, 549–554
  evolving nature of, 3n6
  features of, identifying, 440–443
  gist of, capturing, 512–513
  infringement of patented (*see* patent infringement)
  as inventive step or obvious, 93–97, 185, 581–582 (*see also* non-obviousness requirement)
  joint research agreements on, 96, 100
  one per patent policy, 148–150 (*see also* restriction requirement)
  patent claims for (*see* patent claims)
  problem-solution approach, 20–21, 39–40, 42, 441, 513, 551, 588–589
  reduction to practice, 90–92
  unity of, 150n61, 588–589
  verbal formulations to capture/characterize, 436–448
inventor, defined, 101
IPRs (inter partes reviews), 3n7, 8, 22, 71, 86
IPXL v. Amazon decision, 494–496, 555
ITC. *See* International Trade Commission

Jepson claims, 110–112, 166–169, 175, 586, 587
joint research agreements, 96, 100

key terms, defining, 200–204, 449–450, 454–455, 508–509, 517–518
knockoffs, 219, 223

laws and regulations. See also specific laws and regulations
  anticipating changes in, 53, 56–60
  complexity and challenges with, 5–6
  European (*see* European Patent Convention)
  legal framework for claim construction, 216–249
lay terms, 244, 248
Leahy-Smith America Invents Act. *See* America Invents Act
Lexmark decision, 560–561
licensing. *See* patent licensing
literal infringement. *See under* direct infringement; indirect infringement
litigation. *See* patent litigation
Lizardtech decision, 456–458, 519

machine claims. *See* apparatus claims
manufacture claims
  apparatus claims and, 161
  Beauregard claims, 161–166
  commercial motivation for, 11
  examples and illustrations, 161–166
  mechanics of, 161–166
  patent infringement, 161
  statutory class, 115, 116–118
manufacturing, method of. *See* method of making claims
Markman decision/hearings, 216–219, 221–222, 224, 252
Markush group claims
  advantages and disadvantages of, 405–407
  claim diversity with, 402–409
  composition of matter claims, 159, 183, 412
  examples and illustrations, 407–409
  features of, 404–405
  indefiniteness, 403, 404, 406
Mas-Hamilton decision, 332–334, 547–548
means plus function claims
  advantages and disadvantages of, 339–342
  apparatus-type limitations, 492, 556
  Braun decision, 334–336, 341
  claim diversity with, 328–347
  for component manufacturer, 24–25
  DOE and, 329, 340–342
  EPC standards, 588
  examples and illustrations, 342–347
  functional and structural language, 130, 139, 342–347, 547–548
  indefiniteness, 461
  legal clarification of, 57, 58
  Mas-Hamilton decision, 332–334, 547–548
  for network provider, 49–51, 52
  patent strategy, 24–25, 36–37, 49–51, 52
  statutory foundations, 63, 328–332
  for system integrator, 36–37
  Williamson v. Citrix decision, 336–339
mechanics, 113–214. *See also* claim construction
  overview, 113
  apparatus claims, 119–132
  claim body, 3–5, 113–114, 185–204
  composition of matter claims, 153–161
  grammar rules, 509–510
  improvement claims, 166–169
  independent vs. dependent claims, 204–214
  manufacture claims, 161–166
  method claims, 132–153, 369–371, 385
  patent claims, generally, 113–119
  preamble, 169–175
  transition word, 170, 175–184, 429
medical diagnosis and treatment method claims, 480–483, 578–581
Met-Coil decision, 561–562, 570

method claims
  apparatus claims and, 25–28, 44–46, 132, 147–153, 356, 369–371, 377, 393–394, 491–499, 555–557
  apparatus-type limitations in, 491–494, 496–498, 555–556
  breadth of, 491
  claim diversity with, 26, 37–38, 132, 369–396, 439–440, 555–557
  commercial motivation for, 11
  for component manufacturer, 25–30
  contributory infringement, 277–280
  dependent claims, 140–145, 214, 529–531
  examples and illustrations, 132–153, 371–377, 385–388, 496–498
  inducing infringement, 286–289
  inferential claiming, 195–196, 376
  mechanics of, 132–153, 369–371, 385
  medical diagnosis and treatment, 480–483, 578–581
  method of making (*see* method of making claims)
  method of using (*see* method of using claims)
  for network provider, 42–44, 52
  order of operations, 142–143, 145–146, 377, 385, 492–493
  patent eligibility, 383, 469, 480–483
  patent infringement, 135–136, 138, 145–147, 277–280, 286–289, 369, 379–385, 388–396, 523, 525–526
  patent strategy, 25–30, 37–38, 42–46, 52
  preamble, 173–175, 425–426
  product integration coverage, 37–38, 529–531
  product-by-process claims and, 146–147, 362, 363–365, 367–368, 387
  restriction requirement, 148n58, 150–153
  statutory class, 115, 491–499, 554–557
  step plus function elements, 139, 331, 377, 426
  structural vs. functional limitations, 138–141, 356, 373, 388–396, 400–401
  for system integrator, 37–38
method of making claims
  apparatus claims and, 25, 132, 369–371, 393–394, 493–494
  claim diversity with, 367–371, 385–396, 557
  examples and illustrations, 132–136, 143–147, 385–388
  independent claims, 493
  making device capable of infringing, 388–396
  mechanics of, 132–136, 143–147, 369–371, 385
  patent strategy, 25, 28–29, 37
method of using claims
  apparatus claims and, 25, 27, 132, 369–371, 377, 493–496
  claim diversity with, 369–385, 557
  examples and illustrations, 132–133, 136–143, 371–377
  mechanics of, 132–133, 136–143, 369–371
  new use of old device, 377–379, 493–494
  patent strategy, 25, 27, 37, 52
  product integration coverage, 529–531
  system claim use infringement, 379–385
modifiers
  inconsistent use of, 505
  overly-specific, 268–269
Moore's law, 55–56
multiparty claims, 521, 522–527
multiple claims. *See* claim diversity

negotiation, breadth of claim effects on, 69–70, 270–271
network provider, patent strategy, 39–53
nonce words, 128, 343
nonliteral infringement, 250, 251, 273. *See also* doctrine of equivalents
non-obviousness requirement
  anticipating rejections based on, 516
  double patenting, 151–153
  EPC standard, 581–582
  patent eligibility, 468
  statutory foundations, 63, 81, 93–97, 105
novelty/anticipation requirement
  EPC standard, 574, 581–582
  inherent anticipation doctrine, 377–379
  negation of, 80–81
  novelty searches, 74, 76–77, 581
  patent eligibility, 467
  patent strategy, 16–18
  statutory foundations, 63, 78, 80–81, 82, 87–89, 99

obviousness. *See* non-obviousness requirement
ordinary and customary meaning
  in claim construction, 224–225, 232, 234–241, 242, 244, 258–260
  dictionaries for, 236–241
  specifications defining, 449–450, 455, 517–518
  words in claim consistent with, 258–260

Paris Convention, 573
patent application, sample boilerplate, 595–622
"Patent Claim Construction: A Modern Synthesis and Structured Framework" (Menell, Powers, and Carlson), 249
Patent Claim Drafting Practice (PCDP)
  generally, 1–2
  complexity and challenge, 2–13
  mechanics of (*see* mechanics)
  patent claims (*see* patent claims)
  patent strategy (*see* patent strategy)
  prior art (*see* prior art)
patent claims
  amendment or modification, 54, 72, 81, 298–301, 310–311, 450–451, 460, 502, 517, 585
  apparatus claims (*see* apparatus claims)
  "as a whole," 96–97, 118–119, 185–186, 294–295, 467–468, 480
  Beauregard claims (*see* Beauregard claims)
  breadth of (*see* breadth of claims)
  claim body (*see* claim body)
  commercial issues (*see* commercial issues)
  complexity and challenge of drafting, 2–13
  component claims (*see* component claims)
  composition of matter claims (*see* composition of matter claims)
  construction of (*see* claim construction)
  continuation, 69, 106–109
  continuation-in-part, 106, 108
  contracts vs., 171 (*see also* contracts)
  costs and financial issues (*see* financial considerations)
  defined, 113–119, 176
  dependent (*see* dependent claims)
  diversity of types used (*see* claim diversity)
  divisional, 106, 107, 151, 153, 589
  estoppel, 71–72
  improvement claims (*see* improvement claims)

patent claims *(continued)*
independent (*see* independent claims)
international, 88 (*see also* European Patent Convention; foreign entities)
manufacture claims (*see* manufacture claims)
Markush group (*see* Markush group claims)
means plus function claims (*see* means plus function claims)
mechanics of (*see* mechanics)
method claims (*see* method claims)
mistakes, 5
parts or structure of, 114, 169–170 (*see also* mechanics; *specific parts*)
preamble (*see* preamble)
prior art (*see* prior art)
product-by-process claims (*see* product-by-process claims)
provisional, 88–89
reading or analysis of, 17–18, 81, 115, 488–490, 532
rewriting and revisions, 310–311, 509 (*see also amendment or modification this heading*)
scope of legal rights, 3–5, 65, 68–69, 114, 171–172, 175–183, 235, 413–422 (*see also* breadth of claims; claim body)
software claims (*see* software claims)
statutes vs., 171
statutory classes, 115–118, 491–499, 554–558 (*see also specific classes*)
step plus function claims (*see* step plus function claims)
strategy for (*see* patent strategy)
system claims (*see* system claims)
timing issues (*see* timing issues)
transition word (*see* transition word)
validity, presumption of, 206, 208, 246, 314, 360–361, 461, 489
Patent Cooperation Treaty (PCT), 88, 101, 150n61, 573n1
patent eligibility
avoiding issues with, 461–483, 519
Beauregard claims, 51
breadth of claims and, 478–479
claim diversity and, 383, 466, 478
criteria and exceptions, 462–465, 478–479
medical diagnosis claims, 480–483
method claims, 383, 469, 480–483
patent strategy and, 39, 47, 51
pre-emption of possible solutions and, 470, 480
PTO guidelines, 477–479
software claims, 465–480
patent exhaustion
claim drafting reducing risk of, 558–571
dependent claims and, 448
legal clarification of, 57, 59–60
Lexmark decision, 560–561
patent licensing and, 59–60, 558–571
patent strategy and, 36
Quanta decision, 558, 559–560, 563, 566–571
traditional, 566–567
patent infringement
all elements rule/all limitations rule, 16–18, 191, 250
apparatus claims, 280–284, 289–292, 379–385, 557–558
claim drafting covering variety of potential, 249–292, 519–522, 524–527
claim drafting to increase detection of, 542–546
contributory, 273, 274–284, 524
damages for (*see* damages)
detection and proof of, drafting for, 542–546
direct, 35–36, 38, 249–272, 274, 275, 284, 307, 521, 523–525

doctrine of equivalents (*see* doctrine of equivalents)
elements of, 16
extraterritorial, 30, 39, 136, 146–147, 368–369, 379
imputed, 273n139
indemnity, 12, 34, 324, 383, 448
indirect, 35–36, 250–251, 272–292, 520–521, 523–524
inducing, 273, 275, 276–277, 282, 284–292, 523, 524
injunctions for, 219–220, 321, 532, 535
literal (*see under* direct infringement; indirect infringement)
manufacture claims, 161
method claims, 135–136, 138, 145–147, 277–280, 286–289, 369, 379–385, 388–396, 523, 525–526
multiparty claims, 521, 522–527
nonliteral, 250, 251, 273 (*see also* doctrine of equivalents)
novelty/anticipation, 16–18
patent strategy and enforcement of, 16–18, 30, 32–36, 38–39, 53
prior art, 16–18, 76, 81
product-by-process, 360–369
reading patent claim to determine, 17–18, 81, 115, 488–490, 532
single infringer principle, 124, 138, 145, 147n56, 161, 369, 385, 522–527
system claims, 273–274, 379–385, 526
validity of claim and, 206, 208, 246, 314, 360–361, 461, 489

patent licensing
breadth of claim effects, 71
capture-period, 520
cross-licensing, 15–16, 53, 59–60, 178, 520
defined, 3n7
dependent claims and, 448
"guillotine," 520
implied, 36, 558–571
patent exhaustion and, 59–60, 558–571
patent infringement and, 520
patent strategy and, 15–16, 36, 53, 59–60
revenue or royalties from (*see* royalties)

patent litigation. *See also specific cases and decisions*
breadth of claim effects, 71, 81–82
defined, 3n7
discovery, 220
exclusion enforcement, 15, 220, 222
infringement underlying (*see* patent infringement)
intrinsic vs. extrinsic evidence, 224–249
ITC investigation and, 219–224
prior art searches, 22
remedies (*see* damages; injunctions)

patent misuse, 284, 292

patent prosecution
breadth of claim effects, 81–82, 270–272
cost of, 69
defined, 3n7
estoppel, 71–72, 82, 292, 293–294, 298–301, 421
indefiniteness issues, 460–461
as intrinsic evidence, 227
method of using claims, 378–379
as negotiation, 69, 270–271
validity presumption, 461

patent strategy, 13–62
adding new claims, 47–48, 54
anticipating changes, 53–62
business and market changes and, 60–62
business strategy driving, 13–62
claim diversity as (*see* claim diversity)
clarity of language, 48–49

patent strategy *(continued)*
for component manufacturer, 18–30, 31, 34
examples and illustrations, 16–53, 54–62
exclusion as, 15
hedge strategy as (*see* hedge strategy)
legal changes and, 53, 56–60
for network provider, 39–53
objectives, identifying, 15–53
patent exhaustion and, 36
patent infringement enforcement and, 16–18, 30, 32–36, 38–39, 53
patent licensing and, 15–16, 36, 53, 59–60
patent sale or assignment and, 16, 53n110
reading of patent claims and, 17–18
for system integrator, 31–39
tactics vs., 14
technology changes and, 53, 54–56
trade secrets vs., 14, 30, 38
patent term, 151–153, 188, 438
Patent Trial and Appeal Board (PTAB)
broadest reasonable interpretation, 81–82
inter partes reviews, 3n7, 8, 22, 71, 86
post-grant reviews, 8, 62, 71
PCDP. *See* Patent Claim Drafting Practice
PCT (Patent Cooperation Treaty), 88, 101, 150n61, 573n1
PGRs (post-grant reviews), 8, 62, 71
Phillips decision, 225–226, 227, 229–234, 236–240, 241–242, 252
picture claims, 420–422
plural and singular elements, 501–502
post-grant reviews (PGRs), 8, 62, 71
preamble, 169–175
apparatus claims, 122
Beauregard claims, 162, 398–399
contract, 424
end of, 427–428
examples of, 172–175, 425, 428
improvement claims, 167–169, 175, 586
limitations introduction, avoiding, 424–428
mechanics of, 169–175
method claims, 173–175, 425–426
non-statutory subject matter references, avoiding, 426–427
prior art admissions, 111, 167–168
short, 424–428
theory of, 171–172
precision, 66, 68, 186–188, 507–509
predictable arts
composition of matter claims, 412
enablement, 459–460
inherent anticipation doctrine, 378
Markush group claims, 402, 405, 409
patent eligibility, 465
technology in, 39, 179, 432–433
transition word, 179, 181, 183–184, 428–432, 434
printed publications, 85–87, 92, 103
prior art
generally, 7–9
AIA, 2, 7, 64, 75, 99–109, 452
amending claim, 72
anticipating rejections based on, 514–517
avoiding admissions or characterizations of, 110–112
breadth of claims and, 9, 35, 43, 62–66, 73–112, 270–272, 301, 414, 490–491
claim body distinguishing from, 187–188
claim drafting considering closest known, 483–485, 490
claim drafting reading on known, 488–490
common ownership, 100, 103
cost of searches, 8, 73–75

dependent claims as hedge against, 206, 208
distinguishing new claim from, 64–65, 70n158, 72, 485, 488, 490–491 (*see also* novelty/ anticipation requirement)
DOE scope limited by, 292–293, 304–306
duty to disclose, 75–76, 483n117, 487, 488–491
EPC practices, 104, 111, 574–575, 581–582
improvement claims reciting, 167–168, 587
inequitable conduct related to, 483–490
international, 88, 101
inventive step over, 93–97, 185, 581–582 (*see also* non-obviousness requirement)
known, 9, 43, 64–66, 73, 93, 103, 167–168, 271, 442, 483–485, 488–491, 514, 591
new use of old device, 378–379
novelty searches, 74, 76–77, 581
patent infringement, 16–18, 76, 81
pre-drafting searches, 7–9, 73–78
printed publications, 85–87, 92, 103
product-by-process claims, 361, 362
provisional applications, 88–89
public accessibility, 86, 93, 103–104, 574
public disclosure, 104–105
public use or commercialization, 83–85, 92–93, 103–104, 109, 452, 574
qualification as, 63–64, 78–112
reading claim onto, 17–18, 81, 115, 488–490
rejections based on, 98–99, 514–517
risk of searches, 76–78
searches, 7–9, 22, 73–78, 414, 549, 581
secret, 75
statutory bars, 82–83
statutory foundations for, 63–64, 78–109, 452, 483–484n117 (*see also under* America Invents Act)
timing and priority, 75, 82–85, 87, 89–96, 101–102, 104, 106–109
problem-solution approach, 20–21, 39–40, 42, 441, 513, 551, 588–589
process claims. *See* method claims
product-by-process claims
advantages and disadvantages of, 361–362
claim body, 191
claim diversity with, 360–369
composition of matter claims and, 160
examples and illustrations, 363–369
format of, 361
legal clarification of, 57–58
method claims and, 146–147, 362, 363–365, 367–368, 387
patent infringement, 360–369
validity, presumption of, 360–361
prosecution. *See* patent prosecution
prosecution history estoppel, 71–72, 82, 292, 293–294, 298–301, 421
provisional patent applications, 88–89
PTAB. *See* Patent Trial and Appeal Board
PTO. *See* US Patent and Trademark Office
public accessibility, 86, 93, 103–104, 574
public disclosure, 104–105
public use, 83–85, 92–93, 103–104, 109, 452, 574

Quanta decision, 558, 559–560, 563, 566–571

reading of claims, 17–18, 81, 115, 488–490, 532
ready for patenting, 84–85

redundant terms, 502–503. *See also* double inclusion
reexamination proceedings, 71, 221
restriction requirement, 148n58, 150–153
royalties
  damages, 34, 322, 325–326, 374–375, 532–538
  dependent claims increasing, 448
  patent licensing, generally, 9–10, 15
  reasonable royalty remedy, 322, 325, 533–535

"said," inconsistent use of, 504–505
sale of inventions. *See* commercial issues
Seventh Amendment, 217
single infringer principle, 124, 138, 145, 147n56, 161, 369, 385, 522–527
singular and plural elements, 501–502
sloppy techniques, avoiding, 500–506
smallest saleable unit principle, 34, 325, 537–538
software claims. *See also* Beauregard claims
  commercial motivation for, 11
  EPC exclusion, 575–578, 581
  indefiniteness, 461
  method claims, 369, 469, 556
  patent eligibility, 465–480
  patent exhaustion and implied patent licensing, 571
  structural vs. functional limitations, 347–348, 351–353, 356–358, 395, 453–454
specification(s)
  to interpret claim body, 197–204
  claims drafted before, 444, 448–450
  clarity of, 252–258, 413
  definitions in, 200–204, 449–450, 454–455, 508–509, 517–518
  dependent claim support, 446, 518
  enablement issues, 459–460
  EPC practices, 582–586
  hierarchy of claim terms and, 262–263, 266, 444
  indefiniteness issues, 460–461, 519
  interchangeable terms in, 266
  as intrinsic evidence, 224–233, 235–248
  multiple embodiments, 314–317, 413–414 (*see also* claim diversity)
  patent eligibility issues, 461–462, 469, 472, 474, 477n110
  structural vs. functional limitations, 453–454
  words consistent with understood meaning in, 259–260
  words with broadly understood meanings in, 262
  written description issues, 450–459 (*see also* written descriptions)
statutes, patent claims vs., 171. *See also* laws and regulations
statutory classes, 115–118, 491–499, 554–558. *See also specific classes*
step plus function claims. *See also* means plus function claims
  advantages and disadvantages of, 339–342
  claim diversity with, 328–347
  examples and illustrations, 342–347
  functional and structural language, 139, 342–347
  method claims and, 139, 331, 377, 426
  statutory foundations, 328–332
strategy. *See* patent strategy
structural language
  apparatus claims, 123, 127–132, 356, 393–394
  Beauregard claims, 163–166, 400–402
  claim body, 191–192

for claim diversity, 123, 130, 347–360, 547–549
composition of matter claims, 160–161
DOE, 297–298
means plus function claims, 343–347, 548
method claims, 138–141, 356, 388–396, 400–401
software claims, 347–348, 351–353, 356–358, 453–454
specifications, 453–454
system claims
claim diversity with, 322–328
commercial motivation for, 11
component claims vs., 322–325, 557–558
damages, 325–326
examples and illustrations, 326–327
method of using claims and, 379–385
patent exhaustion and implied patent licensing, 563–564
patent infringement, 273–274, 379–385, 526
patent strategy, 32–36
system integrator, patent strategy, 31–39

technical terms, 244, 247, 248
technology. *See also* inventions
anticipating changes, 6, 53, 54–56
breadth of claims, 6, 66 (*see also* breadth of claims)
component manufacturer, 18–30, 31, 34
computer claims (*see* computer programs; software claims)
network provider, 39–53
patent cross-licensing, 16
patent strategy, 18–53
system integrator, 31–39
terminal disclaimers, 151–153
terms of art, 244–246, 248–249, 548
terms of degree, 244–248, 461
terseness, 507
"the," inconsistent use of, 504–505
Thesaurus of Claim Construction, The, 249
timing issues
claims drafted before specifications, 444, 448–450
EPC filings, 573
filing-to-patent issuance/publication, 10n26, 75, 87
first-to-file patent system, 75, 82n181, 83, 89, 92, 102
first-to-invent patent system, 75, 82–83, 89, 92
ITC investigation, 221, 222–223
one-year grace period, 83–85, 104, 573
patent litigation, 221, 222–223
patent term, 151–153, 188, 438
prior art timing and priority, 75, 82–85, 87, 89–96, 101–102, 104, 106–109
trade secrets, 14, 30, 38, 136
transition word, 175–184
apparatus claims, 122
Beauregard claims, 162–163, 398–399
composition of matter claims, 157–159, 179–183, 410–412, 433–434
"comprising" as, 159, 175–184, 208, 428–431, 433–434
"consisting of" or "consisting essentially of" as, 159, 175, 181–182, 411, 432–435
dependent claims, 208, 210
examples of, 183–184
improvement claims, 167, 169
mechanics of, 170, 175–184, 429

transition word *(continued)*
in predictable arts, 179, 181, 183–184, 428–432, 434
as terms of art, 245
theory of, 176–183
in unpredictable arts, 179–183, 432–435

Unified Patent, 574n4
Unified Patent Court, 574n4
unity of invention, 150n61, 588–589
unpredictable arts
composition of matter claims, 156–158, 179–183, 409–410, 433–434
enablement, 460
inherent anticipation doctrine, 378
Markush group claims, 402, 405, 409
technology in, 179, 432–433
transition word, 179–183, 432–435
US Patent and Trademark Office (PTO). *See also* Patent Trial and Appeal Board
anticipating first action of, 514–517
authority to shift burden, 130
broadest reasonable interpretation, 163, 246–247, 270, 518
correspondence from, affecting patent strategy, 54, 55
database, 73
filing fees, 52, 74–75, 107, 148, 151, 204–205n171, 212, 324
inequitable conduct before, 483–490
one invention per patent policy, 148–150 (*see also* restriction requirement)
patent eligibility guidelines, 477–479
patent interference proceedings, 92
regulatory changes, 6
restriction requirement, 148n58, 150–153
usefulness requirement, 62

vagueness, 66–68, 122, 186–188, 507–509. *See also* indefiniteness
validity, presumption of, 206, 208, 246, 314, 360–361, 461, 489
verbal formulations
for claim diversity, 436–448
dependent claims, 444–448
features identified independently, 440–443
hierarchy of claim terms, 443–445
varying terminology, 436–440
Vitronics decision, 224–225, 226–228, 229, 233–234, 236, 252–253, 259–260

Williamson v. Citrix decision, 336–339
Wilson Sporting Goods decision, 304–306
wordiness, avoiding, 507
World Intellectual Property Organization (WIPO), 88
written descriptions, 450–459. *See also* specifications
avoiding issues with, 450–459, 519
breadth of claims and, 316–317, 414
claim body, 185, 197–201 (*see also* claim body)
claim drafted before specification, 449
definitions, 449–450, 454–455, 517–518
dependent claim support, 518
EPC practices, 582–586
Lizardtech decision, 456–458, 519
negative limitations, 44, 458–459
new subject matter, 106, 108–109
picture claims vs., 421
prior art and, 77, 106, 108–109
statutory considerations, 108–109, 451–454
transition word, 181

About the ABA Section of Intellectual Property Law

From its strength within the American Bar Association, the ABA Section of Intellectual Property Law (ABA-IPL) advances the development and improvement of intellectual property laws and their fair and just administration. The Section furthers the goals of its members by sharing knowledge and balanced insight on the full spectrum of intellectual property law and practice, including patents, trademarks, copyright, design, and trade secrets. Providing a forum for rich perspectives and reasoned commentary, ABA-IPL serves as the ABA voice of intellectual property law within the profession, before policy makers, and with the public.

ABA Section of Intellectual Property Law (ABA-IPL)
Order today! Call 800-285-2221
Monday-Friday, 8:00 a.m. – 5:00 p.m., CT
or visit www.ambar.org/iplbooks.

Qty	Title	Regular Price	ABA-IPL Member Price	Total
____	ADR Advocacy, Strategies, and Practices for Intellectual Property and Technology Cases, 2nd Ed. (5370231)	$149.95	$119.95	$______
____	ANDA Litigation, 3rd Ed. (5370243)	$379.00	$295.95	$______
____	Antitrust Issues in Intellectual Property Law (5370222)	$149.95	$119.95	$______
____	Arbitrating Patent Disputes (5370229)	$89.95	$74.95	$______
____	Careers in IP Law (5370204) (The ebook is complimentary with ABA-IPL Section membership)	$24.95	$16.95	$______
____	Commercialization of IP Rights in China (5370241)	$119.95	$95.95	$______
____	Computer Games and Immersive Entertainment, 2nd Ed. (5370239)	$89.95	$69.95	$______
____	Copyright Litigation Strategies (5370228)	$369.00	$285.00	$______
____	Copyright Remedies (5370208)	$89.95	$74.95	$______
____	Copyright Termination Law (5370226)	$139.95	$109.95	$______
____	Crash Course on U.S. Patent Law (5370221)	$39.95	$34.95	$______
____	The DMCA Handbook, 2nd Ed. (5370234)	$79.95	$64.95	$______
____	The Essential Case Law Guide to PTAB Trials (5370233)	$249.95	$199.95	$______
____	The Essentials of Japanese Patent Prosecution (5370245)	$149.95	$119.95	$______
____	Intellectural Property and Technology Due Diligence (5370236)	$219.95	$179.95	$______
____	The Intellectual Property Law Handbook, 2nd Ed. (5620154)	$139.95	$109.95	$______
____	IP Attorney's Handbook for Insurance Coverage in Intellectual Property Disputes, 2nd Ed. (5370210)	$139.95	$129.95	$______
____	IP Protection in China (5370217)	$139.95	$109.95	$______
____	IP Strategies for Medical Device Technologies (5370238)	$149.95	$119.95	$______
____	IP Valuation for the Future (5370237)	$89.95	$59.95	$______
____	The Law of Trade Secret Litigation Under the Uniform Trade Secrets Act, 2nd Ed. (5370242)	$369.95	$295.95	$______
____	A Lawyer's Guide to Section 337 Investigations before the U.S. International Trade Commission, 4th Ed. (5370240)	$139.95	$109.95	$______
____	Legal Guide to Video Game Development, 2nd Ed. (5370227)	$74.95	$59.95	$______
____	A Legal Strategist's Guide to Trademark Trial and Appeal Board Practice, 4th Ed. (5370247)	$179.95	$144.95	$______
____	New Practitioner's Guide to Intellectual Property (5370198)	$89.95	$69.95	$______
____	Patent Claim Drafting Practice (5370259)	$179.95	$144.95	$______
____	Patent Freedom to Operate Searches, Opinions, Techniques, and Studies (5370230)	$139.95	$109.95	$______
____	Patent Neutral (5370232)	$89.95	$69.95	$______
____	Patent Trial Advocacy Casebook, 3rd Ed. (5370124)	$149.95	$119.95	$______
____	Patently Persuasive (5370206)	$129.95	$99.95	$______
____	The Practitioner's Guide to the PCT (5370205)	$139.95	$109.95	$______

HUSBANDRY AND MANAGEMENT PRACTICES IN FARROWING UNITS I

Farrowing

Emilio Magallón Botaya (coordinator)
Alberto García Flores
Roberto Bautista Moreno
Boris Alonso Sánchez
José Ignacio Cano Latorre
Silvia Almenara Díaz
Patricia Prieto Martínez
Pablo Magallón Verde

SERVET

To Emilio Magallón Salvo, veterinary surgeon,
and father and grandfather of veterinary surgeons.

AUTHORS

Emilio Magallón Botaya (coordinator)

Emilio Magallón Botaya graduated in veterinary medicine in 1978 from the University of Zaragoza, Spain, with a specialisation in animal production and agricultural economics.

After starting his professional career as a large animal veterinary surgeon, he started working in the pig industry in 1981; initially as a technician, later as a team leader and then as a production manager in one of the most important Spanish pig production companies.

For several years he was an associate professor of swine production at the Faculty of Veterinary Medicine of the University of Zaragoza. He also taught economic analysis applied to swine production in the Master's Degree programme in Animal Production and Health organised in partnership by the universities of Zaragoza, Lérida, Barcelona and Madrid.

He has participated in several research projects related to the pig industry and is currently co-leading a project for the genetic improvement of swine funded by the Spanish Centre for Industrial Technological Development (CDTI), in collaboration with the animal production area of the Spanish Institute of Food and Agriculture Research and Technology.

Emilio Magallón has published numerous articles on the Spanish pig industry and has participated in many seminars and panel discussions throughout Spain.

He is a member of Anaporc (Spanish Scientific Swine Production Association) and founding member of the AVPA (Association of Swine Veterinary Practitioners of Aragon), and is currently part of its board of directors.

Alberto García Flores

Alberto García Flores graduated in veterinary medicine from the University of Zaragoza, Spain, in 2000, with a specialisation in animal medicine and health.

After finishing his studies, he went on to take a specialisation course in swine production. He started his professional career as a veterinary surgeon for the control of infectious diseases associated with production animals.

More than 10 years ago, he joined the pig production company of a multinational firm, where he works as a veterinary surgeon in the areas of production, nutrition, diagnosis and treatment of diseases and carries out tasks related to the technical and economic management of farms. He participates in the planning and carrying out of R&D studies on swine production.

He has published several articles and studies on swine. Furthermore, he has participated in several conferences and panel discussions.

He is a member of the Association of Swine Veterinary Practitioners of Aragon (AVPA).

Roberto Bautista Moreno

Roberto Bautista Moreno graduated in veterinary medicine from the University of Zaragoza, Spain, in 1990, with a specialisation in animal medicine and health.

He started his professional career in the sheep sector and worked in the areas of sheep health and production in different livestock companies. He later worked as a sales representative for a pharmaceutical company.

Since 1997 he has been working for livestock production companies, initially in the beef sector as a veterinary surgeon for a company based in the Spanish regions of Aragon and Navarre, and later in the pig sector as a veterinary surgeon for Inga Food, S.A., where he has been in charge of the technical, economic and clinical management of sow farms and fattening units for more than 15 years.

He is a member of the AVPA and is currently a member of its board of directors.

Boris Alonso Sánchez

Boris Alonso Sánchez graduated in veterinary medicine from the University of Zaragoza, Spain, in 1998, with a specialisation in animal production and agricultural economics.

In 1999 he started his professional career as a technician and sales representative for several companies. From 2001 to 2007, he was responsible for the management of pig fattening and breeding farms and since 2007 he has been working for the technical veterinary service of Inga Food, S.A., in the region of Aragon.

He has participated in numerous seminars and training sessions on swine production.

José Ignacio Cano Latorre

José Ignacio Cano Latorre graduated in veterinary medicine from the University of Zaragoza, Spain, in 1990, with a specialisation in animal production and agricultural economics. He holds the official certificate in cooperative company management approved by the Spanish Ministry of Labour (1989-1990). In 1991, he took an advanced course on domestic animal nutrition organised by the INRA in Paris, France.

Since 1992 he has been working as a veterinary surgeon for the swine technical service of a company leader in the animal feed industry, and has carried out and implemented artificial insemination programmes on the company's farms. He specialises in the technical and financial management of breeding, fattening and post-weaning farms. Since 2008, he has served as the team manager of the same company and collaborated with its R&D centre.

José Ignacio has collaborated on several publications and has attended and participated in numerous seminars and national and international conferences.

Silvia Almenara Díaz

Silvia Almenara Díaz graduated in veterinary medicine from the University of Zaragoza, Spain, in 2006, with a specialisation in animal production and agricultural economics.

Her final project towards her Master's Degree in Swine Production and Health, organised in partnership by the faculties of veterinary medicine of the universities of Zaragoza, Barcelona, and by the School of Agriculture Science of Lérida, won a prize awarded by the Association of Swine Veterinary Practitioners of Aragon.

She has done internships in different companies in the sector and since 2008 she has been working for an important animal production company in the area of Zaragoza.

Silvia Almenara has participated in various conferences and training sessions on swine production and health.

Patricia Prieto Martínez

Patricia Prieto Martínez graduated in veterinary medicine from the University of Zaragoza, Spain, in 2006, with a specialisation in animal production and agricultural economics.

She completed her training with practical work experience in different areas of production at the faculties of veterinary medicine of the universities of Lisbon and Costa Rica. In 2007, she took the Master's Degree in Animal Production and Health organised by the universities of Zaragoza, Lérida and Barcelona.

Patricia Prieto began her career in 2008 as a member of the technical veterinary service of one of the most important companies in the pig industry, where she is in charge of several pig breeding and fattening farms.

She has participated in numerous conferences and training sessions on swine production.

Pablo Magallón Verde

Pablo Magallón Verde graduated in veterinary medicine from the University of Zaragoza, Spain, in 2012.

He has done internships in the swine production company Inga Food, S.A., and has taken the Swine Production Medicine Clinical Rotation and Veterinary Diagnostic and Production Animal Medicine training modules at the Iowa State University (USA).

He is currently studying a Master's Degree in Swine Production and Health organised in partnership by the universities of Zaragoza, Lérida, Barcelona and Madrid.

Since 2013 he has been working as a veterinary surgeon in one of the most important livestock companies in Spain.

FOREWORD

Knowledge transmission from one person to another is one of the most important and nobles activities of human beings. The significant progress experienced by the different human societies throughout the ages can be explained to a great extent by the capacity of technology and innovation to transmit knowledge among individuals and from one generation to another. However, this is not an easy task. On the contrary. It is difficult and, in order to be successful, it is essential that the language used to transmit new concepts is understandable to the audience receiving the information. This book is an example of how its authors have been able to overcome this difficulty naturally. It is a scientific work on swine production aimed at the different professionals who work in this sector, and that is why the specialists who have collaborated on this book have used simple, direct and clear language, very close to that of the readers this book is aimed at, to transmit their knowledge and wide experience on the topics addressed. This, of course, does not mean that the explanations given have lost any of their accuracy or clarity. The aim of this book is to provide a tool to help and innovate in the essential aspects of the daily tasks involved in sow herd reproduction today.

The global pig industry has undergone, in the past few years, a true revolution from the point of view of genetic improvement, production quality and efficiency, management techniques, facilities and health, and has become a leading sector. This strategic situation of the pig industry, which is increasingly competitive, requires permanent innovation in production processes from companies and their professionals in order to be more efficient. In this regard, this work can contribute to improving husbandry practices and farrowing unit management, with a focus, in this first volume, on highly relevant aspects such as farrowing and all the factors that affect this process. In a second volume, the authors will address in details the crucial lactation phase as part of the production process.

Finally, I would like to express my most sincere gratitude to all the authors who have participated in this book, in particular to Emilio Magallón, their coordinator, and congratulate them for this excellent initiative.

Dr. José Luis Noguera

President of BDporc,
Data Bank on the Spanish Pig Industry,
and of the Porc D'Or awards

IRTA (Institut de Recerca i Tecnologia
Agroalimentàries, Food and
Agriculture Research Centre)

PREFACE

In our exciting and intense daily work on pig farms, we find that most of the time, the very extensive and wide knowledge available on livestock operation management is not applied or is very much ahead of what we can see in our daily reality. Furthermore, it is difficult to transmit all this information to farmers in a clear and simple way. This is the main reason why we decided to write a book on farrowing management that, with summarised contents but including all the areas related to this topic, would help farmers to acquire the necessary knowledge and be useful to all the professionals involved in the pig industry.

This book is aimed at a very heterogeneous audience, from veterinary professionals to students, and it can also be useful to those team supervisors and personnel specialised in managing and working in farrowing units. And of course, to all the veterinary or animal production professionals who would like to know the latest farrowing unit management techniques on pig farms in a fast and direct manner.

We believe such a book was necessary, in order to gather all the knowledge available on farrowing and the new ways of working on and managing modern sow farms. A book with both rigorous and scientific grounds, but at the same time pleasant to read, which is why we decided to use numerous pictures, tables and summaries.

Furthermore, we, the authors, are veterinary surgeons specialised in the pig industry and are very involved in the daily work on sow farms. By experience, we know that the way knowledge is transmitted is very important, and that is why we have chosen to avoid being overly academic, by using an accessible, clear and simple language so as to make this book easy to read.

We hope to have achieved everything we aimed for.

Emilio Magallón Botaya

ACKNOWLEDGEMENTS

To our families, for being patient with us and for the time we stole from them by writing this book.

To pig farmers, for their work and dedication to such an intense profession as theirs, and for what they teach us every day through their questions and concerns, which we have attempted to answer in this book.

To those veterinary surgeons and professionals who have helped us write this book with their corrections and answers, and particularly to José Luis Noguera and Luis Laborda.

To Grupo Asís for publishing this book and, particularly, to the publishing team for their professionalism and priceless editing work, technical support and trust that we would do a good job.

TABLE OF CONTENTS

Introduction 1

1. Technical and physiological considerations regarding farrowing 3

Natural behaviour of the farrowing sow 3
- Animal behaviour and productivity 3
- Nest building 4
- Placentophagy 4
- Farrowing 5

Physiology of the last stage of gestation 5
- Foetal development 5
- Feeding needs of sows at the end of gestation 7

Physiology of the peripartum period 8
- Duration of gestation 8
- Characteristic signs of imminent farrowing 8
- Hormonal mechanism of farrowing 10
- Evolution of body temperature at farrowing 10
- Mechanism of expulsion of a foetus 12
- Duration of farrowing 12
- Difficult farrowings 13
- Characteristic signs of the end of farrowing 14

Physiology of piglets during the peripartum period 14
- Weight and size of the litter 14
- Mummified piglets 15
- Stillborn piglets 17
- False stillborn piglets 18
- Low-viability piglets 20
- Early postnatal vitality of piglets 21
- Supernumerary piglets and rearing of weak piglets 21

2. Design, structure and types of farrowing houses 25

Introduction 25

The farrowing room 26
- Calculation of the number of pens 26
- Design 27
- Insulation 28

The farrowing pen ... 31
Dimensions ... 31
Orientation of the pens ... 32
The crate ... 34
The floor ... 35
The heated area for the piglets ... 37
Feed and water troughs for the sows ... 43
Feed and water troughs for piglets ... 49
The ideal pen ... 50
Monitoring of environmental conditions in the farrowing rooms ... 50
Temperature ... 51
Ventilation ... 55
Equipment for environmental control ... 61

3. Organisation of farrowing units: batch farrowing 63

Introduction ... 63
Batch farrowing ... 64
Concept of batch ... 64
Weekly batch farrowing ... 65
Two-weekly batch farrowing ... 69
Three-weekly batch farrowing ... 70
Four-weekly batch farrowing ... 72
Five-weekly batch farrowing ... 72
Three-two-weekly batch farrowing ... 74
Turnaround in farrowing rooms ... 75
Farrowing and service targets ... 76
Reaching service targets ... 78
Heat record sheet ... 79
Three-colour system ... 79
Hormonal treatments ... 80

4. Sow feeding during the peripartum period 83

Introduction ... 83
Nutritional goals ... 84
Feeding needs in the last stage of gestation
and during the peripartum period ... 85

Nutritional requirements for maintenance ... 85
Production requirements ... 86
Water needs ... 88
Feeding at the end of gestation and during the peripartum period ... 90
Types of diets for sows during the peripartum period ... 91
Types of feed according to the physiological stage ... 92
Types of feed according to their physical form ... 95
Feeding curves ... 99

5. Sow and piglet management during farrowing 101

Preparation of the farrowing house ... 101
Cleaning and disinfection of the farrowing house and sows ... 101
Arrival of the sows at the farrowing room ... 103
The prepartum period ... 104
Farrowing management ... 106
Ideal environmental temperature for the sow at farrowing ... 107
Administration of oxytocin ... 108
Administration of antibiotics, anti-inflammatory drugs and other drugs ... 109
Care of newborn piglets ... 109
Drying the piglets ... 110
Tying-off and disinfection of the umbilical cord ... 111
Resuscitation of piglets ... 113
Colostrum feeding of piglets ... 113
Artificial colostrum feeding ... 115
Aggressive sows during farrowing ... 116
Programmed farrowings ... 117
Administration of prostaglandins ... 117
Monitoring farrowings ... 120
Non-dystocic problematic farrowings ... 121
Slow farrowing ... 121
Farrowing with constipation ... 122
Farrowing with fatigue ... 122
Farrowing with tetanic contractions ... 123
Farrowing with stress ... 123
Procedure of examination of the birth canal in sows ... 123
Dystocia. Basic obstetrics ... 125
Heavy piglets ... 125

Obstruction of the birth canal 125
Torsion of the uterine horns 125
Sows with a narrow birth canal 127
Performing caesarean sections 127

6. Main diseases in the peripartum period 129

Introduction 129
Main diseases of sows 130
Postpartum dysgalactia syndrome (PDS) 130
Metritis 131
Mastitis 132
Ketosis 133
Osteomalacia 134
Prolapses 135
Nervous sows, attacks to piglets and cannibalism 137
Haematoma of the vulva 138
Shoulder ulcers 138
Main diseases of piglets 139
Dietary origin 139
Management 141
Of infectious origin 142
Congenital malformations 146

7. Work organisation 153

Introduction 153
Personnel needs on farms 154
Qualitative needs 154
Quantitative needs 155
Cost of the workforce and productivity 157
Work organisation 158
List of tasks 159
Task planning 161

8. Conclusion 165

9. Bibliography 168

Introduction

In the last few years, the pig industry in general and sow farms in particular have undergone great changes: increase in the average size of farms, introduction of new more prolific genetic lines, greater qualification of the personnel, changes in feeding patterns, better facilities, etc. All these changes are increasing productivity on sow farms worldwide significantly.

The best farms now wean more than 30 piglets per productive sow and year and some even exceed 33 piglets. Denmark is the leading country in productivity, with farms where more than 38 piglets per productive sow and year are weaned. But let there be no mistake: at a global level, productivity per sow is still very low. There are many inefficient countries and production systems, which, if they wish to remain in the very competitive pig market, will need to undergo profound changes and achieve a dramatic increase in their productivity.

This major increase in productivity entails new husbandry and management practices in all the areas of production, but particularly in farrowing houses; our sows give birth to many more piglets, but with a lower weight, and it is thus necessary to help them survive. This involves changes in feeding programmes, facilities, sow and piglet management, personnel management, etc.

This books aims to provide information about the latest developments in sow farm management, with a focus on farrowing, in order to be used as a tool to help and train professionals of the sector.

The book starts with technical and physiological considerations regarding farrowing and reviews the different types of facilities, the organisation of farrowing houses and batch farrowing management, sow and piglet feeding during the peri-partum period, farrowing unit management and the main diseases of the sow and piglets during this period. Finally, it concludes with work organisation on farms, conclusions and a bibliography.

It should be borne in mind that this book is the first volume on sow farm management and focuses on farrowing. Lactation will be addressed in a second volume.

In addition, considering the practical and accessible approach given to the book and its limited extension, some issues such as body condition monitoring, personnel management or health programmes on sow farms will be addressed in the second volume.

Figure 2 Foetal growth curve.

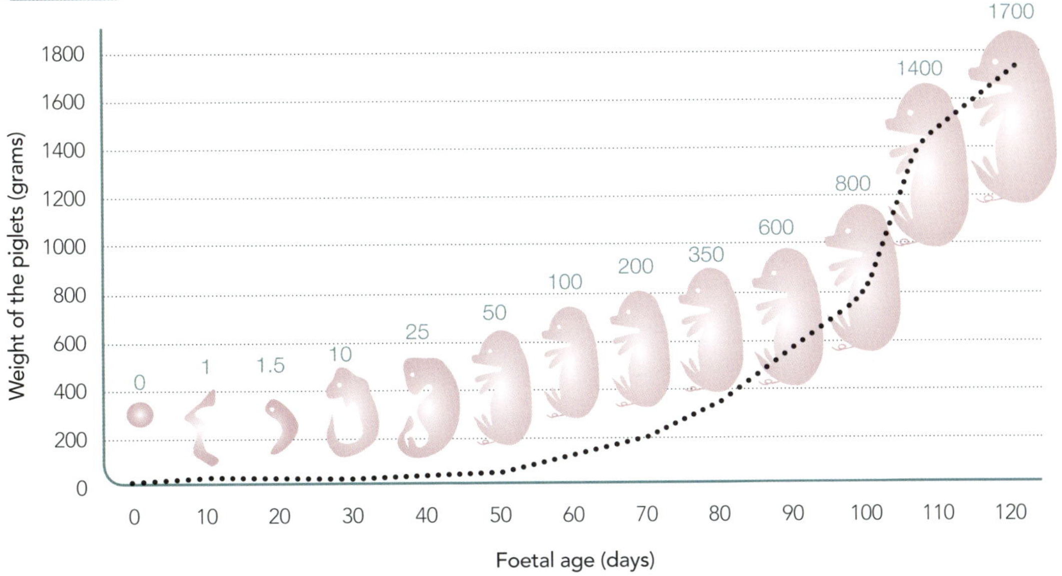

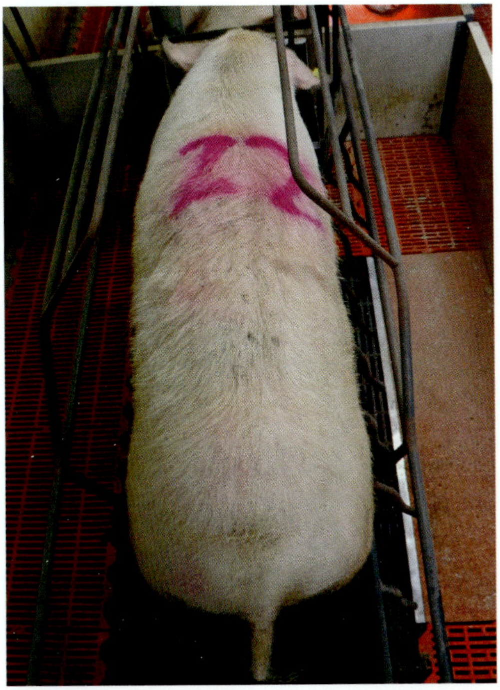

Figure 3 Sow with optimum body condition at farrowing.

Feeding needs of sows at the end of gestation

At the final stage of gestation, sows' energy and protein requirements are greater to cope with foetal development (Fig. 2). However, care should be taken to avoid excessive weight gain and an unwanted degree of fattening, which can increase foot lesions, complications at farrowing, and lead to a voluntarily reduced feed intake during lactation.

A sow that reaches farrowing with an excessive weight gain is also more prone to a longer farrowing duration, greater difficulties to give birth and a higher percentage of stillborn piglets, in addition to a lower milk production. Sows should also not be too thin at the time of farrowing.

Physiology of the peripartum period

Duration of gestation

Gestation in sows lasts for approximately 114-116 days, with a maximum range of 110-120 days. The gestation period in gilts usually lasts about one more day (Fig. 4).

Figure 4 Representation of the gestation period in first-parity gilts and multiparous sows on a farm with hyperprolific sows.

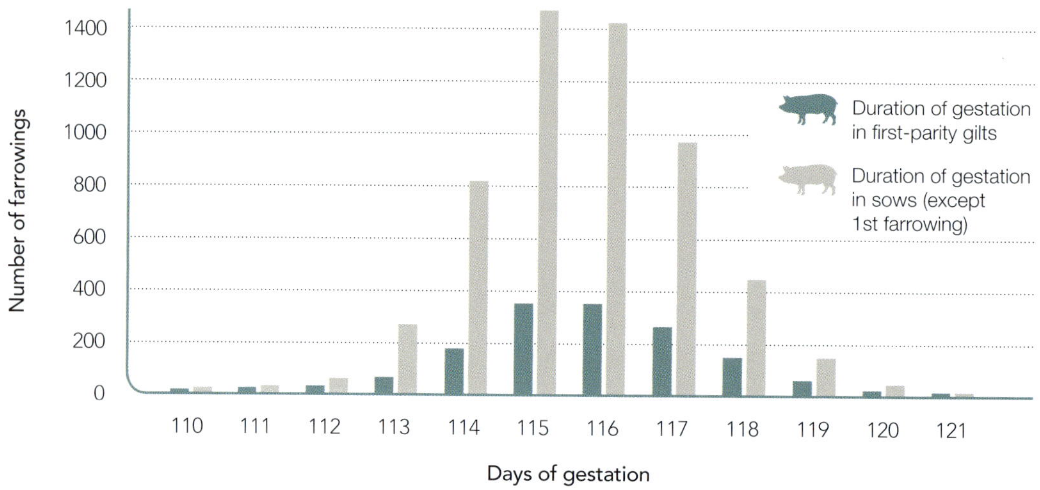

Modern hyperprolific pig lines tend to have longer gestations, as opposed to what occurs in Iberian breeds, which are characterised by their low prolificacy with average gestations of 112-113 days. The duration of gestation also varies slightly depending on the farm, environment, size of the litter and time of the year.

Characteristic signs of imminent farrowing

Before farrowing, very characteristic behaviours and signs can be observed in the sow:

- About 10-14 days before farrowing, the mammary glands and the teats become larger, just as the mammary veins, which become more visible. As the time of farrowing gets closer, the udders are more filled and pinkish and droplets of colostrum come out when massaging them (Fig. 5).

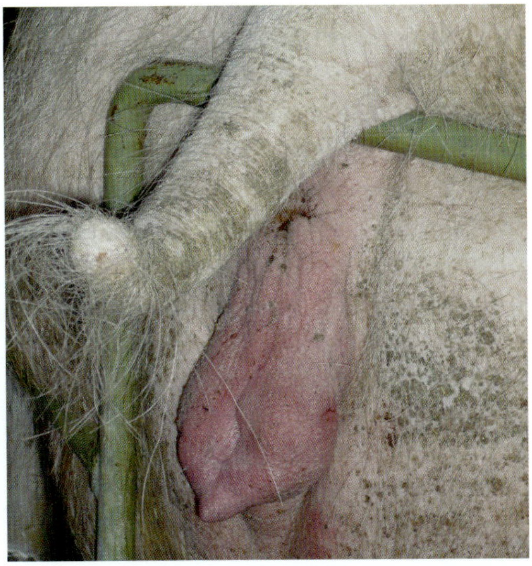

Figures 5 and 6 Swelling of the mammary glands (with droplets of milk) and of the vulva, observed a few hours before farrowing.

- Three days before farrowing at the earliest, the sow may already have colostrum and droplets may be seen coming out of her teats. If a spurt comes out when pressing on them, this indicates that farrowing will take place in the next 24 hours.
- Swelling of the vulva is observed. As a result, the tissues of the vulva are weakened and this area becomes more vulnerable to cuts and wounds (Fig. 6).
- Secretions such as blood, meconium, etc., are observed in up to 60 % of sows.
- The respiratory rate and rhythm are increased. Under normal conditions, the respiratory rate of a sow is 20-25 breaths per minute. Six hours before farrowing, the rate increases to 60-80 breaths per minutes, and goes back down to a normal respiratory rate two hours before parturition.
- Movements of the tail are observed. First, the sow moves it in circles and then holds it straight and up about two hours before the start of farrowing.
- She frequently drinks and urinates, but has less appetite.
- She is restless and frequently stands up and lies down. She kicks her water trough with her head and legs.
- She lies in lateral recumbency and rubs her face against the floor.
- She tries to squeeze under her feed trough or crate. She chews on the bars.
- She displays nest-building behaviour and scratches the floor and feeding trough.

- She swells and contracts her abdomen. The sow pulls her hind legs under her abdomen. She sometimes stretches, extends her legs and is short of breath.
- Three hours before farrowing starts on average, her abdominal contractions become more marked.
- Immediately before farrowing, the sow does not pay attention to the people passing in front of her crate.

Hormonal mechanism of farrowing

Farrowing is one of the most critical steps in pig production. It is very stressful for the sow and there are risks of bacterial contamination of the piglets. Furthermore, this is a key step for the piglet's future development.

The decrease in progesterone levels in the two weeks previous to farrowing, and the increase in oestrogen and corticoid levels one or two days before are among the most important hormonal changes undergone by the sow. The function of oestrogens is to prepare the uterus for contractile activity.

At the time of birth, the corpus luteum releases a large amount of relaxin, which acts together with oestrogens at the level of the uterus to induce collagen remodelling of the cervix. This enables its relaxation and favours the mechanism of expulsion of the piglets.

Farrowing starts with the secretion of the adrenocorticotropic hormone (ACTH) by the piglets' pituitary gland. Foetal corticoids induce the release of prostaglandins, which in turn are in charge of the lysis of the corpora lutea and of the other subsequent mechanisms that trigger farrowing. About 24 hours before birth, progesterone levels decrease, while oxytocin levels, which favour the contraction of smooth muscle fibres and the expulsion of the piglets, increase (Fig. 7).

Evolution of body temperature at farrowing

Approximately 10 hours before farrowing, the sow's body temperature increases by 0.5 °C. During farrowing, her rectal temperature is also high, although significant variations can be observed from one sow to another. These temperature variations seem to be related to the duration of farrowing, the size of the litter and the difficulties at farrowing.

The body temperature of piglets when they are expelled is 39 °C, but it usually decreases to 37 °C in the first three hours of life. This decrease may be due to several causes, which include the evaporation of the foetal fluids that cover the piglets, thus causing their body to cool down. It can also be attributed to the fact that piglets only have a very thin layer of skin and subcutaneous fat, little hair and no glycogen reserves at birth. This means piglets have few resources to face hypothermia, one of the main causes of perinatal death.

Piglets slowly recover their initial temperature of 39 °C. Their body temperature reaches 38 °C after 24 hours and 39 °C after 48 hours, depending to a great extent on the environmental conditions, management practices and colostrum intake. During its first hours of life, a piglet is incapable of avoiding heat losses due to radiation, even if it stays close to the rest of the litter.

Figure 7 Physiological mechanism of the start of farrowing. Adapted from Muirhead and Alexander. *Managing Pig Health and the Treatment of Disease*. 5M Enterprises, UK, 1997.

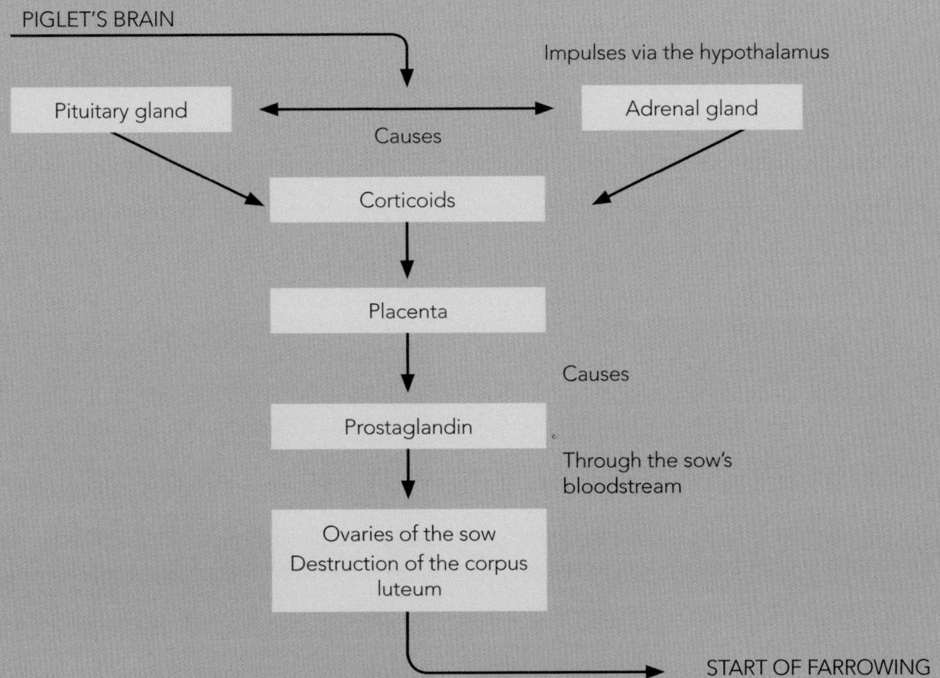

Mechanism of expulsion of a foetus

In the first stage of farrowing, morphological changes occur in the sow's reproductive system, such as the relaxation of the ligaments and tissue of the perineum and vulva. Cervical dilation then starts and the hormone relaxin causes the distension of the cervix, so that the time required for the expulsion is reduced, which favours the birth of live piglets. Vaginal distension takes place in the last stage of farrowing due to the passage of the foetus. Uterine contractions end with the expulsion of the foetuses and placenta.

After birth, as soon as the piglets start to breathe and their umbilical cord ruptures, they become independent individuals. Right after birth, they try to stand up on all fours, totter and slowly take firmer steps (Figs. 8-11).

Duration of farrowing

The duration of farrowing is a factor that determines its difficulty. Although in most cases, parturition lasts between 2 and 5 hours, it should be highlighted that this parameter greatly varies according to the type of sow (genetics, age, weight, size of the litter, etc.). In fact, while some sows expel all their piglets in less than an hour, in others, farrowing lasts for more than 9 hours. The average duration is less than 4 hours.

About 80 % of piglets are born in the first three hours of parturition. The average interval between the expulsion of two piglets is 15 minutes; almost all of them are born within one hour of the birth of the previous piglet.

Expulsion of the foetus and first hours of life of piglets

Figure 8

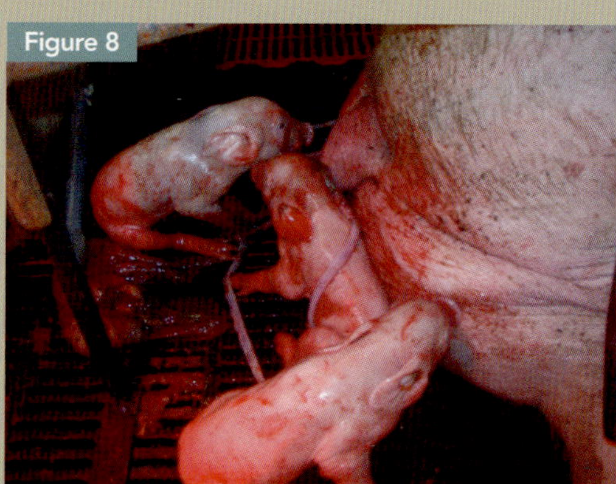

Figure 9

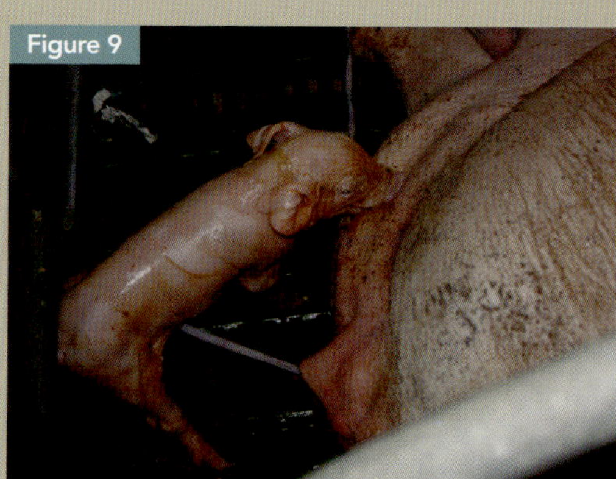

However, 6 % of piglets need more than one hour to be expelled, a very long period of time if we take into account that the average duration of farrowing is 4 hours. Human intervention (manual or pharmacological) may sometimes cause delays or interruptions in the farrowing process, most often with negative consequences that translate into a longer parturition and a higher number of stillborn piglets.

Farrowing conditions affect the survival rate of the piglets so that the rate of stillborn piglets increases in function of the difficulty of the process. Prolonged labour can cause hypoxia in the piglets and manual assistance sometimes causes trauma.

As regards the position of sows at farrowing, they give birth lying down in 97 % of cases, most of them in lateral recumbency and some of them in ventral recumbency; only 3 % of them farrow standing up.

Difficult farrowings

Most sows give birth without requiring the assistance of the farm personnel, which should be given in less than 10 % of cases, except on those farms where farrowing is supervised and intervention protocols are established when the expulsion interval between two piglets lasts longer than expected.

When manual assistance is very common, sow feeding or other management or genetic factors should be revised, since human participation is never recommended as it increases injuries and infections.

Figure 10

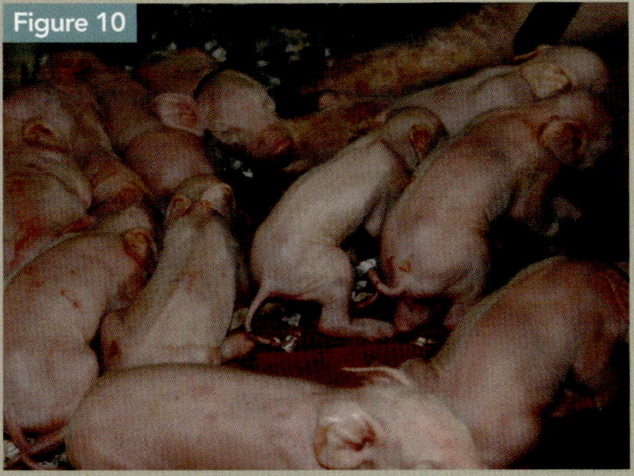

Figure 11

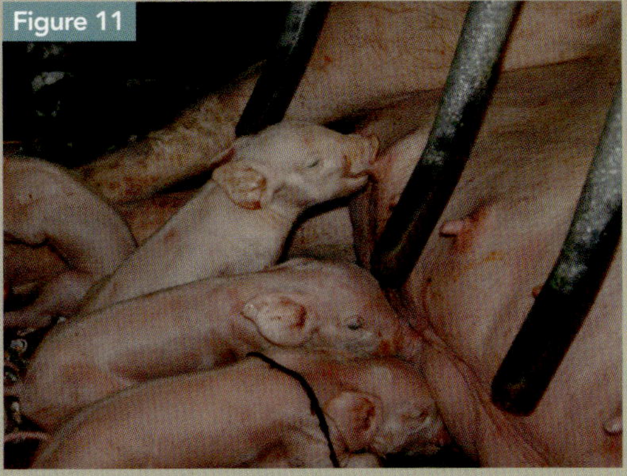

Approximately 70 % of piglets are born in anterior presentation and the other 30 % are born in posterior presentation.

Characteristic signs of the end of farrowing

The expulsion of the placenta occurs within four hours of the birth of the last piglet (Fig. 12). According to the authors' experience, the average weight of the placenta in a batch of 50 sows is 2.45 kg. This value varies from 0.5 kg when it is expelled in parts with some piglets, to up to a maximum weight of 4.60 kg.

Once parturition is over, the sow:

- Calms down, grunts and calls the piglets.
- Stops moving her legs (if these movements do not stop, this means all the piglets have not been borne yet).
- Recovers her normal temperature and eats.

Physiology of piglets during the peripartum period

Weight and size of the litter

The average size of a pig litter is undergoing very fast changes; it varies between 12 and 17 piglets born in total or between 11 and 16 live-born piglets. These figures are exceeded by sows of hyperprolific lines, which produce litters with average values above 16-17 born piglets in total and up to 15-16 live-born piglets on the best operations.

The larger the size of the litter, the lower the average weight of the piglet. According to the authors' data, the mean weight on farms is approximately 1,450 grams in litters of 12 to 14 live-born piglets on average. If the size of the litter increases, the average weight of the piglets decreases by 2 to 7 % per additional piglet born, although it varies depending on the breed, line, environmental conditions and management practices.

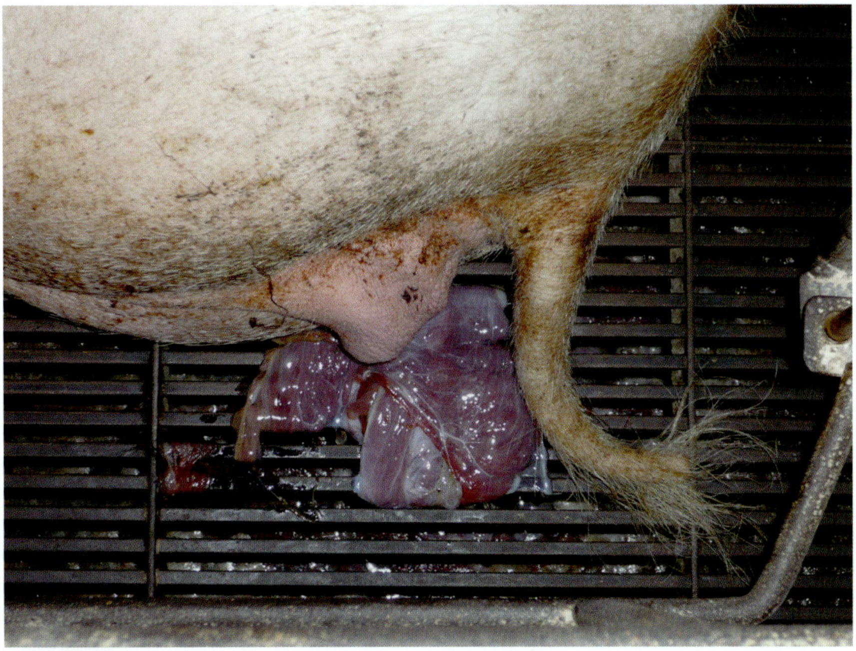

Figure 12 Expulsion of the placenta at the end of farrowing.

When the size of a litter increases, the mortality rate of the piglets increases, especially if no appropriate management measures such as those described in the following chapters are taken. Not only the size of the litter matters, but also its homogeneity. The objective is to obtain very uniform litters, with few weight differences between the live-born piglets, and vigorous animals in order to achieve a greater number of weaned piglets.

The total number of born piglets includes those considered born alive, as well as mummified, dead, false stillborn and low-viability piglets, which are described next.

Mummified piglets

A mummified piglet is that which dies in the uterus in the period comprised between days 35 and 100 of gestation (Fig. 13). The causes leading to mummified piglets may be infectious or non-infectious. A normal value for mummified piglets is about 1-2 %.

Figure 13 Mummified piglets of different sizes.

By measuring the length of the foetuses, it is possible to determine the time of mummification and to know whether the cause of death is infectious, and even what disease has caused mummification (Fig. 14). An infectious disease involving the uterus that does not lead to miscarriage often evolves progressively, giving rise to the formation of mummified foetuses of different sizes.

Figure 14 Relationship between the age and length of the mummified piglets (measurements taken from the head to the base of the tail).

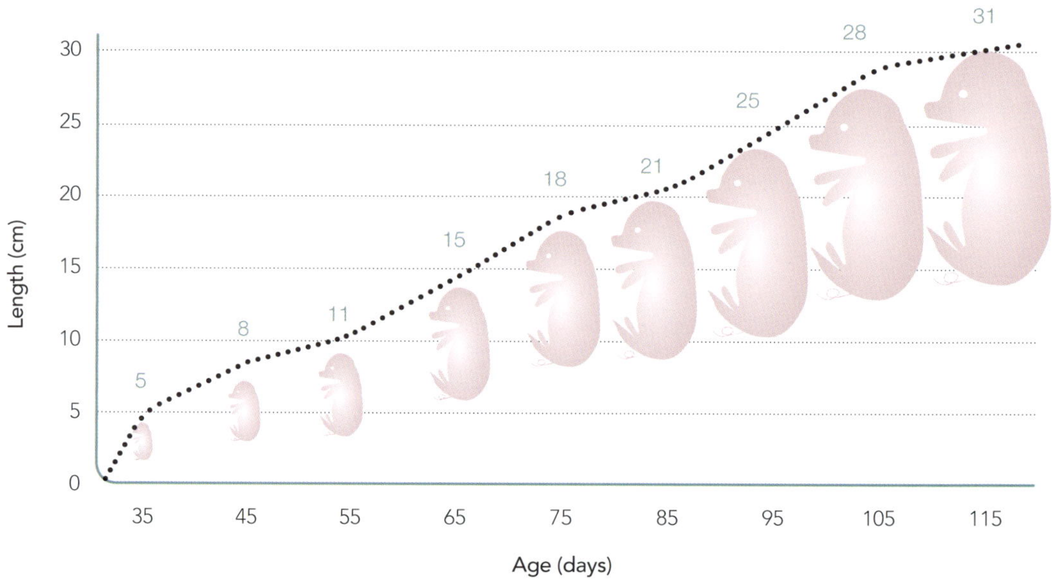

Figure 15 Aspect of a false stillborn piglet (up) and of a true stillborn piglet (down).

Stillborn piglets

These are piglets that died before or during birth. If they died before birth, they can be recognised by their evident dehydration, bad odour and discolouration of their skin. In most cases, they appear covered in foetal membranes (Fig. 15). They should be distinguished from false stillborn piglets.

Most stillborn piglets appear at the end of farrowing. Stillborn piglets are expelled at the end of parturition in 54 % of cases (among the last 20 % of born piglets) (Lallemand animal nutrition, 2012). Apart from the piglet's birth order, other factors also play a role in stillbirths, such as the size of the litter, a longer delivery and a greater interval after the expulsion of the previous piglet. Older sows have litters with a lower survival rate.

Many of the deaths that occur during farrowing are mainly due to anoxia, which appears as a result of an excessively long parturition or due to the occlusion or early rupture of the umbilical cord.

The umbilical cord remains intact in up to 80 % of the piglets that are born in the first positions, while it only does so in 50 % of those that are born at the end of farrowing. Between 70-90 % of stillborn piglets have a ruptured umbilical cord.

The average number of stillborn piglets per litter is 1-1.5, a value that mainly varies in function of the litter size, although it also depends on the cycle of the sow, her body condition and other environmental, health and management conditions. On highly controlled operations where farrowing is induced and monitored, and workers are present 24 hours a day to take care of the sows, the mortality rate can go down to 0.3-0.4 piglets per litter; while on farms with poorer conditions, there can be more than two stillborn piglets per farrowing.

There are stillborn piglets in 51.3 % of the total number of farrowings that take place on an operation, and there are 3 or more stillborn piglets in 14.5 % of the litters. This means a reduced number of farrowings is responsible for a high number of stillborn piglets on pig farms (Fig. 16).

False stillborn piglets

A stillborn piglet is a piglet that was born dead and is not mummified. In practice, the dead piglets that appear on a farm include true and false stillborn animals (individuals that are born alive and have breathed but that farm workers find dead).

The differences between true and false stillborn piglets can be established by means of necropsy. The first difference is the colour of the lungs; in true stillborn piglets, they are dark red (similar to the liver parenchyma), while the lungs of those piglets that have breathed are bright red (Fig. 17). Furthermore, when submerging the lungs in a container filled with water, those of true stillborn piglets sink, while those of false stillborn piglets float (Fig. 18).

The second test is the examination of the stomach: if the piglet has fed from its mother, colostrum is observed in its stomach.

Figure 16 Percentage of stillborn piglets in the total farrowings.
Authors' chart based on data from more than 100,000 farrowings.

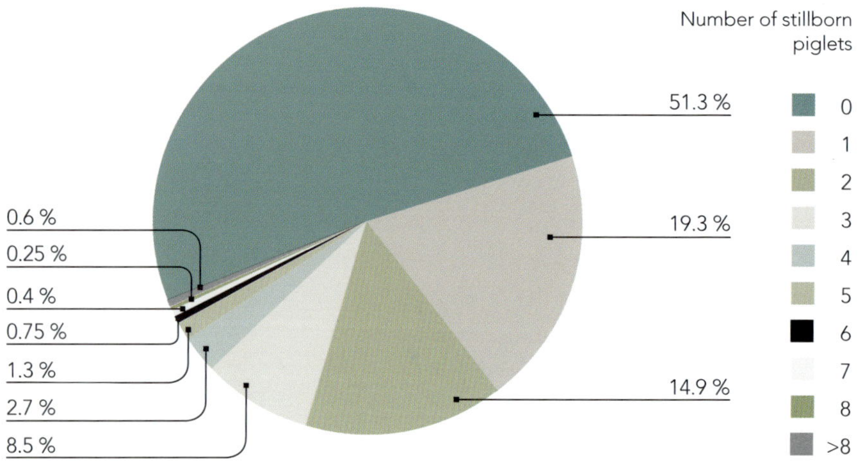

Figure 22 Evolution of the average productive results in Spain from 1990 to 2012. Adapted from Noguera, J.L. et al. Reference data bank for Spanish pig production. 2013. *Boletín BDporc IRTA*. No. 14: 2-3.

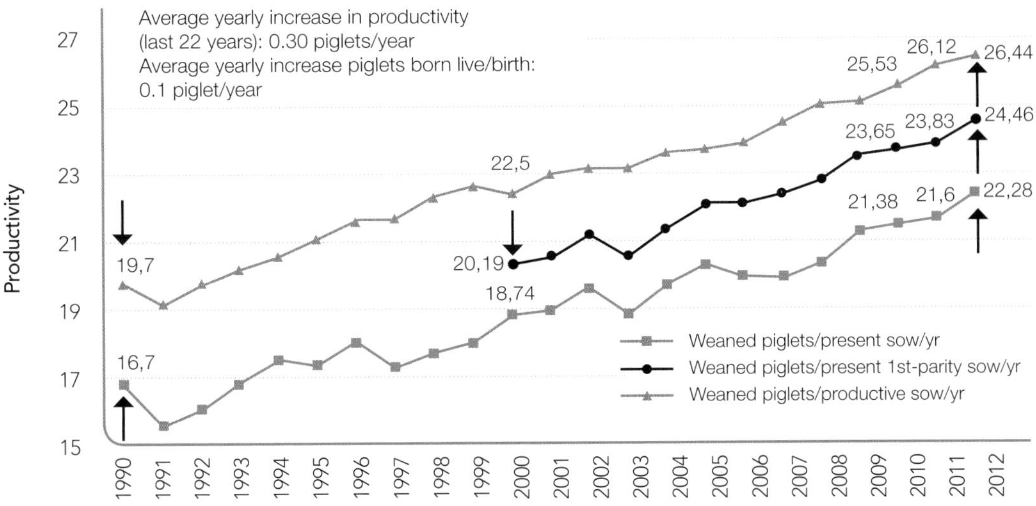

As swine breeds are increasingly prolific, but the rearing capacity of sows has not improved to the same extent, two problems arise. On the one hand, there is an increasingly greater proportion of piglets that are smaller than normal (weak) and on the other hand, supernumerary piglets appear.

- The term weak piglets applies to those whose weight at birth is lower than 75 % the average of the litter (average weight of 1.450 kg). That is to say, a weak piglet is that which weighs less than 1.08 kg at birth.
- The term supernumerary piglets within the same litter is used when the piglets exceed the number of functional teats available. These piglets can be saved by means of cross-fostering techniques.

Vitality is much lower in piglets born after three hours of labour, and on many occasions these piglets require resuscitation.

In a study carried out by Quesnel et al. in 2008, it was observed that the percentage of weak individuals increases to up to 25 % in litters with more than 16 piglets born in total (Table 1).

The increase in prolificacy together with the decrease in piglet weight requires the implementation on pig farms of survival strategies for these piglets. These strategies are based on fostering techniques, segregated weaning and the adoption of feeding systems that are appropriate for both the mother and the piglets.

Table 1 Variables associated with weight at birth in function of the size of the litter. From Quesnel, H. et al. Influence of some sow characteristics on within-litter variation of piglet birth weight. *Animal*, 2008; 2: 1842-1849.

Size of the litter (total born)	≤ 9	10-11	12-13	14-15	≥ 16	Size effect
Average weight (kg)	1.88	1.67	1.57	1.48	1.38	***
Variation coefficient (%)	15	18	21	22	24	***
Percentage of piglets in the litter with a weight 0.75 times lower than the average weight (%)	6	9	12	13	16	***

***: $P < 0.001$.

In very cold areas, a false ceiling is used under the roof. It may be solid (Fig. 4) with adjustable openings for the air to enter the room, or perforated (Fig. 5), to reduce the volume of air in the room, thus obtaining a homogeneous distribution of the air, which is pre-warmed before it reaches the animals. In some countries, glass wool or other insulating materials are used on top of this false ceiling to increase insulation.

Apart from the roof, the four exterior walls complete the building. There are multiple options on the market with a good insulation capacity: thermal clay, expanded clay or cellular concrete (Ytong) blocks, precast concrete walls with a core of extruded polystyrene (to avoid thermal bridges), PVC or polyethylene wall panels, or steel sandwich panels with a polystyrene core.

Once again, the topography and weather characteristics of the area should be taken into account. Depending on the needs, the option that best adapts to these characteristics and provides a satisfactory price-quality relationship should be chosen, without losing sight of the fact that the initial investment in insulation results in a considerable reduction of energy expenses on the medium and long term.

The farrowing pen

Dimensions

The current recommended dimensions for farrowing pens have also increased as compared with the previous ones (sows are larger and the space required for a large litter for 28 days has also increased). As a reference, farrowing pens should ideally be at least 2.5 m long and 1.8 m wide.

Projects carried out with 2.7 m long and 1.9 m wide farrowing pens have already been documented.

Orientation of the pens

In rooms with a single aisle, the short side of the pens (1.60-1.80 m) is usually oriented towards the aisle, so that either the head (Fig. 6) or the rear of the sow may face it (Fig. 7). In the first case, the adjustment of the dispensers, monitoring and cleaning of the troughs, additional supply of water, etc., is made easier for the personnel; while in the second case, having the rear of the sow facing the aisle facilitates handling during farrowing.

However, in rooms with two or more aisles, the longer side of the pen is usually placed parallel to the aisle, so that the personnel can easily feed the animals and conveniently monitor farrowing and the newborn piglets (Fig. 8). In this case, the heating pad is located next to the aisle, so as to give the attendants easy access to the piglets during lactation.

With the coming into force of the EU Directive on animal welfare, and foreseeing possible future measures regarding this matter, trials are being carried out with farrowing pens in which the sow can move around freely during the whole lactation period (Fig. 9).

After looking at farrowing houses as a whole, we will now study **farrowing pens** into more detail.

Choosing the correct size for the farrowing house as well as the appropriate materials and a good design for the pens will allow maximum performance at one of the key points of production. Deficiencies in the design or errors in the choice of materials will reduce animal productivity, mainly because of an increase in the mortality rate from birth to weaning and of a poorer efficiency of the personnel.

> An incorrect design of the facilities may reduce productivity due to an increase in the mortality rate and to a poorer efficiency of the personnel.

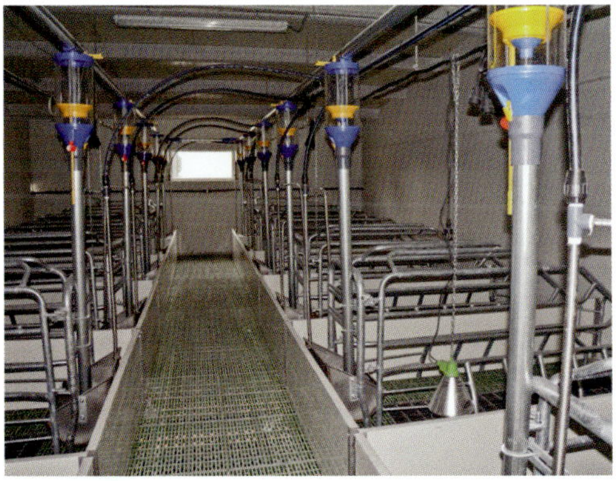

Figure 6 Heads oriented towards the aisle.

Figure 7 Hindquarters oriented towards the aisle.

Figure 8 Unit with several aisles where the sows are parallel to the area of passage.

Figure 9 Farrowing pen in which the sow can move around freely.

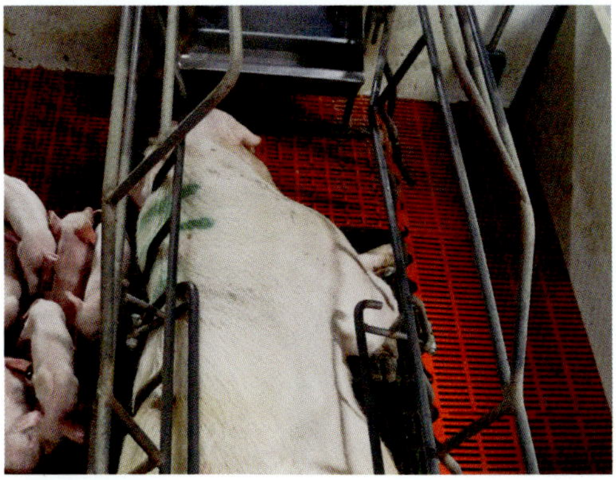

Figure 10 Iron crate.

Figure 11 Galvanised crate.

The crate

There are numerous types of crates and almost all the modern ones work very well. Two types of crates can basically be found: iron crates and galvanised crates (Figs. 10 and 11). Crates with a galvanised frame are stronger and more resistant, but also more expensive.

Recommendations

- Crates should have an easy-to-handle latch, with a bar sufficiently thick to prevent its deformation due to continuous use.
- They should have a system that allows the adjustment of the width at their rear part, depending on the size of the sow that is going to occupy the crate (Fig. 12).
- They should have a system to reduce the space between the two posterior thirds of the crate at a medium height. It may be fixed or mobile **(flip-up bars)**. The recommended space between the two sides of the crate or the two flip-up bars is approximately 40-44 cm (Figs. 13 and 14). This system is of vital importance to reduce the number of crushed piglets in the first days of life, since it forces the sow to lie down slowly, which gives the piglets more time to move away from her.
- It is necessary to ensure that the piglets can easily access the sow's teats and at the same time, to prevent her from "going out" of the space that is allocated to her. Usually, the crates have a side bar that can be adjusted as the piglets grow in size, or **"fingers"** between which the piglets are placed to have access to the teats (Fig. 15).

Figure 12 System to adjust the width of the rear of the crate.

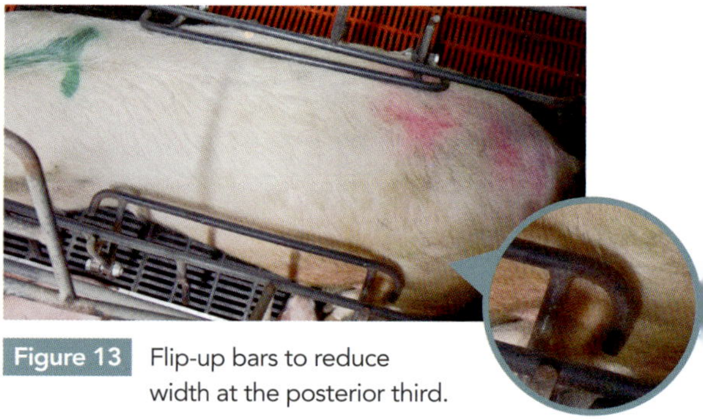

Figure 13 Flip-up bars to reduce width at the posterior third.

Figure 14 Detail of a flip-up bar.

Figure 15 Fingers on the side of the crate to give the piglets access to the teats.

The floor

Two areas should be differentiated: the sow area where the crate is located, and the area for the piglets.

For hygiene and sanitary reasons, the current trend is to use a fully slatted floor (Fig. 16), with a combination of cast iron and plastic slats, or plastic slats only (Fig. 17). A solid concrete area, where the sow can rest her front legs, and where the creep area for the piglets is located, is also used together with slatted floor in the rest of pen, especially in northern European countries (Fig. 18).

In the area of the farrowing pen where the sow is located, plastic slats with a density and supports adapted to her weight and legs may be used.

In areas with high temperatures in the summer, it is recommended to place metal slatted floor (cast or galvanised iron) where the sow lies down, as heat distribution is greater, which allows the sow's body temperature to cool down under thermal stress conditions.

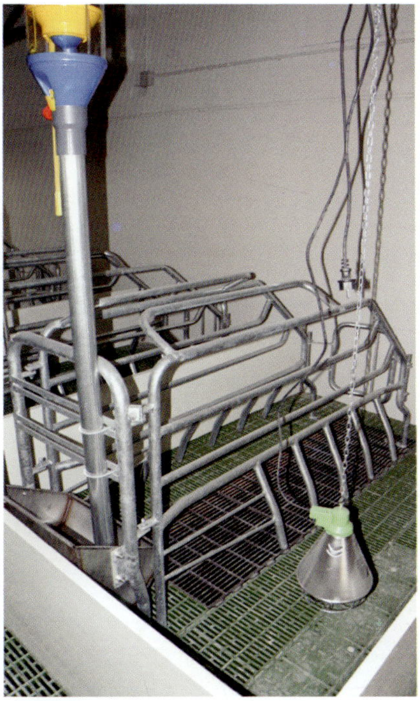

Figure 16 Fully slatted floor.

Figure 17 Slatted floor with a combination of different types of slats.

In areas where the climate is warm, the use of partially-solid flooring is discouraged, as the piglets use it to defecate, urinate... thus increasing the infection pressure of certain pathogens.

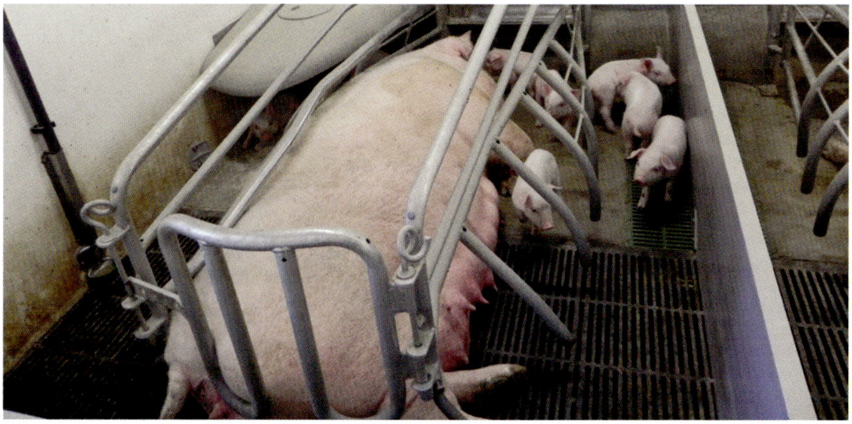

Figure 18 Partially slatted floor.

Recommendations

- Avoid slippery floors. Both cast iron and plastic floorings should have grooves to prevent the sow from slipping when standing up or lying down.
- The areas of passage of the sow (entrance and exit to the farrowing pen), should be fitted with grids suited to her weight.
- Avoid abrasive borders or surfaces that may cause lesions on the piglets' legs or hooves.
- It is a good idea to raise the floor area where the sow lies down by 4-5 cm with respect to the rest of the floor (Fig. 19), so that piglets can access the row of teats located closest to the floor more easily, and at the same time, to make it more difficult for them to enter the space allocated to the sow, therefore achieving a reduction in the number of crushed piglets.
- There are pens with special systems, where the sow's floor area can have a different height from that of the piglets. This way, when the sow stands up, the piglets' area moves down; and when the sow lies down again, it moves back to the same height.
- Cast-iron slatted floors covered with rubber matting provide great comfort to the piglets and work very well, although they are expensive.

Figure 19 Central area raised in relation to the rest of the floor (arrow).

The heated area for the piglets

Another key aspect aimed at reducing the mortality rate from birth to weaning involves preventing hypothermia in newborn piglets. For this purpose, it is essential for the farrowing pen to have a heated area.

Ideal temperature for piglets

The purpose of the heated area for the piglets, apart from preventing hypothermia after birth, is to maintain an appropriate temperature during the first 2-3 days of life. The thermoneutral zone of piglets has a wider range as days go by. After the first week of life, the Lower Critical Temperature (LCT) is already down to 25 °C.

Thermoneutral zone in the pig species. Adapted from Quiles, A. and Hevia, M.L. *Cría y manejo del lechón.* Editorial Acalanthis Comunicación y Estrategias, 2006.

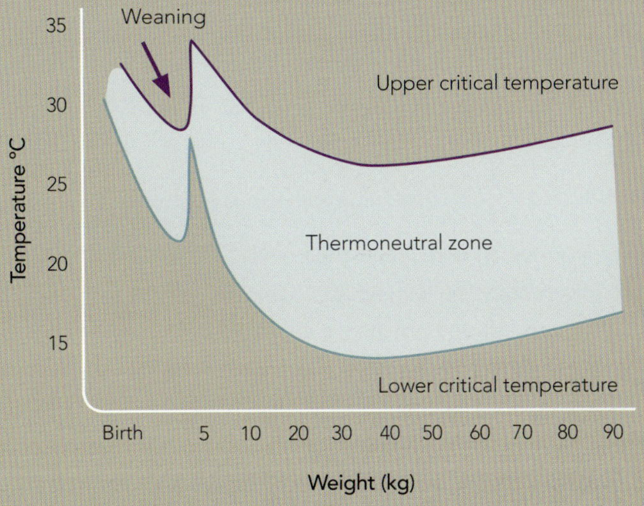

There are different types of systems that provide heat to the piglets, but the most common ones are:

Heating pads

This is the system most commonly used on modern operations. The pad is usually 120 x 40 cm or 120 x 50 cm. These sizes correspond to the space of two flooring grids of 60 x 40 cm or 60 x 50 cm respectively, within the pen.

The surfaces of the pads are made of different materials: polymer concrete, plastic, stainless steel, etc. (Figs. 20, 21 and 22); and they have grooves to prevent piglets from slipping. To avoid heat losses, a layer of insulating material is placed under the pad.

The heating pads should be placed close to the sow's mammary area, normally at the centre in relation to the long axis of the pen. Ideally, a heating pad should be placed on each side of the sow, although this is not usually done as it significantly increases the cost of the facilities.

When covered creep areas are installed, the heating pads are usually placed in one of the front corners. However, the disadvantage of this location is that the pads are very close to the sow's head and may cause a reduction of her feed intake due to heat.

Figure 20 Polymer concrete pad.

Figure 21 Plastic pad.

Figure 22 Stainless steel pad.

> In warm areas, the heating pad for the piglets should be centred, so that the heat it emits does not affect the sow's feed intake.

There are two types of pads:

a. **Electric pads.** With a resistance distributed under the pad's surface. The new-generation pads are low-energy (according to the technical specifications, their maximum power consumption is 85 watts and their average power consumption is 50 watts). This energy has the advantage of being clean and low-maintenance.
   In order to save energy, a switch and a voltage regulator to adjust the temperature are installed with each pad. The ideal temperature of the surface of the panel when the piglets are born is 38-40 °C.
b. **Hot water pads.** The water is heated by means of a boiler. It can be a biomass, propane gas or diesel oil boiler. By means of a pump, the water is distributed through a closed circuit that goes through the pipes of the aisle and different rooms, and then goes back to the boiler.
   In order for boilers to be efficient and to avoid energy wastage, devices are installed in each room to adjust the temperature of the heating water (Fig. 23). They measure the temperature of the water in the return circuit by means of a sensor, and give an order to the valve (Fig. 24) to open or shut off the water supply to the room depending on the temperature that has previously been set.

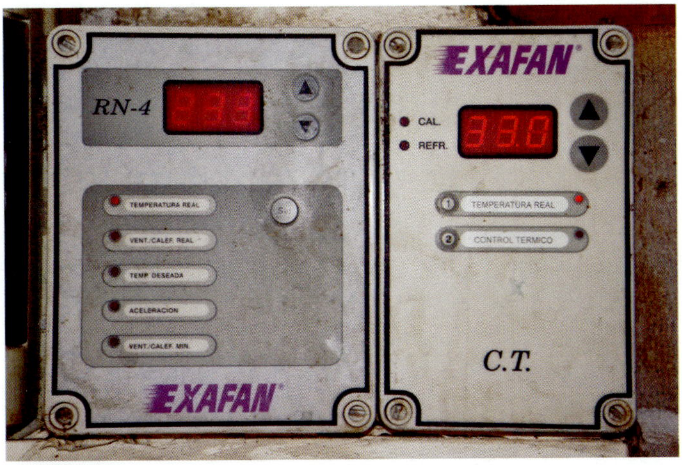

Figure 23 Device for temperature regulation (right).

Figure 24 Valve at the entrance of each room.

Usually, a single device regulates the temperature of the pads for the piglets and monitors the environmental conditions in the rooms (ventilation, temperature, etc.), although these systems can also be installed separately (Fig. 25).

Figure 25 Picture of an environmental controller (left) and heating pad control device (right).

> It should be borne in mind that the heat needs of piglets vary substantially as they grow in age.

Infrared heat lamps

There are many different types: with or without an energy-saving switch, with reflectors of different diameters and with different powers (between 75 and 250 watts). They can be used in combination with a covered creep area or simply placed above the area where the piglets rest.

A **covered creep area** (Figs. 26 and 27) increases the temperature between the upper panel and the floor by approximately 6-8 °C with respect to the same space when it is not covered. Covered creep areas are very effective in cold climates, where they can lead to considerable energy saving, in addition to providing appropriate comfort to the piglets. The crate can be placed diagonally in the pen, thus leaving more space for the resting area of the piglets in the covered creep area.

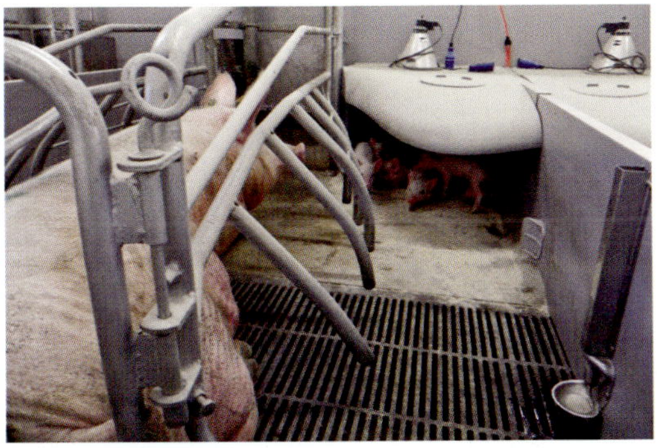

Figures 26 and 27 Different models of covered creep areas.

Recommendations

- In warm areas, it is a good idea to use thick rubber matting or mobile water mattresses, which can be placed under the heat lamp for the first few days and then removed.
- The heat source should always be located on a solid surface (not on slats) to avoid energy losses (Fig. 28). The lamps may not be sufficient in large litters, especially if they are used without a covered creep area. The piglets under the heat source are warmed, but those on the sides receive little heat.

The best option is to combine heating pads with a heat lamp, located at the back of the sow at the time of farrowing (Fig. 29). They should be oriented towards the pad. This way, they provide light so that the piglets move towards this area when they are born.

They are very useful to help dry off the piglets that have just been born. When attendants are continuously present in the rooms, the piglets are picked up, left under the lamp and released once they are dry and warm so they can have their first feed of colostrum. Once farrowing is complete, the lamps are moved and placed above the heating pad, where they are left for the first two or three days of life as a complement of the heat provided by the pad.

> The best system is the combination of heating pads with a heat lamp placed initially at the back of the sow during farrowing, and then moved to the area of the pad.

Gas heaters

They are still used on old farms where there is no electrical installation, but their use is not recommended as they use oxygen and produce carbon dioxide. In addition, when used on farms they become dirty due to the dust, which can lead to deficient combustion (carbon monoxide). This would entail a high risk to the health of both the animals and the personnel, apart from the high risk of fire.

Renewable energies are now being used (solar panels, solar thermal collectors, geothermal energy, etc.) in swine farrowing houses (Fig. 30). The decrease in the cost of purchase, installation and amortisation of these new technologies, combined with an increase in the cost of traditional energies (diesel oil, propane, natural gas, electricity...), seems to indicate that the use of these types of energies will increase on swine operations, depending to a great extent on the future policies on renewable energies adopted by the different countries.

Figure 28 Lamp to prevent hypothermia in the piglets after their birth.

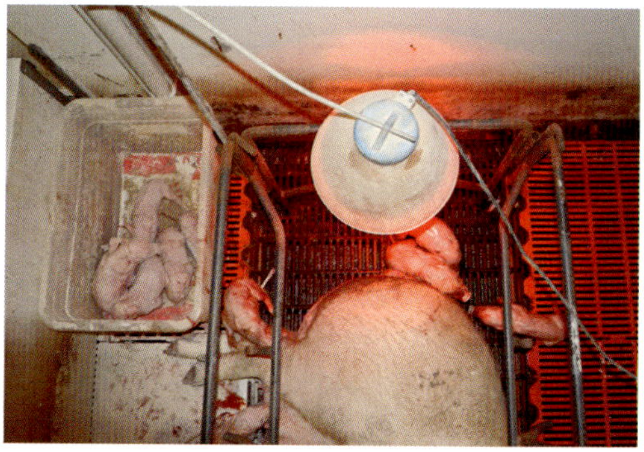

Figure 29 Lamp directed towards the back of the sow during farrowing.

A

B

Figure 30 Photovoltaic installation on a farrowing house. A) Solar panels on the roof. B) Battery storage system.

Feed and water troughs for the sows

The current intensive pig production systems work with genetic lines that are characterised by a high feed-intake capacity and a high milk production. Some sows can eat up to 200 kg of feed and drink 1,000 litres of water during one lactation period. In addition to providing them with optimal environmental conditions, sows need adequate access to and availability of food and water.

Feed troughs

The most commonly used materials are stainless steel or polyethylene with stainless steel frames (Fig. 31).

Recommendations

- The trough should be placed at an appropriate height that allows easy access to the feed and a comfortable position for both young and adult sows. The bottom part of the trough should be placed about 18-24 cm from the floor. This way, the piglets can also pass under the trough without any difficulties.
- The borders should be rounded in order to avoid cuts or lesions on the sow's face caused by the rubbing movement while she is eating.
- They should be strong, sufficiently thick and properly welded so as to prevent breaks or deformations caused by their continuous use, as sows sometimes tend to rest their front legs on them while waiting for the food to come down.

Figure 31 Stainless steel trough.

Figure 32 Feed dispenser.

Figure 33 Dispensers and feeding line.

- They should have rounded shapes and no corners at the bottom, so they can be easily cleaned and the feed that some sows may not have eaten between each feeding can be conveniently removed.
- The front edge should be bent inwards in a right angle to avoid feed wastage, as some voracious sows can become nervous and take part of the feed out of the trough.

On many operations, hopper feeders with different feed distribution systems have been used: push button, swinging sheet of stainless steel, etc., but they have several disadvantages that discourage their use:

- Some sows take a lot of feed out at a time and eat the fresh feed, leaving the meal and remnants of feed at the bottom, which ferment in the summer and therefore need to be removed.
- Their cleaning is more difficult and inconvenient.
- They require more maintenance and individual adjustment of feed flow.
- The sows need more time to eat and take the feed out and in some cases ("lazy" sows) feed intake is reduced.
- In any case, they should be used together with a dispenser that allows the control of what each sow has eaten, and never ad lib.

It is recommended to place the dispensers 5-10 cm from the side of the trough and 10-15 cm from its bottom.

Figure 34 Dispenser system with an extra feed reservoir (white arrow) and a feeding ball. The valve that maintains a constant level of water in the bowl (red arrow) can also be observed.

Dispensers

They are many different models that work well. It is essential that dispensers have a convenient and effective adjustment system, as they are constantly being adjusted. They must allow the ration to be reduced in the days close to farrowing, and the progressive increase of the amount of dispensed feed, knowing what each sow is eating at all times (Fig. 32).

The pipes that go down from the dispenser to the trough are usually made of galvanised steel (Fig. 33). They must be strong and correctly held into place. It is recommended to place them on one side of the feed trough and close to its bottom. This way, when the sow is at the end of the lactation period and eats large amounts of feed, part of it remains in the pipe and comes down as it is eaten. This system may avoid feed wastage; however, there are always some sows that manage to take all the feed out and eat it.

New systems have appeared that allow the combination of the advantages of a dispenser with those of an additional feed reservoir (mini hopper), from which the sow, by means of a push button or ball, manages the amount of food available (Fig. 34), with the feed falling down in the trough in small portions. This system decreases the feed wastage that occurs with some nervous sows, which throw part of the feed out of the trough while eating their ration when the trough is filled all at once.

Automated feeding systems have also recently appeared in farrowing houses, and provide sows with feed in small amounts until the previously set daily intake is reached (according to a computerised feeding curve). They also supply water with programmable dilution values. The trough has sensors at the bottom, which detect whether there is feed and water left. If the sow does not eat, the system does not supply more food. These systems work very well, although the investment necessary is very high. They can be useful on farms where the limiting factor is the workforce.

Drinking systems

Sows lose a lot of fluids during farrowing. Furthermore, they need to drink large amounts of water during lactation to maintain a high milk production. An easy access and sufficient water flow are therefore of vital importance to maximise water and feed intake.

Traditionally, a minimum flow of 2 l/min was recommended for the nipple drinkers or bowl drinkers installed in the farrowing house. With the new productive needs, a minimum flow of 4-6 l/min is recommended. In some companies producing hyperprolific genetic lines, technicians recommend flows of up to 10 l/min. To achieve this, apart from the devices (nipple drinkers, push-button water bowls, etc.) which are already being sold by several distributors, a pressure system connected to the water circuit is required to maintain a constant pressure of 2 atmospheres.

There are different types of drinking systems:

a. **Nipple drinker placed in the feed trough** (Fig. 35). It is the option most recommended by specialised technicians. Its correct placement in the feed trough is very important. The tip of the drinker should be located 15 cm from the bottom of the trough, and thus several centimetres below its border. This way, if the water starts to flow abundantly when the sow is drinking, it will never overflow, thus avoiding water wastage and wetting of the bedding. The nipple drinker must be placed opposite to the pipe that supplies feed from the dispenser.
   The disadvantage is that if a nipple drinker does not work well, it may supply too small amounts of water and this may not be detected; or on the contrary, it may supply too much water, in which case it would be necessary to remove it so as to be able to give the next ration.

> The farrowing house personnel should verify the correct functioning of the nipple drinkers two or three times a week.

b. **Water bowl.** It is placed in the pen close to the floor, on the opposite side to the resting area of the piglets, under the feed trough (Fig. 36).
The disadvantage of this system is that, in the summer, sows sometimes lie down with their snout or leg in the bowl and press the push button continuously to cool themselves down, which causes considerable water wastage.

In newly-built farrowing houses, **auto level-control valves** are installed to maintain a constant volume of water in the feed trough or bowl drinker (Fig. 34). It is a good system; however, its correct functioning must be ensured as the necessary flow may sometimes not be reached, thus limiting the sows' water intake. In addition, the tip of the water pipe should not be placed very close to the bottom of the feed trough (very long pipes), since in the case of sows that do not eat all the feed, this latter may obstruct to the water outlet.

Figure 35 Nipple drinker placed in a feed trough.

Figure 36 High-flow water bowl.

Systems for additional water supply

In some European countries with a long tradition in swine production such as The Netherlands, Denmark or Germany, byproducts are administered to reduce the cost of feeding and automated liquid feeding systems are installed, so feed and water are mixed when supplied (Figs. 37 and 38). These systems achieve very high intakes and performance, although their cost is high.

On most farms, sows eat pelleted feed (dry ration) with a high dry matter content, so they need immediate access to water, both while and after eating.

A good recommendation would be to add 5-10 litres of water about 10-15 minutes after each feeding, so that the sows that eat more slowly or have less appetite and have left some feed increase their intake as the ration becomes "liquid". On some new operations, independent water lines have been installed that supply water to the feed trough automatically through solenoid valves and a timer. It is useful to fit a tap on the pipes to be able to close them in case a sow has already filled the feed trough by herself. On small operations, individual taps are used to fill the trough, or a tap is installed in each room and the additional water is supplied with a hose.

Figure 37 Liquid feeding equipment.

Figure 38 Valves and automated feeding lines.

Feed and water troughs for piglets

Some piglets, when their mother mother has a good milk production, almost do not eat feed or drink water during the lactation period. However, the presence of feed and water should always be ensured, especially from 7-10 days of life, so that post-weaning adaptation is less traumatic.

There are several types of feed troughs: the most common type is a round hopper feeder with dividers that start form the centre of the feeder (Fig. 39). This allows piglets to eat and drink at the same time as their littermates, a situation to which they are used during nursing. These feeders are anchored to the slats with a spring and a hook on their bottom part.

> The mechanism that anchors the feeder to the slats must be practical and easy to remove as feeders should be cleaned daily.

The feed should be supplied twice a day and in small amounts, so that it is always fresh and does not lose the flavours that most attract piglets. The feeders should be cleaned daily and the excess feed they have not eaten removed.

The drinking system is usually a water bowl (Fig. 40), which is placed at the back of the pen, on the opposite side to the heated area for the piglets. It should often be cleaned in order to prevent disease transmission and ensure the piglets do not refuse to drink because it is dirty.

Figure 39 Feeder for piglets.

Figure 40 Water bowl for piglets.

The ideal pen

In accordance with what has been said before, the design of the ideal pen would be that shown in Figure 41, even though it is necessary to bear in mind that it should be adapted in function of the legislation in each country. In this regard, the floor design and materials used will also depend on the geographical area and weather conditions.

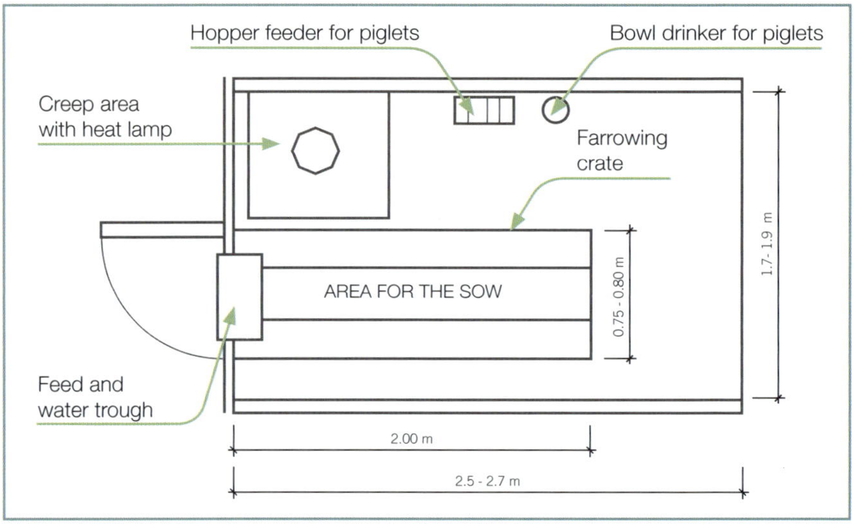

Figure 41 Design of an ideal pen in a farrowing room. Adapted from: Forcada, F. and Viladomiu, I. Cap. 8, Alojamientos para cerdas lactantes. In: Forcada, F., Babot, D., Vidal, A. Buxadé, C. et al. *Ganado porcino. Diseño de alojamientos e instalaciones.* Editorial Servet, Zaragoza, 2009.

Monitoring of environmental conditions in the farrowing rooms

The different parameters to take into account for the correct monitoring of environmental conditions in the farrowing rooms will be addressed concisely next, in accordance with the needs of the sow and piglets at the time of birth.

> The technical and productivity parameters of a farrowing room are conditioned to a great extent by the correct design of the ventilation, heating and cooling systems installed in the farrowing house.

Temperature

The information provided by scientific works carried out by authors from different countries reveals that the thermal comfort zone for a lactating sow is between 16-20 °C. This range can be extended to 12-24 °C, depending on the conditions of the facilities, ventilation and air distribution, without the sows' behaviour being affected drastically. Piglets at birth and during their first hours of life need a temperature of 32-35 °C.

Table 3 Comfort temperature of the sow and piglets. Callejo, A. y Ovejero, I. *Control ambiental de instalaciones de ganado porcino*, 2007.

Type of animal	T (°C)	T (°C)
LACTATING SOW (ambient temperature in the farrowing house)		
Farrowing - 3 days postpartum	20	25
> day 3 postpartum	17	22-25
PIGLETS (creep area temperature)		
Birth - first 3 days of life*	22-34	Will depend on behaviour at rest**
> day 3 of life	Progressive reduction down to 24 °C at 4 weeks of life	

*The ideal temperature of the floor of the creep area during these first few days is 39-41 °C.
**The lateral position (lateral recumbency) of the piglets when resting in the creep area indicates best thermal comfort.

In countries with extreme temperatures in winter, in which the temperature inside the rooms may fall below the LCT **(Lower Critical Temperature)** down to 14-16 °C, the use of heating systems to preheat the air that enters the farrowing rooms is recommended. Radiators in the aisles, delta pipes (aluminium pipes with fins that distribute heat when they are in contact with the air) placed at the air inlet to the rooms, or fan or unit heaters that inject hot air from the aisle, are usually used.

In warmer areas, these issues occur in the summer, when the UCT **(Upper Critical Temperature)** for lactating sows is easily exceeded in the rooms. A temperature much above the UCT may have dramatic consequences on the productivity of the sows and on the piglets as shown in Figure 42.

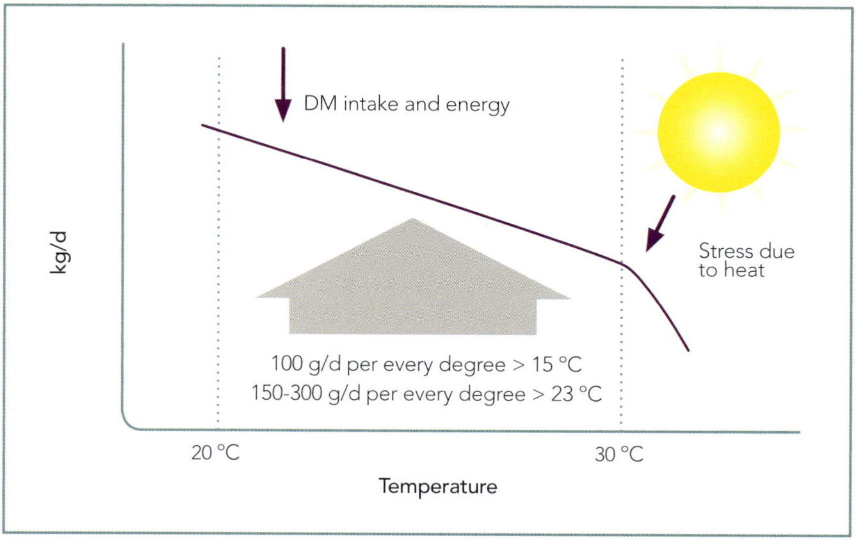

Figure 42 Relationship between temperature in the farrowing room and feed intake. Adapted from Marco i Collell. *Control ambiental en porcino.*

Consequences of thermal stress on sows:

- Sows reduce their feed intake (with great individual differences). For each degree Celsius above 23 °C, the intake is reduced by 100 to 300 g a day.
- The milk production decreases.
- The weight of the piglets at weaning and their subsequent ADG (Average Daily Gain) decrease.
- Body condition at weaning worsens.
- The weaning-to-oestrus interval increases.
- There is a reduction in the size of the litter in the next cycle.

Cooling systems must therefore be installed to reduce or eliminate the effects of thermal stress due to heat in lactating sows.

In warm areas, it is necessary to install cooling systems to prevent the effects of thermal stress due to heat in lactating sows.

The **cooling systems** used on pig farms work by "picking up" heat from the air coming from outside, and cooling it down before it enters the room. This way, a reduction of temperature by 4-10 °C compared to the outside temperature is achieved, if the systems are well designed and correctly sized.

Technically, these are called **"evaporative coolers"** and basically involve putting warm air unsaturated with water vapour into contact with liquid water. The partial pressure difference between the air and the water in the evaporative pads causes the transfer of water to the air in the form of vapour, thus reducing the temperature of the air stream.

The lower the relative humidity of the air that is contact with the water, the better these systems work. If the outside relative humidity is very high, in addition to a reduced performance, an increased number of piglets affected by certain diseases may be observed due to excessive humidity.

The most commonly used cooling systems are:

a. **High-pressure fogging systems.** In farrowing houses, these systems are usually located in the aisle, close to the air inlets to the rooms. They may be used on operations with natural ventilation, but they are much more effective when they are accompanied by an air current provided by the ventilation system. They require regular maintenance and cleaning to prevent clogging or too much water from flowing through the nozzles, which would make them lose their effectiveness.
b. **Cellulose pads.** They are installed in evaporative cooling systems. They are connected to a water tank with an independent closed circuit. They include a float switch to maintain a constant water level and a pump that recirculates the water from each reservoir and distributes it through the pad (Fig. 43).
   The pads are approximately 10 to 15-cm thick and the maximum air velocity through the pad must be 1.25 to 1.75 m/sec in function of its thickness. Depending on the cooling needs, only one pad may be placed, or three pads to form a closed cube and increase the contact surface with the air.

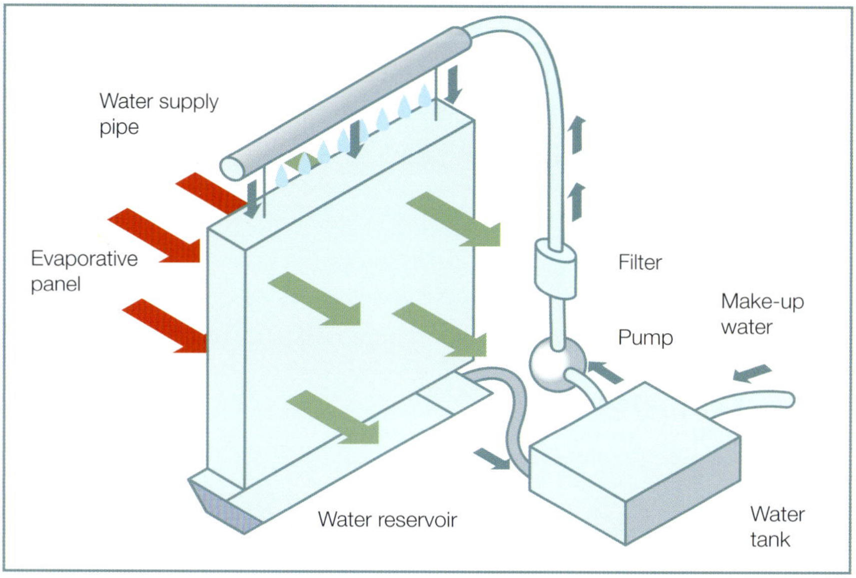

Figure 43 Components of an evaporative cooling systems. From: Blanes-Vidal, V. and Torres, A. G. Diseño y evaluación de la calefacción y de la refrigeración. In: Forcada, F. et al. *Ganado porcino. Diseño de alojamientos e instalaciones.* Editorial Servet, Zaragoza, 2009.

In function of the cooling needs and rooms that should be cooled down, these pads are usually placed on the exterior wall where the door that opens onto the main aisle is located (Fig. 44). When central ventilation is used, they are also placed on the exterior wall of the opposite side, and in buildings with rooms on both sides of the aisle, they are placed on the roof above the aisle.

Figure 44 Cooling pads placed on the exterior wall.

Cooling systems can start automatically when the sensor, located in the farrowing room, detects that the set temperature has been exceeded.
The pads should be regularly cleaned to remove lime deposits and proper maintenance should be carried out, since the pads otherwise lose their efficacy. Some farmers disassemble and store them when the hot season is over. In any case, it is recommended to protect them from direct sunlight and rain.

c. **Drip irrigation systems.** In geographical areas with a high humidity level, evaporative cooling systems are not as effective, and drip irrigation systems are therefore used to **drip water intermittently** (alternation of periods when the system is on with others when it is off) on the sow's neck when she is lying down.

Table 4 Effect of ambient temperature on feed intake and loss of weight in lactating sows. Quiniou and Noblet. *J. ANIM. SCI.*, 1999.

Ambient temperature (°C)	18	22	25	27	29
Intake (kg/d)	5.7	5.4	5.0	4.5	3.1
Loss of weight (kg)	23	22	25	30	35
Loss of dorsal fat thickness (mm)	2.1	1.9	2.7	3.5	3.5
Average daily gain of piglets (g/d)	244	245	233	212	189

As regards the temperature needs of piglets, heating pads, heat lamps and the use of covered creep areas in the case of very cold climates have been described (see The heated area for the piglets, page 37).

Ventilation

Ventilation allows air renewal in the farrowing rooms, thus avoiding excessive humidity and the accumulation of toxic gases harmful to the animals and personnel working in the farrowing house. Moreover, it helps achieve the comfort temperature range for the animals.

The main harmful gases (Table 5) that are generated are:

- Asphyxiating gases: carbon dioxide and methane.
- Irritating gases: ammonia.
- Toxic gases: hydrogen sulfide and carbon monoxide.

In addition to eliminating toxic gases, ventilation eliminates foul odours and dust particles in suspension, which are harmful to the animals from 2.5 g/m^3.

The number of fans that should be placed, their location and technical characteristics are determined in function of the maximum volume of air that needs to be extracted from the farrowing room, in the most extreme conditions. In winter, the minimum ventilation able to renew the minimum volume of air required should be achieved without causing an excessive temperature decrease in the rooms (Table 6).

Two types of ventilation are used on pig farms: **natural and forced.**

Natural ventilation

On modern operations, natural ventilation is not recommended in the farrowing unit, as with this system it is difficult to achieve an optimal temperature with sufficient air renewal, appropriate relative humidity levels and the elimination of harmful gases at all times and under different weather conditions depending on the year, time of the day, etc.

However, some old small and medium-sized farms do not have electricity on a continuous basis or any ventilation system installed and therefore use natural ventilation.

Key aspects to bear in mind for proper **natural ventilation**:

- The orientation and location are key to achieve optimum ventilation (period of sunshine, dominant winds, etc.).
- High degree of insulation and protection from sunshine.
- Correct roof pitch.
- Air inlets (correct size).
- Volume (3 m^3/animal) and sufficient distance from other units.

Table 5 Characteristics and physiological effects of harmful gases. Adapted from Quiles, A. and Hevia, M.L. *Cría y manejo del lechón.* Editorial Acalanthis Comunicación y Estrategias, 2006.

	CO_2		NH_3		SH_2		CH_4		CO	
Type	Asphyxiating		Irritating		Toxic		Asphyxiating		Toxic	
Density (g/l)	1.98		0.77		1.54				1.25	
Specific gravity*	1.53		0.58		1.19				0.97	
Colour	Colourless		Colourless		Colourless		Colourless		Colourless	
Odour	Odourless		Spicy		Rotten eggs		Odourless		Odourless	
Maximum acceptable concentration	1,500-2,000 ppm		50 ppm		10 ppm		1,000 ppm		50 ppm	
Physiological effect on the pigs	Dose	Consequence	Dose	Consequence	Dose	Consequence	Dose	Consequence	Dose	Consequence
	30,000 ppm	Increased respiratory rate	150 ppm	Growth reduction	100 ppm	For several hours: irritation of the eyes and nose	500,000 ppm	Headaches	500 ppm	For 60 min.: no effects
	40,000 ppm	Sleepiness and headache	400 ppm	Irritation of the trachea and throat	200 ppm	For 60 min.: headaches and dizziness			1,000 ppm	For 60 min.: unpleasant but not dangerous
	60,000 ppm	For 30 min.: signs of asphyxia	700 ppm	Eye irritation	500 ppm	Nausea, restlessness and insomnia				
	300,000 ppm	For 30 min.: death	1,700 ppm	Cough and expectoration	1,000 ppm	Unconsciousness and death				
			3,000 ppm	For 30 min.: signs of asphyxia						
			5,000 ppm	For 40 min.: death						

* Proportion of the gas in atmospheric air.

Table 6 Maximum and minimum ventilation recommended in farrowing rooms. Marco i Collell. *Control ambiental en ganado porcino*, 2008.

Days of lactation	Minimum ventilation (m^3/sow/h)	Maximum ventilation (m^3/sow/h)
0-8	40-50	180-250
8-15	50-60	180-250
15-weaning	60-80	180-250

Forced ventilation

The forced ventilation system most commonly used in farrowing units is **negative pressure ventilation** (Fig. 45).

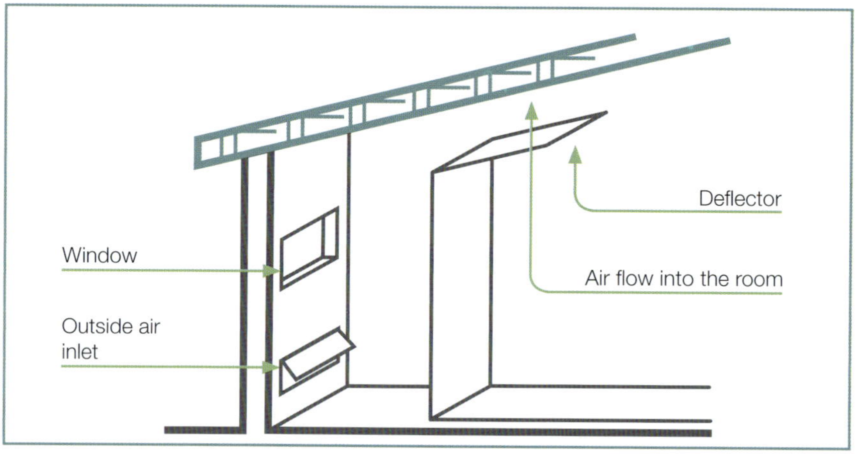

Figure 45 Design of the air inlets. From Escobet, J., Collell, M., and Marco, E. El control práctico del sistema de climatización. In: Forcada, F., Babot, D., Vidal, A. Buxadé, C. et al. *Ganado porcino. Diseño de alojamientos e instalaciones.* Editorial Servet, Zaragoza, 2009.

The air is extracted from the interior of the unit by means of a fan located, usually, in the roof at the back of the room, above the central aisle, or in the back wall (Fig. 46). This way, a negative pressure is created in the room, which lets the air flow in through the inlets designed for this purpose, which are generally placed on the opposite wall (where the aisle is located, Fig. 47). This system is called "**cross-flow system**".

When the room is very wide, the exhaust fans are usually placed in the centre (Fig. 48) and the air inlets on the two side walls of the room (Fig. 49).

Figure 46 Fan in the roof at the back of the room.

Figure 47 Air inlet in the aisle.

Figure 48 Fans at the centre of the room.

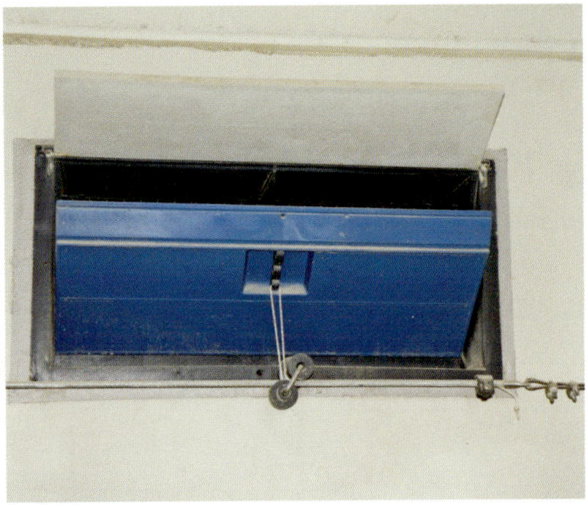

Figure 49 Air inlet in the side walls.

There are systems with which the air is extracted through the manure pits. They have the advantage of eliminating gases and odours, but may create air currents that are harmful to the newborn piglets if they are not properly designed.

In regions with a cold climate, the air is distributed through the porous surface of the false ceiling or through inlets strategically located in it (Fig. 50).

A very precise regulation system is required to avoid gases and condensation, and an effective **safety and alarm** system is necessary in case of failure of the ventilation system, as the air volume is greatly reduced and asphyxiation can occur very quickly.

Figure 50 Air inlets in a false ceiling (arrows).

Ventilation control

It is essential that the location of the exhaust fans and the design and size of the air inlets be appropriate for the whole system to work properly. Ventilation control devices are diverse, as are their characteristics. The help of a specialist is necessary to obtain advice on the location, size and specifications of these elements according to the volume and conditions of the farrowing rooms.

Traditionally, two types of control devices are used:

a. **On-or-off ventilation.** The fan works at maximum speed or is off for set periods of time.

b. **Variable-speed ventilation.** Minimum-speed ventilation is maintained and as the temperature –measured by a sensor placed strategically slightly above the sows (Fig. 51) in the centre of the room– increases, the ventilation speed increases by increments until the maximum ventilation rate is reached.

Nowadays, devices that allow the application of a preset ventilation curve are used from farrowing to weaning and in function of the time of the year (Fig. 52). In addition, these systems can automatically adjust the opening of the air inlets to maintain a constant air velocity (1.5 m/s is the recommended value), as well as the openings of the exhaust ducts.

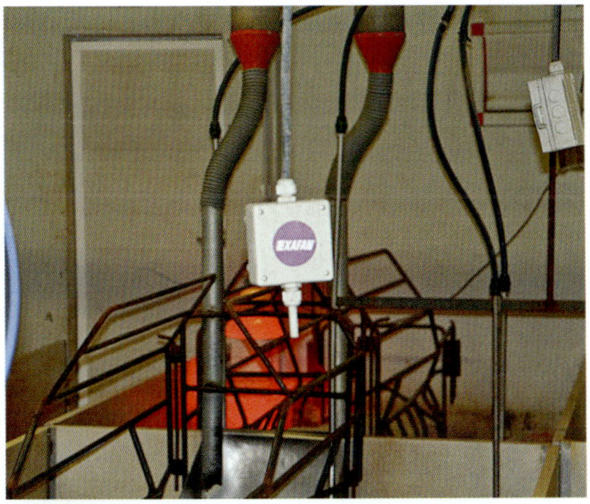

Figure 51 Sensor for temperature control.

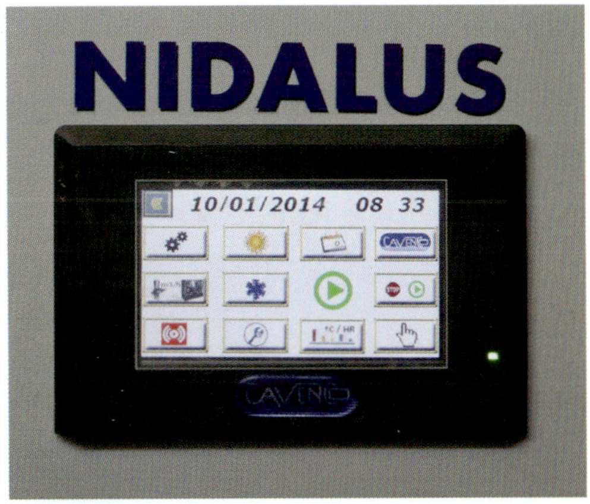

Figure 52 Device for complete environmental control.

If the air velocity increases in excess at the height of the animals, this will cause heat losses in the piglets and a greater incidence of respiratory diseases.

The most sophisticated controllers can also adjust the temperature of the heating pads for the piglets or turn on the cooling system if necessary.

Comprehensive training of the personnel using this type of environmental control equipment in farrowing houses is very important. These controllers work very well, but their use is sometimes complicated and continuous modifications are required as the needs of the animals vary. On some farms, it is possible to find controllers in which the temperature curves or the parameters set for a previous lactation period in one of the rooms have not been modified.

Table 7 Maximum air velocity at the height of the animals. From Martín, C. y Moreno, R. *Producción porcina: aspectos clave*. Ed. Mundi Prensa, Madrid, 1999.

Type of animal	Winter (m/s)	Summer (m/s)
Breeding sows and boars	0.2	0.7
Piglets in farrowing house	0.1	0.3
Piglets in transition	0.1	0.4
Fattening pigs	0.2	0.5

Equipment for environmental control

It is recommended to have some devices available on the farm that are economic and help us ensure periodically that the ventilation and heating systems are working properly.

Infrared digital thermometer

It is very useful in order to measure the temperature of the heating pads for the piglets or resting area (Fig. 53). These procedures allow a better adjustment of the temperature, since there are sometimes differences of several degrees Celsius between the set objective and the real temperature that is obtained.

Figure 53 Measurement of the temperature of the heat pads using an infrared digital thermometer.

Temperature and relative humidity controller

There are several models that work very well available on the market. The controller is left hanging in the room, at the height of the animals. The device measures temperature and relative humidity at specific time intervals (10-15 minutes) and for several seconds. The data can be downloaded to a computer to see the temperature and relative humidity curves for the whole period, so that it is possible to check whether the established settings are effective or not.

Anemometer

It is small and easy to handle, and allows the measurement of the air velocity at the inlets, height of the animals, etc.

Gas analysers and smoke bombs or generators

They can occasionally be used as a complement, to see whether air distribution is correct in the room. This is usually done when a building is going to be used for the first time, but it is not done again later. It should be borne in mind that, with time and intensive use of the devices, there may be maladjustments that are not detected and reduce the efficacy of the systems installed.

It is recommended to thoroughly check the equipment every 6 months, as time and intensive use of the devices may cause maladjustments. The maintenance and daily cleaning of the equipment, deflectors, fans, air inlets, etc. are also fundamental to achieve appropriate heating, ventilation and air conditioning continuously.

3 Organisation of farrowing units: batch farrowing

Introduction

One of the aspects that has revolutionised pig production is the design of facilities specific to each physiological stage of the sow.

Sows, which used to spend their whole productive cycle in the same place, where they gestated, gave birth to and reared their piglets, now have a specific place for each physiological stage.

Furthermore, as farrowing pens are the most expensive facilities on the farm, the need to adjust their number on the operation arises. The farrowing unit becomes a real "bottleneck" on many farms, which often do not have enough farrowing pens to use the most advisable batch farrowing methods, as these require 24 % more farrowing places than the total number of sows. In the case of hyperprolific lines, this figure can increase to 28 % due to the use of nurse sows.

In order to optimise the availability of farrowing pens as much as possible, homogeneous production batches are established and **batch farrowing** is applied.

Objectives of batch production

- Making an optimal use of the facilities on the farm.
- Obtaining a homogeneous production of animals.
- Achieving better work organisation.
- Ensuring that farrowing rooms can be emptied for sanitation (all-in, all-out).
- Improving the general health status of pig farms.

Batch farrowing

Concept of batch

A production batch is a group of animals that are at a similar productive or physiological stage, for example: a group of sows about to farrow; a group of sows about to be weaned or a group of growing animals of a similar age. As can be seen, the concept of batch is associated with a time aspect.

Weaning is the event that determines how a batch is established. Services are carried out taking advantage of the fact that sows come into heat between days 4 and 6 (Fig. 1) after weaning in order to obtain homogeneous farrowing batches. The key is to ensure that most of the sows in a batch are weaned at the same time.

Figure 1 Target weaning-to-service interval (WSI). Adapted from Rodríguez-Estévez. *El anoestro y la infertilidad estacional de la cerda*. Editorial Servet, 2010.

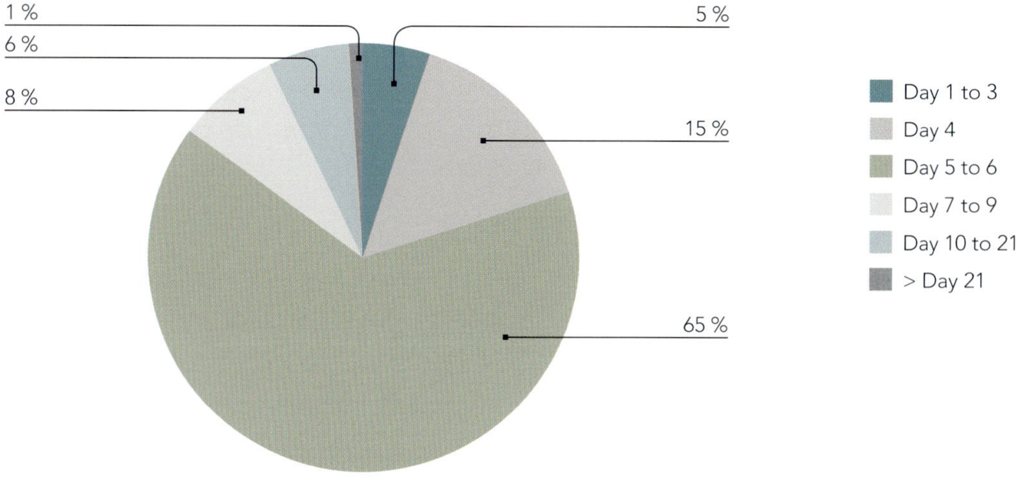

The replacement gilts that the farmer wants to bring in will be added to the batch to obtain the total number of sows of each batch.

Ideally, the size of the different batches should always be similar, so that the facilities of a farm, whose size has previously been calculated, are used in the most optimal manner possible.

Depending on how these batches are grouped, we will talk about 1, 2, 3 or 4-week batch production. The choice of the ideal batch farrowing system for each operation depends on its needs and facilities. It will condition numerous management aspects on the farm, such as the duration of lactation, the management of repeat or nurse sows or the introduction of replacement gilts. In order to calculate the number of batches a farm can work with, the following formula may be used:

$$NB = \frac{G+L+WSI}{i}$$

NB = number of batches, G = duration of gestation, L = duration of lactation, WSI = weaning-to-service interval, i = interval between batches expressed in days.

It is essential to know the number of batches of sows a farm wants to work with for the proper management of a swine operation.

Weekly batch farrowing

The weekly batch farrowing system is the most common system on pig farms. It is used on most large operations. It is the most flexible system, as it allows a certain margin of error in the farrowing target. Moreover, with this system it is possible to wean sows earlier or later than planned.

Characteristics

- The resulting number of batches on the operation is 21-22 (Figs. 2 and 4), depending on whether the lactation period lasts 21 or 28 days.
- It is based on a **weekly service target** in order to obtain a weekly farrowing target (Fig. 3).

- Services, farrowing and weaning in each batch take place within the same week and the day of each task will depend on the day of weaning, generally Thursday, although on very large farms or with few farrowing places, there may be several days of weaning in the same week.
- It allows good work organisation, since all the important tasks on the operation are repeated every week.
- Piglets can be weaned both at 21 and 28 days of age, and it is even possible to choose different weaning ages to achieve, for example, the complete emptying of a farrowing room.
- This is the best system to work with nurse sows if hyperprolific genetic lines are used.
- Sows that repeat will always be served with a batch as services are programmed every week.

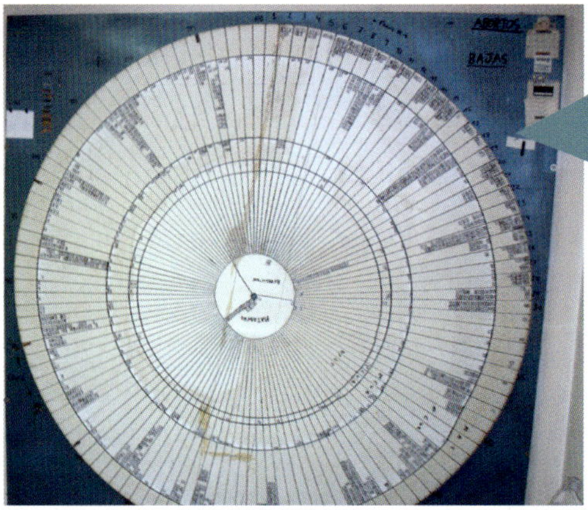

Figure 2 Circular calendar used with a weekly BFS. The outer circle corresponds to sows in the farrowing rooms and the inner one to pregnant sows.

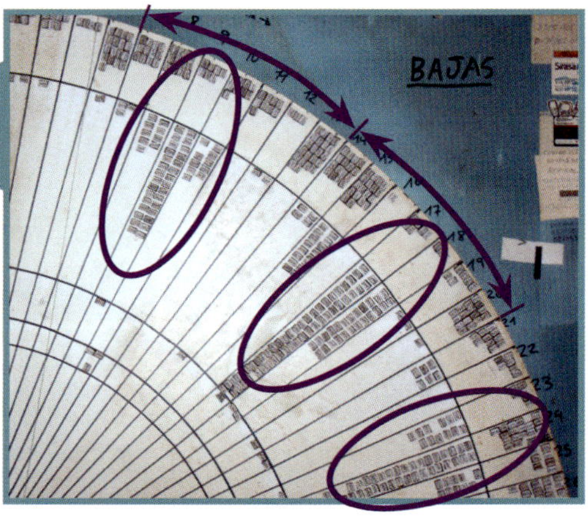

Figure 3 Detail of the circular calendar used for weekly batch farrowing. The arrows show seven-day periods.

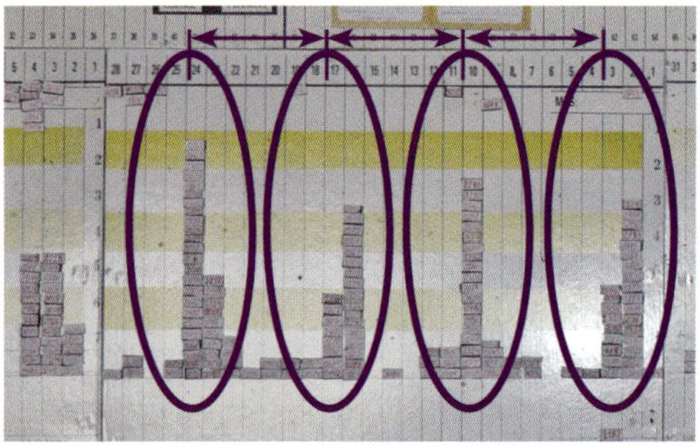

Figure 4 Linear calendar used with a weekly BFS. Every tile on the calendar corresponds to a sow. There is a 7-day interval between each batch. The sows that are going to become part of the batch are served during this period, on two days mainly, due to the weaning-to-service interval.

The current EU Directive on animal welfare requires that piglets are weaned at 28 days of age so they are stronger and adapt better to the transition phase. This, together with the fact that the average size of swine operations is increasingly larger and that new hyperprolific genetic lines have emerged –thus requiring a special management strategy with many nurse sows in the farrowing house–, turn the weekly batch farrowing system into the system that best adapts to the current needs of pig farms.

> Weekly batch farrowing is the system that best adapts to the current needs of pig farms.

Weekly batch farrowing and weaning at 21 days of age

There is a 4-week turnaround in the farrowing rooms (Fig. 5).

- Half a week for the arrival of sows.
- Three-week lactation period.
- Half a week for sanitation.

Weekly batch farrowing and weaning at 28 days of age

There is a 5-week turnaround in the farrowing rooms (Fig. 6).

- Half a week for the arrival of sows.
- Four-week lactation period.
- Half a week for sanitation.

Although weekly batch farrowing is the most common and practical system nowadays, on some occasions it may be interesting to choose a different type of batch farrowing system. This is particularly true on small farms, when a larger number of animals homogeneous in age and size is required to fill a fattening unit or to improve task organisation on the farm.

Batch farrowing at an interval of more than a week generally requires more farrowing and gestation places. However, it usually favours the improvement of the health status of the farm as the farrowing rooms are empty for longer periods of time.

Figure 5 Diagram of a weekly batch farrowing system with weaning at 21 days.

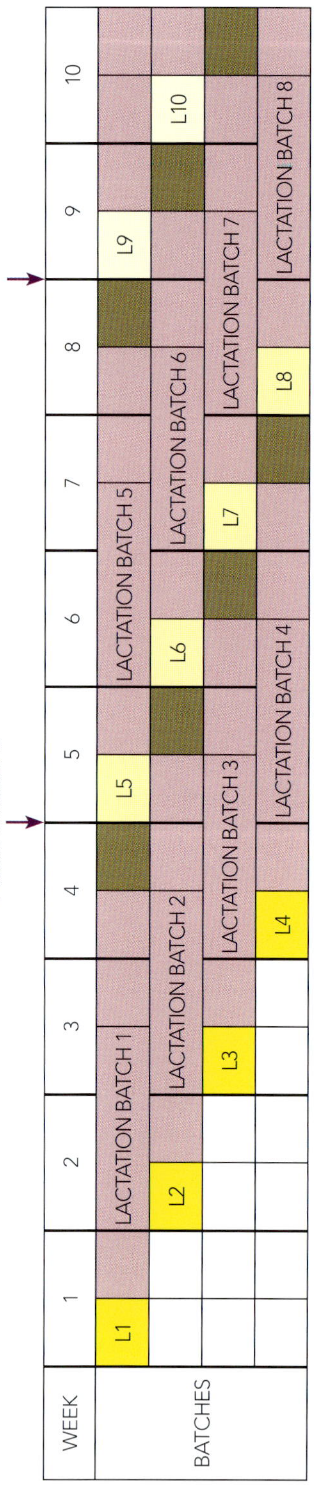

Figure 6 Diagram of a weekly batch farrowing system with weaning at 28 days.

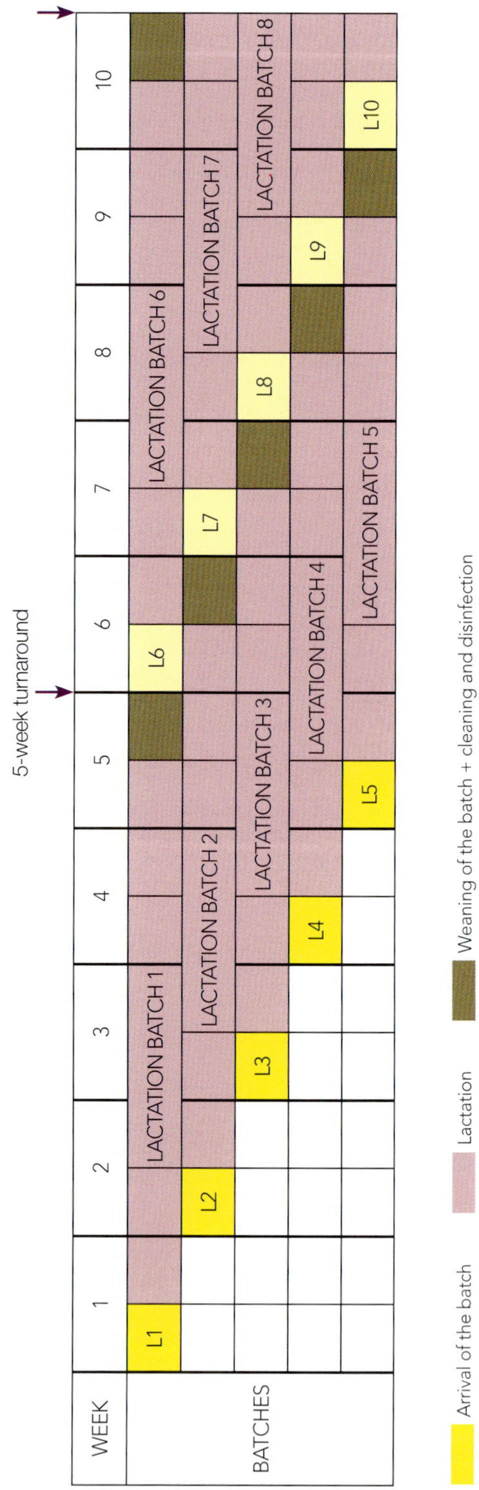

Two-weekly batch farrowing

This system is only recommended on farms with less than 800 sows. The size of the farrowing unit should allow a 4-week occupation. Weaning is performed at 21 days of age. Farrowings take place every two weeks; there will therefore be two batches at the same time in the farrowing unit.

Characteristics

- The resulting number of batches on the farm is 10.
- The work is organised so that the main task is weaning during one week and services and farrowing during the next.
- The main problem with this system is regular repeats (18-24 days), as they do not coincide with a service week (Fig. 7).
- When creating nurse sows, it should be borne in mind that most of the piglets in a batch are 15 days older than those in the next batch. Sows served between two batches or delayed sows are therefore used as nurse sows.
- This system maximises performance in the farrowing rooms, although it requires very short lactation periods and reduces the sanitation period, which is against the current EU Directive on animal welfare and health objectives.
- With this system, it is recommended to use an **extra** farrowing room to create nurse sows and house the sows served between the different batches.

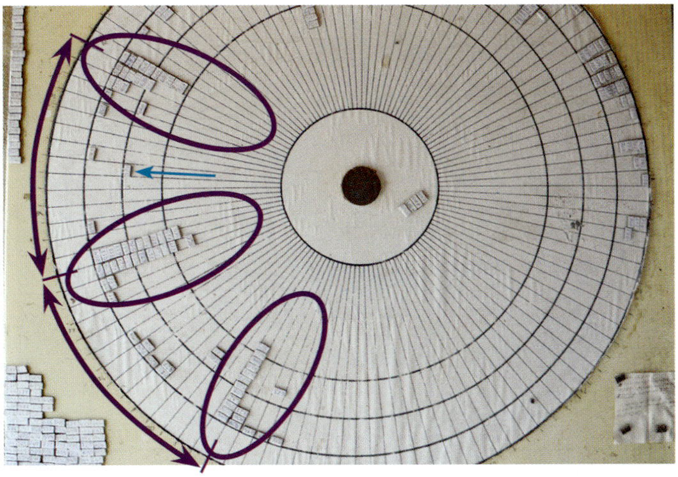

Figure 7 Circular calendar on a farm with a two-weekly BFS. The blue arrow represents one of the sows served out of sequence, normally as a result of regular repeats at 21 days.

With two-weekly batch farrowing, weaning usually takes place at 21 days of age. The farms on which this system is applied are most often old and of a reduced size and they do not usually have farrowing houses adapted to weaning every four weeks (Fig. 8).

The only way of weaning at 28 days of age with this system would be to have enough farrowing places available to be occupied for six weeks. Nonetheless, in this case it is better to use three-weekly batch farrowing, since the same number of farrowing places is necessary and work organisation is much better.

Three-weekly batch farrowing

Of the different batch farrowing systems, three-weekly batch farrowing is **the system with which work organisation is best**, as each week is dedicated to one of the main tasks on the operation: services, farrowings and weaning. Weaning takes place at 28 days of age (Fig. 9).

Characteristics

- The resulting number of batches on the operation is 7.
- The main inconvenient of this system is that it requires a larger number of farrowing places, as there are two batches in the farrowing unit at the same time. Furthermore, as there is a three-week interval between two batches, the total number of farrowing places will be calculated for 6 weeks of occupation. This system also requires a larger number of places for service-control.
- In this case, regular repeats are not a problem, as repeat sows will be served during a service week (every 21 days).
- Creating nurse sows is difficult with this system, and it is therefore very interesting to have an extra farrowing room for this type of management and to house the sows that are served out of sequence.

Figure 8 Diagram of a two-weekly batch farrowing system and weaning at 21 days of age. Farrowing units with 2 batches of different ages.

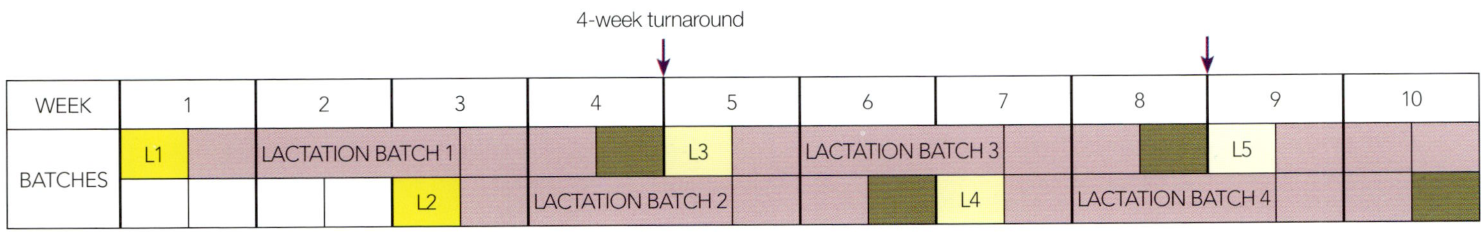

Figure 9 Diagram of a three-weekly batch farrowing system with weaning at 28 days of age. Two batches with a 3-week interval.

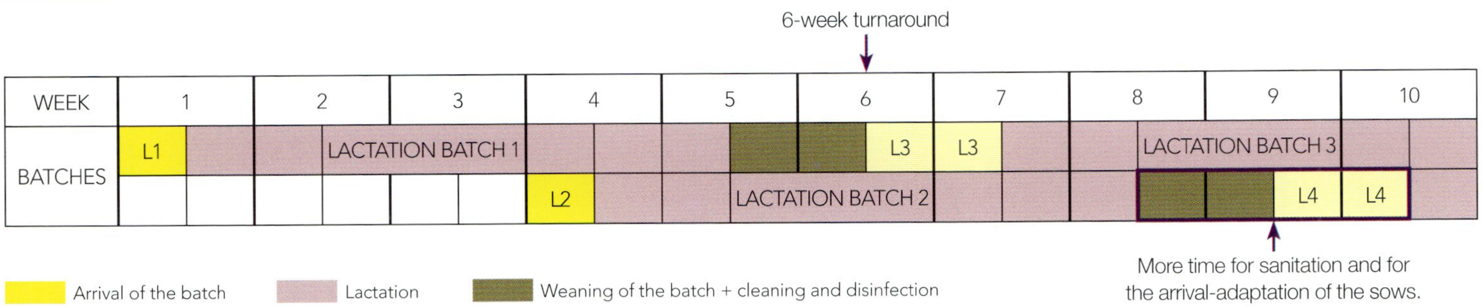

Four-weekly batch farrowing

This batch farrowing system is exclusively recommended to small farms. There is only one batch in the farrowing unit. The whole batch farrows and is weaned at the same time and an **all-in all-out** system is used in the farrowing unit (Fig. 10).

Characteristics

- The resulting number of batches on the operation is 5.
- As regards work organisation, the same as with two-weekly batch farrowing occurs: service weeks coincide with farrowing weeks.
- Sows that repeat within the regular cycle do not repeat during a service week.
- As most farrowings take place at the same time, managing nurse sows becomes very complex as it is not possible to use "**cascade**" or "**shunt**" fostering since there are no sows with different days in lactation*.
- A larger number of places for service-control are required.

Five-weekly batch farrowing

This system is recommended for very small farms. It is similar to four-weekly batch farrowing, with the advantage that it allows more flexibility as regards the age at weaning (Fig. 11).

Characteristics

- The resulting number of batches on the operation is 4.
- Work organisation is the same as with a three-weekly batch farrowing system.
- It allows weaning at 21 and 28 days of age.
- From a sanitary point of view, it is a very efficient system, as it allows longer sanitation periods in the farrowing rooms.
- Working with nurse sows is very difficult with this system.
- A larger number of places for service-control are required.
- Sows that repeat within the regular cycle are served out of sequence.

*A.N. This technique facilitates fostering for piglets of very few days of age, with sows that are at a much more advanced stage of lactation. It involves weaning the piglets of a sow after 21 days of lactation approximately, and using this sow to foster piglets a week younger, and so on, until a sow that has been lactating for a week can foster newborn piglets.

Figure 10 Diagram of a four-weekly batch farrowing system with weaning at 21 days of age. There is only one batch of the same age in the farrowing unit.

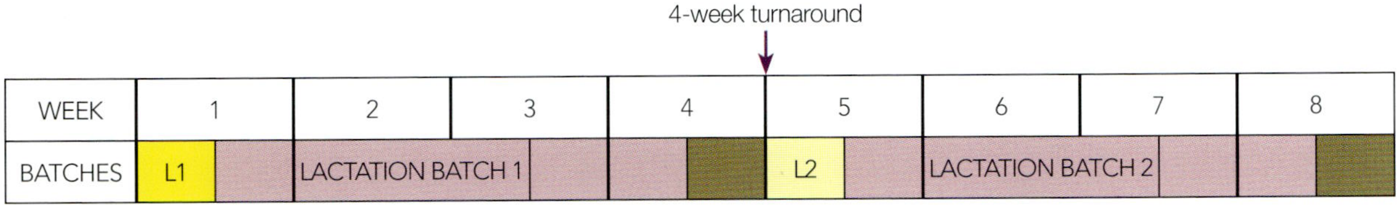

Figure 11 Diagram of a five-weekly batch farrowing system. There is only one batch of the same age in the farrowing unit.

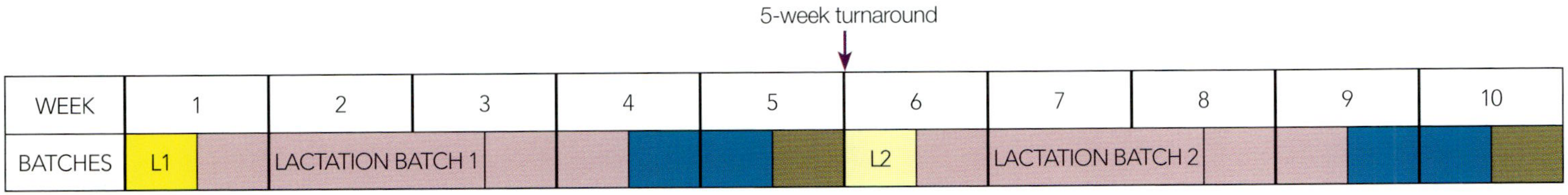

Figure 12 Diagram of a two-three-weekly batch farrowing system.

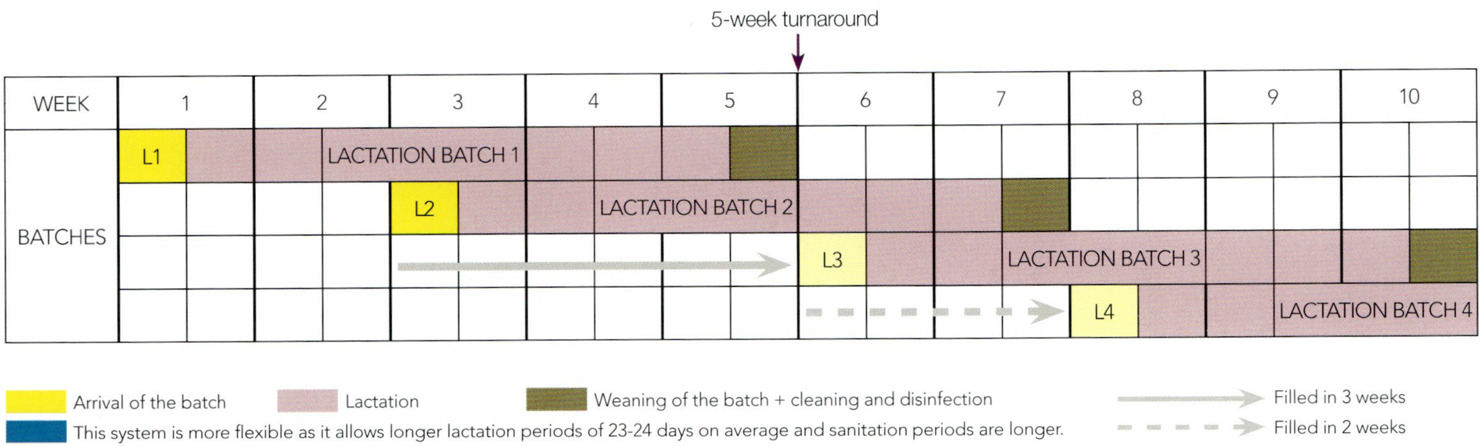

Three-two-weekly batch farrowing

This is a new option for batch management, in which three-weekly and two-weekly batch farrowing systems alternate (Fig. 12). The novelty of this system is that it achieves a 5-week turnaround in farrowing rooms.

Characteristics

- There are 8 productive batches of sows on the farm.
- It allows weaning to be performed every 28 days.
- A better optimisation of the farrowing rooms is achieved as compared with three-weekly batch farrowing.
- It is difficult to prepare nurse sows, as there are two batches of piglets with an age difference of 2 or 3 weeks at the same time in the farrowing unit.
- As regards work organisation, the same as with two-weekly batch farrowing occurs: service weeks coincide with farrowing weeks.

Table 1 shows a summary of the different types of batch farrowing systems (BFS) and the distribution of the main tasks.

Table 1 Task organisation diagram for batch-farrowing. Adapted from Casanovas, C. (2010). www.3tres3.com/manejo_en_bandas/beneficios-del-manejo-en-bandas-superiores-a-una-semana_2997/

Week	BFS 1w	BFS 2w	BFS 3w	BFS 4w	BFS 5w weaning at 21 days of age	BFS 5w weaning at 28 days	BFS 3-2 weaning at 28 days
1	S F W	W	W	W	W	W	W
2	S F W	S F	C	S F	C	S F	S F
3	S F W	W	P		P		
4	S F W	S F	W				W
5	S F W	W	C	W			S F
6	S F W	S F	P	S F	W	W	W
7	S F W	W	W		C	S F	S F
8	S F W	S F	C		P		
9	S F W	W	P	W			W

S: Service; F: Farrowing; W: Weaning.

Turnaround in farrowing rooms

One of the indices that are used to improve the occupation of the facilities on a pig farm is **turnaround** in the farrowing rooms, which is **the time lasting from the arrival of a batch of sows at a farrowing room to the moment when a new batch is moved to the same room.** It includes: filling of the room, farrowing, lactation, emptying and cleaning of the room and sanitation period.

On an increasingly frequent basis, the most efficient pig farms tend to increase the lactation period. Ideally, piglets should be weaned at 28 days of age and with an appropriate growth rate and weight, which will allow a good transition after weaning and greater economic efficiency, as it has been shown that **it is more economical to produce a kilogram of piglet with sow's milk than with feed.** In addition, long lactation periods favour an increase in reproductive efficiency, as they allow better uterine involution after farrowing. All these aspects have a positive impact on the cost of the piglet that is weaned at four weeks of age.

It is considered that ideally, there should be a five-week turnaround in farrowing rooms: four weeks of lactation and one week for the emptying, cleaning, sanitation and filling of the rooms. Thus, the size of a batch on a farm can be calculated by dividing the number of farrowing places by 5 in the case of a weekly batch farrowing system, and by 6 in the case of a three-weekly batch farrowing system. With other batch farrowing systems, prolonging lactation is more difficult without reducing the number of animals or increasing the number of farrowing places.

Many pig farms that work with hyperprolific genetic lines reduce the size of their batches of sows by 15-20 % in order to leave places in the farrowing rooms and introduce nurse sows. In these cases, the best option is to increase the number of farrowing places by 15-20 % so as not to underuse the rest of the facilities on the farm.

Ideally, piglets should be weaned at 28 days of age, with a 5-week turnaround in the farrowing rooms.

Farrowing and service targets

One of the factors with a greater impact on the results of a farm is the capacity to maintain a homogeneous batch size, that is to say, to reach the **farrowing target** of each batch. For this reason, it is essential to reach the service target, in order to subsequently maintain a constant number of farrowings on the operation.

On every operation, farmers should know very well what their service target is, depending on the batch farrowing system they use and farrowing rate of the farm. An example is shown in Table 2.

Table 2 Service target in function of the fertility rate on a farm with 750 productive sows.

Sows that need to be served every week to obtain 36 farrowings according to the expected fertility rate.							
Fertility rate (farrowings/ 100 services)	70 %	75 %	80 %	85 %	90 %	95 %	100 %
Sows to be served per week	51	48	45	42	40	38	36

Thus, the sows available to achieve the service target will be the sum of:

1. **Weaned sows**: easily predictable as the size of the batch is known. The sows that will be sent to slaughter due to low productivity, prolificacy, age, etc., after weaning must be deducted from this group.
2. **Repeat sows**: they usually represent a homogeneous percentage, which will vary depending on the fertility rate on the operation and on the time of the year.
3. **Gilts**: the number of gilts to be served is often going to determine whether the service target is going to be reached or not. It is therefore important to have as much information as possible about these sows (ideal age at first service, weight, previous heat dates, etc.).

The specific management measures applied for this purpose are explained later in this chapter (Page 78).

The service target shows the productive rate of each farm. The following formula is used to establish this target:

$$\text{Service target} = \frac{\text{farrowing target}}{\text{farrowing rate}} \times 100$$

It is advisable for farms to use record sheets on which the service target is shown clearly (Fig. 13).

Farm:												
Month:												
Service target												
		No. of services	Positive ultra-sound		No. of repeats		Abortions		Farrowings		Weaned	
Week			1st (24 d)	2nd (35 d)	REG (21-42 d)	IRREG (30-33 d)	No.	Days G	No.	TB	No.	TPW
	Weaned											
	Gilts											
	Repeat											
	Weaned											
	Gilts											
	Repeat											

Figure 13 Service target plan. REG: regular; IRREG: irregular; G: gestation; TB: total born; TPW: total piglets weaned.

Weekly breeding target: 57

Service week – Week from	to	Batch	No. serv.	Expected value	Expected value (%)
03/01/2011	09/01/2011	2011-1	56	57	98,2 %
10/01/2011	16/01/2011	2011-2	63	57	110,5 %
17/01/2011	23/01/2011	2011-3	51	57	89,5 %
24/01/2011	30/01/2011	2011-4	48	57	84,2 %
31/01/2011	06/02/2011	2011-5	51	57	89,5 %
07/02/2011	13/02/2011	2011-6	54	57	94,7 %
14/02/2011	20/02/2011	2011-7	54	57	94,7 %
21/02/2011	27/02/2011	2011-8	56	57	98,2 %
28/02/2011	06/03/2011	2011-9	55	57	96,5 %
//					
23/05/2011	29/05/2011	2011-21	52	57	91,2 %
30/05/2011	05/06/2011	2011-22	60	57	105,3 %
06/06/2011	12/06/2011	2011-23	65	57	114,0 %
13/06/2011	19/06/2011	2011-24	40	57	70,2 %
20/06/2011	26/06/2011	2011-25	55	57	96,5 %
27/06/2011	03/07/2011	2011-26	57	57	100,0 %
Totals			1438	1482	97,0 %

When the service target is not reached:
- The farrowing facilities are not used in the most optimal manner.

If more sows are served than expected:
- There will not be a sufficient number of farrowing pens available.
- Weaning will have to be performed several times a week or earlier than recommended.
- The sanitation period will be short.

PROBLEMS

If it is much lower than the expected value:
- Program the arrival of a large number of replacement gilts to be introduced in the next cycle.

Figure 14 Weekly service target plan created with a computer programme for the technical management of breeding sows. Consequences of the difference between the real number of services on the farm and the expected values.

Reaching service targets

To reach service targets, various management measures need to be applied regarding replacement gilts. These are explained next.

The availability of gilts is essential to reach service targets and create the necessary batches. The number of gilts needed should therefore be estimated in advance. This is possible by predicting the replacement rate, and to do so an **Annual replacement plan** should be prepared. Many computer programmes for the technical management of sow farms have applications to help calculate this value (Fig. 15).

Once the gilts are on the farm, it is necessary to ensure that they come into heat (the physical exposure to a boar is usually the most effective technique to induce puberty in gilts). Knowing the exact dates at which they come into heat is essential to be able to complete the batches. This way, different strategies, which are sometimes complementary, will be used.

Pigmanager

Service, farrowing and weaning plan (management of replacement gilts)
11/01/2010

Farm 60: Urba Ganadera (067NA064) — Record sheet: 1.2.7 Wednesday January 13, 2010 Page: 1

Week	1	2	3	4	5	6	7	8	9	10	11	12	13	14	15	16	17
Date	11/01	18/01	25/01	01/02	08/02	15/02	22/02	01/03	08/03	15/03	22/03	29/03	05/04	12/04	19/04	26/04	03/05
Expected farrowings																	
Cycle 1	13	8	5	6	4	7	7	11	7	6	10	7		4	9	9	
Cycle 2	6	11	3	8	13	17	3	12	1	9	3	7	2	15	1	6	
Cycle 3	4	10	6	12	3	3		2		9		10		7		8	
Cycle 4	1	8	1	8	4	4		8		6	2	15	1	20	3	10	
Cycle 5		4		9		2		10		9		4		4	1	8	
Cycle 6	1	4		2		1		9	1	3		4		5		1	
Cycle 7		1		7		2	1	3		5		2		6		7	
Cycle 8		4		6	1			4		3		2		4		1	
Cycle 9				1		1		1									
Cycle 10																	
Total	25	50	15	59	25	37	11	60	9	50	15	51	3	65	14	50	
To be replaced*	2	7	2	10	3	5	1	10	1	8	1	8	0	11	1	8	
In prod.	23	43	13	49	22	32	10	50	8	42	14	43	3	54	13	42	
Expected weanings**				23	43	13	49	22	32	10	50	8	42	14	43		
Expected services					23	43	13	49	22	32	10	50	8	42	14	43	
Replacement gilts***						18				32				39			
Gilts available to be served****								34									

* Replacement rate

cycle 1	3.0		
cycle 2	7.0	cycle 7	23.0
cycle 3	10.0	cycle 8	29.0
cycle 4	12.0	cycle 9	32.0
cycle 5	15.0	cycle 10	45.0
cycle 6	19.0	cycle 11>	45.0

** Expected lactation period: 23 days
*** Target no. of services in 4 weeks: 146
**** Target age at first service: 240

Figure 15 Replacement plan created with a computer programme for the technical management of breeding sows.

Heat record sheet

With this sheet it is possible to know the date of first service and the number of gilts that are expected to be brought in the batch. Heat should be induced daily in gilts while they are still in confinement. Usually, ear-tags are placed on gilts when they come into heat and a number is assigned to each of them. The number of each gilt and dates of onset of oestrus should be written down in a notebook (Fig. 16). Gilts will be served three weeks after the second heat. This system is useful on small farms where few replacement gilts are brought into each batch.

Farm:			
Date:			
No. of sows	HEAT 1	HEAT 2	SERVICE
201	06/05/13 (week 19)	28/05/13 (week 22)	week 25

Figure 16 Example of a record sheet with service at the third heat.

Three-colour system

This method is the most visual and easy to apply (Fig. 17). Sows are marked with sprays of different colours every week (red, blue and green) and a number from 1 to 7, which indicates the day of the week on which the sow has come into heat. For example, the sow's back is marked in red on the first week: 1 if she comes into heat on Monday, 2 if she does so on Tuesday, 3 if it is on Wednesday and so forth. Blue is used to mark the number the following week and green the next. This way, it is possible to know visually how many sows can be brought in a batch, what day they will come into heat approximately and whether or not they will need hormonal treatments to be included in the batch.

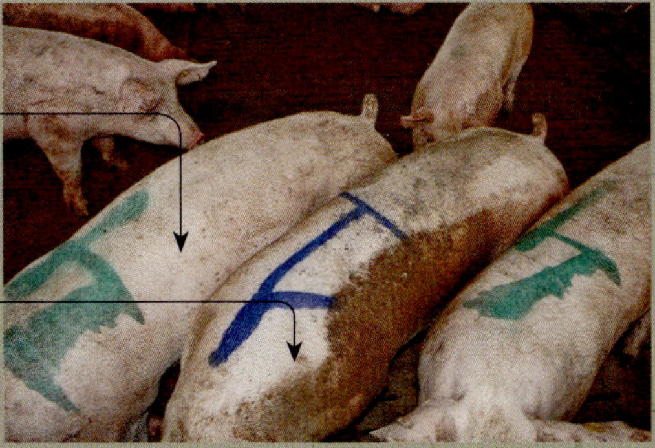

Sow 4: Comes into heat on the Monday of the 2nd week.

Sow 1: Comes into heat on the Thursday of the 3rd week.

Figure 17 Three-colour system.

Hormonal treatments

The best option to introduce gilts in a batch is to do so in a natural way and with the methods that have been explained in the previous sections. Nonetheless, when contact with a male is not effective, or when it is necessary to introduce gilts at a specific time to adjust the number of sows in a batch, hormonal treatments may be used to allow the size of the batch to be maintained. There are two main types of treatment:

Gonadotropin

Seric and chorionic gonadotropins (PMSG and HCG) are hormones responsible for follicular development, which are administered together by intramuscular route. These hormones are used to induce follicular development when it is non-existent or to boost it.

Synthetic progesterone derivatives

Progesterone is in charge of blocking other hormones that cause the maturation of new follicles and therefore the subsequent onset of oestrus in the sow. The function of progesterone is to block the secretion of the follicle-stimulating hormone (FSH) and luteinising hormone (LH) necessary for the growth of new follicles and secretion of oestrogens, and therefore for sows to come into heat. As a result, a few days of treatment with synthetic derivatives of progesterone followed by the interruption of the treatment favour the onset of oestrus in the sow.

These treatments are administered orally.

They may be used when sows need to be introduced in a batch at a specific time so they are served during a service week. These hormonal treatments are used mainly on farms with batch farrowing every two weeks or more.

- If oestrus is not monitored, a treatment of at least 18 days is recommended with the only condition of ensuring that gilts have previously been in heat at least twice. The treatment must therefore start 22-23 days before service. The sows that receive the treatment come into heat in groups 4-5 days after stopping the administration of progesterone.
- If heats are monitored, the treatment should be started before natural progesterone levels start to decrease (on day 13-14 of the oestrus cycle). The follicular phase, heat and ovulation resume when the treatment is interrupted (Fig.18). It is therefore best to end the treatment when the batch of sows in which the gilts have to be introduced is weaned. Gilts come into heat in 4-5 days after stopping the administration of the progestogen. This way, the cost of treatment is reduced.

In order to monitor heats and know clearly when to start and finish the hormonal treatment, the unit supervisor usually records the information on a sheet (Fig. 19).

Figure 18 Use of progestogens.

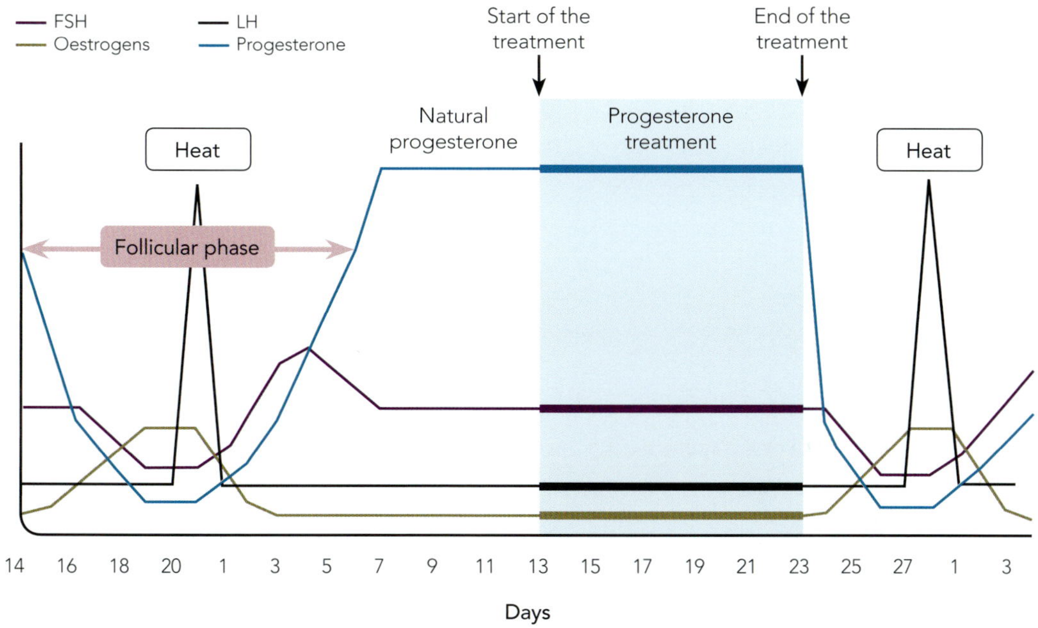

Figure 19 Sheet to record heats and treatment administered.

Farm:							
Date:							
			Expected				
	No. of sows	HEAT 1	HEAT 2	Start date of treatment	End date of treatment	Service	
Monday	461, 435, 423, 412	3/02	24/02	3/03	16/03	26/03	
Tuesday							
Wednesday							
Thursday							
Friday							
Saturday							
Sunday							

4 Sow feeding during the peripartum period

Introduction

The increase in the productivity of modern sows involves a series of changes in their diet. The level of productive demand they are subject to entails an increase in their feeding needs and as a result, traditional sow feeding patterns must be reviewed. On the one hand, as sow productivity may exceed 30 piglets/sow/year, new feeding strategies are necessary in all the phases of production, especially during the peripartum and lactation periods, and on the other hand, feeding costs need to be reduced by means of an increase in the animal's efficiency and feeding management strategies (feed formulation, feeding curves, etc.) to optimise the resources available, which are increasingly expensive and scarce.

Sow feeding is one of the main expenses of swine operations. This concept represents approximately 25 % of the total cost for the production of a piglet. That is why it is necessary to minimise the cost of sow feeding and maximise their productive potential, by means of feeding strategies and the administration of appropriate rations and diets for each productive phase and type of animal, both in terms of age (future breeding females, gilts, multiparous sows), breed and genetic line, using the feeding options that offer the best price/quality relationship at all times.

Appropriate feeding management is essential to optimise the farm's profitability.

The new genetic lines of breeding sows have greater mammary development, a greater milk production and require a good body condition to achieve good results. In the last few years, prolificacy and weight at birth have significantly increased, with litters that weigh up to 20 kilograms, half of which are gained in the last third of gestation. The sows with which farmers work nowadays keep growing throughout their cycles and their age must therefore be taken into account when calculating their maintenance requirements.

Every genetic line has different nutritional needs and feed intake capacities. Feeding curves for sows must therefore be adapted to their real needs.

Finally, the body condition of sows should also be monitored. This is another task that should be performed routinely on farms as one of the necessary measures to optimise feeding management.

Nutritional goals

During the final stage of gestation, it is necessary to follow an appropriate feeding programme that covers the sows' maintenance and production requirements, which have considerably increased in the last few years due to the greater prolificacy of breeding sows.

Objectives of feeding management in this phase:

- Minimising problems and difficulties during farrowing: slow farrowing, constipation, postpartum dysgalactia syndrome (PDS).
- Preventing problems derived from overfeeding, which cause overweight, increase in piglet mortality at birth and reduced milk production by the sow.
- Ensuring an appropriate birth weight of piglets.
- Ensuring the sow's lactation period starts correctly and favouring feed intake during lactation.
- Favouring colostrum production.
- Ensuring an appropriate body condition of sows to prevent catabolic processes, which involve a risk of ketosis.

Feeding needs in the last stage of gestation and during the peripartum period

Sows' nutritional needs have varied over time, in the same way as their genetic type and productivity have evolved. Thus, sows have different maintenance and production requirements. However, these requirements are not the same if the animal is a 160-kg gilt or a 250-kg multiparous sow. They vary in function of the environmental temperature and degree of mobility of the animals, which depends on the production system used (free-access stalls, electronic feeding station, etc.). Farm productivity should also be borne in mind, since feeding requirements are higher if productivity is increased.

During the peripartum period, the changes made in feeding management practices are: an increase in the number of meals (sows go from receiving one single ration per day to receiving 2 or 3), the use of two or three different types of feed instead of one and an increase in the size of the ration to adapt it to the growing requirements of sows. Furthermore, it should be borne in mind that the sow barely eats on the day of farrowing.

Nutritional requirements for maintenance

These are the feeding requirements that provide animals with the energy necessary for their metabolism and to perform different activities, as well as the essential nutrients for the development and maintenance of body structures. They are divided into:

- **Vital feeding requirements.** These are the nutrients required by the animal to survive. In gestating sows, they represent 80 % of the total requirements.
- **Thermoregulation requirements.** They correspond to the nutrients used by the sow to maintain her body temperature. They are highly conditioned by environmental factors such as the temperature of the room where the sows are housed.
- **Requirements for activity and movement.** These requirements are conditioned by the animal's weight and type of housing. With the current European animal welfare legislation and new group housing for gestating sows, it should be borne in mind that sows do more physical exercise than when they were housed in crates. As a result, they need a higher-energy ration, which translates into greater feeding requirements.

Production requirements

These are the nutrient requirements that will provide sows with the energy and nutrients they need for an optimal production. Among these, we can highlight:

- **Requirements for foetal and uterine growth and growth of foetal membranes.** These are the requirements to ensure foetal growth and the development of the placentas and foetal membranes. Approximately 50 % of these nutrients and energy are used in the last 2-3 weeks of gestation, as can be seen in Figure 1. Figure 2 details the growth rate of the different tissues that form the foetus, placenta and membranes throughout gestation.
  These needs represent 4 % of the total required by the animal.
- **Requirements for mammary development.** They represent 1.5 % of the total. This growth takes place at the end of gestation and during lactation. It is important that feeding during gestation does not lead to an excess of fat in the mammary glands, since it should favour the growth of the gland tissue that produces milk at the expense of fat tissue.
- **Requirements for breeding sow growth and recovery of reserves.** These are the requirements necessary for the sow to grow and recover her body condition. These energy and nutritional needs vary in function of body condition at weaning. In the case of gilts, their growth requirements are significant and it should be borne in mind that, in new genetic lines, this growth continues at least until the sixth farrowing (Fig. 3).

A sow's nutrient requirements for foetal and udder development are highest in the last third of gestation, and more specifically in the last 2-3 weeks of this phase in the case of foetal development. This therefore requires the ration to be increased significantly during this period.

A sow's requirements for foetal development are highest in the last 2-3 weeks of gestation and the ration therefore needs to be increased considerably during this period.

Figure 1 Weight evolution of piglets, placentas, fluids and mammary glands during gestation. From: Gil, J. Piglet weight at birth. *Technical seminar MSD-Inga Food*, Lérida. 2014.

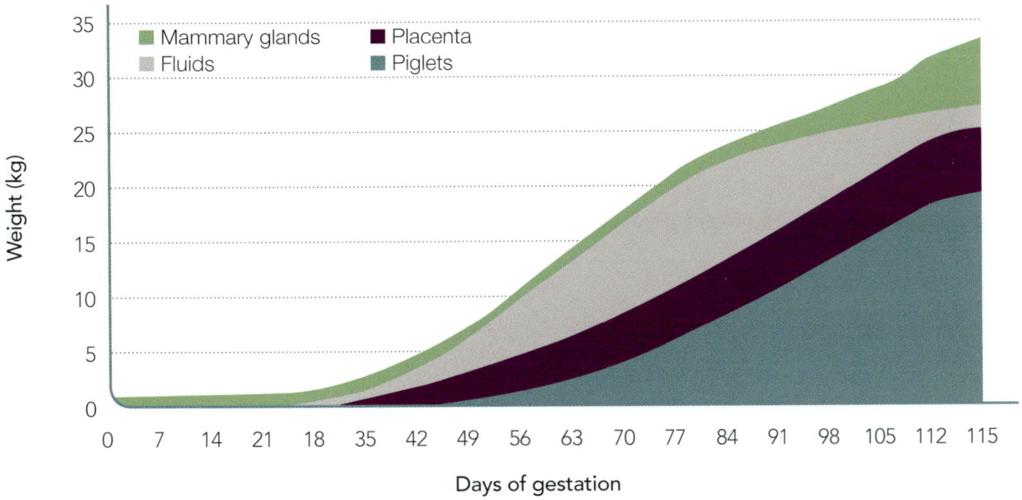

Figure 2 Evolution of the different maternal tissues and composition of the weight gained by the sow during gestation. From Le Treut, Y. *Alimentación y nutrición de la cerda gestante I*, 2006.

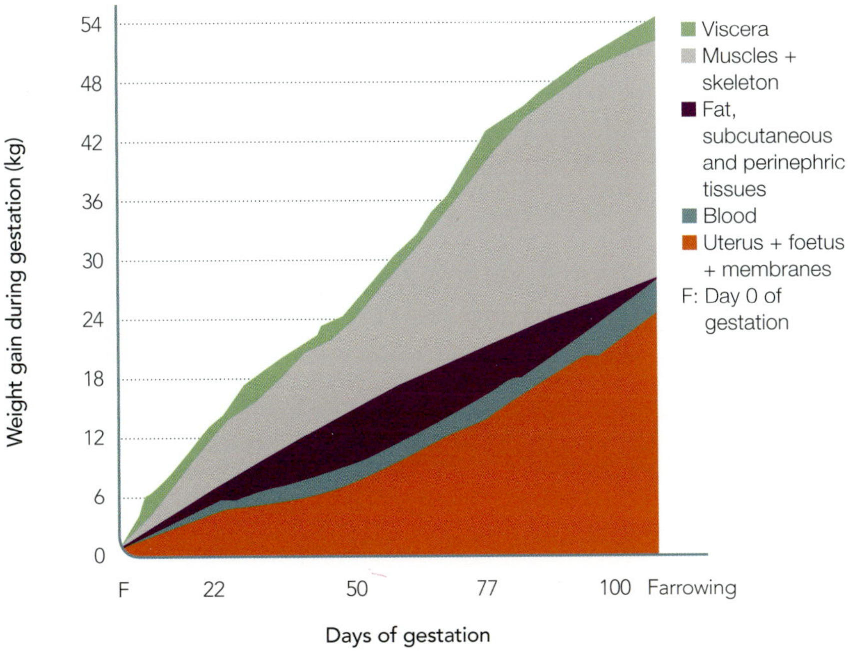

Figure 3 Evolution of sow weight depending on cycle and age. Adapted from Ramaekers, P. *Sow feed formulation and feeding programs*, 2013.

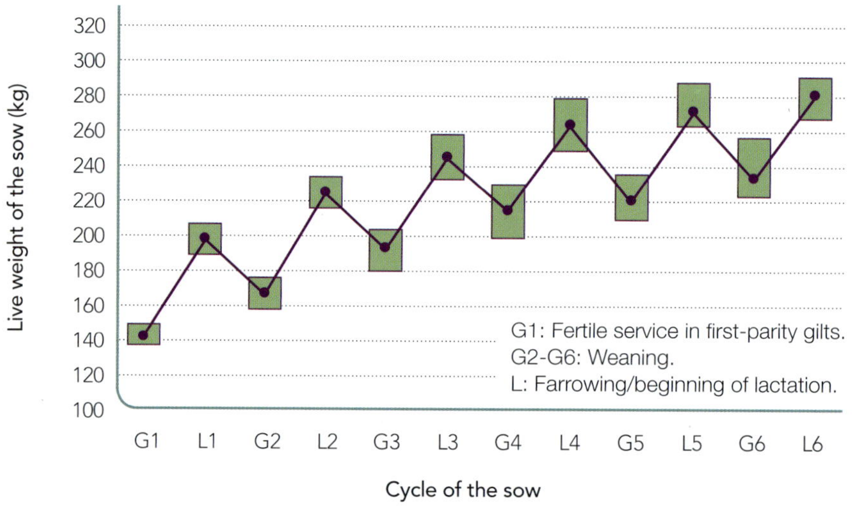

Water needs

It is essential to have fresh drinking water available, with no unusual smell or flavour and at an appropriate temperature, as this helps to achieve maximum water intake. The data available regarding water intake in gestating sows is highly variable, with an average value of 10-12 litres daily, although it can vary between 6 l and 22 l/day, according to the season and above all to the environmental temperature. Once lactation has started, water intake increases significantly to 30-40 litres daily.

A circumstance that must be borne in mind is that there is a directly proportional relationship between water and feed intakes, especially in the case of dry feeding. As a result, a low water intake implies a low feed intake.

> There is a directly proportional relationship between water and feed intakes.

Water requirements are met in three ways:

1. Drinking water. It is the most important source of water.
2. Water in the ration. Very important source of water in the case of liquid feed, with which it can represent 75 % of the total intake.
3. Water of metabolic origin. Water is released as the resulting metabolite in specific vital biochemical reactions. It is of little relevance.

The microbiological and biochemical quality of water has an influence on the health state of sows and special attention must therefore be paid to these parameters to ensure the water given to the animals is safe to drink (Table 1).

Table 1 Reference values for Spain. Source: Annex I. Spanish Royal Decree 140/2003 of 7 February, which establishes the quality criteria for water for human consumption. *BOE*-A-2003-3596.

	Parameter	Value
Physical-chemical quality	pH	6.5-9.5
	Turbidity	< 1 NTU[1]
	Salinity	< 1500 ppm
	Nitrates	< 50 mg/l
	Nitrites	< 0.1 mg/l
	Sulphates	< 240 mg/l
Microbiological quality	*Escherichia coli*	0 CFU[2] in 100 ml
	Enterococci	0 CFU in 100 ml
	Clostridium perfringens (including spores)	0 CFU in 100 ml

[1]CFU: Colony forming units; [2]NTU: Nephelometric Turbidity Units.

Water quality must be controlled, or else some risks are assumed:

- Acid or basic water and hard water: they cause problems in circuits and piping (corrosion, incrustations).
- Water with high levels of sulphates, nitrates, dissolved solids or bacterial contamination: enteric problems.
- Water with high levels of sulphates or nitrites and nitrates, very hard water, water with a high bacterial contamination: they are the cause of general disorders (respiratory problems, abortions, growth delays, etc.).

Drinkers should have an appropriate flow for sows to be able to drink a sufficient amount of water without any difficulty. The minimum flow rate should be 4 l/minute, 8-10 l/minute being the most appropriate range during lactation for the most productive genetic lines. The flow rate of the drinkers should be checked regularly to avoid low flows that would compromise water intake.

Nipple drinkers and water troughs should be accessible to sows so they can easily drink water. Furthermore, it is recommended that the drinking system be similar to the one used in the farm's gestation stalls. Nevertheless, if this is not possible, it is important to help the sows, if necessary, to adapt to and learn how to drink from other types of drinking systems.

It is essential to ensure water is available to the sows during the peripartum period, as on the days close to farrowing their water intake is maintained or even increased. In this sense, it is also particularly important to ensure water is available during farrowing, as sows lose a great amount of fluids at this time. When farrowing is imminent, it is thus necessary to make sure the drinking system is in perfect condition and works correctly.

Feeding at the end of gestation and during the peripartum period

Most foetal development occurs at the end of gestation, and it is therefore necessary to design a feeding curve for each type of sow to achieve the highest possible litter weight at farrowing. The mobilisation of body reserves, especially proteins, should be prevented. The feed ration should thus be increased during this period.

The amount of feed that should be administered to a sow is decided in function of her body condition. On average, in the last third of gestation, 2.5-3 kg of feed should be administered daily. This amount should be reduced to 2 kg on the day of farrowing. Once a sow has farrowed, her ration should be increased in the fastest possible manner to reach 6-8 kg of feed one week later, taking into account that in the lactation phase, the sow should be fed ad libitum to a maximum of 10-11 kg of feed per day.

Rations should be administered once daily during gestation and three or four times daily in the farrowing house. This is due to the fact that, in the farrowing house, it is necessary to ensure maximum feed intake and the feed must therefore be distributed in several meals. When temperatures are high, meals should be given at the coolest times of the day: early in the morning, late in the afternoon and in the evening.

On the day of farrowing, a sow should ingest a maximum of 2 kg of feed, although it is normal for some of them not to eat anything on that day. Due to the circumstances of farrowing, the animal should not be disturbed. If her intake is minimal, the feed should be removed and the feed trough should be cleaned.

Sows undergo a significant physiological change at farrowing. There is a switch from gestation to lactation. It is a crucial time at which considerable metabolic changes take place. Sows start producing milk instead of foetuses and foetal membranes and require greater resources for this process.

Types of diets for sows during the peripartum period

During the peripartum period, sows eat different types of feed depending on their physiological state and on the different feed distribution systems used on the farm (Table 2).

The diets that are normally used during the peripartum period depend on the facilities and location of the sows on the operation. **Gestation diets** are normally used and replaced by **lactation diets** once the sows are moved to the farrowing unit.

Table 2 Different feeding alternatives used short before farrowing.

	Days of the cycle			
	< 100 days of gestation	100-114 days of gestation	Farrowing	Lactation
Type of diet	Gestation diet	Prepartum diet		Lactation diet
	Gestation diet		Lactation diet	
	Gestation diet	Lactation diet		
	Gestation diet			Lactation diet

There are specific types of feed for this production stage –**prepartum diets**–, which are formulated according to the sow's needs and foetal growth at each stage. Their use on farms depends to a great extent on whether it is possible to administer them, as they require a two-loop feed distribution system in the gestation and farrowing units (it would also be useful for other types of feed such as those administered to gilts), or sufficient personnel to distribute the rations manually.

> It should always be borne in mind that feed changes must be made gradually.

Normally, the diet used during the peripartum period is a lactation diet, for reasons related to work organisation and farm facilities, as the sows are already housed in the farrowing room and fed using an automated feeding system. However, on farms where husbandry practices are more sophisticated or with an automated two-loop feed distribution system, sows can eat two or three different types of feed, changing from a gestation to a prepartum diet, or directly to a lactation diet. This is important to bear in mind when formulating the ration in order to prepare diets with similar raw materials and prevent problems of feed rejection.

Types of feed according to the physiological stage

Gestation diets

They should satisfy the needs for foetal and mammary growth at the end of gestation and prevent the mobilisation of the sow's reserves, especially proteins, in the last third of gestation.

They are low-energy and low-protein diets, as the gestation anabolism of sows is taken advantage of at this stage (Table 3).

Prepartum diets

These are designed to be administered from the moment the sows enter the farrowing house (days 100-107 of gestation) until day 3-4 pospartum. These diets facilitate the farrowing process and the start of lactation and reduce the risk of postpartum dysgalactia syndrome.

Characteristics

- High level of proteins.
- High levels of digestible lysine and threonine.
- High palatability.
- High level of high digestible fibres (e.g. beetroot pulp), for a sensation of digestive well-being and to prevent constipation. It also helps to prevent gestational diabetes.
- Low electrolyte balance. With the addition of $CaCl_2$, piglet survival is improved during lactation and urinary infections in sows are reduced. On the other hand, the addition of calcium is made easier, thus preventing problems of sows with posterior paralysis at the end of gestation due to calcium deficiency.
- Other recommended ingredients in these diets:
  - Ω-3 fatty acids. They improve piglet vitality, prolong gestation and speed up farrowing. They are precursors of icosanoids that improve the immune development and intestinal absorption.
  - Flavours, so foetuses or piglets become accustomed to the flavour and smell of the feed through their mother (imprinting*). Anise-derived flavours are used, as well as some essential fatty acids.
- When many constipation problems are observed, the addition of laxatives is recommended, such as magnesium sulphate at 0.75-1 %, or potassium chlorate at 0.75 %.

One of the main factors limiting the use of prepartum diets is their distribution. In the case of small farms, it should be carried out using bags, which greatly complicates daily tasks. On large operations, a two-loop feed distribution system is recommended for gestation and/or farrowing units.

According to the studies carried out by Y-K. Han et al. (2009), a glucose intake of 150-450 g per sow and day for five days before farrowing favours a higher birth weight of piglets and leads to a decrease in the sow's feed intake.

*A.N. Imprinting: This term is used in psychology and ethology to refer to a rapid learning process that takes place at a critical time of development. In this specific case, it refers to the addition of a specific flavour in the sow's diet, so that it passes to her milk and her piglets become familiarised with its taste. This flavour is added in the first feed for piglets, in order to facilitate the adaptation to their new diet.

Lactation diets

These diets are more concentrated than gestation diets as regards energy and proteins (Table 3), as producing milk requires a greater protein and energy intake than producing foetuses. These need to meet the requirements associated with milk production, as these latter have increased considerably with the new genetic lines of hyperprolific sows, and with the maintenance of the sow's body condition during this phase, to ensure she does not end lactation with a poor body condition.

Table 3 Standard nutritional characteristics of diets used during the peripartum period.

	GESTATION DIET	PREPARTUM DIET	LACTATION DIET
NE (kcal/kg)	2,140-2,250	2,290	2,400
CP (%)	12.05-14.50	17-18.50	18.00
CF (%)	6.50-8.00	6.00-8.00	4.00
Ca (%)	0.80	1.00	1.00
DIGESTIBLE LYSINE (%)	0.45	0.78	0.84
Na (%)	0.20	0.20-0.25	0.25-0.30

NE: net energy; CP: crude protein; CF: crude fibre; Ca: calcium; Na: sodium.

Lactation diets may be used during the last stage of gestation, but the ration should be adapted to prevent excessive fattening of the sows.

Feeding management depends on each farm's facilities, and the range of diets administered is that which is most appropriate to maximise production and minimise costs (Table 2).

4

5

Types of feed according to their physical form

On Spanish farms, the feed administered during the peripartum period is nearly always in dry from, although in numerous countries, particularly in northern Europe, liquid feeding is often used as it facilitates the addition of byproducts.

Dry diets

During the peripartum phase, most of the feed administered to sows is in the form of **pellets**, as its distribution is easier and it prevents wastage and facilitates the addition of certain byproducts. An average pellet diameter of 3-3.5 mm (Fig. 4) is recommended.

Feed is sometimes administered in **meal form** to prevent digestive problems or to facilitate the addition of a prophylactic treatment, but its distribution is more complicated since it increases wastage and the intake per sow is lower (Fig. 5).

Another form of presentation for feed is **mash**, when some of the ingredients make the pelleting process difficult, such as fats (Figs. 6).

As a general rule, the particles should have a size of 0.6-0.7 mm; thinner particles may cause ulcer problems as well as an increase in production costs. In addition, some raw materials cannot be ground thinner without causing manufacturing problems.

6

Figure 4 Feed for breeding sows. Pellets.

Figure 5 Feed for breeding sows. Meal form.

Figure 6 Feed for breeding sows. Mash feed.

The feed is usually administered to the sows in the farrowing unit in individual feed troughs. The feed is distributed manually (Fig. 7) or with an automated dispenser (Figs. 8, 9 and 10). It is also possible to make the feed available ad libitum using a hopper feeder, but this system is not recommended because individual intake is not monitored correctly and sows sometimes waste significant amounts of feed when playing with the hopper's mechanism.

It is very important to provide fresh feed in order to maximise its intake during this phase. The feed remaining in the trough from the previous feeding should be removed before the next administration, as on numerous occasions it ferments when mixed with water.

Feed dispensers must allow the ration to be adjusted easily. Their correct functioning must be checked and it should be borne in mind that dispensers regulate the volume of feed; as feed density can considerably vary, it is necessary to regularly weigh the feed used on the farm to adjust the ration. Table 4 shows the relationship between feed volume and density and its weight equivalents.

Feed density is variable and it is therefore necessary to weigh the different types of feed when these arrive at the farm to adjust the volumes in the feed dispensers.

Table 4 Amount of feed (kg) corresponding to the indicated volume, in function of feed density. Adapted from Casanovas, C. (2013).

Raw material	Density kg/litre	Volume of feed dispensed (litres)			
		5	6	7	8
	0.4	2.00	2.40	2.80	3.20
Meal	0.45	2.25	2.70	3.15	3.60
	0.50	2.50	3.00	3.50	4.00
	0.55	2.75	3.30	3.85	4.40
Pellets	0.60	3.00	3.60	4.20	4.80
	0.65	3.25	3.90	4.55	5.20

Figure 7 Manual feeding in farrowing unit with feed trough.

Figure 8 Automated feeding in farrowing unit. The dispensers and feed troughs may be observed in the image.

Figure 9 Detail of the feed dispensers with volume markings.

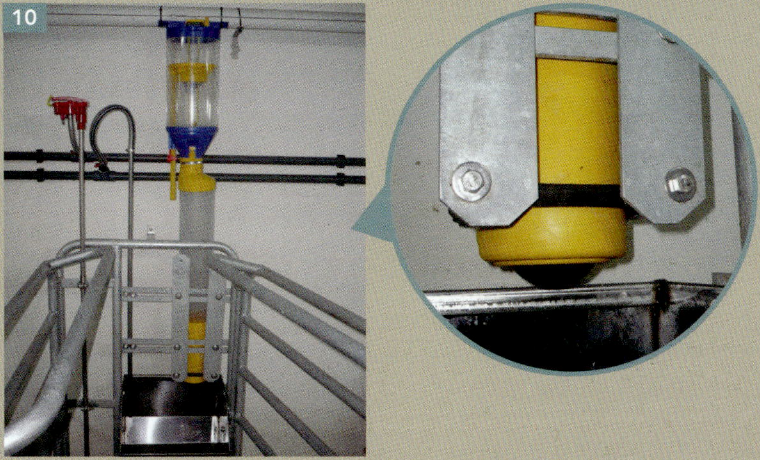

Figure 10 Feeding-ball system in a farrowing unit. In the enlarged image it is possible to see the characteristics of the lower part of the feeder with the feeding ball.

The personnel in the gestation unit should control the dispensers daily in function of the feeding curves for each individual or group of sows. If rations are distributed by means of electronic devices, it must be ensured that the settings are correct and the devices work correctly.

Liquid feeding

Liquid feeding is based on the preparation of a soup with water, feed and byproducts. The range of raw materials that can be used is considerably wider and can include byproducts (e.g. whey, byproducts of beer brewing or of the industrial processing of potatoes, etc.). This system is of great interest in countries or regions where these types of byproducts are available close to farms, since it offers possibilities to reduce the cost of the ration.

This feeding system requires a more expensive infrastructure and has higher maintenance costs than traditional dry feeding systems. It requires careful management in order to avoid problems of abnormal fermentation that may have severe consequences on the health of the animals on the farm. In most cases, it is necessary to add acidifiers to the mix.

The intake capacity of sows increases with this system, which is very interesting in the lactation period, as sows may increase their daily intake of dry matter by up to 10-30 %, especially in warm seasons.

There are new liquid feeding systems for lactation fitted with probes that regulate intakes. This prevents wastage and facilitates the individual feeding of each sow (Fig. 11).

Figure 11 Liquid feeding system in a farrowing room. Picture courtesy of José Andrés Iñigo (INTIA).

Feeding curves

Feeding sows individually in function of their age, breed and physiological state is essential for proper feeding management. It is necessary to feed each sow with her corresponding ration and feeding curves for multiparous sows and gilts must therefore be prepared according to their body conditions.

The feeding curves should be reviewed at least twice a year and the needs of each farm should be assessed in function of the animals' genetics, the facilities, season, technical and economical results and body condition.

Traditionally, feed intake was excessively restricted several days before and after farrowing, which translated into a lower milk production. However, nowadays, a much lower restriction is recommended, as can be seen in Figure 12.

Figure 12 Recommended (multiparous sows and gilts) and traditional feeding curves for the peripartum period in sows with a normal body condition.

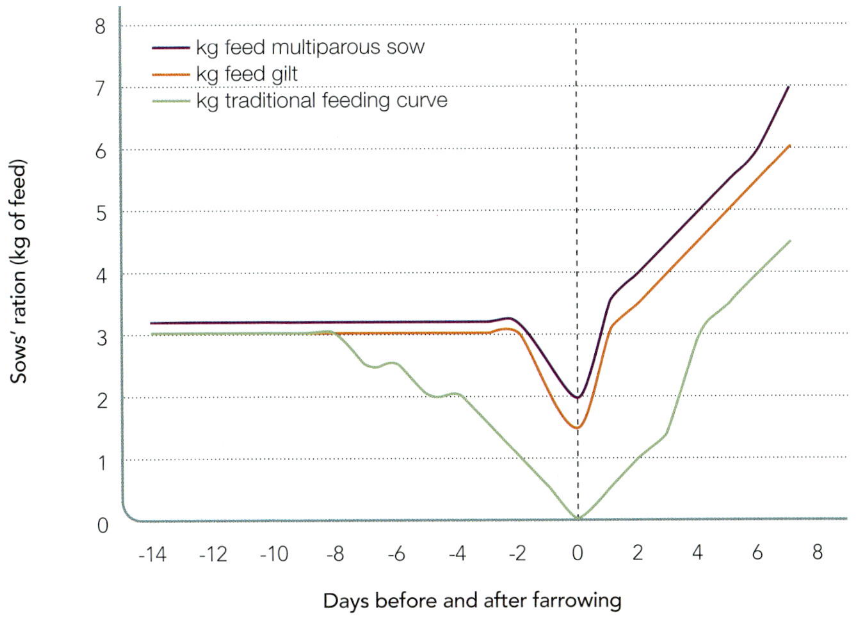

It is also very important to adjust the ration on the days before and after birth, taking into account the changes in the type of feed (gestation diet, prepartum diet, lactation diet) and in the amount fed and daily feeding frequency.

From day 90 of gestation, the ration should be increased by 0.5 to 0.75 kg/day to levels of 3.2 kg in multiparous sows, in order to avoid catabolic states and prevent them from using their own reserves to cover their needs for foetal and mammary growth. Excessive feed intakes should also be avoided so that sows are not overweight when entering the farrowing unit, as the risk of dystocia increases, and it has been demonstrated that overweight sows have a reduced feed intake during lactation, which is vital for milk production.

Feeding should not be excessively restricted in the last third of gestation, as clinical or subclinical ketosis may appear during the prepartum period and compromise the normal farrowing process and start of lactation.

The same feeding recommendations as for multiparous sows should be applied in the case of gilts, with the same factors in mind, although their important growth requirements should also be taken into account. Replacement gilts are the farm's future and they must therefore be fed correctly. Several authors recommend using the **flushing** technique in gilts and increasing the ration to twice the usual one two weeks before the first service, so as to favour a greater ovulation rate and improve prolificacy in the next cycle.

5 Sow and piglet management during farrowing

Preparation of the farrowing house

The objective is to guarantee the appropriate cleaning and disinfection of the farrowing unit before farrowings take place, and to check that the facilities are working properly and all the necessary material to assist farrowings is available. In the same way, it is advisable to ensure that the sows and piglets have all the elements necessary for the farrowing process to take place in the fastest, most natural and most comfortable manner possible.

Cleaning and disinfection of the farrowing house and sows

Prior to the sows entering the farrowing room, any organic matter should be removed from the floor and the manure pits should be emptied and washed. Next, the farrowing rooms should be properly washed, in particular the walls and floors, as well as all the equipment (feed troughs, crates, dispensers, etc.). In order to remove the remnants of organic matter, the use of detergents, which allow a better elimination of dirt, is recommended (Figs. 1 and 2).

Once the farrowing house is clean, it is left to dry. This is a very important process that helps to reduce the infectious and parasitic load in the farrowing rooms, as most germs survive better in humid environments.

Ideally, a farrowing room should remain empty for 3-6 days between the moment when the weaned sows leave and that when new sows about to farrow arrive.

Before moving a sow to a farrowing room, she should be washed and disinfected, either in areas specifically designed for this purpose (Figs. 3 and 4) or failing that, in the farrowing unit.

Sows should be washed with neutral soap and warm water. Special attention should be paid to the cleaning of the teats, abdomen and anogenital region so as to eliminate any remnants of faecal material and other residues, which can act as vehicles for the transmission of infectious agents that may cause pathological conditions in sows and piglets (colibacillosis, exudative epidermitis, etc.). This washing procedure prevents possible reinfections by eggs of parasites (*Ascaris* or coccidia, for example) that may infect suckling piglets.

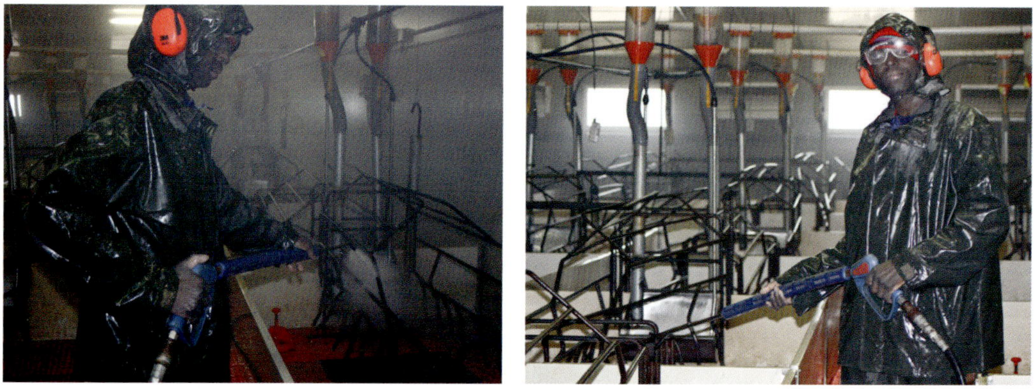

Figures 1 and 2 Cleaning of a farrowing room with a machine.

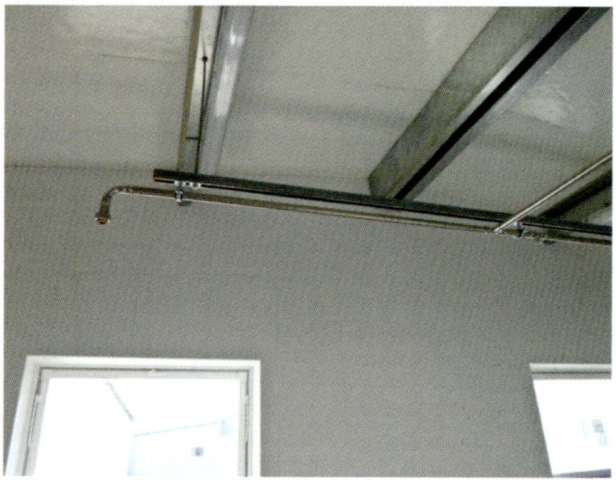

Figure 3 Washing area prior to entering the farrowing unit. Detail of the showers.

Figure 4 Washing area for the sows: detail of the drains.

Washing the sows and a clean environment in the farrowing rooms prevents, to a great extent, urogenital infections and mastitis.

During this phase, it is advisable to ensure that all the equipment in the farrowing room works correctly. It is particularly important to check that the nipple drinkers are fully functional and provide the necessary water flow (minimum 4-6 litres per minute). It should also be ensured that the heating pads for the piglets work properly.

Washing procedure:

1. Removal of organic matter.
2. Washing of the walls, floors, pits and equipment.
3. Disinfection of the farrowing room.
4. Drying of the farrowing room.
5. Sanitation period.
6. Cleaning and disinfection of the sows prior to entering the farrowing room.
7. Inspection of the material, nipple drinkers and drinking troughs.

Arrival of the sows at the farrowing room

As the expected due date of the sows is known, these are introduced in the farrowing room seven days before the expected date of farrowing at the earliest and on day 110 after service at the latest. This way, it is possible to prevent farrowings in the gestation rooms and incidents due to stress problems, which are observed when sows are introduced in the farrowing rooms only 2-3 days before farrowing, as they have not had enough time to get used to the new facilities and distribution of the pens. By doing it as described, sows are calm at the time of farrowing and stress problems –which would lead to a greater percentage of complicated births– are avoided.

With the application of the EU Directive on animal welfare, sows housed in group pens during gestation adapt more poorly to farrowing crates, as they are not used to remaining in a crate. Nevertheless, their capacity to do physical exercise is higher, a fact that results in a better physical condition with easier farrowings and more viable piglets.

The sows are moved to the farrowing room by order of expected parturition date, taking into account, in addition to the date of service, the signs in the teats and vulva indicating that farrowing is close (Figs. 5 and 6, Page 9). Thus, higher performance is achieved in each turnaround in the farrowing room and farrowings are better monitored.

It is necessary to leave empty pens in every farrowing room to facilitate the introduction of nurse sows in order to use fostering techniques. The number of empty pens depends on the prolificacy and on the fostering policy of each farm, and varies from 5 to 20 %.

The prepartum period

In order to facilitate intestinal motility and prevent constipation, which may complicate farrowing, it is advisable to make the sows stand up three or four times a day. This enhances their water intake and reduces urinary infections.

When signs of imminent farrowing are observed, these procedures are interrupted for the sows to remain calm.

At this stage, it is necessary to prepare the farrowing room for parturition. An optimal microclimate must be created for the piglets:

- Place drying paper towels or drying powder so the piglets dry off as soon as they are born.
- It is advisable to use infrared heat lamps, preferably with a red bulb, to ensure piglets dry off quickly when they are born and prevent deaths due to hypothermia, especially during the first 2-3 days of life. It is also recommended to place the piglets in a basket or box under a heat lamp as soon as they are born, so they can dry off properly.
- The different heating systems for piglets should be switched on at least 24 hours before the expected date of farrowing, so the heat pads are warm and the survival rate of the weakest piglets is increased.

If some sows have constipation problems (Fig. 6), magnesium sulphate may be added to the feed (at a dose of 75 grams per sow and day) or the fibre content of the feed may be increased to 6 % in the week previous to farrowing.

A quiet environment in the farrowing room is of vital importance so the sows are not stressed and rear their piglets correctly during their first days of life (Fig. 7).

Figure 5 Aspect of normal faeces.

Figure 6 Aspect of faeces from a constipated sow. Compare with Figure 5.

Figure 7 Relationship between sow welfare and ease of farrowing. Adapted from Lallemand Animal Nutrition, 2012.

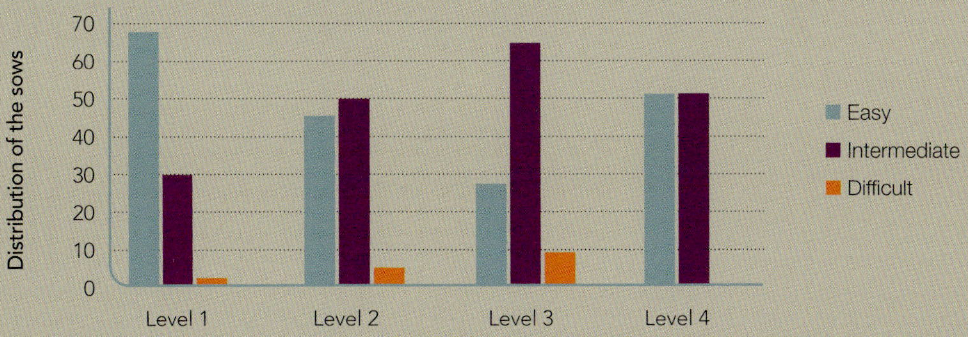

Level 1. The sow is calm. She is lying in lateral recumbency and nurses during farrowing. She ignores her surroundings and pushes without paying attention to her piglets.

Level 2. The sow is lying on her abdomen, thus preventing her piglets from nursing. She pays attention to her surroundings and nibbles the structures of the farrowing crate.

Level 3. The sow is nervous. She is constantly standing up and lying down. She systematically grunts and may crush some piglets.

Level 4. The sow is very nervous and restless. Her own piglets make her nervous and she may try to bite them. She frequently stands up, does not allow her piglets to nurse and is aggressive towards the farm personnel.

Farrowing management

Farrowing is one of the most critical times in pig production. It is characterised by being very stressful for sows, by the high risk of contamination of the piglets and by being crucial for the piglets' future development.

The key is to achieve a quiet environment in the farrowing room so that the sow is comfortable and does not suffer from stress. The most appropriate piece of advice for farrowings **is careful monitoring and little intervention.**

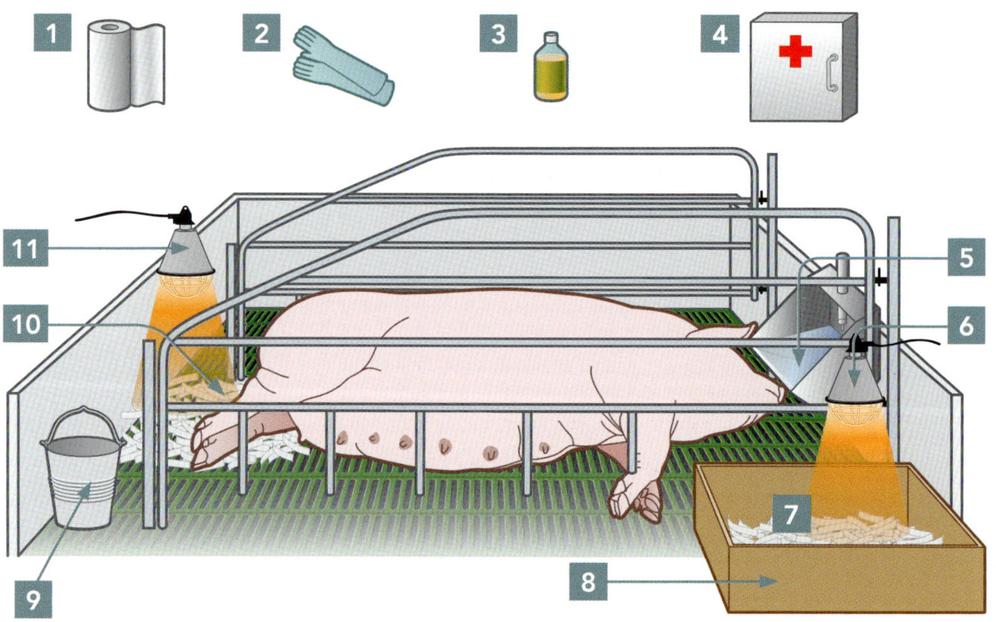

1 **Paper towel or cloth:** drying piglets, more hygienic, better grip on piglets.
2 **Long disposable gloves:** hygienic examination.
3 **Lubricants:** lubricate birth canal during examination.
4 **Small first-aid kit** with oxytocin, analgesics, anti-inflammatory drugs, antibiotics and sedatives.
5 **Plenty of water and very little food.**
6 **Lamp above creep area:** attractive for piglets to lie under.
7 **Drying paper towel/powder for the creep area:** piglets dry off quickly.
8 **Box** for the piglets to dry and to allow split suckling.
9 **Bucket:** removal of placenta, membranes and dead piglets.
10 **Drying paper towel or powder:** reduces heat loss during farrowing.
11 **Lamp behind the sow:** warms piglets during farrowing.

Figure 8 Preparation of farrowing. Elements that must be prepared before farrowing. Adapted from Van Engen, M., de Vries, A. and Scheepens, K. *Pig signals: piglets*, 2011.

On the day of farrowing, the sow almost does not eat; she has no appetite. However, once parturition is over, a high feed intake should be achieved in a few days.

Her water intake is also very important. It should be ensured that the sow drinks at least 25 litres of water a day (three days before and three days after farrowing), since it prevents constipation problems and guarantees a good milk production.

Normally, sows do not require the intervention of a veterinary surgeon to farrow, but the presence of qualified personnel to watch the process is recommended, as it helps to reduce the mortality rate of piglets, not only during parturition but also during the first hours of life.

A sow's feed intake decreases with farrowing, but should be recovered quickly. It is necessary to reach high intakes in a few days.

Ideal environmental temperature for the sow at farrowing

Good environmental conditions in the farrowing room, in particular as regards temperature, have a positive impact on the farrowing process. The ideal temperature in the farrowing room during parturition is about 16-24 °C, the sow's comfort temperature being 16-20 °C.

In hot regions, it is essential for farrowing units to have cooling systems to reduce the temperature in the rooms. Conversely, in very cold geographical areas, low temperatures must be avoided; however, with well-insulated units and the focal heat from the heating pads or other heating systems for piglets, sows are not normally cold.

At times of extreme heat, it may be advisable to reduce the temperature of the heating pads for the piglets in order not to increase the room temperature excessively.

Farrowings must be programmed so they take place very early in the morning, when the ambient temperature is lower. This prevents the sows' lives from being put at risk by the effort of farrowing. Similarly, another option is to program farrowings at night, as long as there are appropriate and sufficient workers to attend them.

> There should not be any draughts above 1.5 m/s in the farrowing rooms and the ventilation airflow should never be directed towards the animals.

Administration of oxytocin

When a farrowing is prolonged, the administration of oxytocin by intramuscular route may be advisable to facilitate uterine contractions. This procedure may be repeated 30 minutes later, but the systematic administration of oxytocin should be considered with great care, as it can complicate the farrowing process and cause an increase in the number of stillborn piglets, by reducing the normal duration of farrowing in excess.

The recommended dose of oxytocin is 5-10 I.U., which are administered by intramuscular route in the muscles of the neck. The doses used should never be higher than those recommended, as the effect of oxytocin is momentary and very fast. Exceeding the recommended doses or repeating the administration without waiting for 30 minutes is counter-productive, because the uterine musculature does not contract efficiently and the farrowing process may be interrupted.

> It is not recommended to administer more than 3 doses of oxytocin per farrowing or to systematically administer long-acting oxytocin analogues.

Once the sow has farrowed, it is necessary to check that she defecates normally, to avoid problems of constipation and observe if there are signs of mastitis-metritis-agalactia syndrome (MMA syndrome), a process better known nowadays as postpartum dysgalactia syndrome (PDS).

Administration of antibiotics, anti-inflammatory drugs and other drugs

The preventive administration of pharmaceutical products, whether by oral (water or feed), intramuscular or genital route is not recommended. There has been an overuse of drugs for this purpose and, on occasions, the only thing that is achieved is the withdrawal of the sow's milk or the alteration of her intestinal flora.

The administration of antibiotics, anti-inflammatory drugs or vaginal cleansing products is only indicated as a preventive measure on farms with frequent specific pathological problems. In this case, their use should be restricted exclusively to the period during which the problems persist (curative use).

Care of newborn piglets

Piglets are normally born covered by thin foetal membranes, from which they free themselves when they are born, as the sow does not lick her offspring after farrowing.

It is recommended to dry the piglets as they are born and ensure they suckle colostrum. On occasions, if there are more piglets than functional teats, it is necessary to put the largest piglets in a box or enclosed creep area for a maximum of 2-3 hours, so that the smallest piglets can suckle colostrum. This is called **split-suckling**.

Remnants of membranes or other fluids may sometimes block the mouth or snout of piglets when they are born and prevent them from breathing easily. In these cases, they should be cleaned with a dry towel so as to ensure they can breathe normally.

It should be remembered that about 70 % of neonatal deaths are due to asphyxia or other causes that occur during the last stage of expulsion and prevent piglets from breathing properly.

It is essential to help the weakest piglets to suckle by placing them close to the sow's teats. On the other hand, in order to reduce deaths caused by hypothermia, it is recommended to dry the piglets and place them on the heating pads as soon as possible, where the focal temperature should be between 32 °C and 35 °C. Infrared thermometers can be used to know whether the piglets are cold.

Focal temperatures under 32 °C increase the likelihood of deaths by hypothermia.

Procedures such as tail docking, teeth grinding, etc. should never be carried out on the first day of life. Cross-fostering should be postponed until 24 hours after farrowing to facilitate the transfer of immunity form the mother to the piglets through the colostrum.

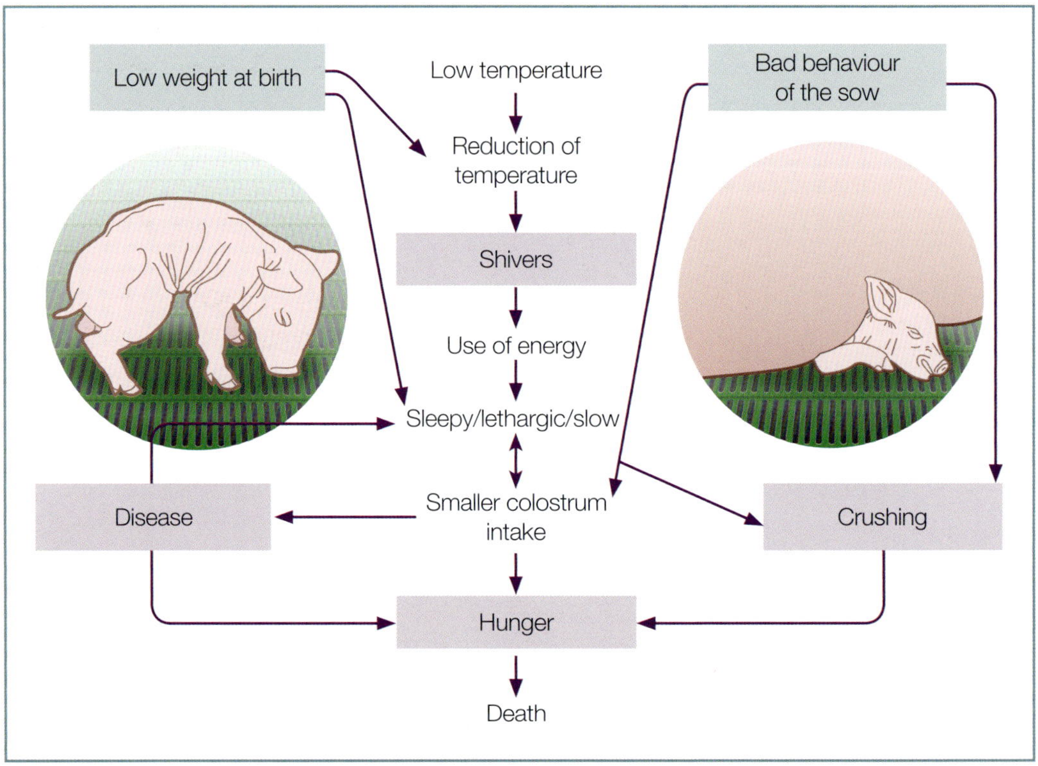

Figure 9 Consequences of hypothermia and of an insufficient colostrum intake. Adapted from Van Engen, M., de Vries, A. and Scheepens, K. *Pig signals: piglets*, 2011.

Drying the piglets

It is very advisable to dry piglets right after they are born with a dry towel or drying powder. This practice saves numerous piglets, as it reduces one of the main causes of mortality in piglets, hypothermia.

The remnants of foetal membranes and amniotic fluids are removed when drying the piglets (Figs. 10 and 11). This procedure involves rubbing the piglets carefully in order to warm them up. It is must be carried out with care so as to avoid microtraumas.

In order to help them breathe, if necessary, the piglets are held by their hind legs and their mouth and snout are cleaned. A sharp swinging movement is sometimes required to clear fluids from the piglet's airways.

Tying-off and disinfection of the umbilical cord

It is very advisable to tie off the piglet's umbilical cord as soon as possible after farrowing. This procedure reduces the risk of umbilical haemorrhages due to the entry of pathogens through the umbilical cord.

On some farms, umbilical haemorrhages are more frequent due to the use of prostaglandins to induce labour. The piglets affected by these haemorrhages are more prone to suffering from anaemia and even to die from this cause.

The umbilical cord should be tied off at about 5 cm from the piglet's body with strings or zip ties, or clamped with self-adjustable clips such as those used for babies. It should not be done too close to the navel so as not to lesion it. Finally, it is cut, preferably under the tied part (Figs. 12 to 15).

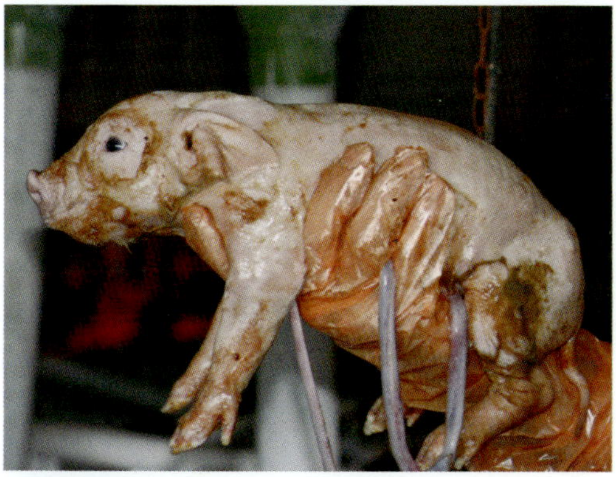

Figure 10 Newborn piglet covered by foetal membranes.

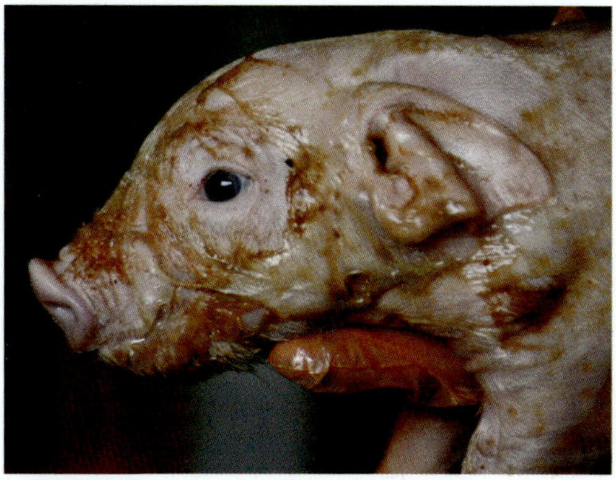

Figure 11 Detail of the previous image.

Procedure for clamping the umbilical cord with a clip

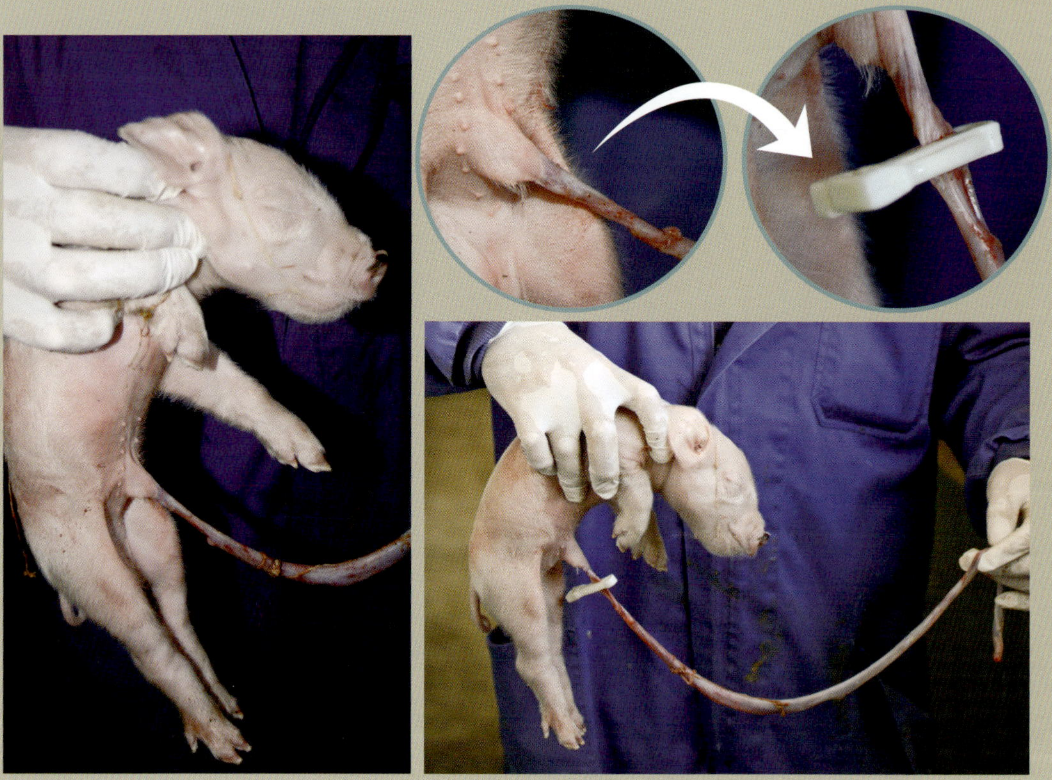

Figures 12 to 15

The percentage of umbilical hernias, which is very high on some farms, decreases with the use of this procedure (tying and cutting the umbilical cord). Hernias are sometimes due to the fact that the piglets' umbilical cord has not been cut. They drag it, sometimes step on it and it may even get trapped in the facilities, which favours the appearance of hernias. Once the umbilical cord is tied, it is preferably disinfected with iodine.

The piglet should not be pulled sharply when it is being born and still attached to the sow's placenta by the umbilical cord, as it increases the likelihood of hernias.

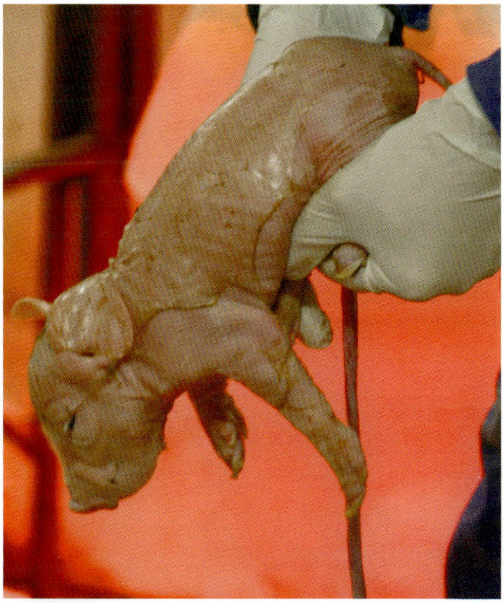

Figure 16 Posture to resuscitate a newborn piglet.

Resuscitation of piglets

Some piglets are sometimes apparently born dead due to asphyxia or birth difficulties.

These piglets can generally be resuscitated. To do so, the entry of air into the lungs must be facilitated. The appropriate procedure is to hold the piglet by its hind legs and bend them towards the abdomen, at the same time as its head is moved down (Fig. 16). This way, the mucus it may have at the back of its throat and in the trachea is expelled and the airways are cleared.

It is advisable to rub the abdomen and in extreme cases, to perform assisted ventilation manoeuvres.

A high number of piglets are disoriented at birth and appear at the front and rear ends of the farrowing pens, far from the heat sources. If they are not dried and placed next to a heat source in time, they often die due to **hypothermia**.

On farms with excellent management of the animals, hypothermic piglets are saved with treatments involving their immersion in warm water.

Colostrum feeding of piglets

Colostrum feeding is key for piglets to receive passive immunity and be able to face certain infectious processes, as they are born in a hostile environment with a high presence of pathogenic agents and almost completely lack immunoglobulins. This lack of antibodies is due to the fact that sows have an epitheliochorial placenta. This type of placenta does not allow the passage of maternal antibodies from the mother to the foetus. As piglets cannot build their immune system during the first days of life, they must acquire passive immunity.

Passive immunity is the result of the transfer of antibodies and specific cells from the mother to her offspring. As the sow's placenta does not allow this transfer before farrowing, it is essential that it takes place immediately after birth.

> Colostrum does not only provide immunity, it is also essential to regulate and maintain the piglets' body temperature, cover their mobility needs and ensure their growth.

It is therefore fundamental that piglets drink colostrum during the first six hours of life. It is important that not only the largest and most competitive piglets, but also the smallest ones, drink colostrum. For this purpose, **split suckling** is applied. The largest piglets are placed in a basket or box for a few hours (2-3 hours), to allow small piglets free access to the sow's colostrum.

> A colostrum intake of at least 100 grams per kilo of live weight is recommended.

It should be highlighted that colostrum contains an inhibitor that prevents piglets from digesting immunoglobulins. Thus, during the first 24 hours, immunoglobulins are absorbed without their structure being altered. It is therefore essential that newborn piglets start to drink colostrum as soon as possible, as the intestinal absorption of immunoglobulins is drastically reduced after the first 24 hours, and is almost non-existent after 48 hours.

Taking into account what has been said before, the optimal colostrum intake is that of colostrum from the mother, as she is the only one able to transmit all types of antibodies and specific cells to her offspring, and her immunoglobulins can cross the piglets' intestinal barrier **without being recognised as foreign**.

Artificial colostrum feeding

This section describes artificial colostrum feeding techniques, which are carried out in extreme cases, when cross-fostering methods cannot be used or when the mother has died.

Sows produce colostrum for the first 24 hours postpartum. During this period, they can be manually milked to subsequently administer this colostrum to the weakest piglets, which cannot suckle due to their low weight or because they cannot stand up (Figs. 17 and 18).

It is recommended to inject a dose of oxytocin of 5-10 I.U. to the sows in order to obtain up to 300-500 ml of colostrum from each sow.

On some occasions, it is necessary to refrigerate and store the colostrum for 48 hours, so as to use it with other litters. However, as has already been explained, the immune protection is much lower for those piglets that have been fed colostrum from a different sow from their mother.

Colostrum can also be frozen to be used over longer periods of time. In this case, it must be frozen as soon as possible and it must previously be filtered with gauze. Thawing is carried out at 39 °C, using a bain-marie, to avoid the denaturalisation of the immunoglobulins.

Normally, the administration of colostrum is done with special feeding bottles, although feeding tubes are sometimes used (3 mm of diameter and 25 cm of length) to intubate the piglets and administer the colostrum directly to their stomach. The tube should never be introduced more 15 cm into the piglet's digestive tract.

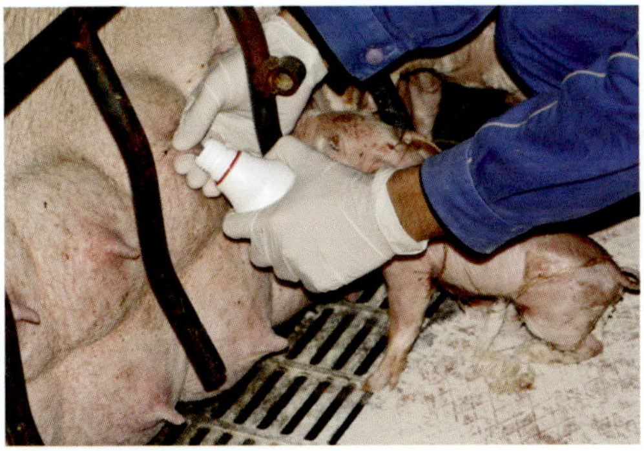

Figure 17 Milking colostrum from the sow.

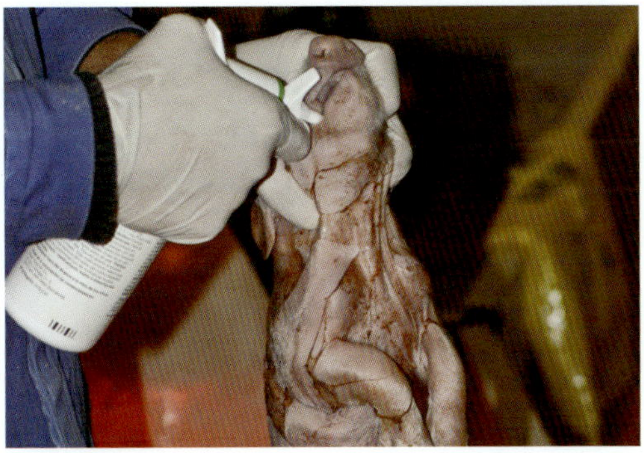

Figure 18 Administration of colostrum to a piglet.

This procedure should always be carried out with the best possible asepsis. It is sometimes necessary to intubate the piglets up to three times at one-hour intervals.

Approximately 20 ml of colostrum should be administered to the piglets at each feeding.

On some farms, post-cervical insemination catheters are used to perform gastric intubation. These practices are almost experimental and are not used on a regular basis on farms, except in extreme cases or on farms with exceptional management practices, since most of these problems can be solved with nurse sows.

Aggressive sows during farrowing

Sows instinctively become more aggressive at farrowing to protect their litter.

Some sows, especially first-parity gilts, get very nervous and even become aggressive towards their litter, to the point of being responsible for situations of cannibalism with their own piglets. The sows that display this behaviour must be euthanised when lactation has finished. In the meantime, they are administered a tranquilliser to make them sleep and achieve a quiet environment in the farrowing room.

Once they are calm, on most occasions they accept their litter. However, proper monitoring is necessary to ensure they accept their piglets when they wake up.

To check whether a sow has recovered her maternal instinct, the mother-child bond has been re-established and she is calm, the piglets are placed next to her teats so they can start drinking colostrum, and the mother's reaction towards her offspring is observed.

This aggressive behaviour is favoured in farrowing rooms with dividers, in which it is possible for the sows and their litters to see the other sows.

In most cases, this behaviour is the result of the presence of noise or other stress factors (unknown farm workers, operations with cleaning machines, noises, etc.) that unsettle the sows, especially, as has been said before, first-parity gilts.

Programmed farrowings

The exact date of service is a very important piece of information for the proper management of sows in the farrowing unit, and facilitates the decision of the ideal time to program the farrowings on those farms that have chosen this option.

It is also very important to know the average duration of gestation on the farm, a piece of data that is highly related to the service pattern of each operation. The average duration varies from 114 to 116 days depending on the farm.

It should be remembered that hyperprolific sows have longer gestations, of nearly 116 days. On the other hand, the Iberian breed, which has a very low prolificacy, has shorter gestations of 112-113 days.

In addition to the expected date of farrowing, it is possible to control the time at which we would like farrowings to take place. This way, they occur during the normal working hours on the farm and parturitions at weekends are avoided.

Administration of prostaglandins

Prostaglandins cause the lysis of the corpus luteum, which leads to the sharp decrease of blood progesterone levels and increases those of **relaxin**, thus causing farrowing.

The induction of farrowing is achieved by administering synthetic prostaglandins (**PGF2α**) by intramuscular route at a dose of 1 ml.

When farrowing is induced, the time interval between the birth of the first piglet and that of the second one is greater. This is due to the fact that the frequency of uterine contractions increases, while their amplitude decreases.

As the duration of gestation varies, as previously explained, from 114 to 116 days on average, the practical recommendation is to administer the product one day before the end of the average gestation period for each farm, that is to say between days 113 and 115, counted from the date of first service.

It is recommended to administer prostaglandins one day before the end of the average gestation period.

Prostaglandins are only injected to sows with a good development of the mammary glands and vulva, to avoid inducing farrowings too early, especially in sows with long gestations. They are normally administered at the beginning of the working day so that farrowing takes place 24-32 hours after the injection. If the sows start to farrow before this interval, this means it was time for them to give birth and the mechanism of farrowing had already been triggered naturally.

It is not advised to induce labour in first-parity gilts and it should be borne in mind that these usually have gestations of up to one more day of duration.

On many farms, farrowing is only induced in sows that have not farrowed after 115 days of gestation. Farrowing problems are thus avoided, as well as delays in the management of the farrowing unit.

A farrowing that is not going to be monitored should not be induced.

Scheduling farrowings

Scheduling farrowings is very useful on those farms with very high mortality rates in piglets at birth that need special monitoring of farrowings. Farrowings can be induced with the administration of prostaglandins so they can take place at times when qualified workers are present.

On the other hand, other farms have very good mortality rates at farrowing and neonatal mortality rates. However, these excellent results can only be achieved if farrowings are induced and qualified workers are present to monitor them 24 hours a day. As a result, farrowings are planned so that those of each batch take place over 2-3 days.

> Farrowings are induced so they can be monitored by qualified workers and take place during the usual farm working hours.

The farrowing induction policy depends on the results of each farm, its size and its working hours. However, it is essential to know the average duration of gestation on the farm so as not to induce farrowings too early, as piglets would have a lower viability.

It has been demonstrated that shortening gestation by a couple of days by inducing farrowing artificially can reduce the piglets' weight at birth by up to 180 grams.

Special care should also be taken when manipulating prostaglandins. As well as inducing labour, PGF2α causes abortion in pregnant females and great care must therefore be taken when administering it.

It is an abortive hormone, so that women using it should always wear latex gloves, as it can be absorbed through the skin. For the same reason, pregnant women should never be in contact with this hormone.

PGF2α is a hormone that may cause miscarriage.

Women must be particularly careful when manipulating prostaglandins.

- They should always wear latex gloves.
- They should avoid any type of contact with the hormone if they think they may be pregnant.

Monitoring farrowings

Monitoring a farrowing involves systematising the parturition process and controlling it by means of a record sheet, on which every event that occurs is noted down at regular intervals of a maximum of 30 minutes (Table 1).

Table 1 Record sheet for monitoring farrowings. Casanovas, C. *Cuadernos del parto de la cerda 1: Parto y preparto*, 2008.

Farrowing process	Time	Piglets	Advice for the record
First part of the farrowing process (up to 2.5 h), monitoring every 45 min approximately	7:30	1	More than one hour passes by between the first and second births. No intervention as it is normal.
	8:35	2	
	9:15	4	Note down the total number of born piglets. No intervention.
Second part of the farrowing process (from 2.5 h), monitoring every 30 min.	10:00	5 hand	No piglet born after 45 min: intervention, a live piglet is removed. Note down intervention "hand".
	10:30	5 hand 0 / Oxytocin	No piglet is born after 30 minutes: intervention, nothing is removed. Note down "hand 0". Inject oxytocin.
	11:00	7	30 min go by and two live piglets are born. Note down total no. 7.
Last part of the farrowing process with one stillborn piglet: monitoring at less than 30-minute intervals.	11:05	9 + 1 Stillborn	Only 5 min go by but a piglet is born dead: intervention, two live piglets are removed. Note down intervention and total no. live and dead
	11:05	11 + 1 Stillborn. Hand	
	11:30	12 + 1 Stillborn	25 min go by and one live piglet is born. Note down total no. 12 + 1 dead.
	11:40	14 + 1 Stillborn / Placenta	20 min go by and two live piglets are born. Note down total no. 14 + 1 dead. Very clear signs of the end of farrowing. Note down END.
END OF FARROWING			

It is very useful to monitor farrowings, especially on large farms where there are shifts in the farrowing unit, as this way the farrowing room attendant who starts his/her shift is fully informed of what is happening and of which tasks are pending. Furthermore, monitored farrowings are better assisted, piglets are dried when they are born and birth-to-weaning mortality rates under 5 % can be achieved.

Monitoring farrowings allows the quick identification of the sows that do not follow the established pace and require special attention.

On farms with monitorised farrowings, very low rates of stillborn piglets are achieved. The authors know of farms with 6,000 breeding sows with stillborn piglet rates under 0.4 %.

Some studies show that when farrowings are monitored, the number of piglets born dead can be reduced by up to 30 %.

Non-dystocic problematic farrowings

The main types of problematic farrowings that may occur are briefly described next, together with advice for their resolution. It should be remembered that this type of farrowings does not require manual assistance.

Non-dystocic problematic farrowings

- Slow farrowing
- Farrowing with constipation
- Farrowing with fatigue
- Farrowing with tetanic contractions
- Farrowing with stress

There should not be any manual intervention in non-dystocic problematic farrowings.

Slow farrowing

A yellowish piglet indicates that this is a slow farrowing. The colour is caused by the piglet having defecated in the amniotic fluid during its expulsion.

Farrowing may be slow due to different causes: obese sow, high environmental temperatures, inappropriate feeding management of the sow or problems of hypocalcaemia.

The slower the farrowing process, the higher the risk of a lack of oxygen for the piglet and the weaker it will be at birth. This will lead to inappropriate colostrum intake and to a decrease in its chances of survival.

Farrowing with constipation

If the sow is not properly fed a few days before farrowing, is administered very concentrated feed poor in fibre or does not drink enough, she may suffer from constipation.

In these cases, in addition to correcting poor dietary practices (incorrect administration of feed or lack of water), a choleretic should be administered to the sow and magnesium sulphate should be added to her diet at a dose of 75 g per day if necessary.

Farrowing with fatigue

It occurs when sows have problems to expel the piglets as a result of a febrile process or due to high environmental temperatures in the summer.

These high temperatures may also be due to the heat sources that are installed for the piglets. For this reason, the use of heaters that heat the entire farrowing room and of propane-based heating systems for the piglets is discouraged, as they can cause excessive heat for the sows.

Most of the time, high temperatures occur in the summer (**heatwaves**), on farms where the cooling systems installed in the farrowing rooms are insufficient to cool the temperature down to appropriate levels.

In these cases, sows may suffer from **heat stroke**, which may even cause their death.

When sows have difficulty breathing, it is recommended to wet their neck or head, provided there is appropriate ventilation in the farrowing room to prevent humidity levels from increasing excessively. In these cases, it is also recommended to treat them with an antipyretic drug.

> The comfort temperature for farrowing sows is 16-20 °C.

Farrowing with tetanic contractions

The abuse or overdose of oxytocin may give rise to tetanic contractions during the farrowing process. This occurs when the birth canal contracts excessively, thus preventing the normal expulsion of the piglets.

It is essential to always be very careful when using oxytocin.

Farrowing with stress

In situations of stress (noise, unusual situations, etc.), sows, in particular first-parity gilts, may be in a state of overexcitement that will slow down the farrowing process and contribute to them being nervous. This may eventually lead to problems of cannibalism and increase problems of agalactia.

These problems may sometimes be related to excessive pain during farrowing, especially in first-parity gilts.

In these cases, the best therapy is to solve the stressful situation and administer a tranquilliser to the sow.

Procedure of examination of the birth canal in sows

The presence of farm workers specialised in the examination of the birth canal and veterinary assistance are only necessary when the time interval between the first uterine contractions and the expulsion of the first piglet or between the births of two piglets is too long. In those cases, it is necessary to examine the birth canal to know the cause of this delay.

> Manual assistance should only be provided when necessary as it can interrupt the farrowing process and cause lesions to the sow.

The examination of the birth canal must be carried out by qualified farm personnel. The farm worker carrying out this task should have small hands and arms so as to introduce them more easily. Furthermore, the duration of this procedure should not last too long to avoid lesions to the sow.

Procedure of examination of the pelvic canal and removal of piglets

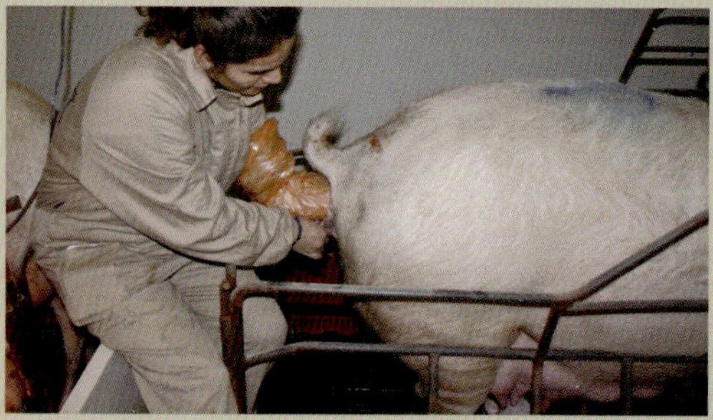

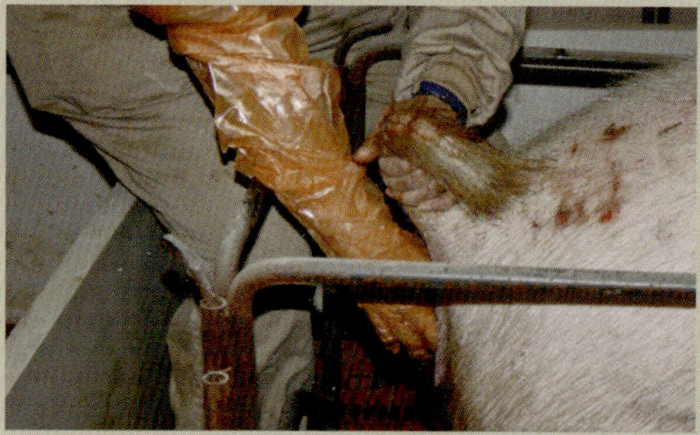

When the examination of the birth canal is necessary because the piglets take too long to be expelled, the procedure will be the following:

- Clean and disinfect your arm.
- Use a plastic glove with an obstetric lubricant that will facilitate the examination and that is not irritating to the sows' genital walls. The use of common liquid soap is discouraged, as it can be irritating.
- Introduce your hand with the fingers joined and progress through the cervix to the bifurcation of the uterus, at the rhythm of the uterine contractions, without applying force.
- When touching the piglet, its position must be determined. If needed, it should be repositioned before being removed.

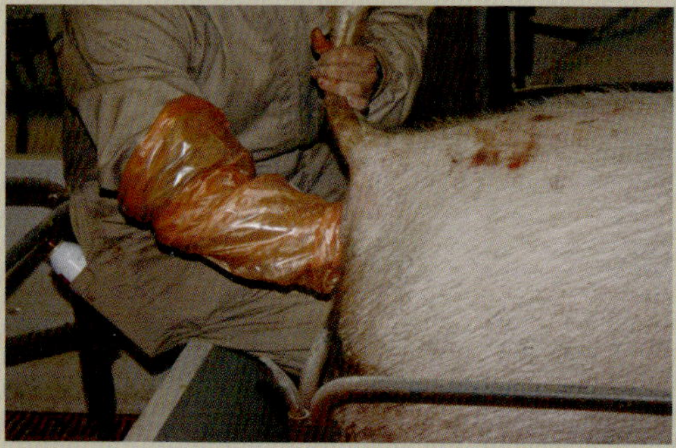

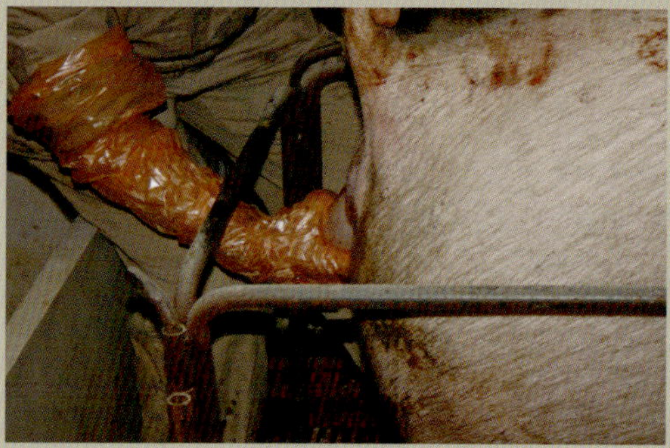

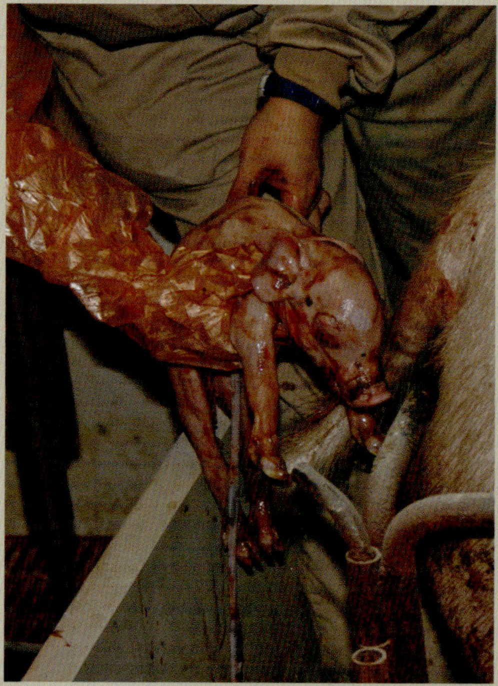

If the examination is long and deep, the administration of antibiotics is recommended.

It is necessary to be careful during the vaginal examination as the sow may move suddenly and hurt the worker's arm. It is advisable to keep the crate open preventively during these interventions.

Dystocia. Basic obstetrics

Although the percentage of manual interventions depends, among other factors, on the protocols to monitor farrowings on each farm and may reach up to 30 %, the cases of dystocia described next usually occur in less than 5 % of cases.

Heavy piglets

The main cause of dystocia lies in the presence of heavy piglets in first-parity gilts. In these cases, forceps or nylon ropes should be used to hold the piglet and pull it out.

The rope, which should be approximately 2 metres long, is cleaned, disinfected and lubricated. It is tied around the third finger and passed through the vagina to the piglet's head. It is then passed behind its ears and under its mandible. The piglet is removed by pulling quickly.

Obstruction of the birth canal

Other circumstances responsible for dystocia are pressure on the reproductive tract by an intestine filled with hard faeces or a bladder filled with urine and uterine torsion. In the first case, the filled intestine causes the narrowing of the birth canal. It is therefore necessary that the sow does not eat on the day of farrowing. If a full bladder is the cause, the sow may be catheterised to urinate if needed. Finally, if dystocia is due to uterine torsion, it is recommended to get the sow to stand up and walk and then to place the uterus back in its normal position manually.

Torsion of the uterine horns

It appears when a litter is large and a uterine horn passes over the other. Torsion occurs and the piglets cannot move forward.

Possible causes of dystocia in the sow and manoeuvres to remove a piglet

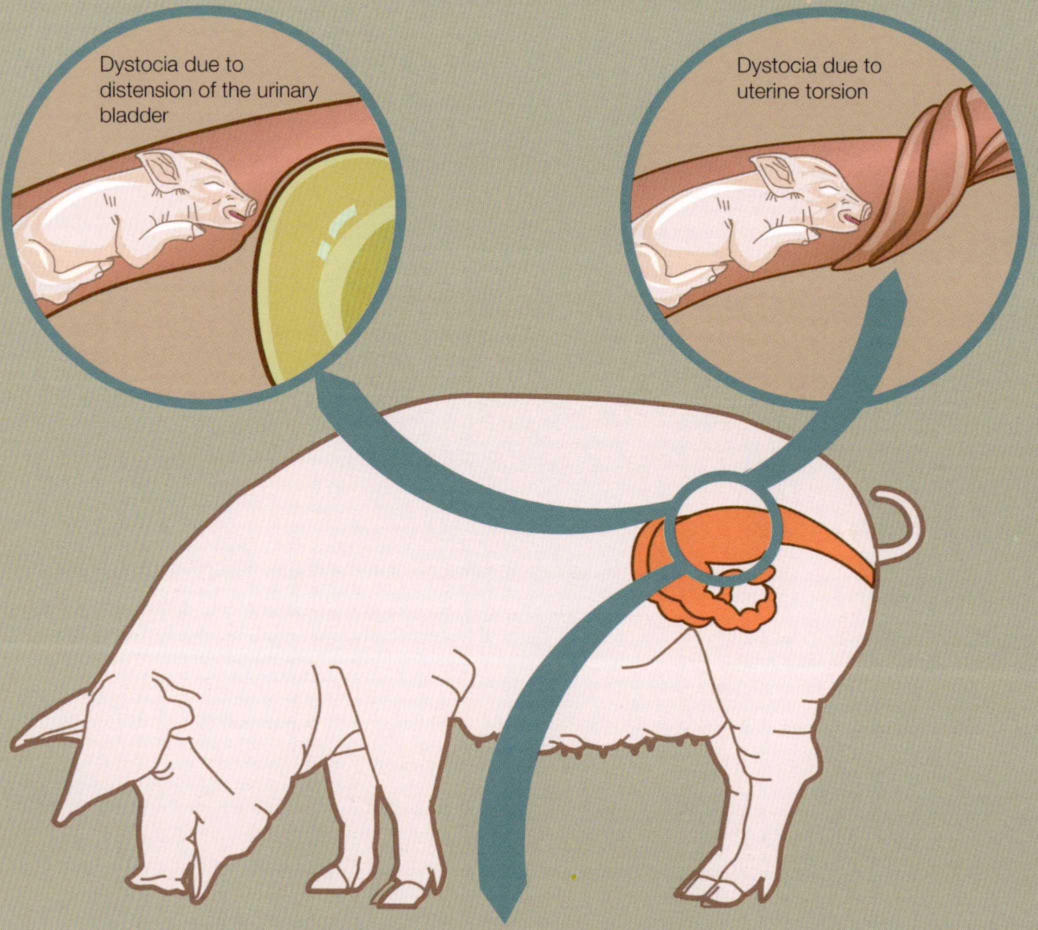

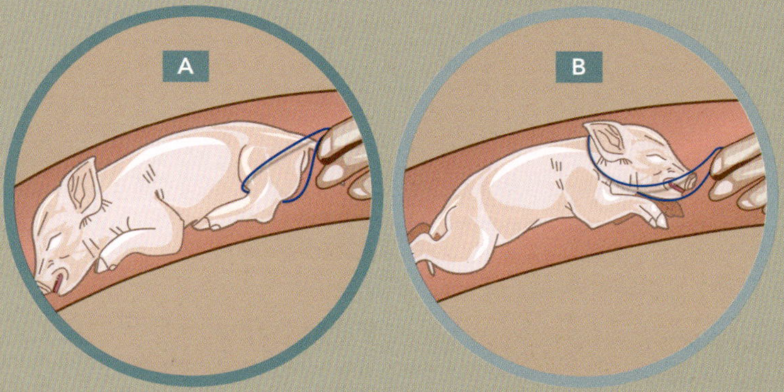

Manoeuvres to remove a piglet during birth by means a nylon string. Posterior presentation (A) and anterior presentation (B).

In order to solve this situation, a hand should be inserted through the cervix, which has become elliptical, and the farm worker should make a downward and backward movement. In these cases, the sow should be standing up and the whole arm should be introduced into the sow to attempt to remove three or four piglets, so that the rest of the litter can be born without any assistance. If this is not possible, the procedure should be repeated.

Sows with a narrow birth canal

In these sows, which are mainly primiparous, it is necessary to use relaxants of the cervix by intramuscular route.

> All gynaecological examinations should be carried out with great care so as not to lesion the piglet or the sow.

Performing caesarean sections

This is a very unusual practice on pig farms. Caesarean sections should only be performed by veterinary surgeons or under their strict supervision.

This procedure, which is termed **planned hysterectomy**, is only of interest when specific-pathogen-free (SPF) animals want to be achieved on selection farms with animals of very high genetic value or in research projects.

This system was considerably used in the past, but it is currently being replaced by more innovative systems of disease eradication with high success rates.

In extreme cases of very complicated farrowings, in which the piglets cannot be removed, the sow is euthanised and the piglets are removed from her uterus. This is termed **emergency hysterectomy**.

Both procedures, planned and emergency hysterectomies, should be carried out in a room prepared for this purpose and under fully aseptic conditions.

Generally, in a planned hysterectomy, the sow is euthanised and her full uterus is removed and taken to a container in an enclosed room, where the piglets are removed to be taken to SPF operations to be fed colostrum and reared by nurse sows.

The piglets survive in the uterus for up to four minutes after euthanisation, so the surgery must be fast in order to remove all the piglets.

6 Main diseases in the peripartum period

Introduction

Nowadays, pig production companies focus their health strategy on the control and/or eradication of diseases within the possibilities given by each operation. Farms of high sanitary status (free from PRRS, *Mycoplasma* spp., haemorrhagic dysentery, atrophic rhinitis and mange) allow a flow of piglets with better productive results, higher average daily gains and reduced expenses in medications. The financial investment to eradicate diseases is recovered rapidly thanks to the good technical and economic results obtained in the fattening unit, provided a high sanitary status is maintained for the longest possible period.

Health objective

In this phase, the objective is to obtain piglets free from most diseases and with a good weight (1,400-1,500 grams), and to prevent them from being infected with diseases during the peripartum period.

The main pathological disorders observed in the peripartum period both in sows and piglets are explained next.

Main diseases of sows

Postpartum dysgalactia syndrome (PDS)

Previously known as mastitis-metritis-agalactia syndrome (MMA). It occurs in sows after farrowing and is characterised by a reduction of milk secretion in one or several mammary glands, which may be partial (hypogalactia) or total (agalactia), and by a fever of variable intensity. These signs may be accompanied by vaginal discharges and often by generalised apathy. The disease has indirect repercussions on piglets. As they cannot suckle enough milk from their mother, their general state and even survival is affected.

The clinical picture usually appears on a more frequent basis in overweight, multiparous sows, after being fed abundantly or with a deficient diet, or after a sudden qualitative or quantitative dietary change during the peripartum period. The main signs shown by the affected sows are usually observed in the mammary glands. The affected sows' mammary glands are inflamed and reddish. In some cases, mammary inflammation partially or totally prevents the milk from flowing.

Sows with a fever have a reduced appetite.

This syndrome appears mainly on farms with poor hygiene, with a greater prevalence of genital and urinary tract infections. Prolonged farrowings and excessive manipulations when assisting them favour this disease.

Vaginal discharges sometimes occur so rapidly that they go unnoticed. They can change from clear and liquid fluids to purulent and sometimes lumpy, white-yellowish fluids in the most severe cases.

In most cases, clinical signs appear early. The affected sows' piglets are weak, have a lower average daily weight gain and may even die due to a lower availability of milk.

Clinical treatment involves the administration to the sow of:

- **Oxytocin** every 12 hours at a dose of 5-10 IU, to facilitate milk production.
- **Broad-spectrum antibiotics** such as beta-lactams or quinolones. In the most severe cases, the sows should be treated every 12 hours.

- **Non-steroid anti-inflammatory drugs** (NSAIDs) to alleviate the clinical signs.
- The piglets should be treated immediately by tube feeding them colostrum or glucose solution so they do not die of starvation.

The main prevention measure is good environmental hygiene and feeding management. Sows should not eat too much before farrowing, so as to prevent constipation, which favours the appearance of this syndrome. Although there are several bacteria related to this syndrome, the main ones are colon bacilli. In case of continuous outbreaks on the same farm, it is therefore highly recommended to correctly clean and disinfect the farrowing rooms, with the corresponding sanitation period. In this sense, a good preventive measure is to clean and disinfect the sows' udders and vulvae with disinfecting products such as chlorhexidine prior to their arrival at the farrowing house.

Metritis

It is a common condition in farrowing rooms. The affected sows eliminate purulent secretions in the form of whitish mucous discharge through their vagina, mainly during 3-4 days after farrowing (Fig. 1).

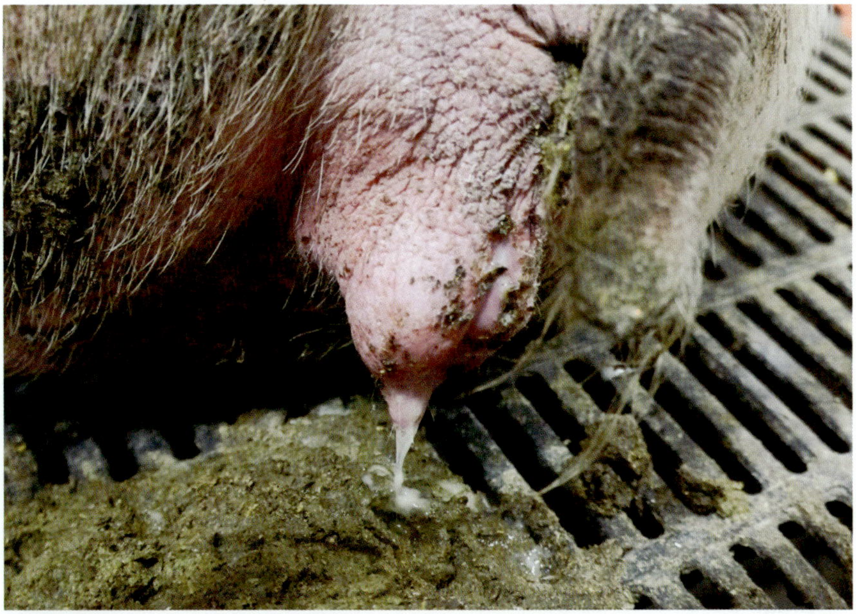

Figure 1 Whitish mucous discharge in a sow with metritis.

This discharge may indicate the presence of metritis. It mainly occurs in prolonged farrowings that have required manual assistance or in which a concomitant infectious process was present. Metritis may be associated with mastitis and causes lack of appetite and fever.

Good hygiene in farrowing rooms reduces the frequency of this condition. It should be differentiated from the whitish secretion caused by urinary problems, such as cystitis, which is also usual on farms with hard water.

Treatment involves the administration of broad-spectrum antibiotics (such as quinolones or beta-lactams).

Mastitis

Mastitis is the inflammation of one or several mammary glands. It is usually due to a wound when it occurs in only one mammary gland and often results in it no longer being functional. It most commonly affects all the mammary glands and is caused by poor management practices or by an infectious agent.

Mastitis usually occurs around farrowing and becomes evident after 12 hours, although on some occasions it appears in the first days after weaning. The administration of a treatment is necessary in order to prevent the process from becoming chronic and to ensure the mammary gland tissue is not replaced by fibrous tissue.

Mastitis is distinguished into two types: acute and chronic mastitis.

Acute mastitis

It usually occurs during lactation and/or after weaning. The udders are increased in size and firmness (Fig. 2), and are painful to the sow when pressed. A sow suffering from acute mastitis normally remains lying down. Her body temperature increases as a result of the infection. In very severe infections, toxins are produced and the sow may eventually die after 24 hours.

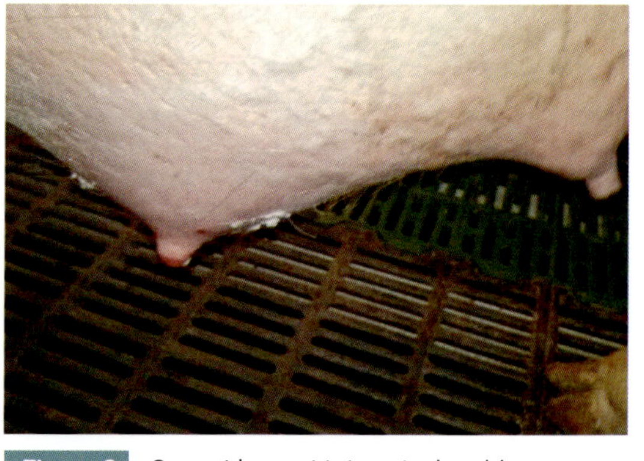

Figure 2 Sow with mastitis in a single udder.

Chronic mastitis

They usually derive from cases of subclinical mastitis in which the clinical picture went unnoticed. In this case, the gland is also increased in size due to the fibrous tissue that has formed. Abscesses that may become ulcerated are sometimes observed.

Treatment involves the administration of an antibiotic and an anti-inflammatory drug. If mastitis occurs during the lactation period, oxytocin should be injected to elicit milk ejection. As the incidence of this disease is associated with poor management practices and deficient hygiene, these factors should be corrected.

Ketosis

Ketosis is an increase in blood ketone bodies manifested by nervous signs, mainly prostration and agalactia. The clinical signs shown by the affected sows in the farrowing house are compatible with subclinical ketosis, such as lack of appetite and hypogalactia.

The high energy demand at the end of gestation, which is increasingly greater in hyperprolific sows, together with the frequent decrease in feed intake during this phase favour a negative energy balance. When the ration's glucose content and the sow's glycogen reserves are insufficient, lipolysis in the fat tissue is activated. The triglycerides stored in the adipocytes pass to the bloodstream as non-esterified fatty acids (NEFAs) and glycerol. NEFAs undergo oxidation in the liver to produce energy. When the oxidative capacity of the liver is exceeded, there is an excess of ketone bodies (ketosis) and an accumulation of triglycerides in the liver (steatosis or fatty liver). As occurs in humans, the production of placental hormones and the increased glucose demand at the end of gestation have a diabetogenic effect that favours lipolysis and the production of ketone bodies in the liver. It is therefore usual to find that ketone body levels are higher than normal in pregnant sows. These ketone bodies, due to the lack of glucose, are used in the short term as a source of energy. However, in the long term, if the glucose deficiency is prolonged, ketone bodies accumulate in the extracellular fluid, leading to a loss of appetite and reduced glucose availability. The sow thus enters into a cycle that progressively exacerbates ketosis; the loss of appetite may be accompanied by more or less severe hypogalactia, which affects the piglets in lactation, resulting in higher mortality rates and weakness. Another important consequence of ketosis is the greater susceptibility to diseases, as high oxidative stress weakens the immune system.

Prevention mainly involves preventing breeding sows from getting excessively fat before farrowing, since there will be a greater negative energy balance. In addition, it is necessary to:

- Administer, in this phase, diets that favour feed intake and intestinal transit.
- Administer a very digestible diet during the peripartum period.
- Use products that promote fat oxidation in the liver such as L-carnitine.

Osteomalacia

It is caused by a calcium, phosphorus and vitamin D deficiency. This deficiency may be due to an unbalanced feed formulation, to the sows' incapacity to absorb the necessary micronutrients or to a low feed intake that prevents the sow from covering her nutritional requirements.

This disorder is observed in the farrowing room, especially in first-parity gilts, about seven days before and after farrowing. It is caused by an increase in the calcium and phosphorus needs for galactogenesis. These minerals partly come from bones, thus causing a reduction in bone density, which leads to an increased risk of lameness and bone fractures.

On farms with this problem, in addition to reviewing and correcting possible dietary imbalances in calcium and phosphorus, and to increasing the affected sows' feed intake, calcium and vitamin AD3 may be injected as a prophylactic measure.

In the most severe cases, the sows' legs may remain splayed out and they are unable to stand up on all fours, which leads to them being euthanised (Fig. 3).

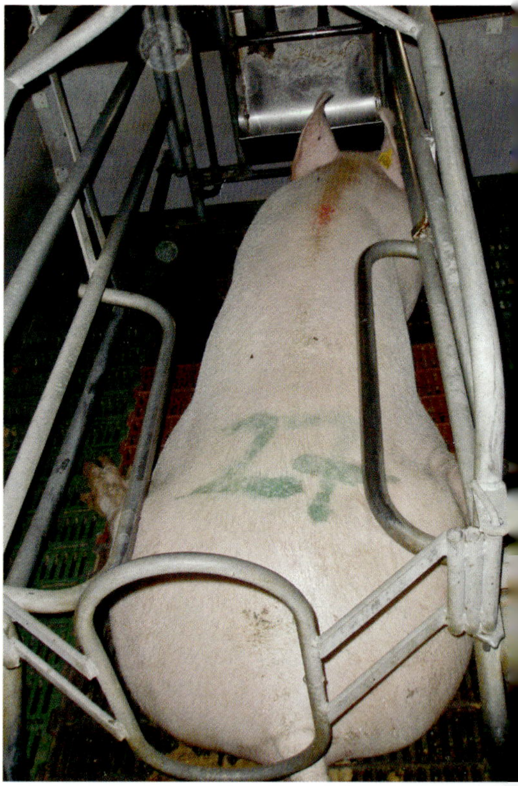

Figure 3 Sow with posterior paralysis.

Prolapses

The most common types of prolapses observed in sows in the peripartum period are described next.

Prolapsed bladder

It is uncommon and characterised by part of the bladder protruding through the labia of the vulva, due to a lack of muscle tone in the sphincter.

Treatment involves placing the bladder back into its natural position, although recurrences are likely and it is therefore recommended to send the animal to slaughter.

Prolapsed rectum

It is a relatively common problem in sows (Fig. 4). Although the exact mechanisms through which this problem occurs have not been described, its predisposing factors are known:

- Oestrus, associated with high levels of oestrogens.
- Constipation.
- Any mechanical factor that exerts pressure on the abdominal area, such as steep slopes in the stables or when the animals huddle together due to low temperatures, will favour this process.
- Diets poor in fibre and mouldy feed that may contain mycotoxins, as well as feed components causing a high degree of fermentation with production of gas in the intestine.

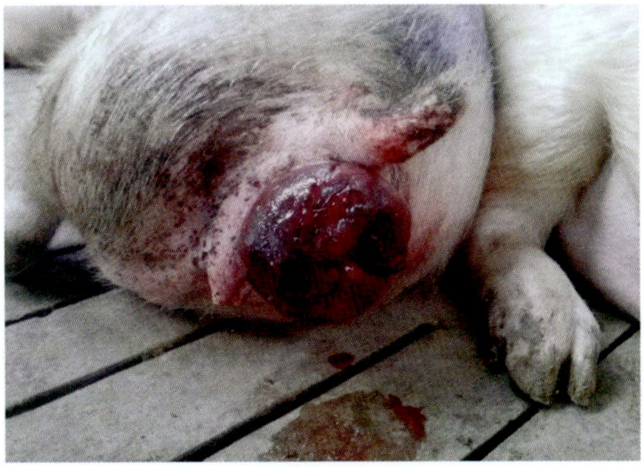

Figure 4 Sow with a prolapsed rectum.

Prolapsed uterus

It is the complete eversion of the two horns of the uterus, which is turned inside out (Fig. 5). It usually happens a few hours after farrowing, due to the prolonged efforts made by the sow, which lead to the uterus protruding outside her vagina as a result of the uterine contractions. It is uncommon and observed in older sows with large litters or heavy piglets, as the structures that support the uterus are weakened, or because the uterine walls have become flaccid.

A prolapsed uterus is difficult to treat and requires a very complicated surgical technique. On a large number of occasions, due to its complexity, the sow eventually dies as a result of severe haemorrhage, and emergency euthanasia is therefore advised.

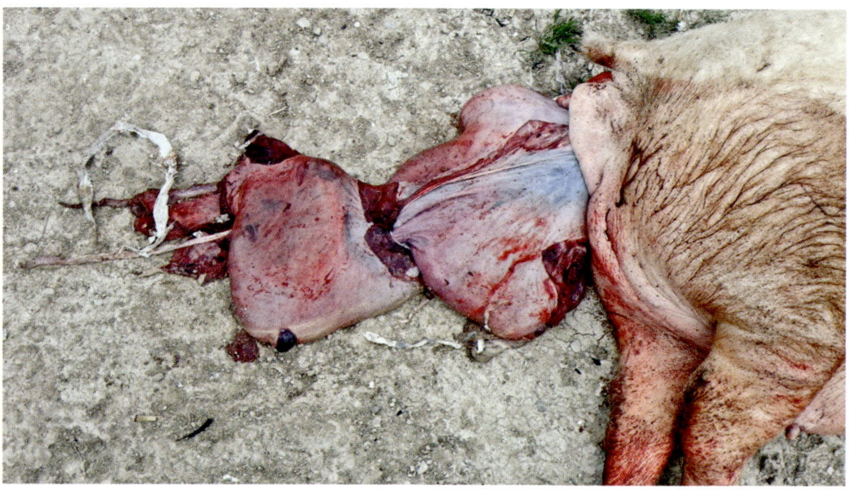

Figure 5 Sow with a prolapsed uterus.

Vaginal and cervical prolapse

Vaginal prolapses are usually accompanied by intense oedema of the perineal area and vulva (Fig. 6). They may sometimes be complicated with a prolapsed rectum.

This process more frequently appears before farrowing and in the last third of gestation. It is more commonly associated with older (more than five farrowings), large sows, with large litters and a good body condition. It is caused by increased abdominal pressure and the relaxation of the internal muscles that support the cervix.

Treatment involves trying to reintroduce the vagina and any other prolapsed structure and placing sutures around the vulva.

A sow that starts to farrow with a vaginal and cervical prolapse has a very poor prognosis, as do her piglets, as the cervix will not fully open.

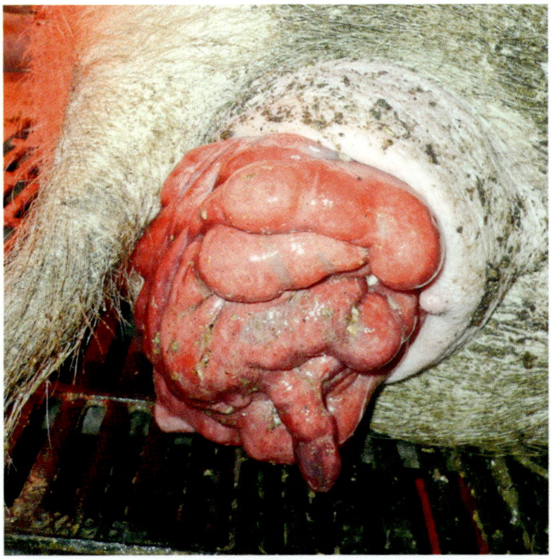

Figure 6 Vaginal and cervical prolapse.

Nervous sows, attacks to piglets and cannibalism

This problem is more frequent in first-parity gilts and may lead to the death of a great part of the litter.

The affected sows are nervous when arriving at the farrowing room and become aggressive. They attack their piglets and may even eat them.

The exact causes of this behaviour are unknown, but the factors that may be involved have been described:

- Individual character and even a certain genetic predisposition. It is thus recommended to euthanise those nervous animals in which the behaviour is observed, especially on farms where selective breeding is carried out. Breed also seems to be a factor.
- Stress due to confinement and above all due to loud noises and/or alterations that lead to the sows becoming nervous.
- Nutritional deficiencies seem to be an unlikely cause.

> Large White purebred sows are more nervous and show a greater tendency to this behaviour than other breeds such as the Duroc or Landrace breeds.

Prevention is quite complicated, as it is difficult to detect what sows are going to develop this behaviour. However, attending farrowings properly and monitoring them is very important to reduce this abnormal behaviour. Observing how a sow reacts with her first piglets may provide some clues as to whether she is going to develop cannibalistic behaviour or not. If she does, an anaesthetic should be injected to calm her down and the farrowing room attendant should wait for the farrowing process to continue and remove the piglets from their mother. Once farrowing is over, the piglets are placed with their mother so they can suckle and the attendant should check whether the sow accepts them.

Haematoma of the vulva

It is a process that occurs after farrowing as a result of the rupture of small blood vessels in the vulva, due to stretching and trauma of the tissues and pressure on them. When this process takes place, the tissues of the vulva become very fragile and easily erode, causing severe haemorrhages. These haematomas can also occur as a result of human assistance at farrowing, especially in first-parity gilts.

In severe cases, a haematoma of the vulva may cause death, as the animal suffers from great haemorrhages and anaemia.

Shoulder ulcers

They occur due to constant trauma on the bony prominences of the scapula. In these situations, the skin opens, erodes and a wound develops in the scapular region (Fig. 7). These ulcers are associated with very thin or poorly fed sows in the lactation phase as well as with inadequate facilities.

In some countries, they are used as an indicator of deficiencies in the sows' welfare.

Treatment involves the application of a healing spray. On farms with optimal management practices, padded bandages are applied on the ulcers or wounds to protect the sows when they lie down.

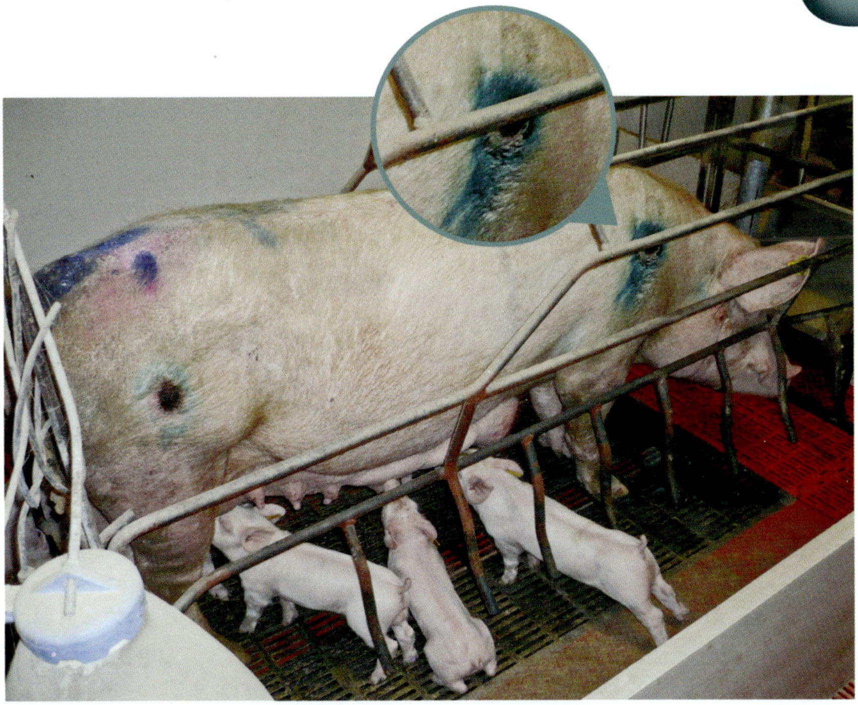

Figure 7 Sow with ulcers in the area of the scapula and hindquarters.

Main diseases of piglets

They are grouped according to their origin, which may be dietary, due to management, or to infectious or congenital diseases.

Dietary origin

Nowadays, the nutritional needs of pigs are very well known and the occasions on which these problems are observed are scarce. However, an incorrect feeding curve during gestation may lead to the sow suffering from vitamin, mineral, energy and protein deficiencies that will affect the development of her piglets.

Hypoglycaemia

In nursing piglets, hypoglycaemia and hypothermia appear together as an energy balance disorder. Although this syndrome may have very diverse causes, at its later stages there is a single clinical picture, in which signs of nervous origin can be highlighted (sensory and motor functions are altered).

It may be due to energy and/or heat imbalances. Newborn piglets are especially sensitive to this condition, since their capacity to regulate their metabolism and body temperature is not fully developed yet. In addition to insufficient heat regulation, they do not have fat deposits that allow them to obtain energy through their oxidation. Their energy needs are covered with maternal milk.

The most important causes of a decrease in the energy available are:
- Agalactia or hypogalactia, postpartum dysgalactia syndrome (PDS) or dietary failures.
- An insufficient number of functional mammary glands, too large litters, congenital injuries or wounds.
- Intestinal absorption disorders in cases of diarrhoea in piglets.

An inappropriate design of the facilities and regulation of the microclimate (lack of focal heat, draughts, humidity, lack of attention during farrowing) favour the appearance of this problem.

Mycotoxicosis
They are more or less severe intoxications due to the consumption of feed contaminated by toxin-producing fungi. They are relatively frequent.

One of the best known toxins is zearalone, which leads to a clinical picture in female piglets characterised by inflammation of the vulva and oedema caused by hyperoestrogenism, and to necrosis of the tail in male piglets (Figs. 8 and 9).

The prevention of the problem includes good feeding management, avoiding its storage during prolonged periods or silos in poor condition that increase the risk of fungal growth. Antifungal agents may be added to the feed during its manufacturing.

When the incidence of cases increases, mycotoxin-sequestering agents may be added to the feed as a preventive measure.

Other conditions
Selenium and vitamin E deficiencies are the best known of the disorders due to intoxications, avitaminosis and other mineral and oligoelement deficiencies. Nonetheless, with modern sow feeding control systems, they are rarely seen.

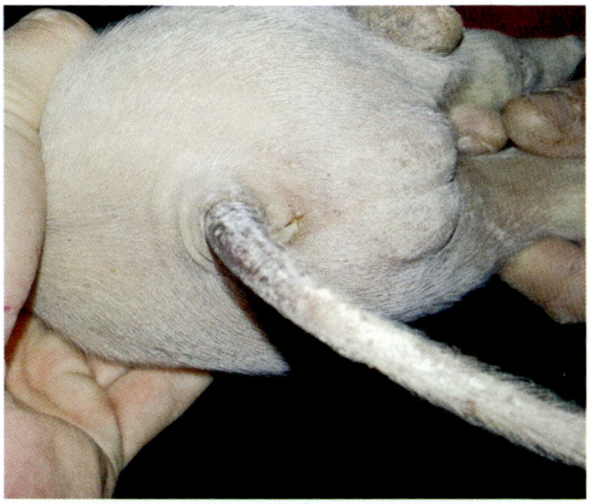

Figure 8 Necrosis of a male piglet's tail.

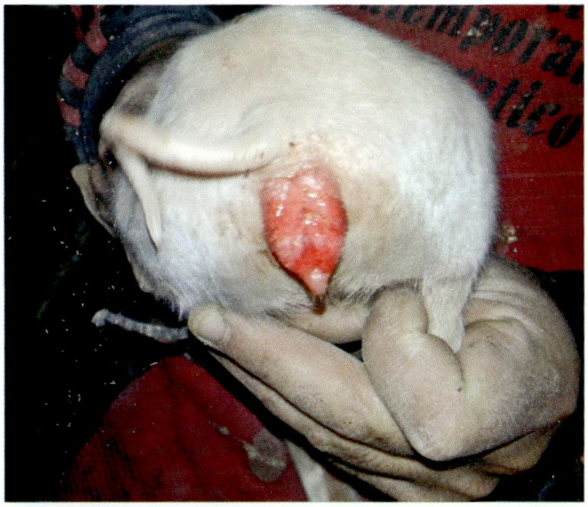

Figure 9 Inflammation of the vulva in a female piglet.

Management

Naval bleeding / pale piglet syndrome

During birth or short after birth, the affected piglets become extremely pale and often die. This can be due to a lack of oxygen caused by trauma to the umbilical cord or its rupture during farrowing, when the piglet is still inside its mother. It is more frequent in large litters and in older sows.

Preventive treatment involves tying off the umbilical cord 2 cm away from the skin after birth. This procedure is carried out using a thread, string or special clip to prevent haemorrhages (Page 111).

If the piglet is very weak, an early iron injection may be administered along with a vitamin K supplement.

Hypothermia

The affected piglets are born weak and with a low body temperature. As they are weak, they are unable to suck and ingest colostrum. Their vitality is thus even more compromised.

They are usually lying down with signs of hypothermia and are dehydrated (Fig. 10).

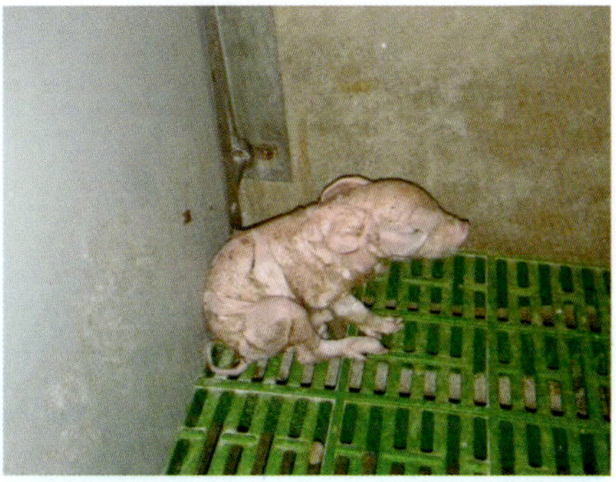

Figure 10 Hypothermia in a piglet.

Treatment should be applied as soon as possible so the piglets survive. Freshly milked colostrum may be administered using a catheter (Page 115). In addition, a significant heat source should be placed in the pen. In severe cases, glucose solution may be administered by intraperitoneal route.

If the incidence of cases increases on a farm without being due to large litters, the protocols for the administration of feed to sows and environmental conditions in the farrowing room (heat sources for piglets) should be reviewed.

Of infectious origin

Diarrhoea

Diarrhoeas are an important problem in farrowing rooms and the main cause of death in piglets during lactation.

> Worldwide, diarrhoeas are the cause of 50-70 % of neonatal deaths in piglets.

During farrowing, the piglet's intestinal tract is microbiologically sterile and has little immunity against disease-producing pathogens. After birth, microorganisms rapidly start colonising the intestinal tract. If the piglet's colostrum intake has not been sufficient, potentially pathogenic microorganisms multiply in the intestinal wall and cause diarrhoea.

In order for piglets to be properly immunised, in addition to a sufficient intake, colostrum should have a high concentration of antibodies, and sows should have healthy mammary glands.

The causes of diarrhoea are numerous and varied, although the most frequent are infections by bacteria and pathogenic viruses and parasitic infections. The term **porcine diarrhoea syndrome** is increasingly used.

In the last years (2013-2014), a new variant of **porcine epidemic diarrhoea** has appeared in America and Asia. Its morbidity and mortality rates in nursing piglets are very high, which decimates the affected pig populations.

Table 1 shows a summary of the main pathogenic agents involved in the appearance of neonatal diarrhoea.

Table 1 Main pathogenic agents causing diarrhoea in piglets during the peripartum period.

	0-3 days	3-7 days	7-14 days	15-21 days	Morbidity	Mortality	I.P.
Clostridial diseases	√	√	√		Moderate	High	< 1 day
Colibacillosis	√	√	√		Very high	Moderada	1-3 days
PED	√	√	√	√	Very high	High	1-8 days
PRRS	√	√	√	√	High	Variable	1-2 days
TGE	√	√	√	√	Very high	High	1-4 days

I.P. Incubation period; PED: porcine epidemic diarrhoea; PRRS: porcine reproductive and respiratory syndrome;
TGE: porcine gastroenteritis virus.

Although there are numerous pathogens that may cause diarrhoea, *Escherichia coli* bacteria are by far the main infectious agent. More than one thousand different serotypes of these bacteria are known. Most of them are apathogenic, as they are very common in the intestinal flora. The strains that cause diarrhoea are those able to attach to the intestinal epithelium and produce toxins.

Enterotoxins pass into the cells of the intestinal wall, cause an increase in the secretion of fluids to the intestinal lumen and block the absorption of electrolytes by these cells. This inversion of natural absorption in the intestine leads to a loss of large volumes of water and minerals that causes severe dehydration in the affected animals and often their death (Fig. 11).

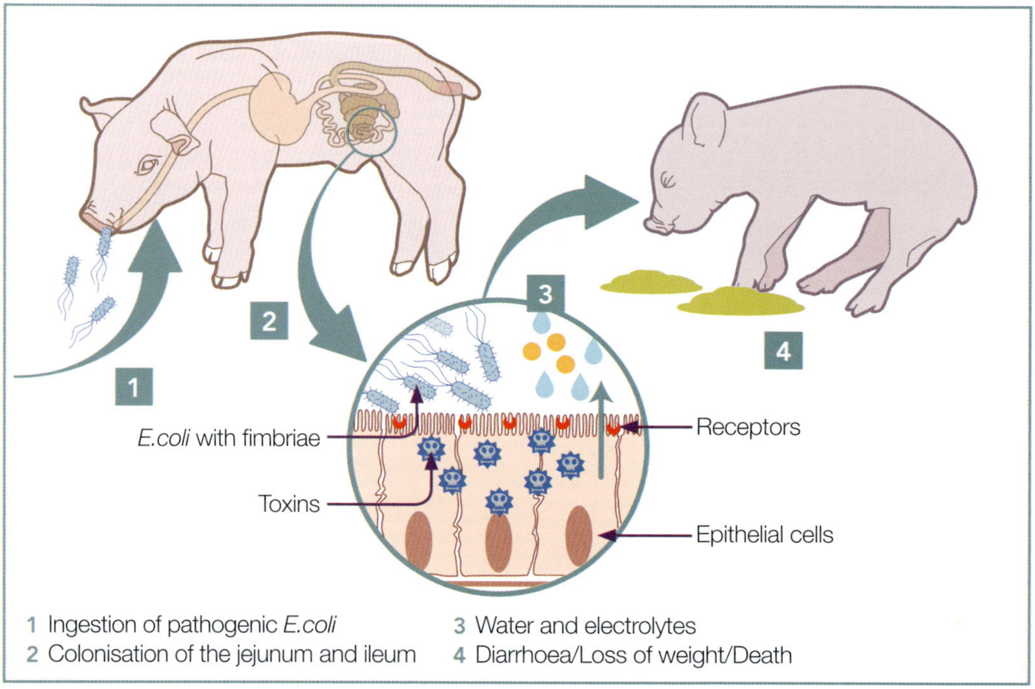

Figure 11 Mechanism of action of enterotoxigenic *Escherichia coli*. From: Fairbrother, J.M. *Escherichia coli en ganado porcino*. Grupo Asís Biomedia, S.L., 2009.

E.coli diarrhoea in piglets in farrowing rooms essentially occurs in the first five days of life. Normally, the whole litter is affected and the piglets suffer from severe watery/creamy diarrhoea with a light whitish colour (Fig. 12). The animals have sunken flanks, are weak and remain apathetic (Fig. 13). A large number of them die of dehydration.

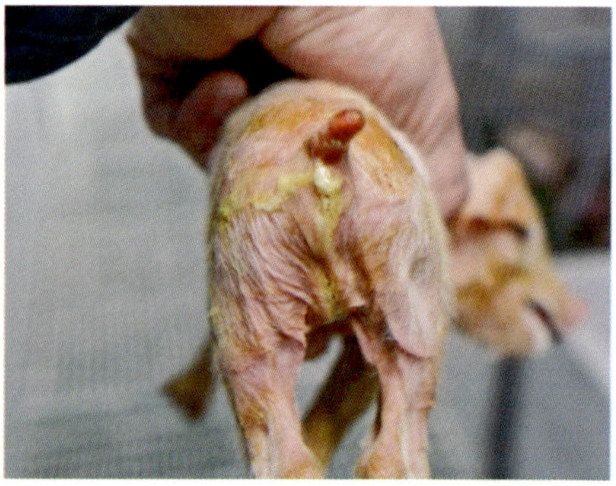

Figure 12 *E.coli* diarrhoea in a piglet with few days of life.

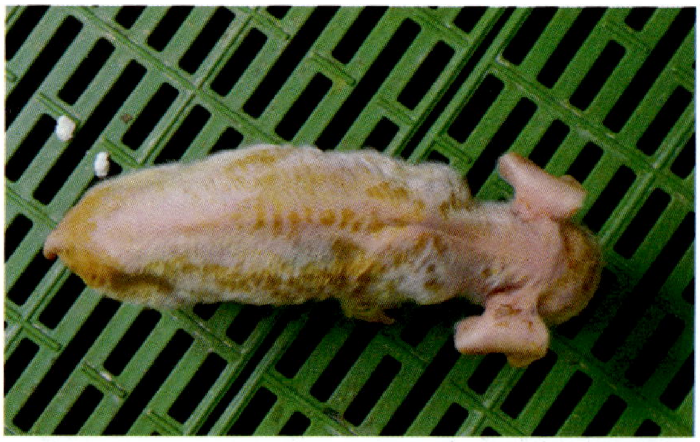

Figure 13 Dehydrated piglet due to *E.coli* diarrhoea.

Curative treatment involves the administration by oral or parenteral route of a specific antibiotic for the *E.coli* strain present on the farm, which requires an antibiogram to be performed. Rehydration of the affected piglets is recommended, but most importantly, adequate prophylaxis should be ensured by immunising the sows, especially first-parity gilts, using an appropriate vaccination programme and feedback with the pathogenic strains of *E.coli* on the operation during gestation. This way, mothers will produce and transmit protective antibodies to their offspring.

What is feedback?

Feedback involves feeding the animals susceptible to develop the disease (nulliparous and first-parity gilts mainly) with faecal material and intestines of piglets that had not been medicated.
A very common method is to collect scours in the farrowing room using a mop with non-treated water, or once chlorine or peroxide has evaporated. Next, the water is diluted and given to the sows at 80-90 days of gestation to ensure piglets are immunised against colon bacilli before birth. Very good results have been obtained on farms with persistent diarrhoeas in the farrowing unit, but feedback entails some risks and knowing the pathological situation of each farm perfectly is essential.

Feedback is a very common and inexpensive method, but it must be carried out correctly and the cases in which it is not advised should be known.

The diseases that manifest with diarrhoeas in the farrowing room and for which this procedure is recommended according to J. Gadd (2006) are detailed next:

- Transmissible gastroenteritis.
- Neonatal diarrhoea.
- Some persistent enteric infections.
- Diarrhoea of litters from first-parity gilts.
- Viral diarrhoeas, porcine epidemic diarrhoea being one of them.

In addition to the infectious and parasitic agents responsible for diarrhoeas in piglets, a series of environmental factors favour their appearance and development.

- Agalactia or hypogalactia in sows, which translates into no or poor milk and colostrum intake by piglets in their first days of life.
- Poor health of the sow. Animals with enteric and respiratory diseases, lameness or mastitis predispose their litter to suffering from this condition.
- Low ambient temperature. Many cases of diarrhoea are due to attempts in reducing energy expenses. It should be remembered that piglets need a focal temperature of 32-35 °C in their first days of life.
- Environmental humidity and inappropriate drainage systems.
- Draughts.
- Lack of hygiene in the pens.
- Drinking water of poor microbiological quality.
- Feed contaminated with bacteria.

To summarise, if environmental conditions are good, the incidence and severity of diarrhoeas will be lower.

Clostridial diseases are another frequent infectious process. They are mainly caused by *Clostridium perfringens* type C and manifest with occasionally haemorrhagic diarrhoeas.

In the last few years, the outbreaks of *Clostridium difficile* have increased and have had higher mortality rates.

Porcine epidemic diarrhoea (PED) and transmissible gastroenteritis (TGE) are viral diseases with high neonatal mortality rates in piglets. In these cases, it is important to adopt proper biosecurity measures and ensure the rapid immunisation of the sows when the first cases appear.

Congenital malformations

In our current pig production system, many sows are inseminated with the same boar, which may as a result give rise to generalised alterations of genetic origin. To solve this problem, the most recommended option is to keep a record of the boars that have inseminated the sows so the problem is rapidly identified 114 days later.

In cases of genetic malformations, it is necessary to check whether these have their origin in the semen used. If this is the case, the donor boar should be sent to slaughter.

Most of the malformations observed and described in piglets at birth are those that can be seen externally (Fig. 14). However, some congenital abnormalities may also cause lesions in internal organs. These are only detected at necropsy. More than 150 congenital malformations in piglets at birth have been described, the most important of which are described in Table 2.

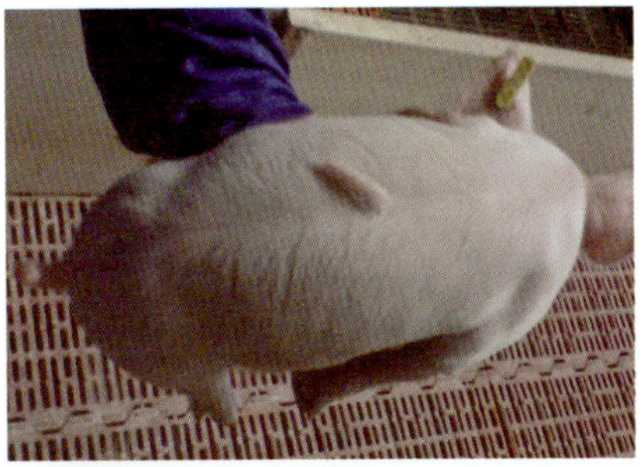

Figure 14 Congenital malformation in a piglet.

Table 2 Aetiology of the main congenital malformations.

	Born animals (%)	Aetiology				Mortality rate in the percentage of affected animals
		Genetics	Toxic-dietary	Management	Infectious	
Abnormalities of the female genital tract	1-2	+				0
Splay leg	0.5-1	+	?		?	50
Heart defects	0.4-0.5	+	?			80
Inguinal hernia	0.4-1	+				10
Umbilical hernia	0.1-1	+		+		10
Skeletal abnormalities (arthrogryposis)	0.3	+	+			50
Cryptorchidism	0.2	+				0
Congenital myoclonus	0.2	+			+	50
Epitheliogenesis imperfecta	0.05	+				5
Anal atresia*	<0.05	+				100
Meningocele	<0.01	+				100
Hermaphroditism	<0.01	+				0

*Greater prevalence in females.

Inguinal and umbilical hernias

Inguinal and umbilical hernias are the most common congenital abnormalities. They are due to a muscle rupture that causes the internal organs to bulge out. On some occasions, they can be related to services performed with a specific boar.

Inguinal hernia

An inguinal hernia is when a portion of intestine protrudes through the inguinal canal out of the abdominal cavity (Figs. 15 and 16). Inguinal hernias do not cause any problems, unless they are large or occur on farms where males need to be castrated. They can be corrected with a simple surgery.

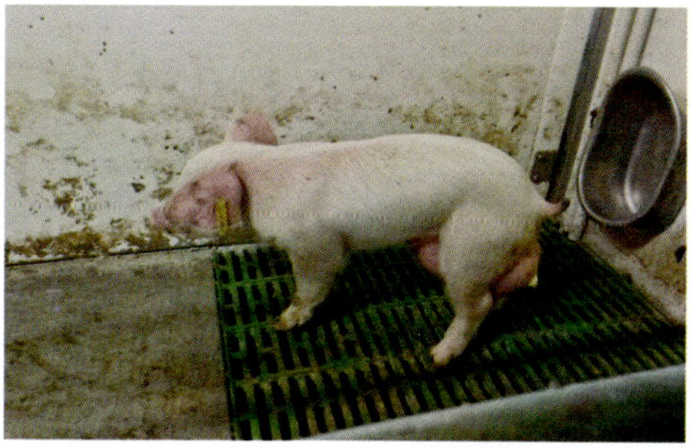

Figure 15 Piglet with an inguinal hernia.

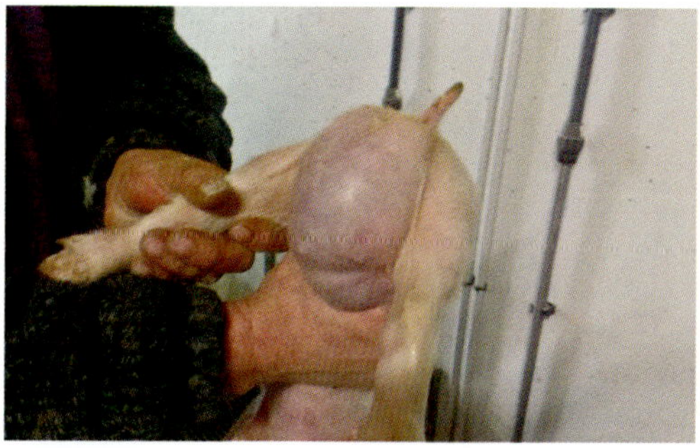

Figure 16 Detail of the inguinal hernia from the previous picture. The hernia contained the intestinal mass.

Umbilical hernia

An umbilical hernia occurs when part of the intestine protrudes in the subcutaneous space through the umbilical ring.

If the incidence of umbilical hernias increases on a farm, piglet management practices should be reviewed:

- During farrowing. The excessive use of prostaglandins causes piglets to be expelled with an overly stretched umbilical cord or umbilical haemorrhages. Inappropriate techniques when attending farrowings may also be responsible for this problem (piglets removed by means of obstetric manoeuvres without ligating the cord).
- Ambient temperature. Cold environments cause the animals to huddle together, causing greater abdominal pressure.
- Procedure to cut and tie off umbilical cords. Not tying the cord or doing it incorrectly favours the presence of hernias (Page 111).

Epitheliogenesis imperfecta

The piglet is born without skin in some body areas (Fig. 17). It is an uncommon condition on pig farms and in most cases, it heals spontaneously as it occurs in a small area. In those cases in which epitheliogenesis is too wide, the piglet should be euthanised.

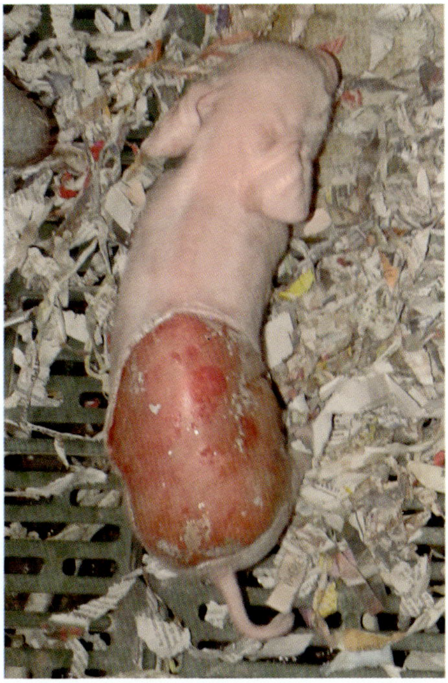

Figure 17 Piglet with epitheliogenesis imperfecta.

Splay leg syndrome

Splay leg at birth is a fairly extended clinical picture that, under inadequate housing conditions, may cause a high mortality rate in piglets.

The cause of the disease is unclear, although it seems that there is a clear genetic component and that some breeds such as the Landrace and Pietrain breeds are affected on a more frequent basis. Its frequency is higher in acute infectious outbreaks such as PRRS outbreaks. This clinical manifestation is due to insufficient muscle maturation, favoured by premature farrowing, as well as to a low birth weight of the affected piglets.

Generally, several piglets are affected with variable degrees of severity in a litter. After birth, they adopt a position in which their hind limbs are splayed out sideways, as if they were sitting. In the most severe cases, the front limbs are also splayed out (Fig. 18).

These piglets usually die of starvation or by being crushed, as their ability to move is hindered. If, despite the clinical picture, the affected piglets manage to suckle adequately, spontaneous recovery will occur.

To correct this defect, the hind limbs may be may be tied together using insulating tape or a rubber band for this purpose, so that spontaneous recovery is accelerated (Fig. 19). It is important that these animals ingest sufficient colostrum to acquire enough strength and be able to survive.

If the prevalence of this condition on a farm is high, it is necessary to look for a possible genetic origin in order to euthanise the boars that carry this alteration.

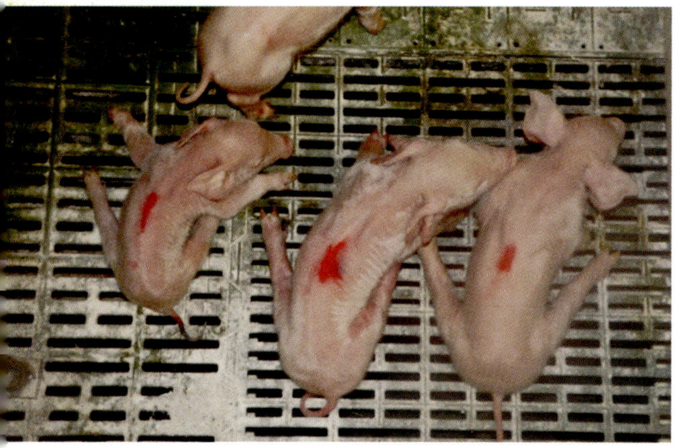

Figure 18 Piglets with splay leg syndrome.

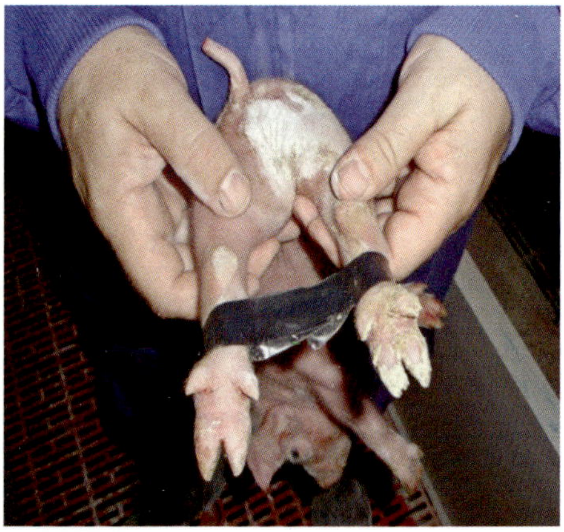

Figure 19 Insulating tape to correct this abnormality.

Congenital myoclonus or congenital tremor

It is a typical disease of the central nervous system, but its aetiology is diverse. The alterations are due to malformations of the cerebellum or to a myelin deficiency.

Different degrees of tremor are observed in the same litter. The affected piglets have clonic spasms of variable intensity and speed. Their head shakes from side to side and drops, their back jerks and contractions may also be seen in the limbs. Tremors, in most cases, start right after birth, which makes nursing difficult and thus leads to death by starvation. If, despite the tremors, the animals can suckle, the signs disappear or are reduced after the first two or three days of life.

There is no known treatment for this disorder. Some variants of this disease are caused by a virus that disappears from the operation a maximum of four months after an outbreak and passive immunisation of the herd. In some cases, the animals have recovered with the rapid immunisation of the herd by means of feedback, using brains from affected piglets as infective material.

Anal atresia

The affected piglets are born with no anus, as their rectum ends in a blind pouch, 5-10 mm from the skin surface (Fig. 20). The incidence is low on pig farms, but it may be more frequent in litters from first-parity gilts. It is a genetic condition. On a problematic farm, records should be controlled so as to ensure the origin is not a boar.

There is no other possible treatment than surgery, which is easy to perform. If a surgical treatment is not applied, the outcome in all cases is death.

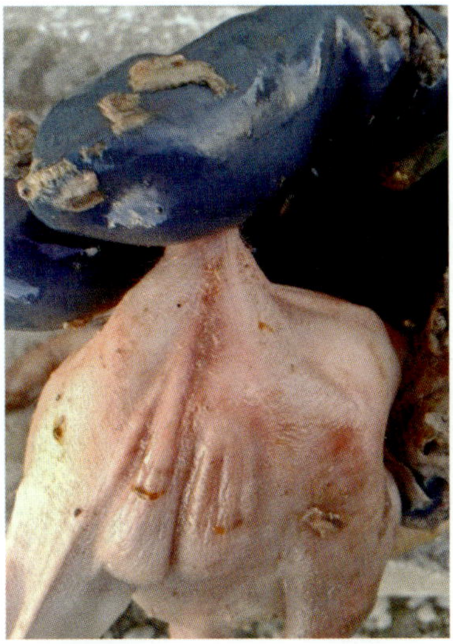

Figure 20 Piglet with anal atresia.

Hydrocephalus

It is an abnormal build-up of cerebrospinal fluid in the brain's ventricles.

It may be the consequence of hereditary genetic alterations or developmental disorders, such as those associated with neural tube defects that may cause spina bifida or encephalocele, or derived from complications in premature births. There is no treatment for this malformation, whose prognosis is death.

Meningocele

Meningocele is the consequence of a protrusion of the meninges through a bone defect in the skull or spine. It may have a congenital or acquired origin. Its clinical presentation is a cyst filled with cerebrospinal fluid (Fig. 21). This disease is lethal.

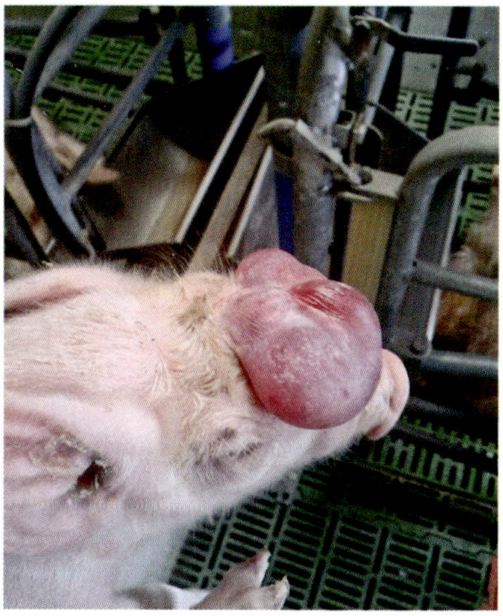

Figure 21 Piglet with meningocele.

Arthrogryposis

It is a combination of joint abnormalities. It involves ankylosis of the joints at several degrees of flexion or extension, which may affect the limbs or spine, resulting in lordosis, kyphosis or scoliosis. Its causes are myogenic or neurogenic and they are associated with spinal cord dysplasia. Its origin is unknown, but it may be associated with vitamin A deficiencies and hereditary factors.

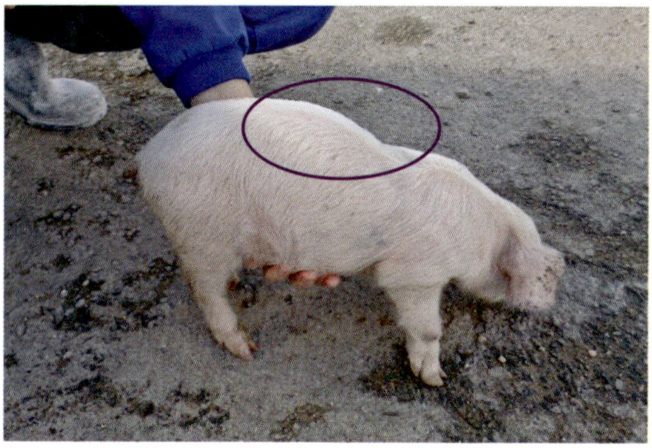

Figure 22 Piglet with arthrogryposis.

7 Work organisation

Introduction

In modern pig production, the workforce, together with genetics, health and nutrition, is one of the fundamental pillars of the success of a pig production company.

Pig production currently allows the production of more than 30 piglets per sow and year, which requires a highly qualified and trained workforce in farrowing units, with a series of well-defined and standardised tasks. The workforce is one of the main factors that influence productivity in farrowing units (Fig. 1).

Figure 1 Influence of the personnel on the size of a litter on the same farm. Extracted from Collell, M., Gestión de recursos humanos, 2006; *Suis* 25: 52.

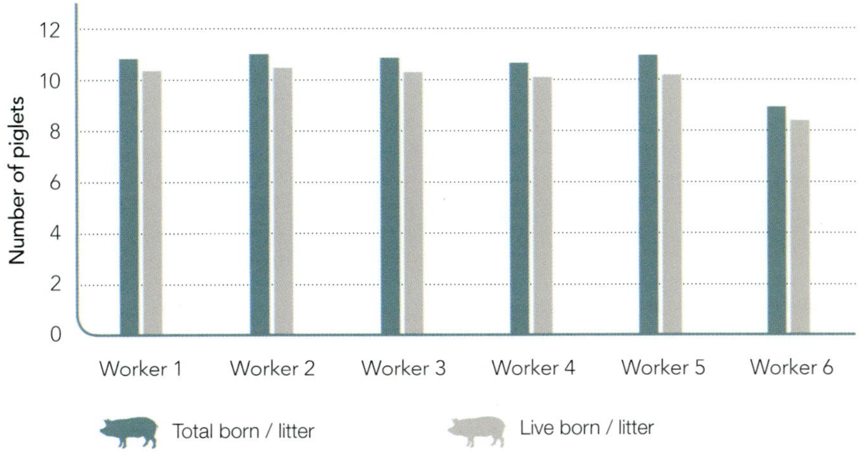

On the one hand, farms are designed to facilitate cleaning and on the other hand, cleaning is highly automated. The farm personnel can thus essentially focus on the management of the different tasks to be performed: farrowings, husbandry practices, services, etc.

A very common sentence in pig production companies around the world is: "**Managing pigs is easy, what is difficult is to manage people**", and experience confirms it.

Personnel needs on farms

When considering the needs of personnel of a farm, it is essential to make a good analysis of the tasks they should carry out and of the specific training required. Both the qualitative and quantitative needs of personnel on the farm therefore need to be established.

- Qualitative needs: skills and training necessary for each position.
- Quantitative needs: number of people necessary.

Qualitative needs

The ideal farrowing room attendant should be:

- **Systematic-meticulous**: on sow farms, the management of the tasks related to farrowing should be highly standardised and systematic.
- **Organised**: the person in charge of attending farrowings should use a system of control of the farrowings in progress (**monitoring**) and note down the data related to the farrowings correctly.
- **Careful-patient**: the people responsible for caring for newborn piglets and attending farrowing sows with pain, nervousness, etc. should be very careful and patient with this type of animals.
- **Clean**: farrowing is a time when the degree of cleanliness and hygiene must be as high as possible.

- **Proactive**: even if everything is highly systematised, problematic farrowings always occur, as well as situations in which it is necessary to make decisions to solve any problems that may arise and to know which ones to prioritise.
- **With an appropriate level of education:** they should know how to use computer tools, personal digital assistants (PDAs) or technical management software, among others.

On many farms and with an increasing frequency, the people dedicated to this function are women, as they fulfil all these requirements.

Quantitative needs

There is a concept used to measure the needs of personnel in an agricultural or livestock company. This is the man-work unit (MWU), which is defined as the amount of work performed over a one-year period by a person dedicated full-time to farm work.

Once the MWUs have been defined, the tasks and work to carry out in the farrowing house should be established (daily, weekly, monthly tasks, etc.).

At the same time, the **time required** to carry out each task should be determined. This will depend on the degree of mechanisation and automation of the operation. The less a farm is automated (automatic feed dispensers, washing, etc.), the longer the time dedicated to these tasks will be (Figs. 2 and 3).

Figure 2 Farrowing room with manual feeding.

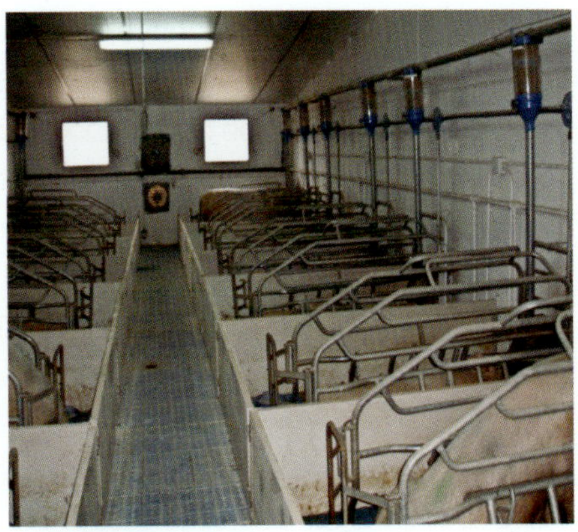

Figure 3 Farrowing room with automated feeding.

As a general rule in Europe, it is established that a farm with phase 1 sows has personnel needs of 1 MWU per 250 sows.

In Europe, a farm with sows in phase 1 (production of piglets until weaning) requires approximately 1 MWU for 250 sows. This amounts to a total of **2,080 hours per MWU per year** (40 hours a week times 52 weeks), taking into account holidays and substitutions.

In other countries where the workforce has a lower cost and the level of automation on farms is reduced, the MWU needs per sow may increase significantly.

Obviously, the personnel necessary on a farm, and particularly in the farrowing house, also depends on the size of the operation. In a very general manner, sow farms can be divided into:

a. **Family farms.** In general, these are small- to medium-sized farms (500-700 sows). The personnel is usually a family (the owner and his/her family), although they sometimes have other employees. The workforce must be very **versatile**, as all types of tasks are usually carried out on the farm (services, farrowing, washing, removing manure, etc.). They usually receive occasional help for different weekly tasks such as weaning, loading animals, etc.
b. **Industrial farms.** These are farms of a larger size with hired workforce and a high level of **specialisation** at work. They have a manager or supervisor for the whole operation, a farrowing unit supervisor and a gestation unit supervisor (Fig. 4). Both the farrowing and gestation unit supervisors have subordinates with perfectly defined positions as far as tasks and times are concerned. It is sometimes advisable to rotate tasks to maintain motivation and prevent the personnel from losing their spirits with certain very repetitive tasks.

Figure 4 Work organisation chart on an industrial farm.

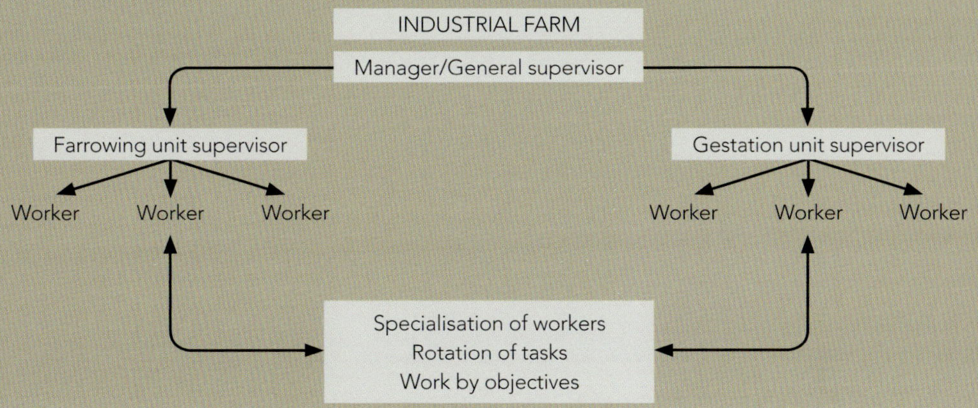

Cost of the workforce and productivity

If the production cost of a weaned piglet is analysed and the total cost is broken down into its different components, the workforce is the second most important item and is only exceeded by the cost of feed (Fig. 5).

Figure 5 Different components of the production cost of a weaned piglet in Spain in the integrated farm system (2012).

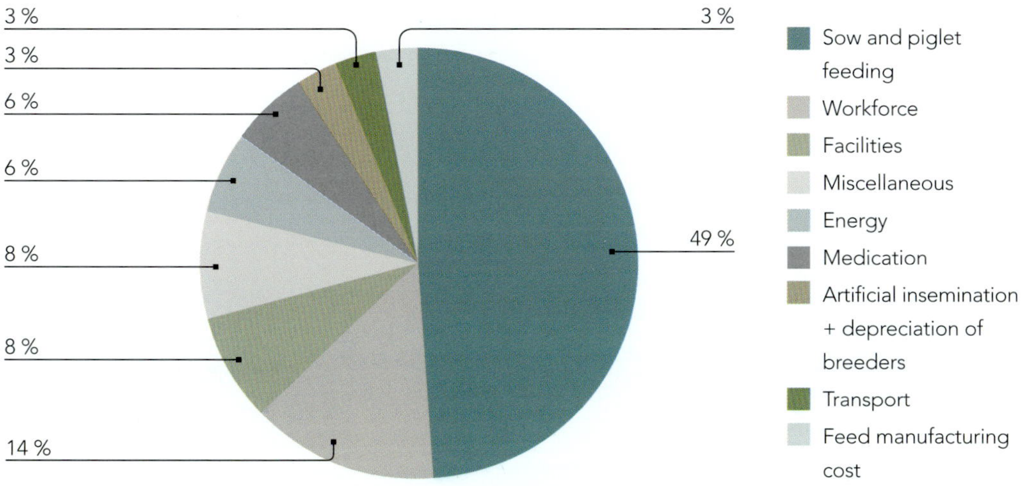

The cost of feed represents a very high percentage, approximately 50 %, of the total cost (it varies sensibly from one year to another depending on the price of raw materials). In order of importance, it is followed by the cost of workforce, which usually represents about 14 % of the total. Without any doubt, it is an important part of the costs, although on many farms there is little personnel working in the farrowing unit, especially if hyperprolific genetic lines are used. It is therefore highly important to have perfectly qualified, trained, motivated, efficient, productive personnel and in an appropriate number.

Normally, productivity on a farm of breeding sows is measured using the parameter **piglets produced per sow and year.** This concept of productivity can be applied to the workforce and several ratios are used to assess its efficiency:

- Piglets produced per MWU and year.
- Piglets produced per hour worked.

As observed in Table 1, the productivity of a farm (piglets per sow and year), considerably influences the cost of the workforce. A greater number of weaned piglets per hour worked reduces the cost of the workforce attributed to each piglet produced.

Work organisation

The first step to achieve an efficient production of piglets is the organisation of the farm, as regards both specific production tasks and its management as a company. Farmers must increasingly change their mindset from that of a traditional farmer to that of a small business manager. They need to dedicate a significant part of their time to managing the operation and give more importance to personnel management.

Although every pig production company is organised according to its own characteristics (size, facilities, genetics, health, type of production, etc.), there are basic guidelines that can be applied to every pig farm. These are described next.

Table 1 Productivity of the workforce according to sow productivity on a farm of 1,000 sows and four MWU.

	PRODUCTIVITY		
Size of the farm: 1,000 sows	20 piglets/sow/year	25 piglets/sow/year	30 piglets/sow/year
Piglets produced/year	20,000	25,000	30,000
Piglets/MWU/year	5,000	6,250	7,500
Piglets/hour worked	2.4	3	3.61

List of tasks

Once the tasks to be performed on the farm, and more specifically in the farrowing unit, have been established, it is necessary to bear in mind the fact that some of them are carried out daily, while others are performed periodically. These latter will depend on the batch farrowing system implemented on the farm (weekly, two-weekly, three-weekly systems...):

- Periodic tasks: the frequency with which these tasks are carried out depends on the batch farrowing system implemented on the farm.
- Daily tasks.

Table 2 shows the different tasks carried out on the operation, according to their frequency.

Table 2 List of periodic and daily tasks to be performed in the farrowing unit.

PERIODIC TASKS	DAILY TASKS
Cleaning and disinfection of the farrowing rooms.	Feeding (several times a day).
Environmental control of the farrowing unit.	Checking the state of the sows and piglets.
Moving the sows to the farrowing unit.	Cleaning the rear part of the farrowing pens.
Administration of antiparasitic treatment to the sows.	Cleaning the aisles.
Attending farrowings (several days).	Data recording.
Processing piglets (identification, iron, etc.).	Maintenance.
Fostering - Nurse sows.	
Vaccination of sows (e.g. parvovirosis).	
Vaccination of piglets.	
Moving weaned piglets.	
Silo control - Feed orders.	
Moving weaned sows.	

On days on which farrowings take place, part of the farm personnel should be in charge of attending farrowings. This involves carrying out a series of systematic tasks:

1. Removing the foetal membranes with which piglets are born and that sometimes prevent them from breathing normally.
2. Resuscitating the piglets that have been born after a long labour or those that are partly asphyxiated.
3. Drying the piglets and placing them under the heat sources, making sure they are sufficiently warm.
4. Providing special care to the weakest piglets, placing them close to the teats and ensuring a proper intake of colostrum (Fig. 6).
5. Ligation and disinfection of the umbilical cords.
6. Ensuring a proper intake of colostrum by all the piglets. Applying split-suckling in large litters.
7. Therapeutic treatment of the sows that behave aggressively towards their litter.
8. Providing obstetric assistance to the sows that need it or when the time interval between the births of two piglets exceed 30 minutes; helping them to expel their piglets.
9. Removing faecal material and farrowing residues from the rear part of the sow.
10. Correcting any health problems by administering the treatments prescribed by the veterinary surgeon (serum and other drugs to piglets with neonatal diarrhoea) and tape the legs of those suffering from splay-leg together.
11. Checking that the sow does not show any signs of mastitis and accepts her litter.
12. Recording any relevant observations in the record sheet, as well as the sows and litter that need to be watched.

As many farrowings take place out of the usual farm working hours, the people in charge of attending farrowings often work in shifts (morning, afternoon, night) in order to ensure that technicians are present for all farrowings.

Figure 6 Care at farrowing: ensuring colostrum intake by the piglets.

Below you will find an example of how shifts may be distributed on an operation.

SHIFT CALENDAR OCTOBER

Jim						
		1	2	3	4	5
6	7	8	9	10	11	12
13	14	15	16	17	18	19
20	21	22	23	24	25	26
27	28	29	30	31		
Dan						
		1	2	3	4	5
6	7	8	9	10	11	12
13	14	15	16	17	18	19
20	21	22	23	24	25	26
27	28	29	30	31		
Steve						
		1	2	3	4	5
6	7	8	9	10	11	12
13	14	15	16	17	18	19
20	21	22	23	24	25	26
27	28	29	30	31		

Holiday ■ Half working day ■ Night

Figure 7 Representation of a work shift calendar for a pig farm.

Task planning

Ninety percent of the events that occur on a farm are predictable and repetitive. By planning them in advance, they can be scheduled on specific dates of the week. This optimises the workforce and, on the other hand, avoids the overlapping of tasks, uncertainty and changes of plans responsible for disorganisation and loss of time.

A weekly work calendar must be established according to the weekly day of weaning on the operation (Table 3). The farrowing room attendants must then be assigned their responsibilities and the tasks to perform for each day of the week (Figs. 8 and 9).

The type of batch management system should always be borne in mind when organising work and assigning tasks and responsibilities.

Table 3 Example of a weekly work plan on a farrowing unit.

MONDAY	TUESDAY	WEDNESDAY	THURSDAY	FRIDAY	SATURDAY	SUNDAY
Feed (3 times)	Feed (3 times)	Feed (3 times)	Feed (3 times)	Feed (3 times)	Feed (3 times)	Feed (3 times)
Check on sows	Check on sows	Check on sows	Check on sows	Check on sows	Check on sows	Check on sows
Check on piglets	Check on piglets	Check on piglets	Check on piglets	Check on piglets	Check on piglets	Check on piglets
Clean back of the pens	Clean back of the pens	Clean back of the pens	Clean back of the pens	Clean back of the pens	Clean back of the pens	Clean back of the pens
Clean aisles	Clean aisles	Clean aisles	Clean aisles	Clean aisles	Clean aisles	Clean aisles
Monitor farrowings	Monitor farrowings	Monitor farrowings	Monitor farrowings	Monitor farrowings	Monitor farrowings	Monitor farrowings
Process piglets	Process piglets	Vaccinate sows	Wean	Wash rooms	Wash rooms	
Load culled animals	Fostering procedures	Vaccinate piglets	Load piglets	Fostering procedures	Move sows to the farrowing unit	

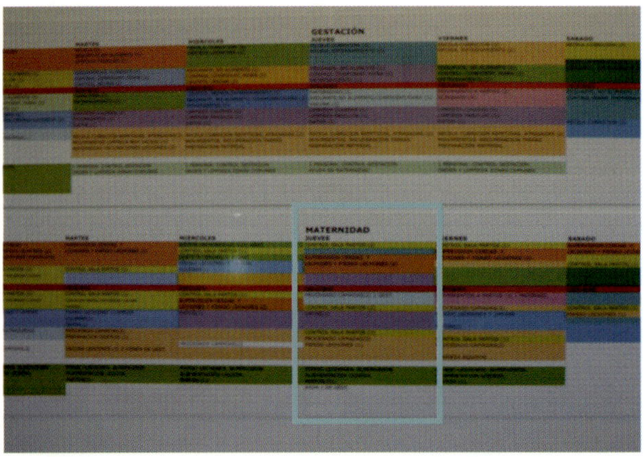

Figure 8 The tasks to be performed in the farrowing and gestation units are assigned to the different farm workers and detailed on boards such as the one shown in this image.

FARROWING UNIT

THURSDAY

- Monitoring farrowing room (2)
- Monitoring sows, piglets and piglet feed (2)
- Break
- Processing litters (2)
- Monitoring farrowing room (2)
- Data recording (1)
- Monitoring farrowing room (1)
- Processing litters (2)
- Piglet feed (1)
- Piglet feed, monitoring farrowings (1)
- Help in gestation unit (1)

Figure 9 Detail of some of the tasks assigned in Figure 8 (box). Each colour corresponds to a task and the number of farm workers necessary to carry it out on this specific day is indicated in brackets.

Once the tasks and the time necessary to carry them out have been determined, it is useful to prepare a **work schedule** (Fig. 10) for the farm. A work schedule is a list of all the tasks performed daily by a farm worker, with the time assigned to carry them out.

A work schedule involves coordinating the different tasks with the people included in the farm's organisation chart.

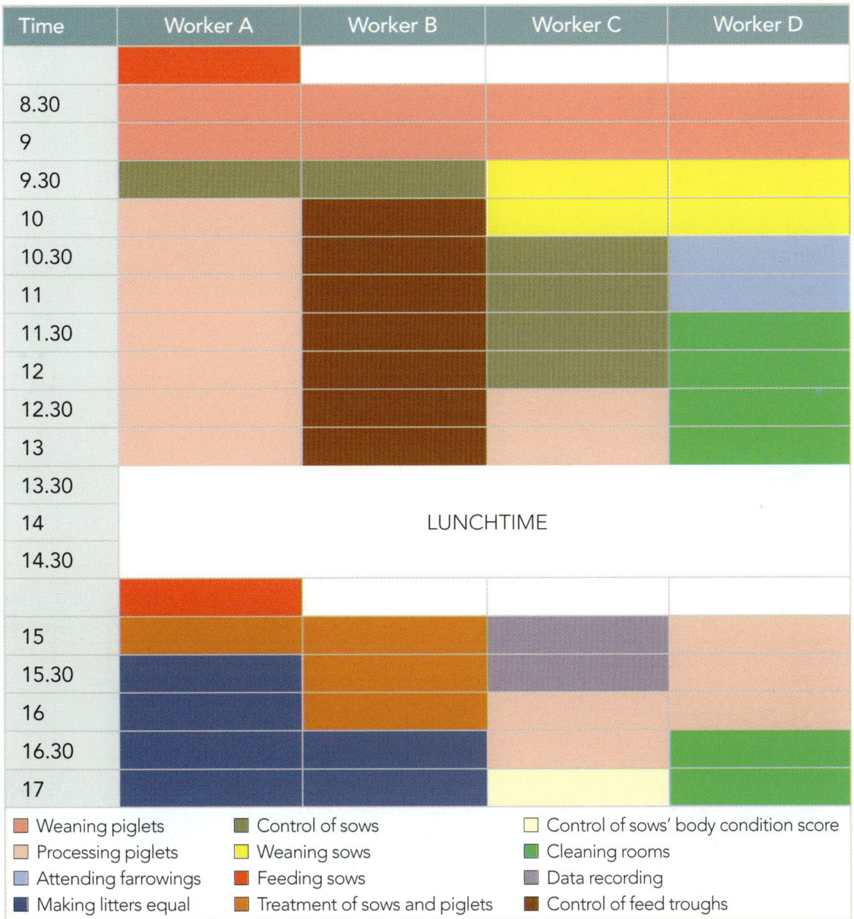

Figure 10 Graphic representation of a work schedule in a farrowing unit corresponding to the day of weaning. Adapted from Collell, M. Motivación y organización del trabajo. *Suis*, 2006; 27: 72.

A work schedule has to be used to optimise the farm's production processes.

The organisation on farms where farrowings take place every two or more weeks is different from that on farms with a weekly batch farrowing system. In the first case, a different series of tasks need to be performed every week (see Chapter 5). Indeed, on a farm with a three-weekly batch farrowing system, there will be three times as many farrowings during the week when these are programmed as on a farm with a weekly batch farrowing system. During this week, other tasks such as inseminating, weaning, etc. will not coincide with farrowings, so most of the personnel will be able to focus on the management of the farrowing house with tasks such as attending farrowings, cross-fostering, etc.

8 Conclusions

As a summary of what has been explained on farrowing unit management and more specifically on the peripartum period, the following conclusions should be highlighted:

- The genetic improvement of productive and reproductive traits and particularly of prolificacy in the last few years has been a real revolution in pig production. The appearance of new lines of hyperprolific sows has given rise to considerable changes in husbandry and feeding practices, farm facilities and in farm and personnel management.
- Although the improvement has been dramatic in the past few years, only a small part of the world's pig industry has benefited from these changes.
- Not all operations or farmers can work with the new more prolific and productive genetic lines. This requires appropriate facilities, a sufficient number of farrowing pens, correct farrowing unit management and more rational and specialised feeding programmes.
- Prolificacy will continue to improve in the future and it is therefore likely that there will be farms with productivity rates above 40 piglets per sow and year.
- Although the technical and physiological characteristics of sows will remain the same, working with thinner and more prolific sows will require major changes in husbandry practices so the animals can express all their genetic and productive potential.

- The variation factors of prolificacy on modern farms are essentially due to genetics, but it is also necessary to take into account the sow's age and cycle, seasonality, feeding, stress situations, semen quality, health status, age at first service, duration of the previous lactation and time of service, among the main factors influencing prolificacy.
- Working with more productive sows requires good organisation and a correct farm design, especially in farrowing units; more and wider farrowing pens are needed in order to wean more piglets with more days of life and a higher weight, and to work with nurse sows.
- Farrowing places should represent 24 % of the total productive sows on the farm, and 28 % when working with hyperprolific sows, so that fostering techniques can be used without any problems.
- New technologies and knowledge on the environmental requirements of sows and piglets at birth allow pig farmers to make the most of environmental control systems, which are completely automated, so as to reach higher productivity rates.
- Feeding during the peripartum period is a key element to work with these increasingly productive sows. It requires an in-depth knowledge of their feeding requirements during this phase in order to prevent constipation problems at farrowing and allow sows to correctly start lactogenesis.
- Good colostrum production and proper colostrum intake by all piglets are necessary for their development and survival. All piglets must drink colostrum from their mother in a sufficient amount in their first hours of life.
- Modern sows farrow many more piglets; however, their birth weight is lower. Piglets therefore require optimal housing and environmental conditions and husbandry practices.
- It is necessary to establish feeding curves in the peripartum phase for each type of sows, taking into account their body condition, genetics, age, productive cycle, as well as the energy content and composition of the feed administered.
- If the farm's husbandry practices allow it, it is recommended to work with specific diets for each productive phase of sows, including the prepartum period, which is a very important phase that requires specialised diets.

- Once a farm has been organised and designed, the chosen work system should be that which allows optimal use of the farrowing rooms, as they are the most expensive facilities on a farm. Weekly batch farrowing is recommended for farms with more than 700-1,000 sows. On small- and medium-sized farms, it is possible to work with batch farrowing every two, three, four or five weeks.
- Farrowing pens, and more particularly crates, should be designed to reduce piglet mortality during the peripartum period, which is essentially due to diarrhoea, crushing and hypothermia.
- A quiet environment and the elimination of stressing factors such as noise and visits are necessary to reduce nervous and aggressive behaviour in sows during the peripartum period.
- Trained and qualified workers are required in the farrowing units of modern swine operations to ensure farrowings are properly attended.
  Monitoring farrowings reduces the percentage of stillborn piglets and contributes to ensuring the weakest piglets start drinking colostrum and nursing correctly.
- With good professionals who manage farms according to the current criteria and recommendations, it is possible to produce a larger number of piglets with optimal costs. This will allow the best pig farmers to remain in such a mature and competitive market as the pig market.
- Good genetics, feeding, facilities and health programmes are necessary, but the farm personnel is the key to successful swine production. Only with properly qualified, trained and motivated personnel willing to work in a team will objectives in accordance with the new possibilities of modern pig production be achieved.
- Knowing the most important diseases that affect sows and piglets allows the establishment of specific prevention programmes in order to reduce the appearance and incidence of these diseases, so these animals express all their genetic and productive potential.
- With the application of biosecurity measures and use of "all-in all-out" systems in farrowing units, the risk of infection is reduced and a better health status of the herd is achieved.

BIBLIOGRAPHY

Aparicio, J., 2013. *Uso de dietas especiales pre y postparto* [online]. 3tres3. [viewed 2013]. Available from: http://www.3tres3.com/alimentacion_cerda/uso-de-dietas-especiales-pre-y-post-parto_32952/.

Barcellos, D., Sobestiansky, J. & Driemeier, D., 2005. *Atlas de patología y clínica porcina*. Goiânia, Brazil: Gráfica Art 3.

Barceló, J., 2009. *Los expertos opinan. ¿Cuál es la mejor edad para destetar?* [online]. 3tres3. [viewed 2013]. Available from: http://www.3tres3.com/los-expertos-opinan/%C2%BFcual-es-la-mejor-edad-para-destetar-i-de-iii_2672/

Barceló, J. & De Paz, X., 2005. Fallo lactacional de la cerda. *Cuadernos de campo Ivomec*. Merial Laboratorios. Zaragoza: Ed. Servet Diseño y Comunicación.

Baxter, E. M. & Edwards, S.A., 2012. *Piglet vitality and neonatal piglet losses. Keynotes and practical talks*. Newcastle University.

Baxter E. M., Jarvis, S., Ross, D.V. et al., 2008 Investigating the behavioural and physiological indicators of neonatal survival in pigs. *Theriogenology*. 69 (6): 773-783.

Belenguer, P., Toledo, M. & Finestra, A., 2014. *Chequeos y árboles de decisiones en reproductoras y lechones*. Barcelona: Editorial Temis Medical.

Bidanel, J.P., Caritez, J.C. & Legault, C., 1990. Ten years of experiments with Chinese pigs in France. 1. Breed evaluation. *Pig News and Information*. Vol. 11 (3): 345-348.

Bizaray, D., 2007. Influencia del comportamiento de la cerda sobre la supervivencia de los lechones. *Suis*. No. 34: 24-31.

Blanes-Vidal, V. & Torres, A. G., 2009. Cap. 5, Diseño y evaluación de la calefacción y de la refrigeración. In: Forcada, F., Babot, D., Vidal, A. Buxadé, C. et al. *Ganado porcino. Diseño de alojamientos e instalaciones*. Zaragoza: Editorial Servet.

Bortolozzo, F. P., Gaggini, T.S., Ferrari, C. V. & Wentz, I., 2014. Lechones momificados en un sistema de producción: cómo interpretar y afrontar distintos desafíos. *Avances en tecnología porcina*. No. 11: 8-19.

Buxadé, C., Marco, E. & López, D., 2007. *La cerda reproductora: claves de su optimización productiva*. 1st ed. Madrid: Ediciones Euroganadería.

Buxadé, C. & López, D., 2005. *Bienestar animal y ganado porcino: mitos y realidades*. 1st ed. Madrid: Ediciones Mundi Prensa.

Callejo, A. & Ovejero, I., 2007. *Control ambiental de instalaciones de ganado porcino*. Barcelona: Merial Laboratorios.

Callén, A. & Lorenzo, J. L., 2007. Reproducción rentable en porcino. *Cuadernos de campo Ivomec*. Merial laboratorios. Zaragoza: Ed. Servet Diseño y Comunicación.

Campabadal, C., 2009. *Guía técnica para productores de cerdos.* San José: Ministerio de Agricultura de Costa Rica.

CAPDEVILA, J., 2010. *Alimentación de cerdas en el parto: consejos prácticos* [online]. Nutrición. 3tres3. [viewed 2013]. Available from: http://www.3tres3.com/nutricion/alimentacion-de-cerdas-en-el-parto-consejos-practicos_2910/

CARR, J., 2004. *Estándares de la producción porcina*. Zaragoza: Editorial Asís Veterinaria.

CASANOVAS, C., 2012. *Puntos clave del manejo de la cerda hiperprolífica*. Nanta-Inga Food Seminar. Zaragoza.

CASANOVAS, C., 2010. *Beneficios del manejo en bandas superiores a una semana* [online]. Manejo en bandas. 3tres3. [viewed 2013]. Available from: www.3tres3.com/manejo_en_bandas/beneficios-del-manejo-en-bandas-superiores-a-una-semana_2997/

CASANOVAS, C., 2008. *Cuadernos del parto de la cerda 1: Parto y preparto*. Ceva Sanidad Animal.

CASANOVAS, C. & CASANOVAS, J., 2006. Manejo en bandas 4ª parte: rotaciones de la sala de maternidad de cinco semanas. *Suis*. No. 28: 38-47.

CASANOVAS, C. & CASANOVAS, J., 2006. Manejo en bandas 3ª parte: rotaciones de las salas de maternidad de cuatro semanas. *Suis*. No. 27: 54-63.

CASANOVAS, C. & CASANOVAS, J., 2006. Manejo en bandas 2ª parte: bandas de producción cada tres semanas. *Suis*. No. 26: 40-51.

CASANOVAS, C. & CASANOVAS, J., 2006. Manejo en bandas 1ª parte: lotes de producción y bandas semanales. *Suis*. No. 25: 40-49.

CEBRIÁN, B. & CERISUELO, A., 2012. Gestión de las reservas corporales de la cerda: aplicación práctica de la medición del espesor del tocino dorsal. *Info Ingaso*. No. 9: 1-14.

CHACARTEGUI, F., 2013. *Alimentación de la cerda. Ventajas e inconvenientes de alimentación líquida en cerdas* [online]. 3tres3. [viewed 2013]. Available from: http://www.3tres3.com/alimentacion_cerda/ventajas-e-inconvenientes-de-alimentacion-liquida-en-cerdas_3255/

COLLELL, M., 2009. *Manejo en calor*. Barcelona: Laboratorios Fatro.

COLLELL, M. y MARCO, E., Marco i Collell. *Control ambiental en ganado porcino*. Merial laboratorios, Barcelona, 2008.

COLLELL, M., 2008. *Manejo en calor. Agua, el elemento imprescindible* [online]. 3tres3. [viewed 2013]. Available from: http://www.3tres3.com/manejo_en_calor/agua-el-elemento-imprescindible_4268/

COLLELL, M., 2007. *Manejo en gestación*. Barcelona: Laboratorios Fatro.

COLLELL, M., 2006. Gestión de recursos humanos. *Suis*. No. 25: 50-58.

COLLELL, M., 2006. Motivación y organización del trabajo. *Suis*. No. 27: 64-74.

CROMWELL, G., 1998. *Presentación de las recomendaciones nutricionales del NRC para porcino. Estudio crítico*. 14th Specialisation Course on Animal Nutrition and Feeding Avances. Madrid.

DE LA FUENTE, J. M., 2004. *Alimentación líquida en porcino. Nutrición.* [online]. 3tres3. [viewed 2013]. Available from: http://www.3tres3.com/nutricion/alimentacion-liquida-en-porcino_779/

DE VALENCIA, J., 1986. *Fisiología de la reproducción porcina*. México: Editorial Trillas.

DOMINGO, M. & SEGALÉS, J., 2005. *Casos de patología porcina (vol. III)*. Barcelona: Editorial Edika Med.

DUNNE, H. M., 1967. *Enfermedades del cerdo.* México: Editorial Hispano-Americana.

EICH, K-O., 1990. *Manual de las enfermedades del cerdo*. Barcelona: Grünland Ediciones.

ENGLISH, P., 2007. Mejora del trabajo en las explotaciones porcinas. *Suis*. No. 43: 54-65.

ESCOBET, J., COLLELL, M., & MARCO, E., 2009. Cap. 7, El control práctico del sistema de climatización. En: FORCADA, F., BABOT, D., VIDAL, A. BUXADÉ, C. et al. *Ganado porcino. Diseño de alojamientos e instalaciones*. Zaragoza: Editorial Servet.

FACCENDA, M., 2006. *Sala de parto*. Barcelona: Laboratorios Fatro.

FAIRBROTHER, J. M., 2009. *Escherichia coli* en ganado porcino. *Monografía Syva*. Zaragoza: Grupo Asís.

FALCETO, M. V., RIVERA, A. CALAVIA. M. & GÓMEZ A. B., 2012. Lactación y etiología del síndrome disgalactia posparto de la cerda. *Suis*. No. 86: 14-22.

FINESTRA, A. & DEVANT, M., 2010. *Calidad del agua en ganado vacuno y porcino*. Barcelona: Merial.

FORCADA, F. & VILADOMIU, I., 2009. Cap. 8, Alojamientos para cerdas lactantes. In: FORCADA, F., BABOT, D., VIDAL, A. BUXADÉ, C. et al. *Ganado porcino. Diseño de alojamientos e instalaciones*. Zaragoza: Editorial Servet.

FORCADA, F., BABOT, D., VIDAL, A. BUXADÉ, C. et al., 2009. *Ganado porcino. Diseño de alojamientos e instalaciones.* Zaragoza: Editorial Servet.

FRAILE, L., 2014. *Antimicrobial therapy in swine*. Zaragoza: Editorial Servet.

FRIGO, E. ¿Qué es la capacitación? In: Foro de seguridad. Foro de Profesionales Lationoamericanos de Serguridad [online]. [viewed 2013]. Available from: http://www.forodeseguridad.com/artic/rrhh/7011.htm.

FRONTERA, E., PÉREZ, E., REINA, D. & ALCAIDE, M., 2009. *Patología parasitaria porcina en imágenes.* Zaragoza: Editorial Servet.

GADD, J., 2006. Retroalimentación e inmunidad. In: *Producción porcina, John Gadd descubre lo que los libros de texto no cuentan*. Zaragoza: Editorial Servet.

GADD, J., 2005. *Guía John Gadd de soluciones en producción porcina*. Zaragoza: Editorial Servet.

GIL, J., 2014. *Peso del lechón al nacimiento*. MSD-Inga Food Seminar. Lérida.

GORRACHATEGUI, M., 2012. *Revisión aspectos nutrición* de la cerda. AVPA Seminar. Zaragoza.

HAN Y-K., WANG, Q., CHO, J-H. et al., 2009. Effects of dietary glucose level during late gestation on littler performance and glucose concentration in sows. *Animal Science Journal*. Vol. 80 (1): 57-61.

Institut technique du porc (I.T.P.), 2004. *Conduite alimentaire de la truie hyperprolifique*. Le Rheu: Editorial ITP Antenne Ouest.

Institut technique du porc (I.T.P.), 1997. *Manual del porcicultor*. Zaragoza: Editorial Acribia.

Lallemand Animal Nutrition, 2012. *Zoom sobre la fase periparto*. Lallemand.

LE TREUT, Y., 2006. *Alimentación de la cerda. Alimentación y nutrición de la cerda gestante I* [online]. 3tres3. [viewed 2013]. Available from: http://www.3tres3.com/alimentacion_cerda/alimentacion-y-nutricion-de-la-cerda-gestante-i_1588/

LEÓN, L., CUBERO, M. J. & GONZÁLEZ, M., 1990. *Síndrome disgaláctico del posparto (síndrome mamitis-metritis-agalactia) de la cerda*. Madrid: Publex Studio.

LÓPEZ, M. J., 2007. *Claves para el control ambiental. Usos en campo*. Barcelona: Merial laboratorios.

MAGALLÓN, E., 2010. *Costes de producción porcina en integración*. AVPA Economic Management Course. Zaragoza.

MANCERA, J. C., 2010. *Controles de alimentación de la cerda hiperprolífica en lactación*. Zaragoza: Inga Food.

MANTECA, X., 2009. *Etología veterinaria*. Barcelona: Multimédica Ediciones Veterinarias.

MANTECA, X. & GASA. J., 2008. *Bienestar en el ganado porcino*. Barcelona: Boehringer Ingelheim Laboratorios.

MARCO, E. & COLLELL, M., 2008. *Control ambiental en ganado porcino*. Barcelona: Merial laboratorios.

MARTIN, C. et al, 2012. Master 2 Know Nutreco.

MARTÍN, C. Y MORENO, R. Últimas tendencias en el alojamiento de reproductoras. En: *Producción porcina: aspectos clave*. Coord. Buxadé, C., Ed. Mundi Prensa, 1999.

MARTINEAU, G. P., 1997. *Maladies d'élevage des porcs*. Paris: Editions France Agricole.

MAZZONI, C., GRADELLINI, S. & TONON, F., 2005. Reducción quirúrgica de la hernia inguinal en el cerdo. *Suis*. No. 20: 30-33.

MERCK & Co., 2009. *El manual Merck de veterinaria*, 4th ed. Barcelona: Editorial Oceano.

MORILLA, A., ZIMMERMAN, J. J. & YOON, K-J., 2004. *Enfermedades víricas emergentes del cerdo*. Barcelona: Multimédica Ediciones Veterinarias.

MUÑOZ, A. & MAROTA, E., 1998. *Porcinotecnia práctica y rentable*. Madrid: Grupo Luzan.

MUÑOZ, A., PALLARÉS, F. J., VILLALUENGA, J. L. & RAMIS, G., 2007. *Práctica clínica en porcinocultura: análisis y abordaje de casos clínicos*. Madrid: Editorial Acalanthis Comunicación y Estrategias.

Muirhead, M.R., & Alexander, T.J.L., 1997. *Managing pig health and the treatment of disease: A reference for the farm*. UK: 5M Enterprises.

Neumann, E. J., Ramirez, A. & Schwartz, K. J., 2009. *Swine disease manual*, 4th edition. USA: A.A.S.V.

Noguera, J.L., López, P., Alòs, N. e Ibáñez, N., 2013. Banco de datos de referencia del porcino español. Resultados por grupos de referencia geográficos, periodo 01/07/12 a 30/06/13. *Boletín BDporc IRTA*. No. 14: 2-3.

Ortiz, E., 2010. *Mitos y leyendas de la alimentación de las cerdas*. Zaragoza: Nanta Optifeed.

Palomo, A., 2013. Síndrome de cerda delgada. Ceva, *Boletín informativo*. No. 4.

Palomo, A., 2013. La importancia de mantener la condición corporal de la cerda. Ceva, *Boletín informativo*. No. 3.

Palomo, A., 2013. ¿Cómo alimentamos para que cada cerda alcance su máximo rendimiento reproductivo? Ceva, *Boletín informativo*. No. 2.

Plonait, H. & Bickhardt, K., 2001. *Manual de enfermedades del cerdo*. Zaragoza: Editorial Acribia.

Pluske, J. R., Le Dividich, J. & Verstegen, M. W. A., 2007. *El destete en el ganado porcino. Conceptos y aplicaciones*. Zaragoza: Editorial Servet.

Quesnel, H. et al. 2008. Influence of some sow characteristics on within-litter variation of piglet birth weight. *Animal*, 2: 1842-1849.

Probst, S., 2008. Gestión de riesgos en la sala de partos. *Suis*. No. 46: 40-51.

Quiles, A. & Hevia, M. L., 2007. *Manejo y alimentación de la cerda*. Madrid: Editorial Acalanthis.

Quiles, A. & Hevia, M. L., 2006. *Cría y manejo del lechón*. Madrid: Editorial Acalanthis Comunicación y Estrategias.

Quiniou, N., 2013. Nutrición de las cerdas de alto potencial. *Suis*. No. 96: 14-21.

Quiniou, N., Brossard, L., Van Milgen Y. et al., 2012. La variabilité des performances en élevage porcin: description et implications pratiques. *INRA Production Animale*. 25(1): 5-16.

Quiniou, N., Noblet, J., 1999. Influence of high temperatures on performance of multiparous lactating sows. *Journal of Animal Science*. 77: 2124-2134.

Remaekers, P., 2013. *Efecto de la alta ingesta de fibra en las cerdas en el preparto sobre la supervivencia de los lechones. Alimentación de la cerda.* [online]. 3tres3. [viewed 2013]. Available from: http://www.3tres3.com/alimentacion_cerda/efecto-de-la-alta-ingesta-de-fibra-en-las-cerdas-en-el-preparto-sobre_32430/

Remaekers, P., 2013. *Sow feed formulation and feeding programs.* Nutreco Swine Academy. Zaragoza.

Remaekers, P., Huerta, I. & van Hees, H. J. M., 2012. *Effect of bird weight and weight gain in the first 24 h on preweaning piglet survival*. Nutreco.

Revuelta, M. & Guillou, D., 2013. El periparto: el gran reto de la cerda y de su microflora intestinal. *Avances en tecnología porcina*. Vol. 10, no. 104: 26-34.

RODRÍGUEZ-ESTÉVEZ, V., 2010. *El anoestro y la infertilidad estacional de la cerda*. Zaragoza: Editorial Servet.

ROTHSCHILD, M. F. & BIDANEL, J. P., 1998. *The Genetics of the Pig*. Edited por Rothschild, M. F. & Ruvinsky, A., USA.

ROTTO, H., 2013. Factores que no se consideran en los diagnósticos: el agua. *Suis*. No. 97: 10-12.

RUTTEN-RAMOS, S., 2008. Optimizar la producción porcina. *Suis*. No. 46: 30-38.

SALÓ, N., 2005. *La comunicación en la empresa*. Barcelona: Editorial Paidós.

SANJOAQUIN, L., 2013. *Alimentación. Manejo alimentario de las futuras reproductoras* [online]. 3tres3. [viewed 2013]. Available from: http://www.3tres3.com/nutricion/manejo-alimentario-de-las-futuras-reproductoras_31880/

SANTOMA, G., 2012. *¿Qué medidas nutricionales tomar ante la productividad de la cerda actual? 2ª parte: periparto y lactación*. 28th FEDNA Specialisation course. Madrid.

SANTOMA, G., 2012. *Alimentar a las cerdas que nos vienen*. 3rd ANAVEPOR Congress. Zaragoza.

SANTOMA, G. & Pontes, M., 2011. *¿Qué medidas nutricionales tomar ante la productividad de la cerda actual? 1ª parte*. 28th FEDNA Specialisation course. Madrid.

SCHWARTZ, K. J., 2005. *Manual de enfermedades del porcino.* Zaragoza: Asís Veterinaria, S.L.

SIMPSON, G., 2013. *Guía de alimentación de Hypor Libra*. Hypor, Hendrix Genetics Company.

Spain, 21 February 2003. *Real Decreto 140/2003, de 7 de febrero, por el que se establecen los criterios sanitarios de la calidad del agua de consumo humano*. Madrid: Boletín Oficial del Estado, no.45, p.7228.

STALDER, K. J., LACY, R. C., CROSS T. L., & CONATSER, G. E., 2003. Financial impact of average parity of culled females in a breed-to-wean swine operation using replacement gilt net present value analysis. *Journal of Swine Health and Production*. No. 11: 69-74.

TAYLOR, D., 1981. *Les maladies du porc*. Alfort: Editions Le Point Vétérinaire.

TORRES, A. & CERISUELO, A., 2013. Necesidades nutricionales en porcino III. *Suis*. No. 94: 34-43.

TORRES, A. & CERISUELO, A., 2012. Necesidades nutricionales en porcino II. *Suis*. No. 93: 44-53.

TORRES, A. & CERISUELO, A., 2012. Necesidades nutricionales en porcino I. *Suis*. No. 92: 34-43.

STRAW, B. E. & D'ALLAIRE, S., 2000. *Enfermedades del cerdo*. Buenos Aires: Editorial Inter-Médica.

VAN ENGEN, M., DE VRIES, A. & SCHEEPENS, K., 2011. *Señales del cerdo: lechones.* Pfizer.

WHITTEMORE, C. T., 1993. *The science and practice of pig production*. Arlington: Harlow Scientific and Technical Editions.

WHITTEMORE, C. T. & ELSLEY, F. W., 1976. *Alimentación práctica del cerdo*. Madrid: Editorial Aedos.

Published by Servet publishing house - Grupo Asís Biomedia S.L.